Interpretive Ethnography of Education: At Home and Abroad

INTERPRETIVE ETHNOGRAPHY OF EDUCATION:
At Home and Abroad

Edited by

GEORGE AND LOUISE SPINDLER
*Stanford University
and University of Wisconsin*

LEA LAWRENCE ERLBAUM ASSOCIATES, PUBLISHERS
1987 Hillsdale, New Jersey   London

Lawrence Erlbaum Associates, Inc., Publishers
365 Broadway
Hillsdale, New Jersey 07642

Library of Congress Cataloging in Publication Data

Interpretive ethnography of education.

Includes bibliographies and indexes.
1. Educational anthropology. 2. Educational
anthropology—United States. I. Spindler, George
Dearborn. II. Spindler, Louise S.
LB45.I58 1987   370.19   87-577
ISBN 0-89859-924-5
ISBN 0-89859-955-5 (pbk.)

Printed in the United States of America
10 9 8 7 6 5

Contents

General Introduction

Ethnographic approaches to the study of education, as a subset of qualitative research, have surged to prominence only in the past decade. They have raised new questions and provided some answers that correlational and experimental research designs did not. As with any new movement there is a tendency to oversell, and to drift away from the disciplinary foundations that make new approaches work predictably and effectively. This volume is intended as a corrective for both tendencies, and it breaks new ground. It samples the ongoing work of eighteen authors grappling with a very wide spectrum of educational processes and problems. Some of these authors are well-established, widely recognized scholars. Some are barely out of graduate training. All are doing innovative, ethnographic, research and writing. They are also all (but one), trained in anthropology, the mother discipline of ethnography. Though ethnography is legitimately practiced by others, its situated history is in the history of cultural anthropology, with some very significant contributions from sociology.

This is not to say that the volume is intended only for educators and social scientists who have an anthropological background. Although organized and written from the perspective of educational anthropology, this book is aimed at a wider and more general audience. A quick scan of the table of contents confirms the breadth of its focus. There are chapters on how the ethnography of schooling is done, written by people who have worked in schools for much of their professional lives. There are chapters on schools abroad, studied ethnographically. There are chapters on immigrants and minorities in our own schools. There are chapters on selected aspects of schools attended by mainstream students. All of these chapters are based on ethnographic fieldwork. But they deal with problems and issues that are of concern to all professional educators and to those interested in education.

Social historians of education will find kinship with the writings of ethnographers of education, for history and ethnography have always been convergent in interests and even in methods. Comparative educationists will find materials and analyses of direct relevance to them, for this book is about education "at home and abroad." Sociologists of education will find the approaches implemented in these chapters congenial, and will encounter significant additions to their understanding of shared problems. Educational psychologists will find this book challenging, for it is consistent in offering cultural rather than psychological explanations for observed phenomena. Philosophers of education will discover a new way of looking at familiar issues. And practitioners of education—administrators, teachers, consultants, supervisors, learning specialists—will find parallels to the situations in which they work and be informed by the ways in which the various authors have gone about the study and analysis of these situations. With these relevancies and applications in mind, it is appropriate to describe this volume as a significant contribution to the social and cultural foundations of education.

There is nothing parochial, anthropological or otherwise, about this volume. Theories, concepts, models, and methods, are borrowed freely from other disciplines, as needed. And most of the contributors are educational anthropologists, scholars whose careers are in schools of education, or conjointly with education. All but two of the chapters have been written expressly for this volume. They are fresh and exciting.

The title of the volume is *Interpretive Ethnography of Education: At Home and Abroad*. This means, first, that we are not limiting ourselves to ethnographic reporting. We are *interpreting* what our ethnographic study has shown us is there, in the situation where the action is taking place. Though ethnographers, particularly those of anthropological persuasion, are more concerned with what *is* than what *ought* to be, the implications for change are close to the surface in every chapter. Interpretive ethnography requires inference, even speculation, but these inferences and speculations must be grounded in observation and inquiry, in depth, in situations, such as school and classrooms, where we have become familiar figures and can be treated casually by our informants.

Our title also makes it clear that we are not confining our observations and interpretations to our own society. Part II of this volume is devoted to comparative and cross-cultural analysis. But unlike more traditional work in educational anthropology, we have made our cross-cultural forays into complex, contemporary societies—England, France, Germany, and China. Our ethnographies of educational situations at home continue this cross-cultural and comparative stance in the chapters on established American minorities, including blacks, Chicanos, and American Indians, and on the new migrants represented by the Vietnamese and Punjabis.

This volume is divided into three parts. The first part, *Issues and Applications in Ethnographic Methods* is not devoted to cookbook procedures. Its six chapters are wide-ranging discussions of ethnographic methods with references to a number of specific research sites. Part I gives the reader a lively exposure to the strengths and weaknesses of ethnography that is essential to an informed appraisal and appreciation of the rest of the volume.

The second part, *Comparative and Cross-cultural,* supports the claim that anthropological ethnographers have often made, that a cross-cultural perspective is always somewhere in their formulations, whether implicit or explicit. This section shows that we can profitably apply the cross-cultural perspective to contexts within complex, modern societies.

The third part, *At Home in the USA,* continues to reinforce a cross-cultural stance, but now in our own multicultural society. This section is divided into two parts, one devoted to migrants and minorities, the other to mainstream USA. We think we gain in clarity by so dividing, for the current problems of education, though they exhibit qualities in common, are not all the same in these two sectors. The volume ends with a chapter on the effects of training for computer literacy on the middle and high school curricula. It shows us that the microcomputerized future, at least for schools, is not problem free.

This volume is complex, variegated, and vexing. It is so because its subject matter is complex, variegated, and vexing. There is so much to be known about so much. This volume is a significant step in the direction of understanding the complex phenomena of education. Every chapter has important implications for educational policy.

The Editors

ISSUES AND APPLICATIONS IN ETHNOGRAPHIC METHODS

EDITORIAL INTRODUCTION

Ethnography: An Anthropological View*

Ethnography has recently become popular in the study of schools, playgroups, bars, business establishments—any place where people gather. Anthropologists have "come home" to do their field research more than they did only a few years ago as remote tribesmen and traditional peasants have become less numerous and less accessible (Messerschmidt, 1981), and this may have accelerated a trend begun for other reasons. This popularity has been a mixed blessing, for false hopes are raised, particularly in education, partly because many people who are quite innocent of anthropology as a discipline, and who have only vague notions of cultural process, claim to be doing ethnography. We have nothing against anyone doing qualitative, field site evaluation, participant or nonparticipant observation, descriptive journalism, or anything else, if it is done well. It will produce some tangible result, and may be useful, but as Harry Wolcott points out in chapter 3 it should not be called ethnography unless it is, and it is not ethnography unless it uses some model of social or cultural process in both the gathering and

---

*A version of this discussion appears in *Educational Horizons,* 1985. 63.4, pp. 154–157.

interpretation of data. This gives us great latitude, but there are boundaries.

What do ethnographers study?

Culture, cultural process, cultural knowledge, appear in various guises. We need to define what we study when we study culture.

We often refer to an "American" culture (Harris, 1981; Merelman, 1984; G. and L. Spindler, 1983). Objections are immediately raised. America is multicultural. America is too diverse to be called a culture. Despite these objections we say there is an American culture, not because we have standardized drug stores, kitchens, cars, clothing or houses, though uniformities in these things do contribute to some patterns that are cultural. We certainly do not claim that there is an American culture because we are composed of at least twenty-four ethnic groups, six social classes, males and females, fourteen major religious groupings and countless sects, many degrees of left and right and extreme factions in both contingents, gays and straights, drug users and abstainers, and hillbillies and city slickers. We claim that there is an American culture because since prerevolutionary times we have been dialoging about freedom and constraint, equality and difference, cooperation and competition, independence and conformity, sociability and individuality, puritanism and free love, materialism and altruism, hard work and getting by, and achievement and failure. We express the dialogue in great and small institutions, political campaigns, expenditures of billions of dollars, schools and libraries, personnel management, business practices, sales pitches, production goals, foreign policy, etc., etc. It is not because we are all the same (we are not), or that we agree on most important matters (we do not), that there is an American culture. It is that somehow we agreed to worry, argue, fight, emulate, and agree or disagree about the same pivotal concerns. Call them values, value orientations, cultural focii, themes, whatever—they are pivotal (G. and L. Spindler, 1983). The fact that these concerns arrange themselves in oppositional pairs is no accident. That is the nature of culture, according to anthropological structuralists (Merelman, 1984). This is the dialogue of American culture. It gives meaning to our lives and actions as Americans. There are other dialogues that give meaning to our personal lives.

Within any social setting, and any social scene within a setting, whether great or small, social actors are carrying on a culturally constructed dialogue. This dialogue is expressed in behavior, words, symbols, and in the application of cultural knowledge to make instrumental activities and social situations *work* for one. We learn the dialogue as children, and continue learning it all of our lives, as our circumstances change. This is the phenomenon we study as ethnographers—the dialogue of action and interaction. We observe behavior and we interview any "native" (student, teacher, boss, housewife, chief) who will talk with us. When we are in classrooms we observe the action and talk to students and teachers, and principals, counselors, parents, and janitors. We observe, formulate questions, ask them, observe some more, and so on, until the patterns of behavior and native explanations for them coalesce into repetitive sequences and configurations. We try to determine how teaching and learning are supported and constrained by understandings, many of them implicit, that govern the interaction of teachers and students. The dialogue around what is to be taught, and how much of it is to be learned, and how the teaching and learning will be conducted, is what we try to record and eventually interpret as ethnographers of education.

What is Education?

We see education as cultural transmission, and of course cultural transmission requires cultural learning, so learning and transmission are separated only by convention (G. and L. Spindler 1982a; Wolcott, 1982). Further, we see that aspect of cultural transmission in which we are most interested—education in the broad sense, schooling in the narrower sense (including initiations, rites of passage, apprenticeships, as well as schools) as a *calculated intervention* in the learning process. We are not interested in all learning that takes place as children grow into adults, get older, and finally die. We are interested in the learning that takes place, whether intended or unanticipated, as a result of calculated intervention. It is our unique subject matter as educational anthropologists and without a unique subject matter as well as a methodology there is no discipline.

Within the focus that we think is useful, there are surface phenomena, the manifest, overt cultural content, and then there are the tacit agreements that make the dialogue of intervention possible.

In our long-term study of the Schönhausen Grundschule (G. Spindler, 1974; G. and L. Spindler, 1982b) and in our recent work in the Roseville Wisconsin school and community we find that the implicit, tacit, and hidden levels of culture are most important. We report on this research in chapter 7, in Part II.

They are what explain puzzling persistencies that are there, over time, under a surface level of manifest change, sometimes even apparently dramatic change. And they are what explain most satisfactorily some startling differences in classroom management and student-teacher behavior between the German and the American schools. Many models for research and analysis used by both social scientists and educators do not permit the study of the very processes that we have discovered are the most important—those aspects of the continuing dialogue between students and teachers that are hidden beneath the surface of behavior.

Good Ethnography

We search for clues to the relationship between forms and levels of cultural knowledge and observable behaviors as the dialogue of intervention and response takes place. The search must follow the clues wherever they lead and cannot be predetermined by a schedule of categories of observation or rating scales. Ethnographic study requires direct observation; it requires being immersed in the field situation, and it requires constant interviewing in all degrees of formality and casualness. From this interviewing, backed by observation, one is able to collect and elicit the native view(s) of reality and the native ascription of meaning to events, intentions, and consequences.

Eventually we must face the task of interpretation and cultural translation. The native view of reality must be directly represented in this interpretation but it can rarely stand on its own. We must translate it into the vernacular of the readers, natives in another cultural system, caught up in a different dialogue, and we must apply some concepts, models, paradigms, and theories from our professional discipline in order to give our findings wider applicability, and, of course, to communicate with our fellow professional natives. As we have said, our persuasion is toward culture and a special canting of it that we have termed dialogue.

Our orientation is idiographic and case study oriented. Idiographic research is widely regarded as incapable of producing generalizations. We take issue with this, and feel that through grounded, case-oriented, open (that is, not predetermined) ethnographic investigation, generalizations can be formulated most effectively. They may be tested, to be sure, with nomothetic methods employing refined statistical models (see G. Spindler, 1978, pp. 31–32 and LaBarre (1978) in Spindler, 1978, 270–275 for a discussion of idiographic versus nomothetic), and often such methods also produce new hypotheses for testing.

There is nothing in what we have said that precludes the use of quantitative data and inferential statistics as a part of an overall research program. We have collected and analyzed such data in every one of our four major research projects (summarized by L. Spindler, 1978). Careful use of statistics defines relationships and parameters in a most valuable way that helps define what must be explored with direct observation and interviewing, and conversely, makes possible the extension of generalizations initially derived idiographically.

Not all anthropologists will agree that what we study is the continuing dialogue that holds a given nation, community, or group together, or tears it apart. It is what we believe we study, though we have not always called it that. Whatever we call it, what we are after is what the native knows and uses in interaction with others in the situations and relationships his society provides for him. We want to discover and record knowledge, meanings and relationships. The power of this position is great and as yet largely unexploited. Education, business, and government will find it very useful, if researchers with the "right stuff" can be employed, and the right stuff, from our point-of-view, is a product of training and discipline in sociocultural interpretation, as well as in research techniques (see also Agar, 1980; Erickson, 1984; Spradley, 1979, 1980; Wolcott, 1983.) For a critique of ethnography that challenges some of the assumptions and methods with which we work and reinforces and extends others, see J. Clifford & G. Marcus, 1986, and G. Stocking, 1983.

The Chapters of Part I

The chapters of Part I demonstrate different but closely related approaches to doing ethnography in and about schools. Solon Kimball's "Method of Natural History" is included because, though first published in 1955, it lays out some of the primary values of ethnography that have proven most useful, and because it lays clear claim to naturalistic inquiry as an anthropological domain of long standing. Our own "Teaching and Learning how to do the Ethnography of Education" (chapter 2) further defines what ethnography is and tells how we have tried to teach it in training seminars at Stanford University and the University of Wisconsin since 1979. In his "On Ethnographic Intent" Harry Wolcott makes a strong argument for ethnography as not only observation and recording of behavior but the interpretation of behavior from a cultural viewpoint. He regards this viewpoint as distinctive to anthropology. Paul Yates, writing from England, brings to this volume concerns about minority and immigrant schooling that will be immediately recognizable to American readers and views these problems in the research context of ethnography. Though the flavor of his methodology is subtly different from ours in the United States it is clear that anthropological ethnography is recognizable as such on both sides of the Atlantic. David Fetterman provides a chapter on educational evaluation that is essential to the balance of Part I. Though every chapter has implications for educational practice, his is most explicit about how ethnography can have a direct effect on educational policy and decision making. The last chapter in Part I, Hugh Mehan's "Language and Schooling" is explicitly sociological, and Dr. Mehan is a sociologist. His chapter is particularly valuable because it describes how discourse can be interpreted in relation to social structure and its tacit rules, and because it also demonstrates unity of purpose and some significant similarities as well as differences between a social and a cultural view. For anthropology the tacit as well as explicit rules are cultural. Social stratification and social process are both governed, though not completely, by cultural principles. These issues go beyond terminology, but they are relatively unimportant in the context of their application to ethnographic interpretation once their common features are understood.

Each chapter in Part I is engaged with the interpretation of behavior as well as its recording and description. All of them, in one way or the other, are concerned with what we have called "cultural dialogue"—the exchange of patterned meanings and significations among actors in social contexts. And they are all focused on understanding the specific interventions in learning that we call education.

REFERENCES

Agar, M. H. (1980). *The Professional Stranger: An informal introduction to ethnography.* New York: Academic Press.

Clifford, J., & Marcus, G. (1986). *Writing culture: Poetics and politics in ethnography.* Berkeley: University of California Press.

Ericksen, F. (1984). What makes school ethnography 'ethnographic'? *Anthropology and Education Quarterly, 15*(1), 51–66.

Harris, M. (1981). *America now: The anthropology of a changing culture.* New York: Simon and Schuster.

LaBarre, W. (1978). The clinic and the field. In G. Spindler (Ed.), *The making of psychological anthropology* (pp. 270–275). Berkeley: University of California Press.

Merelman, R. (1984). *Making something of ourselves.* Berkeley: University of California Press.

Messerschmidt, D. (Ed.) (1981). *Anthropologists at home in North America: Methods and issues in the study of one's own society.* New York: Cambridge University Press.

Spindler, G. (1974). Schooling in Schönhausen: A study of cultural transmission and instrumental adaptation in an urbanizing German village, In G. Spindler, (Ed.), *Education and cultural process: Toward an anthropology of education* (pp. 230–273). New York: Holt, Rinehart and Winston.

Spindler, G. (1978). Introduction to Part I. In G. Spindler (Ed.), *The Making of Psychological Anthropology* (pp. 31–32). Berkeley: University of California Press.

Spindler, L. (1978). Researching the psychology of culture change and urbanization. In G. Spindler (Ed.), *The making of psychological anthropology* (pp. 174–200). Berkeley: University of California Press.

Spindler, G., & Spindler, L. (1982a). Do anthropologists need learning theory? *Anthropology and Education Quarterly, XIII*(2), 109–124.

Spindler, G., & Spindler, L. (1982b). Roger Harker and Schönhausen: From the familiar to the strange and back again. In G. Spindler (Ed.), Doing the ethnography of schooling, *Anthropology and Education Quarterly, XIII*(2), 21–46.

Spindler, G., & Spindler, L. (1983). Anthropologists view American culture. In *Annual review of anthropology,* edited by B. Siegel, A. Beals & S. Tyler. Palo Alto: Annual Reviews Inc., 49–78.

Spradley, J. (1979). *The ethnographic interview*. New York: Holt, Rinehart and Winston.

Spradley, J. (1980). *Participation observation*. New York: Holt, Rinehart and Winston.

Stocking, G. (Ed.). (1983). *Observers observed: Essays on ethnographic fieldwork*. Madison: University of Wisconsin Press.

Wolcott, H. (1982). The anthropology of learning. *Anthropology and Education Quarterly, XIII*(2), 83–108.

Wolcott, H. (Ed.). (1983). Teaching fieldwork to educational researchers: A symposium (A Special Issue), *Anthropology and Education Quarterly, XIV*(3), 170–218.

The Editors

The Author and His Chapter

Solon T. Kimball is one of the founders of educational anthropology and is widely respected for his contributions in that field as well as for his significant works in community studies and applied anthropology. On the faculty of Teachers College, Columbia University, for 13 years, he moved to the University of Florida at Gainsville in 1966 and pursued an active career there until his death from a heart attack on October 12, 1982 (see obituary by A. Moore.)

The paper that is reprinted here was first presented at a working seminar of twelve anthropologists and twelve educators at Carmel Valley, California, in the spring of 1954. This seminar proved to be character defining for the anthropology of education. Though we have gone well beyond it in the decades since the seminar, its influence has been far-reaching and is still echoing in contemporary educational anthropology and ethnography. G. Spindler's address as retiring president of the Council of Anthropology and Education was directed at this influence (Spindler, 1984).

Sol Kimball's description of the method of natural history holds good today. In 1954 it was methodological heresy to recommend anything but correlational and neoexperimental research methods to serious educationist researchers, even though anthropologists had been doing natural history in their fieldwork for about a half a century. Now ethnography, which draws heavily from its natural history base line is virtually a movement in educational circles, though regarded by some with more than lingering suspicion. The suspicion is justified, given the uneven quality of many of its products. Sol Kimball shows us in this chapter that

9

the forté of our method is that we attempt to understand process in context and that, for students of "natural history" the context must be very broad.

REFERENCES

Moore, A. (1984). Solon Toothaker Kimball (1909–1982). *American Anthropologist, 86*(2), 386–393.
Spindler, G. D. (1984). Roots revisited: Three decades of perspective. *Anthropology and Education Quarterly, 15*, 3–10.

The Editors

1 The Method of Natural History and Educational Research*

Solon T. Kimball
Columbia Teachers College and the University of Florida at Gainsville

One of the characteristics which sets anthropology apart from other social sciences is the extensive utilization of the natural history approach as one of its research methodologies. The anthropologist who does field work has as his first obligation the objective recording of human behavior. Although he may have preference for one of the several schools of anthropological thinking, and though his research may be focused toward some theoretical problem, he remains aware that his finished report must be based upon an accurate and complete presentation of the facts. Only thus may he fulfill his obligation to others so that they may utilize his materials in theoretical or cross-cultural analysis.

These requirements dispose the anthropologist to be inductive in his method of analysis. They also demand of him that he look at the total situation. The traditional anthropological monograph includes sections on physical environment, technology, social organization, and religious behavior. Even if an anthropologist chooses to emphasize one of these aspects over the other, his training has taught him that one cannot understand food, clothing, or housing characteristics except as one knows something about the raw materials available and requirements imposed by the environment for group survival. He also knows that the kind and number of social groups is directly related to environmental and techno-

*Reprinted from *Education and Anthropology,* edited by George D. Spindler, with the permission of the publishers, Stanford University Press. Copyright 1955 by the Board of Trustees of the Leland Stanford Junior University.

logical characteristics, and finally that religious expression is also related to these other factors.

Much of the field material on which he bases his analyses is drawn directly from observation or informant accounts of human activity in meeting the tasks of daily life. Almost any anthropological monograph could serve as illustration. The one which first comes to mind is the description by Malinowski of the Kula ring in his *Argonauts of the Western Pacific*. Many other works could serve as examples. Their universal characteristic is the description in time and place of human activities and, in many instances, the derivation of the cultural and social systems which are revealed in the events described.

This method is substantially the same as that used by the biological ecologist. It has as its goal the search for meaningful relationships between the components present in any given situation. It attempts to uncover the nature of equilibrium and the process of change. It may be contrasted with the other major research methods because its emphasis is upon the natural on-going process. As an example of difference the experimental method creates a controlled situation in which the value and quantity of variables present may or may not have any similarity to a situation found in nature, and hence may have limited applicability in control of natural processes. The natural history method does not exclude use of experimental, statistical, or other techniques; it is just that these are subordinate to its main consideration.

The natural historian utilizes two different but complementary and necessary operations in his scientific procedures. He classifies the phenomena of the observable world on the basis of differences and similarities, and he may, in addition, search for the meaningful relationships that explicate the process which he observes. The latter procedure has been called functional and historically appeared with Darwin. Classification is, of course, taxonomy; it had its roots in classical times and was a necessary first step in science to give order to the apparently endless variation of the natural world.

The natural history method has also been used with considerable success in the study of certain aspects of contemporary civilization. In particular, it has been applied to the study of small groups in community and industry. The primitive counterpart of the small group is "band" organization. Anthropologists have reported upon these social groups from their work in many tribes. They did not anticipate, as Harding has pointed out, that they were pioneering in a field which has recently become so popular. As examples of research in this area I refer to the Banks Wiring Room study in the Hawthorne plant of the Western Electric Company as reported by Roethlisberger and Dickson (1939), and to the study of the street corner gang in an Italian slum in Boston described by

Whyte (1943). The emphasis in both researches was the search for relationships within events and thus is illustrative of the functional approach.

Anthropologists who have engaged in the study of modern communities have also utilized the natural history method for some portion of their research activities. Their concern with formal structure, specifically stratification, has led them in the direction of seeking answers to questions which are provided by taxonomic procedures.

Although the natural history method utilizes both taxonomy and functionalism, the distinction between the two is important since the emphasis on one or the other method in any specific research leads to quite different results. Functionalism, as exemplified in the Western Electric and Boston "street corner" studies, gave us a picture of the dynamics of human behavior. There is recorded and analyzed for us the actual behavior in sequential events. On the other hand, taxonomy gives us a classificatory scheme for cataloguing differences in behavior. Both approaches have their uses, but it is suggested that in educational research where it is desired to discover the nature of on-going systems or of the educative process utilization of functional procedures holds greater promise for answering basic questions. Let us consider one problem as an example.

The school system of any specific community is one among several institutions. Its larger habitat is the community, but its specific activities are concentrated within a clearly defined locale. Within each school one may distinguish certain types of persons, related to other persons in certain ways, and carrying out habitual activity. The characteristics alluded to above are commonly known even if they have not been precisely described.

Our central problem, however, is to determine the effect of this system on changes within the child. We are concerned not alone with cultural transmission, but also with cultural acquisition. Some portion of the equipment which the child carries into maturity comes from his experience with school systems. It is our task to determine the character and magnitude of the school influence and to relate it in meaningful ways to other nonschool educative experiences. But the effect of his family and his peers must also be learned.

In ordinary circumstances we would be justified in assuming that the limits of our research could be confined to examining the effect of the events in which the child participates with others. In other societies the socialization process is primarily a function of face-to-face relationships. However, the modern child is subject to a different type of habitat influence. I refer to the mass media of television, radio, and moving pictures. These experiences may be, and often are, of a solitary nature—

or at least people are not in face-to-face relationships in the ordinary sense.

A great deal of effort has been devoted to the area of communication research. Attempts have been made to determine specific effects in terms of attitudes and behavior. Very little, if any, of this research has utilized the natural history method. This area of child experience must also be explored.

It is proposed here that understanding of the educative process can be gained only as we focus upon the child in his total habitat. His activities must be viewed in the context of sequential events accompanied by testing devices which measure change. The results should give us the base from which we may modify the environmental situation, if need be, to facilitate cultural transmission. The method of natural history meets the needs of problems which are dynamic in character and certainly has applicability in educational research.

REFERENCES

Harding, C. F., III. (1953). Current conceptual trends in small group study: Social and applied anthropology. *Autonomous Groups Bulletin,* VIII, 4. New York.

Malinowski, B. (1922). *Argonauts of the Western Pacific.* New York: E. P. Dutton and Company.

Roethlisberger, F. J., & Dickson, W. I. (1939). *Management and the worker.* Cambridge: Harvard University Press.

Whyte, W. F. (1943). *Street corner Society.* Chicago: University of Chicago Press.

The Authors and Their Chapter

George and Louise Spindler have been collaborating in their fieldwork, writing, editing, and teaching since the beginning of their professional career in the late 1940s, when they began field work with the Menominee of Wisconsin. Both have been employed at Stanford University since the early 1950s, and most recently at the University of Wisconsin as well. Their major interests have been in the study of personal, psychocultural, adaptation to culture change and urbanization and in the transmission of culture. They have researched both processes among the Menominee, the Kanai (The Blood Indians of Canada), the Mistassini Cree of Quebec, in Germany, and on the West Coast and the middle west of the United States. They have always done ethnography in these settings but have combined this method with quantitative approaches utilizing various instruments and statistical analyses.

In their chapter they further describe what they think ethnography is and something about how to do it but concentrate mainly on how to teach it. Most graduate students in anthropology went into the field until quite recently with no explicit training in field research methods. Many still do. Neither of the Spindlers had any training in ethnography before they started field work with the Menominee in 1948. In fact it was thought that one could not be taught how to do ethnography. One could only learn through experience in the field.

A keystone of the Spindlers' training seminar is that it is true that one learns through experience, but that experience can be brought into the seminar room as well as acquired outside of it. To this end they use various simulations of field experience in observation, recording, interviewing, analysis, and write-up. Their chapter explains how this is done in the seminar context.

The Editors

15

2 Teaching and Learning How to Do the Ethnography of Education

George and Louise Spindler
Stanford University
and
University of Wisconsin

WHAT IS ETHNOGRAPHY?

In this chapter we have two purposes. One is to state what we think ethnography is and what ethnographers study. The other is to describe how we try to teach it. By trying to teach ethnographic methods and the concepts and values that lie behind them, as well as doing ethnography, we come to an understanding of how ethnography is a certain kind of inquiry, guided by assumptions and purposes that are different than most methods in the social sciences and education.

Ethnographers attempt to record, in an orderly manner, how natives behave and how they explain their behavior. And ethnography, strictly speaking, is an orderly report of this recording. Natives are people in situations anywhere—including children and youth in schools—not just people who live in remote jungles or cozy peasant villages. We and many of our colleagues in educational anthropology have been concentrating lately on schooling as cultural transmission but we do not regard the ethnography of schooling as essentially different than ethnography anywhere.

Credentials

Though our most recent ethnographic field work has concentrated on schools and their contexts in Germany and America (G. and L. Spindler 1982) and will be the focus of our chapter 7, our first field work was with the Menominee Indians of Wisconsin (1948–1954). We did further field research with the Blood Indians of Alberta, Canada (1958–1964) and the Cree of Mistassini Lake, Quebec (1966). Louise Spindler (1978) reviews this research in a retrospective chapter. Our work in Germany began in 1959, resumed in 1967, and has continued intermittently ever since. The earlier phase, centering on "Burgbach," an urbanizing village in the Rems Valley, in southern Germany, an area remarkable for its fine wines, is represented in G. Spindler's case study (1973). Our research in the Schönhausen school in a nearby community began in 1968 (G. Spindler, 1974a) and has continued in field trips in 1977, 1981, and 1985. G. Spindler also did extensive research during the 1950s on California schools with the Stanford Consultation Service headed by Dr. Robert N. Bush.

Altogether we have made 28 field trips, only a portion of which have been represented directly in publication. Like many anthropologists, we would rather *do* field work than write it up. Our field experience, however, is what we teach from as we teach others how to do ethnography.

Toward a Good Ethnography

Teaching anything requires that the teacher have a model in mind for what is taught. Our model of an ethnographic approach has grown out of our own field experience and the influence of our anthropological and educationist colleagues.

This model is not easily classified as "ecological," "ethnoscientific," "semiotic," "psychodynamic," or "interactionist," for it combines, in a pragmatic working combination, elements from all of these current models. We study human behavior in social contexts, so we are interested in social interaction and the ways in which these environmental contexts impose restraints on interaction. We are interested in the meaning that social actors in contexts assign to their own behavior and that of others. We are concerned with the way in which people organize information relevant to their behavior in social contexts. And we try to understand how individuals emotionally load their cultural knowledge, thereby assigning priorities that are not a direct function of the taxonomic ordering of that cultural knowledge.

We have elsewhere (G. Spindler, 1982a) set forth the criteria for a *good* ethnography. They are summarized below.

Criteria for a Good Ethnography

Criterion I.   Observations are contextualized, both in the immediate setting in which behavior is observed and in further contexts beyond that context, as relevant.

Criterion II.   Hypotheses emerge *in situ,* as the study goes on in the setting selected for observation. Judgment on what may be significant to study in depth is deferred until the orienting phase of the field study has been completed. (We assume that the researcher will have searched the literature and defined the "problem" before beginning fieldwork, however much the problem may be modified, or even discarded, as field research proceeds.)

Criterion III.   Observation is prolonged and repetitive. Chains of events are observed more than once to establish the reliability of observations.

Criterion IV.   The native view of reality is attended through inferences from observation and through the various forms of ethnographic inquiry (including interviews and other eliciting procedures).

Criterion V.   Sociocultural knowledge held by social participants makes social behavior and communication sensible. Therefore, a major part of the ethnographic task is to elicit that knowledge from informant-participants in as systematic a fashion as possible.

Criterion VI.   Instruments, codes, schedules, questionnaires, agenda for interviews, and so forth, should be generated *in situ* as a result of observation and ethnographic inquiry.

Criterion VII.   A transcultural, comparative perspective is present though frequently as an unstated assumption. That is, cultural variation over time and space is considered a natural human condition. All cultures are seen as adaptations to the exigencies of human life and exhibit common as well as distinguishing features.

Criterion VIII.   Some of the sociocultural knowledge affecting behavior and communication in any particular setting being studied is implicit or tacit, not known to some natives and known only ambiguously to others. A significant task of ethnography is therefore to make what is implicit and tacit to informants explicit.

Criterion IX.   Since the informant (any person being interviewed) is one who knows and who has the emic, native cultural knowledge the ethnographic interviewer must not predetermine responses by the kinds of questions asked. The management of the interview must be carried out so as to promote the unfolding of emic cultural knowledge in its most heuristic, *natural* form. This form will often be influenced by emotionally laden preoccupations that must be allowed expression.

Criterion X.   Any form of technical device that will enable the ethnographer to collect more live data—immediate, natural, detailed behavior—will be used, such as cameras, audiotapes, videotapes, and field-based instruments.

The most important requirements for an ethnographic approach, as we see it, is that behavior in situations must be explained from the native's point of view, and both the behavior and explanation must be recorded as carefully and systematically as possible, using whatever aids are expedient, such as note taking, tape recorders, and cameras. This obviously requires the ethnographer to be present in the situation (ceremonials, chief's council, school board meeting, classroom, etc.) when behavior is happening, and be able to ask questions of the natives about their behavior. There is a constant interaction between observation and interview. One observes, begins to formulate questions, asks questions and gets some answers, observes some more with perceptions sharpened by new cultural knowledge—refines questions, focusing them on relationships that appear to be particularly critical, observes some more, looking for repetitions of behavioral pattern with more focus than initially, and so on, and on.

Ethnographers Are Pesky People

Ethnographers are pesky people. Resentment and rejection are conditions of life in the field. Sensitivity about and respect for the people one is observing and questioning are essential. One doesn't climb into bed with lovers to observe lovemaking. One might well interview lovers *about* lovemaking—if they can and will talk about it. A lot of ethnographic information is second hand, in the sense that one cannot observe directly what is happening but people talk about something that happened. Validity is affected. One compensates by trying to find a number of people who will talk about the behavior hidden to the ethnographer, hoping to elicit recognizable explanatory elements from some or all of these respondents.

Tacit Rules

There is always the problem that much of behavior is guided by applying tacit, usually undeclared rules. For example, when Americans enter an elevator, they behave in certain predictable ways. They avoid direct eye engagement with strangers. They stand facing the door. Males keep their hands clasped in front of them or straight at their sides, and avoid touching others. Women tend to clasp handbags. People don't start conversations with strangers. Conversations begun by a pair before entering an elevator cease temporarily, or are carried on *sotto voce*. There are more rules for elevator behavior, but these will suffice.

We are rarely conscious of all these rules governing elevator behavior. We know about them, and with skillful interrogation one can usually elucidate them. The ethnographer of elevator behavior can, after riding elevators under varying conditions—crowded, uncrowded, with other persons of the same and opposite sex, several stories' duration, one person, party crowds, business men and women, with an operator and without, etc.—by a skillful combination of casual and more formal interviewing, construct a reliable ethnography of elevator behavior that tells us how people act, and how people explain these actions. We have behavior pattern and native cultural knowledge.

Inferential Interpretation

There is a problem, however. When we interview elevator natives, we find that they can tell us what one does on an elevator. That is, they have the requisite cultural knowledge to behave appropriately in the elevator context under varying conditions, and they know that they have it. When we ask *why* they behave the way they do, our informants are likely to get quite vague; "It makes one uncomfortable," or "I'd be embarrassed," or "It isn't polite," or even "It could be dangerous" (to talk to strangers, eye engage, touch, etc.).

What we don't know is why our informants feel like this. Why are they embarrassed or uncomfortable in elevators when people violate the rules? We don't get the deeper rationale by eliciting the cultural knowledge that informants bring into situations. We find it necessary to infer an explanation, and this is where theory, preference, and prejudice take over.

The rationale that most American anthropologists prefer is cultural. "In Western culture, personal space is important, so people keep a minimum of space between themselves and others. Elevators create situations where personal space may be violated, therefore one takes precautions to reduce that violation to a minimum." Neat enough. But why do Americans need this personal space? "Well, you see, in American culture, independence and privacy are valued, and personal space is an expression of this." But, why Americans and not Arabs or Senegalese? "People in every culture have concepts of personal space, but they differ. Perhaps American concepts of personal space reflect self-expression and individuality that developed with the westward expansion, the frontier, and the space and opportunity." Inference upon inference!

Inference, construction of explanations, and models of explanation that go far beyond the original observations and the elicitation of native cultural knowledge make interesting reading. In fact, this is what we find most interesting. We evaluate our great anthropologists such as Clifford Geertz, Anthony Wallace, Gregory Bateson, Margaret Mead, Clyde Kluckholn, Evans-Pritchard, Malinowski, by the inferences they draw and how they present them to us. Nevertheless, they had a solid base of ethnographic study from which to build their inferential structures of explanation.

The problem is that ethnography provides the raw material for inferencing but inferencing must be minimized while doing ethnography and writing an ethnographic report. The ethnographer collects observations from as intimate a perspective as possible. These observations are collected repetitively—so we are sure which behaviors are patterned and which may be fortuitous one time events. And the ethnographer elicits cultural knowledge from natives who will explain, and perhaps, if occasion demands, defend their behavior. A true ethnography is an orderly compilation of observations and native cultural knowledge. Inference is at a minimum, though some is necessary, even to know what questions to ask our informants. Doing ethnography and making ethnographic reports requires that we hold our inferences in check and use these parsimoniously. Ethnographic interpretation requires us to do more.

Where Are the Ethnographies?

"What are some examples of ethnographies that meet your criteria?" our students ask. Ethnographies, in the pure sense, rarely see the light of day. What we read are mostly case studies with an ethnographic base or significant ethnographic dimension. Most of the chapters in this volume are case studies with a strong ethnographic base. They are case studies in interpretive ethnography. The problem for the reader is often how to separate ethnography and inference.

When we teach how to do ethnography, we stress again and again this separation between ethnography and inference. This separation is an ideal, incapable of full realization, but it guides our behavior as teachers of ethnographic methods.

Inference is necessary. However, the ultimate purpose of ethnography is to provide reliable source material for analysis. Analysis is inference governed by systematic models, paradigms, and theory. We try to teach how to analyze ethnographic data in our training seminars as well. It is impossible to document this adequately in a few short pages. Reading good case studies, including the ones in this volume, with an eye to the distinction between what we have described as ethnography and what we have described as inference will be informative.

We turn now to a description of how we try to teach ethnography in our training seminars.

TEACHING ETHNOGRAPHY

We teach our students to do anthroethnography, meaning that the major concepts, models, techniques, and purposes of "our" ethnography issue from the discipline and theory of cultural anthropology. Anthropology, however, is notoriously eclectic, so we can dip into our neighboring disciplines as needed.

We began collaborative ethnographic training with educators in 1978 with an intensive 2-week seminar for the Milpitas school district near Stanford. Since then we have refined and developed the model that emerged in that very experimental and intensive 2 weeks during seven semesters at the University of Wisconsin at Madison and six summer quarters at Stanford.

Of course, we had taught field methods in our anthropology graduate courses for many years, particularly in advanced seminars in psychological anthropology. Perhaps the most intriguing experience with training novitiates was at the Stanford Center in Germany, where over 400 undergraduates did field work under our supervision in the Remstal (Spindler, 1973). Training graduate students in education, however, has been especially rewarding. These mature and usually professionally experienced people have a clear purpose in learning to do ethnography. They want to use it to gain understandings of education-related phenomena that conventional correlational and experimental research methods have not illuminated.

Our first seminar meeting is devoted entirely to one or two reports by graduate students in anthropology who have recently returned from the field and are writing their dissertations. They are happy to talk about their experiences, and their enthusiasm is infectious. Without any preliminary coaching from us, excepting a very general format, they describe what problem they went to the field with, how the problem changed as they became familiar with the situation, what difficulties they encountered in role taking and responding to the expectations of natives, problems of entré, ethical concerns, sampling procedures, relations with key informants, observing, and recording.

Seminar participants ask questions. As the discussion proceeds, the characteristics of an ethnographic approach to research emerge with great clarity. Researchable problems emerge in the field as one gains experience there. The ethnographer must constantly be on the alert to avoid prejudgement of the significance and meaning of behavior. Repetitious observation over time is necessary. Native cultural knowledge can and must be elicited by casual observation, by eavesdropping, as well as in defined interview situations. One is a participant observer, sometimes intimately involved in native life, but one never becomes a native—not at least as long as one remains an ethnographer.

These inductively derived insights into the ethnographic enterprise are very convincing. Students read the "criteria for good ethnography" appreciatively.

Our second seminar meeting is devoted to a cultural sensitization demonstration (G. Spindler, 1974b). The technique has proved invaluable as a way of showing students, through their own responses to the alien cultural situations exhibited to them with 35mm slides, how their perceptions reflect their cultural experiences. It is humbling to realize that one does not "see" a prominent manure pile in front of a *Bauernhaus* (farmer's house) because there is no cultural category for such a relationship in his or her own culture. It is equally humbling to realize that one has described a terraced German vineyard as a series of defensive barricades against advancing enemy troops because of a cultural category in one's own cultural repertoire that defines things German as militaristic. No respondent ever makes all possible errors, but all respondents make some of them. Each slide is reviewed after the initial administration and the kinds of errors usually made are pointed out. This is a first lesson in withholding judgment, avoiding intuitive leaps, and holding one's cultural categories in check. Our next seminar meeting or two is devoted to a continuation of this lesson in quite a different form.

Consistent with our conviction that a problem of first magnitude for most of us in doing ethnography in schools is that they are all too familiar to us (G. and L. Spindler, 1982), the next demonstration-experiment uses two episodes from a film on aborigines of the central Australian desert. The episodes, lasting about 2 minutes each, are of ceremonial activity involving only adult males, and of subsistence activity using digging sticks and involving only females and young children. The film is run twice, without sound and without introduction except for some general guidelines about observing and taking notes.

Students take notes, then write a one-page summary of them, with only the instruction that they stick to their observations and avoid interpretations of the significance of what they observed. They then exchange their summaries with other students and note differences between them. The summaries are turned in and we analyze them thoroughly, tabulating content, descriptive terms, and, particularly, noting premature interpretations, eticisms and divergences among the students in what was observed.

Students are asked to generate questions for interviews. The interviews follow, usually in the next session of the seminar, with George acting as a knowledgeable old male aborigine and Louise as a recently married woman. Ground rules are established for the conduct of the interviews. The informants' responses are based on indepth ethnographic knowledge of the traditional central desert culture. Both informants behave as informants usually do. They obfuscate, mislead, divert, provide ambiguous answers, get "turned off" by some queries, respond "emically," and so on. Students take notes, get frustrated, hurt, and excited. After an hour, sometimes more, of interview, they write up their second summary, not more than two pages in length. These summaries are analyzed carefully for content, sequence, emphasis, overall integration, and unwarranted interpretive generalizations. Divergences between students' summaries are noted and discussed. A discussion of the relationship between cultural knowledge and behavior follows. The concept of "idioverse" (Schwartz, 1978) is introduced. This concept calls attention to the fact that knowledge held by any one informant is idiosyncratic to some degree and that many natives in different sectors of the cultural topography must be observed and interviewed. We also introduce the problem of cultural translation from the culture of the native to that of the ethnographer.

In several different forms this procedure is followed throughout the seminar. One of the most productive sequences focuses on materials from our long-term field work in Schönhausen (see Chapter 7). We use both slides and Super 8mm films as resources. We start with social settings in the village and its surrounding fields and vineyards, and move finally into the elementary school classrooms. Students are told nothing about the scenes except some general orientation to time and place. Meanwhile, they have had demonstrations of interviews by the instructors, as well as the central desert "experience." They observe, take notes, summarize, interview, observe again, take notes, interview, write up, for as many sessions of about an hour each as we have time for in our semester or quarter format of one 3-hour meeting each week. We term this procedure the "ethnographic interview reinforcement technique." We actively critique each product, both individually and collectively.

The Expressive Autobiographic Interview (E.A.I.)

Another interview technique that we have found very fruitful in our field research in all of our cultural settings, including schools in Germany and America, is the expressive autobiographic interview (E.A.I.). This technique is a cross between a structured expressive interview and a chronological autobiography—in abbreviated form. The interviewer interrupts with questions at critical points, critical to his or her interests (i.e., prepuberty, early school, first contact with the opposite sex, marriage, death, kin relations, etc.), while the interviewee is relating his or her life events.

The emotional atmosphere established in the confidential framework of the life story seems appropriate for questions of almost any type. The respondent introduces you to his or her family, reveals incidents loaded with sentiment, touches upon the main areas of friction and conflict in his or her life, expresses attitudes towards parents, siblings, friends, and authority figures and talks about areas inaccessible to direct questioning.

One purpose in using the technique is to elicit materials concerning a person's special cultural knowledge, beliefs, and attitudes concerning the people and the world around him or her. The informant is often unaware of the kinds of values and attitudes communicated in his or her E.A.I. responses. These kinds of data usually cannot be secured by direct questioning. Answers to direct questions too often refer to the "ideal," what one should do or what it is thought the interviewer would like, rather than to the actual expected behavior of the informant. The E.A.I. is a record of behavioral events plus the informant's attitudes towards them.

Another purpose in using the technique is to elicit materials to help clarify a person's identity, confusion of it, or lack of it. Whether it is male, female, neuter, middle-class American (upper or lower), Native American traditional, modern Chicano, etc., the materials from the E.A.I. help place a person in the larger cultural context. By way of illustration, we cite below two excerpts from interviews conducted by Louise Spindler with Menominee women.

(question): What were you parents like? (The respondent is an elite acculturated woman.)

> My parents believed in self-support, work from sunrise to sunset. They didn't believe in vacationing. If you don't work you can't eat, they said. I'm like that too. I feel these people around here weren't brought up right. My parents always believed in 6 days of work and 1 day of rest.

A culturally transitional Menominee woman replied, in answer to the question: "How did you meet your husband?":

> My mother introduced me to Shumasen's (a shaman) son, John. It always seemed kinda funny that my mother liked all those things—Indian dances and medicines, when my grandmother was a good Catholic (referring to her mother's involvement with a native doctor and learning special native medicines). I don't know where I belong. I don't go to church, and I use Indian cures for different things. I can't go to church now. If I should die I suppose I would be buried out in that potter's field (an unkept area in the cemetery for the "pagans").

It is clear from these two brief excerpts that the first woman identifies with the mainstream American work ethic and that the second is unsure of her identity and is suspended between two cultural worlds. Other matters of a more intimate and potentially threatening nature such as witchcraft, sex, community politics, scandals, crimes, and so forth, are often discussed with an abandon that almost never characterizes other formal interview situations.

There is always the problem of ethics in using personal materials of this type. The interviewer should establish good rapport with the informant before asking intimate questions, and then request permission to use the data. Anonymity must be assured by disguising the identity of the interviewee. Certain intimate details may be omitted, and trivial data disguised to throw curious readers off the track. Still, we have avoided publishing expressive autobiographic interviews in their entirety in outlets accessible to the general public.

We further demonstrate the E.A.I. by role playing Roger Harker, our classic case. Roger is a fifth grade teacher who faces a mix of students of diverse ethnic and social class origins (G. and L. Spindler, 1982). He is a "classic" middle-class WASP. His cultural repertoire is very different from that of about half of his students. He interacts intensively with children who share his cultural background, and almost not at all with children who are significantly culturally deviant from his own. His selectivity is impressive and makes an excellent case for a cultural explanation of behavior.

George Spindler plays Roger Harker and Louise interviews him, using the verbatim transcript of the original E.A.I. collected by George Spindler in the case study of Roger Harker and his classroom. Students in the seminar take notes. Afterwards, the cultural profile of Roger is developed, and predictions of his classroom behavior are made. Then the actual behavior is presented in some detail using extensive ethnographic data and various rating scales developed during the project. One particularly productive exercise is to test retrospectively the predictive power of a psychological model of interpretation as against a cultural model. In Roger's case it is apparent that a cultural model works best. We are able to explain his selective interactions with students. We are able to present the psychological as well as the cultural model since we have not only the E.A.I., but in addition the results of projective tests and psychiatric interviews administered to Roger.

Other Methods

This is not all there is to the seminar, although these are important aspects. These procedures allow us a control over experience and learning that to us seems essential. Because each student is required to write two "miniethnographies" the learning is immediately applied. By the time students do their own ethnographic "sorties" into the local environment they are well-trained in observation and interviewing. More importantly, they have learned to defer judgment, avoid premature interpretation and generalization, and confine *ethnography* to observation of behavior, eliciting the cultural knowledge of natives, and writing "close to the ground."

We also spend the first 30 minutes, sometimes more, of each period discussing questions students have turned in from their reading, both in our text (G. Spindler, 1982b) and from an extensive annotated bibliography. Students write "reactive" rather than critical reviews on each piece read, and we select issues and questions from these reviews for discussion. Much of this discussion centers on theory.

And we present and defend major research projects of our own, particularly on the Menominee, and Schönhausen, with comparative materials from American schools. Though we stress the ethnographic component, we also develop strategies for quantitative design and show how the ethnographic and statistical analyses complement each other.

Quantitative Versus Qualitative

The quantitative versus qualitative argument that has erupted recently is not a valid argument. Some people seem to regard ethnography as in confrontation and conflict with statistically oriented research design. To us this is nonsense. We usually publish results in both forms simultaneously. The chapter on schooling in Schönhausen in this book and in a previous publication (G. Spindler 1974a) are good examples. We used an eliciting instrument, the Instrumental Activities Inventory, to collect comparable data from several hundred "informants." The responses are in the form of declared choices between instrumental alternatives significant in the social setting of the respondent, and also in the form of explanation of the choices made. The choices are easily quantified, the explanations less so, but still entirely possible. The quantification and the application of inferential statistics, testing the probability that a given relationship between distributions of instrumental choice and age, sex, occupation, residence, origin, education, etc., is due to chance, provides us with invaluable generalization that is impossible with ethnographic data alone. The quantitative data, and its analysis and testing, also provide us with parameters within which our ethnography must be understood.

For example, it was imperative that we have I.A.I. data from 1968 and from 1977 in the Schönhausen study. The quantification and statistical testing of these data showed us that perceptions of traditional versus modern-urban instrumental alternatives had shifted radically during the near decade in the opposite direction than our hypothesis had indicated. We had expected a major school reform to produce changes toward urbanization and modernization. Instead the changes were in the direction of traditional lifeways. Our ethnographic data assumed a new significance once this parameter was established. We could understand a growing persuasion on our part that not much had changed in the school at levels of meaning deeper than curriculum, text books, classroom organization, and personnel. Heartened by the confirming evidence of a traditional reorientation we looked deeper into the cultural transactions taking place in the classroom.

The quantitative, statistically analyzed data not only reinforced inferences emerging from our ethnographic work in the school, it forced a rethinking of the significance of dramatic variations in teachers' styles of classroom management, for these styles did not appear to affect student perceptions of cultural alternatives. In fact the quantitative data forced us to rethink the role of the school as an agency of change, the role of the teacher as a cultural transmitter, and in general acted as a needed control on the process of analytic inference from our ethnographic data.

The Menominee case presentation also allows us to demonstrate the relevance of quantification and inferential statistics to establish parameters for ethnographic inquiry. In the context of the training seminar the most important attribute of this study is to show how important it is to establish intracommunity differences and avoid the assumption of homogeneity. The Menominee data also show us how important it is to separate the responses of males and females. Far too often ethnographers have not systematically taken into account the differences between the sexes in their adaptation to the exigencies of everyday life, ideology, and particularly to culture change and modernization (G. and L. Spindler n.d.). We develop this theme in the expansion of the Schönhausen study in chapter 7.

The Menominee case study also demonstrates the relationship between autobiographic data gained from sixteen E.A.I.'s collected from women by Louise Spindler and eight collected from males by G. Spindler, and both the statistical and ethnographic data. It is clear that the autobiographic data bore deep into the strata of personal meaning and experience in the community, where neither quantitative indices nor ethnographic data are as likely to go.

Other Concerns

As a final product, students have two choices—they can expand upon the two miniethnographies they have carried out and written up, doing more fieldwork and developing a problem orientation as they narrow the focus of their work; or they can write a dissertation proposal, well researched and referenced, with a significant ethnographic component.

Throughout the seminar the principles we have stated as criteria for a good ethnography are stressed operationally again and again. We move from observation to interview in order to determine not only what people do in their various social settings but why they do it. The "why," of course, has many dimensions. Situational determinants are always operative. Our focus is upon the relation between cultural knowledge—as it is used *in situ*, its ordering by the informant, and, separately, by the ethnographer—and observed behavior. Behavior, for us, is the "tip of the iceberg," to use Spradley's phrasing (Spradley 1979, 1980).

This viewpoint immediately pulls one into complex and enormously compelling questions about behavior and mental organization that involve the basic questions facing our discipline. We do not fully accept an ethnoscientific or ethnosemantic model of cultural knowledge but we start with it. One of our most productive engagements with the data in our various observation-interview experiments is to show that informants associate cultural domains and their contents in ways that are not predictable from taxonomically ordered domains. They emotionally "load" these associations and they transform the logical structures of taxonomies because of their own personal experiential careers.

Analysis

It would be easier to teach how to do ethnography if we could regard ethnography as a set of techniques removed from theory. It seems to us that there is a tendency in some current "qualitative design" writing to do just that. The result can be a kind of mindlessness that puts neither the theoretical nor applied concerns of educators or anthropologists ahead very far.

We have already sketched the outlines of the theoretical underpinnings of our ethnographic research and for our teaching of ethnographic methods. This underpinning is decidedly eclectic—both an advantage and a disadvantage. We try to make the sources of theory explicit as we proceed through the various stages of our training seminar.

Inference, Analysis, and Generalization. There is a further problem, however, with which we must cope. "What do we do with all this stuff?", students ask. They find that the *analysis* of ethnographic data, beyond its orderly collation and presentation, is the hardest part of the whole enterprise. Analysis, of course, is directed toward goals that are usually shaped by both theoretical and practical concerns. For social scientists the former may be most important. For educators in school systems and classrooms, the latter goals may dominate. In either case it is necessary to take systematic steps to move from data to generalization.

We develop analytic procedures, with examples from our own field work and from the experiences that the students have had as they collected and tried to cope with their own ethnographic data during the course of the seminar. The first step is to generate some *grounded inferences* from collected observations. Grounded inferences are statements of relationships between variables that stay close to the action and frequently become hypotheses for further exploration. For example, a statement about the use of readings about the local environment and the taking of trips to local historical sites in the Schönhausen Elementary School (G. Spindler, 1974a), to the effect that both experiences support a localized identity orientation, is a grounded inference. It is also a hypothesis that can be tested by further analysis and data collection. We collected data on identity, as in our Schönhausen study (G. Spindler, 1974a), to make the connection. In the process of further analysis and data collection, however, we discovered that though the localized identity was strong and apparently reinforced by elementary school reading texts and trips in the immediate locality of the school, this identity did not appear to interfere with the making of pragmatic choices in the direction of urbanization and modernization.

However, we want to go further. We want to produce generalizations that are not limited to our particular community or area of study. For example, in our Schönhausen study, we observed in depth certain parts of curriculum and practice termed *Heimatkunde* (lessons about Homeland). *Heimatkunde* was eliminated in the curriculum in the reform of the 1970s. *Sachkunde* (lessons about current affairs) was substituted as desirably more urban and modern in orientation. Our observations show that *Sachkunde* was reinterpreted by the teachers in actual practice as *Heimatkunde*. We generated from this several generalizations about cultural persistence and about substitute as against transformative change that are potentially applicable to all cultural innovations and all culture change situations. We try to lead students inductively through the mazeway of data presentation in the seminar to grounded inferences and analytic generalizations of this type. For many, this is the most difficult part of ethnographic training.

Analysis and generalization are heuristically difficult, but the difficulty is exacerbated by the fact that the concepts, models, and theory from which we draw in these seminars come from anthropology, and most of our students are unfamiliar with them. This makes it more difficult for us as well, but it is surprising how quickly students acquire an understanding of concepts and theory if they are directly applied to data that have become meaningful to them through a direct experience.

CONCLUSION

No one chapter can completely cover two complex topics such as the nature of ethnography and the teaching of it. There is much else, about movement from opportunistic topographical interviews through several levels of focus, to the highly focused, problem-oriented interview; about various stages in reconnaissance; the differences between ethnography and ethnology; more about interpretation; and particularly, ethics; that we would enjoy discussing. All of our efforts are directed toward understanding what ethnography is, what ethnographic methods can do, and what stands behind them. Through our attempts to teach ethnographic methods to mature professional people with little or no background in anthropology, we have come to see ethnography in a new light. We have discarded some standard assumptions about ethnographic method in anthropology. For example, we are cautious about the use of "key informants." We have, however, retained an essentially anthropological orientation, and have drawn more from culture as a frame of reference than from any other. The training experience in our seminar centers on sensitization to cultural influence on the native behavior and on the perceptions of the observer of that behavior. We look at cultural process in social contexts, such as classrooms, as exhibiting universal features, yet unique to each situation. We see cultural process as a continuing adaptation to the changing conditions of existence for any group. Culture is never static, as we conceive of it. It is ever changing but exhibits remarkable persistence.

We try to create, in each seminar, the conditions for discovery learning. Every seminar session is an inductive learning experience—if we are successful. Our powers of observation and interpretation develop, not from our being told what has to be learned, but from finding out what seems to work. The receptive student, sensitized by this process, is, we believe, not only an ethnographer of human behavior, but a better teacher, administrator, counselor, or supervisor. We think doctors, lawyers, businessmen, and anyone else who deals with people on a daily basis would also benefit from this kind of experience.

In Anticipation

Though not every author of a chapter in this volume holds altogether the same view of ethnography and ethnographic method as the one that we have advanced, every author shares with us some of the same orientations (see also Wolcott, 1983). This shared outlook and the shared sensitivities to social and cultural process are what give the volume a certain unity that seems unlikely, given the wide variety of settings and topics included, and given the diversity in age, sex, experience, and personality represented by the authors. We have taken this space to describe what we think ethnography is and how one can learn to do it because we think that with this introduction, the reader will better understand and appreciate the writings of our colleagues to follow.

REFERENCES

Schwartz, T. (1978). Where is the culture? Personality as the distributive locus for culture. In G. Spindler (Ed.), *The making of psychological anthropology*. Berkeley: University of California Press.

Spindler, G. (1973). *Burgbach: Urbanization and identity in a German village*. New York: Holt, Rinehart and Winston.

Spindler, G. (1974a). Schooling in Schönhausen: A study of cultural transmission and instrumental adaptation in an urbanizing German village. In G. Spindler (Ed.), *Education and cultural process: Toward an anthropology of education*. New York: Holt, Rinehart and Winston.

Spindler, G. (1974b). Transcultural sensitization. In G. Spindler (Ed.), *Education and cultural process: Toward an anthropology of education*. New York: Holt, Rinehart and Winston.

Spindler, G. (1982a). The criteria for a good ethnography of schooling. In G. Spindler (Ed.), *Doing the ethnography of schooling*. New York: Holt, Rinehart and Winston.

Spindler, G. (Ed.). (1982b). *Doing the ethnography of schooling*. New York: Holt, Rinehart and Winston.

Spindler, G., & Spindler, L. (1982). Roger Harker and Schönhausen: From the familiar to the strange and back again. In G. Spindler (Ed.), *Doing the ethnography of schooling*. New York: Holt, Rinehart and Winston.

Spindler, G., & Spindler, L. (In preparation) The problem of women in four changing cultures. In M. Schwartz & D. Jordan (Eds.), *Festschrift for Melford Spiro*.

Spindler, L. (1978). Researching the psychology of culture change and urbanization. In G. Spindler (Ed.), *The making of psychological anthropology*. Berkeley: University of California Press. Paperback edition, 1980.

Spradley, J. P. (1979). *The ethnographic interview*. New York: Holt, Rinehart and Winston.

Spradley, J. P. (1980). *Participant observation*. New York: Holt, Rinehart and Winston.

Wolcott, H. (Ed.). (1983). Teaching fieldwork to educational researchers: A symposium. *Anthropology and Education Quarterly, 14*(3), 171–218.

The Author and His Chapter

Harry F. Wolcott is a professor of education and anthropology at the University of Oregon and received his Ph.D. degree at Stanford. George Spindler was his major professor. He has published four books, three of them in education and anthropology and the fourth on beer drinking. He is a major senior contributor to his discipline and is highly respected as a teacher and researcher. His first field research was with the Kwakiutl Indians of Alert Bay, British Columbia (*A Kwakiutl Village and School,* 1963). His most notable *The Man in the Principal's Office* (1973) was first published by Holt, Rinehart and Winston in the series edited by G. and L. Spindler, *Case Studies in Education and Culture*. MIPO, as the volume came to be known, is a classic ethnography in every sense and is without doubt the most exhaustive account of a school principal's behavior that has ever been written. It has recently been reprinted by Waveland Press (1984), and Wolcott reviews the reception of it in educationist circles in G. Spindler's edited volume, *Doing the Ethnography of Schooling* (1982, Holt, Rinehart and Winston).

Harry Wolcott has taught education graduate students (and others) how to do ethnography and has participated in panels and symposia in methods for many years. His chapter in this volume is partly the result of frustration over how to communicate what ethnography is, rather than what it is not. He concludes that ethnography must be cultural interpretation if it is anthropological and that it is not primarily a method or technique. The former conclusion is not surprising, coming from the mind of an American anthropologist, since our bias towards cultural rather than social-structural or even social-interactional models and interpretative frameworks is well known. The latter conclusion may be startling, for all of us teaching ethnographic methods courses or giving 5-day training sessions in ethnography to teachers seem quite concerned with how-to-do-it.

What Wolcott is saying is very important. It is what divides anthroethnography, at least, from journalistic reporting and naturalistic description, empathetic or otherwise. There are only so many ways to observe, and interview, and record, and collate data. To what one attends during field work and how one interprets the results make an ethnography. This position does make problems for us, to be sure, for we protest that we must do our fieldwork, at least in its early stages, with as little pre-bias as possible, and a cultural stance is a bias.

Fortunately for us, the concept of culture is freewheeling enough to allow us much latitude so that we can attend to a wide range of phenomena. Harry Wolcott's chapter, along with the others in Part I, educates us about what ethnography is and how it is done.

The Editors

3 On Ethnographic Intent

Harry F. Wolcott
University of Oregon

In May, 1981, I was invited to participate in a graduate student seminar hosted by the Department of Educational Administration at the University of Alberta. Our collective mission was to address issues of descriptive research. My assignment was to discuss ethnography.

The University Council for Educational Administration co-sponsored the seminar, and a summary of the sessions subsequently appeared in their newsletter, the *UCEA Review*. In reading that summary, I was reminded of an uneasy feeling I had experienced before and was conscious of during the seminar: here was another well-intentioned effort— on my part to inform educator colleagues about ethnographic research, on their part to become informed about it—that was going awry.

The sessions on ethnography were described as follows (Jefferson, 1981, p. 6):

> Ethnography was addressed in considerable depth, yet neither presenters nor participants were able to state clearly what an ethnography is. Instead, participants tended to fall into the trap of defining ethnography in the negative without really stating how an ethnographic study is distinguishable from other naturalistic inquiries explored through a qualitative methodology.

Although the conference reporter portrayed our failure to define ethnography as a general problem of the seminar in the summary just quoted, I appear culpable as the source of that problem in the more detailed report of the proceedings. Here is what was reported of my particular contribution (Jefferson, 1981, p. 6):

Wolcott described an ethnography by listing what it is not:

1. Ethnography is not field technique.
2. Ethnography is not length of time in the field.
3. Ethnography is not simply good description.
4. Ethnography is not created through gaining and maintaining rapport with subjects.

The only requirement that Wolcott placed on such research is that it must be oriented to cultural interpretation.

We had not been asked to prepare papers for the seminar. Thus, the words ascribed to me and quoted above were gleaned from a combination of brief introductory remarks and the ensuing dialogue. Subsequently, in reviewing my comments as summarized by someone else, I was satisfied that those were indeed the *ideas* I had hoped to convey, but, given another opportunity to express them, I would take greater care to insure that each point was made clearly and to portray ethnography for what it is as well as what it is not. I would like to take the opportunity here to elaborate on my so-succinctly reported comments and to draw attention to what I have come to call "ethnographic intent." I begin by reviewing the points listed above that discuss what ethnography is not.

WHAT ETHNOGRAPHY IS NOT

Ethnography Is Not Field Technique

More fully, I'd like to be on record as saying: *Field techniques in-and-of-themselves cannot an ethnography make.*

A researcher could conceivably use one major fieldwork technique (e.g., participant observation, interviewing), many techniques (the respectable multiinstrument approach or "triangulation") or every field technique ever used by ethnographers, and still not come up with an ethnographic study. True, one would have the stuff from which ethnography is constructed, but that is not much of a boast when ethnography is made of such everyday stuff.

Ethnography Is Not Length of Time in the Field

More fully, I'd like to be on record as saying: *Length of time spent doing fieldwork does not, in-and of-itself, result in "better" ethnography or in any way assure that the final product will be ethnographic.* Time is one of several "necessary but not sufficient" ingredients of ethnography: no sufficient ethnography without it, but no necessary ethnography with it. Based on any one researcher's skill, sensitivity, problem, and setting, optimum periods of fieldwork may vary as much as the circumstances for pursuing it.

If one can make a general observation about the duration of fieldwork in educational ethnography, it is that such research invariably is done in too short a time. Compared with psychometricians who may not actually visit schools or classrooms at all, our hours, days, or weeks of participant observation look respectable enough, but compared to our anthropological tribal elders—particularly the British social anthropologists who sometimes have devoted a major portion of their careers to working among only one "people"—our efforts pale. Yet even amongst educational ethnographers, I was privy to one long-term inquiry when researchers remained on site too long, faithfully satisfying contractual arrangements that failed to recognize that detachment is as important to the ethnographic process as is involvement (Wolcott, 1978; see also Powdermaker, 1966).

Although it is assumed that one will conduct fieldwork over a sufficient period of time to come to know the setting thoroughly, time itself is not the critical attribute. And although there is an unwritten consensus that one ought to remain in the field "at least a year," 12 months in a setting as complex as a contemporary school, even if one's focus is narrowed to a single student, teacher, or administrator, might still result in what has become known appropriately in educational research as "Blitzkrieg ethnography" (Rist, 1980).

Ethnography Is Not Simply Good Description

Those six words seem just right: *Ethnography is not simply good description.* I hope their meaning is clear. Good description can lead to good ethnography, but the good ethnographer is capable not only of good description but of recognizing what elements most warrant attention when ethnography, rather than a novel, a travelogue, molecular biology, or anything else that requires careful and detailed description, is the intended outcome. Some ethnographers perform descriptive obligations rather perfunctorily; more often, would-be ethnographers provide exquisite description but falter in the essential and related task of trying to make sense of what they have observed. Their error lies in the mistaken assumption that observation is scientifically "pure," something apart from scientists themselves, an idea referred to lightheartedly among descriptive researchers as the "doctrine of immaculate perception" (Beer, 1973, p. 49.)[1]

Would-be ethnographers also have the mistaken idea that description is a step that must be completed *before* one proceeds to the next step, analysis. In ethnography, however, data and interpretation evolve together, each informing the other. Additional data provide illustration, test the adequacy of the developing account, and suggest avenues for further inquiry. Fieldwork and interpretation go hand in hand as concurrent, rather than sequential, steps. Michael Agar describes this dialectic process in his informative monograph, *The Professional Stranger, An Informal Introduction to Ethnography* (Agar, 1980, p. 9):

> . . . Glaser and Strauss came up with the elegant statement that in ethnographic research, data collection and analysis are done concurrently rather than being separately scheduled parts of the research.
>
> In many sociological surveys, for example, a questionnaire is designed. Then interviewers go out and "collect the data." The data are then coded and keypunched. Only then does "analysis" begin, with the machine-readable data manipulated according to some statistical procedure. In ethnography . . . you learn something ("collect some data"), then you try to make sense out of it ("analysis"), then you go back and see if the interpretation makes sense in light of new experience ("collect more data"), then you refine your interpretation ("more analysis"), and so on. The process is dialectic, not linear. Such a simple statement, so important in capturing a key aspect of doing ethnography. An anthropologist should have said it long ago.

Even more important is the ethnographer's own sense—hopefully growing more acute as fieldwork continues—of what is relatively more

---

[1]Ethologist C. G. Beer refers to "pure observation" as the doctrine of immaculate perception in an essay entitled "A View of Birds":

There is a view of science that sees the bird watcher's kind of activity as the necessary first step in any field of scientific endeavor. According to Lorenz, "It is an inviolable law of inductive natural science that it has to *begin* with pure observation, totally devoid of any preconceived theory and even working hypothesis." This view has come under attack from philosophers of science such as Karl Popper, who have argued that preconceived theories or working hypotheses must always be involved in scientific observation to enable the scientist to decide what is to count as a fact of relevance to his investigation. I myself have been a critic of this "doctrine of immaculate perception." Each year my students hear why, for both logical and practical reasons, there can be no such thing as pure observation, even for a bird watcher (Beer, 1973, p. 49).

significant to be looking at and looking for in a particular setting. An ethnography is not a mere chronicle of events. As Charles Frake has explained (Frake, 1964, p. 112):

> To describe a culture . . . is not to recount the events of a society but to specify what one must know to make those events maximally probable. The problem is not to state what someone did but to specify the conditions under which it is culturally appropriate to anticipate that he, or persons occupying his role, will render an equivalent performance. This conception of a cultural description implies that an ethnography should be a theory of cultural behavior in a particular society. . . .

The ethnographer's task, as Frake describes it, focuses not on recounting events but on rendering a *theory of cultural behavior.* More recently Ward Goodenough has defined the ethnographic process as one of "attributing" a theory of collective behavior to members of a particular group:

> The culture of any society is made up of the concepts, beliefs, and principles of action and organization that an ethnographer has found could be attributed successfully to the members of that society in the context of his dealings with them (Goodenough, 1976, p. 5).

The idea that culture is "attributed" has proven helpful to me in understanding as well as in explaining ethnography. Culture is not lying about, waiting patiently to be discovered; rather, it must be *inferred* from the words and actions of members of the group under study and then literally *assigned* to that group by the anthropologist. "Culture" as such, as an *explicit* statement of how the members of a particular social group act and believe they should act, does not exist until someone acting in the role of ethnographer puts it there.

Each member of a group has a personal version ("theory," if you prefer) of how things work in that particular group, and thus of its culture or, more helpfully, its "micro-culture." Every society consists of myriad such groups, and everyone in that society needs a personal version of how things work in every one of its subgroups in which he or she has or seeks affiliation. Goodenough refers to these individual versions, these personal constellations of cultural knowledge, as *propriospects* (Goodenough, 1981, p. 111).

There is a difference between culture as perceived by any member of a group and culture as attributed to that same group by the ethnographer. The ethnographer attempts to make *explicit* and to portray in terms of social interaction among *many* individuals—thus the microculture of the entire group, the collected propriospects—what its various members know only *tacitly* and understand *individually.* Ethnographers are rightly accused of making the obvious obvious (or, more kindly, of making the familiar strange, cf. Erickson, 1984, p. 62; Spindler, 1982, p. 15) because, quite literally, their task is to describe what everybody already knows. The catch is, of course, that no one individual, ethnographer included, ever knows it all or understands it all. Ethnographers recognize that they do not have to describe it all, either.

Ethnography Is Not Created Through Gaining and Maintaining Rapport with Subjects

More to the point, I'd like to be on record as stating: *Not even the capacity to conduct oneself brilliantly during the course of fieldwork— with all due concern for building trust, respecting confidences, being privy to people's innermost beliefs and practices, and in every way conducting oneself so that future researchers may further the investigations—necessarily leads to or assures successful ethnography.*

As a matter of fact, the opposite is probably more often the case. Ethnographers who are arrogant, self-serving, and self-centered; who are abominable fieldworkers; who work with seeming disregard for either their colleagues or their "people"; and who have violated a host of ethical canons—sometimes have produced satisfactory ethnographic accounts, whereas other ethnographers (or would-be ethnographers) have been overcome by humanitarian, ethical, and personal considerations that effectively prevented them from ever producing the accounts that everyone encouraged and expected them to write.

Ultimately there is only one test of ethnography: the satisfactoriness of the completed account. We cannot review, critique, cite, or build intellectually upon good intentions or hard-won rapport. There is nothing about ethnography that precludes anyone from acting as a thoughtful, compassionate human being. Commendable as such behavior may be, however, it is neither a prerequisite nor a substitute for ethnography. If you know many ethnographers, you know there are few saints among them!

WHAT ETHNOGRAPHY IS

Recall that the summary of my remarks about ethnography listed points describing what ethnography is not, and concluded with a brief statement treated as though it, too, was part of the trap I had fallen into by defining ethnography in negative terms: "The only requirement that Wolcott placed on such research is that it must be oriented to cultural interpretation."

Happily, that is exactly the idea I hoped to convey: The purpose of ethnographic research is to describe and interpret cultural behavior. The statement is neither negative nor incidental. My tactical error during the seminar was that I did not make that declaration forcefully enough nor often enough, and I did not underscore how it gives a sense of direction to the whole ethnographic endeavor. Quite frankly, prior to the seminar and newsletter feedback, I had not fully realized the implications of how this crux of ethnographic research, the critical attribute that distinguishes it from other qualitative approaches, is taken for granted among anthropologists yet remains virtually unrecognized among nonanthropologically-oriented educational researchers.

This latter statement is far more important than any of the points discussed previously or, for that matter, all of them put together. And any list that begins "Ethnography is not . . ." could be expanded to eight, a dozen, or any number of such negations: Ethnography is not empathy; ethnography is not merely first-person accounting or "Being There"; ethnography is not new-found respect for another culture; ethnography is not "a day in the life"; ethnography is not role study; and so on— although all these may be among its ingredients. If words spoken could appear in neon lights or pyrotechnic displays, my statement would brighten the sky with carefully chosen words: *The purpose of ethnographic research is to describe and interpret cultural behavior.*

Notice that I have eliminated "only" and "requirement" from the statement as originally paraphrased. Cultural interpretation not a "requirement," it is the essence of the ethnographic endeavor. When that concern for cultural interpretation is not evident in an observer's account—either explicitly, through a self-conscious examination of human social behavior and a corresponding effort to "attribute" culture to a group, or at least implicitly, as evidenced by what the observer has selected to observe, report, and discuss—then the account is *not* ethnographic, regardless of how adequate, sensitive, thorough, or insightful it may be. And its "ethnographicness" is not enhanced simply by noting that the researcher borrowed some fieldwork techniques used by ethnographers, spent unduly long at the field site, provided carefully-detailed description, maintained a high level of rapport, or came to a profound appreciation for some other group's resolution of its human problems.

It has been dismaying in recent years to watch educational researchers affix the label "ethnography" to virtually any endeavor at descriptive research. My own position is that the label should be reserved for descriptive efforts clearly ethnographic *in intent*. There are numerous other broad, inclusive terms we can employ to refer to work that is not ethnographic in intent, and care should be given to selecting a broad "generic" label or one that accurately portrays a particular research approach or strategy from among such terms as on-site research, naturalistic research, participant observation study, non-participant observation study, descriptive research, qualitative research, case study, or field study. (See Wolcott, 1982a for a discussion of strategies that share similarities with ethnography without assuming cultural interpretation as the outcome.)

The Ethnographer in Each of Us

In this zealous effort to identify the essence of ethnography, I hope I do not create the impression that it is either so simple that anyone can do it or so esoteric that it can be done only by a chosen few who have already proven themselves. There is something of the perceptive ethnographer in each of us. "The trick in everyday life, as in history or in ethnography," Frake observes, "is to sort out those strands, and discover those events, that have crucial significance for coping with the present situation and anticipating its outcomes" (Frake, 1980, p. 67).

Although few ascribe to the formal role of ethnographer, each of us must succeed as intuitive participant and observer for sheer survival in a social milieu. Each of us must figure out how to cope with the world we encounter, the unexpected as well as the expected.

In our everyday lives personal routines fit like an old glove: we do not have to think about proper forms of address, whether to go to work, how much toothpaste to squeeze out, how much of what to pour or to serve for breakfast, or where to stand or look while talking to another member of the group. Finding ourselves in a new setting, we momentarily become more attentive while we figure out what is expected (and perhaps discern what we can get away with), comforted by the concomitant expectation that those already familiar with a setting may be briefly forgiving while the newcomer learns the ropes. We will be reminded, perhaps gently at first, that this is a setting where we are (or are not) expected to wear a hat, make eye contact, take a larger (smaller) helping than we would prefer, initiate a conversation, or call so many (or few) meetings. We may make some of our newfound knowledge explicit—perhaps by asking "informed" questions or by explaining how things work to someone less experienced than ourselves. How quickly we once became know-it-alls on the school playground, just as today we quickly become "oldtimers" at the baggage claim area, informing others of what we ourselves learned only moments before. For the most part, however, we acquire and demonstrate newfound competence the way we always have, almost totally out-of-consciousness.

Some people display a knack for understanding—or at least for being able to explain to neophytes—how things work in a particular social system. Just as ethnographers seek out such individuals as informants, we ourselves seek them out in everyday life as sources of help and insight. They are "intuitive" ethnographers in terms of the ability to observe, understand, and enlighten. Properly schooled in fieldwork traditions and in ethnographic writing, they conceivably could become ethnographers of their own people, just as they could become historians, novelists, or teachers.

They will not become ethnographers, however, unless their overriding preoccupation is for discerning cultural patterning in the behavior they observe. To accomplish that, they must also engage in a second and related activity, an ongoing dialogue dealing with the nature of culture itself. Thus they need to concern themselves not only with "recounting events" but with how one discerns what qualifies as something of collective social significance as contrasted with the purely idiosyncratic, with personality, with biological determinants and predispositions, and so on. They need constantly to probe the dimensions of culture even as they use the concept to guide their observations and their analyses.

The Culture Concept

It is the absence of self-conscious reflection about the nature of culture that bothers me in reading most educational research of supposed ethnographic orientation. Not that I expect—or ever want—someone to provide the definitive statement of precisely what culture entails, but our gonzo-ethnographers never seem to agonize over (or even acknowledge) how their "working resolution" of what constitutes culture is critical to what they look at, what they look for, and how they are trying to make sense of it.

So basic an issue as whether one is inclined toward the view that culture is best revealed in what people *do*, what they *say* (and *say they do*), or some uneasy tension between what they *really do* and what they *say they ought to do*, poses different strategies for data gathering: whether, for example, one is going to give more credibility to one's skills as participant observer, to words of informants gleaned through one's skill as interviewer, or through some blend of these two seemingly similar but deceptively different ways of pursuing fieldwork. This is why experienced ethnographers are elusive when confronted with straightforward questions such as, "Just tell me what it is that you actually *do* when you are doing ethnographic research" or "What is the first thing an ethnographer does, then the next, and the next?" About all one can say is "You have a look around to get a 'feel' for the setting and the people in it." As often, the answer is simply, "It depends." Ethnography can be talked about in the abstract, but it is not practiced that way. Making the ethnographic process explicit is almost as difficult as making culture explicit.

One of the awkward things about hooking one's career with ethnography (and thus with anthropology more generally) is that its core concept—

culture—is itself intriguing but elusive, all-encompassing yet conceptually weak (for a recent critique see, for example, Wuthnow, Hunter, Bergesen, and Kurzweil, 1984). I have heard some anthropologists deny that the concept holds or even warrants a place in contemporary anthropological thought, but for myself I am sore pressed to contemplate an anthropology without it. Yet when one envisions the intellectual leap from the difficult-enough task of observing and recording behavior in everyday settings to the lofty and even arrogant business of proposing statements about implicit, underlying, mutually-understood-yet-never-examined assumptions and expectations that guide behavior (or even "determine" it—and here again, one's perception of culture's influence in shaping our interactions becomes critical), we realize not only the difficulty of instructing others in how we go about ethnography but also the absolute necessity of involving them in the dialogue of what "culture" is all about.

DOING ETHNOGRAPHY

In a graduate course that I offer entitled "Ethnographic Research in Education," I set for my students the impossible task of "doing" ethnography within the time constraints of an 11-week term. Their assignment includes identifying an informant or setting, completing a series of interviews and exercises in participant observation, and submitting a final paper that transcends these individual field reports and at least points the way toward the development of a full-blown ethnography. The charge I give to help orient them is to try to identify common patterns that seem to account for a large portion of the behavior they have observed or that seem unduly to preoccupy informants' discussions. The relationship of individual to family, the importance attached to reputation, the measures of and routes to success, the nature of external forces that can threaten or smile on one, the qualities admired or feared in others, all offer clues to underlying world views revealing of culture.

The very label one chooses to describe these patterns or preoccupations tends to shape one's search and subsequent analysis. Agar refers to them straightforwardly as "key concerns" (Agar, 1980, p. 164). In my own fieldwork and teaching, the term "themes" has proven useful. It couples nicely with culture to suggest "cultural themes." Although the idea of themes is not used widely by anthropologists (it was introduced in the 1940s by Morris Opler but seems not to have captured the anthropological imagination), neither has it been burdened with definition from other social sciences (see Opler, 1945).

Goodenough's term "standards"—standards for "perceiving, believing, evaluating, and acting" (Goodenough, 1981, p. 110)—provides another organizer, a particularly useful one when informants express their views in terms of what they and others *should* or *should not* do. Educators are inclined toward such proclamations (e.g., "Principals should be instructional leaders," "Teachers should be careful spellers," "Children have a right to read" [although apparently no equivalent right *not* to read]), language highly revealing of the way things are *supposed* to be, the ideal if not necessarily the real.

There are other terms that seem as though they should serve but in practice do not. The concept of "values" is so linked to personal preferences that it is hard to keep students from imposing their own values and value hierarchies on their informants. "Expectations" invite outlining at a level of detail that obscures rather than reveals underlying themes. "Cultural postulates" or "ideological premises" may seem a bit pretentious at the outset, although they do set one on a proper course toward cultural interpretation. "Rules," in the sense of tacit guidelines for social behavior (for example, as Sue Estroff has used them in *Making It Crazy,* 1981), provide another way to identify culture in process. However, my experience has been that students tend to lose sight of the distinction between implicit and explicit rules. They set out to identify tacit guidelines but find themselves listing "laws" and "commandments" instead, in the process also forgetting that it is not usually the breaking of rules (like speeding or being late to work or class) that is of concern, but rather the consequence of being caught at breaking them.

Given the impossibly short duration of time for "fieldwork" in a one-term class, I have found another way to optimize (although not guarantee) the possibility that my students will observe and interpret behavior for its cultural dimensions. Virtually all behavior is influenced by culture, of course, but I want culture to jump out at my students the way it did for ethnographers when anthropology was in its infancy and locating an exotic tribe of one's own was the marching order of the day. I insist that my Americanized students locate an informant from a "dramatically different" society (they may not select a fellow student from overseas, although foreign spouses of overseas students who are not students themselves are okay) or locate a cultural setting or "scene" dramatically different from their previous experience (thus, a class in karate might be acceptable, but a jazzercise, pottery-making, or figure drawing class probably is not). Conversely, my foreign students are welcome to select an American individual or family as informants, or an American cultural scene (a local sorority or co-op, a church group of a different denomination from their native one).

Ethnography Versus Role Study

Students with prior coursework in cultural anthropology or extensive reading in ethnography often have some idea of an individual or a setting they would like to study and are off-and-running as soon as they realize that the essential requirement of the course is to produce a "beginning ethnography." Others are baffled by the vagueness of the task: They don't want to begin until they have a clear sense of where it all is supposed to lead. Still others become annoyed because they came prepared to try their ethnographic wings (perhaps even to test an idea for a dissertation study) but can hardly believe that the author of *The Man in the Principal's Office: An Ethnography* (Wolcott, 1984a) will not allow them to go to a nearby school district—or the one back home—to "shadow" another teacher, principal, or superintendent. As soon as I make culture the critical attribute, they become disoriented. They had understood ethnography to be role study.

Role studies are something that educators and sociologists do so well that ethnographers don't have to join the effort. I doubt that my study of the principalship is of help to students confused about the difference between ethnography and role study, since it is so role-oriented in conception. Conducted as it was under the auspices of the Center for the Advanced Study of Educational Administration, it had to be oriented that way to warrant institutional sponsorship. However, I do think the study provides an adequate model of thoroughness in moving from data to analysis, and, at least in its closing chapters, in providing a modest example of cultural interpretation.[2]

Interviewing an Informant

For students who remain troubled with how to proceed, I can offer a bit more advice based on personal experience as well as the collected wisdom of others who teach fieldwork to educational researchers.[3] I suggest that they work with one or a small number of informants through a series of semistructured interviews. Interviewing an informant has proven to be an excellent starting place for beginning an ethnography. As each interview is completed and transcribed (no small task, it turns out), the researcher begins to accumulate a respectable amount of tangible "data," recorded in informants' own words and amenable to searching and sorting for themes. There is no better way to start this process than by letting people tell their personal "story" to an interested listener.

---

[2]I have discussed the problem of the book as a model for ethnography in a separate article, "Mirrors, Models, and Monitors: Educator Adaptations of the Ethnographic Innovation," Wolcott, 1982b.

[3]See the Fall, 1983 issue of the *Anthropology and Education Quarterly,* Volume 14, Number 3, devoted to the special topic and a bibliography on "Teaching Fieldwork to Educational Researchers." Recent and useful texts on fieldwork include Agar (1980) and Whyte (1984); for applications in educational research, see also Goetz and LeCompte (1984).

Clifford Geertz refers to the process as "the power of the scientific imagination to bring us into touch with the lives of strangers" (Geertz, 1973, p. 16). It is my personal conviction that every human has a story to tell—if a right person comes along to ask and to listen sympathetically.

And what story to ask? Michael Agar suggests two approaches to get the interview process started (Agar, 1980; see also Langness and Frank, 1981); my students find both approaches helpful and seem to move back and forth between the two rather than follow either one exclusively. One approach is to invite informants to tell their life story, with each newly introduced person or event providing the perceptive interviewer a possible topic for future elaboration. The other approach is to ask informants to recount the events of their daily lives and routines. Again, each event offers a point of potential elaboration as the ethnographer probes for underlying themes and patterns. Both approaches provide access and beckon us to view our subjects as people, rather than people as our subjects: to recognize that people live fully contextualized lives in which one is a human being all the time, but a student, or teacher, or administrator only part of the time—and not necessarily the time of one's most interesting or fulfilling moments.

In fieldwork conducted through the years I sometimes have relied more heavily on interviewing, sometimes on participant observation. (I never would want the two in perfect balance; one or the other ought to be the preferred mode for any specific research project as meanings or actions compete for the ethnographer's closest attention.) I encourage students to emphasize whichever of the two approaches, interviewing or observing, "feels right." But for students who lack any intuitive sense of how best to proceed, I point to Michael Agar's bias in favor of interviewing as the primary research activity. Subsequent opportunities for participant observation can serve to check perceptions and to suggest topics to explore indepth during interviews.

Given the time constraints of a term, most students find that their efforts focus on a limited number of interviews with *one* informant. To round out the experience I urge them to join their informant(s) in some activity that might allow them to experience the participant observer role, but that effort frequently proves to be another interview instead, albeit an informal one.

Small Ns and Big Generalizations

Sample size has never been a problem for me: anthropologists ordinarily work with one of whatever they study: one informant (thus, a "key" informant like *Sun Chief*), one family (*Children of Sanchez*), one tribe or clan (*The People of Gilford*), one village (*Life in Lesu*), one society (*We, the Tikopia*). But with our intentionally small Ns, we do confront a critical problem: How do you work with one informant (or family, or tribe) and still manage to move toward *cultural* interpretation?

Knowingly I take the risk that my students will indulge in cultural stereotyping. Abhorrent as that notion has come to be in our newfound and self-conscious pluralism, stereotyping also happens to be the business we all *must* engage in if we are ever to generalize about the expectations or standards that categories of other people hold for us. Ethnographers must engage explicitly in cultural stereotyping if there is to be ethnography.

If the truth be known, ethnographers, like the rest of us, make whopping generalizations from rather modest observations of a few cases. Their forte lies in knowing those cases exceedingly well and in recognizing a critical distinction between generalizing and overgeneralizing (cf. Goodenough, 1981, p. 102), but limits of time preclude my students (like some educational ethnographers) from attaining sufficient information to recognize what degree of generalizing or stereotyping is warranted. The resolution I suggest is that students endeavor to catch themselves in the act of generalizing and stereotyping, and thus to couch their accounts with appropriate tentativeness, rather than allow me to catch them at it with unkind comments scribbled in the margins of their papers. Two cautions seem to help. The first is to stay rather close to what one has actually observed or heard, and to posit how culture *may* be reflected in that behavior, rather than flatfootedly to equate observed behavior with "culture in action." Here again is an opportunity for the reminder that culture is never observed directly; it can only be inferred.

The second caution is to regard and present one's work as the modest *beginning* of an ethnography. Originally I referred to these class projects as "mini-ethnographies," but a student convinced me how much more helpful it was to represent the work as in its *early stages* rather than merely as modest in scope. Ethnographers employ these same caveats, and for good reason. Because of the very processes of human social life that it claims to reveal, ethnography never can be more than partial and incomplete. Even accounts that enjoy a brief moment as definitive works portray at best only part of the total way of life they profess to depict.

Maximizing Differences

Requiring my students to select informants or scenes from societies radically different from their own is a relatively recent condition that I have imposed on the assignment. I imposed it to enhance the likelihood that the differences students identify will be associated with aspects of culture at a national or *macro*cultural level rather than at a *micro*cultural one (cf. Goodenough, 1976), at differences of the magnitude of whole belief systems rather than minor, within-culture variations among teachers in adjacent classrooms or principals in neighboring schools. On a grander scale, that same argument has obtained in the strongly voiced preference for having anthropology (and "anthropology and education") students do their first major fieldwork—typically the dissertation study—in a distant society, or at least with a dramatically different microculture (e.g., migrant workers, gypsies, an ethnic minority, a religious sect) rather than in the all-too-familiar "culture" of the school or classroom.

That raises another of the issues that make school ethnography so difficult and even so unlikely. The people interested in doing it are, for the most part, individuals who have invested virtually their entire lives in school, first as students, then as students of the teaching process, and finally as professional educators. Being so totally immersed in and committed to formal education, they are as likely to "discover" school culture as Kluckhohn's proverbial fish are likely to discover water. The cross-cultural and comparative basis that helps ethnographers identify something they are tentatively willing to describe as culture in someone else's behavior—because it is readily distinguishable from their own—is lacking. These hopelessly enculturated insiders accept as natural and proper the very things an ethnographer from another society—or even an ethnographer from our own society not so totally familiar with schools—might want to question.

Why, for example, do educational administrators have "offices," and usually "front offices" at that? Why do school desk heights change in recognition of physical maturing but door knob heights remain always the same? Why does it seem "natural" that school should be held Monday through Friday, but that school convened on Saturday or Sunday is limited to religious, extracurricular, or punitive reasons? Why are teachers expected to do their preparations in public, rather than in private as administrators (and professors) do? Why are teachers customarily expected to remain after school to do their work and chastised if they try to do that same work in an equivalent period of time before school? How does higher status, or the authority to conduct evaluations, come to be in the hands of people who do not have classroom responsibility? If evaluation is so critical to the educational enterprise (and how have we come to that position?), who evaluates the educational evaluators?

There are clues to educator subculture and to its broader cultural context in the interpretations we might offer for such observations. For example, we make things convenient for children, who attend school fleetingly, as long as we do not inconvenience the adults who inhabit these same schools year after year. Conversely, because we remain unsure how to judge the *quality* of teacher performance, we like to have teachers work where at least we can judge *quantity* (i.e., time). And classroom teachers are far too busy evaluating and adjusting their teaching, and too aware of their own vulnerability, to be preoccupied with systematically measuring and criticizing the performance of their colleagues.

ETHNOGRAPHY IN EDUCATIONAL RESEARCH

The problems inherent in ethnography are not unique to doing ethnography in schools and they are not insurmountable, but they do need to be recognized and addressed. For example, the disadvantages of being an insider, totally familiar with and at home in schools, may be more than compensated for by the understanding a perceptive insider can bring; the same argument is profferred by persons who hold memberships in other groups and wish to study their own people, on the grounds that insiders best understand the total complexity of a system. Some educators have proven astute at identifying pervasive themes, at recognizing cultural influences in their lives, and at analyzing their own professional expectations and their basis for holding them. There are some intuitive as well as some trained ethnographers in their ranks, and many have given attention to the systematic study of anthropology, including voracious reading of ethnography. They comprise a cadre competent to conduct ethnographic research in educational settings and to guide others who would like to pursue that approach. A number of committed educational anthropologists have found opportunities to do cross-cultural fieldwork in addition to turning their attention to schools and educational processes in their own society.

There is still another reason for touting the role and potential of ethnography in educational research with caution. A critical question is: Who really needs it?

Good, solid ethnographic accounts do the very thing they promise. They help us understand how particular social systems work by providing detailed descriptive information, coupled with interpretation, and relating that working to implicit patterns and meanings which members of that society (or one of its subgroups) hold more or less in common. But such accounts do not contain the basis for judging systems to be good or bad, effective or ineffective, except as people within the group being studied express those judgments or reveal frustration in achieving their own purposes, or as the people conducting studies impose judgments of their own. In and of themselves, ethnographic studies do not point the way to how things can or ought to be improved.

For the most part, the kind of information that ethnography is *not* well suited to provide is the kind of help educators most often seek; educational ethnography usually is undertaken with educator preoccupation for improvement (or at least "change") in mind. To paraphrase the late Solon T. Kimball, most so-called educational research is really educational reform in disguise. The ethnographic goal of understanding another way of life is not sufficient for the reform-oriented educator who expects "understanding" to be linked with efforts at improvement. The educator typically wants to swing into action at that very point where the ethnographer may regard his or her work as finished. To the ethnographer's careful rendering of the status quo, a critical insider rightfully may be expected to react, "Of course that is how we do it, but, so what?"

Educators have their own "good customs." The system works; they understand it, at least implicitly; they know how to get their tasks accomplished. For the most part, in managing their daily rounds busy teachers and administrators really *need* studies of school culture (and school roles) about as much as busy Puerto Ricans or Kwakiutl or Japanese *need* studies of their cultures. In that sense, traditional ethnography has been and remains largely "academic" in nature and intent, providing modest increments in our efforts to understand human social life but not providing a basis for discerning what humans should do differently or better. Nevertheless, studies of all these groups, schools included, do exist. Under the very eyes of critics who claim they are still waiting to see it, a substantial literature devoted to the ethnography of schooling, as well as to education more broadly conceived, has been accumulating for years. More encouraging still, anthropologists are reporting successful collaborative efforts in helping educators address pressing problems in ethnographically informed ways (see, for example, Schensul and Eddy, 1985).

Most so-called school ethnography, however, is really quick description (not to be confused with "thick description"), the purpose of which is to reveal weaknesses, point out needs, or otherwise pave the way for change and reform efforts already underway. It is, at best, *ad hoc,* pragmatic, utilitarian ethnography designed to gather evidence rather than to gain understanding. It reveals far more of the educator commitment to what is *possible* (an important aspect of educator world view, I might note), than to the ethnographer's painstaking efforts to document— and even to "respect," in the sense of deferring judgment—what already is.

For years I have been cautioning and urging educational researchers whose purposes transcend (or subjugate, depending on one's point of view) ethnography to recognize and to state forthrightly whenever they are merely *borrowing ethnographic techniques* to accomplish purposes other than those of "pure" ethnographers (see, for example, Wolcott 1975, 1980, 1981, 1984b).[4] In most such endeavors educators are not *doing ethnography* because they do not seek or intend to employ cultural interpretation; rather, they are linking descriptive research to short-term efforts at change and improvement.

By insisting on the distinction between borrowing ethnographic techniques and doing ethnography, I hope that those true ethnographers of education—fewer in number, but with a contribution of their own to make—can continue with the essentially "academic" pursuit of attributing culture both to the smaller social units of immediate concern to professional educators—students at school, teachers in classrooms, administrators of school systems—and to the macro-systems in which they are embedded. Not everybody in education needs to go seeking after culture, but we cannot hope to achieve a full or balanced understanding of what we are up to or how we are going about it if the cultural dimensions of human behavior are ignored or obscured because of our own traditional and psychologically dominated "ways of looking."

Anthropology's major contribution to education in the 3 decades since George Spindler first convened a conference of anthropologists and educators to discuss their common problems (Spindler, 1955) has been a recognition (beginning with a tolerance, expanding in the 70s to an almost too wholehearted embrace) of the contribution of qualitative/descriptive research to a well-rounded educational methodology. I think it is time for anthropologists to take a next step and suggest (with caution at first; more boldly later) that to the ethnographer *method itself is not all that important*: never was, never will be. What ethnographers strive for is to "get it right," and in the long run the elusive "it" of determining in any particular social setting just what constitutes the cultural dimensions of behavior creates more difficulty than the also-elusive rightness of the account.

Ethnographic research does not provide the comforting underpinnings of acceptable levels of significance, adequate rates of return, or Ns sufficient to assure that a value greater than "0" will appear in every box on a matrix. But ethnography comes closer than any other research strategy to explain, for example, why Ed Bell, the key figure in my

---

[4]Apparently I have overdone it a bit: In some circles of educational ethnographers I am known as "Harry the Pure." But at least I (and others of like mind) have been heard, and I believe that educational researchers—doctoral students in particular—boast more frequently and with confidence that they are drawing upon ethnographic techniques in conducting their work where their predecessors felt some misgivings about the claim that they were "doing ethnography." The immodest number of citations to my own writing is intended to identify other articles in which I have elaborated upon aspects of this distinction in my quest to preserve ethnographic purity.

ethnography of the principalship, could rail against having to see that the custodian chased a dog off the school playground or to tracking down which second-grader ate someone else's sandwich during morning recess, yet obligingly went ahead to handle these tasks lest he be accused of failing to perform satisfactorily as an educational administrator. A commitment to cultural interpretation invites (and implores) us to take a broad look at the behavior we are observing and to examine that behavior in its social context. Without attempting to predict, to record, or to recount all the possible "events" of the minisociety of a suburban elementary school, we pretty well know how we expect a proper principal (or teacher, or pupil, or even parent) to act. Organizing and presenting that information explicitly—searching out the "shoulds" and "oughts," the ideals and realities, the satisfactions, contradictions, and paradoxes—is the ethnographer's task. That principals, like other educators, talk about their role as they wish it to be but accept it as it really is, provides more of that "stuff" out of which ethnography is made. Understanding of that sort is unlikely to make principals "better," although conceivably it could make some of them wiser. That is purpose enough.

Let educational researchers of other persuasions do the counting and measuring they do so well. Ethnographers have their commitment and their unique contribution to make within the educational community. That commitment is not to technique per se, to time in the field, to providing "pure" or "complete" description, to gaining rapport, nor to a host of other procedural aspects of fieldwork: it is to cultural interpretation. And the contribution is in helping educators better understand both the little traditions of schools and the big traditions of the larger society. Granted, not all educators seek that kind of understanding, but many do. Education's would-be movers and shakers would be well advised to pay culture more heed if they are ever to fathom how schools remain so remarkably the same in spite of persistent and well-intended efforts to change them.

ACKNOWLEDGMENTS

The earliest version of this article was presented as an invited talk at the Third Annual "Ethnography in Education" Forum, University of Pennsylvania, 21 March 1982. Special appreciation is extended to David M. Smith who extended the original invitation and, with Richard K. Blot, urged me to develop informal comments into a formal article. Subsequently, Emil Haller helped me revise and abridge the article for inclusion in a symposium on research methods that appeared in *Educational Administration Quarterly*, Volume 21, No. 3 (Summer 1985), pp. 187–203.

In *essence* this is the *EAQ* article, but it appears here in its unabridged (and more recently revised) form and intended style.

REFERENCES

Agar, M. H. (1980). *The professional stranger: An informal introduction to ethnography.* New York: Academic Press.

Beer, C. G. (1973). A view of birds. In A. D. Pick (Ed.) *Minnesota Symposia on Child Psychology* (Volume 7, pp. 47–86). Minneapolis: University of Minnesota Press.

Erickson, F. (1984). What makes school ethnography 'ethnographic'? *Anthropology and Education Quarterly, 15*(1), 51–66. (Revised and reprinted from its original publication in the *Council on Anthropology and Education Newsletter,* 1973, *2,* 10–19.)

Estroff, S. E. (1981). *Making it crazy: An ethnography of psychiatric clients in an American community.* Berkeley: University of California Press.

Frake, C. O. (1964). A structural description of Subanun 'religious behavior.' In W. H. Goodenough (Ed.), *Explorations in cultural anthropology.* New York: McGraw-Hill.

Frake, C. O. (1980). Interpretations of illness: An ethnographic perspective on events and their causes. In Anwar S. Dil (Ed.), *Language and cultural description: Essays by Charles O. Frake* (pp. 61–82). Stanford, CA: Stanford University Press.

Geertz, C. (1973). Thick description: Toward an interpretive theory of culture. In Clifford Geertz (Ed.), *The interpretation of cultures.* New York: Basic Books.

Goetz, J.P., & LeCompte, M.D. (1984). *Ethnography and qualitative design in educational research.* Orlando, FL: Academic Press.

Goodenough, W. H. (1976). Multiculturalism as the normal human experience. *Anthropology and Education Quarterly, 7*(4), 4–7.

Goodenough, W. H. (1981). *Culture, language, and society.* Menlo Park, CA: Benjamin/ Cummings.

Jefferson, A. L. (1981). Qualitative research: Implications for educational administration. A conference report. *UCEA Review, 14*(3), 5–6. University Council for Educational Administration.

Langness, L. L., & Frank, G. (1981). *Lives: An anthropological approach to biography.* Novato, CA: Chandler and Sharp.

Opler, M. (1945). Themes as dynamic forces in culture. *American Journal of Sociology, 51,* 198–206.

Powdermaker, H. (1966). *Stranger and friend: The way of an anthropologist.* New York: W. W. Norton.

Rist, R. C. (1980). Blitzkrieg ethnography: On the transformation of a method into a movement. *Educational Researcher, 9*(2), 8–10.

Schensul, J. J., & Eddy, E. M. (Eds.). (1985). Applied educational anthropology. Special Issue, *Anthropology and Education Quarterly, 16*(2), Summer.

Spindler, G. (Ed.) (1955). *Education and anthropology.* Stanford, CA: Stanford University Press.

Spindler, G. (1982). *Doing the ethnography of schooling: Educational anthropology in action.* New York: Holt, Rinehart and Winston.

Whyte, W. F. (1984). *Learning from the field: A guide from experience.* Beverly Hills, CA: Sage Publications.

Wolcott, H. F. (1975). Criteria for an ethnographic approach to research in schools. *Human Organization, 34*(2), 111–127.

Wolcott, H. F. (1978). Small town America in ethnographic perspective: An introduction. *Rural Sociology, 43*(2), 159–163.

Wolcott, H. F. (1980). How to look like an anthropologist without being one. *Practicing Anthropology, 3*(1), 6–7, 56–59.

Wolcott, H. F. (1981). Confessions of a "trained" observer. In T. S. Popkewitz & B. R. Tabachnick (Eds.), *Field-based methodologies in educational research and evaluation* (pp. 247–263). New York: Praeger.

Wolcott, H. F. (1982a). Differing styles of on-site research, or, "If it isn't ethnography, what is it?" *Review Journal of Philosophy and Social Science, 7*(1), 2), 154–169. (Special issue on Naturalistic Research Paradigms.)

Wolcott, H. F. (1982b). Mirrors, models, and monitors: Educator adaptations of the ethnographic innovation. In G. Spindler (Ed.), *Doing the ethnography of schooling: Educational anthropology in action* (pp. 68–95). New York: Holt, Rinehart and Winston.

Wolcott, H. F. (1984a). *The man in the principal's office: An ethnography.* Prospect Heights, IL: Waveland Press. (Original work published in 1973).

Wolcott, H. F. (1984b). Ethnographers sans ethnography. In D. M. Fetterman (Ed.), *Ethnography in educational evaluation* (pp. 177–210). Beverly Hills, CA: Sage.

Wuthnow, R., Hunter, J. D., Bergesen, A., & Kurzweil, E. (1984). *Cultural analysis: The work of Peter L. Berger, Mary Douglas, Michel Foucault, and Jurgen Habermas.* London: Routledge and Kegan Paul.

The Author and His Chapter

Paul David Yates is a lecturer in education at the University of Sussex, United Kingdom, and received his doctorate in 1981 for ethnographic work on a high school and its local Asian population in an English town. This led to the development of his central interests in socialization and schooling, and how these can be described within a broad theory of culture.

In the following chapter he, like others in Part I, tells us what he thinks ethnography is and does. The fact that what he says is entirely understandable, and that we resonate to his prescriptions and caveats, suggests that ethnography as a method and a stance transcends national boundaries and that it is not so exclusively an American product, in its application to education, as to vitiate its cross-cultural relevance and utility.

Paul Yates' analysis of ethnography and its functions is particularly meaningful to us because schools and communities in the United Kingdom face problems very similar to those we face in the United States. "Merry Old England" is today a bustling multicultural society with new as well as established immigrants from countries and places that also furnish migrants to the United States. And in both societies those culturally deviant from the mainstream are viewed with ambivalence, at least, and often with open hostility.

Yates argues for a cross-cultural, comparative approach in the analysis of multicultural relations as a basis for ameliorative measures for problems that schools encounter in adapting to the needs of culturally differentiated minorities. And he supports ethnography as a particularly appropriate method for this analysis.

His chapter is marked by a concern for the underpinnings of ethnographic method in theory and in the philosophy of science. His deliberations should contribute to the maturation of the ethnographic approach.

The Editors

4 Figure and Section: Ethnography and Education in the Multicultural State*

Paul David Yates
University of Sussex, England

> *As an uneven mirror distorts the rays of objects according to its own figure and section, so the mind in forming its notions mixes up its own nature with the nature of things.*
> —Francis Bacon, 1620

There are two objectives I hope to achieve in what follows. First, and this is my major task, I shall describe the nature and methodology of ethnography in educational research. Second, I suggest a possible shift in emphasis which might bring the ethnography of education more firmly into the ambit of multiculturalism.

I begin with a discussion of what sort of thing ethnography is. This is followed by a review of some of the methods and methodologies associated with it. An analysis of some recent work on the perennial epistemological problems associated with the production and validation of ethnographies, provides the final part of the first section. This latter discussion focuses on the question of how the ethnographer stands in relation to the potential field of knowledge.

The second section is more speculative and begins by noting the dominance of sociology in educational ethnography in the U. K. compared to the vigorous anthropology of education in America. This may partly explain the relative lack of interest amongst U. K. ethnographers in

*This chapter was originally published in S. J. Ball (Ed.), *Comprehensive Schooling: A Reader.* Lewes: Falmer Press, 1984. Reprinted by permission.

the description and analysis of cultural groups within the educational sphere. Finally, I suggest the role an ethnography of cultural groups might assume in providing necessary knowledge of ways of life and thought, and crucially, of contributing to an adequate theory of culture on which our multicultural education can be based.

WHAT IS ETHNOGRAPHY?

Ethnography is the study of the world of a people. In the introduction to a recent book on ethnography and education, Woods suggests, "teaching" and "learning" may be "fronts"—dramatic activities designed to cover more significant ones, or merely one kind of activity, and not necessarily the most important, among many (Woods, 1980, p. 9). Similarly, Williamson in a text on the comparative sociology of education suggests that,

> In fact, the classroom and the lessons are perhaps the least significant aspects of school learning, of far greater importance are the great public routines of the school, the ceremonies, symbols and rituals of the school's corporate life. (Williamson, 1979, 6)

Both of these statements point to the signal feature of the ethnographic perspective, that is a willingness to look again at existing categories and emphases which explain educational phenomena, and to re-categorize and re-conceptualize the field of study. This broadens our understanding of our own position in the process of education, and increases our facility for productive action. This is the value of ethnography.

The ethnographic perspective is difficult to reduce to a formula. Rather like the traditional image of a liberal education, its acquisition results in a particular orientation to reality, (what Goodman inelegantly called "crap-detecting") and the propensity to a social analytic mode of thought, rather than the mastery of a set of techniques and the absorption of a specific body of theory. The goals of ethnography are rarely understood as the production of science or truth, but more pertinently understanding, and the personal development of sympathetic imagination free from sentiment.

What the ethnographer attempts is the reconstruction of an observed reality. This requires selection, translation and interpretation. However, an emphasis on the interpretive is not an invitation to idiosyncrasy. Data must be reliable, the product of systematic investigation using methods compatible with the problem, and the constraints of the field. These qualifications are vital, for interpretation by its nature is the product of usually individual, although sometimes collaborative, attempts to redefine, to make new orders from old conceptual categories. This activity is itself social and must have rules, but the rules are to facilitate maximum understanding, and not simply to ensure conformity to any particular model of social science. That would be to put the cart before the horse.

The necessary inclusion of the interpretive intellect in the act of translating social experience into ethnographic accounts may be seen as a weakness from a positivist viewpoint but it remains a prerequisite of ethnographic methodology. Thus from the hard science perspective in sociology Spindler's quoted remark of a state department of education official might seem justified.

> Anything anyone wants to do that has no clear problem, no methodology, and no theory is likely to be called "ethnography" around here. (Spindler, 1982, p. 1)

The point of ethnography is that it can, "as the field arm of anthropology, give fresh insights into perplexing educational problems" (Spindler, 1982, p. III). This may sound rather unspecific and indeed it is, but it is precisely in the recognition and formulation of general cultural propositions regarding education that ethnography can provide a developed and informed context for discussion and a valuable critique of practice. In North America and in many countries in Europe the problem of how to adjust a monocultural educational tradition to a multicultural society is a constant political problem. It is also a complex one.

There is, as Cropley suggests, agreement that immigrant children in the United Kingdom in general, "have lower average marks, obtain lower scores on standardized tests of achievement, are concentrated in the lower ability streams" (Cropley, 1983, p. 34).

The Swann Committee's Interim Report called the expectation of low achievement in West Indian pupils by their teachers, "unintentional racism," H.M.S.O., 1981). Cohen and Manion argue that it is best understood by the notion of stereotyping, that teachers respond to individuals as members of a generic class with generalisable attributes, and in the case of West Indian children these stereotypes are negative (Cohen & Manion, 1983, p. 59). They also quote Tomlinson's report that Asians, "were felt to be supportive of school, keen on education, and their children were viewed as likely to persevere in acquiring some kind of school or work qualifications" (Cohen & Manion, p. 60). If teachers have a high expectation of Asians and a low expectation of West Indians, why does "unintentional racism" only operate against one nonwhite group and not the other? Why are Asians and West Indians differently perceived by teachers? As both can be represented stereotypically can we then go on to ask, is stereotyping morally obnoxious by nature or only when it is negative? And most importantly, what assumptions, information, and habits of perception are teachers' expectations based on, and how far can we attribute pupil performance to teachers' control of the outcomes of schooling, and how far to the demands of the pupils' own culture? Asians may be more likely to be well perceived by teachers than West Indian pupils, but they are also more likely to be victims of racial violence outside of school. Why does race seem to have different meanings in different contexts? These are the sorts of questions where ethnography can provide the necessary context, not only in offering cultural descriptions of groups, but in developing reasoned frameworks which may challenge existing categories and ways of thinking, especially in the areas of race and culture.

Methods and methodologies

Einstein regarded the whole of science as, "nothing more than a refinement of everyday thinking." Social scientific research in education or elsewhere does not produce especially true or more real accounts by virtue of simply being called research. The accounts of researchers are records of events that have been made within the constraints of a set of rules. These rules are not arbitrary but are the application of principles or assumptions to concrete purposes. Methodology is the study of these principles and assumptions. It is logically prior to the problem of methods. The questions addressed by methodology are about the nature of the phenomenon to be studied, and dependent upon the answers arrived at, criteria can be derived by which we can recognize an adequate account. Methodology has regard to the necessary a priori assumptions that the researcher makes about the nature of the world. Methods are the devices by which the data, that is those elements in the events studied which are relevant to the conscious purposes of the researcher, are recognized, apprehended and recorded.

For example, Spindler develops eleven criteria by which we can recognize "a good ethnography of schooling" (Spindler, 1982, p. 7). These criteria cover the assumptions that validate ethnography as a methodology and include reference to ways of obtaining data consistent with the ethnographer's view of the world.

The things that are seen as significant to the educational psychologist, interested in cognitive development, may not be the same as those that signify for the ethnographer interested in the culture of schooling. They may be observing in the same school or classroom but their accounts of the same events could be radically different.

Some methods can be appropriate to more than one methodological perspective. While participant observation is normally associated with anthropology, and more latterly the sociology of education, the interview can be a tool used from several different perspectives and can vary its form in each. For example, a formal interview schedule with set questions, and limited opportunity for divergent response, may be used by a sociologist on a structured sample, to determine teachers' understanding of particular set areas of Asian cultural practice, say kinship and marriage or diet and commensality. This would involve setting the parameters of relevant data quite tightly. The researcher might ask specific questions with factual rather than interpretive answers, such as those related to the geographical distribution of kin, or to intergenerational educational achievement. Resultant data might be processed and represented both qualitatively and quantitatively. On the other hand, if for example information were sought on the comparison of the articulation of education with other institutions among different cultural groups, then quite open-ended interviews might be required. These might elicit the range and nature of possible relationships between education and the marriage market, or education and employment and how recession had affected these conceptions among different cultural groups. More generally the perception of education as a social status could be investigated. In this case the respondent might be encouraged to determine much of the content of the encounter in order for the ethnographer to discover the emic, or folk view, and to provide data for the generation and testing of broad hypotheses about the significance of education to different cultural groups. Turning data into an account in this case would require an emphasis on interpretation rather than quantification.

Ethnography in education takes many forms, micro studies of classrooms, studies of pupils and of teachers, of institutions and of communities and their schooling (Barton & Walker, 1981; Burgess, 1983; Delamont, 1981; Hammersley, 1980; Stubbs & Delamont, 1976; Willis, 1977; Woods, 1980). These different works are written from a range of perspectives focusing on fields of different natures, sizes and complexities. There is no ideological uniformity within them and they employ the full range of ethnographic methods. What unites them is that they provide, in Pelto and Pelto's terms, "true and useful information" (Pelto & Pelto, 1978, p. 1). The quotation marks indicated that the truth was not thought absolute, but that truth and utility were interdependent, "the truth value of our information is best measured by criteria of usefulness—in predicting and explaining our experience in the natural world" (Pelto & Pelto, 1978). I think the confusion of veracity with utility is mistaken. The first is a methodological problem about the status of accounts and the second a concern with their subsequent employment. Nonetheless it points to something important. Ethnography need not be whimsical and provide accounts of the world simply because it is there. It can be adapted to precise purposes, the description of an institution or the investigation of relationships, and can form a part of larger research strategies and problems, for example, what should a multicultural education be premised upon?

Subject and object in ethnography

A perennial problem for all scientists, both natural and social, is what is the proper relationship between the knower and the object of knowledge, and what is the epistemological status of the result? In two recent works Hammersley has brought his considerable experience in the field of educational ethnography to bear on the matter. (Hammersley, 1983; Hammersley & Atkinson, 1983). What Hammersley provides is a critique of naturalism, and in its place he advocates what he refers to as reflexivity.

Positivism and naturalism are the two poles of empiricism. Both see knowledge residing in the object and its extraction as the task of the scientist or ethnographer. Positivism is normally recognized in social science by the attempt to treat the social world in much the same way as inductive empiricist scientists are believed to treat the natural world. Thus the characteristic procedures are the development of hypotheses, and the design of tests, within the experimental model. Survey techniques and quantification may be employed in achieving the desired result, a generalizable proposition having something of the quality of a universal law. This image of social science depends centrally on the logic of the experimental method and the neutrality of the hypothesizing scientist in the face of the real external facts.

Naturalism

What has come to be known as naturalism is equally insistent on the pristine quality of external reality as the source of knowledge, but differs radically from positivism in assumptions about the nature of that reality and how it is to be apprehended. Naturalism, "implies commitment to the observation and description of social phenomena in much the manner that naturalists in biology have studied flora and fauna, and their geographical distribution" (Hammersley, 1983, p. 5). That is to say the stress is on perceiving and representing the social field in a manner that takes account of its special nature, not as with positivism, through the intermediary of an adapted natural scientific method, "Rather than imparting methods from the physical sciences, naturalism argues, we must adopt an approach that respects the nature of the social world, which allows it to reveal its nature to us" (Hammersley & Atkinson, 1983, p. 12). The ethnographer's or participant observer's task here is to reflect, chameleon-like, the cultural world under observation with as little prejudice and artifice as possible. Arguably, however, prejudgment is not only inevitable but forms a major part of the equation.

When we come to understand events, or represent them to ourselves, we necessarily select from all possible interpretations that which satisfies the particular criteria we are operating with. All humans, including ethnographers, symbolize their experience in language. Experience acquires form through subjection to a mediating theory of culture, implicit or explicit.

Perhaps the notion that the social world will reveal itself as long as we do not attempt to distort it with our own theories, should be seen as a dogma within naturalism. That is to say it is a core axiom, held to be true but not susceptible of testing, and upon which the whole enterprise is dependent.

The emphasis on the natural implies the possibility of the artificial, and naturalism is in some sense an antithetical response to the laboratory techniques of some psychology and the standardization of unique events through questionnaire surveys. It is nonetheless the case, however, that, "artificial settings set up by researchers are still part of society . . . they are social occasions subject to all those processes of symbolic interpretation and social interaction to be found elsewhere in society" (Hammersley & Atkinson, 1983, p. 11). The attempt to separate the natural from the artificial in society, violates the unity of the social and suggests that some activities and occasions are in a sense supra-social.

If the task of ethnography is to produce a facsimile of what is observed then the role of social theory seems largely redundant, if not positively pernicious. Also, the intellectual processes of interpretation and representation appear natural themselves, or at least potentially atheoretical. To apply a Marxist or Structuralist framework to the reconstruction of events and experiences would thus be illegitimate, an unwarranted imposition on the real nature of things.

Reflexivity

Reflexivity is the term Hammersley has given to his working out of the effective relationship between the researcher, the objects of research, and any subsequent accounts.

Essentially his ideas are based on the unity of subject and object. The researcher is social, and, "this is not a matter of methodological commitment, it is an existential (sic) fact" (Hammersley & Atkinson, 1983, p. 14). We are also reminded that methods themselves are part of society, "However distinctive the purposes of social science may be, the methods it employs are merely refinements or developments of those used in everyday life" (Hammersley & Atkinson, 1983, p. 15.) For example, we all have conversations with high levels of specificity, with the milkman or our solicitor, which closely resemble the interview. We hypothesize about the nature of society in pubs and on trains, and use comparative method to experimentally test our ideas against reality.

The notion that ethnography is social activity also, "suggests that the researcher's own actions are open to analysis *in the same terms* as those of other participants." (Hammersley, 1983, p. 3). This is an important point, not only does it domesticate and demystify ethnographic research, it also makes it clear that the strategies and tactics of the researcher in the field are governed by her own sociability expressed through the aim of constructing ethnography. However, this notion might sail close to naturalism without the necessary caveat, that although ethnography is social activity, it is specific and conscious in a way that overlays the participation in the field. Thus, I was aware that having to sit on the platform with the President of the Hindu Union, the local priest and other community leaders, during the Diwali celebrations not only dignified me, but more important for the ethnographer, it cut me off from the action. There is a distance between the researcher and the social setting that might be called the ethnographic agenda, which entails the constant awareness of the effect of self as actor, on the field, in the light of the goals of ethnography. Decisions taken in the field close, as well as open, options. The biography and theoretical orientation of the ethnographer will influence decisions and determine what is to be recognized as data, and this in turn constrains the possibilities of any resultant account.

Hammersley and Atkinson (1983) are rather dismissive of cultural description as a purpose of ethnography and assert that,

> In our view the development and testing of theory is the distinctive function of social theory (sic) . . . the idea of relationships between variables that, given certain conditions, hold across all circumstances seems essential to the very idea of theory. (p. 19)

I fear these last strictures rule most social science atheoretical, and their satisfaction would be likely to require of the ethnographer a total access to, and control over the field. However, the criteria for *pukka* theory are further elaborated by Hammersley and Atkinson (1983).

> A theory must include reference to mechanisms or processes by which the relationship among the variables identified is generated. Moreover, such reference must be more than mere speculation, the existence and operation of these "intervening variables" must be described. (p. 20)

The goal of ethnography thus becomes "formalized theory." While this highly refined view is later qualified with some ethnographies being simply, "way stations on the road to theory," this particular description of ethnography bears comment (Hammersley & Atkinson, p. 201).

I think it possible and desirable that ethnography should go beyond the attempt to describe, and to develop and test hypotheses, I think some of the other aims, while admirably rigorous, go beyond the normal possibilities of field based ethnography. The ethnographer can be thought of as an organizing focal consciousness within any particular cultural setting. Although there are ways of maximizing information through the use of informants and the collection of documents, the eventual data can only represent a very partial penetration into the complex reality of the field, comprising, as it does, constantly interacting and developing systems of meanings. Naturalism may rightly be taken to task for employing unrealistic notions of unalloyed transference of the reality under study, in order to preserve its integrity. An over-elaborate machinery for analysis may run the opposite risk of satisfying the demands of theoretical propiety at the expense of authenticity, and incidentally artificially limiting the possible fields of study. It may be the case that the extreme variability of variables in the domain of meaning makes such a view of science incompatible with the practice of ethnography.

The development and testing of hypotheses, however, is an entirely plausible aim of ethnography in education. For example, the literature on differential educational performance between ethnic groups, prompts the question, why should this be so? A reasonable hypothesis from available evidence is that educational performance is a function of culture. This can be broken down into specific areas of investigation around definite questions. Do different ethnic groups hold different images of education? How do these articulate with other aspects of culture? How is education ranked with alternative sources of status and prestige? Such an investigation is possible using participant observation, documentation, and perhaps structured interview in the collection of data, which could subsequently provide both qualitative and quantitative accounts which could be compared along significant variables and relationships. Such research would not necessarily qualify as social theory in Hammersley and Atkinson's terms but may be of great value to policy makers and classroom teachers.

Similarly in vexed and complex local issues, such as the introduction of halal meat in state schools, ethnographic data may provide a counterbalance to implaccable moral assertion. Again this may not necessarily be productive of much in the way of social theory, but may aspire in Pelto and Pelto's terms to be "true and useful."

The necessity of culture

As Burgess reminds us there was a period in Manchester, under Max Gluckman, when anthropology and sociology came together in a joint ethnographic venture, which produced the first generation of school studies in Great Britain (Burgess, 1983; Hargreaves, 1967; Lacey, 1970; & Lambart, 1970). After this initial joint impetus most indigenous ethnography and certainly the ethnography of education has been largely taken up and developed by sociologists, both in the small-scale setting of the classroom and the larger settings of institutions and localities (Ball, 1981; Burgess, 1983; Delamont, 1983, 1984; Stubbs & Delamont, 1976; Willis, 1977; Woods & Hammersley, 1977). The two traditions in ethnography are fully discussed by Delamont and Atkinson (1980).

In America, however, especially through the work of Spindler, an anthropology of education has been developing, in some ways independent of the sociology of education and naturally focused on problems of ethnography (Spindler, 1974, 1977, 1982). On both sides of the Atlantic there has been a move towards a broadening of ethnographic methodology to embrace quantitative method (Hammersley & Atkinson 1983; Pelto & Pelto, 1978, Wilcox, 1982). A significant distinction has been the focus of American anthropologists on the concepts of culture and transmission in education (Bruner, 1968; Cohen 1971; Leacock, 1973; Singleton, 1974; Spindler, 1974a, 1982a).

It is important to note that the accent has been on relatively small-scale studies of aspects of transmission and culture, and is not commensurate with reproduction theory (Bourdieu, 1977; Bowles & Gintis, 1976). The former is mainly concerned with how the younger and elder generations renegotiate the nature and content of culture within a generally conservative social structure. The negotiation refers to the nature of social transactions rather than to radical change (Wallace, 1973). The latter are attempts to explain the persistence of class structures through generations. For Bowles and Gintis, this is achieved through correspondence, the notion that school is organized on a class basis as anticipatory socialization for the workplace (Bowles & Gintis, 1976). Bourdieu uses the concept of cultural capital, which is access to the experience of those elements of French culture on which the schooling system draws, and the consequent ability to discourse upon and within it, which is the means of achieving academic success (Bourdieu, 1977).

Apart from the interest in cultural transmission in the American anthropology of education, which is not absent from U. K. sociology of education, there is a commitment to cross-cultural research and comparative analysis which does not typify British educational ethnography. As Williamson reminds us the development of comparative analysis was seen as a necessary element in the new sociology of education but, "as a strategy to develop further the theoretical framework of the subject these suggestions have not, however, been taken seriously" (Williamson, 1979, p. 3). Currently, comparative analysis is more likely to be a part of social psychology in the study of plural society than of ethnography (Cropley, 1983; Verma & Bagley, 1975, 1979).

The importance of comparative studies of cultural transmission is that the very idea itself demonstrates something of the nature of cultural reality; it is diffuse and differentiated. It is constantly in the process of being maintained and renewed with each human transaction. As with language it can be analysed and recognized on different levels, idiolect, dialect, vernacular, each one a subsystem of culture or language. Neither cultures nor languages are discrete, but are permeable and constantly permeated. Hindi and Punjabi are separate languages but have common antecedents and shared aspects. Hinduism and Sikhism again have the dual quality of similarity and difference, perhaps standing in a similar relation to each other as English Catholics and nonconformists. Hindus and Sikhs share what might be broadly termed Asian cultural characteristics, but conceive themselves, and are so conceived by others, as separate communities. Unity and diversity are the bases of comparative analysis.

I want now to briefly suggest something of the possibilities and potential for ethnographic research within the comparative analysis of culture. Since the publication of the interim report of the Swann Committee the curriculum has become an area of renewed interest, (Cohen & Manion, 1983; Hicks, 1981; HMSO, 1981; James & Jeffcoate, 1981; Lynch, 1981). Much of this work is premised on the notion that the curriculum should in some way reflect the cultures of its participants, rather than academic culture, which is argued to be closer to the culture of middle-class whites than other groups.

Although an area of some confusion, it can no longer be thought of as an area of neglect. Both urban and suburban schools have recently employed a variety of strategies and methods in devising curriculums thought appropriate for a multicultural society (Twitchen & Demuth, 1981). The image of culture, which is very rarely theorized, is often exotic and Eurocentric. That is to say, there is culture (white British) which is unproblematic and taken for granted, and there are other cultures recognizable solely through their difference, or exotic quality compared to indigenous white culture.

Two problems immediately occur which can only have essentially arbitrary answers. First, whose cultures qualify for inclusion and by what criteria? Second, to what precisely in the organization and content of school life should the culture of its participants relate?

The confusion of culture and race is endemic, which goes some way to explain the popular association of West Indians and Asians as solely constituting the other cultures within the U. K. This simple typology is unrealistic and unreliable. It is true that West Indian and Asian cultures are those most frequently discussed in the literature. Is this because they are nonwhites, or because some are immigrants? Should either of these conditions be the basis for rethinking the curriculum? The first leads us into the cul-de-sac of antiteaching, and the second cannot provide any sensible cultural information. We cannot say that the school should take account of the cultures of immigrants, for the U. K. has such a highly variegated immigrant population, most of whom are rarely considered. Are the Poles and the Irish immigrant, populations constituting cultural groups with a right to inclusion? If we agree that West Indian and Asian cultures are definitely candidates, what account is to be taken of diversity within those groups? Are language groups to be considered as distinct culture groups, and if so what levels of linguistic differentiation are to be employed within the complex of contemporary British language types (Stubbs & Hillier, 1983)? For example, a pupil may speak French-based St. Lucian patois and an indigenous dialect, or Jamaican Creole, London Jamaican and standard English, as do many West Indian students in higher education. The West Indian archipelago is not culturally homogeneous indeed, "the term West Indian is itself culturally precarious. The nearest to a factor of cultural homogeneity among the British West Indies has been their love for cricket" (Lashley, 1981, p. 229).

The Asian culture is no less complex, divided by religion, caste, and class. The erstwhile East African Gujarati speaking, Patidar family, with financial and domestic outposts in Germany or Canada, and a land base in Kaira district, may be considered as culturally distinct from the more passive and proletarian Sikh family in Huddersfield (James, 1974; Tambs-Lyche, 1980). These two groups have different histories and patterns of migration and different conceptions of what it means to be immigrant.

If we begin to recognize the complexity of cultural identity then the problem of how culture relates to curriculum becomes more acute. Indeed the cultural identity of particular groups and individuals may be difficult to distinguish in itself. For example, as Cropley (1983) points out West Indian and Asian pupils may be born in Britain and have no first hand knowledge of a homeland, which formed their parents' cultural identity, and thus in some ways determined their own early socialization. Also, in what he describes as "the double bind," children are encouraged to succeed in school, which means taking on British norms and values, while simultaneously living in the shadow morality of the homeland which is antagonistic to British mores (Cropley, 1983, p. 115).

If a particular identified culture is to be recognized in school, what levels and aspects of culture can be included? School is renowned for excluding the cultural lives of most of its participants, the working class. The notion that school alienates minorities is not uncommon, but how is school to authentically include the culture of its participants? Can, or should, the school system include male, working class, West Indian urban street culture? If the answer is yes, should it then be extended to say female, home counties suburban youth culture? This would imply that school should reflect local cultures, but how this might be done and how the content might be turned into school knowledge is not clear. We do know that some cultural groups do not value being schooled, and it is difficult to see a reciprocal relationship between the cultures of school and that of Willis's working class "lads" (Willis, 1977).

School can also be seen as jealous of its own cultural territory. The incursion of nonindigenous cultural behavior is not automatically welcomed. Allowing Muslim girls to wear trousers or opt out of games is sometimes seen as a concession rather than a right, and the proposed introduction of halal meat into Bradford school meals has caused something of a furor. Thus it may be the case that school is capable in some ways, perhaps restricted to the curriculum, of symbolizing the integration of different cultures into its organization, but there is little evidence of the accommodation of actual cultural diversity.

Putting high culture on the curriculum is a possible means of symbolizing inclusion, but Basham's exquisite account of classical India is as remote from the life of modern Asian youth, as Harvey and Bather's account of the British constitution was from political reality for indigenous pupils of a previous generation. This is not to argue that idealized versions of cultural reality have no place in school, but that they require a sympathetic and supportive context if they are to be valued by pupils.

The teaching of comparative religion is now commonplace in secondary school, but on what basis can the comparison be made? For example, is being Hindu in any sense comparable to being Christian? The U. K. is a secular society and its established church has a protestantical bias. Thus, religion may be generally thought of by the indigenous white population as being primarily a matter of the individuals' voluntary belief. Christians can both apostatise and renounce their religion because they have first to ascribe to it as a set of intellectual propositions, found in their most basic forms in creeds. Protestantism is Christian individualism. It is because religion is seen to have this abstracted and external form that we can conceive of religious education as compatible with the notion of a subject on the school curriculum.

The basic categories of caste are communal not individual, and Hinduism is the eschatology of a communal caste society (Dumont, 1980). Verma and Mallick (1981) quote Pandit Nehru on Hinduism, "It is hardly possible to define it, or indeed to say precisely whether it is religion or not, in the usual sense of the word." Individuals are born into a caste and are definitionally Hindu. They do not have to actively intellectually subscribe to any particular articles of faith, they simply are the personification of Hinduism. Because being Hindu is not a voluntary condition it cannot sensibly be renounced. The final complication is that because it is not identified with a specific historical revelation, as is Christianity, it has come to comprise an amorphous and contradictory set of teachings, and to identify it solely with the Bhagavad-Gita and the Upanishads is to distort it on two counts. It is to suggest that it is a religion of the book like Islam and Judaism, and it blurs a central characteristic, that there is a definite distinction between its theology, the Brahmanical tradition, and the local and domestic practices of Hindus, Redfield and Singer's great and little traditions (Marriott, 1972).

It is reasonable to include courses in Hindu philosophy and eschatology in a curriculum because these represent the abstracted intellectual elements of Hinduism. But argueably it is a distortion of the nature of Hindu culture to represent it as items of knowledge on particular propositions. These transformations are nonetheless required if it is to be suitable for inclusion, as school knowledge, on the curriculum.

Rastafarianism as an aspect of West Indian culture presents even greater problems. It has no formal organization, it is raw and overtly millenarian and has many of the characteristics of a youth subculture as well as those of a religion. Whatever its significance for West Indian youth, as a complex of cultural knowledge it is incompatible with formal schooling.

These two short examples are intended to illustrate the following points. First, the cultural lives of groups are complex meaning-making systems which may have a limited potential for inclusion in schooling. Second, a minimal elaboration of the concept of culture provides a tool for the critique of current practice.

Conclusion

I have tried, albeit briefly, to indicate something of the possible nature of the areas an ethnography of schooling might work within. I hope at least to have indicated that multiculturalism requires an adequate theory of culture that can plausibly be generated through the accumulation of ethnographic accounts and comparative analysis. This would require a program of small and larger scale studies of classrooms, institutions, and the communities they serve, and of the people, organizations and networks of those who control and direct the education system.

School is the central state agency of cultural transmission, but we have no clear idea of how culture should relate to schooling. To focus upon the curriculum is in some sense an automatic response of the internal or practitioner view of what school is, especially given its current importance, along with managerial skills, in in-service training. However, it is not at all clear that a multicultural curriculum is what is needed, nor if it is, then what it should be. It may be the case that the social needs of at least minorities would be better served by concentrating on raising levels of certification (Stone, 1981). If, on the other hand school is to reflect the lives of its participants, then prevailing notions of culture need to be submitted to more rigorous analysis than has been the case, and also require a proper empirical grounding. Without this prior basis to innovation, there can be no clear logical connections between the analysis of the problem, the strategy for meeting it, and the criteria for evaluation. How are we to decide in what ways schools should be trying to symbolize cultural diversity? What analytic framework do we currently have for deciding between the exotic view of the otherness of other cultures, which makes Diwali extracurricular and Christmas intra, and the Bullock like notion of culture across the curriculum which tends to founder outside the humanities and religious education.

An ethnography of cultural diversity, which would include indigenous white culture as equally problematic as any other, would provide the necessary context within which hitherto unheard debates could provide us with answers to these most pressing problems, and with them a reliable guide to action.

REFERENCES

Ball, S. J. (1981). *Beachside comprehensive: A case study of secondary schooling*. Cambridge: Cambridge University Press.

Barton, L., & Walker, S. (Eds). (1983). *Race, class and education*. London: Croom Helm.

Basham, A. L. (1967). *The wonder that was Indian*. London: Fontana.

Bourdieu, P. (1977). Cultural capital and pedagogic communication. In P. Bourdieu & J-C Passeron (trans. by R. Nice). *Reproduction in education, society and culture* (pp. 71–106). Beverly Hills, CA: Sage.

Burgess, R. G. (1983). *Experiencing comprehensive education. A study of Bishop McGregor school*. London: Methuen.

Cohen, L., & Manion, L. (1983). *Multicultural classrooms*. London: Croom Helm.

Cohen, Y. A. (1971). The shaping of men's minds: Adaptations to the imperatives of culture. In K. L. Wax, S. Diamond, & F. E. Gearing (Eds.), *Anthropological perspectives on education* (pp. 19–50). New York: Basic Books.

Cropley, A. J. (1983). *The education of immigrant children, a social psychological introduction*. London: Croom Helm.

Delamont, S. (1981). All too familiar? A decade of classroom research. *Educational analysis, 3*(1), 69–83.

Delamont, S. (1983). *Interaction in the classroom* (2nd edition). London: Methuen.

Delamont, S. (Ed.) (1984). *Readings on interaction in the classroom*. London: Methuen.

Delamont, S., & Atkinson, P. (19   ). The two traditions in educational ethnography: Sociology and anthropology compared. *British Journal of Sociology of Education, 1*(2), 139–52.

Dumont, L. (trans.), Sainsbury, M., Dumont, L. & Gulati, B. (1981). *Homo hierarchicus: The caste system and its implications.* Il: Univ. of Chicago Press.

Hammersley, M. (1980). Classroom Ethnography. In *Educational Analysis, 2*(2), 47–74.

Hammersley, M. (Ed). (1983). *The ethnography of schooling: Methodological issues.* Driffield; Nafferton.

Hammersley, M., & Atkinson, P. (1983). *Ethnography, principles in practice.* London: Tavistock.

Hargreaves, D. H. (1967). *Social relations in a secondary school.* London: Routledge and Kegan Paul.

Harvey, J., & Bather, L. (1968). The British constitution (2nd edition). London Macmillan.

Hicks, D. W. (1981). *Minorities, a teacher's resource book for the multi-ethnic curriculum.* London Heinemann Educational Books.

H.M.S.O. (1981). *West Indian children in our schools.* (Cmnd 8273).

James, A. G. (1974). *Sikh children in Britain.* Oxford: Oxford University Press for Institute of Race Relations.

James, H., & Jeffcoate, R. (Eds). (1981). *The school in the multicultural society.* New York: Harper and Row.

Lacey, C. (1970). *Hightown grammar. The school as a social system.* Manchester: Manchester University Press.

Lambert, A. M. (1970). *The sociology of an unstreamed urban grammar school for girls.* Unpbulished M. A. thesis. University of Manchester.

Lambert, A. M. (1976). The sisterhood. In M. Hammersley & P. Woods (Eds.) *The Process of Schooling* (pp. 152–9). London: Routledge and Kegan Paul/Open University Press.

Lashley, H. (1981). Culture, education and children of West Indian background. In J. Lynch (Ed.) *Teaching the multi-cultural school* (pp. 227–250). London: Ward Lock Educational.

Leacock, E. (1973). The concept of culture and its significance for school counsellors. In F.A.J. Ianni & E. Storey (eds.) *Cultural relevance and educational issues. Readings in anthropology and education* (pp. 189–200). Boston, MA: Little Brown.

Lynch, J. (Ed.). (1981). *Teaching in the multi-cultural school.* London: Ward Lock Educational.

Marriott KcKim (Ed.). (1972). *Village India studies in the little community.* IL: University of Chicago Press.

Pelto, P. J., & Pelto, G. H. (1978). *Anthropological research. The structure of inquiry* (2nd edition). Cambridge: Cambridge University Press.

Spindler, G. D. (1955). *Education and Anthropology.* CA: Stanford University Press.

Spindler, G. D. (1963). *Education and culture.* New York, Holt, Rinehart and Winston.

Spindler, G. D. (1974). *Education and cultural process.* New York, Holt, Rinehart and Winston.

Spindler, G. D. (1974a). Schooling in Schonhausen: A study of cultural transmission and instrumental adaptation in an urbanizing German village. In G. D. Spindler (ed.), *Education and cultural process* (pp. 230–72). New York, Holt, Rinehart and Winston.

Spindler, G. D. (Ed.). (1982a). *Doing the ethnography of schooling: Educational anthropology in action.* New York: Holt, Rinehart and Winston.

Spindler, G. D. (1982b). General introduction. In G. D. Spindler (ed.). *Doing the ethnography of schooling, education anthropology in action* (pp. 1–14). New York: Holt, Rinehart and Winston.

Stone, M. (1981). *The education of the black child in Britain.* London: Fontana.

Stubbs, M. (1983). Understanding language and language diversity: what teachers should know about educational linguistics. In M. Stubbs & H. Hillier (eds.) *Readings on language, schools and classrooms* (pp. 11–38). London: Methuen.

Stubbs, M., & Delamont, S. (Eds.). (1976). *Explorations in classroom observation.* Chichester, Wiley.

Stubbs, M., & Hillier, H. (Eds.). (1983). *Readings on language, schools and classrooms.* London: Methuen.

Tambs-Lyche, H. (1980). *London Patidars: A case study in urban ethnicity.* London: Routledge and Kegan Paul.

Tomlinson, S. (1981). Multi-racial schooling: Parents' and teachers' views. *Education 3–13,* 9(1), 16–21.

Twitchin, J. (1981). *Multicultural education: views from the classroom.* London: BBC publications.

Verma, G. K., & Bagley, C. (Eds.). (1979). *Race, education and identity.* London: Macmillan.

Verma, G., & Mallick, K. (1981). Hinduism and multi-cultural education. In J. Lynch (ed.) *Teaching in the multi-cultural school* (pp. 184–201). London: Ward Lock Educational.

Wallace, A.F.C. (1978). Schools in revolutionary and conservative societies. In F.A.J. Ianni & E. Storey (Eds.), *Cultural relevance and educational issues,* readings in anthropology and education (pp. 230–49). Boston, MA: Little, Brown.

Wilcox, K. (1982). Ethnography as a methodology and its application to the study of schooling: A review. In G. D. Spindler (Ed.), *Doing the ethnography of schooling, educational anthropology in action* (pp. 456–88).

Williamson, B. (1979). *Education, social structure and development.* London: Macmillan.

Willis, P. (1977). *Learning to labour: How working class kids get working class jobs.* Teakfield: Saxon House.

Woods, P. (Ed.). (1980). *Pupil strategies.* London: Croom Helm.

Woods, P., & Hammersley, M. (Eds.). (1977). *School experience, explorations in the sociology of education.* London: Croom Helm.

The Author and His Chapter

David Mark Fetterman received his doctorate in educational and medical anthropology at Stanford and was G. Spindler's advisee. At present he is a member of Stanford's administration and conducts qualitative evaluation and audits of management in academic and business departments, the University Hospital, and the Linear Accelerator Center. He has had extensive experience in evaluative ethnography beyond his Stanford position, in his work for the RMC Research Corporation, some of which he describes in his chapter in this volume. He also serves as an assistant professor in the School of Education at Stanford.

In his chapter Fetterman places ethnographic evaluation on the landscape of the ethnography of education and relates it in turn to established interests in anthropology. He then proceeds to an analysis of the Career Intern Program Study that he conducted under the auspices of RMC. He analyzes program ethos, program context, evaluative continuity, the federal context, the qualitative-quantitative dichotomy, the integration of these two different kinds of data and method, the language of ethnography, timeliness, advocacy, and policy and program recommendations.

He takes a clear stand to the effect that ethnographers, as program evaluaters, must hold themselves responsible for going beyond ethnography to make program and policy recommendations. Not all anthroethnographers of education will accept this posture as valid. They will point out that evaluation and ethnography are inherently at odds to begin with and that, further, ethnography can report on reality but not try to change it. Or perhaps one can say that it is not ethnography and evaluation that are at odds but rather the role of the ethnographer and the role of the evaluater. Every ethnography is, in a sense, an evaluation, for it describes how relationships in social contexts "work." Relations with one's informants, however, are likely to be disturbed by any hint of an evaluative or judgmental outlook on the part of the ethnographer. It takes great skill to function as an evaluator but appear not to be evaluating and at the same time retain the trust of one's informants. These questions will not be settled in David Fetterman's chapter. They reflect deep-seated personal persuasion, characterological differences, and differences in research context and purpose. It is useful, however, to have the issues sharpened by someone who has had Dr. Fetterman's extensive experience in ethnographic evaluation.

The Editors

5 Ethnographic Educational Evaluation

David M. Fetterman
Stanford University

Ethnographic educational evaluation is a part of the intellectual landscape of educational research. The roots of this hybrid subdiscipline are firmly planted in the rich soil of educational anthropology. It was nurtured on classic texts in the field.[1]

A hybrid of ethnography and traditional evaluation, ethnographic educational evaluation has contributed to a more complete understanding of both old and new issues in education. It has been used to study desegregation (Hanna, 1982), alternative high school programs for dropouts (Fetterman, 1981a), rural experimental schools (Herriott, 1979a, 1979b; Firestone, 1980), a program for hearing-impaired students (Hemwall, 1984), educational television (Wolcott, 1984), parental involvement in education (Smith & Robbins, 1984), and various other substantive social policy concerns. Ethnographic educational evaluation has come to fruition in my own collection *Ethnography and Educational Evaluation* (Fetterman, 1984), and *Educational Evaluation: Ethnography in Theory, Practice and Politics* (Fetterman & Pitman, 1986).

Ethnographic educational evaluation is the process of applying ethnographic techniques and concepts to educational evaluation. Key elements

---

[1]Spindler's *Doing the Ethnography of Schooling: Educational Anthropology in Action* (1982), and his most widely recognized collection *Education and Cultural Process: Toward an Anthropology of Education* (1974), Robert's and Akinsanya's *Schooling in the Cultural Context: Anthropological Studies of Education* (1975) and *Educational Patterns and Cultural Configurations: The Anthropology of Education* (1976). These and several works of Ogbu and Wolcott were the fertile ground in which this subdiscipline has grown.

of this approach involve conducting fieldwork and maintaining a cultural perspective. Fieldwork in the form of participant-observation may or may not be continuous; however, it is usually conducted over a period of time to identify patterns of behavior. A cultural perspective is used to interpret human behavior on a program, community, and/or sociocultural level of analysis. Additional ethnographic tools are also used such as: key informant, informal, and semistructured interviewing, triangulation, and so on. These methods, traditionally used to understand sociocultural systems, are applied to educational evaluation in an attempt to assess more accurately the relative merits of a given educational approach, setting, or system.

Ethnographic educational evaluation must also adapt those methods it has borrowed from traditional ethnography. Smith and Robbins (1984), for example, combined survey techniques with a structured ethnographic approach to manage the data collection and analysis of 57 sites. Firestone and Herriott (1984) documented similar adaptations in multisite qualitative studies. One of the most significant methodological adaptations is a reduction in the time spent in the field. Typically, ethnographers spend from 6 months, to a year, to 16 years studying a culture or sociocultural system. In marked contrast to this tradition of continuous, long-term fieldwork, ethnographic educational evaluation is characterized by much shorter, often noncontinuous, periods of fieldwork. Moreover, this short-term fieldwork is generally conducted within the ethnographer's own culture. Malinowski (1961) was convinced that participant-observation could only be conducted through long months of residence at the local scene. The quality of data that have been collected and the findings published through numerous ethnographic educational evaluations suggest that Malinowski's position may have been overstated for studies of American subcultures, particularly if site visits are spread out over a period of time. In addition, when the focus of study is a school system we often become, as Wolcott has phrased it, "our own key informant because we know the system so well."

Ethnography has answered some difficult long-standing questions and posed as many new questions. As in the case with many novel approaches in educational research, news of its success has spread quickly. The proliferation of research reports and proposals purporting to use this methodology generated a backlash by anthropologists concerned with the use and abuse of ethnography in educational research (e.g., Fetterman, 1982a, pp. 17–29; Wolcott, 1980, pp. 6–7, 56–59). Educational anthropologists have produced several studies that demonstrate the utility of this approach and establish ethnographic educational evaluation as a legitimate source of inquiry.

CIP: A case study

One of the studies contributing to the acceptance of ethnography in educational evaluation is the Career Intern Program Study (CIP)—a national ethnographic evaluation of an alternative high school program for dropouts. As a model for ethnographic educational evaluation, the CIP study merits closer examination. This study is one of the earliest substantive attempts to apply ethnographic techniques and anthropological insights to a large-scale project, within a time frame established to accommodate a more traditional educational evaluation.

The CIP study focused on an alternative high school program for dropouts and potential dropouts. The CIP schools offer students a high school diploma and a career oriented education. This program was designed to help students make the transition from school to work or college. The CIP was selected for study because it represents one of the few exemplary programs for disenfranchised and economically disadvantaged minority youth. As an important social and educational experiment, the CIP is salient to many kinds of audiences. Policymakers have been interested in the program as a viable response to such serious labor market problems as high school dropout rates and youth unemployment. Social reformers, however, have viewed the program as a vehicle to redress historically based social inequities and promote upward social mobility for minority groups. The program has also been of interest to academicians and researchers because it provided an opportunity to explore the processes of socialization, cultural transmission, and equal educational opportunity in the United States.

The CIP study consists of four sites, three located in major urban centers—(pseudonyms) New Borough, Plymouth, Oceanside—and a fourth in a small city, Farmington (32,000 population). These sites were designed according to a model developed in Philadelphia by an international minority owned and operated skills development organization. The federal government funded and monitored these new programs. A private research corporation was selected to evaluate the four CIP sites.

The study was subdivided into four tasks: (a) implementation, (b) outcomes, (c) interrelationships, and (d) comparison with similar programs. The implementation component involved describing the genesis, the development, and the operation of the program. This first section relied heavily on ethnographic data collection efforts. The outcomes section was somewhat more controversial. It consisted of a treatment and a control group to evaluate the program. Parents resented this part of the study because it randomly assigned some children to the control group, thus precluding their participation in the educational program. The CIP was considered the last chance for many of these dropouts. In addition, the research corporation argued against the use of this design on methodological grounds. The group selected for the control group knew they were being denied an education or "treatment." This knowledge invalidated the double blind assumption of an experimental design, whereby both groups believe they are being treated. The problems resulting from the use of this design led the evaluators to take a strong position against the use of treatment-control designs with these types of social programs. The evaluators' position is reflected in their report recommendations. The ethnographic component of the study focused on the interrelationships and causal linkages between implementation and outcomes. Ethnographic data collection instruments, methods, procedures, and perspectives were employed. The task also relied heavily on information gathered through nomothetic methods and perspectives. Traditional techniques such as participant observation, nonparticipant observation, use of key informants, triangulation, structured and semistructured, and informal interviews, were used to elicit data from the emic or "insider's" perspective. Two-week site visits were made to each site every 3 months for a period of 3 years. In addition, regular contact was maintained by telephone, correspondence, and special visits. The study attempted to be nonjudgmental, holistic, and contextual in perspective. A tape recorder and camera were invaluable in collecting and documenting the data. (See Fetterman, 1980, for details regarding the methodology of the study.) In practice, data collection and reporting activities overlapped for each segment of the study.

The CIP study represents an important shift in emphasis from the urban educational anthropology research of the previous decade because it focused on school success for minority youth rather than on school failure. It differs from the traditional ethnography of schooling in incorporating findings from a multidisciplinary evaluation effort. The research concerned not a single school, but an entire demonstration project in several sites. The analyses examined classrooms, program components, community environments, local and national affiliates, governmental agencies, and evaluators. The study differed also in its multidimensional emphasis, discussing federal involvement, evaluation design, and the role of reinforcing world views. It represented both an opportunity for and a test of ethnography in its emerging role in educational evaluation. The CIP study has contributed significantly to both its parent fields. It has added to educational anthropology's study of cultural transmission and expanded its understanding of the process by which values and ideas are passed on from one generation to the next. In providing educational evaluators with a model of detailed description on several levels, the ethnographic component of the study demonstrates the means of contextualizing the data. By locating data more precisely in a multilevel context, educational evaluators can arrive at a more comprehensive interpretation of its meaning. The study also works to demythologize the qualitative-quantitative dichotomy perpetuated in both fields. By combining both qualitative and quantitative data in an ethnographic description and by analyzing their interaction, the study clarifies the fundamental interdependence of these artificially segregated measures. The CIP study demonstrates as well the difficulties of adapting ethnographic research to the language, timelines, and political concerns of policy makers. Evaluators have a responsibility not only to speak the language of policy, but to add their voice to policy decisions through specific recommendations and a general statement of advocacy.

CULTURAL TRANSMISSION

The study provides a close analysis of the mechanisms of cultural transmission, particularly of the role of program ethos, rites of solidarity and rites of passage. These mechanisms are separated for pedagogical reasons, in practice they are interrelated.

Program Ethos

The CIP credibly transmitted dominant elements of American mainstream culture in an environment where traditional schools fail. The CIP transmits these values by means of the same mechanisms associated with school failure. The school ethos or philosophy rearranges these mechanisms in a manner that "opens doors" to productive participation in the dominant culture: providing a supportive context, maintaining high expectations, and selecting students (called interns) who seek the guidance offered by its "total institution" type rules (Goffman, 1961). These represent the manifest elements of the CIP ethos. Latent functions such as upward social mobility and the transmission of Black middle class values made the educational process credible for dropouts and potential dropouts.

While the focus of the program is to transmit middle class values, this is not accomplished at the cost of one's ethnic identity, as was the case in assimilatory education programs in the early part of this century (Cubberly, 1909). The CIP staff recognize the importance of maintaining ethnic pride and heritage, while teaching interns to function in the middle class work world. One instructor explained it in the following manner: "There is an appropriate way to dress and behave at work; it's like wearing two suits, one at home and one at work."

Interns are aware of the dichotomy and learn to compartmentalize their lives accordingly. The maintenance of ethnic pride is fostered through classroom discussions, relevant assignments, and other means. Interns display partially synthesized value systems in linguistic and behavioral modes by code switching (Gumperz, 1976)—interweaving both street and CIP (middle class) speech and behavior. The interns' pride in their ethnic identity and cultural heritage within the context of the program is most poignantly displayed in intern poetry.

The Black Rose

> I was planted with the seeds of beauty and became a flower determined to be me.
> My petals are colored both front and back, rejoicing in the favor of being black.
> My stems stand straight like a mighty tower with its roots in the soil of soul power.
> Other petals seem to call me names because our petals are not the same.
> But I listen not to what others say because I know I am somebody, you see.
> God gave me wisdom at the beginning of time, a color forever to be mine.
> So I'm shouting with beauty and heaven knows there's nothing prouder than the Black Rose.

The ethos or program climate characterizes the school and also serves as one of the single most powerful mechanisms of cultural transmission. The manifest elements of the program ethos in this study included providing a supportive context and maintaining high expectations. The staff was expected to be "caring but firm." Latent functions included a desire to see these students climb the social ladders of success and to see these former dropouts internalize black middle class values. A complete study of cultural transmission in any system requires an analysis of both manifest and latent functions. These functions operate in a dialectic fashion, inseparable in practice. Too many studies have only documented the existence of the manifest level. This is studying the tip of the iceberg. The core of cultural transmission is the teaching and learning of social and cultural values.

Ethnographic educational evaluation at its best attempts to identify, describe, analyze, and evaluate the social flow of values. Because cultural transmission is an elusive process, attention must be focused on the manifestations of program ethos on several levels, as well as on rites of solidarity and rites of passage.

Rituals

Every sociocultural system has a set of communal rites or rituals. Harris (1971) defines the nature of these communal rites.

> Communal rites fall into two major categories: (1) rites of solidarity and (2) rites of passage. In the rites of solidarity participation in dramatic public rituals enhances the sense of group identity, coordinates the actions of the individual members of the group, and prepares the group for immediate or future cooperative action. Rites of passage celebrate the sociological movement of individuals into and out of groups or into or out of statuses of critical importance both to the individual and to the community. (p. 545)

As a sociocultural system, the CIP has its own set of communal rites. Numerous rites of solidarity are an intrinsic element in the CIP atmosphere. Student council elections are one of the most common rites of solidarity. During elections the sites buzz with excitement. Committees form, interns work on posters and slogans, interns discuss who is the most popular or the most likely to win, candidates make speeches promising some future cooperative event such as school trips or dances, and the entire intern body votes.

Some of the sites have periodic basketball games or other sports events, which serve to bring the entire program together. At one site, the staff played against the interns, both sides wearing CIP T-shirts. Several interns assumed formal cheerleading roles while the majority of the program participants in attendance displayed their involvement in the event by loud booing and cheering. A second type of solidarity rite arises in response to an outside threat. A brief fight between two interns during the game proved to be extremely illuminating in this context. A newer gang affiliated intern threatened to take over the program. One of the older interns felt it necessary to convince him and his gang that the CIP was not going to be taken over. The interns' protective stance, the degree of affiliation and loyalty to the program, and the nature of the undercurrents in the intern world could not have been more clearly demonstrated.

The single most identifiable communal rite of solidarity is the monthly "CIP-is-Hip" day. CIP-is-Hip day is a complex affair that is celebrated or performed slightly differently at each site. It began in one site and as a result of its popularity among participants and external observers spread to the other sites. The typical CIP-is-Hip day is preceded by meetings and preparations for specific events such as interns making a meal for the staff or vice versa. Activities include the awarding of prizes for best attendance, most talkative, best personality, teacher's pet, always on time, enthusiastic about CIP, likely to succeed, class participation, leadership ability, always late, sleeping in class, and so on. The names of award winners are posted, stimulating much joking and arguing about the awards, and general involvement in the excitement.

The instructional supervisor at one site explained how excited the interns were on CIP-is-Hip day:

> We give recognition to interns who are just about any category. And they really like that and the last one, the last one that we had, the second cohort came in, and the attendance was better than the first cohort. You know, they came in while we're having CIP-is-Hip day and that spread the publicity about the program . . . and the enthusiasm that things were going on. . . . So we're going to have another one real soon and we must instead of letting so many go by.

The instructional supervisor also explained more about how the celebration works, how it can be used to improve attendance, and how it helped recruitment when the staff organized the day.

Rituals of solidarity bring the program together. Staff and interns are given more of an opportunity to get to know each other personally and, in the process, the communal ritual serves to establish a bond that links everyone together as a member of the group. These rituals represent the vehicle for producing and maintaining a "little community."

Rites of passage are conducted in various ways at the CIP. Moving from one term to the next marks a rite of passage for some interns. The staff and interns recognize the difference between the "old" and the "new" interns and the transition is considered significant.

When an intern dramatically alters his or her attitude or academic performance, the event is commemorated with a minor rite of passage. The intern may be placed on the honor role, given a specific CIP-is-Hip award or other interns may give the individual a nickname.

The program's most significant rite of passage is, of course, graduation. Interns emphasize throughout the entire program that "your first responsibility to yourself is to get your diploma—that's the purpose for coming." They recognize the difference between passing an equivalency examination and getting a real diploma, both in terms of personal self-worth and employment, and they are in the program to earn the diploma. As one intern explained: "I knew a long time ago about the GED (General Equivalency Diploma), but I wanted a high school diploma." Many refer to this experience as their "last chance."

The graduation ceremony marks the transition from young adult to adult for many, from failure to success for others, and from dropout or "potential dropout" to high school graduate, and either employment or college. The parent organization's newsletter (1979) captures the importance of this rite of passage: "The CIP graduation ceremony, it is worth noting, is taken very seriously by parents and interns. It is a cap on a genuine achievement, and the ceremony affirms that." These mechanisms of cultural transmission function as part of the CIP milieu as well. They provide one of the several structural layers which form the overarching framework or context of the study.

CONTEXTUALIZATION

One of ethnography's most significant contributions to evaluation is its ability to provide the context required to interpret data meaningfully. The ethnographic component of the Career Intern Program study provided contextual information on program, evaluation, and federal levels.

Program Context

The immediate context of the Career Intern Program includes both school facilities and neighborhood environments. A brief description of one site's neighborhood and schools where pimping, drug dealing, gang activity, murder, and arson for hire were routine social activities provided an insight into student lives, and into the challenges confronting the program. Expressive autobiographic interviews (Spindler & Spindler, 1970) focusing on the students' former school experience provided a baseline with which to compare their present attendance rate in the program. A 50% attendance rate had a new meaning when it was compared with a baseline figure of zero or a 20% attendance rate. Similarly, describing the physical structure housing the program, for example a church or an old three story house in disrepair, provides information regarding the educational climate or atmosphere, e.g., religious ties, community support (or lack thereof) for the program, and other contributing factors that account for the social dynamics observed in the program. The old three story house at one site provided a structure that encouraged students and teachers to "disappear into the woodwork."

Evaluation Context

On another level, ethnography captures the roles of the evaluation design and of the research corporation orchestrating the evaluation. An analysis of the evaluation, specifically the effects of the treatment-control experimental design which represents the core of one of the four evaluation tasks, revealed one of the reasons why the program was experiencing recruitment difficulties. The evaluation corporation, in an attempt to economize, decided to test potential students in groups of 15 rather than on a demand basis. Consequently staff members were unable to inform students when testing would occur. Students waiting for four weeks or more often lost interest in the program. The programs already had serious flaws in their recruitment procedures; the implementation of the treatment-control design only made these problems worse. Changing to an on-demand policy for recruiting, testing, and admitting students resolved the problem and, indirectly, validated this finding. Pressure to recruit unrealistic numbers of potential students also forced staff to abandon instruction and counseling to meet the quotas. Playing "the numbers game" resulted in the admission of inappropriate students, which later inflated termination statistics. Moreover, the admission of students with severe learning disabilities, e.g., special education students, significantly contributed to the staff's frustration level. Program instructors were not trained for the special needs of these students and initially were unable to understand why they were unsuccessful. An ethnographic explanation in terms of instruction and tolerance for inappropriate behavior helped to clarify the instructors' difficulties and added to an understanding of the evaluation context in which the program was operating.

Federal Context

The ethnographer's eye also focused on the roles of the sponsor, managing agency, and the President of the United States in attempting to interpret program operations. Federal agency pressure to meet enrollment quotas, for example, resulted in the creative use of attendance statistics by the sites. The evaluation staff identified inconsistencies between their own attendance and enrollment figures and those of the sites. The discrepancy pointed up the fact that the programs had to serve two masters—the federal agency and the evaluation firm. The federal agency was principally interested in the numbers served, while the research firm was primarily concerned with the attendance record. The sites operating in this political context devised a system to meet both concerns. They calculated enrollment figures for federal agencies by counting every individual ever enrolled in the program (total enrollment). They calculated attendance figures by counting only the students that participated regularly (active enrollment). Significant discrepancies in attendance rates between sites were resolved quickly after this formula was identified. Rivalry between sponsoring and managing federal agencies, another contextual variable in the study, explained other observed difficulties in implementing the program. It also suggested how indirect the causal relationships could be as for instance between federal interagency rivalry and student attendance. Interagency rivalry caused a 4 month delay in sending money to one of the sites. During that time the sites had to look for emergency local funding. One site's local affiliate was not financially well endowed and was therefore unable to maintain an uninterrupted program operation. The last minute budget transfers required to meet the payroll lowered staff morale. Moreover, the absence of program funds led staff to question whether the program would continue to operate from week to week.

The inability to purchase supplies had the most significant impact on program operations. "At one point we couldn't even pay for toilet paper," commented one staff member. Instructors ordinarily depended heavily on the use of classroom paper to make the individualized instruction packets for interns. The paper shortage ·interfered with the continuity of the curriculum. Lecturing replaced the packets for a short time. The interns quickly grew bored with the method predominantly used in their old public high school and many stopped attending classes. "Money trickled in (by the 4th month) and saved the program," according to an administrator. "Staff were frustrated to the point of just giving up, and we were beginning to lose our interns." Interns were hanging around outside the building and downtown. The majority, however, returned once the program was restored to a normal operating budget. One of the interns explained his absence:

> There was nothing to do. They were out of packets. The teachers they tell you they don't have any more paper—what kind of school is that? I know it wasn't their fault but . . . I finished my work. I was all caught up. What was I supposed to do?

Another area of concern was the national political context. The relationship between the federal administration and the parent organization of the program was carefully documented, including photographs and tape recordings of exchanges between the founder and leader of the parent organization and the then chief executive of the United States. The economic consequences of this close relationship would have a significant impact on the future dissemination of the program—as does the current political climate.

These are a few examples of how ethnographic research provides evaluators with a multilevel context within which to understand and explain various patterns of behavior. (See Fetterman, 1981b, for a more detailed account of ethnographic contributions to the study of implementation, interrelationships, and outcomes in the CIP study.) This study also offers a model of interdisciplinary description for both evaluators and anthropologists. By dispelling basic disciplinary misconceptions about qualitative and quantitative data, the study alters the shape of the academic landscape.

DEMYTHOLOGIZING: THE
QUALITATIVE-QUANTITATIVE DICHOTOMY

A myth has developed that ethnography is concerend exclusively with the qualitative domain, and educational evaluation with quantitative data. In practice these two measures often work together to explain a phenomenon. Quantitative data can validate or be validated by qualitative observations. Good ethnography requires a qualitative-quantitative mix. The ethnographic component of the CIP study documented both quantitative and qualitative program outcomes. The study examined the quality of the quantitative and qualitative program outcomes. The study examined the quality of the quantitative data and successfully integrated qualitative and quantitative data.

Qualitative Data

There are an infinite number of criteria required to assess a program. Many of the less easily quantified criteria were discussed in detail in the study, ranging from increased attention span to learning to cope with authority. An excerpt of a classroom lecture is presented below to demonstrate how an instructor's attitude towards students and his ability to relate his personal experience to classroom lessons was captured and documented. In addition, his ability to detect intern attitudes through their body language is evidenced.

> I washed dishes my first 2 years off of New Jersey on Long Island, upstate New York. Poughkeepsie. Where those ski resorts are all up there. I did all that because I knew I was in a position of being overqualified for some jobs and not qualified fully for others, because I had not completed my degree, okay. But once you have that piece of paper, then that's a horse of another different color. They can't keep not lookin' at you, turn you down; 'cause you gotta be qualified for somethin' if this piece of paper says you are, you know.

> The college degree is like the high school diploma was 30 years ago. Actually you're in a state in this country, where the college degree really is high school and people better wake up and realize that. All you doing now is getting the skills to go to college. You're not educated, you know it. Long ways from it. For the most part everybody in this room is a functional illiterate. That's the truth. The truth may hurt you. You may get feelings all down in your stomach of anger but that's the way it is. I guess you are very frustrated and you meet with consternation often times with me 'cause I read you so well. You tell me all the answers . . . you say things with your eyes and your expression on your face. What you do with your hands. When someone is guilty usually in my class I can tell, usually tell, whether

they did it or not. You tell me everything and then you get mad at me for knowin' it. So this is what [the film] was talkin' about, body language. So I got this film to show you some of the things that can happen in an interview situation. . . . You can sell yourself to anybody if you practice and to obtain the skill you must practice. That's half the battle—the interview. The other half, as we discussed, is being qualified.

This teacher's motivational techniques were considered controversial but effective, and were useful in developing an insight into the ethos of this program.

The study also documented and reported attitudinal changes. One of the graduates who had made, according to the entire staff of one program, the most dramatic transformation routinely visited the program. This is a typical pattern of behavior for graduates who have developed a very strong sense of identity and affiliation with the program. "He came in smelling like a monster. Thug number one," said one instructor. He was "a hood," according to one of his friends. Another staff member continued: "His hair was long and wild. He wore that big ol' pimpin' hat. Remember him, the one with the Barcelloni (hat). He'd be tearin' up the place, rippin' and runnin' around the neighborhood. Always hanging around with [a former student] and the gang." An instructor commented, "Now look at him. He is a changed man. He smiles now. You would never see a smile on his face before. His hair is cut, he dresses well, speaks politely and he's calmed down. He has truly matured. He's at [the local community college] and he wants to be a mechanical engineer. They say he's got the mathematical aptitude to do it too. We're happy with the change we've seen in him. It's beautiful."

The dramatic change in this intern's apparel and posture was observed and documented photographically by the author over a period of 3 years. In addition, his grades changed from failing to straight A's—honor roll caliber. This particular graduate recognized the transformation he had made; however, he was facing new conflicts and dilemmas which were documented as part of his transition to college life.

I come back to the old neighborhood just to hang out, you know, and they accept me still just like before, except now instead of saying "hey—," they say "hey—the college man," and it's different. Sometimes they won't let me be the same even when I am. Partly because I'm not around that much anymore; before, that's all I used to do is hang out with them. Now I drop by when I can but the other part is the college part. I don't mind too much, I'm meeting some really good people at school and of course I still hang out with [graduates from the CIP attending the same college]. We help each other. If I know something like math and Wilda (pseudonym) needs help after dinner we work on it. When I need help Sammy or Ralph comes by to help me. The tutor is also real good. They explain everything so you can understand. The professors, you know, they don't care, they're just in there busy lecturing, they don't have time for questions with so many people.

When this graduate was asked what he thought about the program and why he returns to visit so often, he said:

How could I forget it? I wouldn't be where I'm at without this place; I'll never forget it. Mr. Smith, I hate to admit it, but he helped me a whole lot. He was tough but that's what it's like out there. It's real. . . . They all helped me and I'll never forget them. I know I'm going to make it now. I know why people were afraid of me before when I had to act "bad." Now I know how to think things through and how it [the system] all works. I'll keep coming back to see my old friends and to try and help the new interns comin' up. Tell 'em how you gotta get serious about all this and how it really pays off.

Interviews with a number of graduates revealed similar experiences and feelings toward the program and the future. An important and interesting manifestation of staff concern for interns was displayed in this intern's case. He had contemplated not accepting the college's offer of admission because he was ashamed of his second-hand clothes. The staff all contributed to a fund to buy him new clothes to enable him to attend.

Finally, a selection of CIP student poetry in their school newspaper offered another means of documenting student attitudes. The selection is entitled: CIP Means.

CIP MEANS

CIP means a home away from home.
CIP means good teachers like you and Ms. Powers.
CIP means having a little fun.
CIP means getting the job done.
CIP means people who care.
CIP means people who share.
CIP means a great deal.
CIP means being for real.
CIP means activity day.
CIP means games that you play.
CIP means meeting a smiling face in the morning.
CIP means no playing around in the corners.
CIP means a stop along the way.
CIP means looking forward to a better day.
CIP means a hop, skip, and jump.
CIP means getting over the hump.
CIP means a new way of life.
CIP means finding a husband or wife.

CIP means eating a good meal.
CIP means they care how you feel.
CIP means seeing a basketball game.
CIP means learning new faces and new names.
CIP means CIP is Hip day.
CIP means Monday through Friday.
But most of all, CIP means success.

Qualified Quantitative Data

These qualitative forms of documentation were balanced by four easily quantified assessment criteria identified as significant by a close study of program operations and participant interviews. They included attendance, turnover, graduation, and placement. The figures reported in the study and in this discussion reflect the conditions of program development and the process of maturation. They are not the product of a program that began fully mature. These quantitative forms of documentation also depended on qualitative investigations. Attendance figures, for example, were not accepted at face value—as reported by the sites. Observations of students signing in at the front door and then racing out the back door were taken into account. Administration attendance "fudge factors" were identified and considered. Classroom head counts by the ethnographer and the evaluators at various points in the day were also used as part of the calculation, as well as unofficial self-reports and estimates by students and staff. Reporting the attendance figures given by the sites and then comparing them across sites would have been grossly misleading and unfair. In fact, official attendance rates would have resulted in a ranking that placed the worst site on top. The recalculated attendance figures were recognized and accepted as the most accurate representation by each site.

The staff turnover rate was highly significant because of the importance of continuity between management and staff and between staff and interns. The development of well functioning CIP components requires continuity of both policies and personnel. Similarly, the development of personal relationships between staff and interns—which promotes attendance—requires continuity in staffing. On-site observations first alerted the ethnographer to a potential problem in this area. Casual observation led to quantification and a pattern developed across sites. Variations in turnover rates were indicative of implementation successes and failures. The reasons for departure represent the links between implementation and a given program's turnover rate.

When the specific breakdown of voluntary and involuntary departures of staff and management was paired with ethnographic observations, two distinct patterns emerged. The majority of the staff left the program voluntarily for career advancement opportunities, while the majority of management personnel left the program involuntarily due to incompetence and/or a lack of appropriate qualifications.[2] The program served as a training ground for the instructional and counseling staff. The lure of additional money, promotional opportunities, better hours, and better fringe benefits in the local schools and in private industry training programs were reported most frequently as the basis for voluntary departures among staff. On the other hand, weak managerial or administrative skills, poor interpersonal skills, and counterproductive communication skills were most often cited as the basis for involuntary managerial terminations. The categories of career advancement, incompetence, and lack of appropriate qualifications were based on the "insider's" or participants' classificatory system. The evaluation did not rely solely on site administrative termination rosters to establish the reasons for departure. Many euphemisms were employed in program operations that unintentionally obscured the reasons for staff departure. Classification of departures, therefore, relied on the following kinds of triangulated information: termination rosters, observation of staff member performance and social interaction with colleagues and interns, key informants, self-reports, casual conversations throughout participants' tenure, follow-up visits and phone conversations with ex-staff members, and so on.

An accurate analysis of the data underscored a simple, widely acknowledged but poorly understood management principle: Securing qualified, talented staff is essential when building and operating any organization. Reporting statistics was important; however, reporting percentages calculated expressly from official channels would have presented a distorted picture of the situation and neglected important insights.

Graduation and placement statistics similarly were investigated thoroughly before reporting any numbers. Because one of the goals of the program was to prepare students for a career—which meant enabling students to earn a diploma rather than a general equivalency diploma (GED)—all GED's were removed from the graduation numbers. In addition, all students expected to graduate who failed to complete all requirements were removed from the graduation lists. In a few instances the

---

[2]The term incompetent was drawn directly from site and disseminator classifications. Bardach's (1977) description of incompetence, however, is one of the most useful definitions of the term:

> It is a description of a relationship between an individual and a particular task or situation: the individual is unable to perform the task or function in the situation up to a given, though ultimately arbitrary, standard of some sort. An individual who is quite competent to do some things will be incompetent to do others. It may not in any meaningful sense by "his fault" that he is incompetent to perform certain tasks—it may well be the fault of the people who assigned him the task in the first place. (p. 126)

ethnographic evaluator contacted a higher number of graduates placed in college than the program had recorded. This was due to poor program record keeping, and consequently served as a manifestation of faulty operating procedures rather than an unsuccessful program. In other instances graduation numbers were reduced after in-depth investigation and analysis of the figures. Similarly, the collection of placement data relied as heavily on peer referral and on-site employee-employer confirmation of individual placements, as on official counselor tabloids and administrative records.

Integrating Qualitative and Quantitative Data

An example on a different level shows how qualitative and quantitative approaches complement each other. Several variations of Program Climate questionnaires were distributed to both staff and interns during site visits. These questionnaires were not developed out of the field experience; however, they served as useful indices of specific attitudes toward program personnel. In fact, preliminary statistical analyses revealed high correlations between on-site observations and the rating scales. The results of standardized reading and math tests (Tallmadge & Lam, 1979) also proved highly illuminating, regarding the school's ability to accomplish its manifest goals. Moreover, high math scores produced by the "quantitative" component of the study were explained by the independent "qualitative" observational data. The presence or absence of those math teachers identified by staff, interns, and ethnographic observation as the most qualified correlated almost perfectly with the math gains and losses.

The use of psychometric test results in the ethnographic analysis as well as the active participation of the ethnographer in gathering, coordinating, and often supervising the procurement of this data illustrates the interrelatedness and interdependence of quantitative and qualitative approaches in the ethnographic educational evaluation endeavor. The integration of these measures was often difficult and occasionally unwieldy, but always productive and revealing. A more difficult undertaking involved the translation of ethnographic findings into the language of educational policy makers.

RELEVANCE FOR POLICY

Ethnographic educational evaluation faces the same obstacles that most academic disciplines and subdisciplines encounter in the attempt to produce findings that are relevant for policy decision making. The CIP

study successfully overcame most of these problems by translating acade-
mese into bureaucratese, internalizing the dynamics of policy decision
making, producing results in a timely fashion, serving as advocates when
appropriate, and providing the type of process information useful to
policy decision makers. In addition, specific programmatic and policy
recommendations were made to enable policy makers to quickly identify
the levers of change (Fetterman, 1981a).

Language

One of the first barriers this study encountered was the language barrier
between ethnographic research and policy decision makers. Learning to
communicate was paramount to the success of the project. As Zander
(1980) explains:

> If we want clients to utilize our research findings, I suggest we extend the
> research process. By extend I mean . . . we would first write the ethnogra-
> phy, then identify the communication patterns within the client culture.
> Lastly, we would translate our ethnographic findings into more emic and
> culturally appropriate styles and formats.

> If we are powerless to teach clients ethnographic literacy, should we learn
> the equivalent smoke signals and talking drums? (Zander, p. 39)

Knowledge is useless if it is presented in an unintelligible manner. An
excess of jargon and a patchwork of patterns and processes can obscure
the most salient research findings. In addition, exhaustive and lengthy
research reports are rarely read by anyone. Ethnographic accounts, in
particular, are noted for their extraordinary length. Even so, it has been
suggested that "ethnographies are, in fact, more likely to be read than a
compiled mass of statistical tables [because] ethnographies have people in
them" (Agar, 1980, p. 35). Moreover, it has been suggested that ethnographies are concise presentations of the ethnographer's observation of
cultural patterns and practices. This may be true; however, I would argue
that the ethnographer's conception of an economy of words is likely to be
perceived as indulgent excess by policymakers, a difference in perspective resulting from the different structures and functions of their respective environments. There is a law of diminishing returns. The criticism,
however, applies to conventional evaluation as well as to ethnographic
evaluation efforts. Cronbach et al. (1980) suggest that "communication
overload is a common fault; many an evaluation is reported with self-
defeating thoroughness" (1980, p. 6). It is true that "when an avalanche of
words and tables descends, everyone in its path dodges" (Cronbach et

al., 1980, p. 184).[3] This observation should not, however, dampen efforts to complete a thorough, scholarly investigation. Detailed findings—whether ethnographic or psychometric in orientation—can be presented in a technical report, while a summary of salient findings or a nontechnical or translated report can be added for policymakers. In fact, many agencies require the inclusion of executive summaries in evaluation reports. These summaries consist of a brief statement of the study's findings and recommendations written in the policy decision maker's own language.

Ethnographers and evaluators interested in effectively communicating their research findings must learn the language or "equivalent smoke signals" of policymakers. Moreover, evaluation research can become more useful if guided by a knowledge of the dynamics of policymaking. The perspective of federal government policymakers is clearly presented in the literature by Mulhauser (1975); Coward (1976); Holcomb (1974); Etzioni (1971); von Neuman and Morganstern (1953); March and Olsen (1976); Acland (1979); Cronbach et al. (1980); Baker (1975); Fetterman (1928b); among others.

Timeliness

One of the most important features of the federal policymaker perspective is timeliness. Knowledge is power, and information is required at prespecified periods to assist in the federal decision making process. Coward warns, "Agencies place themselves in vulnerable positions if they sponsor a research effort that is unable to provide data under constraints imposed by policy deadlines." The inability to address these concerns may leave an agency out in the cold, with little or no future funding. The CIP study attempted to recognize and adapt to these types of constraints.

First of all, the ethnographic component of the study was completed within the specified period of time to allow for maximum policy impact. In addition, interim reports[4] were produced and delivered without jeopardiz-

---

[3]Cronbach et al. (1980) presented an example of "self-defeating thoroughness" in evaluation: "As an extreme example, one recent report on nonformal education in Latin America ran to 900 pages (single space and in English!); perhaps that document found no audience at all" (p. 186).

[4]The ethnographic interim reports were entitled: *Study of the Career Intern Program. Interim Technical Report—Task C: Functional Interrelationships Among Program Components and Intern Outcomes*. Mountain View, CA: RMS Research Corporation; and *Study of the Career Intern Program. Interim Non-technical Report—Task C: Functional Interrelationships Among Program Components and Intern Outcomes*. Mountain View, CA: RMC Research Corporation.

ing the ethnographer-informant relationship or the quality of the work, and without producing any of the associated perils of premature disclosure. Similarly, formal and informal lines of communication between the evaluators, the sponsors and managers, and the sites and disseminators, were maintained on a regular basis without disturbing the delicate web of rights and obligations regarding confidentiality, privacy, and reciprocity. Moreover, the evaluators were able to acknowledge the limited role of research in the policy arena without diminishing their fervor for excellence. The research findings represented a small facet of the input used to make policy decisions. On more than one occasion policy discussions directly related to the program under study were made before the research was either conducted or requested. In addition, drifting tides of political favor or disfavor were taken in stride. The study was a favorite child during one administration and a potential political hazard during the next. A single report would have been either paraded before or hidden from Congress depending on the political ramifications of the research findings.

Advocacy

Although the evaluators were aware of the limited role of their findings in policy decision making, they did not retreat from their political role. C. Wright Mills (1959) distinguished three political roles for social scientists: philospher-king, advisor to the king, and independent scientist. The evaluators selected a combination of the second and third roles. They disseminated the generally positive findings to appropriate individuals in governmental and quasi-governmental institutions. Future funding for the program was dependent on the dissemination of the evaluation findings and the recommendations of various agencies. In addition, the evaluators prepared a Joint Dissemination Review Panel Submission substantially based on the ethnographic findings to improve the program's credibility and its chance of securing future funding. This was accomplished in the

---

The experience surrounding the publication of these reports represents an excellent case example of the role of serendipity in policy decision making. Technical reports are rarely read by more than a handful of individuals. In this case, however, the technical report received greater circulation and produced a greater impact than the nontechnical report. This report received a significant degree of attention because of the unusual unauthorized and unacknowledged use of the work. (See Fetterman, 1981d, for details.) In a dialectic fashion, this attention generated greater interest in the findings within the managing agency. The net result was that a large amount of data was brought to policy decision makers' attention—information that would normally have been skimmed at best. There is no reason to assume that this information necessarily altered policy decisions; however, it produced the potential for shaping policy decisions simply because it was read.

face of significant resistance; it was politically hazardous to favor social programs during this period. These actions were in accord with Mill's (1959) position that:

> There is no necessity for working social scientists to allow the potential meaning of their work to be shaped by the "accidents of its setting, or its use to be determined by the purposes of other men. It is quite within their powers to discuss its meanings and decide upon its uses as matters of their own policy. (p. 177)

The evaluators, ethnographic and conventional, agreed that they had a moral responsibility to serve as an advocate for the program based on the research findings. There is a difference between being an academic and an activist; however, academic study does not preclude advocacy. In fact, often anything less represents an abdication of one's responsibility as a social scientist. (See Berreman, 1968, and Gough, 1968.)

Policy and Programmatic Recommendations

Finally, the ethnographic component of the study produced a set of policy and programmatic recommendations. These recommendations addressed problems in the overall evaluation design, the implementation of the program, and program operations. The study also cast some doubt on the wisdom of replicating experimental educational programs and corresponding research designs, and the value of using conventional school procedures and personnel in alternative educational programs. A few of the recommendations stemming from the ethnographic component of the study are presented below.

Policy Recommendations

We found the use of the experimental design in one part of this study and in this social program to be inappropriate. Ethically, the use of the treatment-control design was problematic because it prevented dropouts trying to reenter the system from taking the first step back through this educational program. Methodologically, there wasn't a true control group. Students who passed the entrance tests, but were selected as part of the control group knew they were not participating in the program or "treatment." In this case, the control group was actually a negative treatment group. In addition, since there was little incentive for the control group students to come back and be post tested, the students that did return represented a biased sample. This produced misleading comparisons with the treatment group. Therefore, we recommend that policy makers:

1. Abandon the use of randomized treatment-control designs to evaluate social programs, particularly when ethical standards have been violated. All available program positions should be filled; individuals should not be excluded from participation in a program for the sake of constructing a control group.

2. Reevaluate the selection of an experimental design when methodological requirements can not be met. The most significant methodological concerns in this case involve: constructing a negative treatment group instead of a control group, and comparing groups without considering the effects of differential attrition at post test time. (See Fetterman, 1982b; Tallmadge, 1979.)

We also found that the goal of replication—expecting clone-like duplicates and triplicates of the original program—was conceptually off-target. Policy makers expected each of the programs to be replicas of the original model.[5] Replication, however, is a biological not an anthropological or sociological concept. Programs take on new shapes and forms in the process of adapting to the demands of their environments. We believe that studying how these programs respond to their differing environments would be more fruitful than noting whether they were in or out of compliance with the model. Therefore, we recommend that:

3. The process of adaptation should be the focus of inquiry. (See Fetterman, 1981c.)

Program Recommendations

We identified numerous programmatic concerns during the course of the study. Two of the most important personnel findings that we documented involved management and staff turnover. The high turnover rate of management was directly attributable to poor screening techniques. The staff turnover rate was often attributable to competing salaries and benefits of local public schools. Therefore, we recommended that program disseminators:

1. Improve screening and selection procedures for management of programs. Focus on administrative experience and educational background.

2. Establsih equitable salaries and yearly schedules comparable with

---

[5]See: J. L. Pressman and A. B. Wildavsky, 1973. *Implementation.* Berkeley, CA: University of California Press, for a classic example of how local level implementation can deviate significantly from federal policy decision makers' intentions.

the local educational agencies to prevent demoralization, burnout, and turnover.

The findings and recommendations of this segment of the study demonstrate ethnography's relevance for educational policy. The relevance of the ethnographic findings and recommendations for policy, however, extends beyond the written word. One of the most important roles of ethnography may be as consultant for policy questions. In the case under discussion, the ethnographer was asked by both government policy makers and program officials for information and advice regarding both short and long term intervention strategies. In addition, information was solicited regarding causal relationships between the quantitative and qualitative study findings. The exchange of information, however, does not presuppose a substantial voice in policy decisions. In fact, often:

> The improvement of research on social policy does not lead to greater clarity about what to think or what to do. Instead, it usually tends to produce a greater sense of complexity. It also leads to a more complicated view of problems and solutions, for the progress of research tends to reveal the inadequacy of accepted ideas about solving problems. The ensuing complexity and infusion are naturally a terrific frustration both to resources who think they should matter and officials who think they need help. (Cohen & Weiss, 1977, p. 73)

Policy decision making is both an art and a craft (Wildavsky, 1979). Moreover, it is an irrational and fundamentally political process. Research represents a pawn in the larger chess game. The insights and findings of the most capably conducted research are useless if researchers abdicate their responsibility and choose not to play the game.

Conclusion

Ethnographic educational evaluation is what ethnographers do in the process of adapting ethnography to educational evaluation. This process had required much innovation. Methods have been altered to accommodate the constraints of contract research. In multisite qualitative studies, innovations have been made to improve the generalizability of the research findings. These innovations have a cost. Flexibility, for example, is often diminished in an attempt to structure data collection efforts in a more systematic fashion. In addition, some control of the research topic is lost in an attempt to respond to policy relevant concerns. Fundamentally, however, ethnographers have been able to ensure that ethnographic educational evaluation remains ethnographic. This has been accomplished by the diligent efforts of applied anthropologists. It has required, minimally: maintaining control of the direction, if not the topic, of one's policy research, consistently employing ethnographic techniques and concepts, and following the basic canons and ethical guidelines of anthropological research.

Ethnographic educational evaluation has increased our understanding of educational issues and the processes of cultural transmission, by clarifying interrelationships and providing added insight into the values that shape human behavior. With careful and conscientious use, this fruitful approach can be applied to the many areas of educational research. Ethnography in educational evaluation has, indeed, found fertile ground.

ACKNOWLEDGMENT

I am indebted to my mentor George Dearborn Spindler for his guidance and insightful criticism in preparing me for this pioneering venture. I am also indebted to Deborah S. Waxman from SRI International for her critical eye and imaginative suggestions in the preparation of this manuscript.

REFERENCES

Acland, H. (1979). Are randomized experiments the cadillacs of design? *Policy Analysis, 5,* 223–241.

Agar, M. (1980). PA comments: Ethnography and applied policy research, *Practicing Anthropology, 3*(2), 35.

Baker, K. (1975). A new grantsmanship, *American Sociologist, 10,* 206–219.

Bardach, E. (1977). *The implementation game: What happens after a bill becomes a law.* Cambridge, MA: MIT Press.

Berreman, G. D. (1968). Is anthropology alive? Social responsibility in social anthropology, *Current Anthropology, 9,* 391–396.

Cohen, D. K., & Weiss, J. A. (1977). Social science and social policy, schools, and race. In R. C. Rist & R. J. Anson (Eds.), *Education, social science, and the judicial process.* New York: Teachers College Press.

Coward, R. (1976). The involvement of anthropologists in contract evaluations: The federal perspective, *Anthropology and Education Quarterly, 7,* 12–16.

Cronbach, L. J., Ambron, S. R., Dornbusch, S. M., Hess, R. D., Hornik, R. C., Phillips, D. C., Walker, D. F., & Weiner, S. S. (1980). *Toward reform of program evaluation.* San Francisco: Jossey-Bass.

Cubberly, E. P. (1909). *Changing conceptions of education* (pp. 15–16). Boston: Houghton Mifflin.

Etzioni, A. (1971). Policy Research, *American Sociologist, 6,* 8–12.

Fetterman, D. M. (1979). *Study of the career intern program. Interim technical report—Task*

C: Functional interrelationships among program components and intern outcomes. Mountain View, CA: RMC Research Corporation.

Fetterman, D. M. (1980). Ethnographic techniques in educational evaluation: An illustration. In Alanson A. Van Fleet (Ed.), *Anthropology of education: methods and applications,* Special topic edition of the *Journal of Thought, 15*(3), 31–48.

Fetterman, D. M. (1981a). *Study of the career intern program. Final Report—Task C: Program dynamics: Structure, function, and interrelationships.* Mountain View, CA: RMC Research Corporation.

Fetterman, D. M. (1981b). *Implementation, interrelationships, and outcomes: Ethnographic contributions to educational evaluation.* Paper presented at the annual meetings of the American Educational Research Association, Los Angeles.

Fetterman, D. M. (1981c). Blaming the victim: The problem of evaluation design and federal involvement, and reinforcing world views in education, *Human Organization, 40*(1), 67–77.

Fetterman, D. M. (1981d). New perils for the contract ethnographer, *Anthropology and Education Quarterly, 12*(1), 71–80.

Fetterman, D. M. (1982a). Ethnography in educational research: The dynamics of diffusion, *Educational Researcher, 11*(3), 17–29.

Fetterman, D. M. (1982b). Ibsen's baths: Reactivity and insensitivity. A misapplication of the treatment-control design in a national evaluation, *Educational Evaluation and Policy Analysis, 4*(3), 261–279.

Fetterman, D. M. (Ed.). (1984). *Ethnography in educational evaluation.* Beverly Hills, CA: Sage.

Fetterman, D. M., & Pitman, M. A. (Eds.). (1986). *Educational evaluation: Ethnography in theory, practice, and politics.* Beverly Hills, CA: Sage.

Firestone, W. (1980). *Great expectations for small schools: The limitations of federal projects.* New York: Praeger.

Firestone, W., & Herriott, R. (1984). Multisite qualitative research: Some design and implementation issues. In D. Fetterman (Ed.), *Ethnography in educational evaluation.* Beverly Hills, CA: Sage.

Geertz, C. (1973). Thick description: Toward an interpretive theory of culture. In C. Geertz (Ed.), *The interpretation of cultures.* New York: Basic Books.

Goffman, E. (1961). *Asylums: Essays on the social situation of mental patients and other inmates.* New York: Random House.

Gough, K. (1968). World revolution and the science of man. In T. Roszak (Ed.), *The dissenting academy.* New York: Random House.

Hanna, J. (1982). Public social policy and the children's world: implications of ethnographic research for desegregated schooling. In G. D. Spindler (Ed.), *Doing the ethnography of schooling: Educational anthropology in action.* New York: Holt, Rinehart, and Winston.

Harris, M. (1971). *Culture, man, and nature.* New York: Thomas Y. Crowell.

Hemwall, M. (1984). Ethnography as evaluation: Hearing impaired children in the mainstream. In D. M. Fetterman (Ed.), *Ethnography in educational evaluation.* Beverly Hills, CA: Sage.

Herriott, R. (1979a). The federal context: Planning, funding, and monitoring. In R. E. Herriott & N. Gross (Eds.), *The dynamics of planned educational change.* Berkeley, CA: McCutchan.

Herriott, R. (1979b). *Federal initiative and rural school improvement: findings from the experimental school program.* Cambridge, MA: Abt Associates.

Holcomb, H. (1974). Tell Congress results of research. *Education Daily, 4,* 313.

Malinowski, B. (1961). *Argonauts of the western Pacific.* New York: E. P. Dutton. (First published in 1922.)

March, J., & Olsen, J. (1976). *Ambiguity and choice in organizations.* Bergen, Norway: Universitets Forlaget.

Mills, C. (1959). *The sociological imagination.* New York: Oxford University Press.

Mulhauser, F. (1975). Ethnography and policymaking: The case of education, *Human Organization, 34,* 311.

Pressman, J. L., & Wildavsky, A. B. (1973). *Implementation.* Berkeley: University of California Press.

Roberts, J., & Akinsanya, S. (1976a). *Educational patterns and cultural configurations: The anthropology of education.* New York: David McKay.

Roberts, J., & Akinsanya, S. (1976b). *Schooling in the cultural context: Anthropological studies of education.* New York: David McKay.

Smith, A. G., & Robbins, A. E. (1984). Multi-method policy research: A case study of structure and flexibility. In D. M. Fetterman (Ed.), *Ethnography in educational evaluation.* Beverly Hills, CA: Sage.

Spindler, G., & Spindler, L. (Eds.). (1970). *Being an anthropologist: Fieldwork in eleven cultures.* New York: Holt, Rinehart, and Winston.

Spindler, G. (Ed.). (1974). *Education and cultural process: Toward an anthropology of education.* New York: Holt, Rinehart, and Winston.

Spindler, G. (Ed.). (1982). *Doing the ethnography of schooling: Educational anthropology in action.* New York: Holt, Rinehart, and Winston.

Tallmadge, G. (1979). Avoiding problems in evaluation, *Journal of Career Education, 5*(4), 300–308.

Tallmadge, G., & Lam, T. (1979). *Study of the career intern program—Interim technical report, Task B: Assessment of intern outcomes.* CA: RMC Research Corporation.

von Newmann, J., & Morganstern, L. (1953). *The theory of games and economic behavior* (3rd edition). New Jersey: Princeton University Press.

Wildavsky, A. (1979). *Speaking truth to power: The art and craft of policy analysis.* Boston: Little, Brown.

Wolcott, H. (1980). How to look like an anthropologist without really being one. *Practicing Anthropology, 3*(2), 6–7, 56–59.

Wolcott, H. (1984). Ethnographers sans ethnography: The evaluation compromise. In D. M. Fetterman (Ed.), *Ethnography in educational evaluation.* Beverly Hills, CA: Sage.

Zander, D. (1980). Ethnography and applied policy research, *Practicing Anthropology, 3*(2), 40.

The Author and His Chapter

Since receiving his Ph.D. in Sociology from the University of California, Santa Barbara in 1971, Hugh Mehan has approached the issue of the role of schooling in society from an interactionist and sociolinguistic perspective. He has examined the construction of classroom lessons, educational tests, and students educational careers within the context of bilingual and special education. He is author of *Language Use and School Performance* (with Aaron Cicourel and others), *The Reality of Ethnomethodology* (with Houston Wood), *Learning Lessons,* "Structuring School Structure," *Harvard Educational Review,* "The Language of Role and the Role of Language in Educational Decision Making," *Language in Society*; "Social Construction in Sociology and Psychology," *Sociologies et Societes; Handicapping the Handicapped* (with Alma Hertweck and J. Lee Meihls) that appeared in 1986.

We are fortunate to have a sociologist of Hugh Mehan's disposition contribute to our book, for his language and concerns, though sociological, overlap with those of anthropology, thus demonstrating common ground that is essential if there is to be any unified attack on educational problems in the social sciences.

The unifying dimension is the concern with language as discourse. The ways in which decisions are made that determine the fate of children as they are channeled into special programs are revealed in the careful diagnosis of the discourse engaged in by the partners to these kinds of decisions. It becomes clear that there are tacit understandings that are constant factors in the exchanges within the discourse and that in turn these understandings reflect and reinforce social stratification. There is no essential disunity in the way Mehan does his analysis and the way an anthropologist would do the analysis, nor are the data collected or the methods of collection essentially different. There are stylistic differences but they do not impede communication.

Dr. Mehan's chapter emphasizes the importance of language, particularly in the form of speech, in ethnographic study. We interview as much or more than we observe. In fact our observations of behavior are largely for the purpose of framing the right (productive) questions to be asked in interview. The responses are delivered in the native language, whether the native is a Dobe !Kung bushman or a fifth-grade teacher in a California elementary school. We learn the language, record it, and translate it into academic language and culture. We also observe and record speech behavior when we are not interviewing, and analyze it in its social context as actors carry on discourses that are a part of the pervasive dialogue of their culture(s). Dr. Mehan's chapter shows us both in a particular application and in the framework of other work in language how important language is to our ethnographic enterprise.

The Editors

6 Language and Schooling

Hugh Mehan
University of California, San Diego

LANGUAGE AND SCHOOLING

In a recent meeting of a committee of educators convened to decide the classification and educational placement of elementary school students, the following dialog took place:

Key: Psy. = Psychologist; S.E.T. = Special Education Teacher; Prin. = Principal; DR = District Representative; Mo. = Mother

EDM   #33

92	Psy.	does the uh, committee agree that the, uh learning disability placement is one that might benefit him?
93	Prin.	I think we agree.
94	Psy.	We're not considering then a special day class at all for him?
95	S.E.T.	I wouldn't at this point//
96	Many	No.

EDM   #47

28	Psy.	Okay, in light of all the data that we have, I think that the program we want to recommend is the learning disability group pullout program.
29	Mo.	Pullout—I don't understand that//
30	Psy.	For Tracy. You know, that's the program we sort of talked about that day, where he would be pulled out of the classroom for specific work on the areas that he needs, that, you know, are identified today.

EDM   #57

35	Psy.	Okay. Now, okay, now then, let's, why don't we take a vote. Um, for the Learning Disabilities Group pullout program. Um, is there anyone, anyone who does not agree? (3) Okay. I think that was unanimous. (soft laughter)

This group of educators decided to place these students in "Learning Disability Groups." The LD group is a "pullout" educational program in which students spend a part of their school day in their regular classroom, and the other part of the school day in a special education classroom. Programs for the learning disabled and their companions such as those for the "educationally handicapped" have been established under the provisions of PL 94-142, "The Education for All Handicapped Students Act." This law, established to provide an equitable education to handicapped youngsters in the least restrictive environment possible, requires final placement decisions to be made by a committee composed of the student's teacher, a school psychologist, a representative from the district office, the child's parents, and in some cases, a nurse. This committee meeting is the culmination of a lengthy referral process which begins in the student's classroom, and involves individual psychological and educational assessment. The referral process studied by my colleagues and me (Mehan, 1983, 1984; Mehan et al., 1981) in a midsize school district in Southern California during the 1978–1979 school year is depicted in Fig. 6.1.

The discourse presented above was recorded in the final phase of this process, called the "Eligibility and Placement Committee." During the school year in which we observed this student classification process, 141 students were referred. Of this number, 53 were considered by the "E and P" Committee. The disposition of students' cases by this committee is shown in Table 6.1.

TABLE 6.1
The Disposition of 53 Cases Considered by Placement Committees

Placement	Number
Educationally Handicapped (EH)	7
Learning Disabled (LDG)	36
Severe Language Handicapped (SLH)	3
Multiply Handicapped	2
Speech	3
Private Schooling	0
No Placement (Returned to Classroom)	1
Placement process Interrupted	1
Total	53

A REPRESENTATION OF THE SPECIAL EDUCATION REFERRAL PROCESS

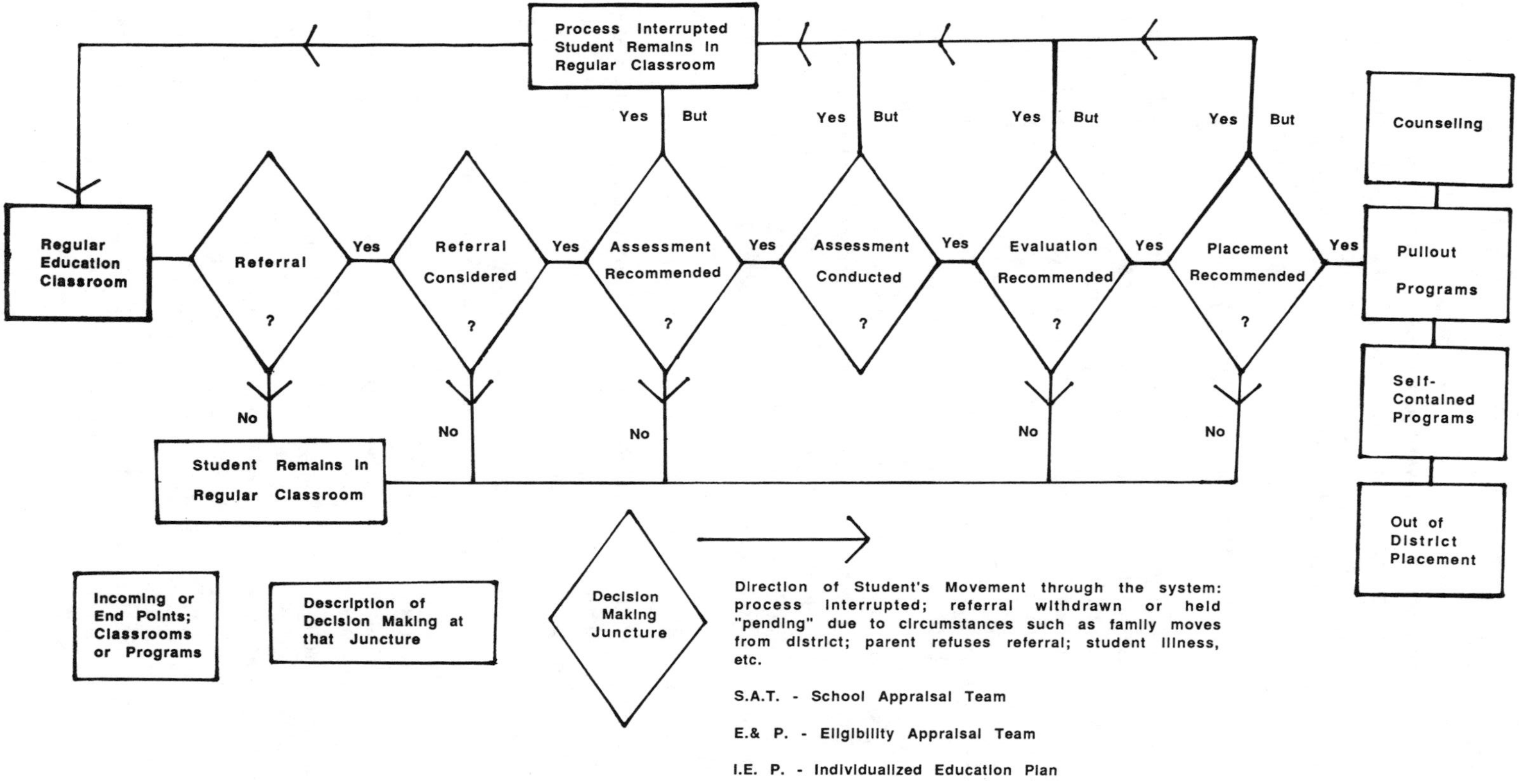

FIG. 6.1.   A Representation of the Special Education Referral Process

The majority of students were placed in the LDG program. EH was the next most frequent placement. Notably, no students were placed in special programs outside the district ("Private Schooling" in Table 6.1), and only one student was retained in his regular classroom.

IDENTIFYING HANDICAPPED STUDENTS

I am interested in *how* a distribution of students in special and regular education programs such as the one displayed in Table 6.1 is produced. In order to determine how a great majority of students were placed in LD and EH, few were retained in their regular classrooms, and *none* were placed outside the school district, we followed the progress of students' cases through the Special Education referral system mandated by PL 94-142 and its particular instantiation in one school district by reviewing official school records, interviewing educators, observing in classrooms and meetings, and analyzing the discourse between participants in key decision making events (indicated by a ⬦ in Fig. 6.1).

We found that a number of discursive and organizational arrangements provided for the statistical pattern in Table 6.1. Some of these practices occurred during the placement meeting itself; other activities occurred in the parts of the referral system that preceded the final placement meeting.

Discursive Arrangements within Placement Meetings

We observed the conduct of placement committee meetings, and when possible, videotaped the proceedings. The committee meetings had a regular and recurrent order:

Information	Decision	Parent	Goals and
Presentation	Making	Rights	Objectives

The first order of business was a discussion of the student's case. In this "information presentation" phase of the meeting, information about the student's record, "problem," and home life was introduced by the school psychologist, classroom teacher, parents, and any one else who had knowledge about the student. This phase of the meeting was followed by the "decision making" phase in which the decision to place the student was made. Next, parents were informed of their rights under the provisions of PL 94-142. Finally, "goals and objectives" for the student in the special education program were written.

The internal order of the phases of the meeting were also regular. During the information presentation phase of the meeting, each of the participants presented information about the child. This presentation of information went in round-robin style, with the school psychologist, classroom teacher, school nurse, and special education teacher reporting what they knew about the student. Information gathered from standardized tests dominated the proceedings (cf. Mehan, 1983; Ysseldyke, 1982). As the discourse from the meetings presented at the beginning of the paper shows, when it came time for the committee to reach a decision, a choice was presented to the committee for ratification. A wide range of alternatives were not discussed or debated (Mehan, 1983).

After the placement decision was reached, parents were told of their rights to placement outside the district for their child:

EDM   #57

35	Psy.	All right. Then what we have to do now is sign. But, um, before we sign I'd like to have uh, Suzanna um, talk about the rights to private schooling and talk about your rights as parents.
36	DR	I think you probably have these two forms but they talk about your rights as parents. I'm going to give you a copy anyway so, um, you are aware.
37	Psy.	I think you received it in the mail before.
38	DR	Yeah. You probably did. I'd also like to inform you of your rights as parents to private schooling for Ricardo [if] the District should not have an appropriate program for the child. Uh, this is the law. However, under the same law, we feel that we [do] have a program for your child that would meet his needs. Okay? So I'm going to ask you to sign this form and you'll keep a copy and I'll sign the form too. And this is [just] only to inform you of your rights. Okay?
39	Par.	(inaudible) (signing) (8–9 sec)

EDM   #33

97	DR	Mrs. Ladd, if we, um after evaluating Shane find that, um, we don't have the proper placement, the classroom available, appropriate placement for Shane, that you can request—or you have rights to private school and you can request that. We've made the decision that we do have a class available for Shane to go into.

The structure of discourse within committee meetings (in which information was presented to committee members and not discussed) and the organization of these meetings (in which information about students was presented first, the decision to place was made second, and, parents rights were discussed third) contributed to the manner in which decisions about student classification and placement were made. This "presentational mode" of decision making (Mehan, 1983), furthermore, contributed to the statistical array of students summarized in Table 6.1.

Organizational Arrangements Outside Committee Meetings

The discursive arrangements that occurred inside committee meetings were matched by organizational arrangements that occurred outside the committee meeting. These arrangements show the influence of circumstances that originate beyond the immediate context of the committee meeting, and outside the control of the district.

The Education for All Handicapped Students Law (PL 94-142) directs school districts to find an appropriate education for all students, including those with physical and educational handicaps, in the educational environment that is the least restrictive for these students. In the event that a school district does not have adequate facilities to educate students within the district, the district is directed to send the students to facilities outside the district *at district expense*. The inordinate expense involved in educating students outside the district influenced the decision making in this and other districts (Moore et al., 1981; Ysseldyke, 1982), and contributed to the fact that there were no out of district placements during the year we studied the district. The organization of the decision making phase of the meeting, and the arrangement of the discussion of parents rights *after* the decision to place students in educational programs within the district reflect the influence of policies drawn up far away from the meeting room on the proceedings within the meeting room itself. In no case was the issue of out of district placement discussed as part of the options presented to the committee for discussion. At most, one or two closely related programs (e.g., EH vs. LDG) were discussed and presented to the parents present at the meeting. The discussion of the parents' rights to private schooling at district expense always occurred after the decision to place the student within the district. This arrangement effectively foreclosed the possibility of the discussion of this option.

Fiscal considerations within the law itself imposed other constraints on the course of decision making which was evident in the discourse of the meeting. PL 94-142 indicates that 12% of the school-aged population will be served by special education programs. The legal incentive to identify a certain percentage of special students is reinforced by financial incentives. School districts are provided funds from state and federal sources for each student in regular classrooms, and a greater amount of money for students in special education programs. They receive more money for students in "pullout" special education programs, and still more money for students in "whole day" programs on a sliding scale. Just as there are incentives to locate and place students in special education in order to receive the maximum state and federal support, so too, there are disincentives to find too many students. Funds for special education are not unlimited. A funding ceiling is reached when a certain number of students are placed in one EH classroom, with one LD teacher, etc. No additional money is provided if more students than the quota are assigned to particular classrooms.

The influence of these financial and legal considerations was evident in the committee's deliberations. The educators took the number of students already assigned to special education programs into account when making placement decisions. Programs that were "full," i.e., had reached the funding ceiling, were eliminated from consideration, while programs that were "open," i.e., had not reached the legally mandated quota, remained subject to consideration.

Vagaries in the school calendar, a consideration within this particular district, also influenced the consideration of placement options. The district operated on a "year round" schedule. Instead of conducting classes from September until June, and designating the summer months as vacation, a staggered schedule of classes and vacations was maintained. Because of this staggered schedule, regular and special education teachers who were to cooperate in the education of certain students often found themselves on incompatible track schedules. This incompatibility of schedules had an influence on placement options.

In the following discussion of the goals and objectives for Shane, the committee members discover that the two teachers who will be responsible for his remediation are on two different schedules:

EDM   #33

324.1   SET: . . . what would be (5) a reasonable kind of—we're on math now Corrine—

325.1   Psy.   Oh

326.1   SET: um to *expect* in terms of growth between now and the end of the year? About 2 months would you say?

327.1   Prin: Well, Carol, what track are you on?

328.1   CLT: A

329.1   Prin: I don't even know when that ends.

330.1   CLT: May. We're the first ones that go off.

331.1   ?:   Oh-oh!

332.1   CLT: And we're going off track for 2½ weeks. Oh, in just another week.

333.1   SET: Oh, I better change this [refers to a goal statement on the form she is completing] to May. And do you [school psychologist] still want to stay with that [goal] on the bender?

This discovery leads the committee to discuss their previous plans, and to revise the goals and expectations for the student's progress while in special education.

The same dilemma confronted another committee trying to decide on the appropriate educational plan for a student:

EDM #47

58.3	SET:	. . . we'll write the goals for June of 1980. We'll review them//
59.1	Mo:	uh huh
60.1	Prin:	//We really can't write//
61.1	Psy:	//The way your track, the way Track D is, John's off track

In the process of setting goals, the committee discovered that the two people centrally involved in the student's educational plan would not be teaching at the same time. This forced the committee to rewrite their objectives for the student's progress.

Summary

Recognizing that "the core of the problem is to link [inter]action and structure without reducing one to the other," (DiTomasi, 1982, p. 15), I have looked at the language of groups of educators as they make decisions about how to classify students. I have tried to show the ways in which circumstances which originate outside the institution (governmental policies, fiscal and legal considerations) interact with local circumstances (the practical project of processing cases, getting done with the work at hand, arranging teaching schedules) to influence the work of formal organization.

In plotting the *reflexive* relations among structure and interaction, I am trying to counter the idea that is so prevalent in sociology that structure and interaction are independent with its consequence that social structure is somehow on a higher plane than interaction. I have attempted to collapse the structure-interaction dualism by showing that a more complete understanding of language and school comes from a close analysis of language use by an ethnographic consideration of the circumstances which surround it.

The school and its subunits are not autonomous configurations, but are influenced by the practical circumstances of bureaucratic constraint, and the society of which the school is a part. Administrative policy concerning student classification (like those influencing curriculum content, textbook choices, teaching methods, and testing practices) are established by school boards, and state departments of education at an organizational level distant from the school. These decisions made in bureaucracies distant from the school impinge upon educational practice in the school, which we see manifest in the language of educators in student placement meetings. Likewise, the demands of the economy for a technically trained, literate, and compliant labor force make the school responsive to external forces. Furthermore, parents, having been to school themselves, voice opinions about what and how their children should be educated.

This ethnographically grounded analysis of discourse shows the way in which social structure exerts a constraining influence on social interaction, while simultaneously considering the interactional mechanisms manifest in language that generate aspects of the social structure (in this case a student's career—as either a handicapped student or a normal student). This reflexive relationship between structure and interaction seems to be more faithful to the organization of social life than a priori assignments of unidirectional causal significance to either interaction or structure.

CONTEXT FREE AND CONTEXT SPECIFIC INTERPRETATIONS OF LANGUAGE USE

This analysis of language in student placement meetings has been presented as an example of a sociolinguistic analysis of language use in the educational institution. In the remainder of this paper, I review a number of similar studies. The goal of my examination is to demonstrate that the study of language use in naturally occurring situations (1) contributes to an understanding of the role of language in education, (2) contributes to an understanding of the role of schooling in social stratification, and (3) contributes to sociological theory by revealing issues not otherwise available for sociological analysis.

The topic of the first set of studies is language use in contrasting settings. The focus of the second set of studies is the language of stratification in schools.

Assessing Language Use in Testing Situations

According to some readings of Bernstein (1971), lower class youth in England fail in school because they fail to master and use the language of mainstream society, the so-called "elaborated code." Their "restricted code" speech restricts their ability to communicate with and understand others. Whatever Bernstein's original intention, this position was imported to the US (Hess & Shipman, 1964), and became an influential explanation of the school failure of lower class and ethnic minority children. For example, Bereiter and Englemann (1966) characterized the language of ethnic minority and lower class preschool children as "inadequate for expressing personal or original opinions, for analysis and careful reasoning, for dealing with anything hypothetical or beyond the present or for explaining anything very complex" (p. 32).

Such statements are comments on the linguistic *competence* of lower class and ethnic minority youth. Bereiter and Englemann are saying that lower class and ethnic minority children have a gap or deficit in their linguistic apparatus which is general, i.e., is not bound by context. This general linguistic deficiency is said to be the basis of the poor school performance of poor children.

Labov (1972) was influential in countering this context-free linguistic deficiency interpretation of school failure with a context-specific view of language use. One of the most provocative examples of situational variability in linguistic performance appears in Labov's analysis of the verbal performance of a black youth from New York City in different testing situations. His interaction with a tester follows:

> The boy enters a room where there is a large, friendly, white interviewer, who puts on the table in front of him a toy and says:
>
> T: Tell me everything you can about this
>   (12 sec of silence
> T: What would you say it looks like?
>   (8 sec of silence)
> S: A space ship
> T: Hmm
>   (13 sec of silence)
> S: Like a je-et
>   (12 sec of silence)
>   Like a plane
>   (20 sec of silence)
> T: And, what would you use it for?
>   (8 sec of silence)
> S: A je-et
>   (6 sec of silence)
> T: If you had two of them, what would you do with them?
> S: Give one to somebody.
> T: Hmmm. Who do you think would like to have it?
>   (10 sec of silence)
> S: Cla-rence
> T: Mmm. Where do you think you could get another of these?
> S: At the store.
> T: Oh ka-ay!

The length and pacing of this student's reply make this student appear extremely dull and to be a linguistically deprived child. However, having knowledge of this child and his peers in other situations, Labov surmised that the reasons for the boy's inarticulateness were to be found in the social situation, not his character or language. His hypothesis was given support when he repeated the testing exercise with a black adult, and the child's verbal production remained much the same, but became quite elaborate when the black interviewer sat on the floor with a bag of potato chips in the presence of his friend, and taboo topics and words were entered into the conversation. In this social context, one in which the power relations between adult and child had been changed, a boy who had previously responded in monosyllables eagerly entered into the conversation. Rather than using language in a minimal, defensive way, he now employed it productively to compete actively with his friend for the floor, to defend his reputation, and to set the record straight regarding a fight in which he had been involved.

Language Use in School and Store

Hall, Cole, Reder, and Dowley (1976) extended Labov's interpretation of language use in different kinds of testing situations to a school and a community setting. Dowley took 3- and 4-year-olds enrolled in a New York City Head Start program to the local supermarket where they discussed the food they saw. Upon returning to the classroom, they were asked to tell the teacher about the trip. Speech in the supermarket was compared to the retelling of the event in school.

The language the students used in the two situations was qualitatively similar in several respects: Neither the form of utterances (questions, commands, statement/assertions), nor the content they expressed differed drastically across the two situations. However, in the informal supermarket setting, the average number of words was greater, the percentage of questions attended to was greater, and the average number of words in response to a question was higher.

Discontinuities Between Patterns of Interaction at Home and School

A companion set of studies examined patterns of interaction at home with patterns of interaction at school (Au & Jordan, 1979; Erickson & Mohatt, 1981; Philips, 1972, 1982). In the hallmark study in this tradition, Philips (1972, 1982) compared the patterns of classroom interaction among Indian reservation children and among Anglo children in the same community.

A reason often given for the difficulties that Native American children face in school is that they lack communicative skills and are nonverbal, i.e., suffer from a linguistic deficit fostered by a deprived cultural environment (Dumont, 1972; John, 1972). Philips, too, found evidence of "quiet Indian children," but, she did not find a *generalized* linguistic deficit; instead, she found that the patterns of communication of Indian children were *context specific,* i.e., varied systematically from one type of situation to another.

Philips found that the Indian children performed very poorly in those classroom contexts that demanded individualized performance and emphasized competition among peers, while they performed more effectively in those classroom contexts that minimized the obligation of individual students to perform in public contexts and the need for teachers to control performance styles and correct errors publically. The classroom contexts in which Indian students performed effectively were similar in organization to local Indian community contexts, where *cooperation* and not *competition* was valued, and *sociality* and not *individuality* was emphasized. Philips attributes the generally poor performance of Indian children to differences in the structures of participation normatively demanded in the home and in the school. The patterns of participation normatively expected in conventional classrooms create conditions which are unfamiliar and threatening to Indian children.

Questions at Home and School

Building on the logic inherent in the work reviewed to this point in the paper, sociolinguists such as Cazden (1979), Anderson and Teale (1981), and Heath (1982), have begun to compare the structure and function of discourse at home and school of middle income and lower income families. These comparisons enable us to see if there is a relationship between language use, language socialization, and differential school performance.

Heath (1982) compared the way white middle income teachers talked to their black low income elementary school students in the classroom with the way in which these teachers talked to their own children at home in a community she calls "Trackton." She found that the teachers relied heavily on questions and language games like peek-a-boo (cf. Cazden, 1979) when they talked to their children at home. The most frequent form of question was the "known information" variety so often identified with classroom interaction (Mehan, 1979; Shuy & Griffin, 1978; Sinclair & Coulthard, 1975). By contrast to "information seeking" questions in which the questioner seeks knowledge presumably held by the respondent when people (notably teachers and testers) ask a "known information" question they have knowledge of the information they seek, and are testing or examining the respondents' knowledge. Middle income parents also talked to preverbal children often. With preverbal children, parents supplied the surrounding context and the hypothetical answers, such that "pseudo-conversations" were a common occurrence:

Mother: You want your bear?
Child: (silence)
Mother: Yes, you want your bear . . .

Heath reports that the children of the middle income teachers were being taught to label and name objects and to talk about things out of context.

These same teachers talked to the students in their classrooms in ways that were very similar to the ways in which they talked to their own children at home. They instructed students primarily through an interrogative format using known information questions, and taught students to label objects, and identify features of things.

However, this mode of language use and language socialization was not prevalent in the homes of low income students. Low income adults only seldom addressed questions to their children at home, and even less often to preverbal children. Where Trackton teachers would use questions, Trackton parents would use statements or imperatives. For example, when talking about a child's poor health, a Trackton mother might say:

"Something is the matter with that boy."

By contrast, a Trackton teacher would say:

"Is something the matter? What is the matter?"

And, when questions *were* asked of Trackton children by their parents, they were much different than the types of questions asked by teachers. Questions at home called for nonspecific comparisons or analogies as answers. They were not the known information or information-seeking questions associated with the classroom.

Heath concludes that the language use in Trackton homes did not prepare children to cope with three major characteristics of the language used in classrooms: (1) they had not had practice in responding to utterances that were interrogative in form but directive in pragmatic function ["Why don't you use the one on the back shelf" vs. "Use the one on the back shelf"], (2) they did not have much familiarity with known information questions, (3) they had little experience with questions that asked for information from books.

But, Heath did not stop her work with a description of home-school differences in questioning. She worked cooperatively with parents and educators to modify the learning environment for Trackton students in ways that were mutually beneficial. It was generally recognized that in order for Trackton students to succeed, they had to learn to use the language of the classroom (cum society), which includes naming objects, identifying their characteristics, providing descriptions out of context, and responding to known information questions. In order to increase the students' verbal skills in these areas, she instructed the Trackton teachers on ways to adapt to the community's ways of asking questions. For example, teachers began social studies lessons with questions that ask for personal experiences and analogic responses, e.g., "What's happening there," "Have you ever been there," "What's this like." These questions are similar to the questions that parents asked their children at home. The use of these questions in early stages of instruction was productive in generating active responses from previously passive and "nonverbal" Trackton students. Once the teachers increased the participation of the students in lessons using home questioning styles, they were able to move them through a zone of learning toward school demanded questioning styles.

We have a model of social change here that stands in stark contrast to those proposed by proponents of linguistic or cultural deprivation interpretations of the school difficulties of students from low income families. Instead of denying the coherence and relevance of the language and culture of the home by eradicating home and community patterns, Heath's work proposes a model of mutual accommodation in which both teachers and students modify their behavior in the direction of a common goal.

Summary

Studies of children's language in different contexts has led to a different interpretation of the language of lower class and ethnic minority children. Instead of being viewed as speaking a deficient linguistic code, these children are viewed as speaking a linguistic code that is every bit as grammatical, rule governed, and logical as the code spoken by their middle class contemporaries.

Cross-context comparisons of language use have thus contributed to a "context-specific" view of cognitive skills and abilities (see LCHC, 1982, 1983 for more details about this perspective). The context specific view proposes that intelligence displays and language use are dependent on context. They are not general abilities that appear uniformly in all contexts; they are specific abilities that vary from one type of situation to another. Therefore, any evaluation of a student that uses information from any single situation, e.g., an educational test, will not have a valid measure of the student.

The implication of this line of research for social stratification is clear: It shifts the source of school failure away from the characteristics of the failing child and toward more general societal processes (Gumperz, 1971). Sociolinguists have argued that school failure cannot be blamed on the child's linguistic code or cultural background. The source of students' problems in school is not to be found in their language; it is to be found in the organization of the school. The problems that lower class and ethnic children face in school must be viewed as a consequence of institutional arrangements which ensnare children, by not being sensitive to the fact that children display skills differently in different situations.

THE LANGUAGE OF STRATIFICATION IN THE SCHOOL

There is a general consensus in our society about the characteristics of good schools. Good schools have modern buildings, well equipped laboratories, large libraries, teachers with advanced degrees, small classes, the most recent curriculum materials. Bad schools lack these resources (Moore et al., 1981, p. 19). Coleman et al. (1966) shook this conventional ideology by indicating that differences in such *tangible* school characteristics as the age of buildings, the average level of teacher training, the number of books in the library, were not correlated with student achievement, once social background was taken into account. Some researchers (e.g., Coleman et al., 1966; Jencks et al., 1972; Bowles & Gintis, 1976) concluded that differences in the characteristics of school environments were of limited consequence in determining students' academic achievement and social mobility. In contrast to this "schools don't make a difference" conclusion, other researchers, including sociolinguists, delved more deeply into the nature of the school environment, developing more sophisticated analyses of school characteristics than these "tangible" characteristics studied by Coleman.

Sociolinguists have paid particular attention to the discourse between educators and students in a number of different school contexts, including the classroom, educational testing situations, counseling sessions, and decision making groups. This attention to detail has shown us how the process of stratification is mediated by language. The ways in which differential educational opportunities are made available in two school contexts, the classroom, and counseling sessions will be described to exemplify the way in which stratification is mediated by language in school contexts.

The Language of the Classroom

The cross-context comparisons of language use reviewed earlier compared the language of the classroom to other social situations familiar to children. Other sociolinguistic studies show how the language of the classroom is a specialized code that students need to master, and is not simply a transparent medium through which the academic curriculum is transmitted.

This line of investigation explicitly parallels the ethnography of communication (Bauman & Sherzer, 1972; Gumperz & Hymes, 1964, 1972), where the basic question is: "What do people need to know to be seen as successful participants in the local community?" (Frake, 1964; Goodenough, 1956). The research question often phrased in the ethnography of classroom communication is: "What do students need to learn to do in order to be seen as successful participants in the classroom community?"

Ethnographically influenced studies of classroom language and communication have been particularly successful in uncovering unspoken classroom rules, and previously unnoticed norms for classroom behavior. These tacit aspects of classroom culture seem to be important for student success, because interpreting social contexts and interpreting classroom rules seems to be a part of successful participation in the classroom community.

Interpreting Contexts.   One important aspect of classroom learning involves learning what context one is in (Erickson & Schultz, 1977; Florio, 1978; McDermott & Aron, 1978). "Contexts" here are not to be equated with the *physical* aspects of settings, but are seen as constructed by the people interacting in them (Erickson & Schultz, 1977). As McDermott and Roth (1979) have put it, contexts are constituted by what people are doing, as well as when and where they are doing it.

In the classroom, as in other contexts, interaction is segmented and to some extent controlled by indirect verbal strategies, systematic shifts in participants' postures, conversational rhythms, and prosody (Cook-Gumperz & Gumperz, 1982; Erickson & Schultz, 1977; McDermott & Gospodinoff, 1979). These changing arrays of postural configurations demarcate the division of the continuous flow of interaction into discrete segments.

Because different contexts demand different behavior, the demands for behavior vary from context to context, even moment to moment within a context. Situational variation in constraints implies that effective participation in the classroom entails recognizing different contexts for interaction, and producing behavior that is appropriate for each context.

Interpreting Tacit Classroom Rules.   While the problem of social order is a theoretical concern for sociologists, it is a practical concern for teachers. However, the rules that are part of this normative order are not communicated directly to the students. They are seldom formulated by the teacher at the beginning of the school year or school day. They are not posted on the bulletin board or stated in so many words at the beginning of a classroom lesson. As a result, classroom procedures are like other normative rules: They are "tacit" (Cicourel, 1973; Cicourel et al., 1974; Garfinkel, 1967; Mehan & Wood, 1975).

This point can be illustrated by referring to the normative rules guiding turn taking in classroom lessons (Humphries, 1980; McHoul, 1980; Mehan, 1979). Access to the floor is governed by different rules at different times. On some occasions, pupils can reply directly (as when the "invitation to reply" rule is in effect), but on others, they must first receive permission (as when the "individual nomination" or "invitation to bid" rules are in effect). However, students are not provided with information about the appropriate ways to gain access to the floor explicitly. The teacher does not say: "When I name a student by name, or nod at him or her, that student and only that student can reply. When I say 'raise your hand' or 'who knows . . .' students are to indicate that they know the answer by raising their hands. When I say 'what is this,' or 'anybody . . .' or trail off a sentence, then anyone can answer the question."

What the teacher does say includes statements like "raise your hand," "who knows," "wait a minute," or "give others a change to think." But these are not the classroom rules per se; they are statements that index the rules. The students have to abstract from the information given in implicit teacher statements and use other contextual cues (Gumperz, 1971) to infer the general classroom rules. Even if the rules of the classroom could be posted, the list would remain "indexical" i.e., be open and incomplete (Garfinkel, 1967), in as much as the rules would have to be interpreted by teachers and students against a constantly changing classroom situation.

Summary.   According to Bourdieu and Passeron (1977) and Collins (1979), schools reward students on the basis of their possession of *cultural capital,* i.e., instruments of symbolic wealth, ways of talking, and acting. The studies just reviewed point out the importance of cultural capital in schooling, but recommend a modification in the way we talk about this concept. Because cultural capital operates as a *cultural style* in the classroom, this concept can be more productively treated as a dynamic process that operates in interaction than as a *thing* that people possess or own. In fact, it seems more accurate to speak of *participation* in status culture than *membership* in status groups (DiMaggio, 1982).

Thus, the language of the classroom is a cultural code, the mastery of which is important for school success, and by implication, for status attainment. To be successful in school, students must indeed master academic subject matter, which involves learning to read, write, compute and the content of such subjects as history, social studies, and science. But, school success is not limited to academic matters. Although it is incumbent upon students to display *what* they know, they must also know *how* to display what they know. This involves knowing that certain ways of talking and acting are appropriate in certain contexts, knowing with whom, when, and where they can speak and act, and interpreting classroom rules that are often implicit.

Ability Grouping

Placing students into small groups for the purposes of instruction seems to be a ubiquitous feature of American elementary schools. Reading and math are the most prevalent subjects in which students are grouped, choices that reflect the society's and educators' concerns for elementary education. Students are placed into heterogeneous and homogeneous groups. In the former case, students of different ability are grouped together, based on the idea that cross fertilization helps students of different ability. In the latter case, students of the same ability are grouped together, based on the idea that students of equivalent ability can be more efficiently taught.

There is nothing inherently sinister or laudatory in such grouping practices; the existing educational research is mixed on the relative merits of the two types of grouping. Basically, it is a practical response to a pressing educational problem in ecological and demographic form: too many students with too little time to teach them. However, an unintended consequence of ability grouping is differential access to educational curriculum, and hence, educational opportunity.

Accounts of differential treatment. There have been many accounts of differential treatment in ability groups reported by researchers who have examined classroom interaction closely (e.g. Cicourel et al., 1974; Eder, 1981, 1982; Gumperz & Herasmichuk, 1975; McDermott, 1976; Michaels, 1981; Rist, 1970). These researchers report that the *distribution* of students to high-, middle-, and low-ability groups seems to be based on characteristics associated with SES—an observation that lends support for the reproduction thesis mentioned at the outset of this paper. Children from one parent households, or from families with an unemployed worker, are more likely to be assigned to low-ability groups.

These researchers also report differences in the *treatment* of different ability groups. Low-ability group students were taught less frequently, and were subjected to more control by the teacher. And significantly for the major point of this paper: Placement into ability groups takes on a caste-like character—once students were placed into ability groups, they seldom left them.

Differential Access to Curriculum and Instruction. Eder (1982), followed in the ethnographic tradition of Hollingshead (1934), Rist (1970), and McDermott (1976), but differed from her predecessors by focusing on teacher-student discourse in ability groups, and hence, gives us insight into the *language* by which stratifying occurs. She examined a first grade teacher's responses to students' interruptions of others' turns at reading, and found differential treatment on the part of the teacher across ability groups. The main activity in the reading groups was taking turns reading aloud. During this activity, the teacher assigned turns at reading to one student at a time. With the two lowest reading groups, the teacher responded to students' interruptions by asking for further information. With the top two reading groups, the teacher discouraged interruptions.

Eder explains these differential responses in terms of differences in expectation about verbal production. Because the high-group students were much more verbal than the low-group members, the teacher may not have been concerned with discouraging them, while she may have been interested in encouraging the low-group members to talk more. Eder finds support for this notion in comparisons of interruptions which were on-topic and interruptions which were off-topic. The teacher ignored or reprimanded off-topic interruptions across all groups, but allowed more on-topic interruptions by low-group members. In fact, topical interruptions were never reprimanded in the low group, and they were acknowledged twice as often.

Eder shows that the teacher's differential responses contributed to different classroom performance across reading groups. While reading turn interruptions became infrequent in high groups, they became increasingly frequent in the lower groups. As a consequence, low-group members did not develop an understanding of reading turns as a speech event in which other members do not speak or engage the reader in discussion—and understanding, which is essential for success in school because reading is so important to all aspects of academic achievement.

The Counselor as Gatekeeper

Erickson and Shultz (1982) studied more than eighty counseling interviews between junior college counselors and junior college students. Their analysis of interaction in these exchanges gives us access to some of the *interactional practices* of social stratification in schools.

Erickson and Shultz found that counselors routinely inquired into students' course grades and degree requirements. More personal information about students also emerged during the course of counseling interviews. The academic information interacted with more personal information to produce differences in counseling treatments, and hence, students' careers. The establishment of "particularistic comembership" was especially important in this regard. Erickson and Shultz found that counseling proceeded differently when students and counselors discovered similarities in interests and common past experiences during the course of a counseling interview, than when students and counselors stuck only to academic (i.e., universalistic) information. Those students who had established a high degree of particularistic comembership were more likely to receive positive counseling, rule bending, and extra help, than those students who interacted with students on a universalistic basis.

The following transcripts from two different counseling sessions videotaped by Erickson and Shultz (1982) illustrate this "gatekeeping" process. The same counselor (designated as "C") appears in both transcripts with a different student ("S") each time.

38 S: Yeah, I guess so. I might keep it up . . . my PE and I wanna go into counseling too see . . . you know have two way . . . like equal balance.
39 C: I see ah . . . what do you know about counseling?
40 S: Nothing
41 C: Okay . . .
42 S: I know you have to take psychology courses of some sorts and counseling.
43 C: Well, it's . . . this is a . . . it'll depend on different . . . it'll vary from different places to different places but essentially what you need first of all, you're gonna need state certification, state teacher certification, in other words, you have to be certified to teach in some area . . . History or English or whatever happens to be your bag, PE. Ah, secondly, you're gonna have to have a master's degree . . . in counseling . . . which you know is . . . an advanced degree [laughs]. That's what you have to do to get a . . . counseling . . . to be a counselor. Uh . . . at least in Illinois and its pretty much the same anywhere you want to go.

The next transcript illustrates the interaction between another student and the same counselor:

29 C: Yeah, uh, . . . are *you* still thinking in terms of two years?
30 S: Ummm, I was, but now the more I'm getting into it the more I'm realizing that I'm starting to like it, if I can catch hold and keep the grasp that I'm goin' at now, I'd like to continue at [name of university] or some other school.

31 C: Okay, this is a good point and I'm glad you brought it up. How much investigation have you done of other schools that offer programs in data processing?

32 S: Not really down to it. I've talked to students over there that's about it.

33 C: At [name of university]?

34 S: Uh, I've talked to one student I know, he . . . never really got into the courses he started them. He said that the courses they offer are pretty good as far as he could see.

35 C: Hmmmmmm. One of the problems that *I* think you're gonna run into is transferability.

36 S: Yeah, I realize that.

C: You know

S: I gotta little biology

37 C: No, I'm not even so much worried about that as I am about these data processing courses

38 S: Why?

39 C: As to whether they'll transfer and accept them at [University]

40 S: Well, if not then I'll just start all over. What can I say?

41 C: Yeah . . . ah, well, one of the things you could say is ah . . . one of the things you could do is check.

42 S: Yeah, I will . . . I'm gonna get in on that.

43 C: Would you . . . Please do that because the sooner you know, the easier it's gonna be for you to make a decision as to whether you wannta continue here and get that two year A.A. or whether . . . you know . . . you're planning on transfering to [name of university].

44 S: Oh oh oh, umn excuse me I thought you meant after, you know, my two years are done here, then go to [name of university]. I wanna get my degree here first.

45 C: You definitely wanna get your . . .

S: Yeah

46 C: Right, make sure though, that if you . . . you plan on going on in data processing, that it will be worth your while to stay here. See there's the key.

The counselor obviously interacted with these two students differently. In fact, he employed two different strategies for describing the educational maze lying between these students and their future goals. With the first student, the counselor began at the student's goal, which lay somewhere in the distant future, and worked back to the present, successively closing doors or laying obstacles in the student's path to a counseling career by explaining that the "first" thing that the student needed was state certification and a master's degree (first transcript, line 43). This is not, however, a first thing; in a temporal sequence, it is a last thing. The information that the student needed first was a list of courses that he should take the following term. These courses would be the ones necessary for transferring to a 4-year college in order to obtain a degree that would eventually lead to a counseling position. The counselor did not provide this information, but instead employed vague terms like "state teacher's certification" and "master's degree." For the junior-college student, these goals must have seemed very far in the future and thus very far removed from his present experience. Without the knowledge of what he must do now to become a counselor, this student could find his options closed in the future.

With the second student, this counselor's strategy was very different. He told the student to be careful in choosing his courses and to be sure that the 4-year college would accept them. The counselor began with the present and continued into the near future (second transcript, line 35), successively opening imaginary doors for the student until the future goal was reached. The counselor treated the student's career in immediate terms, identifying the course of action that would lead from the present to the future goal. As a result of this counselor's different strategies, these students' mobility within the junior college, and we can assume, their access to career opportunities after junior college was affected.

Moving this analysis from a consideration of input and output factors, Erickson and Shultz (1982) report that when behaviors of the counselor and student were synchronized the interaction was smoother, and the counseling more positive. In discovering that smooth interactional synchrony occurred most often between counselors and students who had established a high degree of particularistic comembership, Erickson and Shultz are uncovering an aspect of the machinery that contributes to the assembly of successful counseling sessions. Importantly, this is an *interactional* machinery, not a simple transmission or conveyor belt. And, the grist for this machinery is not simply students' characteristics, including those associated with their social class backgrounds; nor is it individual effort and hard work. Erickson and Shultz demonstrate how these factors enter into negotiation along with such particularistic characteristics as common background and shared experiences which emerge during the course of counselor-student interaction. The analysis of the emergent importance of universalistic and particularistic features in counseling suggests that steps on a student's educational career ladder are *constructed,* and are not the automatic result of SES or achievement.

CONCLUSION

I hope that my goal for this paper has been realized: to demonstrate that the study of language in the social context of schooling is worthwhile in at least three ways: (1) it contributes to an understanding of the role of language in education, (2) it contributes to an understanding of the role of schooling in social stratification, (3) it contributes to sociological theory more generally by revealing issues that would not otherwise be available to our analyses.

The Function of Language in Education

The study of language in schools has revealed underlying patterns of social interaction. A failure to understand the function and purposes of language in schools leaves certain categories of students at a disadvantage—both in that they fail to understand what goes on in classroom, testing, and counseling situations—and that educators may misrepresent the skills and talents of students they evaluate.

The comparison of students at home and at school has pointed out the context specific nature of intelligence and language displays. Displays of competence are context bound. They are not general abilities that appear uniformly in all contexts. Therefore, any unidimensional measure of students' performance is likely to misrepresent the competence of students from certain categories of the population.

Furthermore, language serves as a vehicle for stratification in two ways: (1) stratification is *done* through language, and (2) language use is a basis upon which students are stratified in schools.

The Function of Schooling in Social Stratification

Although sociolinguists only obliquely entered the debate about the contribution of schooling to status attainment, they have made important contributions to this consideration by examining the social organization of school success and failure. They have argued persuasively against characterological interpretations of school failure, i.e., those that attribute the cause of school failure to characteristics of the failing students) whether the characteristics are genetically provided, are associated with home or cultural environments, or are associated with parents' social class. They have also countered reified structural theories (i.e., those attributing the cause of school failure to the "social structure") with more interactionally based approaches (i.e., those which see school success and failure as social constructions by locating the source of students' problems in the social organization of the school in its relation to society and not in students' language).

Sociolinguistic studies in education have also contributed to our understanding of status attainment by showing that what goes on in school makes a difference in the lives of students who attend them. Large-scale surveys may be appropriate for linking input and output variables, but we need more careful descriptions of educational practices in schools and detailed comparisons of life at home and in the community with the demands of the school in order to come to grips with the processes of social stratification. If it can be said that schooling facilitates mobility or reproduces the existing status and class arrangements in society, then sociolinguistic studies are important for showing *how* these activities are carried out.

Students are sorted and stratified in such a way that differential educational opportunities are made available to them. However, this stratifying is not always based on students' measured abilities or their background characteristics. The operation of race, ethnicity, social class and other "social origin variables" has not been accorded the same importance when researchers have started with details of everyday life in schools as it has been when researchers have made correlations between SES and status attainment. Ethnographers are as likely to point out that teachers and students are making sense, synchronizing behavior, and conducting identity struggles as they are to say that students are being stratified. While SES and school achievement are important, schools are also places where cultural capital matters and decisions are made on the basis of particularistic considerations (cf. DiMaggio, 1982, p. 189).

As a result of such findings, it seems prudent to make further inquiries into the *mechanisms* of stratification in schools. Doing so will probably reveal the wisdom of observations about sense making and stratifying, because life in schools is at least complex enough that at least those two processes are occurring simultaneously. Doing so will also move us away from simple correlational models of background variables and attained status and toward models which include descriptions of the processes of stratification.

The Importance of Language for Sociology

In most general terms, we have with sociolinguistic studies of language in education a parallel between what Grimshaw (1981) once characterized as the difference between treating language as an *obstacle* to sociological research and treating language as *data* for sociological research. Although G. H. Mead (1959) pointed out the relevance of language to sociology 60 years ago, language, a preeminently social phenomenon, has been somewhat ignored by sociologists. As Gusfield (1981) has pointed out, the prevailing view of language in sociology is analogous to a windowpane. It is something to be looked *through* while looking *at* something else. Thus, the language of people has been treated as a window into people's attitudes and life patterns, or into correlations between one aspect of the social structure and another. By treating language as a mediating force in people's lives, sociolinguists have pointed out the importance of looking at the window of language and not just looking through it. Here, language as a mediator is not meant in the statistical sense of a variable that intervenes between independent and dependent variables in a correlational equation; it is used in the communicative sense that the acts of speaking and listening enable people to make sense of the world. That is, using language transforms the world, changing nature into culture.

It is for this reason that the specification of language as data for sociological research rather than as an obstacle to it can be valuable to sociologists. What Grimshaw said over a decade ago is still true today. Language is important for social research because it "lays bare the mutual implications of cultural meanings and linguistic usages . . . [and] . . . provides an approach to the complex causal relationships between language structure and social structure" (Grimshaw, 1981, p. 321).

ACKNOWLEDGMENT

I appreciate the comments that Courtney B. Cazden, William Corsaro, Donna Eder, Allen Grimshaw, Ray McDermott, George Spindler and Jürgen Streeck provided on earlier drafts of this paper. Portions of this chapter appeared in *Sociology of Education;* permission to reprint is greatfully acknowledged.

REFERENCES

Anderson, A. B., & Teale, W. H. (1981). *Literacy as cultural practice.* Paper presented at Simposio Internacional: Nuevas Perspectivas en los Procesos de Lectura y Escritura. Mexico City.

Au, K. H., & Jordan, C. T. (1978). Talk story in Hawaiian classrooms workshop. *Ethnographic and Sociolinguistics Research in Classrooms Symposium.* American Sociological Association Meetings. Los Angeles.

Bauman, R., & Sherzer, J. (Eds.). (1974). *Explorations in the ethnography of communication.* Cambridge: Cambridge University Press.

Bereiter, K., & Englemann, S. (1966). *Teaching the disadvantaged child in the preschool.* Englewood Cliffs, NJ: Prentice-Hall.

Bernstein, B. (1971). *Class, codes, and control. (Volume 1): Theoretical studies towards a sociology of language.* London: Routledge & Kegan Paul.

Bourdieu, P., & Passeron, J. C. (1977). *Reproduction in education, society and culture.* Beverly Hills, CA: Sage.

Bowles, S., & Gintis, H. (1976). *Schooling in capitalist America.* New York: Basic Books.

Cazden, C. B. (1979). Peekaboo as an instructional strategy: Discourse development at home and at school. *Papers and Reports on Child Language Development, #17,* Stanford University, Department of Linguistics.

Cicourel, A. V. (1973). *Cognitive sociology: Language and meaning in social interaction.* London: Penguin.

Cicourel, A. V., Jennings, S. H. M., Keiter, K. H., MacKay, K. C. W., Mehan, H., & Roth, D. R. (1974). *Language use and school performance.* Orlando, FL: Academic Press.

Coleman, J. S. et al. (1966). *Equality of educational opportunity.* Washington, DC: U.S. Government Printing Office.

Collins, R. (1971). Functional and conflict theories of educational stratification. *American Sociological Review, 36,* 1002–1019.

Collins, R. (1980). *The credential society.* Orlando, FL: Academic Press.

Cook-Gumperz, J., & Gumperz, J. J. (1982). Communicative competence and educational practice. In L. C. Wilkinson (Ed.), *Communicating in the classroom.* Orlando, FL: Academic Press.

Cooper, H. M., & Good, T. (1983). *Pygmalion grows up.* New York: Longmans.

DiMaggio, P. (1982). Cultural, capital and school success. *American Sociological Review, 47*(2), 189–201.

Dumont, Jr., R. V. (1972). Learning English and how to be silent: Studies in Sioux and Cherokee classrooms. In C. B. Cazden, V. P. John, & D. Hymes (Eds.), *Functions of language in the classroom.* New York: Teachers College Press.

Eder, D. (1982). Differences in communicative styles across ability groups. In L. C. Wilkinson (Ed.), *Communicating in the classroom.* Orlando, FL: Academic Press.

Erickson, F., & Mohatt, G. (1982). Participation structures in two communities. In G. Spindler (Ed.), *Doing the ethnography of the classroom.* New York: Holt, Rinehart and Winston.

Erickson, F., & Shultz, J. J. (1977). When is a context? *ICHD Newsletter, 1*(2), 5–10.

Erickson, F., & Shultz, J. J. (1982). *The counselor as gatekeeper.* Orlando, FL: Academic Press.

Florio, S. (1978). *Learning how to go to school.* Unpublished doctoral dissertation, Harvard University.

Frake, C. O. (1966). Notes on queries in ethnography. *American Anthropologist, 66*(3), Part 2, 132–145.

Garfinkel, H. (1967). *Studies in ethnomethodology.* Englewood Cliffs, NJ: Prentice-Hall.

Goodenough, W. (1956). Componential analysis and the study of meaning. *Language, 32,* 195–210.

Griffin, P., & Humphrey, F. (1978). Task and talk. In R. Shuy & P. Griffin (Eds.), *The study of children's functional language and education in the early years.* Arlington, CA: Center for Applied Linguistics.

Grimshaw, A. D. (1981). *Language as a social resource.* Stanford: Stanford University Press.

Gumperz, J. (1971). *Language in social groups.* Stanford: Stanford University Press.

Gumperz, J., & Herasimchuk, E. (1975). The conversational analysis of meaning: A study of classroom interaction. In M. Sanchez & B. G. Blount (Eds.), *Sociocultural dimensions of language use.* Orlando, FL; Academic Press.

Gumperz, J. J., & Hymes, D. H. (Eds.). (1964). The ethnography of communication. Part 2. *The American Anthropologist, 66*(6).

Gumperz, J. J., & Hymes, D. H. (1972). *Directions in sociolinguistics: The ethnography of communication.* New York: Holt, Rinehart and Winston.

Gusfield, J. (1981). *The culture of public problems.* Chicago: The University of Chicago Press.

Hall, W. S., Cole, M., Reder, S., & Dowley, G. (1977). Variations in young children's use of language: Some effects of setting and dialect. In R. Freedle (Ed.), *Discourse production and comprehension.* Norwood, NJ: Ablex Publishing Company.

Heath, S. B. (1982). Questions at home and school. In G. Spindler (Ed.), *Doing the ethnography of schooling*. New York: Holt, Rinehart and Winston.

Hess, R. D., & Shipman, V. C. (1965). Early experience and the socialization of cognitive modes in children. *Child Development, 36*(4), 869–885.

Hollingshead, A. B. (1949). *Elmstown's youth*. New York: Wiley.

Humphries, F. M. (1979). *'Shh!' A sociolinguistic study of teachers' turn-taking sanctions in primary school lessons*. Unpublished doctoral dissertation, Georgetown University.

Jencks, C. et al. (1972). *Inequality: A reassessment of the effect of family and schooling in America*. New York: Basic Books.

Jensen, A. R. (1969). How much can we boost I.Q. and scholastic achievement? *Harvard Educational Review, 39*(1), 1–123.

John, V. (1972). Styles of learning, styles of teaching: Reflections on the education of Navajo children. In C. B. Cazden, V. John, & D. Hymes (Eds.), *Functions of language in the classroom*. New York: Teachers College Press.

Laboratory of Comparative Human Cognition. (1981). Culture and intelligence. In W. Sternberg (Ed.), *Culture and intelligence*. New York: Cambridge University Press.

Laboratory of Comparative Human Cognition. (1982). Culture and cognitive development. In W. Kesson (Ed.), *Handbook of Psychology. Mussen Handbook of Child Development* (Volume 1). New York: Wiley.

Labov, W. (1972). *Sociolinguistic patterns*. Philadelphia: University of Pennsylvania Press.

McDermott, R. P. (1976). *Kids make sense*. Unpublished doctoral dissertation, Stanford University.

McDermott, R. P., & Aron, J. (1978). Pirandello in the classroom. In M. Reynolds (Ed.), *The future of education*. Reston, VA: Council for Exceptional Children.

McDermott, R. P., & Gospodinoff, K. (1979). Social contexts for ethnic borders and school failure. In A. Wolfgang (Ed.), *Nonverbal behavior*. Toronto: Ontario Institute for the Study of Education.

McDermott, R. P., & Roth, D. R. (1979). The social organization of behavior: Interactional approaches. *Annual Reviews of Anthropology, 321*–345.

McHoul, A. (1978). The organization of turns at formal talk in the classroom. *Language in Society, 7*, 183–213.

Michaels, S. (1981). Sharing time: Children's narrative style and differential access to literacy. *Language in Society, 1*, 423–442.

Mead, G. (1979). *Philosophy of the present*. Chicago: Open Court.

Mehan, H. (1979). *Learning lessons*. Cambridge, MA: Harvard University Press.

Mehan, H. (1983). The role of language and the language of role in practical decision making. *Language in Society, 12*(3), 1–39.

Mehan, H. (1984). Practical decision making in naturally occurring institutional settings. In B. Rogoff & J. Lave (Eds.), *Everyday cognition: Its development in social context*. Cambridge, MA: Harvard University Press.

Mehan, H., & Wood, H. (1975). *The reality of ethnomethodology*. New York: Wiley Interscience.

Moore, D. R. et al. (1981). *Student classification and the right to read*. Chicago: Designs for Change.

Philips, S. (1972). Participant structures and communicative competence. In C. Cazden, V. John, & D. Hymes (Eds.), *Functions of language in the classroom*. New York: Teachers College Press.

Philips, S. (1982). *The invisible culture: Communication in classroom and community on the Warm Springs Indian reservation*. New York: Longmans.

Rist, R. C. (1970). Education, social science, and the political process. In J. Karabel & A. H. Halsey (Eds.), *Power and ideology in education*. Oxford: Oxford University Press.

Shuy, R., & Griffin, P. (1978). *The study of children's functional language and education in the early years*. Final Report to the Carnegie Corporation of New York. Arlington, VA: Center for Applied Linguistics.

Sinclair, J. M., & Coulthard, R. M. (1975). *Toward an analysis of discourse*. New York: Oxford University Press.

Treiman, D. J., & Robinson, W. R. (1981). Introduction. *Research in Social Stratification and Mobility, 1*, 1–2.

Wilcox, K. (1982). Differential socialization in the classroom: Implications for equal opportunity. In G. Spindler (Ed.), *Doing the ethnography of schooling*. New York: Harcourt-Brace-Jovanovitch.

II COMPARATIVE AND CROSS-CULTURAL

EDITORIAL INTRODUCTION

The ethnography of education was born as a part of the anthropology of education and many of the early works in this emerging discipline, by people such as Jules Henry, Margaret Mead, Dorothy Eggan, Mark Watkins, C. W. M. Hart, Melford Spiro, and John L. Fischer, were about education and/or schooling in remote non/Western cultures. This was a natural orientation for a field emerging from anthropology, the discipline whose major claim to distinction has been and will continue to be studies of cultures other than ones own. Despite the "return home" by significant numbers of anthropologists who are working in some segment of their own society, the *sine qua non* of cultural anthropology is its command of cross-cultural data and knowledge of whole cultures or parts of large, complex cultures, that is deeper and more complex than that controlled by any other discipline. More than 3,500 individual cultures or segments of complex cultures have been studied and recorded by anthropologists during the relatively short span of time since the emergence of their discipline in the late 19th century. The Human Relations Area Files, initiated by George Peter Murdock and initially housed at Yale University provides an organization of cross-cultural data that is unparalleled by any other source.

The cross-cultural orientation in the anthropology of education is less prominent than it was only a decade or so ago. Educational anthropologists were among the first to come "home" (and some have never been away from it). Though the value of a field experience away from home is still held as an ideal by most educational anthropologists training graduate students, the political barriers to work abroad, particularly in schools, have become more and more difficult to surmount, and supporting funds for such work more difficult to obtain. Small wonder, then, that students and their professors have both turned to studies of multiculturalism and minority groups in the United States in relationship to the educational scene.

Though there have been gains in this focus on the problems and processes of education in the U.S.A. there have also been losses. The anthropology of education, of all things, is in danger of becoming parochial! We have not even informed ourselves about ethnographic work in England or Europe, according to complaints heard now and then from colleagues overseas. Part II of this volume is intended as a corrective for this tendency to lose our cross-cultural and comparative interests, and supports our claim to being a discipline for which a cross-cultural perspective is essential.

Though it would be possible to do so, and indeed we will in another publication, we have not included any chapters on tribal communities, where some of our norms for educational practice are most severely challenged. We have, rather, included reports on field research in Germany, France, England, and the People's Republic of China. The educational objectives in each reported situation are recognizable for each is a part of a complex contemporary national society. The methods of instruction are not radically unfamiliar. Nevertheless, there are enough differences to give us perspective on our own practices and beliefs about effective education.

George and Louise Spindler describe and interpret their long-range study of the elementary school in Schönhausen, Germany and end with a comparison to certain salient features of a comparable school in Wisconsin that they have worked in recently. The two schools, in their different cultural contexts, provide invaluable perspective on each other. Paul Yates reports on an English middle school with a multi-cultural student body. We see mirrored in that school many of the problems faced in our own, but with differences issuing from English culture and social class structure. Kathryn Anderson-Levitt describes the cultural knowledge that French elementary school teachers use in the teaching of reading and tries to account for how they acquire it. This kind of knowledge will be recognizable to American readers but is different enough to put our own in perspective. Norman Chance provides us with a rare look inside the educational system of the People's Republic. The cultural revolution and its aftermath loom large in his discussion. Though China is far off and exotic for many of us, we can quickly grasp the problems encountered, and their remedies, but they are different enough to be interesting.

The Editors

The Authors and their Chapter

Since the authors have been introduced in chapter 2, we need only to say here that we began to get interested in Germany as a field site when we first went to the Stanford center in Germany in the Rems Valley near Stuttgart in 1960. We conducted ethnographic studies of the area with our undergraduate students, concentrating on culture change and urbanization, during the nine times we taught there between 1960 and 1976, when the study center closed. The results are presented in Burgbach: Urbanization and Identity in a German Village (1973).

In the following chapter we report on three field studies in a nearby community, Schönhausen, also in the Rems Valley. Though our studies in Schönhausen began while we were at the Stanford study center they continued well beyond its termination, spanning 25 years altogether. Long-term studies of changing communities are rare enough in the social science literature, and long-term studies of single schools even more rare.

This chapter describes the Schönhausen community and its school, summarizes some of the results of the first field study in 1968, and describes the results of the field studies of the school in 1977 and 1981. Our most recent field research there, in 1985, is footnoted but not reported. A comparative dimension is provided by certain results from our study of an American school in the middle west that we initiated in 1983.

The objectives of the research shifted during this long period, and so did the research methods. Though ethnographic study was carried out in all field visits, and can be considered the base method, we were strongly oriented toward instrumentation and quantifiable data in the 1968 and

1977 studies. The data thus obtained proved invaluable, alerted us to shifts toward cultural conservatism and provided us with specific, comparable data for each time period. We used standard inferential statistical procedures to analyze these data.

By the end of the 1977 field trip (and moreso in 1981 and 1985) we had moved toward a more and more qualitative, "natural history" approach, using films both as a record of behavior and as evocative stimuli for interviews with teachers, and of course, toward ethnographic standbys such as participant observation. In the process, though we had never laid aside the concept, we rediscovered culture as a pervasive determinant of observed behavior. Though we view culture as the major process of human adaptation, and therefore responsive to environmental, demographic, and other conditions antecedent and external to culture, it is clear that in the short run of decades or even centuries, culture tends to have a kind of life of its own. It does not covary with other variables, such as technological development, in the predictable way we often assume.

The Editors

7 Schönhausen Revisited and the Rediscovery of Culture

George and Louise Spindler
Stanford University
and
University of Wisconsin

In this extension of the Schönhausen study begun in 1968 (G. Spindler, 1974) we report and interpret the results of two subsequent field researches there (see Appendix for a description of Schönhausen), one in 1977, the other in 1981, and the beginning of a new field study in the United States in 1983. We take note of some results from our 1985 field trip but cannot include a thorough report since the analysis is not complete (see Appendix). In 1977 we administered the Instrumental Activities Inventory (IAI) to a sample of children, parents, and teachers comparable to the 1968 sample (see Appendix). We were interested in the question of change and response to mandated reform. What had been the effect of a sweeping educational reform mounted, as far as the Schönhausen school was concerned, about the time we were leaving Germany in the spring of 1968? Had the choices of instrumental activities shifted toward urbanization and modernization—the intended outcome of a sweeping mandated reform? The answers to our questions surprised us and raise questions about reform, culture change, and cultural persistence.

In 1977 we also for the first time used film to record behavior in the classroom. As we observed and so recorded we were struck by the dramatic differences in classroom style among the teachers. We could literally say that with six regular classroom teachers (one male) we had six different teaching and management styles. This raised disturbing questions for us. How could we claim any uniformity in cultural transmission if each teacher was so different from every other teacher, even in this little school in a small community with a strong traditional orientation? It wasn't until we analyzed the films upon our return home that we discovered that the differences did not run as deep as they appeared, and that there were significant commonalities.

In 1981 we returned to do more filming and to pursue the question of commonality despite differences, and to interview the teachers in some depth about this very problem. We shared the films we had taken in their own and their colleagues' classrooms with the teachers and found them to be useful evocative stimuli.

In the fall of 1983 we extended our research to a semirural community and school in the middle west. Its position as a mediator of rural-urban life styles, its size, and even its ethnicity, are comparable to Schönhausen. The experience has sharpened our understanding of what it is we are working with. The differences between Roseville (the U.S. school) and Schönhausen are pervasive and deep and they are cultural.

In the pages to follow we present data about each of the research forays mentioned above and will discuss how these data contributed to our understanding of education. Our first discussion is about the new IAI data collected in 1977.

A DECADE OF CHANGE

During the nearly ten years since our first intensive study of the school (1968) and the collection of our first IAI sample and the 1977 revisit and collection of new IAI data much had happened. A sweeping educational reform had been implemented at both federal and provincial administrative levels. The effects of this reform had just begun to surface at the Schönhausen Grundschule during our 1968 field study. New reading books for the third and fourth grades had appeared that stressed modern life, high technology, and the realism of contemporary urban life. They were in sharp contrast to the romanticized stories about life in the country and village that children had been reading for several generations.

This initial surfacing of reform soon extended to every sector of school life. The curriculum for all grades was completely revised, new textbooks, readings, work manuals were supplied, a stream of directives to school personnel "clarifying" the new objectives were issued from the ministries of education, and the new teachers, fresh from the teacher training institutions appeared in numbers.

The *Bildung Reform* (educational reform) was only a part of a vast effort to modernize and urbanize. Though West Germany had experienced the *Wirtschaftwunder* (economic miracle), and thanks to the necessity of rebuilding bomb-shattered industrial plants had an essentially new production technology and industrial plant, the administrative structure of nonurban areas, the methods of agricultural production, transportation facilities, and residential construction had lagged in development. The great increase in the population of West Germany due to the tidal wave of migrants and escapees from the Soviet zone created problems of accommodation that had never been entirely resolved.

The population of the Remstal had increased three-fold overnight, and rural areas and idyllic *Weinorten* (wine-producing villages) such as Burgbach and Schönhausen were inundated, tripling and quadrupling in size. The final phase of accommodation to these dramatic changes was taking place during the near-decade between our 1968 and 1977 studies. The *Weinberge* (hillside vineyard plots) had been "rationalized." Small separate holdings had been consolidated by legal means. Drastic physical recontouring of the slopes to maximize exposure to the sun, minimize erosion, and make it possible to use large-scale cultivating and spraying machinery had been completed.

Accompanying these demographic and land use changes there were abrupt changes in the labor force and particularly in the land-based sectors. The traditional, family-worked Weinberge had been eliminated by *Rebflurbereinigung* (rationalization by legal and physical means). The tiny plots of vineyard and the strips of flatland, fractionated and distributed noncontiguously over the area through a tradition of inheritance without primogeniture, were no longer. With them went the extended family of whole or part time land working relatives, the great Bauernhäuser, in fact the whole traditional pattern of rural nucleated land-oriented village life. When we first observed the Remstal area in 1959 there were dozens of functioning Bauernhäuser in every village. By 1977 most of them had been converted to duplexes or apartment houses, or torn down. In 1968 there were 203 persons listed as *Hauptberufliche* (major occupation) Weingärtner in Burgbach. By 1977 there were 23. Only 8% of the adult population of Schönhausen indicated any relationship whatsoever to agricultural land in their town hall records. In 1968, 23 years after the end of World War II, these communities were still defined as *Ausgesprochener Weinorten* (emphatically wine-producing villages). Though no less wine was produced from the grapes grown on the rationalized slopes, the continuity of generations of interlocking relationships between land-humans-livestock-production-habitation had been broken. We have referred to this traditional pattern as an ecological "lock-in" and the *Fluhrbereinigung* process as the key to that lock (G. Spindler, 1973). Extended families that had been "locked" into the land for generations became suburban nuclear families, still maintaining ties of relationship to wider kin but nevertheless quite different in composition, residence, and style of relationship than before.

The administrative structure of the whole Remstal was also rationalized. In the immediate area of Schönhausen there were five historically separate villages, all of them wine producing, but each distinctive in character—even to significant dialectical shifts from one village to another in the Swäbish spoken by those born in the village. Each village had its own *Bürgermeister* (mayor) and *Gemeinderat* (town council). Each had its own distinctive harvest festivals and its own church. This distinctiveness, albeit on a small scale, was a matter of pride. The administrative reform eliminated the separation of the five communities, eliminated their mayors, town councils, even their names, and welded them into one great urbanized unit called *Weingarten*.

The decade between our first (1968) study and (1977) restudy was one of great change and sweeping intentional modernization. The purpose of our restudy was to try to pin down the consequences of these changes in the functioning of the school as a mediator of change. The school is mandated as such. Its purpose is to prepare children for the conditions of life they will experience in an urbanizing and modernizing environment.

We again administered the IAI and carried out an intensive ethnographic study of the school and its immediate community context. Our assumption was that the changes, particularly the intentional educational reform, would affect the perceptions of instrumental alternatives in the intended direction—toward a more modern outlook. The Remstal IAI had been designed with this in mind. The choices respondents can make are all between traditional-village and modern-urbanized instrumentalities, as they are construed in the Remstal. We were jolted by the results, though we didn't appreciate their full significance until we had thoroughly computerized the data upon our return to Stanford.

THE NEW REMSTAL SAMPLE

The 1968 IAI sample included 278 children in grades 3 through 9 (age approximately 9–16 years), 31 parents (9 males) and nine regular teachers (one male). In 1977 we collected responses to the IAI from 233 children (grades 3–9), age range 9 to 16 years, of whom 122 were again male, 65 parents (16 males) and nine teachers, of whom six were regular classroom teachers. Innovations in sampling included the use of a control sample of 65 additional respondents from a nearby urban elementary school.

Both samples included representation of all occupational, educational, cultural, and region-of-origin categories and degrees of urbanization present in the Schönhausen community.

Again the responses were sifted for associations and differences between these background factors and IAI (instrumental) choices. Again age and sex produced the most statistically significant results, with sex producing the most consistent differentiations. The differences *within* the new sample by sex were fewer than in 1968, for reasons we will clarify. The new (1977) sample was also tested against the old (1968) sample. And here were the surprises.

The Old and New Sample Compared by Sex

The first surprise revealed by our data analysis was that the 1977 sample as a whole, excluding the teachers, produced choices of instrumental alternatives that were more traditional land-village oriented than the 1968 sample produced. The overall sample trend towards more traditional choices, e.g., village residence, traditional dwelling (Fachwerk Haus), old church, Weingärtner was significant. There are many comparisons between the old and new sample, and within the new sample between age groups that would be interesting to interpret. We will concentrate on the 102 children in the Grundschule, who are our core group, and their mothers. Because sex is the single most important antecedent variable in our data matrix, we focus on these differences.[1]

First, let us take a look at the old sample of Schönhausen girls. Within the 1968 sample there were statistically significant differences in the distributions of choices: boys and girls ranging from .01 to .007 (using chi-square) for instrumental choices of village vs. city; Fachwerk vs. modern row house; Weingärtner vs. white collar work; factory vs. independent small shop; technical draftsman vs. small farmer; traditional vs. modern church; party at home vs. party in a tavern (Gasthaus); participation in the Weinlese; and living in a Bauernhaus. In each instance the girls chose the modern, urban instrumentalities more frequently than boys did. As we compare boys and girls *within* the new sample (1977) from Schönhausen we again find differences, but their direction is *reversed*. Girls make more tradition-oriented choices; boys make more urban-oriented choices (than girls do), and don't want to live in the Bauernhaus. The differences between sexes are weaker than within the 1968 sample, for the sample as a whole is more traditional. Nevertheless, the fact that the direction of choices is reversed for the two sexes is startling.

The most interesting differences appear when we examine the distribution of IAI responses for new (1977) girls as against old (1968) girls. The new (1977) girls, as compared to old (1968) girls chose the village over the

---

[1]We have expanded on differences by sex in relation to culture change in the Schönhausen study, in the context of a broad discussion of such differences in our Menomini, Blood Indian, and Cree research, in relation to comparable issues in studies of the Israeli Kibbutzim, in a chapter for the Festschrift for Melford Spiro (G. and L. Spindler, in preparation).

city; the Fachwerk over the modern house; Weingärtner over working in an office; independent shop owner over factory worker; small farmer over machinist; large-scale farmer over technical draftsman; traditional over modern church; a party at home over one in a tavern and participating (as against not participating) in the harvest.

There is no question, statistically speaking and with reference to choices made within the instrumental activities framework that we presented respondents with, that the girls in 1977 made an abrupt swing toward traditional instrumentalities. We must remember again, however, that the majority of choices in both 1968 and 1977 (with some notable occupations) were traditional. These are shifts in frequency of choice, shifts in *distributions* of responses.

When we examine the differences in distributions of responses for new (1977) as against old (1968) boys we find a pattern that is statistically much weaker than for the girls, but that is in the opposite direction. The new boys more frequently choose modern instrumentalities than the old boys do.

Particularly startling to us is the fact that in three instances the new girls almost totally reversed the distribution of responses, as compared to the old girls. The three instances are the Fachwerk Haus, Weingärtner, and Party at home. Nearly 100% of all new girls responding to the IAI made traditional choices in these areas, where a slight to heavy majority had made modern choices before (in 1968). These traditional/modern reversals are particularly significant because they are at the core of the village-land-domestic complex. They are a statement of apparently near-universal agreement within the 1977 sample of girls that the traditional instrumentalities, particularly as they are related to domesticity and village-land life style, are more desirable than modern instrumentalities in the same areas.

Comparisons of the distributions of IAI responses for older students (through the ninth grade and including several kinds of schools) show the same general trend towards more traditional choices for the 1977 sample, but the responses are less consistent, and the differences less marked. The realities of instrumental choices in an urbanizing environment have forced themselves upon the consciousness of these young people. In contrast, the Grundschule children in the third and fourth grade can express the "pure" sentiments, largely unaffected by practical considerations, that in muted form are distributed throughout the sample as a whole.

The same statement can be made about the parents. Again the 1977 sample tends toward more traditional instrumental choices than the 1968 sample of parents. New mothers are more traditional as a group. We also compared the sixteen working mothers with those who did not work and found no significant differences between the two groups.

The Teachers. In 1977 there were still only six regular teachers in the school, including the Rektor (principal). Since 1968 three teachers had been replaced. The newcomers were all young women.

An examination of the IAI responses for all teachers in 1977 showed little change from 1968. Only one teacher opted for life in the big city as against life in the village. She cited better shopping facilities, better medical services, and more "culture." All of the others extolled the virtues of village life, such as cleaner air, safe places for children to play, friendly relations with neighbors, pleasing landscape and less traffic. But all agreed that they wanted to live (and all did) in a village near a big city, where the advantages of city life would be available.

Responses to other IAI choices showed a strong pragmatic orientation. A Fachwerk house, for example, is perceived as romantically pleasing but requiring a lot of upkeep and as being expensive to heat. All appreciated the values associated with the harvest, the evening at home, the Bauernhaus, the independent worker and the Weingarten, but none would choose to live in a Bauernhaus or be a Weingärtner permanently.

As cultural agents the teachers can be characterized as pragmatic and moderately conservative, seeing both advantages and disadvantages to most instrumental relations but appreciating the values of the small community and the countryside.

Summary of statistical differentiations for the Remstal data

We have chosen a prose style of reporting the results of statistical tests to avoid pages of charts and columns of figures. To clarify the relationships we discovered we summarize the main findings for the Remstal data.

1. A major mandated reform effort to modernize the agricultural, residential, administrative sectors in West Germany reached its major phase of implementation in the Remstal in the period between our first study of Schönhausen in 1968 and our restudy in 1977.

2. The Schönhausen sample as a whole in 1977 made more traditional instrumental choices than in 1968; the opposite effect than the one we had predicted.

3. Sex differences within the 1968 sample were highly significant, with females choosing modern instrumentalities more frequently than males.

4. Males chose more modern instrumentalities and females made more

traditional choices in the 1977 sample, than in 1968, thus reversing the distribution of choices by sex.

5. Females in the 1977 sample chose traditional instrumentalities much more frequently than females did in 1968.

6. Particularly significant, in both a statistical and interpretive sense, is the fact that three "reversals" occurred in distributions of instrumental choices for the females that relate most directly to the traditional land-village-domestic complex.

Discussion

The IAI data just presented are not proof that the sweeping and very expensive educational reform made no difference, nor does it show that the reform caused a conservative swing in sentiments. What these data do demonstrate is that the reform did not result in a clear swing in perception of goals and the means to them in the direction in which the reform was intended. There is a difference, too, between sentiment and behavior. There is no doubt, as we have said, but what Schönhausen, and in fact the whole Remstal, changed considerably in the decade between studies. We make the assumption, however, that "sentiment," in the form of preferential instrumental choices and the cognitive ordering of relationships between goals and the means to them influenced both short- and long-range adaptations. We assume also that identities are expressed in life style choices that are persistent and also influence behavior. In addition to the basic knowledge and the skills taught in schools we hold that it is these instrumental relationships that are presented and defended. They are a part of the culture being transmitted in the school at any given time.

The IAI responses from Schönhausen show us clearly that despite the reform, sentiments and identities did not shift in the direction of modernization, but, rather, shifted in the direction of traditional values and life styles. It should be sobering to planners of culture change and reform, educational or otherwise, to observe this result. It is a phenomenon that is not limited to Schönhausen or the Rems valley. Conservative and traditional sentiments are surfacing in many parts of the globe, particularly in the United States, in attitudes and behavior concerning sex, marriage, work, achievement, religion, and patriotism. It seems that the processes of culture change are not under our direct control and occur in ways we do not fully understand.

It is especially interesting that it is the females in the Schönhausen sample who have made the most dramatic shift toward traditional goals and instrumentalities. In 1968 they were more urban and modern than the males. In 1977 they were more traditional in choices than the males. We have to go beyond the old sexist saw that it is a woman's prerogative to change her mind. It is the family and home, and the complementarity of male and female roles in the traditional cultural framework that are most threatened by urbanization and modernization. The new roles available to women in the work place, the small city apartment, and in public life, do not, it appears, make up for the loss of stable neighborhoods, rewarding work relationships, extended kin networks, and complementary male/ female responsibilities in agricultural production. Females responded again and again in their defenses of their IAI choices to the effect that they feared isolation and a breakdown in familial and domestic relationships as a concomitant of urbanization. Their explicit choices of instrumental alternatives and goals expressed this fear as well.

Something of the same kind has been described for the kibbutzim of Israel by several researchers such as Melford Spiro (1979). It seems that when a point in change is reached where family and domestic values are deeply threatened these women have opted for more traditional life styles. The reasons for this go well beyond the scope of our discussion. As we interpret the phenomena it is a cultural, not biological process, but it has an ultimate biological base that is culturally translated (see G. & L. Spindler, in preparation).

We see in the IAI response patterns described an indication that culture is not easily shaped to fit explicit human intentions. This does not seem a revelation, particularly to anthropologists, but it is easily overlooked in studies of schooling. The cultural dimension, particularly in the form of cultural knowledge (assumptions, norms, expectations, as well as specific information) persisting through surface change is a constant theme in the rest of our discussion. Though we had never strayed from culture as an explanatory variable, we had given it less attention than it deserved. We "rediscovered" it in unexpected ways.

TEACHERS' STYLES

When we started filming classroom behavior in the 1977 field visit our objective was to secure a permanent record of behavior, centering on the teacher and her or his interaction with children. We were interested in both the presentation of information and the organization of learning experiences and in classroom control. We had taken hundreds of 35mm slides in the 1968 visit and had continued to take more in 1977. They had been of help but lacked the vivid quality that only sound and movement can provide. Further, they were even more selective than film, for the action frozen in a still picture has a duration in real life of only a fraction of a second.

Our film technique was based on the notion that we did not want to record everything. We had already done intensive ethnographic observation when we started filming and had developed a keen sense of the timing and pace of each classroom. We were interested in critical sequences of action in instructional management and classroom control. We managed to film 4,000 feet of such sequences, sometimes lasting only a few seconds, some lasting a minute or two, during the 2 weeks of intensive filming.

Since we had already done much ethnographic observation in each classroom and had developed a construction of teachers' styles, our filming, quite naturally, tended to emphasize behavior that distinguished the teachers from each other. We soon began to use a kind of descriptive shorthand to refer to these styles and use them in the descriptions below. They are in no sense intended to be pejorative. These were all excellent teachers who had developed methods of handling their subject matter and maintaining control of their classroom that suited them best. They were all professionally trained and had learned a variety of techniques in their teacher training institutions from which they could draw. All but one, not included in the typologies below, had more than 5 years of experience. We present three stylistic types that represent the range of styles for all six teachers.

Stylistic Types

The Orchestra Leader. This middle-aged male was one of the most dynamic and active teachers we had ever seen in action anywhere. He was what the Germans called a *Frontal Unterrichter* (one who instructs from the front of the room). Unless he was circulating around the room helping individual students with workbook exercises, he was almost always up front. Maps of his classroom movement show that he used the space in the center of the front most of the time and rarely left it during an instructional episode. He used maps, pictures, diagrams, and some ingenious self-designed demonstrations, as well as verbal exposition, to get his lessons across. He involved children by calling on them and they frequently came to the front of the room to complete a math exercise, an incomplete grammatical sentence, discuss the elements of a picture, or manipulate one of his ingenious demonstration devices. He stirred up great enthusiasm. Children would snap their fingers while raising their hands and utter little moans of eagerness to get his attention. During our observation of him, both in 1968 and 1977, we never saw him turn the class over to his students but once—for a weights and measures experiment. During that time he sat at a student's desk on the window side of the room but he could not sit there quietly. He kept on directing the experiment and the movement of the children from his seat with comments, hand gestures, and "body English."

After his demonstration-exposition, of grammar, math, natural science, or current affairs, he had the children working on workbook exercises at their desks. Though the children sat at tables together, they worked alone. Herr Steinhardt would walk about the room examining the work of individual students. When he thought the work was lagging or some mistakes were being made he would admonish, correct, or ask questions, as he thought were needed to get the student on track.

When the workbook assignment was finished the children would find Herr Steinhardt up front again and they would bring their completed work to him for approval. He would glance through the work and make a comment. The child would leave the room or return to his or her seat depending upon what time it was.

Herr Steinhardt never relinquished control of his classroom while he was in it and he directed the activities in it from the frontal position. His gestures were sweeping and dynamic, his voice loud and clear, his manner pleasant but authoritative (but not authoritarian), and stimulating. He was the director, the conductor, of the symphony in his classroom.

The Fader. This attractive young woman of 26 years, dressed more often in jeans than the other teachers and carried herself with a faintly countercultural air. She was what the Germans called a *Gruppen Unterrichter* (group teacher) and *Role Speiler* (role player). She occupied the frontal position only to set up a class interaction or demonstrate a specific lesson. Most of the time she was somewhere in the back of the room, usually standing, leaning against the wall in a corner or on a window sill. She was so inconspicuous at times that we came to call her the "fader" for she would "fade" from our view, particularly as we were filming. She circulated freely among students at their tables when they were working on workbook exercises or art work, of which there was a great deal. Her classroom was quieter than Herr Steinhardt's and she responded to disruptive behavior of any kind with a quick look, a finger to the lips, or a small, sharp exclamation with a quick, close-to-the-body gesture. She never left her position to admonish a child who was misbehaving, where Herr Steinhardt would move decisively to a miscreant and lay a firm hand on his or her (more often his) shoulder, or tweak an ear, usually with a half humorous air.

She used role playing to engage the children in activity demonstrating some aspect of what the lesson was about. For example, the discussion one day was about town government and how it worked. There had been preliminary discussion and reading about its structure and history, and a trip to the local *Rathaus* (town hall). Frau Schön began the lesson sitting on the edge of her desk on the left front of the room. "I want you to think about how one could petition a change of some sort in the community that the town government could bring about. What would you like to see happen? How would you plan it? How would you make your proposal?" Without further ado she divided the class of twenty-six children into working groups and left her position in the front to circulate from table to table to listen and make a few quiet suggestions. After 20 minutes of such activity the groups were ready for action. She appointed one group of eight as the town council and mayor, another as proposers of the park, and the rest as concerned citizens.

With the stage set the children quickly occupied the front of the room, the council arranged in a half circle, the petitioners in another group facing them, with their spokesman in front. After the *Bürgermeister* (mayor) explained what the meeting was about the spokesman made the proposal, explaining where the park would be, its size, and that it would have benches facing into the park area rather than towards the street so that the "old people" could sit and watch the children play, because "old people like to see children playing." The Bürgermeister and council members asked questions and raised objections that the spokesman, after brief consultations with his group, would answer. The "concerned citizens" watched the proceeding eagerly, some standing on their seats in order to see better and making *sotto voce* comments.

Frau Schön had "faded" into the rear corner nearest the windows. As matters proceeded she raised an eyebrow or pursed her lips now and then. We thought these gestures unnoticed by the children at first, but as time wore on, we could see that both actors and spectators were glancing at her repeatedly and seemed to "catch" her (to us) subtle communications. But she never left her position until the role playing was over and the children had returned to their seats. A brief followup discussion of the proposal, its presentation, and the response of the *Gemeinderat* (town council) was held, with Frau Schön now leaning against a window sill about midway to the front of the classroom. Later, a workbook exercise on town government was completed.

Role playing was used by Frau Schön to demonstrate almost anything, and her behavior was consistently low key. She never overtly directed the role-playing action, and consistently reinforced the children's efforts to organize their own activities. She never, however, really abdicated her control of the classroom, but her control was quite subtle.

The Grasshopper.   This short, wiry, middle-aged teacher, Frau Hahn, was neither a "fader" nor an "orchestra leader." She never stayed in one place long enough to be either one. She had no customary location in the classroom. After the first attempts we gave up trying to do location and movement maps. She was in constant motion, her wiry body could jump, twist and turn, roll, and sit cross-legged on the floor with the most agile of her students. Her regular class consisted of the first and second grades combined. Her music sessions included the third and fourth graders.

A typical hour in her classroom of first and second graders began with a story telling session. She started the session sitting on a chair in a half circle, but soon as the story warmed up she was on and off the floor, carrying on with the story line but now acting it out, gesticulating, bending, leaping, bringing the children along with her as the action unfolded and the characters developed. After the story had been told, or rather lived, she conducted a free wheeling discussion and administered a specially prepared recognition exercise. But never did she work from the front of the room. She was always in motion, in the midst of the children, even when giving directions or setting up the activity.

In her music lessons she was, if anything, even more active. The children were seated on chairs along a north and an east wall, each with a percussion instrument of some kind; triangles, simple xylophones, drums, cymbals, wooden sticks, rasps. She played the melody first on her flute, with foot stamping and body movement to demonstrate and accentuate the rhythm. Then she would have each "section" (drums, xylophones, etc.) accompanying her separately, finally combining them together in one grand orchestration. She leapt from group to group, from individual to individual, admonishing, demonstrating, correcting, accompanying all with the greatest intensity and involvement. When the orchestration was under sufficient control to show how such a miracle could be achieved and each child had participated vigorously in the achievement, she played a lively tune on the turntable, demonstrated a dance step, and quickly brought each child into first a hand-to-hand circle and finally to free, individual expression.

It was exhausting simply to watch her work, but she would confess no fatigue. Her energy and determination seemed unbounded. She was indeed a creative and lively grasshopper.

Common Features

We were so impressed by the apparent differences among the Schönhausen teachers that we questioned our assumption that we were studying teachers as agents of cultural transmission. Immersed in the school and its activities, and in the community as well, we had gradually lost our "distance" from what we were studying. The culturally "strange" had become all too familiar (G. and L. Spindler, 1982).

It was not until we returned home, after the 1977 trip, and had begun to view our films again and again, that we began to see some common features of instructional organization and classroom management. We reexamined our notes from the same classrooms and time periods and found them supportive of generalizations emerging from the film viewings. To see whether or not others would perceive some of the same features we showed selected films of all three teachers to several groups of graduate students, totaling 120 persons in all, mostly from education, without any directions or introduction excepting for some general background on the area and a brief statement of our research purposes. Viewers were asked to describe each of the three teachers, then sum up the salient differences and commonalities. The level of agreement between what the viewers reported and what we saw was startling.

First, we agreed that there was an invariant sequence of steps for every lesson, irrespective of what the lesson was about. It was difficult to see the sequence in certain lesson contexts, for there was so much activity and the markers between elements were not at all obvious in some instances. Further, it was impossible for some of our viewers to discern the sequence in some film episodes because the filming had been too episodic and selective. Consequently the validity of our assertion that the sequence below held good for most lessons rests upon our classroom notes, slides, and tapes, as well as upon the film strips. The sequence was more explicit in some lessons than in others and at times certain steps in the sequence were left out or combined differently than we are presenting them. We believe, however, that the listing below is a fair characterization of the sequence in most instructional units.[2]

The Sequence.   1. Presentation and definition of task. The teacher explains what the lesson is about: learning telephone behavior, petitioning town government, making complete sentences, listening to and discussing a story, doing multiplication, recognizing and naming local flowers, learning about magnets, or about the metamorphosis of a butterfly, etc.; and tells the class what is going to happen.

2. Demonstrations by the teacher. The teacher does correctly something that is going to be learned, such as showing how to multiply, complete a sentence, name some flowers, etc.

3. One or two children participate with the teacher in the demonstra-

---

[2]There is a significant and expanded literature by our educationist colleagues on classroom behavior, control, teacher styles, and characteristics and processes underlying surface phenomena that is too voluminous to cite. We have found Larry Cuban (1984) and Robert Tabachnik et al. (1982) particularly relevant to our concerns. Though their objectives and analytic paradigms are different than ours, we seem, quite independently, to be heading in the same direction.

tion. This may occur simultaneously with step two but is often a second stage of demonstration.

4. The whole class practices whatever is being taught, in small groups, one by one, or as a whole.

5. A workbook or comparable exercise is provided that requires each child to do some writing, diagramming, checking, sums, etc.

6. When the exercise is finished the child takes the completed work directly to the teacher and expects to get some acknowledgment from the teacher.

Classroom Management and Interaction.   The second area of agreement concerning common features cross-cutting teacher differences was more diffuse and problematic, but for our purposes, as they were emerging by then, of greater significance. All of us could see certain commonalities in classroom control and the interaction among children and between teachers and children even though there was variation and difference in emphasis. The observations by the viewers and by ourselves merged into the following generalizations. Again, the validity of the generalizations rests upon all of the data we collected from the classrooms, not the films alone, though the films and their viewing with others gave us invaluable leads.

1. Classrooms are noisy and boisterous when the teacher is out of the room. Children rarely continue working (tests are an exception) when the teacher leaves for a while. The level of physical activity and the noise level are usually quite high during these times. Children run, shriek, wrestle, play tag, jump off desks. In general, even when they are quiet and working, children give the impression of exuberance and vitality.

2. When the teacher is in the classroom there is pervasive control, though the means of communicating the limits of behavior to children varies considerably from teacher to teacher.

3. Control of the classroom or any part of it is never relinquished by the teacher, even when the children are carrying out what appears to be self-directed activity. The control may be verbal, overt, and frequent, or may be expressed nonverbally, by gestures or expressions, sometimes very subtly.

4. All children do essentially the same things at the same time, even when the amount of activity would lead one to think otherwise. Though there is individual work, as in workbook exercises, all of the children are working at the same exercises at the same time.

5. There is feverish competition for teacher approval. Children groan, grunt, moan, snap their fingers, wave arms, to get the teacher's attention.

Children show the teacher their work in progress to get reinforcement, and when finished, literally shove it in the teacher's face to get some nod of recognition or approval. Children carrying out role playing and class demonstrations keep glancing at the teacher to catch nods, raised eyebrows, pursed lips, and other gestures, expressions, or signs of approval or disapproval of what is going on.

6. A uniform and, in our view, a high standard of expectation concerning product is maintained and, on the whole, met. Third graders asked to draw the inner area of Schönhausen, around the Rathaus, produced drawings remarkable for their uniformity and for their excellence. Nearly all third graders wrote complete sentences explaining their choices of instrumental alternatives, and cited the same advantages and disadvantages. Even though the actual choices made might differ, the elements of the rationale were uniform.

7. All classrooms were strongly teacher-centered, with little observable attempt to reinforce independence, autonomy, or individual creativity.

The first level of generalization concerning sequence management of instruction can be interpreted as describing a product of teacher training, though we have no clear evidence that this is the case. The second level of generalization concerning classroom management and interaction is of a somewhat different order and takes us closer to culture and farther from pedagogy. Though pedagogy is not acultural, it is a specialized subset of culture that is distinctive from the broad stream of national, class, community, or folk culture. Though student teachers may acquire the points of view and behavioral patterns that they manifest in Schönhausen classrooms, as summarized above, during teacher training, it is doubtful that they are intentionally taught in the training institutions. In fact teachers explained that their training in group instruction and role playing was designed to free their teaching from the lock step of the formal, authoritarian, traditional classroom.

CULTURE IN THE CLASSROOM

Schönhausen and Roseville, U.S.A.

When we returned to Schönhausen in 1981 we continued filming and classroom observation but focused on interviewing teachers. We had interviewed each teacher informally a number of times as we inquired about the reasons for behavior we had observed in the classroom. But now we sat down with each teacher to talk for as long as the teacher was able to stay with us. We had an agenda, centering on one's philosophy of education, one's feelings about Schönhausen and its school, and the instructional program.

We also showed teachers the films of their classrooms, both individually and to all the teachers as a group. The three teachers who had left the school returned to see the films of their classrooms taken in 1977. These sessions were all taped. The individual viewings were not particularly productive. Teachers remarked about their appearance or how quiet the class seemed but were not stimulated to any revealing expositions. The group sessions were very different. Teachers talked fast and incessantly about individual children, teaching techniques, difficulties and successes, philosophies of instruction, educational objectives, and needed changes. It was the first time, they said, that they had seen each other in action, and one of the few times they had talked with each other in any depth about matters of common professional interest. The conversations were recorded and we worked a long time to unscramble the rapid exchanges, with fair but not complete success. But it was clear that films as evocative stimuli for discussion had worked well.

The interviews and the film viewings and discussions took us further into an understanding of the cultural knowledge teachers brought with them into the classroom and the ways in which it was implemented in instructional management and social control. It was not, however, until we had done some field work again in a comparable American school, that the full impact of this understanding was felt.

We entered the Roseville elementary school in the fall of 1983. The Roseville school and community were comparable in that both Schönhausen and Roseville were semirural. Both schools were mediating, for students, changes from a traditional agricultural base line to a more urbanized environment. Both were small communities and schools, and both were predominately ethnically German. Our purpose in the Roseville school was to collect films of classroom activity that we could show to the Schönhausen teachers. After our film viewing session with these teachers they had earnestly requested that we bring some films of a comparable American school back with us on our next visit. The Roseville principal and teachers graciously invited us to film any and all activities in and around the school and to observe their classrooms, and ask questions about what we saw. Again, we filmed episodes of behavior that seemed criterial to us on the basis of our ethnographic observations.

We also showed the Roseville teachers films of the Schönhausen classrooms. Their responses were similar to those already described. They were particularly impressed with the intense activity of the Schönhausen children and reflected that perhaps they (Roseville) kept "the lid on" children's spontaneous activity. The energy and vitality expressed in the behavior of the Schönhausen children led more than one observer to wonder if their diet was different. As a matter of fact there is a great difference between "squeezin' soft" American white bread and the dense dark (and tasty) Schönhausen Bauernbrot (farmer's bread).

From all of these interactions, from our filming, and from our ethnography, we have begun to understand that beyond all of the overt, observable behaviors, including responses to the IAI, that we have collected so much useful data on, there are some very pervasive and basic cultural orientations. That there were significant cultural factors influencing behavior was not surprising to us, but we did not see them clearly until we had returned to observe in the Roseville school. Certain salient features of basic cultural assumptions, norms, and expectations for Schönhausen and for Roseville emerged. We can scarcely claim them as representing the whole of either German or American culture but the differences are suggestive and relate well with other observations of both cultures (G. and L. Spindler, 1983). In any event they seem to explain a great deal about Schönhausen and Roseville.

To check our perceptions against those of others we again asked graduate students to view our films and record their interpretations. Eighty-five graduate students, again predominately in education, produced, with a high level of agreement, certain characterizations of the Roseville classroom activity. Their perceptions matched ours and we present them below. Since many of the students had also viewed the Schönhausen films their responses are often implicitly comparative, though not always phrased that way.

The Roseville Elementary School

1. There is a diversity of activity in every classroom. One group will be reading and discussing a lesson, some children will be reading at their seats, others working on art projects (it was approaching Thanksgiving), and a small group in the back of the room will be using flash cards to drill each other in math.

2. The teacher sits more (than at Schönhausen), even when conducting a lesson. The teacher often sits at her desk while children come up singly or in groups of two or three to get some help or further direction.

3. The room is orderly, quiet, almost "somber." There is none of the relatively chaotic, "feverish" activity of the Schönhausen classrooms.

4. Children work independently much of the time, without even looking at the teacher. They seem absorbed in their own tasks.

5. Children interact with each other as they work, or move from one task to another, and peer approval is sought.

6. Art work is popular, as in cutting out and pasting on turkey tails or making a poster.

7. The teacher appears to act as a coordinator rather than a director of activity.

In general, our observations and the film viewings produced a picture of classrooms much less teacher centered, much more orderly and quiet, and with far more independent, apparently self-regulated activity that took place without teacher monitoring excepting when sought by the child, than in the Schönhausen school. Our observations of the two schools, our interviews, and the viewings of the films lead us to a final statement of cultural orientations that as an aspect of teacher cultural knowledge underlie many specific features of instructional and classroom management and seem to be strongly accountable for the differences between the two schools.

Teacher Cultural Knowledge

Schönhausen: "Katzenjammer Kids" assumption: Children are naturally lively, destructive, mischievous, all hell will break loose when external authority (teacher) is not present.

Roseville: Teachers expect classrooms to stay in order when they are absent from the room. Misdemeanors are regarded as an exhibition of immature behavior and as a violation of an understanding between teacher and child.

Schönhausen: Authority is external and imposed upon the individual.

Roseville: Authority is internal and imposed by the individual upon one's self.

Schönhausen: Individuals are members of groups accomplishing standard tasks competitively but uniformly. The individual "is very important but must work in the group." Attention is given to the individual to bring the individual up to group standard.

Roseville: Individuals are the end goal of teaching and learning. The group exists in order to make individual life and achievement possible—as contexts with sufficient order to permit the pursuit of individual goals and satisfactions. Attention is given to the individual so that he or she may develop to the fullest possible extent as an individual.

Schönhausen: The teacher is regarded as responsible for learning, including stimulating motivation. The teacher organizes all activities in order to attain instructional goals.

Roseville: The teacher is responsible for coordinating various activities and various forms of self-development. The teacher tries to reinforce the individual's attempt to improve. Individuals vary with respect to both quality and quantity of production.

There are other cultural assumptions and orientations as a part of teacher cultural knowledge that will emerge more clearly with further work but these listed items indicate the direction of the cultural differences between Schönhausen and Roseville as they directly influence instruction and classroom control.

Teacher cultural knowledge does not work in a social vacuum. This knowledge is constantly reinforced and adapted as interaction takes place. The "dialogue" that takes place in the classroom requires also that the children share at least the key assumptions and tacit rules embedded in this cultural knowledge. When classroom behavior breaks down, as in certain urban classrooms, it is often because teachers and students are not bound by the same cultural "contract," or the students know what the teacher's cultural expectations are and purposely violate them for reasons external to the classroom. In Schönhausen and Roseville teachers and children are bound by the same contract and share cultural knowledge that makes the classroom dialogue consistent, and consistently different, for the two schools.

FINAL COMMENTS

We have pursued our interpretive ethnography of the Schönhausen elementary school, and finally the Roseville school, through the presentation and discussion of the IAI results, the description of teachers' styles, the analysis of the underlying features held in common, and the differences between the Schönhausen and Roseville classrooms and the cultural knowledge of the Schönhausen and Roseville teachers.

In all of the various settings and interactions we have discovered a cultural dimension that appears to be pervasively determinant of complex behavior. We found that despite massive and expensive attempts at reform the sentiments of those to be reformed swung in the opposite direction from that intended—toward traditional goals and the means to them. We found that despite dramatic apparent differences in the ways teachers presented instructional materials and controlled classrooms there were underlying features that were held in common in both the sequence of instructional management and the management of classroom activity and interaction. We found that surprising differences between the Schönhausen and Roseville schools seemed well explained by differing cultural orientations and cultural knowledge respectively German and American—or at least Schönhausen and Roseville. Interpretive ethnography, using concepts and models from cultural anthropology, will lead us in the directions pursued in this analysis. The results appear to be useful, both as a contribution to knowledge and as a route to understandings that can influence educational policy, modify expectations, and influence attempts at reform. It would seem imperative that planners should become knowledgeable about the key cultural dialogues carried on in the intended arena of proposed change.

ACKNOWLEDGMENT

We take this opportunity to thank the National Institute of Mental Health, the Wenner-Gren Foundation, the Spencer Foundation, the North Atlantic Treaty Organization, and the Center for Educational Research at the University of Wisconsin, Madison, for financial support for the research. Further, we would like to thank our colleagues at the Center for Behavioral Sciences at Stanford, and in the Department of Anthropology Colloquium Series, for the opportunity to test out our interpretations in a receptive, but critical, context.

APPENDIX

Schönhausen and its Setting

Until the beginning of World War II, Schönhausen, a village in southern Germany and the setting of the study, was almost entirely devoted to the cultivation of wine grapes and subsistence farming. It is near a large city and is part of a rapidly urbanizing area, the Rems River Valley (henceforth Remstal) in Baden-Württemberg, Federal Republic of Germany. More than twenty separate villages and small towns of the Remstal are coalescing now into one more or less continuous urban complex. At present Schönhausen is one of several smaller villages with a total population of around 2500, an increase from a pre-World War II population of around 1300. Two kilometers in a northeasterly direction separate it from the next village and one kilometer in a southwesterly direction from a town of about 7000. Schönhausen is surrounded by terraced hillsides where nine different varieties of wine grapes are grown. Grains and vegetables are grown in the valley flat lands. There are also factories and machine shops within a short distance built on what was until recently agricultural land. Custom furniture, machine parts, women's sandals, map globes, metal cabinets and cases, electrical equipment, soft drinks, leather goods, and many other items, not to mention thousands of liters of bottled wine, are produced in these factories and shops. Most of the operations involved in this production require skilled labor. Though Schönhausen is part of this rapidly urbanizing and industrializing complex, it has retained a fairly traditional appearance. The ancient *fachwerk* houses are protected by law from significant exterior change, and new houses, apartments, and other buildings have been constructed so as to blend harmoniously with existing structures. A number of large houses, some very old, shelter both human beings and animals—cows, pigs, rabbits, and fowls—under one roof.

The rather traditional appearance of Schönhausen can be misleading. The village has increased almost 100 percent in population since before World War II, due largely to a massive influx of population resettled in West Germany from 1945 through the fifties. Before the war the village was almost entirely agricultural, of the type known as *ausgesprochener Weinort* (a village devoted to the cultivation of grapes and the making of wine). It was almost entirely Protestant and almost entirely composed of people born in the area who spoke the Schwäbisch dialect as their native language, though they learned standard High German in school. Today Schönhausen is still a Weinort (a place where wine grapes are grown), but only a small minority of people are full-time Weingärtner (vintners). Most of its inhabitants work in nearby factories built since 1950 or in the nearby city. Some maintain small plots of land and are part-time Weingärtner, even though they work for wages. Only a bit more than half are natives and speak the Schwäbisch dialect—the rest are migrants from what was the east zone (now the German Democratic Republic) or from the outlying prewar German minorities, such as the Sudetenland and Bessarabia, or from other parts of Western Germany. There is also a group of *Gastarbeiter* (workers from other countries).

Until recently, Schönhausen was a homogeneous agricultural folk community. Today it is a heterogeneous, only partly agricultural, largely suburban community. Some of its people are Catholic, many do not speak the native dialect (but have dialects of their own representing the linguistic diversity of Germany), and only a few work the soil. Schönhausen is being incorporated, both physically and symbolically, into the emerging metropolis, though this process will take more than a decade.

It is precisely these conditions that make Schönhausen a significant site for a study of the role of the school as a culture-transmitting agency in a rapidly changing community. The community is changing from folk to urban, and the divergencies in backgrounds between natives and newcomers set the stage for potentially explosive confrontations. This is especially true since the newcomers were at first simply assigned to various homes in Schönhausen (as in other communities) during the resettlement, until new housing could be constructed, and were then given various advantages, among them loans at relatively low interest rates, in order to help them recoup the losses incurred by fleeing the east zone or occupied lands. The children of these people are now, and have been for some time, in the Schönhausen School, as well as in the more advanced schools to which the children from Schönhausen, and elsewhere, graduate. All the children in the village attend the Schönhausen School for four years. This attendance is irrespective of the eventual educational and occupational routes they will take after finishing the first four grades. It is also irrespective of their origins—whether native or newcomer, born of parents whose work ties them to the land or to parents whose work takes them to the city or whether their families migrated from an urban or a rural area. Particularly intriguing is the fact that on the whole this great influx of diverse (though Germanic) population was assimilated without any apparent disturbance. The low incidence of crime, suicide, and juvenile delinquency suggests that there has been no substantial increase in the social and psychological ills that often accompany rapid urbanization. Schönhausen and the area around it give every appearance of social and economic health.

The 1985 Field Trip

We returned to Schönhausen in May, 1985, to pursue further the general problem of classroom control and to try to specify in greater detail the differences between German and American culture as they affected classroom behavior. We brought with us films that we had taken in the Roseville classrooms. The two schools were similar in degree of urbanization, proximity to an urban center, size, and even national origin—the vast majority of the Roseville children are German-American. We showed the films to all the Schönhausen teachers and children. A special showing was arranged for the Director of Education for the area and his staff. His position is roughly equivalent to the Superintendent of Schools for the district of which Roseville is a part. We also had films from 1981 and 1977 and new (1985) films from the Schönhausen classrooms to show the teachers. Every interview with school personnel was bracketed by the films from Roseville and from Schönhausen so that respondents always had concrete behavioral points of reference for their expressed feelings and opinions. The procedure was productive and we learned many things, some of them clarifications of what we already knew and some breaking new ground. The differences noted between Roseville and Schönhausen in this chapter hold good, but one observation should be added now, and that is a concern for the organization of resources and time for *collective productive efficiency* in the management of all classroom (and other) activities in the Schönhausen school. It wasn't *discipline,* as such, that concerned these teachers, or their pupils, it was the efficient use of time and resources. As they perceived the Roseville classrooms where individual children pursued, for part of every hour, a variety of activities (reading, listening to tapes, playing with the library computer, using flash cards on each other, etc.) according to individual persuasion, they were not sufficiently coordinated around central objectives that could only be obtained by energetic, efficient work. This central observation was related in turn to a number of other matters, such as self-discipline, externalization of authority, performance expectations, and so forth. Until all of the data are analyzed this is as far as we can go.

The IAI Technique

The Remstal IAI is a collection of 37 line drawings in its long form and 17 in its short form. The drawings depict "activities," such as living in a Bauernhaus or traditional Fachwerk Haus, going to a modern church, participating in the grape harvest, working as a Weingärtner, or as a white collar worker, etc., that are instrumental to a more traditional, small village and land-based or to a more urbanized life style. Respondents choose instrumental activities and explain why they so choose. The IAI was developed in our Blood Indian research on culture change (G. and L. Spindler, 1965). We have used it among the Blood, Mistassini Cree, and in Germany. It is adapted to the cultural milieu anew in each usage but the principles of its organization and the model directing them remain constant. It can be administered to individuals or to groups. In the Schönhausen study we showed pairs of line drawings on 35mm slides simultaneously, using two projectors, and three drawings (on slides) singly. The objective, in all instances, was to discover how children, teachers, and parents chose instrumental activities contrasting in degree of urbanization and traditionalism, and how they defended their choices. By "instrumental activity" we mean an occupation, a habitation, use of a possession, school attendance, recreation, etc. that supports a given life style—in our case a life style more traditional or more urban. See Spindler (1974) for a complete description of the technique as applied in Schönhausen in 1968.

REFERENCES

Cuban, L. (1984). *How teachers taught: Constancy and change in American classrooms, 1890–1980.* New York: Longman.

Spindler, G. (1974). Schooling in Schönhausen: A study of cultural transmission and instrumental adaptation in an urbanizing German village. In G. Spindler (Ed.), *Education and cultural process: Toward an anthropology of education* (pp. 230–273). New York: Holt, Rinehart and Winston.

Spindler, G., & Spindler, L. (1965). The instrumental activities inventory: A technique for the study of the psychology of acculturation. *Southwestern Journal of Anthropology,* *21*(1), 1–23.

Spindler, G., & Spindler, L. (1982). Roger Harker and Schönhausen: From familiar to strange and back again. In G. Spindler (Ed.), *Doing the ethnography of schooling.* New York: Holt, Rinehart and Winston.

Spindler, G., & Spindler, L. (1983). Anthropologists view American culture. In B. Siegel, A. Beals, & S. Taylor (Eds.), *Annual review of anthropology* (pp. 49–78). Palo Alto: Annual Reviews Inc.

Spindler, G., & Spindler, L. (in preparation). The problem of women in four changing cultures. In M. Swartz & D. Jordan (Eds.), *Festschrift* for Melford Spiro.

Spiro, M. E. (1979). *Gender and culture: Kibbutz women revisited.* Durham, NC: Duke University Press.

Tabachnick, B. (1982). Illusory Schooling. In T. S. Popkewitz, B. R. Tabachnick, & G. Wehlage (Eds.), *The myth of educational reform: A study of school responses to a program of change.* Madison: University of Wisconsin Press.

The Author and Her Chapter

Kathryn Anderson-Levitt is an assistant professor of anthropology in the Department of Behavioral Sciences at the University of Michigan, Dearborn. She received her doctorate in anthropology at Stanford and did postdoctoral study at the University of California at Los Angeles in the Mental Retardation Research Center.

Her chapter describes the professional knowledge that Madame Jeanette Durand, a teacher in a French elementary school, uses to guide her teaching of reading. This professional knowledge can be regarded as cultural knowledge shared, with small modifications, among teachers teaching reading in French schools. How the precise components of the knowledge are acquired is somewhat of a mystery, as they are not replicas of anything taught in professional teacher training.

We know that similar categories of cultural knowledge are acquired by American teachers though their content may be quite different as well as the methods of conveying them in classroom practice. This chapter takes a significant step toward understanding cultural knowledge and its influence on teaching.

Dr. Anderson-Levitt explains herself and her purposes.

A stint as a teacher's assistant in South-Central Los Angeles during my undergraduate years gave me unfailing admiration for schoolteachers' skills in human relations as well as pedagogy. The experience also convinced me to enter a tamer profession.

I went to Stanford to study the way culture shapes perception, especially in the classroom. My first research efforts were an ethnographic evaluation of a school for dyslexic adolescents, and a case study of diverse models of learning problems used in the diagnosis of a "dyslexic" boy. Cultural models intrigued me from the beginning.

Wise counselors talked me into doing my dissertation research overseas, where I would look less the fool asking teachers obvious questions like "What do you mean by 'sounding out'?" and "How do you know that Johnny can read?" I returned to a city in France where I had already studied the language as an undergraduate, and conducted the study of first-grade teachers described in this chapter. I had expected to track, with the aid of a video camera, nitty-gritty cues in ongoing classroom behavior by which French first-grade teachers made judgments about their pupils' progress in reading. Instead, I found that the teachers' interpretations of classroom incidents depended less on specific cues than on their prior theories about the children. When I began to wonder how a teacher shaped early impressions of a child into a predictive theory, I was led back to the study of cultural models—models of the child and cultural models for teaching expressed in this chapter.

Eventually I will have to face the Big Question about the relation of cognition to behavior: Do cultural models really guide a teacher's decisions, or simply serve as *post hoc* accounts? Meanwhile, stimulated by postdoctoral study at UCLA's Mental Retardation Research Center, I have been doing research with mentally retarded adults and their care providers in sheltered workshops (Anderson-Levitt, 1983; Anderson-Levitt & Platt, 1984). The same issues arise again: What are the cultural models of the kind of treatment that should be provided? What is the relationship of cultural models to actual behavior?

The Editors

8 Cultural Knowledge for Teaching First Grade: An Example from France

Kathryn M. Anderson-Levitt
University of Michigan—Dearborn

INTRODUCTION

Some studies of schooling reveal the private world of students; some dissect the hidden curriculum. This chapter examines something less exotic—the professional knowledge of teachers and the overt curriculum. Yet even in the mundane, obvious facts about schooling—or *especially* in the mundane facts, perhaps—an anthropologist discovers how people organize life in cultural terms.

My research took place in France, and focuses on reading instruction in French first grades. Other social scientists have done participant observation in French schools to learn something about French culture (Wylie, 1964), rural social organization (Spiegel, 1978), or political behavior (Schonfeld, 1976). Although this study, too, identifies values, norms, and assumptions peculiar to French culture, my main purpose is not to describe the French but to make American readers reflect on the cultural nature of knowledge for teaching in the United States. A description of French schoolteachers makes a good mirror, for the French teachers' professional knowledge differs just enough from American teachers' knowledge to "make the familiar strange" (Spindler & Spindler, 1982).

In this chapter, "professional knowledge for teaching" refers to whatever a schoolteacher has to know, and know how to do, in order to carry on everyday classroom activities. Consider, for example, the following reading lesson which I witnessed in France. What did the teacher have to know in order to teach it?

A Lesson on the Letter *V*

In a first-grade classroom in an urban school in France, the children settle in their seats to begin the morning's work. The classroom is large and well lit from the windows forming most of one side wall. Homemade flashcards and children's artwork decorate the other side wall, and the children sit in double desks oriented toward the chalkboard at the front of the room.

It is the end of November in 1978, 2½ months into the school year. The teacher, Madame Jeannette Durand,[1] begins to *raconter,* to exchange news with the students. During the discussion she pauses twice to write on the chalkboard fragments of stories students have volunteered. Then she questions several children who have remained quiet. When David responds, she writes on the board the essence of his report: *"J'ai été voir le Père-Noël à Monoprix"* (I went to see Santa Claus at Monoprix [a department store]).[2] She remarks in an aside to the visiting ethnographer how David said *"J'ai été voir"* perfectly, whereas at the beginning of the year he couldn't pronounce *v* at all.

Soon after, the teacher ends the discussion and turns to a revision of syllables containing the vowels *é* and *è*. After morning recess and a mathematics lesson, Jeannette returns to the sentences she elicited from the children in the morning's discussion. She erases all but David's sentence, and leads the class in "reading" it several times from memory. After lunch, the class reads this text on the board again, and the teacher begins a new reading lesson on the letter *v*. She has the class think of words with the *v* sound in them, then dictates words from David's sentence to the children, who attempt to reproduce the words in chalk on individual slates. Afterwards, she has the class manipulate small slips of paper on which the same words have been dittoed. The children paste the slips into the reading notebook which serves as their primers, and illustrate the text.

The following morning, after listening to the children's volunteered remarks, Jeannette has the class read a text she has written on the chalkboard (in printing and cursive writing) using words from David's sentence, *v* words the class had learned earlier, and syllables beginning in *v*. David arrives late, and before he comes in the teacher complains privately to the ethnographer, "You go to the trouble of taking his sentence for reading and everything, and he's not there." She dictates *v* syllables for the children to write on their slates, and teaches formation of

---

[1]All proper names are pseudonyms.

[2]As discussed later in the text, most first-grade teachers in France avoid using upper case letters. Jeannette actually wrote on the board, *"j'ai été voir le père-noël à monoprix,"* that is, "i went to see santa claus at monoprix."

the *v* in cursive writing for the writing exercise. That afternoon, the class reads aloud from a dittoed text of *v* words and syllables, then pastes it into the reading notebook. The lesson on *v* continues that afternoon and the next morning with further slate dictations, reading text on the chalkboard, and review of the text pasted in the reading notebook.

An Innovative Teacher

Before discussing Jeannette's knowledge for teaching, it is important to note that other French teachers would *not* have considered her typical of the profession. I observed over forty schoolteachers in France, including fourteen first-grade teachers. Jeannette was one of the least conventional. She was the only teacher I knew personally who used student-composed sentences as the class's primary reading text, although I had read and heard of the technique. This technique, loosely referred to as *la méthode naturelle* (the natural method) in France and as "language experience" in the United States, draws a child's first reading texts from the child's own speech.

Jeannette took *la méthode naturelle* a step further than most of its practitioners. As she once explained, not all the children have interesting experiences to recount. Therefore, she arranged a number of experiences for the class as a whole, and these often led to reading texts. During the year in which I studied her class, she organized a bus trip to a farm with milk cows and a walking tour to a dairy near the school. The class also walked to a local bakery, then baked bread at school. Later they visited a children's art exhibit, the local botanical garden, a housing project, and other interesting locales within the *quartier*.

Jeannette was also unusual, though not unique, in the time she devoted at the end of the school day to *atelier* (workshop), various individual and group projects in arts and craft. Many of the projects, particularly albums of captioned illustrations about the fieldtrips, were informal extensions of the reading lessons.

STUDYING CULTURAL KNOWLEDGE

Despite Jeannette's innovative methods, most of the knowledge she used in conducting lessons like the lesson on *v* is cultural knowledge. The word *cultural* specifies knowledge that is learned from and shared with other people (D'Andrade, 1981; Goodenough, 1971; Spradley & McCurdy, 1972)—although in this case exactly what is shared and exactly how it was learned will be at issue. Cultural is the opposite of idiosyncractic.

"Knowledge for teaching," as mentioned above, means whatever a teacher has to know or know how to do in order to teach. It does *not* refer to teachers' familiarity with scientific theories of reading instruction. Nor does it refer to teachers' behaviors per se, although some knowledge is so taken for granted (e.g., the assumption that first graders can learn cursive writing) that one must infer it from the teachers' behavior. (For that reason this chapter occasionally resembles a description of behavior.) Rather, this report concerns teachers' practical professional knowledge, their *savoir faire* or "know-how": neither what they think nor what they do, but *what they think as they are doing what they do*. Knowledge, then, is a shorthand term for the beliefs, values, expectations, mental models, and formulas for doing things which the teachers use in interpreting and generating classroom events.

Recently, American researchers have taken an interest in describing teachers' practical knowledge for teaching. For example, Yinger (1980) has described how one first-grade teacher did her yearly, weekly, and daily planning. McNair (1978–79) has identified what teachers were thinking as they taught reading lessons, and Pittman (1985) diagrams a teacher's macroplan and microstrategies for handling students who are off task. Leiter (1976) discusses the thoughts running through a teacher's head as she interpreted students' test scores. Studies like these provide rich information about how teachers really think, but they tend to ignore what I emphasize here: the cultural part of cognition.[3]

This chapter employs two strategies to make visible the cultural nature of knowledge for teaching. First, Jeannette Durand's formulas for reading instruction are examined to show that, despite Jeannette's personal creativity, almost everything she did in the classroom reflected knowledge shared with other French teachers, hence cultural knowledge. Second, informal comparisons are made between French teachers' and American teachers' knowledge to point out differences that come from different cultural assumptions.

Where I refer to practices in American classrooms, my remarks derive from American studies of teachers' practical knowledge and from my own observations of six California first grades—public and parochial, middle class and working class—in the spring of 1978. My brief visits hardly qualify as ethnography, but at least they prevent facile references to a falsely idealized notion of American teachers (cf. Hsu, 1979).

The description of French first-grade teachers comes from 13 months of fieldwork in France, during which I conducted participant observation in three first-grade classrooms for the first 6 months of the 1978–79 school year. Jeannette Durand's class was one of those. The second was taught by Madame Berger, the third by Paul Alain. In addition, I spent a day of

---

[3]This phrase is borrowed from D'Andrade (1981).

participant observation in eleven other first grades and recorded interviews with eight of the teachers observed. To place the study of first grades in context, I also observed twenty-nine classes at other grade levels, from nursery school through vocational secondary school.

Additional information about French teaching comes from conversations with local elementary school inspectors, administrators whose duties include supervising the quality of instruction in their districts, instructing teachers in pedagogical methods, and grading teachers for the purpose of certification and pay raises. I also draw on two conversations, one of them tape recorded, with groups of teachers attending in-service workshops. The interview I recorded in June with eighteen first-grade teachers and their professor is referred to as the June workshop, and the less formal conversation held in September with eighteen teachers and a school inspector is referred to as the September workshop.

All the fieldwork took place in a middle-sized city and surrounding villages in a *département* in west-central France. Jeannette Durand taught in an urban school serving a predominantly working-class population, although a few of her students had parents in the liberal professions. Madame Berger's school drew a mixed middle class and working class student body from a residential *quartier*. Paul Alain's school, in a new *quartier* on the edge of town, served an upwardly mobile working-class population. While these, my principal informants, all taught in urban public schools, other participant observation took place in Catholic schools and in rural public schools.

FRENCH KNOWLEDGE IN PERSPECTIVE

The Variety of Possible Formulas for Teaching Reading

French teachers' recipes for teaching reading, when described in isolation, seem so reasonable and coherent that one is tempted to ask, "But how else *could* one teach reading?" Let me put the French formula in perspective by suggesting the wide range of possible techniques for reading instruction.

Anyone who follows the "great debate" over reading method knows that in contemporary Western schools two distinct formulas are conceivable, at least in theory. In a pure *phonics* method, which defines reading as decoding, the teacher would begin with letter-phoneme correspondences and, once students has mastered several of these, would introduce the decoding of simple words (e.g., Rawson, 1975). In France this approach is called the *synthetic* method, because a child learns to synthesize syllables from individual letters, or the *syllabic* method, because students learn to decode (usually meaningless) syllables before facing whole words. Only one teacher I observed in France, in an upper-middle-class Catholic school, used a nearly pure form of the synthetic method.

In a pure *global* or *sight word* method, which defines reading as extraction of meaning from the page, the teacher would create an environment in which children want and need to learn to read (e.g., by setting up a library corner, by placing name labels on coat hooks) and would then provide individual help to the would-be readers (e.g., Foucambert, 1976). Eventually students should make discoveries about letter-phoneme correspondences in words which they can already read by sight. In France, this method is referred to as *global-analytic* when the teacher leads students through the analysis of syllables and sounds in sight words systematically, rather than leaving the discovery entirely up to them. Featherstone (1971) found classrooms in some British schools where teachers favored a modified version of the global approach, and Ashton-Warner's (1963) distinctive formula for teaching reading through students' "key vocabularies" derives from the same philosophy. However, I never found a French teacher using a strictly global method in first grade, and teachers who use it in its pure form are rare (Saltiel, 1979, p. 10).

Examination of pedagogy in other eras and other cultures reveals many other possible recipes. The Japanese language does not have an alphabet, and Japanese children learn to read the syllabic script *kana* before facing ideographic *kanji* characters (Sakamoto & Makita, 1973). Conceivably, one could learn to read any spoken language by decoding syllables rather than phonemes, although it would be awkward to memorize all the possible syllables in a language like English.[4] A global approach without meaning is also possible. In Quranic schools in Morocco, students who have little or no understanding of classical Arabic learn to read the Qur'an by chanting the characteristics of each Arabic letter, tracing words, and copying the words from texts they have memorized (Wagner & Lofti, 1980).

As pedagogical method can vary, so can the physical and temporal organization of instruction. In English and French *monitorial* or *mutual* schools of the early 19th century, a thousand students assembled in a

---

[4]The Japanese case raises the issue of other, more subtle relationships between the structure of a particular language and the method of reading instruction. In French, for example, there is a tendency toward syllables which begin with a consonant sound and end with a vowel sound (Gregg 1960, p. 68), so that the French equivalent of the phonics approach stresses the pattern *consonant + vowel (la, ma, me)* whereas early phonics lessons in English stress the short vowel pattern *consonant + vowel + consonant* (bat, man, Dad). French primers also introduce multisyllabic words *(papa, petit, Valérie)* earlier than English primers, evidently because French contains fewer one-syllable words.

great hall took instruction from a single teacher assisted by a hierarchy of monitors (Léon, 1967, p. 79). In rural schools of the same era, small class size and frequent absences might force a teacher to give individual instruction (Prost, 1968). Of course, a class is not necessary at all, nor need reading be learned in childhood. Among the Vai people of Liberia, when a young man chooses to learn the Vai script—typically when he is in his teens or twenties—he studies at home for a few months with a literate friend or relative (Scribner & Cole, 1981).

French Knowledge for Teaching

Reading Method.   Officially, the decision about how to teach reading was up to Jeannette. The Ministry of Education, a branch of the national government, specifies only what should be learned and the amount of time a teacher should spend on each subject; for the 1978–79 school year, the Official Instructions required 9 hours of reading, writing, and oral expression out of a 27-hour week in first grade (France, 1977). Any discussion of teaching method in the Official Instructions is strictly advisory. Teachers are free to choose the instructional method and the textbooks they prefer, subject only to unofficial pressure from an inspector or principal and to budgetary limitations. The thirteen first-grade teachers I observed in addition to Jeannette used seven different primers, no more than four using the same one.

Jeannette's preference for student-composed texts over published primers placed her in the minority among first-grade teachers. Nonetheless, the way she used those texts to teach reading was utterly conventional. With the great majority of French teachers, she employed the *mixed method* of reading instruction, which combines elements of two archtypal methods described above, the global-analytic and the synthetic.

In the mixed method, Jeannette Durand and her colleagues begin by teaching the class to read a limited number of words and sentences globally. Some letters are abstracted from these texts and their sounds learned. So far, the method resembles the global-analytic approach, but at a crucial moment the teacher introduces the technique of decoding. From that point, instruction resembles the synthetic approach: The sounds of individual letters are taught, and the children practice decoding syllables and words which combine the new letter with letters previously learned.

While Jeannette's use of student-composed texts was less conventional than her use of the mixed method, it was the conventional way to be unconventional. That is, rejection of a published primer is common enough to carry a label *(la méthode naturelle)*. Teachers who use the natural method belong to a minority, but a large and visible minority. Although popularity varies with the age of the teacher, the inclination of local school inspectors, and the students' social class, some districts report that 25, 50, or even 70% of the first-grade teachers do not use a primer (Saltiel, 1979, p. 10).

Moreover, along with the label, the natural method carries cultural connotations beyond Jeannette's control. Jeannette told me that she used student texts simply because the primer bored her and the children. However, whatever her private motivations and despite the fact that Jeannette combined the use of student texts with the mixed method of instruction, many people in France associate the natural method with global reading instruction. The global method, in turn, is associated with radical politics, for both the natural method and the global approach grew in part from the work of Celestin Freinet, who developed specific global techniques of *natural* reading instruction in the 1920s for the purpose of liberating working-class children from an allegedly rote education. More recently, several informants claimed, global techniques became the rage in public schools for a certain period while the Catholic schools, which generally serve a politically conservative population, maintained allegiance to the synthetic method. These political connotations still linger. For example, a first-grade teacher quoted in a recent journalistic study argued, "In my opinion, the syllabic method is old hat, reactionary. The natural method seems more liberal, closer to my idea of the child" (Saltiel, 1979, p. 11).

Timing.   In addition to a broad plan for reading instruction based on the mixed method, Jeannette shared with other teachers a clear sense of the proper timing of instructional stages. The Ministry of Education's Official Instructions (France, 1973) make no mention of a timeline for reading instruction (except to recommend, contrary to prevailing practice, that knowing how to read no longer be a rigid criterion for passing first grade). In contrast, the teachers I interviewed in the June workshop expressed a clear consensus about when to move from global instruction to decoding. I asked how long the global stage lasts and they chorused: "until November," "the beginning of November," "to the end of October, around All Saints." (The professor running the workshop was a little surprised— whether because this struck her as too early for decoding or because she didn't expect such clear agreement, I don't know.) All Saints is a week-long school vacation which occurs in both Catholic and public schools around All Saints' Day, November 1, a Catholic holy day marked in France by visits to the cemetery. Evidently the teachers planned their teaching more or less within the blocks of time provided by the school calendar, a calendar based on the agrarian year and Church holidays.

In accord with this consensual timeline, Jeannette introduced the concept of decoding just before the All Saints' Day vacation, when she taught the letter *f*, the class's first consonant. Prior to that point, she had taught eighteen words by sight and then, beginning in the third week of the school year, had taught the sounds of five vowels taken from sight words. The introduction to decoding consisted of blending the *f* with each of these vowels to decipher nonsense syllables.

Madame Berger followed nearly the same schedule. She started the class with about seventeen sight words from their primer *Daniel et Valérie*, the French equivalent of Dick and Jane. As Jeannette, she introduced the first isolated letter, *i*, 2 weeks into the school year, and after teaching several other vowels, she introduced the first consonant and the concept of decoding immediately after the All Saints' vacation. Paul's primer took a slightly different tack. It began with fifteen sight words, but placed more formal emphasis on the analysis of syllables within those words. Still, in the fourth week, Paul had taught the first lesson on an individual letter, *l*, followed by the study of several individual vowels. Just after All Saints, his class, too, was decoding a limited number of syllables.

After introducing decoding, each teacher taught lesson after lesson on individual letters, repeating in each lesson instruction on how to decode. The teachers who used primers followed the sequence of lessons in that primer, progressing from sounds considered easier (e.g., *p, t*) to more difficult sounds (e.g., *on, eu*). Jeannette made her own decisions about the sequencing of lessons, usually waiting to hear the sentences offered by the students before selecting a new letter to be studied. However, she referred occasionally to a copy of *Daniel et Valérie* for general ideas about what to cover when. Thus, she selected David's sentence about Santa Claus for a reading text in part because she knew a lesson on the letter *v* was appropriate for that time of year.

Grouping.   Another decision first-grade teachers face is whether to separate the class into small groups for reading instruction, and if so, when. For most of the year, Jeannette taught reading to the class as a whole. After Christmas, (which she thought of as the year's midpoint even though the objective midpoint fell in February), she began to say, "I must make two groups soon." By January, her seating plan tacitly acknowledged two reading levels in the class, with children who needed remedial help in the front near the board. However, it was not until mid-March that she officially separated eight students, who would do remedial work, from the fifteen who already "decoded well" and would read a published storybook.

The other first-grade teachers I visited also hesitated to divide the class into groups, and if they did, did so sometime after Christmas. Madame Berger taught reading to the class as a whole throughout the year, although she seated the children having difficulty together, gave them simpler versions of written exercises, and occasionally took them aside for supplementary oral reading. Paul Alain took problem students aside for individual reading without ever forming a distinct remedial group. Of the other teachers I observed, three taught joint first/second or joint kindergarten/first and grouped accordingly. The six teachers with regular first grades whom I visited before Christmas had no reading groups at that time, although at least one planned to group later. Of the two visited late in the school year, one vehemently refused to group by ability while the other had formed three groups.

The French teachers who formed groups tended to talk as though they were forced into doing it. As teachers at the June in-service workshop explained, "There comes a moment when there's a group that isn't following any more, and you are obliged to separate them." They added later, "In first grade, it's rare that one can, until the end of the year, keep a single group." One teacher in the June workshop suggested that they hesitated to use small group instruction because, with twenty-five students and no aides in the classroom, "it's simply easier to work with the whole class than to individualize the work." However, teachers in the September workshop expressed the issue in terms of teaching philosophy, admitting that they "almost" grouped because they "can't help it," but arguing that to really divide at the beginning of the year would be to "catalogue" students. They echoed the words of a teaching principal who explained that, while she would eventually group her first graders by level of "maturity," "we don't have the right to group too much, for fear of 'cataloguing.' "

Chalk, Pens, and Organization of the Lesson.   Jeannette did not know until the morning of a new lesson what her next reading text would be nor even which letter the new lesson would concern. However, once she selected the text and the letter from the students' remarks during *raconter* period at the beginning of the day, she followed a familiar recipe for conducting the lesson.

Teachers using a published primer take the same steps Jeannette took in her lesson on the letter *v:* (1) In some kind of discussion, the teacher elicits sentences—probably about a picture from the primer—which resemble sentences which will be found later in the primer. (2) The teacher writes these on the chalkboard, in lettering and cursive but without upper case letters, and leads the class in "reading" the text from memory. (3) Through repetition, the children come to "read" the individual words by sight. When the class is so reading the text, the teacher encourages them to analyze the words, that is, to identify familiar letters or syllables. (4) The children take out slates and the teacher dictates words from the text. (5) The teacher identifies the letter to be studied, has the class think of words which use the letter, and puts further text on the board with words and syllables using this letter. (6) There are more slate dictations of syllables and words using the letter. (7) The class reads aloud from the primer or, in Jeannette's case, dittoed text. (8) Within this sequence, the teacher intersperses other activities such as the reading of large flashcards, the manipulation of words on little slips of paper, or exercises in silent reading. Eventually students are encouraged to compose sentences themselves. (9) Later in the school year, the lesson ends with a final dictation in ink in students' notebooks. The entire lesson is completed in 2 or 3 days.

From an outsider's perspective, French reading lessons are organized neatly around the materials at hand. The French teachers cannot afford the workbooks or programed materials that one finds in some American classrooms, but they do have ample chalkboards—chalkboards that slide or open like shutters to reveal multiple surfaces—and plenty of multicolored chalk. The children bring slates, chalk, and damp sponges as well as ballpoint pens and blank notebooks in their school bags. These materials work beautifully for lessons that place considerable emphasis on dictation and other writing skills.

Whether slates and notebooks became traditional teaching tools because of strong French interest in writing, or whether teachers came to emphasize writing because of the tools available, it is clear that today's French teachers tend to consider writing skills as important or more important than reading skills. For example, in a survey of 120 elementary teachers in diverse settings, one team of the researchers asked, "Is there one discipline of French [i.e., within language arts] which is more important than the others?" Half of the teachers were willing to rank one discipline above the rest, and of these, 42% cited written expression as the most important, another 22% cited grammar and 12% cited spelling. Only 12% cited reading as most important, while the remaining teachers cited vocabulary (6%) and oral expression (6%) (Isambert-Jamati et al., 1977, pp. 64–65).

Teachers share not only the same attitude toward writing but several cultural assumptions about how to teach it. Whereas kindergarten students generally learn only printed *(détaché)* letters, first graders learn printed and cursive writing *(attaché)* together. The very words *attaché* and *détaché* suggest that printing and cursive are just two variants of the same script, one with attached letters and one with detached. In the United States, in contrast, cursive writing is postponed until after children can read. On the other hand, while Americans teach both upper and lower case from the beginning, the French teachers delay upper case letters until the very end of first grade.

French first graders generally write in chalk and in ballpoint pen, two media very different from each other and from the pencil of American first graders. Teachers have the children take dictation in chalk on a slate for practice. The children write in a large hand on the slates, and they can easily erase and revise the mistakes they make in chalk. However, when the teachers assign writing and copying exercises, and when they give a final dictation at the end of a reading lesson, they have the children write in ink in their notebooks. The students use fine point Bic pens to write between narrow lines. In the classes I observed, teachers started the children on lines ruled for lower case letters 3mm high (Fig. 8.1), and allowed students to graduate to lines ruled for 2mm letters (Fig. 8.2) when they were ready. The French teachers did not share my American preconception that 6-year-olds lack the fine muscle control for this writing. Indeed, some informants hinted that it was not French children who wrote like adults, but American adults who wrote like children, with their large and rounded hand.

Writing in ink permits no chance to revise errors. When Madame Berger once discovered one of her problem students using a pencil and an eraser for a writing exercises, she described this as a "bizarre but logical reaction." Her use of the word *bizarre* reveals how completely she had taken for granted that children use pens in first grade. Nonetheless, she conceded the logic of using pencil for a boy who made frequent mistakes.

"Reading" the Students. As Madame Berger's remark suggests, knowledge about students is a crucial part of knowledge for teaching. When Jeannette chose David's sentence for a text on the letter *v*, she was obviously thinking about more than the sequence in which consonants should be taught. In such moment-to-moment teaching decisions, she drew on her knowledge of 6-year-olds in general and her own students in particular.

One thing that attracted her to David's sentence was the topic of Santa Claus, which she expected to kindle great interest among any group of first graders. To be able to capitalize on the students' own interests was,

Fig. 8.1. First grader's writing on wide-ruled paper (actual size, excerpt from the first dictation of the year, in November).

Fig. 8.2. First grader's writing on narrow-ruled paper (actual size, excerpt from the first dictation of the year, in November).

after all, her explicit reason for using the natural method. The other attraction of David's sentence, which she made explicit in asides to the ethnographer, was that in telling his story David had correctly pronounced the *v* of *voir*. Salient in Jeannette's repertoire of knowledge about her students was the idea that David *parle mal* (speaks poorly), particularly when pronouncing letters like *v*. She also knew that David was having difficulty learning to read and faced a dim academic future because he was *un cas* (a "case"), a child with real problems. Operating by the theory that a student who doesn't learn anything else will learn the text he volunteers himself—a theory she once expressed to me when discussing a different problem student—Jeannette chose David's sentence in hopes that it would clinch the pronunciation of *v* for him and give him a general boost in learning to read.

Speaking poorly, *un cas,* and most of the other concepts and theories with which Jeannette organized her knowledge of particular students were part of the cultural knowledge she shared with other teachers. The themes in Jeannette's talk about students closely paralleled themes in Madame Berger's and Paul Alain's talk. (These parallels are examined in more detail in Anderson-Levitt, 1983). Although Madame Berger put more stress on the children's background in kindergarteen, Paul on their affective development, and Jeannette and Paul on their creativity, all three teachers emphasized such concepts as age and maturity, speaking poorly, working well, making an effort, working by oneself, participating, having psychological or behavioral problems, being timid, being babyish, having problematic older siblings, and having serious family problems.

It is true that Jeannette differed from Madame Berger, Paul, and most other French first grade teachers because she passed her problem students on to second grade rather than making them repeat first grade. The traditional response to a child who has not yet learned to decode has been to retain him; thus Madame Berger held back 6 of her 27 students and Paul held back 4 of his 27. In deciding not to do likewise, Jeannette seemed to be responding in part to recent Official Instructions from the Ministry of Education, which urged that children be given the chance to learn to read over the course of 2 years, in first and second grades (France, 1973).

However, despite her resistance to retaining students and despite the differences in her teaching method, Jeannette had students who were having difficulty learning to read in about the same proportion as Paul and Madame Berger had. At the end of the year, she expressed serious reservations about the future academic success of 4 of her 23 students. Within 3 years, three of the four were a year behind their classmates.

Moreover, despite her progressive policy on grade retention, Jeannette interpreted academic problems in the same way as Madame Berger and Paul. All three blamed traits within the child (e.g., lack of maturity, poor speech, psychological problems) for every one of the twelve children in serious trouble in their classes. For about half the problem children, the three teachers placed additional blame on familial problems (e.g., a recent divorce, poverty, alcoholism). In only one case did a teacher (Paul) explicitly attribute some of the blame to the school system (Anderson-Levitt, 1983).

As other first-grade teachers, Jeannette found the notion of *un cas* particularly useful for organizing her impressions of children like David, who presented the most serious problems. At the very beginning of the year, she referred to David and a couple of other students as *les cas*. One of these children turned out to be a "case" only in the sense that he was "messy" and "agitated." However, the others, including David, were *cases* almost in the sense of *cas social* (social workers' cases)—a term Madame Berger once applied literally to one of the cases in her classroom. These were children who, in addition to serious academic difficulty, faced serious problems at home. David, for instance, was the poorest reader in Jeannette's class and his parents were unemployed and alcoholic. At the end of the year Jeannette described David vividly as "still fragile."

This attribution of learning problems to problems at home belongs to the cultural pool of knowledge shared with other schoolteachers in France. In Isambert-Jamati's study (1977, pp. 78–79), 29% of teachers interviewed attributed differences in language skill among their pupils to, among other things, *climat familial* (family climate). The authors refer to this notion as that of " '*cas particuliers,' avec des circonstances familiales données*" ('particular cases,' with specific family circumstances), and they note that practically the same proportion of teachers cited it in middle-class schools and in working-class schools.

Comparison with American Knowledge for Teaching

At a general level, one could make several abstract statements about the French teachers' pedagogy which would hold equally true for American teachers. For example, the French teachers seem to let instructional materials (in their case, slates, basal readers, teachers' guides) guide their planning for instruction much as American teachers let teachers' manuals, textbooks, and workbooks guide theirs (McNair, 1978–79; Peterson & Clark, 1978; Peterson, Marx, & Clark, 1978; Yinger, 1980). Both French and American teachers organize instruction around the blocks of time provided by their respective school calendars (see, for example, Sarason [1971, pp. 152–54] on American teachers) rather than according to some hypothetical internal calendar guiding their students' development. The great majority of both French and American teachers adopt the same general "mixed" method of reading instruction, and, judging from my limited observations, in both France and the United States, teachers in private schools are likely to give more emphasis to phonics than their public school colleagues. Finally, when reading instruction does not go smoothly, both French and American teachers tend to blame something about the child rather than their own teaching or situational factors (see Hertweck, 1982).

On the other hand, in terms of practical knowledge about how to carry on a lesson, the French teachers' formulas differ from American formulas in many ways. Even if there were no language barrier, a French teacher would not walk into an American classroom and produce a typical American reading lesson. While both French and American teachers synchronize instruction with the school calendar, the school year (as well as the school week and school day) are organized differently in France and the United States. Instructional materials differ, as I have noted, and so do assumptions about the children's capacities for using them. While French teachers expect their first graders to write in ballpoint between narrow lines, and to learn both printing and cursive—but not upper case—American teachers expect children of the same age to produce large letters with thick pencils between wide lines, in printed script only—though in both upper and lower case. The organization of the reading lesson differs, too. Although both French and American teachers spend a lot of time listening to oral reading, it is my impression that French teachers require much more writing during reading lessons, especially in the form of dictations.

Finally, beliefs about dividing the class into reading groups differ dramatically. In the six American first grades I visited, the teachers seemed to take for granted that small groups should be formed for oral reading. They formed two to four reading groups (homogeneous by ability in all but one classroom) on the basis of tests or a "readiness program" given early in the year. Only one of the American teachers formed heterogeneous groups because she, as the French teachers, feared the effects of labeling the children. Whereas most of the French teachers believed in taking aside one remedial group relatively late in the year on the basis of actual classroom performance, the American teachers seemed to believe in early, systematic grouping on the basis of predicted performance.

Innovation in Perspective. These differences between French and American knowledge for teaching reading put Jeannette's innovations in perspective. Her reliance on student texts and her use of field trips and workshop projects made her an unusual and interesting teacher. Yet on a world scale Jeannette's practical knowledge varied little from that of other French teachers. She shared with traditional teachers like Madame Berger the same formula for conducting a lesson, the same vision of the progression of reading instruction, the same interpretations of children having trouble learning to read.

WHY TEACHERS TEND TO THINK ALIKE

In a study of American families with alternative lifestyles, Weisner, Bausano, and Kornfein (1983) make a similar point. While the *pronatural* families they studied differed in many ways from conventional American families, the differences were very small on a cross-cultural scale. Pronatural caregivers breastfed their babies longer, carried them more, or kept the babies in the parents' bed more often than average American couples, but within the range of possibilities for those behaviors encountered world wide, their innovations represented no more than variations on the American theme. It is not easy to escape constraints of the system (what Weisner, Bausano and Kornfein call the eco-cultural niche) nor to avoid drawing on the cultural knowledge which predominates in a setting.

Constraints on Thinking

Why should French teachers think alike, or at least think much more like each other than like their American counterparts? How is it that a group of teachers comes to share so delimited a body of cultural knowledge?

Consider first the constraints of the setting in which the teachers work. We saw that in a number of general ways, French teachers' thinking resembled American teachers' thinking. One reason this would be so is that teachers in all industrial societies operate under similar sets of constraints. They develop their particular recipes for teaching within fixed environments: There is a fixed school year, a fixed (and, teachers feel, very large) number of students per class, a rigid age-graded system for those students, general public expectations that the students be able to read at the end of first grade, and a limited, largely predetermined set of instructional materials with which to work. Of most significance, there is the unyielding fact that schools are part of the mechanism through which social stratification is reproduced (Baudelot & Establet, 1971, 1975; Bowles & Gintis, 1976; Sewell & Hauser, 1976).

Given such constraints, it would be very surprising to find such teaching formulas as a strictly tutorial system, 20-year-olds in first grade, or the complete absence of tracking in any Western school.

If the general constraints of any industrial educational system explain similarities between French and American pedagogies, then the specific limitations of the French school system must explain quite a bit about why French teachers tend to think alike. For example, age grading in French schools has traditionally been rigid. Children must start first grade in the year they turn six, and if they do not move on to second grade a year later they will probably carry a handicap with them the rest of their lives (Baudelot & Establet, 1975). Little wonder that first-grade teachers provide direct reading instruction, introducing decoding only a few weeks into the school year rather than simply placing the children in a literate environment and letting the desire to read develop in its own time.

Similarly, it may be that France's highly competitive examination system at the secondary level as well as the pressure on elementary teachers to make judgments about passing or retaining individual students at the end of the year discourage instructional systems built on peer tutoring or group evaluation.

One must also consider constraints as subjectively defined. American and French class size is about the same. However, only French teachers consider the size of their classes, legally limited to twenty-five children for first grade, too large to permit small group instruction. Many elementary teachers interviewed by Isambert-Jamati et al. (1977, p. 60) pointed out that, although the Official Instructions for language arts actually presuppose small group instruction, this is a near impossibility in large classes.

The Effect of Cultural Transmission

The constraints of the setting within which teachers work place boundaries on what teachers are likely to think, but do not predict in any positive sense what kind of knowledge for teaching will develop. Constraints are negative; they merely rule out formulas entirely incompatible with the system. To understand why French teachers settle on one rather than another of the teaching formulas which would be thinkable within the setting, we have to look at the positive effects of cultural transmission.

In France, formal transmission of knowledge for teaching takes place in a network of Normal Schools. If Jeannette Durand, Madame Berger, and Paul Alain had all followed the same curriculum in Normal School, we would probably attribute the similarity of their approaches to their formal pedagogical training. However, such an explanation would be too easy, especially if one can believe the school inspector who told me that "after 2 years in the classroom [beyond Normal School] they forget everything they learned there."

In fact, such an explanation is impossible, since neither Jeannette, Madame Berger, nor Paul—nor a majority of the teachers I studied—had ever attended Normal School. During the baby boom from the 1950s to early 1970s when my informants entered the profession, Normal Schools could not produce enough teachers. Because the law allowed anyone with a *baccalauréat* (a degree from an academic secondary school) to teach elementary school, thousands of young people began teaching without any training in pedagogy, entering the profession as substitute teachers. More than half the teachers practicing in the district during the time of my fieldwork had become teachers by the substitute route.[5] Eventually they had to pass a written examination on pedagogy and an inspection of their actual teaching, and some of them have taken brief in-service courses, but their training was much less intensive and much less uniform than that given *Normaliens*.

How, then, is cultural knowledge for teaching transmitted informally? French teachers have little or no opportunity to observe their colleagues in action. Even *Normaliens*, who are sent to work with Master Teachers, tend to do the teaching themselves under the Master Teacher's guidance rather than to observe the Master Teacher at work. A couple of informants who began their careers as substitutes remembered arriving in an absent teacher's classroom to find that the day's lesson plans were locked in the cupboard, safe from the novice's eyes. In general, the teachers I met considered the classroom a private area. Few of them had ever given thought to having aides or parents in class, let alone a colleague.

Many French teachers, then, teach themselves how to teach. At first it is hard to imagine why, if each is reinventing pedagogy in isolation, the reinventions should vary so little. But D'Andrade (1981), Wallace (1970, p. 109), and Wolcott (1982, pp. 89–91) remind us that cultural knowledge does not have to be passed along *en bloc* in order to get reproduced. Only a few clues from veteran teachers—a label to hang on a certain kind of

---

[5]No one could give me statistics on the proportion of teachers who had and had not attended Normal School, for once non-*Normaliens* passed their certifying examinations, they became indistinguishable from ex-*Normaliens* in official records. Staff at *l'Inspection Académique* made a rough guess that about half the teachers in the district were non-*Normaliens*. Of the teachers from whom I collected professional histories and who were sampled either at random or because they had been recommended as good teachers, only six had attended Normal School while twelve had become teachers through the substitute route.

A questionnaire given by Ida Berger to 800 teachers in the Paris region in 1974 indicated that only 27% had passed through Normal School. The percentage is generally higher in the provinces. Still, "the great majority of elementary school teachers were trained on the job with the aid of *des Conférences Pédagogiques* [conferences with the inspector or the inspector's aide], of course, but without systematic preparation. Various types of in-service training *(recyclage)* have affected only 20% of schoolteachers . . . ex-*Normaliens* in the same proportion as the others" (Isambert-Jamati et al., 1977, p. 61).

Hiring of non-*Normaliens* stopped only around 1978, when the reduction in the school-age population sharply cut the demand for teachers.

student behavior, a political attitude to associate with a certain instructional method—may suffice to guide novice teachers into independent rediscovery of approximately the same knowledge that veterans use.

French teachers facing their first, difficult assignments draw from several sources for those occasional clues about how to teach. Few of the Normal School graduates, my informants claimed, look to the "beautiful lessons" of Normal School for solutions to real classroom problems. Instead, despite the occasional locked cupboard, some teachers remembered getting help as newcomers or substitutes from the principal of a school. Even where colleagues are close-mouthed about their own teaching methods, new teachers can learn about methods for handling students as I did, by listening to anecdotes swapped among faculty members during recess.

Expectations of persons the teacher deals with face-to-face, particularly when expressed in the context of judgment about the teacher's work, will have special influence. The local school inspector, who makes decisions about certification and salary scale, may promote a specific teaching method; in any case, the inspector or the inspector's deputy, the *conseiller pédagogique*, will probably offer general advice before or during the certification examination. Support or lack of support from one's principal can influence a teacher's enthusiasm for one method or another. Meanwhile, the second-grade teacher, who expects to see certain skills in the students arriving from first grade, may have to be appeased. Not least in importance, parents have expectations. In two schools I visited, parent groups had mounted successful campaigns to quash attempted teaching innovations.

There are also written sources of information. Marchand (1971, p. 29) reports that teachers rely to some extent on the teacher's manual for reading and mathematics textbooks and on suggestions published in practical professional magazines. Occasionally I observed a teacher referring to a teacher's manual, and Jeannette once mentioned that she had begun to pick up a book on pedagogy once in a while. There are also the Official Instructions to consult. Since 1972 the Official Instructions have been distributed directly to all elementary teachers (Isambert-Jamati et al., 1977, p. 52). I witnessed information from the Official Instructions being transmitted orally at the beginning of the year from principal to teachers and from teacher to teacher, much as prepublished information is transmitted orally in the world of nuclear physicists (Traweek, 1982). Finally, teachers also study written materials on curriculum and instruction before passing the certification examination, although I did not find out what they study.

Meanwhile, even lacking all these sources of ideas, teachers surely refer, consciously or not, to their own memories of elementary school—

as models to emulate or as patterns to avoid. Jeannette, for example, indicated once or twice that she wanted to avoid repeating the duller aspects of instruction in the Catholic school she attended as a child.

Room for Creativity

It jolts our pride to discover the narrow range within which innovations occur. Hard as we work to produce fresh ideas for teaching (or preparing meals, or solving physics problems), in cross-cultural perspective the new ideas hardly diverge at all from the knowledge already shared with our peers. In this sense, it is almost true that "there is nothing new under the sun," as the author of Ecclesiastes noted so long ago.

Yet, in another sense individuals produce new creations all the time. Although we cannot think without the cultural ideas we share with our fellows, the ideas do not control us—we control them. We are not cultural robots (or "cultural dopes," as Garfinkel [1967] puts it), preprogrammed to follow the prevailing cultural recipes. Although we draw from a common pool of cultural knowledge, we continually put that knowledge to use in novel situations. Lévi-Strauss (1966) calls us *bricoleurs,* Rube Goldbergs who improvise new solutions to new problems with the limited stock of cultural themes on hand.

Jeannette Durand's idea for teaching reading were as creative as one could ask within the narrow range of probable variation in French knowledge for teaching. Where Jeannette really shone, though, was in the moment-to-moment conduct of class. In concert with her students— monitoring and taking into account their signals about what was going on—she made lessons happen. Drawing on her cultural knowledge about reading, the school year, David's speech problem, and a thousand other things, she repeatedly created events called "reading lessons."

In the same manner, every individual in whatever professional or nonprofessional situation is busy creating the world, using practical knowledge as raw material. Discovery of the cultural nature of that knowledge, a discovery which Jeannette's story can facilitate, is one step toward mastery of that creative process.

REFERENCES

Anderson-Levitt, K. M. (1983, November). *French schoolteachers' model of the six-year-old.* Paper presented at the 82nd annual meeting of the American Anthropological Association, Chicago.

Ashton-Warner, S. (1963). *Teacher.* New York: Simon and Schuster.

Baudelot, C., & Establet, R. (1971). *L'école capitaliste en France.* Paris: Maspero.

Baudelot, C., & Establet, R. (1975). *L'école primaire divise.* Paris: Maspero.

Bowles, S., & Gintis, H. (1976). *Schooling in capitalist America.* New York: Basic Books.

D'Andrade, R. G. (1981). The cultural part of cognition. *Cognitive Science, 5,* 179–195.

Featherstone, J. (1971). *Schools where children learn.* New York: Avon Books.

Foucambert, J. (1976). *La manière d'être lecteur.* Paris: Sermap.

France, Ministry of Education. (1973). *Instructions relatives à l'enseignement du français à l'école élémentaire.* Circulaire no. 72-474 du 4 décembre, 1972. Paris: Imprimerie Nationale.

France, Ministry of Education. (1977). *Réforme du système éducatif. Contenus de formation à l'école élémentaire: cycle préparatoire.* Nancy: Centre National de Documentation Pédagogique.

Garfinkel, H. (1967). *Studies in ethnomethodology.* Englewood Cliffs, NJ: Prentice Hall.

Goodenough, W. H. (1971). Culture, language and society. *McCaleb Module in Anthropology.* Reading, MA: Addison-Wesley.

Gregg. R. J. (1960). *A student's manual of French pronunciation.* Toronto: Macmillan of Canada.

Hertweck, A. (1981). Educators' accounts of students' behavior. In Hugh Mehan et al. *Final report: NIE educational decision-making study.*

Hsu, F.L.K. (1979). The cultural problems of the cultural anthropologist. *American Anthropologist, 81*(3), 517–532.

Isambert-Jamati, V. et al. (1977). La réforme de l'enseignement du français à l'école élémentaire. *Actions Thématiques Programmées no. 14.* Paris: Centre National de la Recherche Scientifique.

Leiter, K.C.W. (1976). Teachers' use of background knowledge to interpret test scores. *Sociology of Education, 49,* 59–65.

Léon, A. (1967). *Histoire de l'enseignement en France.* Paris: P.U.F.

Lévi-Strauss, C. (1966). *The savage mind.* Chicago: University of Chicago Press.

Marchand, F. (1971). *Le Français tel qu'on l'enseigne à l'école élémentaire.* Paris: Larousse.

McNair, K. (1978–79). Capturing inflight decisions. *Educational Research Quarterly, 3*(4), 26–42.

Peterson, P. L., & Clark, C. M. (1978). Teachers' reports of cognitive processes during teaching. *American Educational Research Journal, 15*(4), 555–565.

Peterson, P. L., Marx, R. W., & Clark, C. M. (1978). Teacher planning, teacher behavior, and student achievement. *American Educational Research Journal, 15*(3), 417–432.

Pittman, S. I. (1985). A cognitive ethnography and quantification of a first-grade teacher's selection routines for classroom management. *Elementary School Journal, 85*(4), 541–557.

Prost, A. (1968). *Histoire de l'enseignement en France, 1800–1967* (2nd ed.). Paris: Armand Colin.

Rawson, M. B. (1975). Developmental dyslexia: Educational treatment and results. In D. D. Duane & M. B. Rawson (Eds.), *Reading, perception and language.* Baltimore: York Press.

Sakamoto, T., & Makita, K. (1973). Japan. In J. Downing (Ed.), *Comparative reading.* New York: Macmillan.

Saltiel, M. (1979). Apprendre à lire à l'école primaire. *Le Monde de l'éducation, 46,* 8–14.

Sarason, S. B. (1971). *The culture of the school and the problem of change.* Boston: Allyn and Bacon.

Schonfeld, W. R. (1976). *Obedience and revolt: French behavior toward authority.* Beverly Hills: Sage Publications.

Scribner, S., & Cole, M. (1981). *The psychology of literacy.* Cambridge, MA: Harvard University Press.

Sewell, W. H., & Hauser, R. M. (1976). Causes and consequences of higher education. In W. H. Sewell, R. M. Hauser, & D. L. Featherman (Eds.), *Schooling and achievement in American society* (pp. 9–27). Orlando, FL: Academic Press.

Spiegel, S. J. (1978). *Education and community in a French village.* Unpublished doctoral dissertation, University of California, Berkeley.

Spindler, G., & Spindler, L. (1982). Roger Harker and Schönhausen: From the familiar to the strange and back again. In G. Spindler & L. Spindler (Eds.), *Doing the ethnography of schooling: Educational anthropology in action.* New York: Holt, Rinehart and Winston.

Spradley, J. P., & McCurdy, D. W. (1972). *The cultural experience.* Chicago: Science Research Associates.

Traweek, S. (1982, December). *Gossip in science.* Paper presented at the 81st annual meeting of the American Anthropological Association, Washington, D. C.

Wagner, D. A., & Lofti, A. (1980). Traditional Islamic education in Morocco: Sociohistorical and psychological perspectives. *Comparative Education Review, 24,* 238–251.

Wallace, A.F.C. (1970). *Culture and personality* (2nd ed.). New York: Random House.

Weisner, T. S., Bausano, M., & Kornfein, M. (1983). Putting family ideals into practice: Pronaturalism in conventional and nonconventional California families. *Ethos, 11*(4), 278–304.

Wolcott, H. F. (1982). The anthropology of learning. *Anthropology and Education Quarterly, 13*(2), 83–108.

Wylie, L. (1964). *Village in the Vaucluse* (2nd ed.). New York: Harper and Row.

Yinger, R. J. (1980). A study of teacher planning. *Elementary School Journal, 80*(3), 107–127.

The Author and His Chapter

Paul Yates is already known to us through his chapter in Part I. As an Englishman, educated in English schools and teaching at an English university, his outlook is somewhat different than that of any American counterpart. The middle school he has studied is quite similar to its American counterpart.

The United States is believed to embody the ideals of individual achievement, freedom, and equality. It is conceived as an open society. And schools are intended as instrumentalities serving these ideals.

We know that schools in America are struggling with the seeming inability of many minority group members to succeed on mainstream terms. The explanation for academic failure and school dropouts, exceeding 50% for some minority populations, range from blame the victim to blame the school. In any case, both the students and their schools fail.

In the United States we are currently experiencing a surge of new immigrants from Southeast Asia, Cuba, Haiti, India, and Pakistan. To the surprise of everyone, many of the newcomers do better in school than indigenous minorities in the United States. Chapters in the next part of this volume by John Ogbu, Margaret Gibson, and Christine Finnan explore this phenomenon selectively. Those of the new immigrants who are successful in school surmount great obstacles of language and cultural differences and they do so because they believe that schooling is the vehicle that will carry them to success in life. Many of our indigenous minorities do not believe this to be the case.

Success and failure in schools are products of a complex of interactions among administrators, teachers, parents, and children. The racism so deeply embedded in Anglo-Saxon and American mainstream culture is surely a significant factor. The real cultural differences are important as well. But the self-perceptions and the perceptions of each other by the various actors on the scene are certainly major factors. Schools reinforce the ordering of social classes in England as firmly as or more so than they do in the United States. Students determine their own fates by the perceptions of school, and of themselves, just as they do in the United States. And teachers, administrators, and educational specialists define the channels to success and select the people who will go in to those channels just as they do in the United States.

The comparisons that Dr. Yates' ethnographic research in an English school provide are illuminating.

The Editors

9 A Case of Mistaken Identity: Interethnic Images in Multicultural England

Paul David Yates
University of Sussex

INTRODUCTION

Britain has a continual history of immigration. In the 16th century there were significant numbers of Walloons in Norwich, and in the 17th century there were 80,000 Huguenots in Britain (Mullard, 1973). In the 18th century the Irish immigrant connection with Britain began, and throughout the 19th century there was a "steady influx of East European Jews" (Cropley, 1983).

The present plural state is largely a result of immigration due to the labor shortage in the U. K. after the second world war. At this time immigration was encouraged from the New Commonwealth, that is, the West Indies especially Jamaica, and from India and Pakistan, all formerly part of the British Empire. It is currently estimated that "the total number of colored residents is expected to rise to at least 3 million by the year 2000, even if there is no further immigration" (Cropley, 1983, p. 25). Of this segment of population approximately 2 million will have been born in the U. K. This minority *colored* population of approximately 3 or 4% is a novel and now permanent feature of British society. Both the West Indian and the Asian communities are culturally heterogeneous, with those of Jamaican origin numerically dominating the former, and Pakistanis the latter.

The Asian community with which I worked in the middle and late 1970s were largely from East Africa, mainly Uganda, and had been forced to leave by the Africanization of the economy by Idi Amin. Immigration from this source reached its peak in 1972 when Amin expelled the Asian community. Trade between East Africa and the Gujerat peninsula in north west India has gone on for a millennium (Tambs-Lyche, 1980). The dominant land-owning Patidar caste of Kaira district in Gujerat began their modern commercial links with East Africa with the establishment of British protectorates, and the European settlement of present day Kenya and Uganda, towards the close of the 19th century. From then until recent times the Hindu Patidars formed part of an entrepreneurial merchant class, maintaining strong and constant links with families and family land in India (Pocock, 1972).

The town of Broadmere (this is a pseudonym) had distinct advantages as a place of settlement for the dispossessed incomers from East Africa. It was an expanding town, based on local light industry, near to London, and with a ready supply of good quality housing. The postwar economic boom was over by the early 1970s but Broadmere suffered very little unemployment and has maintained its prosperity throughout the current recession. The Asian community in Broadmere also included a smaller group of East African Gujerati speaking Nayees, a ritually inferior caste of barbers, also originally from Kaira district, and a few Sikh families from the Indian Punjab and Muslim families from Pakistan. My fieldwork in both the community and school focused on the majority Gujerati speaking Asian community.

As Kirp (1979) details in his aptly titled *Doing Good by Doing Little,* the U. K. educational system has largely tried to absorb the new cultures within existing conceptual frameworks. Thus, the headmaster at Broadmere Comprehensive aimed to "treat all pupils equally," which was seen as morally correct in that it avoided discrimination. Cultural difference was only recognized by allowing Sikh boys to wear their traditional turbans, and Moslem girls trousers.

However, there are some recent changes which may prove salutary, for example the introduction of antiracist policies in London and Bradford schools. Also, the Rampton report (DES, 1981) on West Indian children has prompted a good deal of interest in the multicultural curriculum (Cohen & Manion, 1983; Hicks, 1981; James & Jeffcoate, 1981; Tierney, 1982). There is still very little attempt to work through, in general and theoretical terms, the problems of teaching in the newly multicultural state, although Lynch (1981) is a welcome exception. Most pertinently, there is no developed anthropology of education to take in the theoretical issues of culture and transmission within an ethnographic framework (Yates, 1984). This paper is a contribution to that task.

In the next section I draw on ethnographic material collected through observation and interview of pupils and teachers in Broadmere secondary comprehensive school. In this account I concentrate on how each group understands the other. In the final section I draw on the ethnography to develop the concepts of cultural dissonance and the cultural contract.

THE ETHNOGRAPHY*

Broadmere school is strongly academically oriented and because of the limited scope of local employment it is homogeneous in social class terms. The school is divided into lower, middle and upper schools, all separately housed but on the same site. The school covers the age range 12 to 16 + years, each subschool cohort containing two-year groups.

Multiculturalism as a problem for schooling is normally seen in terms of the relative underachievement of members of ethnic minority groups (Driver & Ballard, 1979). What I want to suggest is that the causes of performance may not be located in theories of cultural deficit, but may initially be understood within the complex cultural configurations of different groups.

Cultural developments within the curriculum may simply be signaling the existence of other cultures from a particular cultural standpoint without actually incorporating other cultures or affecting pupils' general understanding of culture and ethnicity, either their own or that of others.

Much of what follows covers the description and analysis of the one dimensional quality of ethnic groups images of each other in schools, and the poverty of the cultural information available to both teachers and pupils.

Let me begin with an example of the sort of dissonance in mutual understanding which typifies the problem. For historical reasons physical prowess in athletic games has become an important part of schooling in Europe and America. Both boys and girls can achieve high social status through being recognized as physically proficient. This is not a universal of human society but a culturally specific fact. In the culture of the Asian immigrants, for example, sporting ability is not generally recognized or valued. It is particularly irrelevant to the status of girls.

To participate in sport requires the development and refinement of certain motor skills. For example, basic to many team games is the ability to throw and catch balls, or otherwise control their movements. Again I stress that this is not a natural human activity but limited to specific cultures and contexts. The development of such abilities depends on their being recognized as socially significant and as necessary to the establish-

---

*The ethnography of Broadmere School was initially published by S. Modgil et al. (Ed.), in *Multicultural Education: The Interminable Debate*, 1986, Falmer Lewes, Press Ltd.

ment of a particular valued status. However, neither the indigenous pupils and teachers, nor the Asian immigrant pupils were likely to make a cultural analysis of sport in developing their own understanding.

Thus, while it was generally understood that Asians were likely not to be good at sport, the only explanation used by the English teachers was ethnocentric and in terms of cultural deficit. It was thought that the Asians lacked the necessary physical coordination to play games well, especially the girls. This is particularly interesting as a culturally specific judgment based on a very slender knowledge of the group involved, because had the teacher seen the grace and precision with which the Asian girls danced at the Diwali festival celebrations, then the fact that physical ability is a matter of cultural emphasis would have been very well illustrated.

Other factors that might help explain the performance of Asian girls in sport tend to be left out of the account by all groups, but may be crucial to the recognition of cultural identity in school. First, much of school sport is team based and the relational structure of teams, involving both competition and collaboration, with a group of people whose social ties need not extend outside of the purposes of the game, is a difficult complex of ideas to translate within the values of a communal, kin-oriented social structure. Running about with balls may be a meaningless activity in some cultural contexts. More specifically sporting activity can induce a sense of absurdity or a feeling of impropriety in some girls. That is to say that far from enhancing their self-image sport can produce and sustain a sense of cultural alienation.

Thus, the difference in evaluative criteria employed by the English and by the Asians means that mutual understanding does not occur, because neither group appreciates the necessity of building in cultural context to explanations of school performance. This means that a level of consensual understanding that would facilitate the productive schooling of both the majority and minority cultural groups fails to be achieved.

I shall now go on to further illustrate the case and look more generally at teachers' understanding of Asian pupils, especially in the remedial section of the school where newcomers go to bring their English language ability to a level where they can join the main school. I include a vignette of a racialist teacher to illustrate the ease with which a liberal institution can accommodate, or fail to control, individual teacher's prejudices becoming the basis for their professional conduct. Finally, I turn to the description of pupil cultures as ethnic cultures, and discuss the negative stereotypes that pupils use to make sense of those from outside their ethnic groups.

The vast majority of the teachers I spoke to did not have what could be described as a conscious formulated attitude towards the Asians in school, because they had not become an object separated from the body of pupils which demanded thought. This is readily understandable. Teachers outside the remedial area only came into contact with those Asians sufficiently anglicized to cope with life in the school. As a group within school the Asian presence was small, at most 5%, not highly developed, and they were conformists. They generally seemed to be thought to represent the normal spectrum of school intelligence but as a group were probably more hardworking than the English (Vellims, 1983). Thus they were ideally suited to moving through the school entirely unremarked by the teachers because they did not cause them any problems.

Mr. Steel was a teacher with responsibility for the pastoral care of pupils in the middle age range. His wife was involved in a local scheme to teach immigrant women English at home. He seemed generally sympathetic to the Asians because their behavior, as he understood it, was laudable. He told me of an Asian couple that he and his wife knew, who had got both their son and daughter into university. Here we must note that in 1981 in the U. K. only 22.4% of the relevant cohort entered higher education, compared to 42.8% in the USA. Mr. Steel saw this as making it socially through one's own efforts, something he felt himself to have done and something that he admired in others. His final comment on the success of the children was "good luck to them I say, if they are willing to grasp the opportunities the lazy English kids won't take." Thus he chose to react to, and characterize the Asians on a level at which he could value them, a reasonably positive form of discrimination.

The head of Physical Education said that the Asians were not "highly motivated" in sports, occasionally a good spin bowler would come along or a bat for the cricket team, and there was Pramit who was an excellent rugby forward, but he was very exceptional. He did say that from time to time an "all black" ladies hockey team had been assembled but internecine wrangles had meant the venture was short lived. He explained that there was not one at the moment because there was no hockey specialist on the staff. He thought Asians lacked esprit de corps and the necessary competitive edge to be good at sport. A female Physical Education teacher I spoke to found the Asian girls "pretty hopeless," her explanation of this being that they lacked coordination; for example they would be incompetent if a game involved catching or controlling balls. She thought perhaps it might be something in their background that caused this. I have already commented on this particular problem, but it is interesting to note that not one Asian girl I interviewed actually enjoyed games lessons, but several had a positive dislike of them.

One Asian girl who was considered very bright by her teachers and who was particularly conscious of being discriminated against on the grounds of her color, dreaded Physical Education because when the teacher asked for captains of teams it was always white girls, and when they picked their teams the Asian girls were always left till last and sometimes the teacher had to put them onto a team. If the Physical Education teacher who told me that Asian girls were not very efficient was voicing a generally held view then the logic of not including them in one's own team can be seen to be based on sporting rather than ethnic criteria. However, if one were using discrimination on grounds of ethnicity as a primary source of explanation then it could simply look like racism.

Of the two Asian boys who excelled in a sporting activity, one, Dipak, was the son of a divorcee and had little contact with the Asian community and the other, Pramit, was determined, and consciously so, to integrate himself into English society. He was not considered to be particularly clever academically and had remained in the remedial unit for the 4 years since his arrival in the U. K. He had asked to be included in a rugby trial; had succeeded in gaining a place and this had proved a very fruitful avenue of recognition and allowed him to see himself as valued by the institution and obliquely by English society.

Dipak had been in England for 11 years, spoke no Asian language and talked and behaved like an English boy though evidently physically of Asian origin. He was very confident in his manner, even aggressive, and was considered to be potentially a first class sportsman. The head of Physical Education mentioned him to me and said that he did not know whether or not he was an Asian "but he was definitely a something or other," this presumably referred to his color although his ethnic origin was undecipherable from his speech or behavior.

Although generally it was unnecessary for teachers to make radical adjustments to the presence of immigrant pupils, this was not the case in the remedial unit. There are three points to make here regarding the structure of the unit that made ethnicity a sufficiently important concept as to demand that the teacher held a view. First, and most obvious, the remedial unit had to deal with those incoming Asians who had a language difficulty; and it was children in this category that initially formed the bulk of the Asian school population. Nearly all the remedial teachers had first hand experience of teaching Asian children. Second, the remedial unit was separate from the school proper, and the staff formed, for others and themselves, a small recognizable group with particular conditions and problems. Finally, in a school that was very highly academically oriented the remedial teachers and their charges had a low if worthy standing within the school. This may partly have been due to the fact that their work did not require a high level of subject expertise.

In each year group there were two remedial forms. The teachers described below taught pupils in the middle age range. Mrs. Bushel, a comfortable looking middle-aged woman, took the "top" form as it was recognized that she was a successful remedial teacher and that if anyone was capable of coaching the remedial children through a couple of low grade certificated examinations, it was she. Indeed her form had some limited success in examinations and this was a strong factor in her high standing in the group. It is interesting to note in passing that this fact underlines the dominance of the academic ethos, which was still seen as providing the only criterion of success even in a group whose existence presumed that academic success was not universally achieved.

Mrs. Shard, slightly built and in early middle age, took the second fifth form. Mr. Gordon, a man in his late thirties took a fourth form, and Mr. Less, a young English teacher with an English as a Foreign Language (EFL) qualification, a degree in English Literature, and teaching experience in Nigeria, took a special form of immigrant children with particularly chronic language difficulties.

One of the teachers, Mrs. Shard, was perniciously prejudiced against her Asian pupils, and indeed against Asians in general. A garrulous woman, she paraded her opinions very readily, and over many many conversations I came to understand the nature though not the springs of her attitudes.

Mrs. Shard would talk of the general run of remedial children as though they were half-wits, "Of course the poor little dears won't know what's hit them when they leave the shelter of the school." She had the embarrassing habit of talking about children in their presence in the third person, even to me, an outsider. Most children, unless they had some other obvious handicap, were simply described as being in various stages of thickness, "He, of course, is very thick; she is not as thick as some." If I went into her classroom she would always turn what I expected to be a private discussion into a declamation. I went into her class one day to arrange some interviews and she immediately began declaiming. Turning to a young Sikh boy she said, "Daljit is finding out how true is everything I've said," (apropos of employment difficulties for the unqualified fifth form leaver.) Daljit simply nodded. Inspired, she went on to explain the obvious virtue of reducing the school leaving age to 14 after which age she thought schools would only have those interested in learning staying on, the rest could be "maturing" at work. Her use of other people seemed to be only in terms of reflectors for her unnegotiable picture of social reality. I was tolerated as I was a willing audience although she expressed no interest in what I was actually doing at the school.

Mrs. Shard had a folk history of the origins of her attitudes to Asians which she blamed on the school. Before coming to school she had nothing against Asians, "My husband used to think I was soft," but what she had learned since then had changed her mind. She would tell the usual mutually contradictory stories of all Asians being simultaneously rich in their own right and also a drain on the welfare services. This was substantiated by the story of a family who were living on welfare and "getting everything," while the father was a substantial property owner in India and regularly flew out to collect his rents.

Mrs. Shard only had one overt supporter in the staffroom and that was Mrs. Bushel, who had taught in Africa and South America and had a rather old fashioned colonialist view of Asians as being perfectly normal intellectually but a little less than perfectly developed spiritually. Pantheism for her was a sign of moral ignorance if not turpitude. Thus, Mrs. Shard gained some general support from Mrs. Bushel though the latter was never in my hearing openly racist in her views.

Mrs. Shard disliked Mr. Less and would often suggest that he was lazy, and imply that what he was doing with the immigrant children was "a scandal" on account of their being, "far too thick to learn anything anyway." Speaking of a child she had taught from Mr. Less's form, she said, "Admittedly he's Asian but he can't even spell his name." Later in the same conversation she described the contents of Mr. Less's school bag as being "running shorts mixed up with curry and old sandwiches." She once asked me what I thought of Mr. Less. I replied, noncommitally, allowing her to tell me what she thought, which was what I had been set up for. She went on to be very critical in a personal way about Mr. Less in front of me and her colleagues. This was an unusual way for a teacher to behave, but the community of the staffroom was too loosely knit for any effective control of a member, also this same looseness mitigated any desire for control of social attitudes amongst the staff.

If a teacher finds he is not in sympathy with colleagues, it is very easy simply to avoid them in a large institution and focus attention and energy on relations with pupils, other aspects of the school world, or with something entirely outside the school. It is possible for the classroom teacher to fulfil his role without developing any particular commitment to pupils or the institution.

Mr. Less, for his part never actually personally attacked Mrs. Shard though he did recognize that she was less than sympathetic to the group that he was most interested in.

It was suggested to Mr. Less that he pick about a dozen of the children having most problems with English and set them up in a small form-room of his own. When I arrived at the school for my second period of fieldwork there were eight children in Mr. Less's form, all Asian immigrants, excepting one West Indian boy. The curriculum timetable of the form included science, math, and drama although these first two subjects were taught at the most rudimentary level, and drama not at all. Their teaching was simply cobbled together; because they were outside the examination system there were no criteria upon which to decide whether, with the exception of English, they should be taking one subject rather than another.

Mrs. Shard complained that the class was "all black" and said that she and Mrs. Bushel had been in favor of a mixed form because both thought that segregation was bad. When I asked Mr. Less why the form had no indigenous English pupils in it he said that the Deputy Headmaster had been against it in case the white parents complained.

For Mr. Less, whose family had a tradition of humanitarian colonial service, racism in its modern form was simply not part of his conceptual world. The guiding concepts for Mr. Less were cultural continuity and the British Commonwealth of Nations. His overt motives for teaching immigrants were public spirited. The notion of duty to society was real for Mr. Less. This was not, however, a consciously political stance as he would rarely make any abstract comment about his role in the life of the immigrant community. Apart from a vague notion that developing world cultures should be taught to the children, to help different ethnic groups understand each other better, he had made no analysis of the potential role of education in sustaining a multiethnic community.

Mr. Less was very conscious however of how his interest in a group which was not considered very important in the school made him a marginal person and vulnerable to criticism. In my estimation this was probably not the case; the fact that the school had employed an EFL teacher was the salient point in terms of public relations and what he actually achieved was regarded as a problem of a lower order. This, of course, was as far as the school, or more properly the Headmaster, was concerned; to Mr. Less, however, to succeed in the eyes of his colleagues was important and he saw his being given the immigrant class as a strong public recognition of his expertise. Mr. Less was nominally a member of the English rather than the remedial department. The next academic year the Head of English was giving him some ordinary teaching for the first time, about which he remarked to me, "It will be interesting to teach some ordinary Asians."

In many of his attitudes to immigrants Mr. Less held views representative of the teachers. He knew there was a problem, and used his expertise to alleviate it, but otherwise did not try to understand the implications of a multicultural society on the community or inside the profession of teaching, except through vague notions like the family of the Commonwealth, which may well have meant even less to his immigrant charges than to the population as a whole.

There is a problem in discussing teachers' attitudes to race relations in the school because many teachers did not come into contact with immigrants and avoided the necessity of acting on their opinions in their professional capacity. There were a few to whom it was an issue, and here attitudes and opinions differed.

English was the only subject taken by the whole school where social values can be legitimately scrutinized. The head of English, an intelligent young man with mildly progressive theories of his subject and its teaching, would not have race discussed in his classes. He took the same line as the British political parties, to make race an issue would be to exacerbate a potentially disruptive situation. His private opinion was that the white children "are for the most part probably racist." He was against classroom debate of race because he believed that the children would simply trot out the racialist platitudes learned from their parents and reinforce each other's racism. Several of the children I interviewed would preface a racist remark with, "Well, my mum says that . . ." However, this generalized racism need not, and did not, stop children from having friendships with members of other ethnic groups.

In comparison with the head of English, another senior member of the department, Mr. Winch, took an opposite view that the discussion of racial problems in the school had a possibly cathartic effect, and at least brought the problem into the realms of conscious thought where it might be subjected to the illumination of reason. Despite this moral purpose, Mr. Winch who had previous experience of ethnically mixed schools in America, thought that the English children were racist in their attitudes "to a frightening extent."

Mr. Winch surprised me with his ignorance of the school. Although he had taught there for over a year, and was one of the most vivacious members of staff, he had not realized that the majority of immigrants were in the remedial unit nor that the remedial unit was separately and comparatively poorly housed. His perceptions of immigrants were limited to his experience of them in the classroom, and what sort of professional challenge they represented, for example in teaching drama.

The fact that Asian children found the role playing that is central to school drama impossibly embarrassing was a social fact that forced itself upon the attention. In a drama lesson that I observed the Asians were allowed to sit out and not take part in the acting at all. When asked why they did not find drama easy the answer was that they did not see what good it did or what they could learn from it. This certainly was part of the explanation, that expectations of school were confounded by drama being presented as a lesson rather than a diversion: a problem of different cultural values and of ideas of what constituted legitimate school knowledge. The teacher's choices are not easy, either pupils are forced to participate where they do not understand the nature of the game, or they are excluded, which reinforces their own sense of being alien, and their alienness and incompetence in the eyes of others.

Mr. Winch's understanding of his task in relation to the immigrants typified the general liberal stance of the English department. Society for Mr. Winch was mainly a series of communications the most important of which were through language; thus to promote the awareness of the potential of language in communication was seen as the major objective, whether a child was an immigrant or not. This illustrates the tendency to put new problems into old categories where the fit may not be exact but is sufficiently undisturbing to allow one to proceed as if it were. For while the language needs of immigrants may in some senses be similar to those of the indigenous child, the fact that there is also a lack of cultural understanding behind the lack of ability in the immigrant child might be usefully taken into consideration, at least by the teacher being conscious of the fact. For Mr. Winch the inability to communicate would have serious repercussions for the child's intellectual development, emotional relationships, and more mundanely the ability to perform in job interviews. He hoped that the Asians "would be able to effectively function in all the various aspects of language when they leave . . . we expose them to more language than they would otherwise see and try to make them aware of language as a tool." Mr. Winch was optimistic about the future in comparison with his experiences in America. He said that the English were already eating curry and that he recognized a broadening of British culture. He saw the role of the school as very important in assimilating immigrants into British culture, teaching them the "nonverbal cues," as well as the verbal. Mr. Winch saw eventual intermarriage as the inevitable result of this exchange. He voiced a common complaint against the immigrant community, that they did not in his opinion organize to help themselves to adjust to life in Britain. This is an interesting point for I think there was a noticeable (in comparison with English children) passivity amongst the Asian children at Broadmere which was the result of their attitude to authority and belief in the legitimacy of school. Mr. Winch suggested that the Asians should make their aspirations and needs known within the school, and teachers should know more about the background of immigrant pupils. He also thought that positive discrimination was not necessarily to the good as it confirmed the differences between the races and institutionalized it. Positive discrimination in favor of immigrants, he suggested, would always run the risk of an adverse reaction from the indigenous community on the ground of maintaining parity of provision.

Mr. Winch was a particularly aware teacher, and if any action from the school were to be initiated then he would most likely be the instigator. Despite having a higher than average consciousness of immigrants and their problems, it was a consciousness that only resulted in the formation of an attitude rather than in action. This is only to be expected, because the institution itself kept quiet about its immigrant population and this may have been because of the fear of gaining a reputation amongst the white community as a school with a high proportion of immigrants, or a school which favored immigrants.

When asked about the Asians in school, teachers would often answer by saying that particular Asians were very bright. Two individuals were continually mentioned as representing the top-ability Asians. One young science teacher, Mr. Hume, spoke of a phenomenon which seemed to him almost exclusively Asian and certainly fitted with my general understanding, that was of the child who was conscientious and diligent but whose educational aspirations exceeded his ability to pass examinations. Mr. Hume mentioned particular Asian children as typifying the child in whom intelligence was seen to be imbalanced with aspiration and motivation. These were thought to be usually, though not invariably, matched amongst the indigenous population.

Apart from the judgments that specifically related to school, casual inquiry was likely to produce a stereotypical reaction from the whites regarding the Asians. "The women don't speak English, they believe in all these gods—they don't eat meat." To the majority of the English, Asians were an undifferentiated mass of people. The low level of general information about the Asian population and their way of life that existed amongst the indigenous English might be thought surprising given their mutual proximity. If the immigrant population was being prejudged to their detriment, then one might expect a community of active prejudice to involve some attempt to know about the disfavoured group in order to give substance to the prejudicial image. I asked the white children at school where they thought the Asian immigrant population came from? Most children thought they came from India, some children mentioned Pakistan and a minority some East African country. Ignorance at this level seemed not to relate to the child's position in the school; the elite sixth form were as ignorant as the remedial children. Much the same picture emerged from the question, what religions are practiced by the immigrant community? Not a single child made the connection between Pakistan and Islam. Some thought the Asians were all Buddhists, others Muslims. Few children seemed to have heard of Hinduism and a minority could not name a single Asian religion.

There was clear prejudgment on the part of the white community, who held inherited opinions about the social and moral qualities of the Asian community they were not based on any personal empirical evidence. This in itself is unremarkable. In order for a change in social structure to make sense it must perforce be given an interim meaning before interaction can moderate and deepen the social understanding in the host community. In other words the process of prejudgment would seem unavoidable, a necessary part of the dialectic of the maintenance of social reality, and the fact that this prejudgment is unfavorable in many cases is a separate problem relating to historical relationships and particular judgments of reality.

The first part of the relational design, the prejudgment, might be expected to be part of the Asian consciousness of the English if it is as I suggest a structural social process. This is in fact the case. The knowledge of U. K. culture amongst immigrants, many of whom had been in this country a decade or more was as shallow as that of the host community's knowledge of them. This was in some ways more surprising in a group that was having to learn to operate in a new culture, and is probably explained through the dominating importance of the small group, the family, in the self and social conceptions of Asian immigrants. In matters related to the public world of work and relations with the local economy the Asian knowledge of the scene was excellent. The average male immigrant could tell one where to buy the cheapest remoulds and classify local firms in terms of their wage rates and prospects for advancement, and would have met and spoken to a good many English men, but would still think that the English do not love their children and that divorce is the inevitable result of English moral laxity.

The mutual ignorance between the two groups suggests that attitudes and behavior may rest upon a view of society that has no empirical basis. This is not unusual insofar as we can all understand, and incorporate into our conceptions of the world, attitudes and opinions based on very scant knowledge and no direct experience. English people will have a fairly detailed personal image of America and will form judgments about American society, its moral tone, its standards and way of life. This will be done for the most part without recourse to visiting America to check attitudes against reality. When this same orientation is used to make statements about the people living next door, to incorporate them without directly relating to them, then this reticence requires some social explanation.

One element might be the inherited racism of the imperial decline. Another might simply be the apprehension about outsiders which is a fairly constant feature of human societies, though not invariably so. This would be intensified if accompanied by feelings of being in competition with the newcomer for scarce resources. Another feature of social structure that would work against interrelations is the quality of reserve which characterises both English and Asian culture. People are often made meaningful by being put into a family context, in Asian social relations, classificatory kin abound. Often a boy would say "We are going to London on Saturday to see my cousins." On being questioned about the relationship further, it may transpire that he does not know whether he is related by marriage or blood to the people he will visit but just calls them cousins. In this primary relational arena which depends on the fiction of kinship as a criterion for inclusion it is obviously difficult, generally, to bring in members of the English community at this level because of the simple categorical incongruity.

There is nothing inherently sinister about communities maintaining social distance while sharing the same physical space. If one thinks of the operations of class in the English community then it would seem possible for class cultures to remain discrete yet mutually tolerant in the main. Both in suburbia and urban England it is possible to live in a house without knowing anything about one's direct neighbors. In school, however, avoidance is not a possible option because of the social organization of school activities. This does not mean that proximity fosters tolerance through continuous exposure.

For example, the idea of involuntary repatriation of the Asian community was very much favored by the white children, who expressed concern within the usual range of employment, housing, and social security, although locally none of these were acute problems. Mr. Winch said that the white children would often refer to the Asian community as "Paki's," used as a general derogatory term. This illustrates the lack of desire to form an accurate or realistic picture of the newcomer. Mr. Winch also suggested that it was not only color but also manners and behavior that made the Asian an outsider in school. The fact that they had special uniform regulations was resented; for example the few Muslim girls were allowed to wear trousers, when the rest of girls would dearly have loved to wear them but were not allowed. This was an obvious cause of grievance and separation.

From observation of children in and around the school, girls tended to associate in pairs or in large fragmented and stationary groups of ten to fifteen. The boys, outside of games playing, tended to be seen less in pairs or large groups but in smaller groups of around four to six. I noticed no real difference in this pattern between the indigenous English and the Asian children. Obviously, though, five Asian boys together amongst a majority of white boys will stand out.

What is undeniable is that the Asian boys and girls spend most of their time out of class with other Asians. The main reason for this was the legitimately grounded fear of rejection by the white children, which was sometimes covered by professions of superiority of manners and sensibility on the part of the Asians. A common Asian perception of the English at school is that they are frivolous and do not really want to succeed. This is in contrast to the Asian self-perception as hardworking and serious in their studies, an orientation to school which they regard as virtuous. The rather sophisticated English view of academic success, that if you have to sweat to succeed, then the success is in some sense devalued, is not part of the Asian view. This rather aristocratic view that only innate rather than achieved ability is authentic was not in that pure sense obvious at Broadmere, although a strong value was put on work avoidance, or at least ostensible work avoidance, by the majority of the school. The Asian attitude to study made them look like grinds to the English, and grinds had a low social value.

There were also gender culture differences that kept the ethnic groups apart. It was difficult to observe natural playground behavior at close quarters as my presence as an adult authority was inhibiting. Most of my conversation observations were made at periods when children were on the move through the school. Much conversation between the English boys was dominated by sport and mutual insult in a general aura of aggression and potential physicality. There were obviously many who did not belong to this world, but it represented standard and approved behavior. Very few of the Asian boys fitted this model with notable exceptions. In general demeanor they were not ebullient, they did not appear to develop the mock aggressive joking relationships of the English boys. They were generally much quieter in their manner and more reticent in their relationships. Conversation in school was mostly about aspects of school life and work and other members of the Asian group. There was also a qualitative difference between Asian and English relationships which was very hard to define. Perhaps it could be characterized by suggesting that English relations evolve and develop through shared experience, while Asian boys, who may well see very little of each other outside of school, are friends by declaration and are referring to a set of mutually binding emotional responsibilities towards each other, rather than saying he is my friend therefore we will do things together.

There is one other major factor which separated the Asians in school. A proportion of the Asian children spoke very little English. They therefore naturally sought out those they could talk to in their Indian language; thus they appeared cliquish and emphasized their ethnicity.

The Asian girls were not only distinguished by their color but also by their distinctive hairstyles and in the case of the Muslim girls by their trousers. They were effectively cut off from the culture of the English girls, in a way in which other ethnic minorities are not, by their lack of interest in English fashion, make-up and boys. The conversations of the girls revolved around the doings of members of their families, and to a lesser extent happenings at school.

There were varying degrees of closeness to and interactions with, English culture among the Asian pupils. Some few Asian boys were at ease with the English boys through their success as sportsmen or their English manners. There were a few Asian girls born in the U. K. who were able to live through the medium of English culture while at school, who did not wear long plaits, and who spent their time with the English rather than the Asian girls.

Just as the Asians thought of the English children as homogenous, so the English failed to differentiate among the Asians. However, between a boy who was born in Broadmere town, of educated westernized Asian parents, and a boy recently arrived from the Punjab countryside, there was very little in common. Criteria for inclusion in an Asian group were first, sex, then religion, and third, class or caste, although caste was a very vague concept to most of the Asian children, who thought that it was merely a matter of endogamous restriction. Thus the Sikhs in school knew all the other Sikhs, at least by sight, and were likely to choose their friends from this group. The Hindus, not being sectarian in the same sense, did not have so strong a notion of themselves as a religious community; this was most strong among the Muslims who tended to be the most orthodox and the least interested in engaging with European culture. However, perhaps by default rather than design Hindus formed friendships with other Hindus.

Thus, there were within the Asian school community distinct groups. These groups were to an extent autonomous. The Asians did not behave or conceive themselves as a general category although they were seen as such by the English. In Asian friendships there was also a divide between those in the remedial units and those in the school proper. To the extent that this division also reflected the length of time spent in England then the difference may be between those more or less adapted to English life.

These differences that existed within the Asian community were not recognized by the English just as the Asians did not know sufficient about English culture to make any complex judgments themselves. Neither community, English nor Asian, had any necessity to find out one about the other. Social judgments at the level of the cliche are sufficient to furnish the barest meaning, and unfortunately motivation to develop this meaning is more likely to be fueled by antipathy than a real desire to increase understanding of what it is to live in a multiethnic community.

This may partly be for reasons of history and the specific relations between white and other races. There is also the point to be made in the case of the English that the major social theory still operating would seem to be social Darwinism and the hierarchy of cultures. Implicit in many of the casual conversations that I had with English adults and children was the idea that the Asians were fresh from the jungle, that they lacked civilized habits. The major empirical proofs of this were the facts that their food smelled different from English food, that their women insisted on *native* dress, the sari or pajamas, that they could rarely speak very good English, and they put their children to work. These differences were perceived as evidence that the Asian community was below the English on the cultural ladder. The Asian habit of having large families was also cited as evidence of a bucolic backwardness.

Finally, what I have briefly tried to illustrate is the general lack of cultural awareness of other groups, and the constant resort to one-dimensional images in understanding other cultures. What this means in the comprehensive school is that judgments tend to be made ethnocentrically, to the detriment of other groups, by pupils and teachers alike. This may not affect the academic performance of indigenous pupils because their natal culture is also that of the school. For ethnic minority pupils, their ability to perform successfully within the culture of school, in part depends on their understanding of the host culture, particularly in relation to their own culture.

LANGUAGE AND CULTURE

It became clear to me during the fieldwork phase at Broadmere that the complexities of the linguistic environment in school went largely unrecognized. Simple referential and folk cognitive models prevailed. They were all that had been required in a monolingual environment. The new categories of bilingual pupil or of pupils without English were absorbed into existing notions of deficiency. Also the fact of cultural diversity was only recognized marginally in dress regulations or sometimes in Home Economics. This is in no sense an abnormal state of affairs.

In this last section I shall broaden the debate and discuss language and culture and how they may help explain performance in multicultural schools and communities.

Mother tongue teaching is an area where the linguistic elements of schooling are currently being debated (Rosen & Burgess, 1980; Mercer, 1981). This has partly arisen from the recognition that some Asian communities especially are maintaining their vernacular languages generationally. Thus, English born children of Asian parents in Bradford may arrive in school speaking Punjabi as a first language, and with little knowledge of English. This may be thought less of a problem with West Indian pupils, whose languages are mainly English based creoles, and the relatively new vernacular, London Jamaican. There is also renewed interest in indigenous minority languages, in Welsh medium primary schools and in Scots Gaelic (Davies, 1983).

Languages, like cultures, are neither constant nor discrete. Both change over time and through space. For example, American English and British English have a long history of mutual trading and English and French continually interpenetrate. Also, my father's idiolect, or personal language, is both lexically and syntactically distinct from mine, as is my son's. There are also constant and subtle changes of meanings within the stable lexicon. The English word buxom, for example, moved from meaning pliant and submissive in the 14th century, through bright, healthy, and vigorous in the 16th century before acquiring its present connotation of pneumatic beauty. Word concepts take their meaning, and are mediated by, their context. Contexts differ both syntactically and socially. "I love bagels" and "I love mother" use the same word love to refer to very different emotional states. The word love in Asian English rarely has the romantic connotation often present in British usage.

I am using language and culture partly as analogous because in investigating their formal connections the nature of culture and transmission can be modeled. They have something of the image of techtonic plates, the invisible slabs on which our continents rest. Like them they are in perpetual, but rarely perceptible movement, and changes in one cause correspondent shifts in another. Similarly, in relations between communities each group assimilates the life of the other into its own patterning of cultural perceptions, as I have tried to illustrate.

Thus, the English in general are horrified by the notion of arranged marriage (though not by computer dating) because they map the notion of marriage in British culture onto Asian culture. In Asian culture the socially objective criteria for nubility are explicit in the negotiation of a marriage, in British culture they are implicit, and the negotiation is conceptualized as free choice. However, what the British might choose to think of as compatibility can be translated as meeting objective social criteria, of age, class, level of education, and ethnicity, for these are the actual conditions governing indigenous British marriage. Equally the general view of English marriage arrangements amongst the Asian community I worked with, was of an unstable system based on transient affections, evidenced by the high divorce rate. It was concisely put by a young friend as, "You have the love before the marriage, but with us it grows slowly afterwards." This is the key to the notion of cultural dissonance, it is the inevitable product of cultural contact, it is not a mistranslation.

The problem can be located in the nature of culture itself. Cultural groups are not necessarily characterized by consensus; they do not exist by virtue of agreeing about the nature of themselves and things, but by the capacity to interpenetrate each others meanings. Again, the analogy with language can be made. In the U. K. many languages are spoken, one of which is English. This can be subdivided into different vernaculars, which are expressed by groups and individuals. Each individual's language, or idiolect, is the unique live point at which meaning has to be generated through interaction. Every human exchange involves a cultural translation, the reconceptualization of someone else's cultural reality through language. This is most often a spontaneous and unconscious capacity, for pupils in their peer groups or teachers in the staffroom. Because levels of shared conceptions can be assumed, including shared identity as pupil or teacher, the fact of translation does not impinge, or present any problem. However, the further one goes from the potentiality of idiolect mapping idiolect, or more precisely, from the implicit belief in this as a possibility, the more the fact of translation becomes apparent.

New cultural forms can be forged within recognized existing languages, this emphasizes that sharing a symbolic system does not insulate against the possibilities of dissonance. The student political movement in American universities in the 1960s is an example of this. Roszak (1969) describes it as representing ". . . a culture so radically disaffiliated from the mainstream assumptions of our society that it scarcely looks to many as a culture at all, but takes on the appearance of a barbaric intrusion" (p. 42). This graphically describes another aspect of understanding other cultures, our own may appear to us as natural and correct and other cultures as aberrant. Dumont and Wax (1971) in their account of the schooling of Cherokee Indians note the implicit official assumption that the ultimate goal should be "total ethnic and cultural dissolution." That is to say success would be achieved when the Cherokees were culturally indistinguishable from white Americans. This idea can be seen in its genesis in President James Monroe's request in 1819 to the newly established Office of Indian Affairs that Indians should be introduced to "the habits and arts of civilization" (Button & Provenzo, 1983, p. 149).

Domination by cultural inclusion is a plausible task for educational systems. In a different analysis Ogbu (1978), following Cox (1945) uses caste as a model for American society and argues that while it is clearly the work of schools to transmit the dominant white culture to its inheritors, "Success in regard to blacks and other castelike minority groups is to be measured by the extent to which they equip the latter with knowledge and skills for their low social and occupational positions" (Ogbu, 1978, p. 40). To return to the linguistic analogy, everyone must speak English but in the vernacular, or dialect, which demonstrates their relative position in the hierarchy of cultural groups.

THE CULTURAL CONTRACT

In the U. K. and the U.S.A. the idea of home background as a causal factor in educational performance has been common for at least 2 decades (Douglas, 1964, Little & Smith, 1971). The commonest formulation of the home school relation is some version of deficit or its absence. Minorities, and in the U. K. the indigenous working class, do comparatively less well in school because they lack the cultural attributes, both psychological and material, of the white middle classes. This would seem to be a permanent and intractable problem. What the ideal outcome would be we do not know, it would be absurd for instance for everyone to graduate from Harvard and William and Mary or from Oxford and Cambridge, but certainly success would be measured in higher levels of academic achievement.

The promotion of equality of educational opportunity has long been a potent motivation of innovation and intervention in education (Coleman, 1969). Implicit in it is the idea that everyone would like to compete, that if more opportunities were available they would be welcomed by the oppressed minorities. Seen from a cultural perspective this may not be an adequate formulation.

In a Marxist cultural analysis of ethnographic data on a group of working class boys in an English secondary school, Willis (1977) suggested that the boys understanding of schooling in their lives was directly related to its role in the maintenance of culture. Academic failure was a necessary part of becoming a member of "the lads" working class community. It is as important for some people to fail in school as it is for others to succeed, depending on the meaning of schooling for a particular cultural group. Thus, what can be seen from one point-of-view as the absence of motivation to succeed, may be the result of a partly objective analysis of the relevance of education to the maintenance and reproduction of cultural groups.

In the U. K., the upper classes and the working class are antiintellectual and indifferent to education. It is Bernstein's (1975) "new middle class," whose social position derives from work, not the ownership of property, who give a high value to academic success because it is vital to the reproduction of the group, and the maintenance of its position within the social hierarchy.

It is possible to see school as culturally separable from its clients, pupils, and their parents. It has an enduring form, and a set of roles, that remain more or less constant as individuals move through the process. Each individual arrives at school as a member of a cultural group, and children with similar cultural characteristics tend to form peer groups, which like all human groups act to sustain particular meanings. Every child that is schooled has to accommodate school in relation to the values of her culture. This entails making sense of the relevance of schooling to the life of the group, and by this largely unconscious mechanism, levels of engagement, motivation, and achievement are determined. Thus, Ogbu's "successful" school which reproduces inequality and maintains the dominant position of whites, may actually be functional in maintaining black cultural identity.

It is important to remember that nondominant cultural groups may inadvertently be jealous of precisely those characteristics that ensure and reproduce their subordinate social position. The high value placed on macho behavior by Willis's "lads" drew its meaning from their acceptance of the inevitability of manual labor.

Thus, children make a contract with the institution of school according to the test of cultural relevance, and their understanding of their own life chances. There is an equation between the cultural meaning of school and levels of performance. This may help to account for differences within as well as between cultural groups.

There is increasing evidence in the U. K. that West Indian girls perform better than boys (Bagley & Verma, 1980; Fuller, 1980). Possible explanations of this are that teachers have lower expectations of boys than of girls. Also students interviewed by Tomlinson (1983a) "were all of the opinion that boys got a 'worse deal' from school than girls." In a London study Rosen and Burgess (1980) found girls to have higher levels of literate skill than boys and to be more likely to speak Standard English in school. However, it can also be argued that gender cultures are exclusive and distinctive among adolescent West Indians. What both the media and social scientists refer to as *black youth* is more usually male West Indian working-class culture. Although there is very little available evidence on gender cultures, Tomlinson (1983b) did ask her small sample of West Indian female university students to account for the superior performance of girls, in spite of what Wallace (1979) had referred to as the "double oppression" of being black and female. In response they referred sympathetically to the greater levels of prejudice experienced by males, but were also critical of aspects of masculine culture which mitigated against academic achievement.

Men seem to be in the forefront of discrimination but the peer group also is an important influence on them—they want immediate gratification and to keep up a good front with their friends.

Black boys stagnate—they are into having fun—drinking—girls—girls aren't so rowdy.

Black women . . . don't cause the same amount of trouble—but boys do have more pressure from their peer group to misbehave. (Tomlinson, 1983b, p. 89)

There is also evidence that Asian pupils perform better than West Indian pupils, a fact that came to general attention with the publication of the Interim Report of the Rampton Committee (DES, 1981). The London Times in a leading article neatly outlined the problem, how could differential performance be explained when, "Asians also suffer from poverty, overcrowding and discrimination, that is worse in some ways, and many of them have the additional handicap of speaking English as a second language" (Times, June 18, 1981).

This was in one sense not news, studies by the Inner London Education Authority between 1966 and 1976 "demonstrated overall that pupils from India and Pakistan do better on tests of attainment than other 'immigrant' groups" (Tomlinson, 1983a, p. 48). In the 18+ 'A' level examinations, which are the culmination of English schooling and generally required for matriculation, Rampton reported 13% of Asian pupils achieving 'A' level passes against 12% of other leavers (DES, 1981).

There is a folk cultural understanding of the performance of Asian pupils, perhaps mainly based on the everyday evidence in the U. K. of Asian small businesses, or traders staying open longer and working harder than indigenous whites. What the British see as their lost Puritan virtues are often projected onto the Asian community, who are characterized as industrious and self-reliant.

Asian success can also be understood as a function of the relevance of education to the reproduction of the cultural group. The extended family, and not the individual, is the status unit. Individual action is interpreted within the context of the group, and is judged according to whether it enhances or detracts from the standing of the extended family, within the local community or the caste. This is the context of education. Qualifications are negotiable status.

The experience of the process of education was differently evaluated by the Patidar and the indigenous English. The liberal philosophy of education, which largely legitimates the process for Europeans and Americans, was entirely absent from the Asian community's understanding. Education was not seen as something that inhered in the individual or changed the person in any way, so that being educated was not seen as a social status in itself, it was more simply a resource at the command of the group.

This was partly clear from the mechanics of choice. I took part in several discussions about the postschool educational careers of individuals. The decision would be a group one, with the person concerned having a voice, but neither the power nor the desire to make an individual decision. The discussion would be probably informally chaired by an eldest brother, and aimed at achieving a consensus on how the subject's further education could be used to maximize the resources of the group. For boys, electronics or business studies were currently favored, for girls commercial training or preferably pharmacy. Education was seen as equally important for girls as for boys, partly because level of education was a factor in negotiating marriage. Purely intellectual subjects, philosophy or history, or expressive subjects, literature or fine arts, never entered discussions. I suspect that this is not because they have no utility, but that they require an individual sense of the intellect operating in the world, which was alien to Patidar communal culture.

Thus, the differential educational performance of minority groups might be partly understood by seeing how education articulates with other cultural complexes and particularly its role in the maintenance and transmission of culture. These are the structures that determine the nature and qualities of dissonance between groups, and provide the ground rules for the cultural contract with schooling. In the textbooks Saraswati is the goddess of wisdom, but in Broadmere she had become the goddess of education.

REFERENCES

Bernstein, B. (1975). *Class, codes and control* (Vol. 3). Towards a theory of educational transmission. London: Routledge and Kegan Paul.

Button, H. W., & Provenzo, E. F. (1983). *History of education and culture in America.* Englewood Cliffs, NJ: Prentice-Hall.

Cohen, L., & Manion, L. (1983). *Multicultural classrooms.* London: Croom Helm.

Coleman, J. (1968, Winter). The concept of equality of educational opportunity. *Harvard Educational Review* special issue, *38*(1), 7, 22.

Cox, O. C. (1945). Race and caste: A distinction. *American Journal of Sociology, 50,* 360–368.

Cropley, A. J. (1983). *The education of immigrant children: A social psychological introduction.* London: Croom Helm.

Davies, C. (1983). Ysgolion Cymraeg. In M. Stubbs & H. Hillier (Eds.), *Readings on language schools and classrooms.* (pp. 82–91). London: Methuen.

Department of Education and Science (1981). *West Indian children in our schools, A report of the committee of enquiry into the education of children from ethnic minority groups.* (The Rampton Report), HMSO.

Douglas, J.W.B. (1964). *The home and the school: A study of ability and attainment in the primary school.* London: McGibbon and Kee.

Driver, G., & Ballard, R. (1979). Comparing performance in multiracial schools, South Asian pupils at 16 plus. *New Community, 7,* 2.

Dumont, R. V., & Wax, M. L. (1971). Cherokee school society and the inter-cultural classroom. In B. R. Cosin et al. (Eds.), *School and society: A sociological reader* (pp. 77–85). London: Routledge and Kegan Paul.

Fuller, M. (1980). Black girls in a London comprehensive school. In R. Deem (Ed.), *Schooling for women's work.* London: Routledge and Kegan Paul.

Hicks, D. W. (1981). *Minorities, a teacher's resource book for the multi-ethnic curriculum.* London: Heinemann Educational Books.

James, H., & Jeffcoate, R. (Eds.). (1981). *The school in the multicultural society.* London: Harper and Row.

Kirp, D. L. (1979). *Doing good by doing little. Race & schooling in Britain.* Berkeley: University of California Press.

Little, A., & Smith, G. (1971). *Strategies of compensation: A review of educational projects for the disadvantaged in the United States.* Paris: OECD.

Lynch, J. (Ed.). (1981). *Teaching in the multicultural school.* London: Ward Lock.

Mercer, M. (1981). *Language in school and community*. London: Edward Arnold.

Mullard, C. (1973). *Black Britain*. London: Allen and Unwin.

Ogbu, J. U. (1978). *Minority education and caste. The American system in cross-cultural perspective*. Orlando, FL: Academic Press.

Phillips, C. J. (1979). Educational under-achievement in different ethnic groups. *Educational Research, 21*, 2.

Pocock, D. F. (1972). *Kanbi & Patidar: A study of the Patidar community of Gujarat*. Oxford: Clarendon Press.

Rosen, H., & Burgess, T. (1980) *Language and dialects of London school children: An investigation*. London: Ward Lock.

Roszak, T. (1969). *The making of the counter culture*. New York: Anchor Books.

Saifullah Khan, V. (1983). The mother tongue of linguistic minorities in multicultural England. In M. Stubbs & H. Hillier (Eds.), *Readings on language schools and classrooms* (pp. 113–138). London: Methuen.

Tambs-Lyche, H. (1980). *London Patidars: A case study in urban ethnicity*. London: Routledge and Kegan Paul.

Tierney, J. (Ed.). (1982). *Race migration and schooling*. Eastbourne: Holt, Rinehart and Winston.

Times (1981, June 18). Looking the facts in the face. (p. 15).

Tomlinson, S. (1983a). *Ethnic minorities in British schools*. London: Heinemann Educational Books.

Tomlinson, S. (1983b). Black women in higher education—Case studies of university women in Britain. In L. Barton & S. Walker (Eds.), *Race, class and education* (pp. 66–80). London: Croom Helm.

Vellims, S. (1983). South Asian students in British universities—A statistical note. *New Community, 10*(2) 202–212.

Wallace, M. (1979). *Black Macho and the myth of superwoman*. New York: Dial Press.

Willis, P. (1977). *Learning to labour: How working class kids get working class jobs*. Teakfield: Saxon House.

Yates, P. D. (1984). A case of mistaken identity: Inter-ethnic images in the comprehensive school. In S. J. Ball (Ed.), *Comprehensive Schooling: A reader*. Lewes: Falmer Press.

The Author and His Chapter

Norman A. Chance is professor of anthropology at the University of Connecticut. He was born in Lynn, Massachusetts, and studied anthropology at the University of Pennsylvania before receiving his Ph.D. degree from Cornell University in 1957. He taught previously at the University of Oklahoma and McGill University, where he also served as Director of the Programme in the Anthropology of Development until 1968, when he moved to Connecticut to head the newly formed Department of Anthropology. Prior to developing an interest in China, he undertook research in the southwest United States and in Alaska, Canada, and Mexico.

Soon after the "Ping Pong Diplomacy" of 1971 Norman Chance applied to the Chinese Embassy in Ottawa, Canada to undertake a brief study of changing patterns of education resulting from the Cultural Revolution policies then being implemented. In April and May of 1972 he and his wife toured five major cities and many towns, visiting schools, research institutes, and so forth. He was treated as an honored guest. But it was not until the fall of 1979 that he could once again visit the People's Republic to do an ethnography of a Beijing commune—Half Moon Village. This commune is described in his case study *China's Urban Villagers* (1984) in our series, *Case Studies in Cultural Anthropology* published by Holt, Rinehart and Winston. As a participating resident of Half-Moon Village he was able to acquire intimate knowledge of everyday peasant life and through his more than fifty interviews with leaders, factory workers, students, teachers, and many others, extend his understanding of contemporary life in China far beyond the boundaries of his resident community. His chapter reflects this knowledge. His objective analysis, neither as glowingly positive as some reports would have it, nor as dour and negative as others, furnishes us valuable insights into both the promise and the problems of schooling in contemporary communist China.

The Editors

10 Chinese Education in a Village Setting

Norman A. Chance
University of Connecticut

Interwoven into China's educational policies of the past 30 years are two contrasting strategies. One focuses on the question of equality and has as its correlary the effort to increase the availability of education as broadly as possible. The other focuses on quality and has as its correlary the concentration of available resources on a smaller number of "better" schools. The tradeoff between breadth and depth is obvious—one approach reduces the differences between the people at the expense of quality. The other emphasizes quality at the expense of the majority. In China's case, this majority includes 800 million peasant farmers that comprise 80% of the population.

Needless to say, questions of quantity and quality in educational opportunity are characteristic of other countries too—a well-known American example being the debates carried on in the 1960s and 1970s over the issue of "open education" in contrast to today's emphasis on increasing the quality of primary and secondary education—particularly in the areas of science and mathematics. However, in the United States such discussion has largely reflected different aspects of one unified educational strategy, whereas in China conflicts between these approaches have been so intense as to suggest to many that two quite distinct strategies are at work.[1]

---

[1]Suzanne Pepper (1980) in a highly stimulating article, divides these strategies into two categories—"egalitarian" and "hierarchical." The egalitarian approach was characteristic of the so-called Great Leap Forward in the late 1950s, and most dramatically during the 1966–76 decade of the Cultural Revolution. The hierarchical approach characterized the policies of the early 1950s, the early 1960s, and those currently in effect.

221

Two related questions of educational policy have also concerned China's leaders over the past 30 years. One is how to insure that the people become ideologically committed to the new socialist society. The other is how to train China's youth in technology and science in order to build a highly productive society able to substantially improve the living standard of the people.

During Mao Zedong's period of leadership, he emphasized that these two qualities should be nurtured within each individual, with "red-ness" guiding "expert-ness." Because, in his view, the existing society did not adequately provide this nurturance, he tried to change its structure so that it could. This effort was most pronounced during the Cultural Revolution. In 1966, all schools were closed. When primary and secondary schools opened again 2 to 3 years later, a major effort was made to universalize primary education and expand secondary schools. To do this, length of schooling was reduced from 12 to 10 years and course materials were correspondingly condensed and simplified. Traditional rote methods of teaching were critizised. Examinations were temporarily eliminated. Tracking systems were abolished. All students and teachers were required to increase their participation in physical labor. Upon graduation from middle school, many urban "educated youths" were encouraged and later required to go to work in the countryside. Governmental authorities who saw the major purpose of education as that of serving the state bureaucracy were attacked—and at the same time, the capabilities and skills of peasants and workers were given maximum ideological emphasis.[2]

Wanting to learn about these innovative efforts in education, I undertook three field trips to China in the 1970s, the most significant of which was the opportunity to live and work in Half Moon Village in the fall and early winter of 1979.[3] This community, one of 116 villages comprising Red Flag Commune, is located on the rural periphery of Beijing Municipality, about an hour's bicycle ride from the capital city's urban center. The analysis that follows describes the process of education in Half Moon—including the social and cultural as well as intellectual relations between teacher, student and parent.

Pervading this common interactive pattern are the political undercur-

---

[2]A large body of literature is now emerging on this period of dramatic change in Chinese education. See, for example, Gardner (1982), Pepper (1978, 1980), Shirk (1982), Unger (1982), and Zweig (1978).

[3]Appreciation is gratefully acknowledged to the Chinese People's Association for Friendship with Foreign Countries for their invitation to undertake the 1979 field study; to Nancy Chance, for sharing her research on education in Half Moon; to Peter Seybolt, Julia Kwong, and Nancy Chance for their helpful comments on an earlier draft of this article; and to the University of Connecticut Research Foundation for their financial assistance from 1979 to 1983.

rents described earlier. Educational administrators, concerned more with quality than quantity of education, actively support the upgrading of existing programs and amount of study time. Parents, on the other hand, looking back several decades when there were no schools at all for their children, are drawn to the universalization of educational opportunity. Tied as they are to the agricultural cycle, these peasants have difficulty perceiving how advanced schooling can be of real benefit to village youths soon to join them in the fields or in local sideline industries—occupations requiring little more than the most basic of elementary education. And finally, relocated urban educated youth, some of whom feel they are the "lost generation" of the Cultural Revolution, try to adjust to a new political reality in which socialist values they once readily identified with are now sharply challenged by the country's leaders. In the concluding section of this chapter, we examine the perceptive evaluation of one such sent-down youth in which she traces her experience using "society as the classroom."[4]

A VISIT FROM THE TEACHER

Su Shitou, 10-years-old, attends third grade in a primary school near Half Moon Village. Though bright and full of wit, he doesn't like to study. For him, working with figures and characters is boring, especially when he can spend time with his father in the fields or collecting different kinds of insects by the irrigation ditch at the edge of the village.

In class, Su doesn't listen to his teachers either, preferring to talk with his nearby schoolmates. For this reason, his teacher recently reassigned him to share a desk with a girl in the hope that his classroom behavior might improve. Yet just the other day, Su got into trouble again. He put a broom on top of the half-open classroom door, expecting it to fall on a student walking into the room. Only this time it fell on the teacher. There were a few giggles from his friends, but that was all. Every set of eyes focused on the tall man standing, broom in hand, at the front of the room. In a calm but firm voice, Teacher Wang addressed the class.

"Students, who is responsible for this?" he asked, gently waving the broom before him.

The room was still. Then, as Su Shitou rose from behind his desk, the other students turned in his direction.

"I'm sorry, teacher. I did not expect the broom to fall on you. I was playing a joke."

---

[4]The material that follows is largely drawn from (Chance, 1984). Chapter 5 of *China's Urban Villagers: Life in a Beijing Commune*.

"Su Shitou, you and I will have a little talk after school." With that remark, the teacher turned, walked toward a small platform at the front of the room, and sat down behind his desk. Reaching into a drawer, he pulled out a black notebook. As the students watched, he wrote a few comments on a back page under the name Su. Then, looking at Shitou once again, he closed the book, returned it to his desk, and addressed the class, informing them that it was time to begin the day's language lesson.

In midafternoon, at the close of school, Shitou stood before his teacher, waiting for the pronouncement.

"Xiao Su, I want you to inform your parents I am coming by the village this evening before dark to talk with them."

It was the answer Shitou expected. He had been forewarned the last time he got into trouble. There are two reasons why a teacher might come to a student's home. One is simply to inform the parents how the child is progressing and answer any questions they have about the school. The other is the more dreaded *gaozhuang,* in which a complaint is lodged about bad behavior. Unfortunately for Shitou, this definitely appeared to be a *gaozhuang* type of visit. As teachers are highly respected in Half Moon, as in other villages of Red Flag Commune, a complaint expressed by them about a student is taken seriously. But that's not all. Such a criticism also casts shame on the whole family. As a result, Shitou knew that, at the very least, he would get a good dressing down. More likely, it would be a good beating.

That evening, shortly before sunset, Teacher Wang arrived at the Su courtyard gate.

"Hello. May I come in?"

"Oh yes, Teacher Wang," responded Mother Su. "Come in and have a seat. Have you had your dinner? Please, let me give you some here."

Father Su added, "You must be tired, I'm sure. Have a seat. Shitou, make some tea for your teacher." As a solemn-looking Shitou turned toward the kitchen, his father admonished him: "Shitou, say hello first."

"Hello, Xiao Shitou," the teacher said. "I've already had my dinner, so just some tea will be fine. I simply dropped by to visit a little with your parents."

"Thank you, Teacher Wang," responded Mother Su. "You are always so busy attending to the students. Sometimes they don't understand very well. And other times, they are naughty. How is our Shitou doing in school? Does he cause any trouble in class?"

"Oh, no. He is a good boy. He has made real progress recently."

"Around here, he likes to play and run around. Can't sit still even for 5 minutes. He must give you a lot of headaches, I suppose?" inquired the father.

"Boys get restless easily. Shitou used to talk with other students in class, but he doesn't do that anymore. Is he reading at home and doing schoolwork by himself?"

"He reads picture books quite a bit. Stories about various heroes. But he doesn't like homework. When we force him, he does it with friends.

During this whole exchange, Xiao Shitou was sitting quietly on a *kang* in the back of the room, observing everything and saying nothing.

"I see. He likes to read story books. Good. What we have to do now is show him that he can't just learn from pictures. He must do well in schoolwork too."

"You're right. Mother Su and I are sorry we don't pay enough attention to his schoolwork. It's important to learn things. Children don't know that. Whenever I get angry with Shitou, I give him a good slapping."

"That's no use. It's not the way to put him on the right track. Remember, he is still young. Teachers and parents need to cooperate to train the younger generation to be useful to the country."

While addressing the teacher, Father Su kept glancing at his son. "Teacher Wang, what you say is correct. Whenever Shitou does anything wrong in school, tell him I support whatever punishment you give him."

"Punishment is not the best way to educate students. We do reasoning. The result is better. That way he will understand. Actually, Shitou is making progress. That's all that counts. Of course, sometimes he forgets. It is best if he listens to the teacher. Children are like small trees. It takes careful nurturing for them to grow straight and tall."

"You are right again, Teacher Wang. We should do more with Shitou. We don't pay enough attention to his schoolwork."

"I should do more too. But he is making some headway. Don't worry about him too much. Well, it's getting late. I must be going. Thanks for the tea."

"Good-bye, Teacher Wang. Thank you for coming, and for all the work you are doing with Shitou. We appreciate it."

This portrayal of Teacher Wang's visit to the Su family, described in detail by a perceptive key informant, illustrates both continuity and change in the education of village children like Su Shitou. Teacher Wang, aware of the impact that his high status has in the village, chooses to underplay his problems with Shitou. He knows that his presence in the Su household is indication enough that the son is in difficulty at school. Such a visit is usually followed by punishment handed out by the father: a slap or beating if the child is in primary school, and at least a severe verbal reprimand if the student is older. In this case, the father not only indicates that he supports that course of action, but goes even further, giving blanket approval to the teacher to impose any punishment he deems advisable while Shitou is at school. Today, this common parental response is more likely to be challenged by modern teachers like Wang. That is, the family is encouraged to become involved in the child's education, rather than simply treating the offending son (almost never a daughter) as an object bringing shame to the household.[5]

The history of Su Shitou's and Teacher Wang's school began in 1952 when the villagers of Half Moon and other nearby communities first constructed it. Prior to that time, no educational facilities were available to the largely poor peasants living in the area. Not surprisingly, for the next 2 decades, student enrollments were relatively small, most parents questioning the importance of all but the first few years of schooling. At that time, knowledge gained in the classroom was seen to having little bearing on how to plant, weed, and harvest crops. For young girls having to care for younger brothers and sisters at home, there was even more reason to either delay entrance into primary school or drop out early. Boys, on the other hand, not only had fewer tasks to complete in the home, but were not expected to begin work in the fields until their early or midteens. Relatively free of daily work responsibilities, they were better able to take advantage of what school had to offer. Furthermore, peasant parents, most of whom were illiterate, at least wanted their sons to be able to read newspapers and perhaps even simple books. Today, over 90% of the children, both girls and boys, complete their 5-year primary school education—a substantial achievement in 3 decades. Exactly what does that education entail?

PRIMARY EDUCATION

Children begin their formal education at age seven. Half Moon doesn't have its own primary school. So, depending on the students' ages, they attend one of two schools shared between several nearby villages. The total population of the two institutions is 416, less than 4% of Red Flag Commune's overall primary school enrollment of 14,000. Each of the five grades contains approximately 40 students each. There are ten teachers, one for each classroom. Other members of the staff include a director and

---

[5]This belief that the shame of an individual (and also the honor) is shared by the family and lineage has a long history in China. Under the emperors, a well-known principle in the penal system, called *lianzuo,* stated that the whole family was to be held collectively responsible for serious political crimes committed by any one member. Even close relatives of the given family, such as the wife's patrilineal kin, could be executed along with the criminal—all pointing to the fact that within the traditional Chinese cultural framework, individuals were not seen as independent beings, but as members of the larger kinship network.

a physical education instructor who share their time between the two facilities.

Classrooms are arranged quite simply. In some, each student has his or her own table or desk, while in others they are shared. The much larger flat-topped desk at the front of the room is reserved for the teacher. On the wall behind the teacher's desk hangs a large blackboard, and above that, eight large Chinese characters are painted in bold red colors: *tuanjie, jinzhang, yan su, huopo,* meaning "Be united, alert, earnest, and lively." For the class, it is a reminder that all students should work together as one, not be lazy, be serious in study, and be energetic. By looking carefully high on the wall between the two sets of characters, one can also see a large, relatively clean rectangular space—the one remaining physical legacy of an earlier time in school history, when a picture of Mao Zedong hung in every classroom.

At the back of each room are "study gardens" (bulletin boards), where students post their better compositions. Other spaces are reserved for the names of students who have been helpful cleaning up or assisting others. Still another location in the "garden" contains a list of all the students and their success in recent personal hygiene inspections, in which hands, front and back, neck, and ears are checked. Those who do well receive a small red flag beside their names. Those who do not receive nothing. For this age group, negative evaluations are not considered helpful, especially when they are made publicly.

The primary school curriculum begins with a concentrated focus on Chinese language and arithmetic, followed by courses in music, physical education, drawing, and calligraphy. From grade three on, depending on the availability and skill level of the teachers, courses are offered in common knowledge (elementary science), geography, history, and painting. Most classes meet for 40 minutes. Lunch break is from 11:30 to 2:00, followed by two more class periods. Though school is over at 3:30, students are encouraged to remain longer to complete their homework or receive additional help from a teacher. Physical education is also included in the daily curriculum. Following an early-morning jog around the school yard, students participate in regular exercises during 10-minute intervals between two class periods throughout the day.

What is sometimes called "moral education" is a vital part of learning in both primary and middle school. Although the subject is not formally taught, it pervades school activity both in and outside the classroom. In meetings with teachers, in summaries of the semester's work, and in various outdoor activities, actions of students are utilized to illustrate important moral precepts such as "being responsible to others." Common illustrations include children who, on finding an object like a pen or workbook on the school playground, return it to the teacher, or children who find pieces of scrap metal and turn them in at the local state-run recycling center. Praise for such action is not given immediately, but reserved for a class meeting, where other children can learn what is good and proper behavior.[6]

Training in social responsibility is further developed through student committees. In the lower primary grades, such committees rely heavily on the teacher's guidance although even here, children elect a monitor to organize simple group tasks. Classes in advanced primary grades elect committees that assume responsibility for leading morning exercises, supervising study periods, collecting homework assignments, and preparing class performances for holiday occasions.

Similar moral education occurs outside the classroom. In harvest season, primary school children are taken out to the fields to watch their parents and neighbors working. Older brothers and sisters from middle school also help with the harvest, as do retired peasant men and women. While there, the children husk small ears of corn left behind by their parents; or, if brought to the threshing ground, they sweep up gleanings of wheat for later storage. Such activity not only instills in the student the value of work, it also emphasizes the importance of being thrifty with what one produces. In all these efforts, the child is reminded to cooperate with teachers, parents, and "grannies," to follow instructions, and to share what one has with others. The values conveyed in such an environment—respect for age, cooperation in work, and generosity—are extensions of similar themes inculcated at home.

Of course, moral education is sometimes overdone, as the parents of one young student found to their chagrin. In the early 1970s during the Cultural Revolution, one son learned at school about a selfless hero named Lei Feng, who spent his whole life helping others rather than concentrating on his own interests and those of his family. The eager pupil, deciding to follow the hero's example of "devoting his life to the collective effort," proceeded to take some manure set aside for his family's courtyard plot and spread it over the adjacent collectively owned brigade land. His family was not impressed.

For the most part, this kind of education is not only pervasive, but effective. Students continually learn proper behavior from teachers, parents, textbooks, radio, newspapers, and television. In all these instances, they are encouraged to help each other, care for each other, learn from each other, and "take each others' happiness as their own." In contrast, activities that cause embarrassment or remarks that emphasize a

---

[6]In this instance, face is "given" rather than "lost" (Hu, 1944, p. 56; Stover & Stover, 1976, p. 206).

negative attribute are discouraged. Envision, for example, a Chinese child's participation in a game like "musical chairs." In an American school, such a game encourages children to be competitive and to look out for themselves. But to young Chinese, the negative aspect is much more noticeable. That is, losers become objects of attention due to their having lost their space—and therefore "face." In China, winning is fun, too. But it should not be achieved at the expense of causing someone else embarrassment. In all kinds of daily activity, including study as well as games, Chinese children are regularly reminded that they must work hard and be sensitive to the needs of others, for only through such effort will their own lives become truly meaningful. Of course, Shitou's classroom behavior is a reminder of the distance that separates reality from the ideal.

Self-discipline encouraged through moral education is also applied to "the three R's." For example, in a second grade classroom, a great deal of effort is spent learning to read Chinese. American children have only 26 letters to memorize and a system of phonetics to assist in recognizing new words. Chinese students have no comparable system to assist them in learning an immensely larger set of characters that are needed to transcribe the Chinese language. Memorization, and its application through intensive reading, is the only way to master the many hundreds of ideographs that children must know in order to read and write effectively. And that takes considerable self-control.

On a typical day, the teacher enters the classroom and puts on the blackboard four words written in *pinyin,* the romanized form of standard Chinese. In primary school, this system is used to help children learn how to pronounce characters, a practice similar to the way in which phonetic systems are used in the United States to assist in learning English pronunciation. Next to each word is placed the corresponding ideograph. The teacher points to the written word and the ideograph, pronouncing it each time. Then, the character is broken down into its subparts and interpretations made.

Finally, using a pointer, the teacher demonstrates the correct steps for writing the ideograph—the stroke order—naming each part at the appropriate moment. Following this demonstration, a volunteer is asked to repeat the process. After being selected, the child stands straight up beside his or her desk and responds by drawing the Chinese character in the air with a finger. Next, the teacher asks the whole class to go through the same procedure. If a volunteer makes an error in answering, the teacher usually does not comment negatively, since any possible embarrassment to the student is to be avoided. Instead, another volunteer is quickly selected. Finally, flash cards are brought out with *pinyin* on one side and the Chinese character on the other. In sequence, the teacher and a volunteer, followed by the rest of the class, all recite what is inscribed on the card held in the air. Blackboard and cards are then used to reinforce each other. The quick pace of the lesson easily holds the attention of most children as they repeat over and over again the drill necessary to retain the new words.

This type of rote learning, while most pronounced in language classes, is not limited to such subject matter. In early primary grades the child is regularly expected to follow the instructions of the teacher. The idea of the child developing individual initiative or creative expression on his or her own or in "free" classroom periods is not a part of the educational process. Art classes, for example, are common in primary school, but the usual tasks involve paper cutting or copying drawings made on the blackboard by the teacher. They do not tap possible artistic talent of the student. So too, in Chinese literature classes, students are expected to respond briefly to precise questions posed by the teacher or participate in group recitation of selected passages of text, rather than discuss or debate possible interpretations of the author's meaning in the selected passage. This cultural patterning in the classroom is consistent with similar learning in the home. Teachers, parents, and other authority figures are knowledgeable. Students and children are not. Therefore, they must listen, study hard, and emulate their elders, so that they too will have that knowledge in the future.

Such an approach to education instills a feeling of group solidarity among students. However, it does little to develop in the child a sense of inquiry, creative challenge, or deductive reasoning. Wanting to explore more deeply the relationship between group-oriented, rote-focused learning so common in the primary school and the more individual oriented, problem-focused approach characteristic of middle-class America, I asked the director of the school near Half Moon Village if I could attend a class and then meet with him afterwards. He expressed his pleasure at my interest and welcomed me to attend any class I wished.

OBSERVING AT SCHOOL

A few minutes before 7:30 on a chilly morning in early December, I arrived at the low one-story adobe and brick buildings that housed the school. The school director, who had been waiting for my arrival, greeted me warmly and then introduced the fourth grade teacher who was to be my host for the morning. Together, we entered his classroom, and I sat down in the back trying unsuccessfully to be inconspicuous. Still, after a few brief stares and whispers, the class began to settle down. The 42 students were about evenly divided between boys and girls. Remembering the story of Su Shitou, I wasn't surprised to see several couples sharing small desks and benches. Young girls, who rarely misbehave in school, were used to help the teacher keep order in this classroom too.

Of the 42 students in the room, 12 wore red scarves indicating their participation in the Young Pioneers, a loosely organized group of children (somewhat similar to the scout movement in the United States) whose activities include those of a helpful nature—cleaning streets, assisting the elderly, and aiding teachers. Although most children between eight or nine and fourteen belong, it was obvious many hadn't bothered to wear their scarves on that day. Only a few children defined as "bad" or "consistently naughty" are excluded from the organization.[7] Needless to say, such naughty children are urged to improve their ways so that they too can become Young Pioneers.

As the teacher began the lessons, first in math, then in language, I watched the children's response. It was difficult, of course, to determine the extent to which my being in the room influenced their behavior. Most were attentive, sitting straight and fairly still unless they were writing, drawing, holding a notebook, or reciting. As the morning progressed, and one set of lessons and exercises followed another, some children began using their pencils and paper for play. A few others simply stared out the window. All sat quietly, however, and only infrequently did anyone disturb the tenor of the class by whispering loudly or getting up and walking around. On such occasions, the teacher first looked sternly at the child and asked that the whispering stop. If that tactic was unsuccessful, he then walked down the aisle and firmly tapped his pencil on the student's desk, at which time all inappropriate activity at the desk quickly ceased.

By midmorning, the old pot-bellied coal stove was laboring rather unsuccessfully to heat the drafty and still cold classroom. Most students wore padded jackets, and a few, mittens or gloves, the latter only being removed when the student wrote in a notebook or on the blackboard. When the next bell rang, indicating an outdoor exercise break, all filed out the door quickly, seeking to throw off the chill brought on by sitting so long in the drafty room. After thanking the fourth grade teacher, I too walked briskly around the schoolyard and then headed for the director's office at the end of the long building. After stepping into his considerably warmer room, we chatted informally for a short while. Then he offered his view of the present educational system. It was one I had heard on several earlier occasions that year while interviewing officials from the Ministry of Education in Beijing.

---

[7]Until 1980, children from landlord, rich peasant, or "class enemy" households could also be excluded.

"Education is improving now." commented the middle-aged director, speaking in a friendly but slightly bored manner.

"Before (meaning during the decade of the Cultural Revolution from 1966 to 1976) . . . the children had no discipline. They didn't behave properly and couldn't learn anything. Now that is all changed. We have ten rules and regulatons for behavior, and they have settled down. Now they are learning very well."

I remembered the large poster I had seen on the classroom wall showing several students happily reading their textbooks. Below the picture was a statement urging everyone to study hard, work diligently, and help the teacher and others when needed.

"What changes do you envision for the future?"

"We want to help the teachers improve their skills. This coming year the commune will hold special enrichment classes for fifth grade teachers under the direction of the Ministry of Education. Unfortunately, our level of teacher training is quite low. Even in communes like this one, close to the city, funds for advanced training of our staff are very limited."

I was reminded of an earlier discussion with the Deputy Vice Minister of Education for Beijing Municipality, who had emphasized that education could not be disconnected from the development of the region as a whole. Given the overall limitations of the country's economy, funds to upgrade educational quality had to be weighed against other modernizing efforts. Because rural students are still the vast majority of the total student population—over 100 million—the costs are immense. To spend one more dollar per student, the government official reminded me, would cost an additional 100 million dollars!

My thoughts returned to the more manageable Half Moon Village. The primary school director continued:

"The Ministry of Education plans to improve rural education in two ways in the next 2 or 3 years. First, we must raise the level of training of those teachers presently in the classroom. This will be done by setting up training centers. Teachers who pass examinations after taking the new courses will be given a more senior status. Second, we want to establish more 'spare-time schools,' so that the new illiteracy that has reemerged over the past ten years can be eliminated. Finally, I hope we will be able to reinstate the 6 years of primary school education that we had before the Cultural Revolution. But, unfortunately, that will not be soon, given the cost involved."

Both primary and secondary education had expanded significantly throughout the commune by the early 1970s. Much of this activity, closely linked to the educational policies of the Cultural Revolution, emphasized the importance of utilizing local initiative. And indeed, many villages established new primary (and junior middle) schools by using local people and urban-trained "educated youth" to staff them. Wages for these new teachers were largely paid by the villagers themselves, through brigade-based work points. In order to obtain additional teachers for the new facilities, the earlier system of 6-year primary schools were reduced to 5—justification for the step being summed up in the slogan "less but better."

This dramatic educational effort put forward during the Cultural Revolution brought the benefits of expanded primary and secondary education to many commune youth, a real achievement, given the large increase in population between 1950 and the 1970s. Yet it did so at the expense of improving educational quality. The local primary school director was obviously identifying with the quality side of this equation. After obtaining some data on the history and size of the school, I expressed my appreciation for his efforts and took my leave. Walking home, I thought about how far the primary schools serving Half Moon and other nearby villages have come from their small beginnings in the early 1950s. Given that progress, it wasn't surprising that attention had now shifted to the junior and senior middle school which still has considerably fewer graduates.

MIDDLE SCHOOL

Of Red Flag Commune's 22,200 students, approximately 8200 are in secondary or middle school. Of the latter, the large majority are enrolled in three-year junior middle schools. The commune also has a few two-year senior middle schools, whose total enrollment is about 2000. However, only one, located near the commune headquarters, offers sufficiently high-level courses (including English) that it can even consider preparing its students to take the nationwide examinations for advanced technical school or university. Not surprisingly, most of these students are sons and daughters of middle-level commune officials or senior-level state workers who live nearby. The highest-level commune officials (whose income is received from the state) usually maintain their residence in Beijing City, thereby enabling their children to have an even better, urban education.

Today, about 80% of all primary school graduates in the commune begin middle school, although less than 30% finish. Of those who do, almost none enter higher education. In 1979, for example, of the senior secondary school students in the commune who chose to take the nationwide examination for entrance to a technical school or university, only eighteen passed.[8] A few went on to university, but the large majority

---

[8]Unfortunately, the number of students taking the examination could not be obtained.

were admitted to a less competitive lower-level technical school. Educational quality at even the best commune school is simply not adequate to meet the competitive standards now set by the Ministry of Education for entrance to higher education. This is true even though nonurban students can receive a lower passing score on the entrance examination than their city counterparts. As a result, the gap between educational opportunities for urban and rural (or in this case, the urban periphery) students is still very much an issue.

Why do so many middle school students drop out before finishing? There are several reasons, most of which pertain in one way or another to economic problems. From the point-of-view of the commune, secondary education costs more to support and requires more highly trained instructors. Furthermore, such teachers usually live in urban areas and have little or no interest in moving to more rural locations. Second, education is not compulsory. Many families feel they cannot spare their sons' and daughters potential income after age fourteen, fifteen, or sixteen. This is particularly true in the poorer villages of the commune. Third, middle schools, and especially the very few senior middle schools, are located quite some distance from those aspiring to attend. With poor roads and lack of bus transportation, some students are unable to attend the school on a daily basis and unable to pay the cost of having someone house them away from home.

Given the unlikelihood of receiving a passing examination grade for university or technical school entrance, most students and their parents see little reason to spend more than a year to two furthering their education. True, some say that fourteen may be a little early to begin work in field or factory. But if the children continue in school, their parents must pay for notebooks, clothing, and other related costs. Poorer peasant families find this difficult. Furthermore, such expenses are always weighed against the gains. Not uncommon is the question: Why waste time in school if the training doesn't help in the future? Especially so when the time can be better spent bringing more income into the household. And finally, some young people do not have either the interest or the ability to complete five additional years of school. Today, students must receive a passing grade of at least 60 to enter both junior and senior middle school. Failures always occur, whether through lack of commitment or ability.

The junior middle school that Half Moon students attend is located several miles from the village. It offers a large range of courses, including Chinese language and literature, algebra, chemistry, biology, physics, agricultural machinery, politics, and Chinese and Western history. In 1979, a young teacher from the school was sent to Beijing Normal College to learn English, and upon her return that subject was added to the curriculum.

The school has one other distinguishing feature: a two story-high classroom, library, and office building—a feature that sets it apart from all other structures for miles around. The over 600 young people who attend this school have use of the enlarged facility due to the efforts of earlier students and staff. In 1971, as part of the "self-reliance in education" phase of the Cultural Revolution, the district government, with the active assistance of students and their parents, built a small pharmaceutical factory and print shop, which was then partially integrated into the school. Throughout China at this time, all students were expected to "combine mental and manual labor," spending at least part of each school week in constructive work.

Once construction was completed, Half Moon and other village students from the area worked part-time in factory or print shop for the 42 weeks of the school year. Eventually, they, together with newly hired local workers, produced enough chemical products for sale to the state that the school was able to pay off its loan for building materials and purchase much-needed equipment and supplies. By 1976 (the last year for which records are available), the annual profits of the factory, all of which are allocated to the school, had reached 100,000 (Chinese) dollars. The total income earned in this educational sideline industry since 1971 is a substantial 530,000 dollars.

For peasants in the area, their junior middle school is a source of real pride. Furthermore, they perceive the effort to provide a middle school education for all eligible students, rather than a selected few, as basically sound. As several parents put it: Fifteen years ago, who thought our children could attend middle school? Now, anyone can go. When local people were asked what positive gains were made in the commune during the Cultural Revolution, this middle school was often given as an illustration.

Today, with educational policy strongly emphasizing the latter side of the quantity–quality equation, one might assume that the earlier Cultural Revolution focus would be completely rejected. But such an assumption is not quite accurate. For example, in the academic year 1978–79, students in the district middle school were divided into two groups, rapid and slow learners, and then placed in different classrooms according to their designation. Within a short period of time, serious problems began to emerge, leading eventually to a discontinuation of the tracking scheme. What happened? Evaluating the change at the end of the year, the principal reported, "It didn't work. It undermined the students' spirit and stereotyped their behavior. Therefore, we have gone back to the earlier system of mixing fast and slow learners in the same classes. Now, the faster ones are given more work and the slower ones more help. The result appears to be much better for everyone."

Most of the revised policies are supported by middle school teachers.

Those almost universally acclaimed are regulations for proper behavior, stricter academic standards, with corresponding emphasis on grades, and removal of "revolutionary" (that is, rhetorical) content from the subject matter. Student responses to these changes are also significant. Academic study is taken much more seriously than when I first visited middle schools in the area in 1972. At that time, political study and manual labor accounted for a much larger portion of the student's time. Academic study, as such, had less appeal.

In Half Moon Village today, the greater commitment to studying is seen everywhere. Younger siblings regularly ask older ones for help in solving basic mathematical problems, writing a short essay, or classifying plants. Students speak positively of their elderly literature teacher, who joyfully uses old Chinese classics as basic reading material—now that they are no longer branded as unacceptable due to a lack of revolutionary content. And they worry about their examinations. Gone is Mao's famous quotation, once used to challenge the educational bureaucracy: "To take an examination is to participate in one's own ambush!" For those seeking positions requiring educational knowledge, examinations are vital. For the rest, simply necessary.

Does education have much influence on one's later employment? The question is an important one in Red Flag Commune. Interestingly, in at least one instance, the answer appears to be negative for young men and affirmative for young women. Commune statistics for the year 1978, reveal that there were 3202 male junior middle school students and 3037 female. However, senior middle school only had 859 young men, while 1035 were young women. Given the approximately equal balance between the sexes in the commune and equal access to school facilities, what is the reason for the difference?

Unfortunately, data was unavailable from the commune for further study. However, in Half Moon, information from a village-level census showed that while there is a strong relationship between having at least some junior middle school education and occupation for young men, its effect on income is not a positive factor. Whereas, for young women, the correlation between education and income is pronounced. It seems, therefore, that young men can enter the work force early without financial penalty, while young women only benefit financially by remaining in school.

PORTRAIT OF AN EDUCATED YOUTH

Not all young people living in Half Moon and surrounding villages have been educated in local schools. A few received their middle school education in Beijing City and other urban locations, following which they were assigned to Red Flag Commune as "sent-down educated youth." This movement, most closely associated with the Cultural Revolution, actually has a longer history—beginning on a small scale in the mid-1950s, increasing gradually from 1962–66, and then expanding dramatically from 1968 to 1976 before finally being concluded in late 1979 (see Bernstein, 1977). Although difficult to estimate, it is probable that between 18 and 20 million urban middle school graduates were sent to the countryside from 1956 to 1979. In this time period, over 7000 were assigned to Red Flag Commune alone, most to work in the state sector.[9]

The goal underlying this effort was threefold: first, to alleviate urban unemployment, which by 1957 had become a problem, particularly in the placement of recently graduated middle school students; second, to enable city youth to bring to the countryside their recently acquired modernizing skills, and in so doing to help reduce the gap between urban and rural populations; and finally, to enable urban youth to live with, contribute to, and learn from the peasants in such a manner as to become ideologically "remolded" in order to assume the role of China's revolutionary successors.

The first aim was largely accomplished. Large-scale unemployment of urban youth did not become a serious problem in China until the late 1970s. The other two aims were successful only in particular instances in which sent-down youth were able to integrate themselves economically and socially into the life of the countryside. For the most part, while the experience of living in villages deepened the urban youths' understanding of the economic poverty and social problems of rural life, it did little to help alleviate that condition for the villagers. At least, that latter point was the characteristic response of Half Moon villagers asked to comment on this massive experiment. In the peasant's view, urban youth lacked the experience, physical stamina, and commitment to be able to work effectively in the fields.[10]

Interested in the innovative nature of the movement to send urban youth "Up to the Mountains and Down to the Villages," while at the same time wanting to learn more of the problems that seriously weakened its effectiveness, I sought out several relocated youth who still lived in the commune. Of those interviewed, one individual stood out as having the

---

[9]Red Flag is fairly unique in having a large state-owned sector as part of its enterprise as well as the usual collective and individual/family ownership of the means of production (see Chance, 1984).

[10]Of course, village residents also wanted to place their own children in better paying jobs such as that of a brigade accountant. As a result sent-down youth not infrequently found themselves relegated to the life of an unskilled field worker even though they had more education than their local counterparts.

special kind of maturity, objectivity, and sensitivity that an anthropological fieldworker always seeks in a key informant. In my case, that person was Zhang Yanzi, a local tractor driver.

Actually, most of her life as a sent-down youth was not spent in the commune. Rather, she had originally volunteered to go to a state farm in China's Northeast. However, the fact that she had discussed her Northeast experiences with Half Moon Village and other commune members is important, for only by such means are local residents able to deepen their knowledge of the sent-down youth movement elsewhere in China. Wanting to learn what other villagers already knew, I asked if she would be willing to share that part of her life history. After some initial hesitation, she agreed.

It wasn't until late fall that she was able to arrange some time in her busy schedule for our get-together. We met at the home of some common friends, who, after offering us tea in the courtyard, excused themselves to clean up and prepare for the evening meal. Sitting on two straight-backed wooden chairs, facing the warm rays of the late afternoon sun, we chatted for a few minutes, sipping our tea and commenting on Half Moon's efforts to obtain a new tractor. It wasn't easy for her, having to exchange her role as tractor driver for that of social historian and analyst. I watched carefully as she tried to relax, leaning forward in her chair and blowing gently into a metal teacup held in both hands. A smudge of grease on her strong angular face helped communicate her occupation as mechanical worker, just as her muscular body spoke of a decade of outdoor work in the countryside. Only one incongruous feature gave any evidence of her earlier life as an urban youth: the slightly waved set of her dark hair.

"Zhang Yanzi, when did you decide to join the movement to the countryside?"

"I first heard about the Going to the Countryside and Settling Down with the Peasants campaign when I was in middle school and decided to apply. After graduation, I was assigned to a state farm in the Northeast and left Beijing on December 5, 1967. Really, it was run as an army production unit, but it was no different than a state farm except for the army. When I arrived, there were only 200 students, but in the following year 3000 more arrived. They came from all over, including Beijing, Shanghai, and Hangzhou. Many educated youth went to the Northeast— in all, about 300,000. Some of the farms had as many as 70, or even 90% youths in each unit. Before we came, there were only a few older cadre and workers. Some had been reassigned in 1955–56, after the Korean War, and others had come from Shandong province in 1958. They were the only older people in the area. Having been in the army, they had a good work history and tradition.

"When I arrived at the farm, my first job was as an agricultural worker. Then I was a primary school teacher for a while. I was only 16 then, and some of my students were older than me. I didn't feel much like teaching them because my parents were intellectuals. During the Cultural Revolution, my father was badly treated by his students, so I didn't want to be a teacher in the school. I complained a lot and finally got transferred to a production unit. The conditions were pretty bad. I fed pigs for a while and then worked as a cook. Finally I became a tractor driver. Then, for health reasons, I went back to teaching in 1976, and was finally transferred here in 1977."

"Were you under any pressure to go to the Northeast?" I asked Zhang.

"In the beginning, no pressure was put on anyone to go. It was all on a volunteer basis. Each individual had to pass the Three O.K.'s. One was from the actual student, one from the family, and one from the school. If there was any disagreement, then the person wouldn't go. Even if you hesitated just before climbing on the train you could stay. But we didn't do that. We were all very enthusiastic.

"Only later was the policy changed. Then, instead of volunteering, every urban family with three educated children had to send two of them to the countryside. Only one could stay behind. If you didn't go, your parents would be organized into a study group. Before my brother went, they had my parents in a study group. When the parents agree that the children can leave, then they stop. Otherwise, they have to continue."

"Were other means also used?"

"If a family still didn't agree, neighborhood committees would come out to the street and beat big gongs, hang up 'big character posters,' and use other kinds of propaganda to persuade you to let your children go. They would just keep on coming back, trying to talk to you over and over again until you finally agreed.

"But in the beginning it wasn't like that. It was different. We went because we were filled with the spirit of conquering difficulties. We knew the countryside was backward and life would be hard. Actually, except for the weather, it wasn't as bad as we thought it was going to be. We had good preparation, and we wanted to make a contribution. But it was cold. We were told that if you went outside in winter without a hat your ears would fall off. Nobody lost their ears, but a few lost some fingers and toes.

"We all ate together in the public dining halls with some of the older workers. Even though conditions were hard, they took pretty good care of us, giving us easier jobs and better housing. There were a few peasants at the farm, and they too were helpful. But not long afterward, the political factionalism began. It started among some of the older workers and soon spread throughout the farm. We got involved, and the younger workers did too. Because we dared to speak up, we were sometimes used as a tool by one faction against another. And more and more students arrived. After a while, all you could see on the farm were educated youth. We were supposed to learn from the peasants, but the only ones around were the storekeeper and a few others. Pretty soon the young people began talking down to the peasants, saying they were dirty and uncultured. They called them 'countrymen.' It sounded good, but it was really sarcastic, sort of like 'country bumpkin.' In units where there were few educated youth, the work was done better, but where they were the majority, the problems became severe."

"Looking back on the overall policy, what is your evaluation of it?"

"I think educated youth going to the countryside was sound. It enabled them to learn more about the good qualities of the peasants and also some production skills. The problem was in the method used during the Cultural Revolution. Some locations didn't really need any more workers. In those places, rather than help the local cadre to do their jobs better, it actually caused a lot of trouble. On the surface, people supported it because Chairman Mao said it was a good thing to do. People agreed publicly, but not privately. That was especially true in the army units. There were few organized plans to open up new areas for agriculture, light industry, or sideline production. In many areas, this lack of planning meant that more labor power had to be used to solve problems rather than mechanization. This is not really the way out for agriculture. It is very tiring and low in efficiency. After a while, a lot of young people began to feel discouraged.

"In all those years, no machines were brought in to improve mechanization or open up new lands. Everyone looked to industry because it was developing faster. Eventually, the educated young people felt that anything was better than working in agriculture. Lots of empty slogans but no increase in production. So they began to talk about returning home. They said, 'If so little can be done here, we should be allowed to return to the city.' I, too, thought about returning. It wasn't an easy decision, and after I came to it, I found it was very hard to accomplish."

"What made you to decide to go home?"

"I have two younger brothers. Both of my parents went to a May Seventh Cadre School early in the Cultural Revolution for political reeducation. One younger brother was still in primary school, and the other had just begun middle school. The whole city was pretty much in chaos, and no one was really able to care for them. My parents were quite concerned about having to leave the two children in the city by themselves, but there was nothing they could do about it except come back from the cadre school and visit them once a month.

"Soon my 11-year-old brother began to running around with some bad kids. He learned to smoke and pretty much stopped going to school. The neighbors tried to help, but he wouldn't listen. My father still calls him illiterate. He thinks London is the capital of the United States and Spartacus is French. He is always confused about these things. Now, he is supposed to be a middle school graduate, but he sure didn't learn much of anything in all those years of school. That's what they got in the way of education during the Cultural Revolution. Anyway, when my older brother graduated and went to the countryside, that left my younger one home alone. So my parents thought I should return. Also, my health wasn't very good. So I applied to go home."

"Was it approved?"

"Going through the 'front door' is very difficult.[11] There are many procedures at different levels of government. And no one cares about you. First, they tell you to wait. Then you have to have a physical examination at the local hospital, followed by a check-up at the higher hospital. They just keep on delaying. They delayed my request for a year and a half, and still nothing happened.

"Some had their requests for going back to the city approved really fast. That raised many questions with the others. How did they do it? What did they depend on? Well, they depended on the 'back door.' At that time, the only way to get anything done was through the back door. My parents were once opposed to going through the back door. They didn't like that style of work. They told me that before the Cultural Revolution,

---

[11]In China, a commonly heard expression is *zou houmen*, which means "going through the back door." The history of this custom is as old as China's bureaucracy. It enables leaders, civil servant cadres, and others to benefit themselves, their kin, and groups they represent through personal ties, contacts, and behind-the-scenes dealings, often to the detriment of the larger population of which they are a part. Going through the "front door" is to follow proper procedures.

backdoorism wasn't so common. So they asked themselves, if the Cultural Revolution is so good, why are there so many back doors now?"

"What happened then?"

"They didn't understand the change. They tried all the approved ways to get me back to the city, and nothing worked. They finally realized that if they didn't use the back door, nothing would happen. That had become my decision too. Others had submitted requests to return later than me, but all were approved except for me. They said my method was no good, that what was needed were cigarettes and wine to send to the right places. 'Go through the back door or it won't work,' they told me.

"I was hesitant. In some ways I wanted to stay in the Northeast. I had already been there almost 10 years. I saw all the changes. On arriving, there were only nine units. By the time I left, there were over 40. I was personally involved in the construction of several new units. It was just grassland before we started. We built a lot of houses, a storage barn, and a day care center. We also reclaimed some land. There is a lot of my work and sweat in that place. So I really loved it.

"Most of the educated youth didn't think about how the peasants had to work that hard all their life. They didn't compare themselves with the peasants at all. They just thought that if they had a way to return to the city, why should they suffer there? Finally, in our company, there were only two educated youth left. All the others had fathers who were able to get them out. Then I began to think, 'How come my parents can't get me back to Beijing? I must not have a good father or I would be back there now. That was my thought at the time. But still, I hadn't really made up my mind. Other things finally helped me to decide."

"What were they?"

"There were two reasons actually. On four different occasions, I applied to go to a university, once to Beijing and three other times in other parts of the country. There were tests then, but it was just a formality. The results didn't make any difference. Who went to school was still based on political requirements and one's class background. Whether one was qualified academically didn't make any difference. When I applied, each time I was approved by my local leadership. On three occasions I was almost admitted, but it fell through because of the political department. I was not a Party member. Secondly, my parents were not workers or peasants or cadres. For these reasons, I was seen as politically inferior, and therefore never was admitted to college. I wanted to learn mechanization, machine building, things like that, or go to agricultural school. I did a lot of self-study and I wanted a university education. But it wasn't going to happen. So I felt very pained, very disappointed.

"The other reason why I finally decided to leave was that the Party branch was trying to train me and educate me. I was hard-working, sincere, and very active. I never complained about the work or that it was difficult and tiring. Also, I felt free to express my ideas. Two times I filled out an application form for Party membership at the local Party branch. Each time, they discussed it with me and then reported to the higher leadership. Neither time did they get approval. The higher leaders told them I was not determined to stay in the countryside. My boyfriend had joined the PLA for 5 years. He was in radar. After his service, he went back home. Because he returned to Beijing, I was in trouble. If my boyfriend is there, people will think I'll want to return also. A person without the determination to remain in the countryside cannot join the Party.

"Then my boyfriend asked his unit if he could be transferred to the Northeast, but it wasn't approved. His family opposed it strongly. So did his friends. The reputation about Heilongjiang (Province) was really pretty bad, especially among Beijing people. Since his family and friends were opposed to his coming, it made me think about why everyone hated the Northeast and the army production unit. Finally, I decided I didn't want to stay there any longer. It was not for me any more.

"It was under these circumstances that I wrote my parents. Before I first left Beijing, my father told me something that made a deep impression on me. In his heart he didn't want me to leave home, but because he was a teacher, a 'bourgeois' intellectual, he couldn't say anything. If he opposed my going, a bad label would be put on him for trying to stop the revolutionary action of youth. So he could only support it. What he said was, 'We are not afraid to have you go now, but we are afraid you won't come back later.' He meant, if I were to go he still wanted me to come back. I have remembered his words all these years.

"After receiving my letter asking if he could get me home, my father wrote back and criticized me, saying I shouldn't think in such terms. I should not go through the back door. I should believe the Party's policy would solve my problems. Of course, I knew these were empty phrases. So I waited. A little later, a close friend of my parents who worked in the Education Ministry visited their home and told them they shouldn't be so honest. 'It won't work,' he said. Then he went on, 'Listen to me. I won't ask you for money. I won't ask you for anything else, not for cigarettes or liquor. Just find a good teacher for my children so they can be well tutored. If you do that, I will make a recommendation for your daughter to be transferred to the countryside near Beijing in Hebei Province. From there it is not difficult to transfer to the city. You can even help me write the recommendation letter.' My parents finally agreed.

"For me, that was great news. In the past, my parents had always helped other people but never asked for help in return. Now they were going to help me. During Spring Festival, my father asked me to come home. He then told me the whole story. I could either be assigned to the countryside in nearby Hebei or I could come home and wait for an assignment there. But I did have to return to the Northeast until the formal transfer and teaching certificate had been approved. It wasn't very long before I was home.

"While at home, I met my uncle who lives in Shijiazhuang. He is also an intellectual, an engineer in the city fire department. Because of his educated background and being a leader in the city, he too was hit during the Cultural Revolution. He was beaten up, and one of his legs was broken. He had three children, just like our family. Two went to the countryside. They both married local people and never came back again. My uncle once praised my father, saying that as a result of the Cultural Revolution, he had become an 'enlightened' intellectual. His remark actually had several meanings. On the one hand, he was telling my father that he was smart to have learned these tricks. Of course, he also knew that it could be dangerous if an intellectual was caught using the back door. But mostly, he was criticizing the Cultural Revolution for corrupting people. My uncle had been a Party member in Shijiazhuang and had had his membership taken away from him. Now, of course, it has been restored. But all during the Cultural Revolution, he never did use the back or side door for his kids. His wife cursed him, saying he was dumb, that he was a stubborn intellectual while my father was the enlightened one. But he never changed. Now he is doing research at an institute in Hebei.

"And you?"

"As for me, after staying home for a while, I had an opportunity to come here, not as a teacher but a tractor driver. After 2 years I could have gone back to Beijing. Still, if I accepted a transfer then I could only receive eighteen dollars a month, whereas if I decided to remain I could get thirty. So, I decided to stay. I like it here driving a tractor. It is a good life."

I looked up from my note-taking. Having been immersed in her story, I was not quite prepared for its abrupt conclusion. And yet, as the cold chill of the late afternoon air replaced the fading rays of the sun, I knew we should stop. So did our friends, who called from inside the house to their two young children who were playing on the other side of the courtyard.

It was time for their dinner and that of the rest of the family. I expressed my appreciation to Zhang for her assistance, said goodbye to our hosts, and took my leave.

Walking down the long lane to the other side of the village, I thought about the interview and how illuminating it was. In one sense, it was simply Zhang Yanzi's story told in her own words. But in another, her life experience and the insights she brought to it had a larger proprietorship, due to the many who could learn from it.

Zhang had committed herself to the same political ideal that guided the self-reliant construction and funding of the middle school near Half Moon. But the material success of this effort was not equaled in the movement of sent-down youth to the Northeast. Poor planning, increasing political factionalism, and corrupt management eventually led her to question the implementation of the whole project, and, therefore, her contribution to it. Like many Chinese youth with similar experiences (see Siu & Stern, 1983; Liang & Shapiro, 1982), she became disillusioned and eventually returned to Beijing. However, what struck me most in listening to the story was not the adversity she overcame or the clarity she brought to her analysis, though both were considerable. Rather, it was Zhang Yanzi's ability to cast her experience in the context of the society's larger goals that gave her commentary such quality—that, and her sense of humanity.

This same orientation guided both the self-reliant building of the middle school near Half Moon Village and frustrated the local principal and teachers, who were no longer able to follow their regular course of instruction. This same political ideal first led Zhang Yanzi to commit her life to helping build a socialist society in the Northeast, and later, to turn away in discouragement, accepting help through the back door that she had earlier rejected. Indeed, through the course of this period, the commitment to being "red" became mired in factionalism defined as purity, while the effort to develop "experts" deteriorated into a decrying of educational standards in general. And the youth, in whose name much of the struggle was fought, were left distrusting many of their leaders, and some, the cause of socialism itself.

Today, China is turning in a new direction, seeking a political approach to education that stresses expert-ness over red-ness, and quality over quantity. Such decisions significantly benefit urban students and teachers at the expense of China's much larger rural based peasant population. Can such a policy be maintained by a government committed to building an egalitarian society? Apparently not, for the present leadership now rejects the egalitarian goals once espoused by Mao Zedong and his associates as being unrealistic in light of the country's low level of economic development.

Such a decision may be expected to draw a sharp response from those dissatisfied with such a course of action. These individuals include peasant youths locked into unskilled labor due to their being unable to pass newly reinstituted nationwide examinations required for entrance to higher level technical schools and colleges; students taught during the "ten lost years" of the Cultural Revolution; and others without adequate training needed to attain higher level positions in the country's technologically oriented drive toward modernization. Can such disparate individuals and small groups ever become unified in their opposition to the existing policy? The answer to that question bears watching in the future.

REFERENCES

Bernstein, T. P. (1977). *Up to the mountains and down to the villages: The transfer of youth from urban to rural China.* New Haven, CT: Yale University Press.

Chance, N. A. (1984). *China's urban villagers: Life in a Beijing commune.* New York: Holt, Rinehart and Winston.

Hu, H. C. (1944). The Chinese concept of face. *American Anthropologist, 46,* 45–64.

Gardner, J. (1982). New directions in educational policy. In J. Grey & G. White (Eds.), *China's new development strategy.* London: Academic Press.

Liang, H., & Shapiro, J. (1982). *Son of the revolution.* New York: Knopf.

Pepper, S. (1978). Education and revolution: The Chinese model revisited. *Asian Survey,* 847–890.

Pepper, S. (1980). Chinese education after Mao: Two steps forward, two steps back and begin again? *China Quarterly, 8.*

Shirk, S. L. (1982). *Competive comrades: Career incentives and student strategies.* Berkeley: University of California Press.

Siu, H., & Stern, Z. (1983). *Mao's harvest: Voices from China's new generation.* New York: Oxford University Press.

Stover, L., & Stover, T. (1976). *China: An anthropological perspective.* Pacific Palisades, CA: Goodyear.

Unger, J. (1982). *Education under Mao: Class and competition in Canton schools, 1960–1980.* New York: Columbia University Press.

Zweig, D. (1978). The Peita debate in education and the fall of Teng Hsiao-p'ing. *China Quarterly, 73,* 140–158.

III AT HOME IN THE USA

EDITORIAL INTRODUCTION

Part III of this volume consists of two groups of chapters: one, Group A, on specific immigrant or minority groups and the ways in which each relates to schools, the other, Group B, on certain dimensions of the mainstream engagement with schooling. They both reflect the recent "return home" of anthropologists alluded to in the introduction to Part II.

Part III begins with John Ogbu's chapter on variability in minority responses to schooling, in which he compares nonimmigrants to immigrants, and ends with a chapter by Susan Jungck in which she describes the effect of computer literacy training upon the curriculum and upon instruction in a middle school and a high school. These two chapters bracket discussions on Punjabi immigrant youth in a California high school, the Silicon Valley Vietnamese community and its reinforcement of Vietnamese occupational adaptations, discontinuity in the home and school environment encountered by Mexican-American children, Papago Indian strategies for mitigating cultural discontinuity in early schooling, the emergence of sexist behavior in nursery school and kindergarten, student/teacher relationships in lower track classes in an academically oriented high school, and the social cliques in the middle school and high school and the criteria for participation in them.

This wide range of concerns serves the purpose of Part III well, and that purpose is to consider as thoroughly as is possible in relatively short compass, significant dimensions of contemporary American school life in relation to its context in American culture. This is a tall order, given the complexity of the American setting. Part III cannot represent all of this complexity but it samples significant aspects of it and does so with the depth and richness that interpretive ethnography makes possible. Part III is a demonstration of what ethnographic methods, informed by a cultural perspective, can do when they are applied to the study of education in our own society.

Part III also showcases the importance of a cross-cultural, comparative perspective. Parts II and III of this book are quite connected, even though the first is about education in other cultures and the second is about education in the United States of America. A cross-cultural perspective acknowledges the validity of lifeways different than one's own, finds them interesting and worthy of attention, and endeavors to understand the difference.

What our colleagues did in Part II and what they do in the first chapters of Part III exhibit all of the characteristics of a cross-cultural, anthropological approach, but there is a difference. In the situations described and analyzed by Ogbu (Black), Gibson (Punjabi), Finnan (Vietnamese), Delgado-Gaitan (Mexican-American), and Macias (Papago Indian) there is not only the culture of whatever minority group is being discussed to consider. The major focus is on the interaction between the mainstream and the minority group. This is where the culturally phrased American dialogue becomes particularly obvious.

The indigenous minorities in the United States—black, Mexican-American, and American Indian—interact with mainstream institutions in ways predetermined by history. Blacks came and endured as slaves. Indians were a militarily conquered minority (though the Papago themselves were among the peaceful people). The Mexicans were both a conquered minority as the Southwest became U. S. territory, and a source of low caste, transient labor. The history of the relations of these minorities with the mainstream left a heritage of bitterness and hostility that in varying degrees is a factor in relationships between them and mainstream institutions and persons now. Much of the American dialogue about freedom and equality seems hollow to them, in the shadow of this heritage. And yet, indigenous American minorities have always held to the hope that in the end they, too, could participate without prejudice in the process and rewards of our productive mainstream culture. Their hope has found its counterpart among many, perhaps now the majority, of mainstream Americans. The American dialogue, carried on in shifting but recognizable forms since Independence, has been and is preoccupied with mainstream/minority relationships in one form or another. A fair and just solution to the problematic aspects of this relationship are essential to the continuing health of our society.

The solutions cannot be created alone by mainstream institutions, including schools. The heritage of bitterness and hostility acquired from slavery, conquest, and exploitation, and nourished by racism and prejudice, must be overcome on *both* sides.

The relations between the new immigrants and the mainstream, as displayed in Gibson's, Finnan's, and Ogbu's analytic interpretations shed light on the situation of indigenous American minorities. The new immigrants do not have the heritage of the indigenous minorities as a handicap. For this and other reasons, such as the strong educational background of the Vietnamese refugees of 1975, the new immigrants have done relatively well in mainstream schools despite great cultural and linguistic differences. They do well because they regard schools and schooling as essential instrumentalities to success in their new life, and because their home cultures provide them with familial security, sources of self-esteem, and value orientations toward success in both material and idealistic terms, irrespective of cultural differences.

There is no necessary conflict between a minority home culture and the mainstream. If we were to know the full variety of home and family cultures in the mainstream we would understand that better. The instrumentalities of mainstream business, professional, and social culture can be acquired by anyone with the application of intelligence and willing hard work. Increasingly, in American life, one's personal life, one's personal culture, is regarded as one's own business, and the multifaceted nature of American life makes it possible for virtually anyone to find like-minded peers.

The chapters on the interaction of mainstream schools and culture (Group B) are focused on quite different issues from those in Group A of Part III. Canaan's chapter on cliques in middle school and high school underlines how important social life is among American adolescents and how the school is a major setting for its happening. In fact, Gibson's description of the Punjabi adjustment in a California high school suggests that the main business of mainstream adolescents, unlike the Punjabi youth, is learning to get along in the peer group, rather than learning math and science and becoming literate.

Goodenough's chapter shows us how sexism, so deeply ingrained in mainstream culture, emerges in nursery and kindergarten groups, with little boys excluding little girls from their play, or exploiting them when they are admitted. She also shows us the conditions of nonsexist behavior, in the same context.

Page's analysis of lower track classrooms in an academically oriented upper middle class mid-western high school exposes a routine of interaction based on tacit understandings held by both the teachers and students that makes a mockery of teaching and learning. And finally, Jungck's report on computer literacy in a mainstream middle school raises hard questions about the immediate and long-range future of computer-oriented and computer-influenced schooling.

Part III raises questions and defines problems with which we will be struggling for some time to come. The chapters within it raise the questions but also detail the basic processes of which they are an expression. Our understanding of these processes is deepened. Through this level of complex understanding, afforded by interpretive ethnography, solutions to our problems can be generated.

The Editors

GROUP A:
MULTICULTURALISM, IMMIGRANTS, AND MINORITIES

The Author and His Chapter

John U. Ogbu, a native of Nigeria, is a professor of anthropology at the University of California, Berkeley. He received his A.B., M.A., and Ph.D. in anthropology at Berkeley. His major fields of research include education and culture, cross-cultural problems in minority education, social stratification, and contemporary United States society. Professor Ogbu has done field work in Malawi, Nigeria and in Stockton, California. His major publications include *The Next Generation: An Ethnography of Education in an Urban Neighborhood* (Academic Press, 1974), *Minority Education and Caste: The American System in Cross-cultural Perspective* (Academic Press, 1978). His articles have appeared in several journals, including *Child Development, Comparative Education Review, American Ethnologists, Africa,* and *Anthropology and Education Quarterly.* He is currently doing a cross-cultural research on the school experiences of immigrant and nonimmigrant minorities.

In his chapter he discusses the school experience of immigrants and nonimmigrants in the United States. Though he acknowledges the effect of cultural discontinuity between home and school he points to other factors as being more important in their adjustment. Immigrants hold a different model of school and the relationship of schools to success, than do indigenous minorities. This model influences behavior in ways advantageous to the immigrants. How this happens is a subject of his chapter.

Dr. Ogbu's far-reaching and substantial analysis is essential to an understanding of not only the situation of the new immigrants but also that of the indigenous minorities in the United States. His chapter supplies necessary background for the analyses to follow, of the Punjabi, Vietnamese, Mexican-American, and Papago Indian engagement with schooling.

The Editors

11

Variability in Minority Responses to Schooling: Nonimmigrants vs. Immigrants

John U. Ogbu
University of California, Berkeley

INTRODUCTION

In anthropological study of minority education in modern urban industrial societies like the United States, it is conventional to compare minority children's cultural adjustment in school and their academic achievement with the adjustment and achievement of majority or dominant-group children. In the area of academic achievement—the substantive focus of this chapter—there is evidence that the minorities do considerably less well. We have generally tried to explain the lower academic achievement of the minorities in terms of cultural discontinuities. That is, we often say that minority children do not do well in school because the curriculum materials and teaching methods of the schools are different from the cultural content and teaching and learning styles of the children's cultures. We tend to stress not only the importance of differences in cultural contents and styles of teaching and learning, but also differences in values, communication styles, learning styles and styles in social interaction and social relations.

Furthermore, we have generally compared only those minority groups who are doing poorly with the majority groups. We have done less in terms of comparing the minority groups who do well in school with the majority groups. If we had, we might have found that the successful minorities do not necessarily initially share the same cultural attributes with the dominant groups. Knowing this probably would have forced us to revise our explanations of why other minorities are less successful.

Even rarer is the effort to compare various minority groups them-

selves. Yet, such a comparison appears to have theoretical and methodological significance for anthropology of education. Furthermore, it is the
kind of study that will certainly provide some useful insights to those
engaged in improving the academic achievement of the less successful
minorities. It is with the consideration of the theoretical, methodological,
and practical value of this kind of comparative approach that this chapter
is written.

VARIABILITY IN MINORITY ACADEMIC ACHIEVEMENT

There is plenty of evidence from studies in Britain (Brake, 1980; Ogbu,
1978; Parliamentary Select Committee Report, 1973), Israel (Lewis, 1979;
Ortar, 1967; Rosenfeld, 1973), Japan (DeVos, 1973; Rohlen, 1983), Sweden (Skutnabb-Kangas & Toukoma, 1976, cited in Cummins, 1982),
Canada (Kahn, 1983) and the United States (Coleman et al., 1966; Ogbu,
1978; Slade, 1982) that minority groups do less well in academic achievement than dominant groups. But the evidence also suggests that the lower
academic achievement of the minorities is *disproportionate* and *persistent*
only among some minority groups, while it is *transitory* among others and
almost nonexistent among still other minority groups. Let me briefly
review some of the cross-cultural evidence of this variability in the
academic performance of the minorities, beginning with my own findings
in Stockton, California.

From 1968 to 1970 I studied the academic records from the kindergarten through grade 12. These were black, Chinese, Filipino, Japanese,
Mexican-American and white students. I found that the Chinese, Filip-
pino, and Japanese students did considerably better than black and
Mexican American students. I also found that in one junior high school
the ethnic representation in the honor roll was the reverse of the ethnic
populations. The rank order in the honor roll was Chinese, Japanese,
Filipino, white, black and Mexican American. That is, three minority
groups ranked above the dominant white, while two ranked below. This
variability predated my research. For example, a survey of Stockton
schools in the 1930s found that many Mexican-American students and
Asian students were experiencing learning difficulties due to language
differences/nonfamiliarity with the English language. But another survey
in 1947 revealed that the Asian students no longer had language problems;
in fact, they were by this time doing better than whites as indicated by the
fact that their proportional representation at the junior college level
(grades 13 and 14) far exceeded that of the whites, being about 250% of
their expected rate. In contrast, only 5% of the blacks who were in the 7th
and 8th grades made it to the junior college level. The Mexican Americans
closely followed the blacks (Sears et al., 1938; SUSD, 1948).

For the United States as a whole, this variability in the pattern of
minority school performance has been documented in numerous studies.

The Coleman Report (Coleman et al., 1966), for example, found that Asian-American students did considerably better than black Americans, Mexican Americans, American Indians and Puerto Ricans in reading, verbal ability and math tests. Educational Testing Service's report on the performance of various ethnic groups on the SAT for 1980–81, published by *The New York Times* of October 24, 1982, showed the same variability (Slade, 1982). A review of the ability testing by a committee of the National Academy of Sciences published in 1982 also found that Asian-American students were doing better than blacks, American Indians, Mexican-American and Puerto Rican students (Wigdor & Garner, 1982, pp. 71–78).

A similar variability in the pattern of minority school performance is found in other countries as well. In *Britain,* for example, *West Indians* do far less well in school than East Asian and other minorities (Ogbu, 1978). Cummins (1982) reports that in *Ontario, Canada, French Canadians* do less well in school than Canadian-born children of immigrant minorities and that the latter tend to do "as well or better than equivalent SES Anglo students." In *New Zealand,* children of immigrant Polynesians tend to do better in school than the *native Maoris,* another Polynesian population with similar language and culture (Penhoe, personal communication).

Studies of the same minorities in two or more different settings reveal some interesting patterns: A minority group doing poorly in one country in regular school academic work and in standardized tests is often found to be doing quite well in another country where it has an immigrant status. A good example is the case of the *Japanese Buraku outcaste.* In Japan itself, Buraku students continued to massively underperform when compared with the dominant Ippan group. But in the United States where Americans treat the Buraku exactly the same way they treat other Japanese immigrants, the Buraku do at least as well in school as their other Japanese counterparts (Ito, 1967; Shimahara, 1983). Another interesting and instructive case is that of the Finns. The academic performance of Finnish children in Sweden is reported to be very low; whereas Finnish children in Australia are reported to be doing very well in school. It should be noted that the Finns were for a long period colonized by the Swedes (Skutunabb-Kangas & Toukomaa, 1976, cited in Cummins, 1982). The *Koreans* are yet another interesting example. In Japan where the Koreans originally migrated to as colonial subjects, their school performance continues to be very poor when compared with the school performance of the dominant Ippan group. However, in the United States where the Koreans are voluntary immigrants, they are doing just as well in school as other Asian-American students (DeVos, 1983; Loo, Schneider, & Werner, 1984). Finally, I mention that while West Indian children in Britain (which they regard as their "motherland") are at the bottom of the academic totem pole, they appear to be relatively successful in American schools. In the United States they view themselves as immigrants (Fordham, 1984).

One conclusion from this brief survey of variability in minority school performance in the United States and elsewhere is that the minorities who are doing relatively well in school appear to be immigrants or those who regard themselves as immigrants; while the minorities who are not doing well in school appear to be indigenous minorities or subjects of former colonial territories. Furthermore, the school performance of an indigenous minority or a former colonial subject people tends to improve when the same minority group becomes an immigrant group in another society. Why do the immigrants generally do relatively well in school? Why do the indigenous minorities not do so well in school? These are the questions we attempt to answer in the remainder of this chapter.

My main argument in comparing the two types of minorities may be summarized as follows. For historical, structural, and psychological reasons, the two types of minorities, even within the same educational system, perceive, interpret, and respond differently. That is, they have different folk models of schooling which encourage different patterns of behavior. The nonimmigrant minorities tend to equate schooling with one-way acculturation or assimilation into the dominant group which they consciously and unconsciously resist. Consequently they do not behave in a manner that maximizes academic success. In fact, they are generally characterized by what may be called low-effort syndrome or lack of persevering academic effort. The immigrant minorities, on the other hand, do not equate schooling with acculturation or assimilation and feel freer to adopt behaviors that enhance school success. Unlike the nonimmigrants who see schooling as one-way acculturation, the immigrants adopt what may be called an alternation model which permits them to behave one way in the school setting and another when they are at home or in the community.

In the following pages I try to describe and explain these differences in models of schooling and responses, focusing on black Americans and Chinese.

NONIMMIGRANT MINORITIES

There are two types of indigenous or nonimmigrant minorities, namely, autonomous minorities and castelike minorities. *Autonomous minorities* are primarily minorities in a numerical sense. They may be victims of prejudice but not stratification. They are not usually characterized by persistent disproportionate school failure. They are, therefore, not the focus of this presentation.

Castelike minorities are minorities incorporated into a society more or less involuntarily and permanently through slavery, conquest, and colonization. *Black Americans* are a good example because they were brought to the United States as slaves and after emancipation relegated to caste-like status through legal and extralegal devices (Berreman, 1960, pp. 120–127, 1967, pp. 308–324; Myrdal, 1944; Davis, Gardner, & Gardner, 1965). *American Indians,* the original owners of the land were incorporated through conquest and then forced into reservations; and initially *Mexican Americans* in the Southwestern United States were also incorporated through conquest and displacement from power; those who later immigrated from Mexico were accorded the subordinate status of the conquered group. Membership in a castelike minority group is usually acquired at birth and permanent. That is, however, much less true for American Indians, Mexican Americans and Puerto Ricans than it is for black Americans partly because of the wide range of color differences within each of these groups which varies from pure white to pure black (Nava, 1970; Senior, 1972; U.S. Department of Interior, Bureau of Indian Affairs, 1974). With the structural subordination of the minorities firmly established, both the exploitation by the dominant group and the responses of the minorities combine to produce "secondary cultural differences" in contrast to primary cultural differences characteristic of immigrant minorities.

Dominant-Group Exploitation.   Dominant-group members usually rationalize their exploitation of castelike minorities by what DeVos (1967, 1984) calls "caste thinking," which he says always involves the belief that there is some unalterable biological, religious or social inferiority that distinguishes members of the minority group from those of the dominant group. They emotionally and strongly believe in this indelible mark and take steps to prevent the minorities from contaminating them by instituting appropriate barriers, such as prohibition of intermarriage, residential segregation, and the like. All these forms of treatment are clearly exemplified by the experience of black Americans.

The exploitation by the dominant group is both instrumental (e.g., economic exploitation through job ceiling) and expressive (e.g., use of the minorities for scapegoating). There are many ways in which the minorities are exploited instrumentally, but in the context of formal education economic exploitation is primary. Black Americans have, for example, until recently been relegated to menial jobs and denied chances of working at more desirable and better paying jobs based on individual training (education) and ability (Norgren & Hill, 1964). The concept of *job ceiling* probably best describes the economic exploitation of blacks and similar minorities. A job ceiling consists of formal statutes and informal practices that limit the access of the minorities to more desirable occupations, truncate their opportunities, and narrowly channel the potential returns that the minorities could expect to get from their education (Mickelson, 1983). At the same time the job ceiling allows dominant-group members to compete more easily and freely above that ceiling for the more desirable jobs on the basis of individual training (education) and ability. The instrumental exploitation usually becomes incorporated into the cultural beliefs and practices of the dominant group in the course of time.

One result of the job ceiling and similar barriers is that castelike minorities have fewer resources and opportunities for upward social mobility or opportunity to achieve "middle-class" status. Their upward social mobility within the universe open to them in the wider society moreover, often requires some additional criteria, such as clientship, that is not required of members of the dominant group. Another result of the job ceiling is that most individual members of castelike minority group remain relatively poor or at the level of margin of subsistence. As a result, and as is indicated below, the minorities' perceptions of the job ceiling greatly influence their instrumental responses which, in turn, generate attitudes and competencies that are not necessarily compatible with those required to do well academically in school.

Caste thinking—the belief that castelike minorities are inferior—permits members of the dominant group to exploit the minorities expressively, too, such as using the minorities as scapegoats. Dominant-group members tend to project onto the minorities alleged inborn and societal traits they do not like. According to DeVos (1967), different castelike societies project onto their minorities different impurities. For example, in Japan the Ippan dominant group consider as most reprehensible Buraku Outcastes' supposed violent and aggressive behavior. The Ippan also think of the Buraku as disease-ridden. White Americans, on the other hand, emphasize the supposed primitive sexuality of black Americans and to some extent the latter's "dirtiness" and "aggressiveness." Dollard (1957) points out that in southern United States projections of sexual fantasies enabled white men to maintain their image of ideal white womanhood while exploiting black women sexually. DeVos (1984) suggests that scapegoating and other projections generally serve to relieve the intrapsychic stress of dominant-group members which arises in times of social, political, and economic crisis. Eventually the projections achieve "autonomous functioning," i.e., they continue to exist after the crises that initially brought them into existence have been resolved. The projections, together with the feelings of aversion, revulsion, and disgust they evoke come to be incorporated into the culture of the dominant group and children learn them "naturally" as they learn other aspects of their culture. It is for this reason that expressive exploitation tends to persist even after the instrumental exploitation like the job ceiling has been formally abolished.

Castelike Minority Responses. Castelike minorities do not accept their denigrated status or dominant-group's rationalization of their subordination and exploitation. On the other hand, they do not totally escape the effects of the denigration and rationalization (Berreman, 1967, p. 314; Tuden & Plotnicov, 1970). And they, in turn, usually develop their own version of the rationalization. Furthermore, they develop appropriate instrumental and expressive responses to cope with their subordination and exploitation.

One aspect of the rationalization of the minorities relevant to the problem of schooling is their epistemology—their explanation of how their society works and their place within it—which is different from the epistemology of the dominant group. Not only do the minorities reject dominant group's rationalization of the existing social order, but they also develop what may be called *an institutionalized discrimination perspective* (Lewis, 1981; Ogbu, 1974), whereby the minorities argue that they cannot advance into the mainstream of society through individual efforts in school or by adopting the cultural practices of the dominant group. That is, on the basis of their repeated personal and group experiences the minorities have come to believe that they cannot "make it" simply by following the rules of behavior for achievement that "work" for the dominant group. Consequently they tend to develop what black Americans call "survival strategies" to cope with economic (e.g., job ceiling), social, and political subordination and exploitation by the dominant group.

In the economic sphere, for example, black Americans have developed several "survival strategies" to *circumvent, raise,* or *eliminate* the job ceiling. These strategies include clientship or "uncle tomming," collective struggle or "civil rights activities," and hustling. Note that among the minorities collective struggle includes rioting and other activities not necessarily legitimated by the dominant group but which nevertheless call attention to the grievances of the minorities and sometimes increase their access to better education, jobs, housing, and the like. Other minorities may employ these and other strategies according to their own circumstances. The survival strategies tend, however, to become institutionalized in the minorities' cultures in the course of time. They also give rise to norms, values, and competencies which may differ markedly from those of the dominant group. These developments have many implications for the schooling of the minorities.

Castelike minorities also respond expressively, such as by developing oppositional collective identity systems and oppositional cultural systems. Specifically, black Americans, for example, developed their sense of peoplehood or collective social identity from their collective experience of subordination and exploitation, from the fact that even though they may have initially been members of different groups or different tribes in Africa with different cultures and identity systems, and, even though they lived in different parts of the United States, they experienced similar encompassing and enduring exploitation and derogation from white Americans. That is, regardless of their place of origin in Africa, their place of residence in America, and, regardless of their individual abilities and training, their individual economic status and physical appearance, black Americans learned in the course of their history that they could not easily or freely escape from their birth-ascribed membership in a subordinate, disparaged group. They also realized that they were not assimilated and could not expect to be assimilated like various white immigrant groups for whom the door of assimilation was open; nor could they return to their "homeland" as some nonwhite immigrants did. Furthermore, castelike minorities recognize that their demeaning experiences, their lack of opportunities for advancement, and their generally unsatisfactory life situation were and are due to dominant group's exploitation and not because of anything inherently wrong with them. Even for those who have the option to pass only a few may do so successfully because of the social and psychological costs to the individual attempting to pass (see Burma, 1946, pp. 18–22; Warner, Junker, & Adams, 1941, especially chap. 4, in the case of black Americans). Under this circumstance, blacks and similar minorities (Spicer, 1966, 1971; Castile & Kushner, 1981) respond by what DeVos (1967) calls "an ethnic consolidation" or collective sense of identity (Apel, 1970; Green, 1981; Mullings, 1978).

Collective oppositional identity system serves some major functions for individual minority-group members. For example, it promotes formation of peer groups which tend to satisfy their affiliative needs that are apparently not met by the family and other institutions. DeVos (1984) suggests that effectiveness of castelike minority families to satisfy the affiliative needs of their members is weakened by a castelike stratification system which denies minority-group males material and other resources needed to perform adequately the husband-father role. In the case of black Americans, however, it also appears that peer groups are important historically because they served as a survival institution during slavery when black families were frequently broken up. According to Rawick (1972, cited in Fordham, 1984), blacks adapted childrearing practices that emphasized the importance of affiliation with more enduring groups outside the family, such as peer groups and the "community"; this resulted in developing a kind of "fictive kinship" links with the feelings with one's peers.

Closely associated with the development of a collective oppositional identity system is the evolution of an oppositional cultural system with several mechanisms to protect and maintain the identity system. These mechanisms include collective struggle, deviant behaviors (i.e., deviant from the point of view of the dominant group), collective hatred for the dominant group, and cultural inversion. I say more about cultural inversion because it is a mechanism more manifested by minority students in school setting.

Cultural inversion is the tendency for members of one population (e.g., black Americans) to regard certain forms of behaviors, certain events, symbols and meanings as *not appropriate* for them because they are characteristic of members of another population (e.g., white Americans); at the same time, however, they claim other forms of behaviors, other events, symbols, and meanings as appropriate for them *because these are not* characteristic of the members of the other population. Thus what is appropriate or even legitimate behavior for the in-group members is defined in opposition to the practices and preferences of the members of an out-group.

Cultural inversion is sometimes used to repudiate negative stereotypes or derogatory images attributed to the minorities by members of the dominant group. Sometimes it is used as a strategy to manipulate dominant-group members or for "getting even" with them, or, as Holt puts it in the case of black Americans, "turn the table against whites." Cultural inversion may take several forms. For example, it may include hidden meanings of words and statements (Bontemps, 1969); different notions of time and its uses (Weis, in press); or different emphasis on language dialects and communication styles (Baugh, 1984; Holt, 1972); or it may be an investure of positive values on negative images and the like (Holt, 1972). It may simply be an outright rejection of the other group's preferences or what they consider appropriate behavior in a given setting like the school (Petroni, 1970).

Cultural inversion along with other oppositional elements result in the coexistence of two opposing cultural frames of reference or ideals orienting behavior, one considered appropriate for the minorities and the other for the dominant group. Cultural frames of reference or behavior models are strongly associated with both the minorities' emotional attachment and their sense of collective identity. Consequently, those who try to behave like the dominant group or who try to cross cultural boundaries may encounter opposition from other minority-group members, especially from their peers. Peer group members oppose crossing cultural boundaries partly because of their collective animosity against the dominant group and partly because it threatens their cohesiveness as a group which serves as a source of their affiliative gratification and sense of collective social identity (DeVos, 1984). Individual minority-group members trying to cross cultural boundaries also experience internal and discouraging conflicts from a shared sense of social identity and from uncertainty of being accepted by the dominant group. It should be pointed out, however, that cultural inversion is practiced selectively, that is, it occurs in some areas but not in other areas. Why some aspects of culture are selected for cultural inversion is a matter that deserves further study.

Cultural Consequences

These developments—minorities' epistemological, instrumental, and expressive responses to their subordination and exploitation—have distinctive cultural consequences for the minorities. In the case of black Americans, for example, the interlocking of the job ceiling, social, and residential segregation and their lack of political power and influence, created for blacks a special type of physical, sociocultural, and psychological environment. Within this environment blacks developed adaptive lifestyles different in many respects from the adaptive lifestyles of white Americans. As indicated earlier, black Americans' encounter with the job ceiling and similar barriers in other areas of opportunity structure probably gave rise to a high degree of disillusionment about future opportunities; it probably led to somewhat different "folk theories" about success and failure; longstanding conflicts with the schools and other institutions controlled by white people gave rise to distrust of these institutions. The survival strategies gave rise to norms, competencies, and behaviors that are distinct.

However, what makes the cultures of castelike minorities like black Americans truly different from mainstream culture is not that the contents of black culture are derived from African sources, as some investigators tend to claim; nor is it that the manifest contents of black and white cultures are different, as some others try to claim. Differences in contents per se are not the overriding problem. Rather, it is that black culture is characterized by elements of opposition and ambivalence in its relation to white culture or mainstream culture. At the ideational level the opposition is embodied in the belief among blacks that the black cultural frame of reference is different from the white cultural frame of reference as noted earlier. At the psychological level the ambivalence and opposition lie in the "double consciousness" of cultural dualism which DuBois (1903) noted at the turn of the century. It is this oppositional and ambivalent quality creating for the individual what DeVos (1967, 1984) refers to as "affective dissonance" and permeating various domains of black culture, that clearly makes black culture different from white culture; it is this that distinguishes castelike minority culture from the cultures of immigrant minorities; and it is this aspect of castelike minority culture that is most relevant to their academic performance because of the tendency of castelike minorities to equate the culture of the schools with the culture of the dominant group and to equate schooling with acculturation.

Social Change.   The castelike situation I have described is not static or uniform. In the United States, for example, efforts have been made since the mid-1960s to abolish the statutes and informal practices through which blacks and similar minorities have been exploited (Ogbu, 1978). Polls taken since the mid-1960s show that caste thinking among whites has also been decreasing. However, vestiges of subordination and exploitation remain, as evidenced by occasional media reports, findings of research or special investigations (see, for example, Governor's Task Force On Civil Rights, State of California: *Report On Racial, Ethnic And Religious Violence In California*, 1982), and occasional rulings by state and federal judges.

The minorities have not always responded to subordination and exploitation uniformly. Moreover, the changes in the beliefs and practices of the dominant group that have occurred since the mid-1960s have also affected the responses of the minorities. For example, among blacks, some segments, especially the young college-educated, middle-class blacks have benefited disproportionately from the changes in the opportunity structures. They now have more access to jobs above the job ceiling and to desirable social and political positions in the wider society than they had before the mid-1960s. Their new positions and opportunities often require and enhance white middle-class type of education and cultural know-how. It is, therefore, likely that many of these blacks and their children are freer from the logic of black cultural frame of reference and identity system.

On the other hand, for a larger segment of the black population, especially among inner-city blacks, no significant improvements in social, political, and economic opportunities of the type described earlier have taken place. In fact, their economic opportunities and conditions seem to have become worse (Hunter, 1980; Jones, 1984). Among these blacks and similar segments of the other castelike minorities, the cultural beliefs and practices described earlier still prevail and their implications for schooling are still evident. I now turn to suggest how these beliefs and practices influence the academic achievement of the minorities.

Response to Schooling.   Although there are bound to be differences in the way various castelike minorities have historically responded to education, it can generally be said in the case of black Americans that they have always desired education. Several reasons have been given for the high and persistent educational aspirations of blacks. According to Powdermaker (1968, p. 392) who studied blacks in Mississippi in the 1930s, most blacks believed that education would give them equal status with whites and thereby resolve the "race problems." Blacks are also reported to view education as the route to escape from their menial tasks because it would give them access to "clean jobs." Warner, Havighurst, and Loeb (1944) say that education was historically one of few available routes open to blacks for upward social mobility. As a result blacks looked to education for self-advancement long before whites began to do so in the 1930s when the latter found other avenues (e.g., cheap land, expanding frontiers, and expanding businesses and industries) shrinking. Thus, blacks have long regarded education as very important in their attempt to improve their material and social conditions. They have generally interpreted their initial exclusion from the public schools, their subsequent segregation and inferior education as *designed* by white people to prevent them from qualifying for the more desirable jobs open to the whites and to prevent them from attaining equal status with the whites. Consequently, a significant part of their collective struggle has been devoted to gain more access to education and to convince or force white people and the schools they control to provide them with *equal* and *quality* education.

In spite of their faith that education would solve their material and social or racial problems, and in spite of their collective struggle for equal access to good schooling, it appears that there are other aspects of their responses to subordination and exploitation by the dominant group that adversely affect the chances of black Americans to succeed academically in school. I briefly suggest how these responses contribute to the *problem of persistent disproportionate school failure.*

Low Effort Syndrome and Other Factors Producing Minority School Failure. My main argument is that some of the responses by castelike minorities to their subordination and exploitation described earlier produce some group and personal attributes, including psychological states, which discourage them from maximizing their academic efforts. As a result their achievement is low. For example, among black Americans the responses to the job ceiling include differential folk theories of success and failure in American society. These theories, in turn, generate disillusionment and ambivalence about schooling that discourage exerting sufficient academic efforts. Although black parents verbally stress the importance of education and may endeavor to support their children's education materially, they also convey to the children subtly and unknowingly contradictory messages powerful enough to cancel out much of their educational encouragement and efforts. They do so through the actual texture of their own lives and the discussions of the textures of the lives of other adult blacks characterized by unemployment, underemployment, and discrimination. From these powerful messages and cultural knowledge, even young black children begin to form their image of the connection or lack of it between school success and future occupational status of black people. The children's own subsequent experiences of failure to obtain part-time jobs or summer jobs only confirm in their minds the validity of these contradictory messages. Eventually they learn to blame the system, including the schools, for failure on their parents' part and for their own failure, and become fatalistic, failing to develop serious attitudes and persevering efforts toward their schoolwork (Ogbu, 1984a).

I pointed out earlier that blacks interpret their initial exclusion from the public schools and subsequent segregation and other differential treatment as designed to prevent them from qualifying for good jobs open to whites. They therefore have generally "fought" rather than "worked with" the schools "for better education." This perpetual fighting or conflict with the schools has resulted in deep distrust, permeating many aspects of the relationship between blacks and the schools. The general feeling among blacks is that the public schools cannot be trusted to educate black children like they educate white children. I have suggested that parents, the black community, and the media communicate these conflicts and distrust to black children and that the existing conflicts and distrust make it difficult for the children to accept, internalize, and follow school rules of behavior for achievement.

The survival strategies in many ways ameliorate the burden of exploitation and subordination of the minorities. But they also encourage attitudes and competencies or behaviors that are not necessarily compatible with doing well in academic school work. For example, clientship teaches black children the manipulative attitudes, skills, and behaviors used by their parents and others in dealing with white people and the institutions like the welfare agency they control rather than task-oriented attitudes and effort facilitating academic accomplishments. Collective struggle to which black children are well exposed from infancy teaches them to blame the system for high unemployment and other problems facing their community, including academic problems. And hustling teaches them, among other things, that one should "make it without working," especially working for white people. In some cases work for white people or "the Whiteman's thing" includes academic or schoolwork (Foster, 1974; Silverstein & Krate, 1975).

Differences in norms and competencies and behaviors generated by these survival strategies might be seen by the anthropologist as a good case of cultural discontinuities or cultural conflict. But one should go further to note that this is a special kind of cultural discontinuity arising from *secondary cultural differences* (Ogbu, 1982). Secondary cultural differences arise from responses of subordinate minorities to their treatment by the dominant group. As a result they are a part of *boundary-maintaining mechanisms* which do not readily change through contact between the minorities and majority-group members. They differ from the *primary cultural differences* accompanying immigrant minorities from outside their host society. The primary cultural differences are not a part of boundary-maintaining mechanisms and are less resistant to change in contact situations.

The secondary cultural differences are further distinguished by the attribute of *style,* whereas the primary cultural differences have more to do with *content.* For example, most writers on the problem of cultural discontinuities in castelike minority schooling generally stress the problem of style: cognitive style (Shade, 1982), communication style (Gumperz, 1982; Kochman, 1982), interaction style (Erickson & Mohatt, 1982), and learning style (Boykin, 1980; Philips, 1976). Studies of immigrant minorities (Gibson, 1983; Guthrie, 1983) like studies of non-Western peoples receiving Western-type schooling (Gay & Cole, 1967; Lancy, 1983) suggest differences in content as the problem.

The boundary-maintenance function and the attribute of style of the secondary cultural differences are sometimes expressed by the minorities in the form of cultural inversion. All these are really aspects of a wider phenomenon, namely, persistent oppositional cultural frame of reference or behavior model, which is affectively associated with the minorities' collective oppositional identity. There is a tendency on the part of castelike minorities, for instance, to equate the schools' "style" with the white American or mainstream style that is in opposition to the minorities' styles (see DeVos, 1982a). For this reason minority students who adopt the school style in communication, interaction, or learning may be accused of "acting White." Even more serious a problem is that castelike minority students may define academic effort and success as a part of the white cultural frame of reference or white way of behaving. When this is the case a bright minority student faces a difficult choice: He or she is punished by peers for behaving in a manner that enhances academic achievement; on the other hand, conforming to peer pressures not to behave that way leads to academic failure.

There is some ethnographic evidence (Ogbu, 1974; Petroni, 1970) of those instances where black adolescents appear to define academic tasks and certain extracurricular activities traditionally dominated by whites as "White" and therefore not appropriate for blacks; at the same time they define sports and other extracurricular activities traditionally dominated by blacks as appropriate for blacks. Under this circumstance black students who try to excel in academic work or become involved in certain traditionally white-dominated extracurricular activites are ridiculed as "Uncle Toms" or as "acting White." On the other hand, it is appropriate and praised for black students to excel in sports. Petroni has suggested, and I agree, that the fear of being called an "Uncle Tom" or of being accused of "acting White" may prevent bright black students from making the necessary effort to do well in school.

The epistemology or group logic that sustains the oppositional cultural frame of reference is learned more or less unconsciously by castelike minority children as they grow up. It is therefore not subject to conscious analysis by the actors. As a result even when black students genuinely express interest in doing well in school their actual behaviors may produce results quite the opposite of their intentions (Ogbu, 1974; Weis, 1985).

In summary, these responses to exploitation and subordination—folk theories of success and failure, disillusionment arising from knowledge of and experiences with the job ceiling, ambivalent attitudes about schooling, incongruent competencies, conflicts with and distrust of the schools, and an oppositional cultural frame of reference—make it difficult for blacks and similar minorities to learn and demonstrate persevering academic attitudes and efforts required for success in school. Instead, these responses lead the minorities toward ambivalent attitudes and to a low-effort syndrome with regard to academic work.

Of course, not all black or all castelike minority students are caught in the web of these responses contributing to poor academic work. Middle-class black students who are not encapsulated in peer group pressures do quite well in school; so do children from certain "church families," and children from families with academic attitudes similar to those of immigrant minorities. In addition, minority students who "escape" from peer group encapsulation and group logic at some point in their school career. In general, it appears that what distinguishes castelike minority students who do well in school are that (a) they adopt pragmatic academic attitudes and apply themselves more seriously to their schoolwork; (b) they escape from or remain more or less outside peer-group encapsulation and oppositional group logic; and (c) they invest more effort into their schoolwork (see Clark, 1983; Ogbu, 1984b; Weis, in press).

IMMIGRANT MINORITIES

Immigrant Minority Origins, Domination And Exploitation.   Immigrant minorities are those who have moved more or less voluntarily to their host society for economic, social, or political reasons (Mabogunje, 1972; Shibutani & Kwan, 1965).

Immigrant minorities often suffer the same kind of subordination and exploitation endured by castelike minorities. They are, for example, subject to economic exploitation in the form of a job ceiling, to residential segregation, school segregation and inferior education, and to political manipulation and exclusion. Elsewhere (Ogbu, 1983), I have used the case of Chinese immigrants to the United States to illustrate the subordination and exploitation of the immigrants and the pattern of their responses. The following discussion draws from that work.

Immigrant Minorities' Responses.   The responses of the immigrants to their subordination and exploitation are in some ways similar to those of castelike minorities and in some other ways different. For example, the "survival strategies" of the immigrants may include clientship, collective struggle, and hustling that I described for castelike minorities; but these activities do not necessarily mean the same thing for the two types of minorities because the immigrants (a) may be forced into these activities by different circumstances; (b) tend to perceive their involvement in these activities as temporary; and (c) have other options outside their host society that are not open to castelike minorities. Therefore the activities do not produce the same effects on the two types of minorities. Moreover, as I argue later, there are mitigating factors that do not permit development of persistent conflicts with and distrust of the schools. Finally, the expressive responses of the immigrants are different, enabling them to retain their *different* collective social identity and cultural frame of reference *rather than develop an oppositional* identity and cultural frame of reference.

A useful way to understand the immigrants' situation is, therefore, to examine how some of their distinguishing features, as well as some external factors, influence their perceptions of and responses to domination and exploitation. I also point out some of the potential barriers to the immigrants' school success and how they try to overcome them. In this discussion I refer mainly to the Chinese Americans, although my analysis applies in varying degrees to other immigrant minorities.

Distinguishing Features Of The Immigrants.   Immigrant minorities are usually not influenced to the same degree as castelike minorities by the caste thinking and denigration of the dominant group because they do not consider themselves a part of the prevailing stratification system, but as strangers outside it. They may thus initially occupy the lowest rung of the occupational ladder, lack political power, and possess low prestige, but this objective structural position does not reflect their overall status in the social hierarchy because the immigrants do not usually think of their position as their hosts do. The immigrants may not, in fact, understand the invidious definitions the dominant group members attach to their position. But even when they understand them the immigrants may reject such definitions because they are strangers and are not a part of the local status system. Many immigrants, on the other hand, may view their menial positions in America as somewhat *better* than what they were prior to emigration (Shibutani & Kwan, 1965, p. 119). Then, too, even though the immigrants may be subject to pillory and discrimination, they have not usually had time to internalize the effects of discrimination or have those effects become an ingrained part of their culture, at least during the first generation.

A second distinguishing feature of the immigrants is that their reference group is back in their "homeland" or in their immigrant neighborhood and not in the dominant group of their host society. That is, the immigrants tend to measure their success, failure, or worth by standards of their homeland, and their reference group is usually their peers back in their homeland or in the immigrant neighborhood. When they compare themselves with their "own" people the immigrants often find much evidence of their own achievement and/or good prospects for their children because of "better opportunities" (Shibutani & Kwan, 1965, p. 517). Immigrant minorities do not generally measure success solely or primarily by the standards of their host society, as do nonimmigrant minorities; nor do the immigrants usually try to compete for equal status with the elite members of their host society, as nonimmigrant minorities are inclined to do. This is because, in the past at least, the nonwhite immigrants came first and foremost to accumulate wealth or other means of achieving self-advancement "back home" or in the host society, not to seek equal status. More recent immigrants have come as refugees or for similar economic reasons. In general, whether in the past or among the more recent immigrants, the goal of self-advancement is uppermost in the minds of the immigrants and acts as a strong incentive to exploit antici- pated and unanticipated opportunities and to maintain pragmatic attitudes toward economic and other activities, even in the face of prejudice and discrimination. I do not mean, of course, that immigrant minorities do not occasionally protest against maltreatment by their hosts (Cather, n.d.; Melendy, 1972; Sung, 1967).

A third factor influencing the responses of immigrant minorities to subordination and exploitation is the diplomatic and economic ties be- tween the immigrants' countries of origin and their host society. Such ties sometimes make the immigrants' subordination more rigid, sometimes more flexible (Sung, 1967).

Furthermore, unless the immigrants are political emigres, they have at least a symbolic option to return to their "homeland" or to reemigrate to other societies if circumstances in their host society become intolerable. This option means that the immigrants can export academic and other skills to some other societies for more desirable use and benefits (Ogbu, 1983; Sung, 1967). Reemigration is not always possible for all nonpolitical emigres, but this option is more available to them than to castelike minorities.

Potential Barriers To School Success. We can appreciate how the above features of the immigrants and their perceptions of and responses to their status in general affect their perceptions of and responses to schooling when we examine some potential barriers to school success and how they are dealt with.

Historical documents and some ethnographic studies suggest that there are at least three groups of factors that could adversely affect the school performance of immigrant minorities. To some degree they do; but apparently their effects are often temporary. As a result, the immigrant minorities are not, like castelike minorities, characterized by persistent disproportionate school failure.

One potential barrier to academic success is the inferior education given to the immigrants. It is reported that some immigrant minorities, such as the Chinese in San Francisco and elsewhere in California, were initially denied access to the public schools. Like blacks, they were also given segregated and inferior education later. In some cases the immigrants protested against their treatment. But on the whole segregation and inferior education did not discourage them from trying to maximize their academic achievement. One reason why they were not discouraged was that some immigrants came to American from countries where they themselves knew that educational opportunities were even more limited, and education in general more inferior. For instance, it is reported that some Chinese immigrants came to America primarily because they wanted their children to benefit from American free public school education. Moreover, such immigrants may not know that their children are attending inferior neighborhood schools, or that their children are receiving differential treatment in school. Instead, they tend to evaluate the free public education in the United States positively and encourage their children to take advantage of it (Ong, 1976; Ow, 1976).

A second potential problem is the lack of opportunity for the immigrants to derive benefits commensurate with their educational accomplishments because of employment discrimination and other barriers in adult opportunity structure in the United States. To understand the potential adverse impact of such barriers it is important to recognize that in contemporary industrial Western societies formal education has usually been structured on the commonsense idea of preparing children for future adult employment. Parents encourage their children to do well in school and children strive to do well when from repeated experience people come to believe that there is a good link between school success and later adult opportunities in the labor market. In this kind of situation people develop a folk theory of success which incorporates school success and a strong pursuit of educational credentials through effort investment as important elements.

However, immigrant minorities are usually successful in school even though they have not yet benefited from schooling in their host society. The incentive for the immigrants to work hard and succeed in school in the absence of this experience lies in the fact that they anticipate that school success will enable them to get good jobs and wages; and partly because they have not yet experienced discrepancies between educational achievement and lack of employment opportunities because of their ascribed group membership. Immigrant parents who are relatively well educated from their country of origin, but have low-status jobs in the United States, tend to attribute the discrepancies to the fact that they do not speak good English or that they were not brought up in America. Such immigrant parents generally accept the dominant group's criteria for success in school and society and encourage their children to follow suit (Ong, 1976; Ow, 1976). There are those immigrant parents educated and raised in America who have experienced discrepancies between educational attainment and employment status. These parents may still perceive schooling positively and encourage their children to do well in school, *if* they see options for their children to get good jobs in the immigrants' neighborhoods (i.e., within the economy of the ethnic enclave), in the immigrants' homeland, or elsewhere outside the United States. In other words, immigrant minorities who have alternative opportunities for educational rewards develop coping strategies and competencies enhancing academic pursuit and success even though they face dismal conventional educational payoffs in their host society. The Chinese immigrants are a good example (Sung, 1967).

The immigrants' culture and language constitute a third potential factor that could adversely affect their school performance. Chinese immigrants, for example, brought to America a learning style that emphasizes external forms and rote memorization rather than observation, analysis and comprehension; a language that is very different from English; and an authority structure of the family that discourages training children in independence and autonomy.

Another example of cultural differences between the immigrants and the dominant white Americans and the public schools is found in Gibson's study (1983) of the education of Punjabi immigrants in Valleyside, California. Gibson sums up the Punjabi situation by saying that, "In many areas the Punjabi way is simply not the Valleyside way. This causes resentment (among whites). There is a feeling that (the Punjabi) should conform to the dominant group way."

Until recently the schools generally ignored Chinese and Punjabi cultures and languages as they ignored the cultures and languages of other minorities. Yet, both Chinese and Punjabi students are relatively successful academically. It seems that these immigrants are successful partly because they are willing and determined to cross cultural and language boundaries in order to obtain school credentials for future employment and other benefits. And they are reported to perceive and interpret schooling largely as an investment. Ethnographic studies reveal that Chinese and Punjabi parents make it clear to their children that it is very important for them to work hard to succeed in school in order to improve their employment and economic chances in the future. And the parents also take steps to see to it that their children learn to work hard and *actually* work hard toward these goals.

CONCLUSION

I conclude by pointing out that ultimately the wider society is responsible for persistent disproportionate school failure of castelike minorities. Schools are implicated because they tend more or less to treat minorities so as to prepare them for subordinate positions in the prevailing stratification system. I have shown elsewhere (Ogbu, 1974, 1978), how both society and schools in the United States and other places contribute to the educational failures of castelike minorities.

In the present chapter I have been primarily concerned with explaining the differences in the academic responses of castelike and immigrant minorities and the resulting differences in achievement. In accounting for these differences I have stressed the importance of the diversity in their perceptions, interpretations, responses, and the reasons behind them although both types of minorities face similar problems in school and society.

Of particular interest among the many differences between castelike and immigrant minorities are the twin-phenomena of *identity* and *cultural frame of reference*. Among castelike minorities both the *identity system* and the *cultural frame of reference* are in opposition to those of the dominant group. Castelike minorities, furthermore, tend to equate school culture with dominant-group culture, so that the cultural frame of the school is also in opposition to that of the minorities. The result appears to be *a model of schooling* in which the minorities *view schooling as a one-way acculturation or assimilation process*. That is, castelike minorities like black Americans view schooling as learning white American culture and identity. But because blacks have a collective identity and a cultural frame of reference that are in opposition to those of white Americans, the acculturation model is problematic. There is, therefore, the possibility of conscious and/or unconscious opposition and an "affective dissonance" (DeVos, 1982b) toward learning in school or "acting White." The dilemma for an individual black student or other castelike minority student is that he or she has to *choose* between academic success or "success in the White way" and being a member of his or her group.

The collective identity system and cultural frame of reference of the immigrants are different but not oppositional. And due to the circumstances surrounding their emigration, the immigrants do not necessarily equate school culture with white American culture. At least they appear to separate those aspects of the school culture which facilitate academic success and learn to conform to them in ways considered essential for school success within general white American culture. However, they appear to resist giving up their own culture to learn to conform to white American culture (Gibson, 1983). In general, immigrant minorities do not equate schooling with a one-way acculturation or assimilation. Rather, they perceive schooling as an investment to obtain credentials for employment. The immigrants, therefore, tend to develop what may be called *an alternation model of schooling*. The essence of the alternation model is that it is possible to participate in two different but not oppositional cultures simultaneously. The immigrant child does not, therefore, equate behaving according to school norms or according to school requirements with giving up his or her own culture and identity. Rather, he or she learns to behave in school as the school requires and when at home or in the community he or she conforms to the ethnic or community expectations. That is, the immigrant student learns to switch back and forth between two different (home and school) but not oppositional cultural frames of reference (Ogbu, 1984). This situation and ability to alternate without crisis of identity greatly enhances the chances of the immigrants to succeed academically in school.

REFERENCES

Apel, J. H. (1970). American Negro and immigrant experience: Similarities and differences. In L. Dinnerstein & F. C. Jaher (Eds.), *The aliens: A history of ethnic minorities in America*. New York: Appleton-Century-Crofts.

Baugh, J. (1984). *Black street speech: Its history, structure, and survival*. Austin: University of Texas Press.

Berreman, G. D. (1960). Caste in India and the United States. *American Journal of Sociology, LXVI*, 120–127.

Berreman, G. D. (1967). Concomitants of caste organization. In G. DeVos & H. Wagatsuma (Eds.), *Japan's invisible race: Caste in culture and personality* (pp. 308–324). Berkeley: University of California Press.

Bontemps, A. (1969, Summer). *A lecture given at a workshop on black history and culture*. University of California, Los Angeles.

Boykin, A. W. (1980, November). *Reading achievement and the social-cultural frame of reference of Afro-American children*. A paper presented at an NIE Roundtable Discussion on Issues in Urban Reading, Washington, DC

Brake, M. (1980). *The sociology of youth culture and youth subculture*. London: Routledge and Kegan Paul.

Burma, J. H. (1946). The measurement of Negro passing. *American Journal of Sociology, 52*, 18–22.

California, State of. (1982). *Governor's Task Force on Civil Rights: Report on Racial, Ethnic and Religious Violence in California*. Sacramento: State and Consumer Service Agency.

Castile, G. P., & Kushner, G. (Eds.). (1981). *Persistent peoples: Cultural enclaves in perspective*. Tucson: University of Arizona Press.

Cather, H. (n.d.). *History of San Francisco's Chinatown*. Unpublished M. A. thesis, University of California, Berkeley.

Clark, R. (1983). *Family life and school achievement: Why poor black children succeed or fail*. Chicago: University of Chicago Press.

Coleman, J. S., Campbell, E. R., Hobson, C. J., McPartland, J., Mood, A. M., Wernfield, F. D., & York, R. L. (1966). *Equality of educational opportunity*. Washington, DC: U.S. Government Printing Office.

Cummins, J. (1982). *Working draft: A report (on bilingual education) prepared for The Ford Foundation,* (chap. 2) Academic achievement of minority students: Fitting the facts to the policies. Unpublished manuscript, The Ontario Institute for Studies in Education.

Davis, A., Gardner, B. B., & Gardner, M. R. (1965). *Deep south: A social anthropological study of caste and class.* (Abridged ed.). Chicago: University of Chicago Press.

DeVos, G. A. (1973). Japan's outcastes: The problem of the Burakumin. In B. Whitaker (Ed.), *The fourth world: Victims of group oppression* (pp. 307–327). New York: Schocken Book.

DeVos, G. A. (1982a). Adaptive strategies in U.S. minorities. In E. E. Jones & S. J. Korchin (Eds.), *Minority mental health* (pp. 74–117). New York: Praeger.

DeVos, G. A. (1982b). Adaptive conflicts and adjustment coping: Psychocultural approaches to ethnic identity. In T. Sarbin & K. E. Sheibe (Eds.), *Studies in social identity.* New York: Praeger.

DeVos, G. A. (1983). Achievement motivation and intra-family attitudes in immigrant Koreans. *The Journal of Psychoanalytic Anthropology, 6,* 25–71.

DeVos, G. A. (1984, April). *Ethnic persistence and role degradation: An illustration from Japan.* A paper prepared for the American-Soviet Symposium on Contemporary Ethnic Processes in the U.S.A. and the U.S.S.R., New Orleans, LA.

DeVos, G. A., & Wagatsuma, H. (Eds.). (1967). *Japan's invisible race: Caste in culture and personality.* Berkeley: University of California Press.

Dollard, J. (1957). *Caste and class in a southern town.* (3rd ed.). Garden City, NY: Doubleday.

DuBois, W. B. (1903). *The souls of black folk.* Chicago: A. C. Clurg and Co.

Erickson, F., & Mohatt, G. (1982). Cultural organization of participant structures in two classrooms of Indian students. In G. D. Spindler (Ed.), *Doing the ethnography of schooling: Educational anthropology in action* (pp. 132–175). New York: Holt.

Fordham, S. (1984, April). *Afro-Caribbean and native black American school performance in Washington, DC: Learning to be or not to be a native.* Unpublished manuscript. A paper given at Graduate School of Education, Harvard University, Cambridge, MA.

Foster, H. L. (1974). *Ribbin', jivin', and playin' the dozens: The unrecognized dilemma of inner city schools.* Cambridge, MA: Ballinger.

Gay, J., & Cole, M. (1967). *The new mathematics and an old culture: A study of Learning among the Kpelle of Liberia.* New York: Holt.

Gibson, M. A. (1983). *Home-school-community linkages: A study of educational equity for Punjabi youth. Final Report.* National Institute of Education, Washington, DC

Green, V. M. (1981). Blacks in the United States: The creation of an enduring people? In G. P. Castile & G. Kushner (Eds.), *Persistent peoples: Cultural enclaves in perspectives* (pp. 69–77). Tucson: University of Arizona Press.

Gumperz, J. J. (1982). Conversational inferences and classroom learning. In J. Green & C. Wallat (Eds.), *Ethnographic approaches to face interaction.* Norwood, NJ: Ablex.

Guthrie, G. P. (1983). *An ethnography of bilingual education in a Chinese community.* Unpublished doctoral dissertation. College of Education, University of Illinois, Urbana. Champaign.

Holt, G. S. (1972). Stylin' outa the black pulpit. In T. Kochman (Ed.), *Rappin' and stylin' out: Communication in urban black America* (pp. 189–204). Chicago: University of Illinois Press.

Hunter, D. (1980, August 18). Ducks vs. hard rocks. *Newsweek,* pp. 14–15.

Ito, H. (1967). Japan's outcastes in the United States. In G. A. DeVos & H. Wagatsuma (Eds.), *Japan's invisible race: Caste in culture and personality* (pp. 200–221). Berkeley: University of California Press.

Jones, T., & Yu, P. (1984). Black men, welfare and jobs. *The Washington Post,* May 11.

Kahn, L. (1983). *From minority to majority group? Social change and schooling in Quebec.* Unpublished manuscript, Department of Anthropology, University of California. ley.

Kochman, T. (1982). *Black and white styles in conflict.* Chicago: University of Chicago Press.

Lancy, D. F. (1983). *Cross-cultural studies in cognition and mathematics.* Orlando, FL: Academic Press.

Lewis, A. (1979). *Power, poverty and education: An ethnography of schooling in an Israeli town.* Forest Grove, OR: Turtledove Publishing Company.

Lewis, A. (1981). Minority education in Sharonia, Israel, and Stockton, California: A comparative analysis. *Anthropology and Education Quarterly, 12*(1), 30–50.

Loo, Y. Schneider, B. L., & Werner, O. (1984). *Asian American educational success: Cultural and structural explanation.* Unpublished manuscript, Department of Anthropology, Northwestern University.

Mabogunje, A. L. (1972). *Regional mobility and resource development in West Africa.* Montreal: McGill-Queens University Press.

Melendy, H. B. (1972). *The Oriental Americans.* New York: Twayne Publishing.

Mickelson, R. (1983). *Race, gender, and class differences in youth academic achievement attitudes and behaviors.* A dissertation proposal. Graduate School of Education, University of California, Los Angeles.

Mullings, L. (1978). Ethnicity and stratification in the urban United States. *Annals of the New York Academy of Sciences, 318*, 10–22.

Myrdal, G. (1944). *An American dilemma: The Negro problem and modern democracy.* New York: Harper.

Nava, J. (1970). Cultural backgrounds and barriers that affect learning by Spanish-speaking children. In J. H. Burma (Ed.), *Mexican-Americans in the United States: A reader* (pp. 125–134). New York: Schenkman.

Norgren, P. H., & Hill, S. E. (1964). *Toward fair employment.* New York: Columbia University Press.

Ogbu, J. U. (1974). *The next generation: An ethnography of education in an urban neighborhood.* Orlando, FL, Academic Press.

Ogbu, J. U. (1978). *Minority education and caste: The American system in cross-cultural perspective.* Orlando, FL: Academic Press.

Ogbu, J. U. (1982). Cultural discontinuities and schooling. *Anthropology and Education Quarterly, 13*(4), 290–307.

Ogbu, J. U. (1983). Minority status and schooling in plural societies. *Comparative Education Review, 27*(2), 168–190.

Ogbu, J. U. (1984a). *Understanding community forces affecting minority students' academic efforts.* Unpublished manuscript, prepared for The Achievement Council of California, Oakland, California.

Ogbu, J. U. (1984b). Stockton, California, revisited: Joining the labor force. In K. Borman (Ed.), *Becoming a worker.* Norwood, NJ: Ablex.

Ong, C. (1976). *The educational attainment of the Chinese in America.* Unpublished research project, Department of Anthropology, University of California, Berkeley.

Ortar, G. R. (1967). Educational achievement of primary school graduates in Israel as related to their sociocultural backgrounds. *Comparative Education, 4*, 23–34.

Ow, P. (1976). *The Chinese and the American educational system.* Unpublished research project, Department of Anthropology, University of California, Berkeley.

Parliamentary Select Committee on Immigration and Race Relations (1973). *Education, 1: Report.* London: H. M. S. O.

Petroni, F. A. (1970). 'Uncle Toms': White stereotypes in the black movement. *Human Organization, 29*(4), 260–266.

Philips, S. U. (1976). Commentary: Access to power and maintenance of ethnic identity. In M. A. Gibson (Ed.), *Anthropological Perspectives on Multicultural Education. Anthropology and Education Quarterly,* Special issue, 7(4), 30–32.

Powdermaker, H. (1968). *After freedom: A cultural study in the deep south.* New York: Atheneum.

Rawick, G. P. (1972). *From sundown to sunup: The making of the black community.* Westport, CT: Greenwood Publishing Co.

Rohlen, T. (1983). Education: Policies and prospects. In C. Lee & G. DeVos (Eds.), *Koreans in Japan: Ethnic conflicts and accommodation.* Berkeley: University of California Press.

Rosenfeld, E. (1973). *A strategy for prevention of developmental retardation among disadvantaged Israeli preschoolers.* Jerusalem: The Henrietta Szold Institute. Research report No. 173.

Sears, J. B., Almack, J. C., Davidson, P. E., Brown, W. H., Neilson, N. P., Bayley, N., & Green, D. G. (1938). *Stockton School Survey.* Stockton: Board of Education, Stockton, California.

Senior, C. (1972). Puerto Ricans on the mainland. In F. Cordasco & E. Bucchiono (Eds.), *The Puerto Rican community and its children on the mainland* (pp. 182–195). Metuchen, NJ: Scarecrow Press.

Shade, B. J. (1982). *Afro-American patterns of cognition.* Unpublished manuscript, Center for Educational Research, University of Wisconsin.

Shibutani, T., & Kwan, K. M. (1965). *Ethnic stratification: A comparative approach.* New York: Macmillan.

Shimahara, N. K. (1983). *Mobility and education of Buraku: The case of a Japanese minority.* Unpublished manuscript, Graduate School of Education, Rutgers University, New Brunswick, NJ.

Silverstein, B., & Krate, R. (1975). *Children of the dark ghetto: A developmental psychology.* New York: Praeger.

Skutnabb-Kangas, T., & Toukomaa, T. (1976). *Teaching migrant children's mother tongue and learning the language of the host country in the context of the socio-cultural situation of the migrant family.* Helsinki: The Finish National Commission for UNESCO.

Slade, M. (1982). Aptitude, intelligence or what? *The New York Times,* October 24, pp. 22–23.

Spicer, E. H. (1966). The process of cultural enclavement in middle America. *36th Congress of International de Americanistas, Seville, 3,* 267–279.

Spicer, E. H. (1971). Persistent cultural systems: A comparative study of identity systems that can adapt to contrasting environments. *Science, 174,* pp. 795–800.

Stockton Unified School District. (1948). *Community survey: In-school youth.* Unpublished manuscript. Research department. Stockton Unified School District, Stockton, CA.

Sung, B. L. (1967). *Mountain of gold: The story of the Chinese in America.* New York: Macmillan.

Tuden, A., & Plotnicov, L. (1970). Introduction. In A. Tuden & L. Plotnicov (Eds.), *Social stratification in Africa.* Pennsylvania: University of Pittsburgh Press.

U. S. Department of Interior, Bureau of Indian Affairs. (1974). *Statistics concerning Indian education.* Washington, DC: U.S. Government Printing Office.

Warner, W. L., Junker, B. H., & Adams, W. A. (1941). *Color and human nature: Negro personality in a northern city.* Washington, DC: The American Youth Commission.

Warner, W. L., Havighurst, R. J., & Loeb, M. B. (1944). *Who shall be educated? The challenge of equal opportunity.* New York: Harper.

Weis, L. (1985). *Between Two Worlds: Black students in an urban community college.* London: Routledge and Kegan Paul.

Wigdor, A. K., & Garner, W. R. (Eds.). (1982). *Ability testing: Uses, consequences, and controversies, Part 1: Report of the Committee.* Washington, DC: National Academy Press.

The Author and Her Chapter

Margaret Gibson began her career teaching in Latin America, first as a volunteer for the American Friends Service Committee in rural Mexico, then as a first grade teacher in a bilingual school in Panama. She has also worked for an international exchange organization in Philadelphia, the Eisenhower Fellowships, and served as a Project Officer for the National Center for Educational Research and Development—the predecessor of NIE. Her work in the latter position convinced her of the need for further research on group differences in educational performance.

After receiving her Ph.D. from the University of Pittsburgh in Education and Anthropology, Gibson joined the faculty at California State University, Sacramento, where she taught courses in educational anthropology and served as research coordinator for the newly formed Cross Cultural Resource Center. She there learned of the rapidly growing Punjabi immigrant community described in this chapter. A recent article on collaborative educational ethnography (1985) describes the evolution of the Punjabi Education Project. A book, *Accommodation without Assimilation: Punjabi Sikh Immigrants in an American High School and Community,* is forthcoming. Another related volume, *Minority Status and Schooling: Immigrants vs. Non-Immigrants,* is also nearing completion. The latter, coedited with John Ogbu, includes comparative case materials from the U.S. and abroad.

Gibson has recently returned from a year of research and teaching in South Asia and in England. Currently adjunct professor of anthropology at CSUS, Gibson is devoting full time to research and writing.

The Punjabi students in Valleyside high school were far more successful in school than preliminary data on them or the data on indigenous American minorities would suggest. Their academic success does vary with how long they have spoken English and recent immigrants are therefore severely handicapped. Nevertheless most stay in school through the twelfth grade. Those who were born in the United States do well academically—as well or better than Valleyside natives who experience no discontinuity with mainstream culture.

The difference between Punjabi immigrant and American mainstream family culture is indeed substantial. Differences in concepts of proper behavior for teenagers are particularly telling for high school students and they center on norms and values concerning independence. At precisely the time when Punjabi parents feel their children need the most guidance, mainstream parents are letting go and encouraging independence. Mainstream adolescents make their own decisions. And their social life and extracurricular activities are usually more important to them than high academic achievement.

The cultural differences between Punjabi and mainstream youth are explored in this chapter, as well as the social problems Punjabi students encounter due to the prejudice of at least a significant minority of Valleyside mainstream students.

The Punjabi experience in Valleyside is not too different from that of recent immigrants elsewhere in the United States. Their struggle to succeed, the problems they encounter in doing so, and their successes, highlight features of mainstream American culture, some positive and some negative. As we are informed about the Punjabis, Vietnamese, and others who have recently come to our country, we are informed about ourselves.

The Editors

REFERENCES

Gibson, M. (1985). Collaborative educational ethnography: Problems and profits. *Anthropology and Education Quarterly, 16*(2), 124–148.

12 Punjabi Immigrants in an American High School

Margaret A. Gibson
California State University, Sacramento

OVERVIEW

Researchers interested in minority education in this country have generally focused attention on those groups whose school performance lags furthest behind that of the white majority, showing how cultural and structural barriers impede academic progress. The present paper, while also directly concerned with barriers to educational opportunity, focuses on a minority group which fares comparatively well academically, the Punjabi Sikhs, and shows how aspects of Punjabi culture contribute directly to success in school. The setting for the study is a small agricultural town in California's Central Valley where Punjabi immigrants constitute about 13% of the total student population.[1] I call the town "Valleyside."

The impetus for the research was the local school district's need for information about the Punjabi community and the problems faced in school by Punjabi youth. Standardized tests administered by the district in October, 1978, had revealed a serious disparity between the academic achievement of Punjabi high school students, as a group, and the rest of

[1]Although Sikhs constitute the overwhelming majority of Valleyside's Asian Indian population, there are also a few Hindu and Moslem families living in the area. Like the Sikhs, they, too, are Punjabis. Punjabi is their mother tongue, Punjab their homeland. While differing in religious beliefs, their cultural heritage is in most ways similar to that of the Sikhs. Punjabi, thus, is a regional identity. I use the term "Punjabis" both when referring to Valleyside Sikhs, all of whom have their origins in Punjab, and when referring to the total Asian Indian population attending Valleyside High, Sikh, Hindu, and Moslem alike.

281

the student body. District officials were concerned, furthermore, by mounting tensions between "Valleysiders" (my term for Valleyside's white majority) and Punjabis, both in school settings and in the community at large. The Punjabi Education Project was launched in 1980 to help address these problems.

The project was a collaborative effort, involving a Punjabi community organization, the school district, parents, students, and community members (see Gibson, 1985). The collaborative and comparative nature of the project was reflected in the makeup of the research team, which included two Punjabi Sikhs, one male and one female, and two white Americans, both female. I served as project director and principal investigator. The fieldwork discussed here took place between 1980 and 1982.[2]

We concentrated our attention on the school performance and experiences of students in their final year at Valleyside High, the District's only comprehensive high school. Research samples included all 44 Punjabi seniors (Class of 1981) and 46 Valleysider seniors, selected by random sample. All Punjabi parents and all but three Valleysider parents gave permission for their children to be involved in the study and agreed themselves to be interviewed.

Members of the research team were able to participate in and observe community and school affairs over a 2-year period. Interviews with the Valleyside High seniors, their parents, and their teachers form the heart of the project's data base. Almost all interviews were tape recorded and later transcribed. Those conducted in Punjabi were translated into English. The analysis draws, additionally, from student and teacher questionnaires, student themes, school documents, and academic performance data for some 600 Punjabi, Mexican American, and Valleysider students, grades 9 through 12.

Systematic analysis of standardized test scores confirmed the disparity in achievement between Punjabi high school students *as a group* and the rest of the student body. It revealed, also, that the overwhelming majority of the Punjabis who scored poorly were recently arrived from India and weak in English. From these and other data we realized that it was necessary to distinguish new arrivals from those raised in the United States.

Second generation Punjabi students, together with those who had arrived in Valleyside as small children, in spite of facing cultural, linguistic, and social difficulties in school, did quite well academically. Recent immigrants fared far less well. Although most recent arrivals persisted in school through 12th grade, they never broke out of a remedial track.

───────────────

²I gratefully acknowledge the contributions of fellow research team members, Amarjit Singh Bal, Gurdip Kaur Dhillon, and Elizabeth McIntosh, and the many parents, students, and educators whose ideas are reflected throughout this paper.

Valleysider students contrasted with the Punjabis. They faced no cultural or social barriers of similar magnitude, yet their school performance on the whole was rather mediocre. In this paper we shall compare the two groups, Valleysider majority and Punjabi minority, showing how the cultural background of each bears directly on academic performance and social relations.

VALLEYSIDE

Settled initially at the time of California's gold rush. Valleyside grew slowly until the 1960s. Between 1965 and 1980 the county population increased by approximately 40%, to a total of 50,000. Many of the newcomers were Punjabi immigrants. At the time of fieldwork, about 70% of the population were Valleysiders, 12% Punjabis, 12% Mexican Americans, and 4% other minorities.

Valleysiders

Few Valleysider adults are themselves native to the area, but a majority of their children are. Those whom we interviewed enjoyed the rural, small-town atmosphere and considered it a good place to raise children. Oldtimers felt the county was becoming too populated. Newcomers complained, occasionally, about the lack of "cultural advantages" and the town's "provincial" nature. Both groups agreed, however, that its smallness made it a safer place to live than larger, metropolitan areas, and made it easier to deal with problems when they did arise.

In years past most Valleysiders had depended directly on farming for a livelihood, but times have changed. Not only has the overall population grown, creating more job alternatives, but many small farmers have sold out. In recent years, Valleysiders explained, it has become increasingly difficult to make a decent living from the small, family-run farm. In 1981 an acre of good peach land cost upwards of $7,000. Walnut and prune acreage ran even higher.

Valleyside is a comparatively wealthy town, but much of its wealth lies in the land. The median income for Valleysiders in our sample, all parents of high school seniors, was $30,000, excluding children's earnings. About a third of the fathers ran their own businesses. The rest were equally divided between public and private sector positions. Almost all of the mothers were also employed for at least part of the year. Although they held relatively low-paying positions, their salaries were an important part of the family income. Most Valleysider parents were satisfied with their employment and had no plans to change. They noted, however, a general lack of opportunity for advancement and lower wages than in nearby cities. Young people, parents observed, could always find summer employment in Valleyside because of agriculture, but for full-time, permanent employment the opportunities were limited.

Quite a few Valleysiders, especially those whose families had moved to the area a generation or more ago, had many relatives throughout the county. Others had no kin nearby. Regardless, family was important to Valleysiders. Some noted, however, that they found it increasingly difficult to maintain a strong and united family. It was hard, they pointed out, to do things together on a regular basis. Even family meals could be difficult to arrange, as each member of the family had a separate schedule.

Valleysiders spoke proudly of this country's greatness. Most especially they valued their freedom and the economic opportunities available in America. They supported free enterprise and believed that initiative pays off. They appreciated the right not to conform. "Perhaps we do conform," one woman observed, "so as not to be viewed as weird. But it is our right to do what we want, so long as we are not infringing on others and not causing problems." The combination of freedom and opportunity was the reason, Valleysiders noted, that people from all over the world wish to immigrate to the United States.

Punjabis

Most Valleyside Punjabis have entered this country under the terms of the Immigration and Naturalization Act of 1965. This Act, which removed the race limitations of earlier immigration laws and abolished the national origins quota system, has resulted in a dramatic increase in Asian Indian immigration to the United States. Indians today are one of America's fastest growing immigrant communities. Between 1965 and 1985 the number of Asian Indians in America grew from only 10,000 to more than a half million (Gibson, n.d.). During this period the Valleyside Punjabi community increased tenfold, from about 700 (Wenzel, 1966) to 7,000 or more, by local estimates. Several thousand visas are issued each year through the American Embassy in India to Punjabi Sikhs. Many of these emigrants state Valleyside to be their destination in the United States.[3]

More than 80% of Valleyside's Punjabis are Jat Sikhs. They are followers of the Sikh religion and members, by birth, of a traditional farm-owning group in India known as Jats. Most come to California direct from rural Punjab. They come because they believe economic and educational opportunities to be far better here than in India. They believe also that they can adapt relatively easily to life in Valleyside because it is an

---

[3]This information comes from Nicholas MacNeil, American Consul, New Delhi, and members of his staff (personal communication, February 29, 1984).

agricultural community, similar in a number of respects to village Punjab. They know, furthermore, that they can turn to family members already settled in Valleyside for assistance.[4]

Although most Punjabi immigrants consider themselves "better off" in America than they were in India, those who settle in Valleyside have left behind a family farm and a life where they employed others to work for them. Most had only small holdings in Punjab, but they had the security of owning their property outright and being able to raise the food needed to feed a family. Jat Sikhs have farmed for generations in Punjab and take great pride in their agricultural skills. In Valleyside, however, they farm because they have no other option. Most of those who come to Valleyside lack fluency in English. Many, especially the women, have had little or no schooling. The men must work, at least initially, for minimum or near minimum wages as laborers in Valleyside's fruit orchards. The majority work with their hands—pruning, thinning, and picking peaches. During the summer months Punjabi women work alongside their husbands picking and sorting peaches. A few women, mostly long-term residents, are hired seasonally by the local canneries. Most families count on summer income to tide them through the year.

In spite of low wages and back-breaking work, a significant number of Valleyside Punjabis had, by 1981, been able to buy their own farms. At the time of fieldwork, Punjabis owned an estimated 50% of the county's peach acreage (La Brack, 1982a, 1982b), plus additional acres of prunes, walnuts, almonds, and pears. A few Punjabis had done very well in farming, but most of those settled in Valleyside had only small ranches (about 25%), or worked as farm laborers (50%). More recent arrivals, if they had a high school education and some knowledge of English, had shifted to factory work in nearby cities (20%). The price of land was too high to make a profit, they believed, and the future of orchard farming had become increasingly bleak. Punjabi youngsters, for their part, could testify to the drudgery of agricultural labor. Few wished to farm for a living.

Like Valleysiders, Punjabis considered their new home a good place to raise children. They appreciated the rural atmosphere, good weather, and "clean air." For many Punjabis the drawbacks of life in America related to the quality of human relations. Life was busier, they said. There were more worries and less time to enjoy themselves. Punjabis, when they did get together socially, did so at home, or at the *gurdwara* (Sikh temple). Most Punjabi adults felt uncomfortable socializing in public places, in

---

[4]I discuss Punjabi immigration and adaptation patterns more fully in a forthcoming volume entitled *Accommodation without Assimiliation: Punjabi Sikh Immigrants in an American High School and Community* (Gibson, n.d.).

part because of the hostile attitudes of many Valleysiders toward them. For a few, the clash between cultures was sufficiently troublesome to cause regret about leaving India. One man expressed his feelings as follows:

> Their culture does not mix with ours. Secondly, they don't consider us as part of the people of this country. They are prejudiced toward us. . . . Sometimes we even think that it would be a good idea to go back to India, as we do not feel happy.

In spite of the prejudice, most Punjabis were positive about life in America. They, like their Valleysider neighbors, valued the personal freedoms of this country and the economic opportunities they believed it offers.

ACADEMIC PERFORMANCE AT VALLEYSIDE HIGH

Academic achievement at Valleyside High compares favorably to that at other comprehensive high schools across the nation. Valleyside seniors, for example, have consistently scored from 25 to 50 points above state and national averages on the math SAT; verbal SAT scores have surpassed the state and national averages in 5 of 7 years recently, but by a smaller margin. Scores on competency tests in reading, writing, and mathematics, given to all junior high students attending schools in the Valleyside district, show a range and distribution similar to that of a national sample of 8th graders.

Meeting national averages, however, is no necessary sign of educational excellence. Less than 70% of the students who entered Valleyside High in 1977 received their diplomas 4 years later. About one-third of the total student body left school without taking a single high school level class in math or science. Less than 20% pursued increasingly more advanced courses each year in English. Only 12% of those who graduated were expected to complete 4 years of college.

Valleysider Patterns

Valleysider parents, for the most part, commended the educational program at the high school. Even those whose children had done poorly praised the high school faculty and curriculum. Parents noted that the system worked well for those who arrived in 9th grade with the requisite basic skills and who know what they wanted and needed from high school. Many Valleysider parents explained, however, that their children either were bored by their classes, were too shy to ask for assistance, or lacked motivation. Some pointed out, in addition, that their children were simply unable to handle the academic demands of high school due to poor language and math preparation.

Teachers and administrators noted similar problems. They explained the root cause as a lack of parental support for education. More specifically, they cited too little discipline and supervision at home and a general failure by parents to be involved in their children's education in meaningful ways. Many other problems, they believed, related to these.

Most Valleysider seniors were themselves pleased with their high school experience. They reported that they had taken the courses of their choice and that they were satisfied with the grades they had received. Many admitted that they had deliberately selected "easy" courses once basic requirements had been met. Only those who planned to enter directly into a 4-year college felt the need to take increasingly advanced academic courses every year. These courses were viewed as "college prep" and other students simply saw little reason to take them. They also knew that should they later decide to attend college, they could make up missing courses by attending community college. The only requirement for admission to a community college was graduation from high school or a minimum age of 18.

One Valleysider student explained that he had not taken any math course beyond 1st-year algebra because he did not feel the more advanced courses would prove useful in the future. The "peak" of his education, he reported, had come in 10th grade, when he had taken algebra 1, biology, and English 2. After that his interests and energies had turned away from school to an after-school job, musical interests, and activities with friends. Following high school he hoped to support himself through a lawn maintenance business.

Many other Valleysider students, especially the boys, expressed similar attitudes. One college-bound senior, well liked by peers and teachers, noted that getting an education meant more than just going to school. He reported:

> I go fishing and skiing a lot. I get my work done, and to miss school and do these other things is educational to me too. . . . Obviously there are people that never cut school, and what if something did happen and you are stranded some place out in the wild somewhere? You wouldn't know how to survive. So it is a different type of education. I don't miss [school] because I'm lazy. I miss it and do something worthwhile.

This student was absent 10 days his senior year, 4 less than the typical senior in our Valleysider sample. He also worked close to 40 hours a week in the family business, played two varsity sports, and participated in a variety of social activities both in and out of school. He was far from lazy. His senior year, however, he deliberately took the minimum course load. Only one of his four classes, senior English, required homework, and this he was taking because the college of his choice required it. Senior year, he explained, was "kick back time."

Valleysider Success Theory

Valleysider parents, and teachers too, saw high school as preparing young people to go out on their own. Parents wanted their children to master the "basics," which for most meant passing all required courses, and to graduate from high school. They were extremely disappointed if one of their children failed to graduate. Most placed equal emphasis on vocational and academic classes. Many were particularly pleased with the vocational classes that provided work experience and job-related skills. They wanted their children to be ready following high school to earn a living. It would be nice, some said, if their children were to finish college. Most, however, did not expect their children to do so, nor, they reported, had they stressed higher education as either a goal or a necessity.

Other qualifications beyond formal education were at least equally important to their children's ultimate success as adults, Valleysider parents believed. Initiative, drive, a willingness to knuckle down and do the job were basic. Opportunity, they said, was also essential, by which they meant being in the right spot at the right time in order to receive a chance to get ahead. Connections, too, they believed were important. A college education was simply one more ingredient and not necessarily the most significant one. While some parents saw college as a means to help one advance, others observed that even a college degree was no guarantee of a job. It depends on what you want, one parent commented, noting also that hard labor jobs paid well. Another observed pointedly that mechanics made more money than school teachers.

The median years of education for the Valleysider fathers in our sample was 13 (excluding kindergarten) and for the mothers 12. Although 15% of the fathers and 26% of the mothers had never finished high school, more than half the fathers (56%) and almost half of the mothers (44%) had pursued some postsecondary education. Few, however, had completed 4 years of college (23% of the fathers and 12% of the mothers) and many of those with some college education had attended a community college as adults, often years after finishing high school.

Most Valleysider students said they would be pleased to have their father's job and income. Over half of the girls reported that they would be happy with their mother's job and even more with her income. Valleysider students, by and large, believed their parents had done well in their jobs, even without a college degree, or, in a number of cases, without a high school diploma. One student explained his father's views as follows:

> He feels that if you get straight A's and work really hard, that doesn't mean you are going to be successful. But he says, "Just give it your best. You prove yourself when you work hard and don't let anyone down."

Almost every Valleysider youth, by the time he or she was finishing high school, had worked in several jobs. These students felt confident of the skills that they could apply to new positions. Most frequently they noted their ability to get along with others.

The ability to get along in society was stressed by teachers as well as parents, many of whom placed social criteria for success ahead of academic ones. In defining a successful high school experience, teachers avoided ascribing success to intelligence or academic achievement. Academic achievement, some said, was based largely on innate ability, and was no necessary predictor of adult success. Valleysider parents agreed. More important, teachers explained, were social skills and a sense of self-worth. For them, the nonsucceeder was not the one with poor academic skills. It was the student who could not "fit in," who did not "feel part of it," and who did not value many of the things that other students enjoyed at school.

Taking part in extracurricular activities was considered particularly important. The school stressed it. Parents encourage it. Students enjoyed it. Almost every Valleysider boy in the senior sample had participated in at least one school sport. In almost equal numbers the girls had been involved in some school activity, a sport or more generally one of the high school's many clubs. Top students continued their participation throughout high school, often involving themselves in multiple activities each year. Students in the bottom half of the class were more inclined, during their junior and senior years, to spend their time in nonschool activities and working in part-time, after-school jobs.

Valleysider parents supported both part-time work for their children and a good social life. Parents wanted their children to enjoy themselves during these years before they had to take up full adult responsibilities. Jobs provided teenagers with the money to go out with friends, attend movies, keep up with the latest clothing styles, and even to purchase and maintain a car. Jobs, thus, provided independence. From the parents' perspective they also taught young people responsibility and the realities of the working world.

Self-reliance was the goal. Parents pointed out that their children soon would be 18 and legally adults. Parents assumed, furthermore, that following high school, or 2 years of college, their children would leave home to live on their own. To prepare them for this day, Valleysiders encouraged their offspring, from the time they were small, to make decisions independently and to take responsibility for their actions. By late high school most Valleysiders placed few controls on their children. The parents' role, at this point, they believed, was to counsel and guide. Their children had to make their own choices in matters of friendship, education, jobs, use of time, place of residence, and marriage.

Throughout the interviews Valleysider parents emphasized the importance of raising girls, as well as boys, to be independent. Valleysiders wanted their daughters to be able to support themselves and, if necessary, their families. It would be up to their daughter, they said, to decide if she would maintain a career while also raising a family. They wanted her to be prepared, however, to make it on her own and to feel confident in her ability to earn a good living.

Punjabi Success Theory

Punjabi parents encouraged no similar independence in their offspring. Like Valleysider parents, they wanted their children, as adults, to be able to support themselves. Unlike Valleysiders, however, they placed no emphasis on preparing young people to leave home and to live on their own. Self-reliance, Punjabi style, meant taking one's place and pulling one's weight within the family group. Punjabis call it "standing on your feet," a phrase frequently used by those whom we interviewed.

All Punjabi parents expect the younger generation to defer to elders for direction and approval. Adolescence, from the Punjabi perspective, is a time when young people need especially strong parental supervision and guidance. Teenagers, parents explained, naturally "question everything," including their parents' values, but they lacked the maturity to make wise decisions for themselves.

For Punjabis, decision making is a joint process. This maintains family unity and reduces the risk of children getting into trouble. Punjabi parents were much disturbed by what they perceived to be the American emphasis on encouraging young people to question adult advice and to make decisions on their own. "American people," as they saw it, were "ruining their kids." One Punjabi, a long-term resident of Valleyside, explained his views as follows:

> They are not making the right life for the kids. NO, NO. The poor kids. They have no sense, what to do, where to go, or who to meet. We were talking a minute ago about that, that it is a bad stage—you know, 16, 17, 18. . . . I don't want to ruin their life. NO. So I tell them, "Do this, it is better. Do that, no good." They listen, too.

Most Punjabis believed they could make better decisions than their children and that it was their duty to do so. The children would learn by example and, after they had studied and were married, they would be able to shoulder responsibility for their own decisions.

Not all agreed with this approach. Remarking that Punjabi adults, typically, were very arrogant, always discounting their children's advice, one man stated strongly that children should be consulted and their viewpoints considered. If children demonstrate that they can make good decisions, another commented, then they should be given "full freedom." Both parents were referring to their sons.

Valleyside Punjabis encouraged no such freedom for their daughters. Parents felt typically, that they should make almost all decisions affecting their daughters. Young people themselves described how boys had far more opportunity than girls to make everyday decisions in such matters as clothes, hair style, and activities with friends. Boys, for example, were free to join friends after school for a game of soccer or hockey, or to go out with friends in the evening to the movies. Girls, by contrast, were expected to return home directly from school. Only rarely was it possible for them to get together with girlfriends outside of school. Most of their social activities revolved around the immediate family, or cousins and other relatives living in Valleyside.

The actions of any family member may damage a Punjabi family's name, but it is a daughter's behavior that most readily brings disgrace. If a teenage girl "steps out of the house, goes out to play, or is seen sitting with other girls," one parent explained, it brought a loss of respect. Another, the father of an 18-year-old girl born and raised in Valleyside, objected to his daughter having a driver's license. Even a trip to the county library was cause for concern since, as he pointed out, his daughter might meet up with friends and start "fooling around."

Not all parents were as traditional as these. Most agreed, however, that gossip about one's daughter was a serious embarrassment. It damaged family honor and could have a negative impact on marriage arrangements, not only for the girl in question, but for unmarried brothers and sisters.

Arranged marriages and the value placed on maintaining family honor are central to the Punjabi Sikhs' system of cultural maintenance. Valleyside Punjabis saw it as their duty to choose a mate for each of their children. They believed that they could find better matches than their offspring could find for themselves. They were older and had more experience, more contacts, and better judgment about what makes a marriage successful. They expected, without question, that their children would marry other Sikhs of the same caste background. Beyond that, family reputation and the young person's education, looks, and personality were considered important.

For Punjabis arranged marriages do not conflict with "standing on your own feet." Through careful selection, Punjabi parents felt that they not only could secure their child's future, but their own. They were helping to put the child "on his feet" and, at the same time, assuring that they themselves would be cared for in later years. Punjabis, like other Asian groups, remain closely tied to their parents, even as adults, each dependent on the other in a relationship which serves the mutual benefits of both.[5]

Punjabi Home-School Linkage

Valleyside Punjabis in the present study had taught their children to be diligent in their school work. Schooling came first, ahead of housework, jobs, and most especially social activities. "The main thing is to study," one mother said, "nothing else."

Parents expected their children to do well in school. Children were instructed to do as their teachers said, to follow the rules, and to get home without any criticism of their behavior. They were urged to acquire the skills and credentials necessary for competing in mainstream society, but warned at the same time to do nothing that would shame their families. "Dress to please the people," Punjabis frequently said, "but eat to please yourself." Accommodation without assimilation was their strategy.

Only rarely did parents involve themselves directly in school affairs. They were reluctant to visit the schools or to attend school meetings, nor did they see any reason why they should do so. Parents in India, they explained, were only asked to go to school when a child had refused to obey those in authority. Their responsibility, as parents, was to see that this did not occur.

Most parents had little understanding of the American system of education. Few were able to help with homework or course selection. Newer arrivals, moreover, simply had no time to get involved in school matters. Their entire lives were consumed by the myriad problems of adapting to life in America and by the realities of sheer economic survival. Even long-term residents had little knowledge of what their children were actually doing in school and whether or not they were progressing satisfactorily. "We send the children to school and leave the strings to

---

[5]Francis Hsu (1981) has noted that majority youngsters nearing adulthood shift their relationship with their parents away from obedience and deference to self reliance and a striving to get ahead on their own. They do not reject their parents, as some immigrants, including Punjabis, mistakenly assume, but they do wish to be their equals, free from supervision even by the teenage years.

God," one farmer reported. Himself illiterate, this man relied on more educated family members to deal directly with school officials.

Parents recognized that some children had neither the interest nor the ability to excel in school. They saw little point in keeping such children in school. "If the child does not wish to study, then what can the teacher do?" one parent remarked. "Those that are only interested in play and clothes, or who wander around with the baddies, cannot become successful," commented another. Punjabis rarely blamed the educational system, or the teachers, for a child's difficulties. Responsibility for learning, in the Punjabi view, rested with the individual. Those who wished to learn, would learn.

Parents were not naive about the difficulties their children faced in school. They simply brooked no excuses for poor performance. Those who squandered their chances bore the consequences. With only a "simple education," children were reminded, they could expect only a "simple job."

All Punjabi young people could cite examples of culturally deviant students who had been withdrawn from school, first for a few days and, if the misbehavior was not corrected, then permanently. Punjabi youngsters realized that if they themselves got out of line their parents might well arrange an early marriage or put them to work in the fruit orchards. This was a known system.

Punjabi youngsters avoided problems in school which might be reported to their parents. Regardless of the cause, they knew their parents would fault them for getting in trouble. Only rarely was a Punjabi student at Valleyside High suspended from school. The importance of upholding family respect served as a strong incentive to good behavior.[6]

Punjabi students, by and large, had a more serious orientation toward school than their Valleysider classmates. Teachers and administrators, even in the elementary grades, noted their "sense of purpose" and "direction." High school faculty were likewise impressed by their willingness to work hard. Punjabi students spent much more time on homework than their Valleysider counterparts. The difference was especially striking between the two groups of boys. While over half of the Valleysider boys sampled said they "almost never" did homework, three-quarters of the Punjabi males reported doing an hour or more of homework nearly every day. Punjabi males, furthermore, earned better grades and graduated from high school in larger numbers, proportionally, than Valleysider males.

---

[6]See Gibson and Bhachu (1986) for further analysis of the incentives and sanctions used by overseas Sikhs to promote success in school.

Analysis of attendance patterns revealed a similar contrast between the two groups. While no Valleysider students in our random sample had perfect attendance during their final year in school, one in five Punjabis never missed a single day. The median number of days absent for Valleysiders was 14, for Punjabis only 3.

Punjabi teenagers not only liked school, they had a definite sense that they were learning things valuable to their future. A good command of English, they believed, together with the vocational and academic skills they were acquiring, would make them more competitive in the job market, or in college. Many of these youths aspired to technical and professional jobs, occupations that, for the most part, require postsecondary education. Three out of four hoped to finish at least 2 years of college. Almost two-thirds wanted a 4-year degree.

Punjabi Performance Profiles

Of the 232 Punjabi students attending Valleyside High in October, 1980, only 30% had begun their schooling in the United States. Only 12% were American born. Sixty percent had been in the U.S. 6 years or less. In analyzing Punjabi school performance patterns, age on entry into English-medium schools and proficiency in the English language were the two most important factors influencing academic performance patterns. The two were closely related.

Punjabi boys educated from 1st grade in Valleyside took more college preparatory classes in high school than their Valleysider counterparts. Punjabi girls educated for all 12 years in the U.S. also performed well in the academic classes which they took, although few enrolled in college preparatory courses for all 4 years of high school. Over one-third of the Punjabi boys who started school in the U.S. completed 4 years of science and math, and nearly half completed 3 years. This was in keeping with their aspirations for careers in electronics, computer science, and engineering. Proficiency in English was a critical factor in the comparative success of these students.

Those Punjabi students who never mastered English in the early primary years were severely handicapped in their ability to compete academically at the secondary level. An alarming near 90% of those who transferred into the American system from India after 4th grade continued to be weak in English throughout high school. While almost all of these students, through perseverance and hard work, eventually did receive a high school diploma, they graduated with far less than a "high school education." Home-school cultural differences, together with the prejudice which new immigrants from India faced at Valleyside High, accounted for part of their difficulties, but important, too, was the quality of the instructional program.

BARRIERS TO SCHOOL SUCCESS

Punjabi is the home language of almost all Valleyside Punjabis. Less than 5% of the Punjabi students who attended Valleyside High in 1980 had learned English as their first language. Most of those raised from early childhood in the U.S. had entered first grade knowing little or no English. Nor had they received any special assistance with English as a second language during their elementary or junior high years. By high school, however, three-quarters of these students were classified by the school district as "fluent-English-speakers."[7] They had learned English through participation in the regular school program.

Standardized test scores suggest that the English skills of the American-educated Punjabis were not as strong, in many cases, as those of their Valleysider peers. The Punjabi students, nonetheless, proved themselves competitive in high school, not only in the required courses but in the most advanced academic classes offered at Valleyside High. Other factors, beyond English language proficiency, promoted their success.

The failure of almost all newer arrivals, together with a significant minority of those arriving before 5th grade, to acquire enough skill in English to be competitive in high school reveals an unquestionable need for special language instruction for these students. Our research findings raise a number of questions, however, about the unintended effects of the ESL program offered by Valleyside High. These effects relate both to the structure of the program and to the social segregation it produced.

The ESL Program At Valleyside High

At Valleyside High limited and non-English speakers were segregated for much of the school day. First-year ESL students spent five out of six periods daily in classes which, by their own appraisal, were far "too easy." While first-year students felt that they needed ESL, most second- and third-year students believed they would have learned more in regular academic classes. Teachers and administrators were reluctant, however, to move them out of the ESL program, in part because the district had been required by the federal Office for Civil Rights to increase its special services to language minority students (Gibson, 1985).

District policy permitted limited-English-speaking students to meet high school graduation requirements in math, science, and English through ESL classes, even though the instructional level and content of these classes was, at best, equivalent to that of the upper elementary

---

[7]The school district tests all students whose home language is other than English, using criteria established by the Office for Civil Rights, U.S. Department of Education.

grades. The policy was designed to enable immigrants, whose schooling had begun in a non-English-speaking country, to graduate from high school in the same number of semesters as their American born and educated age-mates. Many limited-English-speakers received one-third or more of all their high school credits from ESL classes. The remainder of their credits came from a combination of general education and vocational classes. Limited-English-speakers were moved along through the system with little opportunity to take either solid basics or college preparatory classes.

A number of Punjabis were themselves critical of Valleyside High's ESL program. One noted bluntly that the low reading level of ESL materials, which he called this "dog in the park stuff," just "won't do." Another expressed outrage that Punjabi students received good grades and high school credit for classes which did not prepare them to be competitive in the job market: "Our children are placed in ghettos and remain there for the whole time spent in school," he said. A few Punjabis accused school officials of "racist" intentions, noting that the outcome of the current program was to "perpetuate second-class status for Punjabi students." Others felt that the ESL track had become an unintentional "trap."

Teachers explained that success in even the slower-paced mainstream classes required at least a 6th grade command of English. Students arriving with very little English, no matter how bright and well prepared, simply could not make the transition from Punjabi to English in one, or even two, years. Some of the students, furthermore, had received inadequate preparation in Indian schools and were totally unprepared to undertake high school level work. Separate classes for new arrivals was the best solution, most teachers believed.

Teachers themselves noted additional difficulties with the ESL program including their own lack of specialized training in ESL and the scarcity of proper instructional materials. Most of their ESL materials were written at a very elementary level and were not stimulating for secondary students. Instructional personnel also cited as a fundamental problem the absence of an overall ESL curriculum at either the high school or district level.

Although Punjabi parents and students concurred with the necessity of special instruction in English for limited- and non-English speakers, they felt that students needed to spend more time interacting with non-Punjabi classmates. Both the formal and informal instructional milieu tended, however, to keep Punjabi students, especially new arrivals, separated from the rest of the student body. In trying to provide for their needs, some instructional personnel "babied" the ESL students and, instead of encouraging competition and self-reliance, created an environment in which ESL students came to rely on extra help. The high school's tracking system for mainstream students was part of the problem, as was the pervasive negative attitude toward recent arrivals from India.

Tracking

Students were placed for their regular academic classes into two tracks— one slow, one fast. Students moving out of ESL, because they could not keep up with the demands of fast-track classes, were placed in the slower track. Yet some ESL teachers considered the slow track a potentially negative learning environment. A majority of the slower-track students were characterized as "lower ability." Some slow-track students simply refused to comply with school and classroom standards regarding work and behavior. Absenteeism was an additional problem. Teachers had lower expectations for slow-track students. Valleysider youngsters in the slower-track classes, furthermore, were felt to be less tolerant of Punjabi classmates than higher ability students. "It goes back to rednecks, the poor white trash types looking for another group to put down," one teacher explained. For all of these reasons, there was a tendency to keep Punjabi youngsters in the secure environment of ESL, even when they were ready to move forward.

Cultural Barriers

Most children, Punjabis included, learn to juggle the differential demands of home and school (Cazden, 1982). Valleyside Punjabis, for example, were taught by their parents to defer to their elders and to remain respectfully quiet in their presence. When Punjabis first entered American schools they were reluctant to speak in class, except to respond with factual information to a teacher's direct question. They were particularly uncomfortable, one Punjabi educator observed, with the "American technique of brainstorming" and fell silent when expected to express their own ideas. Yet, by high school, most Punjabi students, especially those who had been raised from early childhood in Valleyside, had learned to behave one way at home, another way at school, and to meet most demands of American classrooms.

The coeducational nature of schooling in America posed the greatest difficulty for the Punjabi immigrants. In village Punjab, traditionally, teenage boys and girls avoid conversation in mixed company, and even eye contact. In Indian schools girls are not faced with the necessity to mix with boys, or to speak up in their presence. Classroom interaction is structured differently and, in most cases, secondary schooling is segregated by sex. At Valleyside High the Punjabi girls, including those born and educated in America, participated only with great reluctance in coeducational activities which appeared competitive. They did not wish to draw attention to themselves in the presence of the opposite sex.

Physical education (PE) classes at Valleyside High highlighted cultural differences. Students received full credit for PE if they attended regularly, changed into gym clothes, and made reasonable effort to do what was asked of them. Although requirements seemed straightforward, most Punjabi girls in the senior sample lost credit for wearing street clothes to class and for not participating. Punjabi girls were taught that in adolescence they should not be physically active, especially in the presence of males, and that they should keep their legs fully covered. "Our people don't think it is right for girls to wear shorts and run around," one parent noted. Another explained that in village Punjab older girls would never be seen playing outside. Instead, he said, they would be seen walking "with their heads low." Right or wrong, he concluded, Punjabi parents expected the same from their daughters in Valleyside.

Ironically, the federal regulations (Title IX) designed to bring about equal opportunities for women in sports, and all other aspects of education, have worked to the disadvantage of Punjabis. Title IX goals include "the elimination of within-class segregation" and "role models of both sexes."[8] To comply with the letter and the spirit of the regulations when they were first mandated, Valleyside High instituted coed PE classes, except for contact sports. More recently the high school returned to all-male and all-female gym classes because teachers found that the coed classes simply did not work. Coed sports caused many girls, Punjabis in particular, to participate even less than before.

Another problem related to Punjabi standards of modesty. Punjabi youngsters had been taught not to undress in the view of others, but the openness of the locker rooms at Valleyside High made this difficult. For privacy some changed in the toilet stalls. Valleysider students, lacking knowledge of Punjabi culture, became annoyed by the inconvenience. Punjabi girls "used to bug me," one Valleysider explained.

> Like in PE and stuff, some are a little strange. They go and change in the bathroom stall and no one can go to the bathroom. This is kind of irritating. Everyone else changes out where they are supposed to.

The American-educated Punjabi girls were the subgroup of Punjabi students that had the most difficult time reconciling their two worlds, Punjabi and American. Be independent; make your own decisions; go as

---

[8]Cited in "Complying with Title IX Regulations," ERIC/CUE Fact Sheet Number 2, March, 1981. New York: Clearinghouse on Urban Education.

far as you can with your education; postpone marriage and children until your career is begun. These were the messages they received at school, through the media, and from most non-Punjabis with whom they had contact. But their parents told them, all our respect is in your hands. Uphold Punjabi standards; do nothing that will reflect poorly on your family. Many of these young women were indeed pulled in two directions. They wanted more freedom to mix with friends, more support for their ideas, and more opportunity to pursue their educational and occupational goals.

Some of the girls felt that whatever they did, they were criticized. They were faulted by Valleysiders for not dressing American and by their parents for dressing up. Their parents asked, "Why does she have to wear different clothes everyday and wear her hair out [unbraided]?" "She's asking for trouble," they assumed. It was improper for teenage girls to attract attention to themselves. When boys took notice, the girl was blamed. Even Punjabi peers were critical when a girl's behavior deviated from traditional norms.

Conflicts between the two cultural systems had a direct bearing on the girls' social life at school, as well as their academic performance. Punjabis discouraged their children, girls in particular, from mixing with Valleysiders fearing that such contact would alter their children's values. As one parent noted, "When our children get together with the white children, they start doing things which affect our family honor."

One senior, a girl who had come to the U.S. as a small child, expressed frustration with her lot:

My parents don't like my clothes, my hair, the way I talk. They don't like my future plans. They don't like anything about me. They don't like my philosophy about marriage. You should marry an East Indian, yes, but you should pick your own husband. . . . My aunt understands. She went to Valleyside High. But my parents say, "Don't talk to anybody. Don't go anywhere. Come straight home," and that's it. I don't know how I can [ever] get it through their heads that I want to go out with a guy, if they won't even let me go out with a girl.

This young woman was especially bitter about the constant gossip, and the pressures placed on her family to make her conform.

Due to their parents' restrictions, some Punjabi students, most notably girls raised in America, felt the only way to arrange time with friends, males as well as females, was to cut their classes. While the median number of days absent for Punjabi boys was 2, and for recently arrived Punjabi girls just 1, for the American raised and educated girls it was 8.5.

These girls tended to be less than satisfied with their overall performance at Valleyside High. Of the Punjabi students educated since first grade in the U.S., boys were more than three times as likely as girls to pursue college preparatory courses for all 4 years of high school. This was true even though 90% of the girls aspired to a college degree. In high school the girls took business courses instead of advanced classes in math and science because they simply did not believe their parents would permit them to go to college.

Many Punjabi girls felt constrained by a traditional set of values characteristic of village Punjab which places less emphasis on education for women than men.[9] Some Punjabi parents opposed any higher education for women. They noted that too much schooling could cause a woman to become too independent in her life style and decision making, which in turn could create difficulties in arranging a good marriage. The husband's family might worry about such an educated woman fitting in. Those parents who did want their daughters to attend college and graduate school usually insisted that they defer their higher education until after marriage. At that point the decision of college attendance could be made jointly by the young woman, her husband, and her husband's family.

Punjabi parents' attitudes were changing, however, in recognition of the employment opportunities available to women with postsecondary education. Punjabis showed themselves to be quite flexible and receptive to changes which served their interests and tied into their theories of success. They were unwilling to change, nevertheless, simply to conform to mainstream American values and life style, especially in matters touching religion and marriage customs.

Prejudice

Valleyside Punjabis embraced the concept of people intermixing with those of different class, caste, and racial backgrounds. They believed that all children should be offered the same education. "We all belong to the same God," one woman explained. "Even in India," she said, "there is no separation [in school]." Parents also believed that their children, if they were to live and work in America, needed to learn about other cultures, be exposed to different ways of thinking, and acquire the skills to deal effectively with all types of people.

Parents were deeply concerned, however, about their children becoming "Americanized." An Americanized Punjabi, to them, was one who had forgotten his or her roots and who had adopted the life style of white peers. Punjabi praised America for the fairness of its institutions and the laws safeguarding individual rights. They welcomed the opportunities to

---

[9]The patterns described here are those shared by the large majority of Punjabi families living in Valleyside.

work and to save, the modern conveniences, and the chance for children to be well educated. But they were sharply critical of the dominant culture and its effect on their children. Punjabi ways were best, they said, at least for them. Learn from the "Americans," Punjabis instructed their young, but don't become like them.

Many Valleysiders were equally adamant that Punjabi immigrants should change their way of life once in America. Valleysiders supported freedom of religion, but had little tolerance for cultural differences. They equated "being American" with conforming to the norms of the majority.

Interviews with Valleysiders revealed that they associated clothing styles with both cleanliness and patriotism. One young man, who commented that "we are really patriotic now in the U.S.," pointed out that those Punjabi students who dressed like their white peers were those whom he "considered Americanized." These were also the ones, he said, who didn't "smell." Negative attitudes related to Punjabi hygiene pervaded almost every segment of the Valleysider community. Statements such as, "They smell like a dead horse," or "You go into their homes and you can't breathe," were common. Even more widespread was Valleysider discomfort with the Punjabi Sikhs' turbans and beards, their diet, and their family structure.

A climate of prejudice permeated the high school experience of all Punjabi students. Although no Valleysider students said Punjabis caused difficulties for them personally, many Punjabi youngsters cited the prejudiced attitudes and actions of Valleysiders as their main problem at school. Punjabi parents were troubled by the negative social climate and its impact on their children's development. "If you are always worried in case some white child is going to say something to you, . . . then obviously it is going to interfere," one parent commented. Another explained that when children are "teased and picked on . . . they cannot concentrate on their education." Still another observed that "instead of the child being successful, he becomes weak and afraid, saying 'Why study?' and goes to work in the fields or the factory."

Valleysiders and Punjabis agreed that ethnic relations at Valleyside High needed improvement. There was little agreement, however, regarding the causes of the problems, or the solutions. Valleysider students said that if Punjabis would learn to speak English, and would dress and act like other Americans, then there would be more mixing across ethnic lines and less hostility. Punjabi students, on the other hand, said it was the prejudiced attitudes and behavior of Valleysiders that deterred them from mixing and restricted their opportunity to learn English.

Punjabi students wanted to fit in at school, but it often proved difficult to reconcile the expectations of Valleysider classmates and teachers with those of the Punjabi community. Dress was one example. In an effort to please both peers and parents, some girls would leave home with hair tightly braided and, on their way to school, don jewelry and makeup, and let their hair fall loose. When high school teachers suggested that skirts were preferred for job interviews, Punjabi girls would borrow a skirt at school and change back to slacks before returning home. At home and at the *gurdwara* they wore a *salwaar-kameez* and *dupatta* (the traditional Punjabi dress of loose pants, long overblouse reaching to the knees, and a scarf-like piece of cloth, 2 to 3 yards long, worn around the neck and shoulders, or over the head).

Punjabi teenagers were attracted to many aspects of mainstream American culture. They enjoyed the latest rock music. They wore designer jeans and Vaurnet sunglasses. They loved french fries and ice cream. They watched the Super Bowl on TV. They pressed their parents for more independence, more freedom to make decisions on their own. Their values were changing, but at the same time Punjabi youth remained firmly and squarely anchored in their Punjabi identity. "Being in America," one senior explained, means "you have to compromise a little," but "we are not saying that we want to become like whites."[10]

Valleysider students believed in religious freedom and the individual's right not to conform, but, in practice, they penalized those whose standards were different. "We have numbers on our side," explained one Valleysider, a bright, popular student.

> Numbers mean power, and you get 100 Anglos and 10 Punjabis, and you know that the Anglos can overpower the Punjabis. So they can say that my way of living is right and yours is wrong and get away with it.

To this Valleysider youth, and many others, being "American" meant "acting like white people."

Only a majority of Valleysiders participated actively in the harassment of Punjabis. The majority, however, either condoned their classmates' behavior or felt powerless to alter the situation. Verbal jibes, such as "you stink" or "you goddamn Hindus," and milder forms of physical abuse, such as food throwing, were common. More offensive but less frequent incidents included Valleysiders spitting at Punjabis, sticking them with pins, and throwing lighted cigarettes at them. Punjabi boys, who wore their hair long and in a turban, in keeping with Sikh teachings, were constantly teased.

Two Punjabi seniors reported far more serious incidents, one a criminal offense. In this case a girl's long braids were deliberately set on fire:

---

[10]Punjabis generally refer to the majority group as "whites" or "Americans."

I was walking along with a friend of mine after I finished my class and a boy lit my hair with a lighter. I had to cut a lot of my hair off. . . . One girl who was coming behind me quickly put my hair out with her hands. If she hadn't done that, all of my hair would have been burned.

The girl, a limited-English-speaker, had been in the United States for only 2 years. In the second case another girl, again a limited-English-speaker and a recent immigrant, was put off a school bus taking students to their summer employment at the nearby air base. The bus driver later reported that some non-Punjabi students had told him the girl had lice. The girl was simply put off the bus miles out of town without an explanation.

Those Punjabis who spoke the least English were preyed upon the most. Fluent-English-speakers had learned to respond to Valleysider cracks with a quick comment of their own. Racial prejudice, however, affected all Punjabis.

In keeping with their parents' advice, most Punjabi youngsters tried simply to ignore the hostilities. Immigrants, as one Punjabi youngster explained,

don't want to cause any trouble. They want to adjust. They want to get ahead and they want to learn something. They tend not to be aggressive. They tend to overlook things.

Such an approach did little to deter the offending Valleysiders.

Some Valleysiders spoke freely about their actions. One explained how he and his buddies hassled the "Hindus . . . just for the hell of it." Another boy told of throwing food at Punjabis to make his friends laugh. This student also described how a classmate would pass daily by a group of Punjabi students who were sitting on a low wall and "slap each of them on the head." His reaction: "It was pretty tight, but it was pretty funny." No Punjabis reported amusement at such antics.

Punjabi youngsters raised in the U.S. were less willing than newcomers to say "never mind" and "let the time pass," as their parents instructed, even though they knew their parents would blame them if a fight erupted. Several incidents suggested an increasing willingness to turn to force, even weapons, if pressed too far.

Sikhs, throughout history, have shown their toughness and their willingness to resist forcefully when pushed. There is a strong Sikh military tradition and outward symbols of it in religious and personal life. Sikh males are instructed that they must defend their honor and the honor of family and community. "Turn the other cheek twice," Sikhs say, "but the third time you must fight."

Valleyside High faculty recognized the explosive nature of the situation. They dealt sternly and swiftly with serious offenses. They were less effective, however, in addressing the underlying causes of the problems. Most believed that the troubles would persist until Punjabis became assimilated culturally into the mainstream of American life. This would take time, they realized, but, in their view, it was both inevitable and desirable. Oddly, some of the Punjabi values which contributed most to Punjabi success in school, such as the emphasis on group decision making, placing family interests ahead of personal wishes, and providing strong parental supervision for adolescents, were the very qualities most misunderstood and disturbing to many Valleysider educators.

COMMUNITY FORCES AND SCHOOL PERFORMANCE

The Valleyside case study points to a direct and strong relationship between home and community forces and the school adaptation patterns of both Punjabi and majority-group students. With the Punjabis the focus here has been the role of family and community in promoting academic success. We have shown, too, however, how values characteristic of village Punjab can thwart girls' educational ambitions.

Asian American students are said to do well in school, in part at least, because of cultural traditions which promote academic achievement (see Schwartz, 1971; Sung, 1979). Such a case may certainly be made for the Sikhs of Valleyside. Children are instructed to respect and obey those in authority and to bring honor to their family. They are taught also that no person is better than another and that an individual will rise, or fall, on his or her own merits and initiative. It is assumed that through hard work and cleverness any Sikh can become a successful and important person. Within traditional Punjabi Sikh society great emphasis is placed on individual achievement, little on inherited status (Pettigrew, 1972). The egalitarian principles of Sikhism act as an equalizing influence on the Sikh community and weaken the potential development of restricted educational categories and socioeconomic groups. Sikhs believe that all children should be entitled to equal educational opportunities.

Cultural and religious factors alone, however, cannot explain the academic accomplishments of Sikh immigrants (Gibson & Bhachu, 1986). In India, Jat Sikh farm families have traditionally placed no great emphasis on all their children becoming educated. Secondary and postsecondary education for females not only has not been considered a priority, it has been discouraged. In rural Punjab, furthermore, formal education for Jat Sikh women has had little function as there were, and still are, no jobs apart from household chores which they can perform. Nor has education been a priority for all Jat Sikh males. Only those who were expected to earn their livelihood apart from farming were encouraged to remain in school.

The Valleyside case points, therefore, to the importance of contextual as well as cultural variables in shaping school performance patterns. In America a great many more employment opportunities exist, for women as well as men, than is the case in India. Employment in this country, furthermore, is more open than in India. Valleyside Punjabis recognize that prejudice and discrimination can hinder their employment opportunities, but they still believe their chances to compete based on skills and credentials to be far better here than in most other countries. In such an environment formal education takes on greater importance than was the case in rural Punjab. Schooling, furthermore, is more readily available and of a higher quality than in village India. Valleyside Punjabis can attend high school and community college without leaving home. Older students, by holding after-school and summer jobs, can even pay their own way. In India students have no similar opportunity to be wage earners.

Important, too, is the Punjabis' situation as voluntary immigrants, who have chosen freely to come to this country. America for them is like a promised land. They are willing to work hard and to make great sacrifices to get ahead. Their reference point, moreover, is India. A comparative perspective helps them to see the many advantages that life in this country holds. Children are reminded of this constantly and reminded, too, that if they fritter away their opportunities they will have only themselves to blame.

Many different immigrant groups have been found to do well in school, not only those of Asian descent (Ogbu, 1983; Ogbu & Gibson, n.d.). Cultural explanations fail to explain why immigrant youths from distinctly different cultural backgrounds, such as Turks in Australia, Central Americans in San Francisco, and British West Indians in St. Croix, have similar school response patterns (Gibson, 1983; Inglis & Manderson, n.d.; Suarez-Orosco, n.d.). These students, by and large, do well in school even in the face of major cultural and social barriers. Immigrant minorities have a different relationship to the dominant group than indigenous minorities and a distinctly different perception of the opportunities available to them.

The school-performance patterns of a particular minority group, or subgroup, are tied closely to the group's theory of success (Ogbu, 1974). Such theory is shaped not only by the cultural preferences of the group, but also by the historical context of settlement in the host country, and the group's response to its present situation. Valleyside Punjabis realize their children face many difficulties in schools. They are especially concerned about prejudice, on the one hand, and pressures to American-ize, on the other. They believe, nonetheless, that compliance with school demands is their best alternative. Educated Punjabis who have become economically successful, while also maintaining strong ties to the commu-nity, serve as role models for the younger generation and reinforce the overall Punjabi Sikh strategy of accommodation without assimilation. Sikhs are not merely accommodative, however. If a time comes when accommodation proves ineffective, it may be anticipated that Valleyside Sikhs will turn to other means.[11]

The present study also shows how the cultural preferences and success theories of the white majority influence the school performance of major-ity youth. Although Valleysiders view a high school diploma as essential, most slight academic work and give comparatively greater attention to the acquisition of social competencies. The most studious Valleysider stu-dents are labeled "brains" and, unless they balance their bookish orienta-tion with social and athletic skills, they are considered peculiar. The students described as "most outstanding" by their peers are those who excel socially.

The focus of education in America today, at the secondary level in particular, has "more to do with conventional standards of sociability and propriety than with instrumental and cognitive skills" (Collins, 1979, p. 19). Few majority-group parents urge substantial academic performance from their children. Neither, by and large, do their teachers and coun-selors. There is an assumption, shared by Valleysider parents, students, and teachers, that the more advanced academic courses are only for college-bound students. Those students who do not expect to go on to a 4-year college see little point, therefore, in taking math, science, and English classes beyond those required for graduation. They are not viewed as part of a basic education or as necessary for those who plan to enter the work force directly from high school. Thus, for the last 2 years of high school, the typical Valleysider student turns his or her attention to part-time jobs and social activities. Majority parents and educators are disturbed when teenagers choose to take it easy in school, but they see little that they can do to alter the situation.

School success is often correlated with parents' jobs, income, and education. In the Punjabi case, however, none of these variables proves critical. Far more important are parents' and students' beliefs about the value of formal education, combined with a system of sanctions which serves to press deviant students back into line.

---

[11]The current activist Sikh radicalism in India and abroad, and the Ghadr Party Marxism of American Sikhs earlier in the century, show the Sikhs' readiness to resist their oppressors when they feel no other alternative exists (Singh, 1966).

We need to learn more about why subordinate status promotes "compensatory striving" for some, while for others it contributes to persistent academic difficulties (DeVos & Romanucci-Ross, 1975, p. 379). The answers lie neither in cultural nor in structural explanations alone, but in the dynamic interactions which exists between them.

REDUCING EDUCATIONAL INEQUITIES

The comparative success of Punjabi students in meeting school demands suggests no cause for complacency in addressing the barriers. The most serious impediments relate to the structure of school programs and the prejudiced attitudes and actions of majority youngsters, both areas over which the Punjabi community has little or no control. Home-school cultural and linguistic differences pose difficulties also, but these difficulties are exacerbated by the social structure and tracking system at Valleyside High.

The ESL program, although instituted to help language minority students move rapidly into the high school's regular academic program, tended instead to move students up and out as part of a remedial track. The high school's tracking system, in general, served to pigeonhole and stereotype the students, majority as well as minority. Students in the slower tracks tended to lower their expectations and succumb to peer pressure to take it easy in school.

It is unreasonable to assume that non-English-speaking immigrants. who arrive in this country in the midst of their school career, will be able to meet the regular requirements for high school graduation while also learning English. It is even less reasonable to suppose that they can compete in college preparatory classes. Such students need a system which permits them to take more than four years in high school, or which teaches them English first and then places them into the high school's academic program in accordance with their ability and prior preparation in other countries.[12] Immigrants also need a rigorous program in English as a second language, far more rigorous than that at Valleyside High, together with a curriculum and social climate that promote mixing across ethnic lines.

One of the major drawbacks of the ESL track, as it existed in Valleyside, was that it tended to keep limited-English-speakers socially separated. Not only did this slow their learning of English, it contributed

---

[12]Valleyside High now requires language minority students to fulfill the same English requirements as majority-group students. It also now permits students to spend more than eight semesters in high school, if necessary, to meet graduation requirements.

to Valleysider stereotypes about Punjabis. These included the Valleysider assumption that Punjabis were unwilling to adapt to their new surroundings.

Punjabis, like other minorities, do adapt, and would adapt all the more readily were their own identity not challenged in the process (cf. Philips, 1976). Like other minorities they resent the presumption of their inferiority and the suggestion that they are less American because their cultural traditions differ from those of the majority. Nor do Punjabi immigrants believe that cultural assimilation will guarantee them equal opportunities or open doors to positions of power and privilege. Cultural conformity, from their perspective, can only contribute to their downfall.

School administrators at Valleyside High often seemed more concerned with how well Punjabi students were fitting into the mainstream social scene than with how they were doing academically. All too often Punjabi students were judged deviant for nonparticipation in school dances, clubs, and class picnics, while their academic diligence was less frequently cited. A definition of school success that hinges on cultural assimilation contributes to the problems of minorities in America's schools.

Valleysiders, like many white Americans, demonstrate a cultural parochialism which educators would do well to address in school programs. Most majority students are quite unaware of their own cultural assumptions. They assume, for example, that anyone who looks and dresses differently "smells bad," and that an extended family all living under one roof must be living in filth and poverty. Majority students, and their teachers, are equally misled when they argue that arranged marriages are wrong and that young people who feel obliged to accept their parents' matchmaking are to be pitied.

Valleysiders worry about job competition and about Punjabis becoming, as indeed they have, a major economic force in the community. This is another dimension of the prejudice. Yet Valleysiders themselves have little interest in orchard farming. They insist, moreover, that individuals should be hired on the basis of objective qualifications, rather than out of consideration for race or ethnic background. They acknowledge, too, that Punjabis are good workers. What appears most troublesome for many Valleysiders is that Punjabi immigrants are becoming economically successful while maintaining many of their traditional Punjabi ways.

White Americans, by and large, believe strongly in the rightness of cultural assimilation. They believe ethnic relations would improve if Punjabis would only try harder to blend in. Few seem to recognize that the racial difference would remain, or that the changes they ask for would undermine the very strength of the Punjabi family system and community.

The issue for educators is not whether immigrants change their way of life, or how fast, but whether schools foster an instructional and social climate that helps students to pursue their educational and vocational goals. If teachers and administrators continue to believe that cultural assimilation is the single and simple quid pro quo for school success, we shall make little progress in promoting equal educational opportunities for minority students. By pressuring minority students to conform to majority standards, schools devalue their cultural traditions and contribute to an oppositional climate, a sense of "us verses them," which can do much to undermine the instructional process. If we are to eliminate the problems of racial prejudice, as they exist on school campuses today, we need educational programs which are dedicated to providing students with a cross-cultural and comparative perspective. All will benefit, majority and minority alike. To improve academic performance we need to identify and to create learning environments encouraging to just those values and attitudes of Punjabis and other immigrants which support their success in the American system of public education.

ACKNOWLEDGMENTS

The National Institute of Education funded this research project from 1980 to 1982 and encouraged its progress during that period. The opinions expressed here, however, do not necessarily reflect those of the Institute.

REFERENCES

Cazden, C. (1982). Four Comments. In P. Gilmore & A. A. Glatthorn (Eds.), *Children in and out of school* (pp. 209–226). Washington, DC: Center for Applied Linguistics.

Collins, R. (1979). *The credential society: An historical sociology of education and stratification.* Orlando, FL: Academic Press.

DeVos, G., & Romanucci-Ross, L. (1975). Ethnicity: Vessel of meaning and emblem of contrast. In G. DeVos and L. Romanucci-Ross (Eds.), *Ethnic identity: Cultural continuities and change.* Palo Alto, CA: Mayfield.

Gibson, M. A. (1983). Ethnicity and schooling: West Indian immigrants in the United States Virgin Islands. *Ethnic Groups, 5*(3), 173–197.

Gibson, M. A. (1985). Collaborative educational ethnography: Problems and profits. *Anthropology and Education Quarterly, 16*(2), 124–148.

Gibson, M. A., & Bhachu, P. (1986). Community forces and school performance: Punjabi Sikhs in rural California and urban Britain. *New Community, 13* (Spring/Summer).

Gibson, M. A. (n.d.). *Accommodation without assimilation: Punjabi Sikh immigrants in an American high school and community.*

Hsu, F. L. K. (1981). *Americans and Chinese.* Third Edition. Honolulu: The University Press of Hawaii.

Inglis, C., & Manderson, L. (n.d.). *Education and reproduction among Turkish families in Sydney.* Unpublished manuscript, Department of Education, The University of Sydney.

LaBrack, B. (1982a). Occupational specialization among rural California Sikhs: The interplay of culture and economics. *Amerasia, 9*(2), 29–56.

LaBrack, B. (1982b). Personal communication, University of the Pacific, Stockton, California, November 28.

Ogbu, J. U. (1974). *The next generation.* Orlando, FL: Academic Press.

Ogbu, J. U. (1983). Minority status and schooling. *Comparative Education Review, 27*(2), 168–190.

Ogbu, J. U., & Gibson, M. A. (Eds.). (n.d.). *Minority status and schooling: Immigrants vs. non-immigrants.*

Pettigrew, J. (1972). Some notes on the social system of the Sikh Jats. *New Community, 1*(5), 354–363.

Philips, S. W. (1976). Commentary: Access to power and maintenance of ethnic identity as goals of multicultural education—Are they compatible? *Anthropology and Education Quarterly, 7*(4), 30–32.

Schwartz, A. J. (1971). The culturally advantaged: A study of Japanese-American pupils. *Sociology and Social Research, 55*(3), 341–353.

Singh, K. (1966). *A history of the Sikhs: Volume 2, 1839–1964.* Princeton, NJ: Princeton University Press.

Suarez-Orosco, M. M. (n.d.). Immigrant adaptation to schooling: A Hispanic case. In J. Ogbu & M. Gibson (Eds.). *Minority status and schooling: Immigrant vs. non-immigrant.*

Sung, B. L. (1979). *Transplanted Chinese children.* Report to the Administration for Children, Youth and Family, Department of Health, Education & Welfare, Washington, DC.

Wenzel, L. (1966). *The identification and analysis of certain value orientations of two generations of East Indians in California.* Unpublished doctoral dissertation, University of the Pacific.

The Author and Her Chapter

Christine Robinson Finnan is a cultural anthropologist at SRI International, a nonprofit research institute in Menlo Park, California. She received her Ph.D. in education and anthropology from Stanford University in 1980 under the supervision of G. Spindler, and an M.A. in anthropology from the University of Texas in 1974.

She became interested in refugee settlement issues in 1976 while working at a refugee settlement agency in San Francisco. At that time, she was primarily interested in the adaptation of children to life in the United States, but as her involvement with refugees deepened, and issues surrounding resettlement grew more complex, she became increasingly concerned with the adjustment of adult refugees. Since completing her dissertation, she has worked on several projects at SRI focusing on refugee settlement issues. This chapter reflects both research conducted for her dissertation and her current work on the role of the refugee community in refugee adjustment.

Finnan attends to the development of an occupational identity among Vietnamese refugees and the support in the community of these refugees for this identity. This support helped the refugees survive not only the usual exigencies encountered by refugees but also some very poor instruction in the electronics training course they took to prepare themselves for employment in Silicon Valley.

The ways in which the image of the electronic technician's role became a positive one, and the ways in which the Vietnamese refugee community contributed to the development of this identity tells us much that is also relevant to understanding the adaptations of other refugees and immigrants to the United States. Dr. Finnan points out some of these relationships in her discussion.

The Editors

13

The Influence of the Ethnic Community on the Adjustment of Vietnamese Refugees

Christine Robinson Finnan
SRI International, Menlo Park, California

INTRODUCTION

When considering the rapid economic advances made by many of the newer migrants to the United States a great deal of credit is usually given to the strength of their belief in education as a route to success. Education does play a critical role when adaptation is examined over several generations; however, it often plays a less important role in the adjustment of first generation migrants. School does not necessarily provide a route to success; rather, it can provide short-term training and instruction that enables newcomers to enter into occupations that are sanctioned by their ethnic community.

Most adult refugees and some immigrants enroll in training or education because they must change their occupation when they arrive in the United States. For many, the new occupation is lower in status than that previously held. The newcomer must not only learn new skills but also develop a new occupational identity. The school environment is an obvious influence on the development of a new occupational identity. This research shows, however, that the process of training can do do little more than provide access to equipment and a credential. In the situation described in the following section, the students' ethnic community was the primary influence on their occupational identity development.

This chapter examines the process of occupational identity development within a group of Vietnamese refugees[1] and focuses on the role of the Vietnamese community in helping Vietnamese refugees shape a new occupational identity. The study is based on field work conducted in 1978–1979 with a group of Vietnamese refugees enrolled in an electronics technician training program in Santa Clara County, California.

The chapter describes occupational identity development as a process of shaping one's self-image to fit an occupational role, while creating an image of the role compatible with one's self-image. Although this process is influenced by the training process and the individual's personality and aptitude, I emphasize the importance of the ethnic community in this process. Two issues related to the role of the ethnic community in taking on a new identity are explored. The first concerns the kinds of roles played by the ethnic community in influencing refugee adjustment. The second concerns the relative importance of the ethnic community as an influence in shaping an individual's occupational choice and occupational identity.

I first present a description of the research context followed by a presentation of the findings. The discussion of these findings explores the role of the community in adjustment.

THE RESEARCH CONTEXT

I attended a 6 month job training program designed to train electronic technicians. I began the research with the goal of better understanding the relationship of job training and occupational identity development. I attended the course as a participant, but not as a student. I worked on assignments with students and talked informally with them. Data were collected primarily through observations and informal interviews at this one program, although I also augmented my data with interviews with Vietnamese refugees at other job training centers, in refugee help centers, and with refugees working as technicians.

The particular class I attended began in October, 1978, with an enrollment of 30 students. Students were in class for 7 hours each day. Mornings were devoted to lectures on electronics and to work on prob-

---

[1]The fact that this description of Vietnamese refugees is based on refugees arriving in 1975 and 1976 skews the nature of their backgrounds. The 150,000 Southeast Asia refugees that fled Southeast Asia in 1975 were primarily the elite and were better educated than most refugees that came later. These later arrivals, often referred to as "boat people" often came from rural backgrounds, and a large number of them were ethnic Chinese, as opposed to the predominantly ethnic Vietnamese that arrived earlier.

lems in simple physics and mathematics. Afternoons were devoted to lab work. The training center maintained an intentional ethnic heterogeniety; there were six Vietnamese students among a class of whites, Hispanics, blacks, Filipinos and Koreans. When the class ended in April, 1979, twelve students received technician certificates, four of whom were Vietnamese.[2]

The high drop-out rate for this training cycle can be explained by the demands of the training and by the quality of instruction. Electronics technician training demands a level of understanding of math and science that many students did not have. Students with English language limitations were especially disadvantaged unless they had considerable formal schooling, especially in the sciences. Many of the American students said that they never liked school, and some had not finished high school. Of those who finished high school, few took many math and science classes. Students from Mexico and Central America were even further disadvantaged by their educational and language limitations.

Many of the students who did not finish the program might not have dropped out if the instruction had been better. My observations coincided with the introduction of a new teacher into the program. She was hired because she is bilingual in English and Spanish. Despite the good intentions of the training center, the first months of the course are best described as chaotic. The instructor left the room for extended periods of time, leaving students without adequate assignments to occupy their time. Students who understood the material worked over the same problems several times, while those who did not understand, talked, complained, and day dreamed. When the instructor lectured, she was rarely prepared, and she covered material too quickly for many students. Few students were happy with the course, and many quietly dropped out.

The Vietnamese students, however, remained excited about becoming electronics technicians. How is this possible when the instruction was poor? First, the Vietnamese students were able to keep up with the lessons because they all had formal training in math and science in high school or college in Vietnam. Schooling in Vietnam was patterned on the French system and demanded a solid grounding in basic skills. The poor quality of the program was a problem for the Vietnamese not because they were unable to keep up with the material, but because they became bored with the lack of challenge. Second, and possibly more important, the Vietnamese refugee community encouraged its members to see themselves as technicians before they started the training course. The Viet-

[2]One Vietnamese man dropped out to take a job as a technician. Another man did not complete the course because he felt he was too old (about 60 years).

namese community helped individual Vietnamese feel that electronics technician "is a good job for me" because the community held that "it is a good job for us Vietnamese."

FINDINGS

The Dynamics of Occupational Identity Development

Occupational identity development describes the process of molding an image of self to fit a role, while also molding an image of the role to fit one's self-image. Occupational identity can be defined as a response to and influence on a social role, usually in the world of work. There are two key phrases in this definition. *Response to* describes how a person molds his/her self-image to fit the role. *Influence on* describes how a person shapes an image of the role to complement his/her self-image. This process applies to all workers as they maintain a balance between their self-image and their image of the occupation, but it is especially important as refugees or immigrants adjust to new roles in a new culture. Table 13.1 summarizes how Vietnamese refugees created compatibility between their self-image and electronics technician jobs. As the table shows, there are a number of components that, combined, make up a person's self-image and a person's image of the job. Following, I illustrate how the Vietnamese students and their community mold each component so that, in the end, the components comprising self-image and those comprising the image of the occupation are compatible.

Adjustments to Self-Image

Compatibility of Background and Interests With the Demands of the Job.   Many refugees emphasized aspects of their background and interests that were consistent with the demands of electronics technician jobs. Most, in fact, realized that they were overqualified for technician jobs. The students I observed either had college degrees or were in college when they left Vietnam; many of their American classmates had high school degrees at best.

Not only were these Vietnamese refugees well educated, their education was oriented toward math and science, areas basic to electronics technician jobs. Vietnamese students in the training program repeatedly said that the material covered in class was easy because they studied math and science in college. Several of them taught math and science in Vietnam.

The students explained that most high school graduates in Vietnam

TABLE 13.1
The Process of Occupational Identity Development

The Vietnamese community encourages members to develop an occupational identity as electronics technicians by:	
Encouraging members to mold their sense of self to fit the role.	*Helping members shape an image of the job consistent with their self-image.*
—They emphasize the compatibility of their background and interests with the demands of the job.	—They see the electronics industry as an advantageous occupational environment.
—They recognize that they possess limitations that prevent them from taking many other jobs.	—Electronics technician jobs have an image of being middle class jobs.
—They believe that Vietnamese and Americans share the same attitudes toward work.	—Electronics technician jobs are male jobs and help maintain status hierarchies in the home.
—They feel financially responsible for their families.	—Electronics technician jobs are adequately challenging to refugees.

learned basic electronics theory in required math and science classes. They described the high school curricula as rigid and rigorous. All students had to take prescribed courses, despite their interests. For example, although one woman was studying to become a lawyer in Vietnam, she took physics and calculus in high school.

Vietnamese in the United States displayed evidence of continued interest in electronics. In the Vietnamese community in Santa Clara County, one self-help organization and some individuals offered classes in electronics to those interested in becoming technicians or learning new skills. In addition, Vietnamese students flooded public and private training programs. In 1978, private training programs in electronics technican training (charging about $2,000 for an electronics technician certificate) were composed of between 40% and 90% Vietnamese students. Many Vietnamese read electronics books at home to improve their performance at work or in school. One man explained that each night he would read ahead in an electronics book so that he would understand what was presented in lecture. He had no trouble with the concepts behind electronics, but he did not understand all of the English terminology.

The behavior of Vietnamese students in classes also illustrates their interest in electronics. At the job training center, the Vietnamese students participated actively; they asked questions, and worked ahead of the class whenever possible. The Vietnamese students were so interested in the subject they were accused of "hogging" the equipment, and of preventing others from learning.

Limitations Preventing Refugees from Regaining Their Former Occupation. One might ask why such well educated and ambitious people settled for futures as electronics technicians. Most refugees saw themselves as having limitations that prevented them from taking jobs similar to jobs they held in Vietnam. Inability to speak English fluently was the most serious limitation for most refugees. All of the Vietnamese students in the training classes were far from fluent in English, and they would have had trouble competing for jobs demanding fluency. It was not unusual for Vietnamese refugees arriving in 1975–1976 to have limited English-speaking ability. For example, in a telephone survey of refugees, only 25.2% of those arriving in 1975 reported speaking English well or fluently, and 30.6% reported speaking no English on arrival (U.S. Department of Health and Human Services, 1983).

Another limitation refugees mentioned was their age. Many felt that they were too old to pursue a career demanding extended training. In addition to being older, many refugees had children, and they felt that it was more appropriate for them to take a job and let their children train for careers. For example, one man said:

> My future is nothing, and my present is nothing. I want my children to be better than my life. I think they can get through if I work and save money. They would like to go to school.

Finally, some refugees said they are too small and weak to work at many jobs. They thought electronics technician jobs were good for them because the jobs do not demand physical strength. One refugee said that fellow trainees for a machinist job doubted that he could do the job because of his size. He said that he told them, "I may have a small body, but I have a big mind." He proudly related that he was promoted before all of the other trainees.

Compatibility of Vietnamese and American Attitudes Toward Work. The Vietnamese also saw their cultural attitudes toward work as consistent with life in the United States and with the demands of the job. Vietnamese described themselves as hard working, diligent, and patient. They explained that these traits have made Vietnam as a country a formidable foe to larger nations such as the United States and China. They believed that these traits will help Vietnamese advance in the United States and that these traits are especially well-suited to the electronics industry. For example, one man explained that Vietnamese become technicians because they are patient, and can memorize things easily. Another Vietnamese said employers like Vietnamese because, "they are patient, industrious, and clean. They come early, and work twice as fast as Americans or Mexicans." Vietnamese believe that these traits are rewarded in the United States and that they will be given the opportunity to contribute to what they see as America's greatness. For example, one man said that America is rich because people work hard, are intelligent, and they cooperate. Other refugees remarked that their neighbors are always working, which makes it difficult to form friendships. Vietnamese also see themselves as hard working. One man explained that they learned to work hard because they come from a small country where they had to work hard to survive. Many Vietnamese refugees saw the United States as an open society, thriving on diversity and rewarding hard work and enterprise. A student explained why he thinks the United States is a rich country:

I can say American life is very good because this land is not American land. Everyone came from another country from all over the world, so they have different ideas, and they collect good ideas. The bad ideas, somewhat less. That's why the culture has the best skills, scientists, pharmacists, doctors, everything. . . . They have new idea, maybe new idea is better than old. So it makes the culture better than the old.

Underlying this statement is his belief that Vietnamese will also contribute to America's greatness.

Influence of a Feeling of Financial Responsibility for Family. The Vietnamese students interviewed felt strongly that refugees should work to support themselves and that they should not rely on welfare. Refugees liked electronics technician jobs because the training period was short (usually 6 months) and the starting pay was adequate. More extensive training, even if it was for better jobs, would have kept them financially dependent too long. Electronics technician jobs paid a good enough salary ($5.00–$10.00 per hour in 1978) to come at least close to economic self-sufficiency. Refugees said that they wanted to work, and they knew that Americans resented them taking welfare.

Self-sufficiency in a Vietnamese family involves parents caring for their children, children caring for their parents and people in the United States caring for relatives in Vietnam. Vietnamese parents care for their children out of love, responsibility and a feeling that their children are their future. Grown children also assume responsibility for their parents. Vietnamese are shocked by the treatment of the elderly in the United States. They said that they would never send old people to rest homes or let them sit alone on park benches. Children rarely question their responsibility to their parents. In addition, many Vietnamese refugees left family members in Vietnam, and they feel responsible for their financial and emotional well-being. For example, one young man said he wants to become an engineer because:

> My mother wrote that I must find my life to brighten my family. Sometimes I am lazy or tired, but I think about my family. After I was in prison with the Viet Cong, my mind was not well. It is easy to be tired.

Sacrifice for the family may not always be positive, especially when desires for immediate economic security rule out efforts to advance. For example, some Vietnamese community leaders are concerned about the future of young people who forego college to work to support their family. A community worker said:

> I'm really concerned about the family of six; the father is 55; the oldest child, 25. They ask the children to go to work rather than to college to gain economic security. The need to survive [in Santa Clara County] is so much.

Summary of Adjustments Refugees Make to Their Self-Image.   In sum, Vietnamese refugees' self-image supported their decision to become electronics technicians. They saw themselves as hard working, well educated, ambitious, and diligent. They felt these traits would be rewarded in the United States, particularly in the electronics industry because it rewards people with middle class attributes and aspirations. On the other hand, they acknowledged having limitations which prevented them from training for a number of jobs in the United States. They also saw themselves as motivated to work because they were responsible for themselves and for the welfare of their families.

The training program did little to help the students identify as electronics technicians. The instructor, through her lack of organization and preoccupation with matters outside of the class served as a negative role model for the students. The high dropout rate shows that many students chose not to shape their self-image to fit the job. The following describes how the Vietnamese students created an image of the job consistent with their image of themselves as middle class and ambitious.

Creation of a Positive Image of the Job

Advantageous Occupational Environment.   Refugees saw the occupational environment in Santa Clara County as conducive to their efforts to become self-sufficient, even though the cost of living in the county was one of the highest in the country. To the Vietnamese community, the electronics industry contained: many jobs, good jobs, skilled jobs, opportunities to advance in jobs, and good potential for more jobs in the future. The electronics industry was a symbol of opportunity. Even though many of the refugees arriving in the United States in 1975 were the elite in Vietnam, and the upper rungs of the occupational ladder in Vietnam were theirs, some of the refugees interviewed said they preferred working in the United States to working in Vietnam because there is more potential for advancement here.

The electronics industry represented opportunity to many Vietnamese refugees. They saw the industry growing, and they felt there was room for them to advance within it. At the time this research was conducted, their perceptions were supported by many others in the industry. For example, in 1979, the Santa Clara Manufacturing Group estimated a 24% increase in jobs between 1979 and 1981 and a 20% increase between 1982 and 1985 (Santa Clara Manufacturing Group, 1979[3]).

Vietnamese in Santa Clara County saw many opportunities within the electronics industry to better their futures. First, they recognized the opportunity to make quite a bit of money by either working overtime or working at two jobs. Many refugees were eager to work as many hours of overtime as possible. In fact, some chose jobs for their overtime potential. Other refugees worked two shifts each day, usually one shift at one company and another at another company.

Second, the industry was capable of providing jobs for entire families. Most refugee households relied on at least two salaries. Typically, the husband worked as a technician and the wife as an assembler. Older children often worked full or part-time in electronics-related jobs.

Third, refugees saw several ways to advance as technicians. For example, they could advance in terms of salary by switching to a company that was willing to pay more money. A placement counselor said that Vietnamese were notorious for "job jumping" in order to make 10 cents an hour more money. They could also move into a job with more responsibility and a higher salary. Many of them tried to become engineer's assistants, or they found other positions with more responsibility after starting with an entry-level job. Finally, they could move from a small company to a large company. Working for a company like IBM carried a great deal of prestige.

Fourth, for refugees choosing to continue their education, the industry had many job openings for engineers. Many of the technician students planned to study engineering while they worked as technicians. Engineers were given quite a bit of respect within the community, and they were seen as refugees that had "made it."

---

[3]These estimates were made prior to the economic recession in the early 1980s that slowed growth in the electronics industry.

Fifth, many refugees saw the electronics industry as a source of employment for their children. Even people with young children said that they would like their children to become engineers and technicians. In other words, the industry was seen as appropriate not only for the first generation but for the more Americanized second generation.

Few refugees were worried about the future of the electronics industry, and few questioned the advisability of clustering in one industry. In the late 1970s there was little reason to worry about the strength of the industry, and even if there was reason to worry, many refugees felt they were equipped to survive change. For example, when asked what Vietnamese would do if the bottom fell out of the electronics industry, a community worker said:

> The Vietnamese are known to be adapting to any situation. If the bottom falls off from the electronics industry, it is nothing like the bottom falling off from Vietnam. If they could get it made, they will. If they need to change their trade, they'll change again. Why put all eggs in one basket? I say, "let's do it while it's still good." After that, so what? I don't think that's still a concern.

Vietnamese refugees' attraction to the electronics industry was strong enough to enable them to justify living in an area of the country with a very high cost of living. Most Vietnamese felt that the occupational advantages of the area outweighed the economic disadvantages. For example, one student and her husband visited friends in rural Oregon. When they returned, she talked at length about the beautiful house her friends bought for $40,000. She thought the house would cost $200,000 in Santa Clara County. The friends tried to convince them to move to Oregon, but she said they refused. She said she wanted to have a good job; she did not want to "pull up vegetables" like her friend. Vietnamese refugees generally are willing to sacrifice material comforts, such as large homes, for white collar jobs, in part because the jobs carry more status, but also because they appear to have more potential for advancement.

Electronics Technician as a Middle Class Job.   Vietnamese have given electronics technician jobs a middle class image. The requirements needed for the job, the work environment, and options for advancement have characteristics Vietnamese associated with middle class occupations. Vietnamese liked the technician jobs because the requirements were mental, not physical. The refugees' educational backgrounds were utilized in technician jobs more than in many jobs other refugees held. To the Vietnamese, the mental/physical distinction separated working class from middle class occupations. Vietnamese were willing to work for less money at a job demanding education than to do manual labor. The community worker cited above added:

> Vietnamese find electronics technician suitable to their liking. Vietnamese are very conscious of status. To them, hard labor, manual work is not good. They would take an assembly job at $5.00 per hour over carpenter at $8.00 per hour because it is manual work. They like a clean job; it is the culture.

The industry also helped them recreate class boundaries; middle class, educated men became technicians, while the poor and less educated became assemblers.

The industry has an image of the future, which the Vietnamese also associated with middle class jobs. It is technology in its most advanced form. Some Vietnamese felt they were getting in on the ground floor of what will be the industry of the future. People cited examples of well known Vietnamese lawyers and important government people who trained in electronics because "this is an electronics country." The products developed in the industry contributed to the image that the industry symbolizes the future.

The work environment has characteristics of middle class work as well. Electronics companies are very clean. Workers often wear sterilized gowns, hair nets, and gloves to prevent contamination of the components. To many Vietnamese, a clean job is a good job, and electronics jobs are the epitome of clean jobs.

Another characteristic of middle class jobs, the opportunity for advancement, has been described above. The Vietnamese image of unrestricted advancement opportunities in the electronics industry allowed them to project a positive image of their future as middle class workers in the United States.

Electronics Technician Jobs Are Male Jobs and Help Maintain Status Hierarchies in the Home. The majority of Vietnamese training to become electronics technicians were men. The absence of women from the training would have been more understandable if few women worked, but most men said that their wives worked, often as electronics assemblers. This occupational hierarchy was so prevalent, it became the central focus of a song, extolling the virtues of Santa Clara County, that circulated among Vietnamese refugees:

> O day, chong Tech vo Ly
> Cung lam mot xip con gi xuong hon.
>
> Here, the husband is a technician, and the
>   wife is an assembler

Together, working the same shift, nothing is
happier.

Refugees suggested several reasons for this hierarchy. First, many
women did not speak English well. In many Vietnamese families, the
husband studied English while the wife stayed home with children.
Second, women moved into the labor force more slowly than men,
primarily because of the demands of raising small children. Third, some
Vietnamese said that women are not interested in math. Although all
students in Vietnam studied math, women tended to emphasize history
and literature.

It also appears that many men did not want women to work as
technicians. For example, tension arose between a Vietnamese man and
woman in the training program. The woman said that the man would not
help her with problems, although he helped the other men. She thought
that he would not help her because he thought that technician was a man's
job. If her assessment of the situation is correct, it illustrates how
Vietnamese have used electronics technician and assembly jobs to maintain a traditional status hierarchy between men and women.

Electronics Technician Is Adequately Challenging to Refugees. Electronics technician jobs offered enough challenge to make refugees feel
they were doing something skilled and productive. The job used their
educational background and had the appearance of a middle class job.
The job, however, was not so challenging that it was threatening to people
trying to adjust to a new life. Most refugees faced serious hardships in
Vietnam and in flight, and they had to adjust rapidly to a new culture,
language, and labor market since coming to the United States. To expect
them to seek challenging, professional jobs immediately is unrealistic.

Electronics technician jobs gave them a chance to gain work experience, improve their English and learn about a new industry while they
were working. It also helped them cope with their problems. The students
said that while they were in training, they were too busy to be homesick
or sad, and that their work helped them think about the future, not the
past. The electronics industry gave them hope for a better future. They
needed to believe that they will advance in order to counteract the effect
of the hardships they have endured.

Summary of Creation of a Positive Image of the Job. In sum,
Vietnamese refugees not only molded their self-images to fit the job, they
focused on aspects of the job that made it seem like a good job. They
emphasized the availability of jobs and of advancement opportunities in
the industry while they downplayed the economic sacrifices they had to

make to live in Santa Clara County. They saw the job as especially attractive because it had the image of middle class work; it was mental not physical work; it was clean, and at the forefront of a state-of-the-art technology. In addition, the occupation's demand for some English language ability and mathematical training, helped maintain a traditional hierarchy between men and women. Finally, the job helped people focus on the present and future, and relegate hardships to the past. The job was neither too hard to be threatening and discouraging, nor too easy to be menial and demeaning. As electronics technicians, refugees could feel like skilled, productive workers, while they adjusted to life in the United States.

The Vietnamese community was the refugees' primary source of information on the characteristics of the occupation. Most refugees had friends or relatives already working in the industry and information passed freely about it. The staff at the training program also tried to create a positive image of the occupation, but the poor quality of the instruction detracted from their message about the industry.

DISCUSSION

The preceding illustration of a group of Vietnamese refugees altering their self-image to fit the requirements of electronics technician jobs, while creating an image of the job that was consistent with their self-image emphasizes the role the Vietnamese ethnic community had in this process. As the following discussion shows, shaping members' occupational identity is only one part of what ethnic communities do. It is easy to recognize the importance of ethnic communities in adjustment, but their importance, relative to other influences, is rarely examined.

Role of the Ethnic Community

In the job training program just described, the Vietnamese community played a number of roles in shaping the occupational identity of its members. First, it provided a positive image of the fit between the job and individual skills and limitations. The community projected a positive image of the job as adequately challenging, clean, and skilled. Even the Vietnamese song presented earlier portrays electronics technician as a perfect occupational choice. Not all ethnic communities in Santa Clara County, however, shared this image of electronics technician work. Many non-Vietnamese saw the job as tedious, monotonous, and potentially dangerous. People worried about eye strain, back problems, and other potential health hazards associated with the job.

Second, the community provided many role models for refugees interested in becoming technician. When asked if people had friends in the electronics industry, most refugees laughed and explained that all of their friends were in the industry. New arrivals to Santa Clara County saw Vietnamese technicians buying cars and houses and displaying other visible signs of relative affluence. They also saw people that had held prestigious jobs in Vietnam working, seemingly happily, as technicians.

Third, the Vietnamese community helped its members enter the occupation by offering classes in electronics and by providing job referrals. For example, a refugee self-help group offered training in Vietnamese to Vietnamese wanting to become technicians. The instructors were Vietnamese engineers or technicians who volunteered their time to teach classes in the evening. Individuals also offered similar services for a small fee. Friends and relatives told refugees about job openings at their companies. In many cases, companies were eager to hire friends of Vietnamese employees because employers tended to be pleased with the performance of Vietnamese. Vietnamese job developers in refugee help centers also focused on the electronics industry in searching for jobs for refugee clients.

This kind of role for the ethnic community is not unusual. For example, in a study of the role of refugee communities in resettlement, SRI International found that Southeast Asia refugee communities provide both tangible and intangible support to their members (Finnan & Cooperstein, 1983). Tangible supports include financial assistance and services such as assistance finding jobs, and educational services such as employment training and English language instruction. Intangible supports are more closely related to the above discussion. They include the emotional, cultural, social, and spiritual support often sought by refugees when they try to make the transition from their old culture to a new one. Intangible supports also include the interpretive framework the community provides that manifests itself in refugees' atttitudes about their relation to society and in their new social, ethnic, and occupational identities.

Research on Cuban refugees illustrates that the Cuban community played a similar role in the adjustment of its members. In a study of Cuban refugees in New Jersey, Eleanor Rogg (1974, p. 14) found that the interpretive framework provided by the community functions in at least two ways. First:

> The ethnic community acts as a prism through which the new values of the absorbing society are refracted in such a way as to make them more acceptable to the immigrant and more compatible with his cultural heritage.

Second, the community acts as a screen or membrane, letting members absorb just as much about the host society as they are able to at any given time. This slows acculturation, but does not stop it. As Rogg (1974, p. 14) continued:

> Little by little, new elements of American culture filter in through the community and slowly the immigrant becomes gradually assimilated without the shock of cultural collision.

Rogg (1971) also suggests that the community provides a reference base where the values, attitudes and cultural patterns of the refugee are considered worthwhile; that is, although other Americans may serve as a normative reference group in setting standards, fellow refugees serve as a comparison reference group against which refugees evaluate success.

The ethnic community plays many roles in the overall adjustment of refugees and immigrants, as well as in their occupational adjustment. The supports provided by the community help refugees overcome culture shock experienced on arrival in the United States. In the case of occupational identity adjustment, the community helps members accept the reality of downward occupational mobility. Some researchers (Stein, 1979) have expressed concern about the effect of downward occupational mobility on refugee adjustment. This concern, however, underestimates the important role played by the community in shaping images of appropriate occupations.

Relative Importance of the Community in Occupational Identity Development

Although the foregoing discussion focused on the role of community in shaping the occupational identity of students, there are other influences, such as the influence of the training or schooling process, and the personality and aptitude of the individual student. Considerable research has been conducted investigating these influences. For example, there is a large body of literature on the influence of training on occupational identity development. In studies of medical students (Becker, Geer, Hughes, & Strauss, 1961; Huntington, 1957; Preiss, 1968), law students (Carlin, 1966), and music students (Kadushin, 1969) researchers concluded that students are more likely to identify as full members of their occupational group as they progress through school and display competence in the area of their training. They also found that students identify with a profession once they have invested time in it.

Other researchers focus on the fit between a student's aptitude and personality, and available occupations. The emphasis has been on applying a personality and occupational inventory to people seeking occupational counseling. People are directed toward occupations that are most compatible with their personality type (Holland, 1966).

The influence of the training process, and personality and aptitude are undeniable, but to exclude social influences, such as that of the family and community removes occupational decision making from its social context. Vietnamese refugees may illustrate the importance of the community more clearly than would other groups because they are recent arrivals to the United States and because the ethnic community is particularly important to most new arrivals. However, their uniqueness as a group does not prevent them from serving as an example of a group of people involved in a process that occurs for everyone who must make sense of the relationship between self-image and occupation. Outside influences similar to an ethnic group (e.g., family, peer group) influence everyone's occupational identity development. Most people look to friends and family for some kind of guidance or approval while selecting and pursuing an occupation. The situation for the Vietnamese was merely more extreme in that a large number of adults had to make occupational choices quickly and the community channeled most of them into the same occupation.

For the Vietnamese studied, the community influence appeared to be greater than the influence of schooling or individual attributes. The training process discouraged identification with the occupation, and the Vietnamese students reconciled themselves to the fact that they could not pursue occupations more suited to their personalities and aptitudes. In fact, they emphasized aspects of themselves that were compatible with electronics technician jobs. The balance between these influences for non-Vietnamese students may be different, but the influence of their social context (e.g., community, family, peer group) is still present.

SUMMARY AND CONCLUSIONS

This chapter describes the process of occupational identity development among a group of Vietnamese refugee students. The process involves students molding their sense of self to fit the occupation while simultaneously creating an image of the job compatible with their self-image. This process is heavily influenced by the students' social context. In the case of the Vietnamese students, their ethnic community plays a major role in helping them develop an occupational identification with their chosen job. The chapter further explores the many roles of ethnic communities in refugee and immigrant adjustment and assesses the relative importance of the social context (e.g., community, family, and peer group), occupational training, and personality and aptitude on occupational identity development.

The process of occupational identity development presented in this chapter describes little dissonance between the image the Vietnamese community created for electronics technician jobs and the attributes of individual Vietnamese. This fit will not necessarily remain. For example, in recent years, new refugees have arrived that do not share the same background characteristics as the first arrivals. For them, electronics technician jobs have been unavailable. In addition, electronics technician jobs have been more difficult to find because of the economic recession in the early 1980s and because of electronics companies' decisions to move out of Santa Clara County.

Even those refugees who once easily identified as electronics technicians may not always do so. As they adjust to life in the United States, and the novel becomes familiar, the balance between their image of themselves and of the job will change. When this happens, the line, "Together, working the same shift, nothing is happier" may no longer hold, and they will look for new jobs. It is likely that Vietnamese refugees in Santa Clara County will begin to lose some of their interest in electronics technician jobs. Their interest in other occupations should be seen as a positive symbol of successful adaptation rather than a sign of instability. Adaptation involves change, a trait some Vietnamese feel is a characteristic of their people. A community worker said:

> One thing though, Vietnamese are adaptable to change. That's why the Vietnamese are poised. Unlike Americans, when faced with a terrible situation, they go crazy. But Vietnamese have made themselves adaptive. Western people try to cope with situations, try to fight it, and if they can't fight it, they try to control it. If they can't, two things happen: they become resigned or become crazy. Not so with Vietnamese; they try to adapt to the environment, try to work with it.

REFERENCES

Becker, H., Geer, B., Hughes, E. C., & Strauss, A. L. (1961). *Boys in white*. Chicago: University of Chicago Press.

Carlin, J. E. (1966). *Lawyers' ethics: A survey of the New York City Bar*. New York: Russell Sage Foundation.

Finnan, C., & Cooperstein, R. A. (1983). *Southeast Asian refugee resettlement at the local level: The role of the ethnic community and the nature of impact*. Menlo Park, CA: SRI International.

Holland, J. (1966). *The psychology of vocational choice: A theory of personality types and model environments*. Waltham, MA: Blaisdell Publishing.

Huntington, M. J. (1957). The development of a professional self concept. In R. K. Merton, G. G. Reader, & P. L. Kendall (Eds.), *The student physician*. Cambridge, MA: Harvard University Press.

Kadushin, C. (1969). The professional self concept of music students. *American Journal of Sociology, 5*, 389–404.

Preiss, J. (1968). Self and role in medical education. In C. Gordon & K. Gergen (Eds.), *The self in social interaction*. New York: Wiley.

Rogg, E. (1971). The influence of a strong community on the economic adjustment of its members. *International Migration Review, 5*(4), 474–481.

Rogg, E. (1974). *The assimilation of Cuban exiles: The role of community and class*. New York: Aberdeen Press.

Santa Clara County Manufacturing Group. (1979). Report on estimates of job growth and building expansion of sixty Santa Clara County companies. 1979–1985.

Stein, B. (1979). Occupational adjustment of refugees: The Vietnamese in the United States. *International Migration Review*, Vol. *13*, No. 1:25–45, Spring.

U.S. Department of Health and Human Services, Office of Refugee Resettlement. (1983). *Report to Congress: Refugee Resettlement Program*. Washington, DC, January 31.

The Author and Her Chapter

Concha Delgado-Gaitan received her Ph.D. from Stanford University in 1983. She was on the faculty at the University of California, Davis, and is now an assistant professor of education at the University of California, Santa Barbara. One of her major concerns is ethnographic research in education and its implications for policy, practice, and educational reform. These directions have been significantly influenced by the many years that she served in the field of education as an elementary school teacher, school principal, language program director, teacher trainer and researcher. She has focused her work on the analysis of behavior and the role that language and culture play in the acquisition of knowledge.

Her chapter expresses the combination of her interests well. She is concerned with the discontinuities between home and school experienced by Mexican-American children and regards them as a significant factor in the low academic achievement of many of them. In her chapter three major forms of discontinuity are analyzed: cooperative-competitive; authority; and dimensional complexity. The latter refers to the relative complexity of experience in the home versus the school. She studies these discontinuities as an ethnographer should, by direct observation , extensive interviewing, and when possible, participant observation. Her results are convincing in their detail.

Discontinuities of the type described by Delgado-Gaitan are present in any situation where home and school operate with different cultural guidelines. The Punjabis and Vietnamese described in previous chapters experienced them acutely but their academic performance is relatively good. The reasons for this have been explored in previous chapters.

It seems clear that discontinuities in management and expectation will always be a factor wherever there are significant cultural differences separating home and school environments. That they are a factor in academic performance cannot be denied and recognition of this should lead to changes in classroom practice. What the new immigrants have taught us is that their negative effect can be overcome if there is sufficient motivation, and if there is a positive expectation of success. Accommodations can be made on both sides of the relationship between home and school.

The Editors

Traditions and Transitions in the Learning Process of Mexican Children: An Ethnographic View

14

Concha Delgado-Gaitan
University of California, Santa Barbara

INTRODUCTION

This chapter investigates discontinuity between the home, community, and the school. I examine specific areas of continuity-discontinuity of Mexican children's interaction at home relative to their classroom instruction in Oakgrove school, Los Portales, California.

The disharmony between home practices and classroom expectations, particularly for minorities, has been of interest to others. Among the most pointed research on the relationship between home and school culture are Philips, 1983; Au & Jordan, 1980; Au, 1980; and Heath, 1980, 1982, 1983.

The ability of Warm Spring Indian children to "hold the floor" is one of the important factors identified by Philips (1983). Philips observed that the Indian children experience discord in their classroom interaction. The difference between the Indian and non-Indian community is manifested in the classroom where the teacher selects individuals as the sole speakers to hold the floor. Non-Indian children generally jump to the occasion to hold the floor while Indian children are reluctant to do so because in the Indian community adults minimize the extent to which some persons have more control as addressors (p. 192).

Similar discontinuities to those raised by Philips are examined by Au and Jordan (1980). The major hypothesis in the Kamehameha Early Education Program (KEEP) proposes that greater academic success is a result of continuity between children's home environment and classroom practices. The home interactions of Hawaiian children provide an opportunity for collectivity evidenced in the way children perform tasks with siblings (Galimore, Boggs, & Jordan 1974). The collective orientation of Hawaiian children suggests well-developed strategies within the group for teaching peers, learning from each other, and being resourceful (Au & Jordan 1978).

Continuity between the home and school cultural practices of Hawaiian children is maintained through reading lessons. Reading lessons in the KEEP program are organized to resemble the Hawaiian "talk story" in the way that children take mutual turns in relating their personal experiences. The success of children's reading achievement is attributed to the minimal pressure placed on children to individually produce correct answers. The reading objective is to encourage children in the comprehension process of reading as opposed to the phonetic decoding of the words (Au, 1980).

Differences of literacy between Roadville and Trackton children contribute to the wide gap in achievement scores between the two groups at the reading readiness level (Heath, 1980). Children from the Roadville community begin school prepared to engage in reading activities that require systematic interaction with the written text. However, these children are not skilled in decontextualizing information from the text to the social setting. Conversely, black working-class children in the Trackton community are reinforced and rewarded for verbal ability to tell stories about their daily events. Heath suggests that the school needs to offer Roadville children an opportunity to produce narratives of real events while Trackton children must be taught to take meaning from books in a way that is congruent to their creative ability to fictionalize (Heath, 1980, pp. 43–45).

The uses of questions in the Trackton community, homes, and the school discussed by Heath (1982), shows that black children acquire a different strategy for working and responding to questions in their home and community as compared to the functions of language in the classroom. In Trackton homes and within the community children were more talked "at" than "with" (Heath, 1982, p. 115), and their responses to questions required nonspecific comparisons of item or event. Questioning in the classroom by teachers required confirmation of certain skills necessary to indicate comprehension of material. Teachers often asked questions that required descriptors or labels. Trackton children did not respond because these types of questions were unfamiliar to them.

Heath concludes that the Trackton childrens cultural verbal skills need to become a part of the daily classroom curriculum and in turn, the students need to be trained to the appropriate classroom questioning strategies.

Ethnographic studies such as those of Philips, Au, and Jordan and

Heath, eloquently illustrate how children respond to socialization within their home and community, and face conflict in the classroom when teachers expect different behavior without understanding their home background and the native competencies fostered by it. Solutions are complex but some educational reform is possible. Teachers must utilize children's special native skills as well as teaching them the new competencies.

The study of discontinuity in the educational process suggests a combination of theories that appropriately define the various dimensions of the problem. My study in Los Portales unites the mismatch theory (Florio & Schultz, 1979; and Schultz, Florio, & Erickson, unpublished manuscript) with Ogbu's (1978, 1981, 1982) cultural-ecological theory. The discontinuities that Mexican children manifest in the classroom raise many complex issues. The mismatch theory specifies differences in culture as the source of interaction conflict. Although the discontinuity described in this paper can be attributed to differences in culturally patterned socialization practices between the home, community, and the classroom, we must recognize that other important factors may be in operation. Such factors as social class and immigrant status of families are accounted for in the cultural ecological theory. They help explain the discontinuities between recent immigrants to the U. S. and members of the majority Anglo mainstream culture.

THE STUDY

Three features of the Los Portales study on discontinuity are discussed here: cooperation-competition, authority-egalitarian, and multidimensional-unidimensional. The discussion of these attributes is not intended to dichotomize these findings nor to imply that Mexican children are competent in only one skill as opposed to the other. The study is designed to examine the function of these points of discontinuity as they affect classroom interaction and create miscommunication between teacher and student and between student and student.

Research Strategies in Los Portales

Prior to collecting interaction data on home, play, and classroom events, I gathered demographic data on the social and ethnic organization of the community as well as the use of language in Los Portales' businesses and public service institutions. Several informants, who had resided in Los Portales over 20 years, provided me with invaluable ethnohistories which revealed personal accounts of the data collected from the community at large.

Following the demographic research, I moved into the public school domain and contacted the district bilingual education director. She suggested that I contact the Oakgrove School principal. As a result of my interview with him I received permission to observe children during recesses. My affiliation with school, I felt, would give me more legitimacy with the parents and families. I began by observing play groups during recess. This afforded me the opportunity to make friends with many of the children who lived in the neighborhood around the Oakgrove School. These children became participants in the research. I focused on children in grades 1–3 as this age group engages in more group play than the upper grade students. After I had observed the students over a period of a few weeks, the students recognized me and expected my daily visits. A group of seven children played on the playground rather consistently and they and their four families eventually became the main subjects throughout the 18 months of fieldwork in Los Portales, California.

The data were collected through observations and interviews. I observed the children around their home, at their play, and in their classroom tasks. Once the children, parents, and teachers adjusted to my presence, I was able to take notes and tape record as I observed their play, their tasks at home, and their classroom lessons with minimal interruption of the normal routine. My observations in the children's homes consisted of lengthy visits during the day. In the summer visits were all day and during school time. I spent mornings in the school and afternoon in the homes. During the visit, I could always expect that I would be drawn into the children's activity either in play or some household task. In addition to collecting data, I became a convenient social worker for the families, which made sense, given my position and their situation.

Classroom observations were rather different. Most of the time I did not participate in classroom lessons as much as I did in the home tasks and play events. However, I did make myself available if the teacher requested my assistance. I usually followed the tone of the classroom. At times the tasks were flexible and allowed for my participation while other tasks were arranged so that the teacher alone directed the class. Most of the classroom tasks centered around ditto worksheets in math, reading, and language arts. Thus, my role was limited to answering questions for students when I was allowed to participate. Spontaneous and unstructured interviews were also collected. They included reenactment of hand claps after a play activity ended, or questions to a teacher regarding an observed pattern during a lesson. Structured exit interviews were collected at the end of the research study.

CHILDREN'S NATIVE COMPETENCIES

Children of Los Portales display many more competencies than those highlighted in this paper. I have selected to deal only with three salient areas which affect meaningfully the instructional dimension in the classroom: cooperation-competition, authority, and multidimensional-undimensional levels. Historically, Mexican children have been considered submissive because they respect adult authority. In some instances, children have even been referred to as nonlingual. The Los Portales data, for example, reveal that Mexican children learn to obey adult authority at home. It is a form of respect for children to listen and perform what is expected of them without defying their elders. While they are accustomed to complying with adult directives, they are also taught to be resourceful in performing tasks, as data support in later sections of this paper. Children's willingness to accept direction cannot be interpreted as a lack of self-motivation, it is an industrious attitude which children display in response to the work ethic communicated in the home.

Language and social competencies are inherent in cultural tasks performed by children in Los Portales. Spanish is spoken almost exclusively by the children in this community. They have full command of the authority and expressive aspects of their language. These competencies are traditions that are shaped and transformed as children participate in different settings. If children are capable of learning new behaviors, why is it necessary for schools to provide continuity in the children's learning process? A complete response to this question is complex and too involved for this paper to deal with adequately. However, I will demonstrate the importance of continuity, and of social interaction practices relative to the schooling process of Mexican children in Los Portales.

Cooperation and Competition

As expected, tasks and play events in the home are characteristically different than tasks in the classroom. Egalitarian modes of interaction are dominant among children in play events and between adults and children at home. Although children do work and play individually and do behave competitively in Los Portales, we note that more frequently they cooperate in collective ways with others. Cooperation is encouraged by adults and it is exhibited in children's willingness to accept tasks, as well as collectivizing with others in mixed play groups, (age, sex). Every event offers an opportunity for children to demonstrate their leadership as well as their ability to follow. The examples cited in this section illustrate how the cooperative ethic functions in the home, including play, and the extent to which children respond to a classroom orientation of competition.

Home Interactions

Text 1.   (On a Saturday morning Mrs. Islas leaves Yolanda and Pedro with instructions for cleaning the house.)

Mother: Ándale Pedro, me voy, y para cuando regrese, quiero que limpien esta casa y no se descuiden de Sabrina. Y tu (pointing to Yolanda) no la hagas llorar. (Mother exits). *Allright, Pedro, I'm leaving and when I return, I want this house cleaned and don't leave Sabrina unattended. And you, (points to Yolanda) don't make her cry.* (Pedro picks up Sabrina and sits and rocks her while he orders Yolanda to wash dishes.)

Pedro: Tu tienes que fregar platos. *You have to wash dishes.*

Yolanda: No, tu hazlo y yo cuido a la niña. *No you do it and I'll take care of the baby.*

Pedro: (Sits Sabrina on Yolanda's lap and goes to sit down again for a minute.) Yo nomás voy a darle leche a Sabrina y tu tienes que lavar platos o no puedes jugar. *I'm just going to give Sabrina milk and you have to wash dishes or you can't play.*

Yolanda: (Pouts) Nostros vamos al parque y tu no vas. *We're going to the park and you're not going.* (She pushes a kitchen chair up to the sink and washes the dishes. Pedro sits Sabrina on his lap and feeds her after heating warmed-up oatmeal. He cuddles and teases her as he feeds her. When Yolanda finishes the dishes, she started out the door to go outside.)

Pedro: Todavía no puedes salir, tienes que barrer. *You still can't go outside, you have to sweep.*

Yolanda: ¡No, tu hazlo! *No you do it!* (She walks over to Pedro and takes Sabrina from Yolanda and she runs outside. Pedro yells:) Tienes que entrar antes de que venga mamá. *You have to come in before mother gets back.*

In this sample, Mother entrusts Pedro, the oldest of the three children, with full responsibility. He must oversee Sabarina's well being and assist Yolanda in housework. He willingly accepts this responsibility and follows through with his mother's instruction. We notice, too, his assertive leadership in delegating work to Yolanda. He knows just how far to push to get Yolanda to work, and Yolanda also knows at what point she can refuse to work, she negotiates her assignment. Inspite of the apparent effort to dodge unpopular work, like dish-washing and sweeping, Pedro and Yolanda verbally negotiate the division of tasks and the completion of their chores. One observation in this event is that the children prefer to care for Sabrina than to wash dishes or sweep. Although Yolanda and Pedro do not collectivize on one single task, they share in the total work load. The next example depicts children working collectively on a single task.

Text 2.   (Herlinda has arrived from school and her father arrives about an hour afterwards. He sits down on the couch. Herlinda and I sit on the back doorstep. The younger sister runs in and out of the living room.)

Father:	Mi hijita quiero que tu y tus hermanos salgan a limpiar la yarda. Hay mucha basura. *Dear, I want you and your brothers to go outside and clean the yard. There's a lot of trash.*
Herlinda:	(Goes to stand by father who is on the couch.) Ay, papa, yo no quiero hacerlo ahorita. Quiero hablar con Concha. *Oh dad, I don't want to do it now. I want to talk with Concha.*
Father:	Pues si te apuras horita acabas pronto y luego puedes hablar. *Well, if you hurry up and finish it fast then you can talk.*
Herlinda:	(Gets up from the couch and yells at the boys from the hallway.) Oígan, ustedes tienen que ayudarme allá afuera. *Hey you guys, you have to help me outside.*
Father:	Mira mi hijita, ahí abajo del lavaplatos hay bolsas grandes— meten todas las hojas muy bien para que no se rieguen. *Look dear, there are large bags so you can put the leaves in them so they don't scatter.*
Herlinda:	(Walks to the bedrooms and screams at the boys)¡Chava, Jaime! ¡Vengan ayudarme! *Chava, Jaime! Come and help me!*
Chava and Jaime:	(Come out of the bedrooms, doors slam.)
Father:	Oye mi hijo vayan a ayudarle a tu hermana. *Hey son, go help your sister.*
Chava and Jaime:	(Rakes the leaves and sweeps.)
Herlinda:	(Stuffs the bags—when the bags get too full, says to Chava:) Tu haz esto, está muy pesado. *You do this. It's too heavy.* (She proceeds to hand him the rake.)
Chava:	(Goes to stuff the bags.)
Herlinda:	(Comes to me.) ¡Ya, ya hice! *I did, I did it.*
Chava:	(Calls to father:) ¡Papá, Herlinda ya dejó el trabajo! *Dad, Herlinda left the work.*
Father:	(Gets up and goes to inspect work in the yard.) Jaime, mi hija. *Let's see, dear.*
Herlinda:	Mira, papá yo ya limpié eso y eso, y lleve algunas bolsas pero ellos trabajan más despacio. *Look, dad, I've cleaned that, and I took some bags, but they work too slow.* (She walks back into the house and says to me:) Vamonos. *Let's go.*

Parents often encourage children to assist each other as in the above example. Herlinda is observed resenting yet complying with her father's commands. Mr. Parra expects the children to work at maintaining a clean house. Herlinda assumes leadership in organizing her brothers to help her. She assigns herself and her brothers to appropriate parts of the task according to their ability. Herlinda also consciously balances the work in a fair way, and she involves her father in negotiating her involvement in the task. Throughout the task, the father's role remains one of an authority supporting the children in working harmoniously.

Collectivity is also practiced by children in play activities separate from adults as evidenced in this next play event.

Text 3. (In the apartments by the carport Nora, Yolanda, Efren, Laura, and Anita hang around on a warm summer afternoon.)

Nora: Yo tengo un juego es "Gorrión, Gorrión". Vamos a jugar. *I have a game. It's "Gorrión, Gorrión." Let's play.* (Nora forms the circle and shows the actors what to say. Walks around the circle saying "Gorrión, gorrión" with a towel in hand.)

Efren: (Squatting inside the circle.) Diga usted, Señora. *Yes, m'am.*

Nora: ¿Fue usted al campo ayer? *Did you go to the country yesterday?*

Efren: Sí, sí fui. *Yes, I went.* (He begins chasing Nora around the outside of the circle.)

Nora: ¿Quién vió? *Whom did you see?*

Efren: Al Gorrión. *The Gorrion.*

Nora: (Chases Efren with the towel trying to hit Efren until he runs inside the circle.)

(Efren chooses another person to be chased by Nora around the circle. They play two rounds until Efren falls on the cement slick with oil and cries—the game ends.)

Circle games like Gorrion-Gorrion symbolize a type of collective preference. While Nora introduces the game and instructs them on the rules, other children participate equally as persuers. The game continues for only a few rounds; and, although not all the children get a chance to be in the circle or to chase, they all hold hands and provide shelter for the person being chased and to keep out the persuer. This aspect of collective behavior differs from the type of collective behavior expressed in the following card game.

Text 4. (This card game takes place in Nora's living room with Laura, Nora, Yolanda, Herlinda, and Pedro as players. Nora brings out the cards and the others sit around her.)

Herlinda: First!

Nora: Second, second, second.

Yolanda: No, I can't.

Herlinda: OK, yo soy first, you second, el third. *OK, I'm first, you second, he's third.*

Mother: Jueguen callados. *Play quietly.*

Pedro: Wait a second!

Herlinda:	Ahora voy yo. *It's my turn.*
Pedro:	Me toca a mi. *It's my turn.*
Yolanda:	No, a mi. *No, it's my turn.*
Herlinda:	She's last!
Concha:	¿Quién es primero? *Who's first?*
Pedro:	¡Yo! I am first, second, third.
Concha:	¿Y quién decidió quien es primero? *Who decided who's first?*
Yolanda:	Pedro. El pidió primero. *Pedro, he asked first.*
Yolanda:	Five. (Looks at the number of pairs she has.)
Nora:	Cuatro pares. (Counts her pairs.) *Four pairs.* (End of one game and beginning of another.)
Herlinda:	¡Soy first! *I'm first!*
Yolanda:	Second . . . Ey Herlinda. Ve tu tienes los pares ahí, los moviste. *Herlinda, look you have your pairs over there. You moved them.*
Pedro:	¡No! Deja!¡ Que dejes! *No, leave them alone! I said leave them alone!*
Nora:	Pero es que yo quiero jugar. *But it's that I want to play.*
Yolanda:	El los esconde aquí. Cheater! *He hides them over here. Cheater!* (Referring to Pedro.) (The game continues with each one picking matching pairs.)
Pedro:	Ella lleva seis pares. *She has six pairs.*
Yolanda:	Ándale, Pedro, Yo ya seguiá. *Come on, Pedro. It was my turn.*
Pedro:	(takes his turn) Ah, nada. *Oh, nothing.*
Herlinda:	(takes her turn) Ah, 'ira, dos pares. Yolanda toma un par. No más tienes pocos. *Oh look, two pairs. Here Yolanda take one pair. You only have a few.*
Yolanda:	(takes the cards Herlinda offers her.)
Nora:	(takes her turn) Oh mira otro par. *Oh look another pair.* (As she picks up a pair, she looks at her stack and counts her pairs then hands Yolanda one pair.)
Yolanda:	(Accepts the pair and takes her turn. She doesn't match a pair)
Herlinda:	¡Fin! Ahora yo tengo 8 pares, y Nora 7 pares, y Pedro seis y Yolanda, cuatro. Así es que yo soy primera y ustedes ganaron segunda tercera, y cuarta. *The end! Now, I have 8 pairs, and Nora 7, and Pedro 6, and Yolanda 4. So, I'm the first winner and you won second, third, and forth.* (The four players began another game of matching cards and their turns coincided with their winning place in the previous game.)

The most interesting point about games is that it begins with the children negotiating their turn in the game, but Pedro wants to take control of the situation and tries to manipulate the game. As the game unfolds, however, we see how the children take a competitive situation and turn it into an opportunity to share their gains with each other. Another aspect of a collective spirit in this game is evident at the end of the game when Herlinda claimed four winners and not just one. She assigns a winning place to all four players.

Classroom Interaction

The focus of classroom interactions are tasks or lessons. The four classrooms observed assign small group work, however, the group arrangement is usually for the teacher's convenience. Children are grouped according to academic ability levels. These structures generally reveal a competitive orientation as opposed to the collective ethic practiced in home activities. Children, when left to work independently, attempt to share information in various ways while they endeavor to meet the classroom expectations of working individually. At times, teachers specifically discourage children from working together for fear that they will copy answers from each other. Children seem to want to share answers and they usually find a way to do so even if the teacher disapproves. Children are not trained to teach or explain material to each other, therefore, they resort to giving each other the answers on fill-in workpages. Unfortunately, collectivizing efforts can sometimes lead to more work if the teacher catches students copying as illustrated in the following example.

Text 5.   (Following opening exercises, flag salute and sharing.

Teacher:	A sus grupos. *To your groups.*
	(One group went with the teacher to a corner table. Another group went with the teacher assistant to another corner.)
Boy₁:	(threw a box of crayons to a girl)
Teacher:	No se los avientes, dáselos con cariño. *Don't throw them, give them to him with love.*
	(teacher assistant works with one group where she gives further instructions)
T.A.:	(counts 1–20 in English/Spanish)
Student Group:	(They all sit listening and watching.)
Yolanda:	(sat in back looking forward)
T.A.:	(called one student at a time to respond to her question:) ¿Cual numero es más grande? *Which number is greater?*
	(The girls in back of the group braided each other's hair. T. A. calls Yolanda to the front of the group and gives instruction to the group.) We're going to put an "X" on the one circle that has more. Luego los que no hicieron esto bien, tienen que corregirlo—Ustedes se sientan juntos. *Since you didn't do this right, you have to correct it. You sit together.*
	(This group of four girls and two boys sat together.)
Boy₁:	'Ira, este tiene mas. *Look this one has more.*

Boy₂:	¿Qué le pongo aquí entonces? *What do I put here, then?*
Boy₁:	A este le pongo "X." *On this one I put an X.*
Boy₂:	Then do the back of it.
Boy₁:	I didn't need those (pushes away those pieces of paper, to use for counting) Eek, tu también no lo acabas. Yo ya lo acabé. *Eek you're not finished either. I finished.*
Girl₁:	Yo ya voy acabando, yo ya hice todo esto. *I'm finishing. I've already done this.*
	(Students relied heavily on their fingers to count.)
Boy₁:	I didn't need tose (pushes away those pieces of paper, to use for counting) Eek, tu también no lo acabas. Yo ya lo acabe. *Eek you're not finished either. I finished.*
Girl₁:	Yo ya voy acabando, yo ya hice todo esto. *I'm finishing. I've already done this.*
	(Students relied heavily on their fingers to count.)
Boy₁:	(gives Boy₂ answers of 1st two problems on back side of page) Llega ya hasta aquí, cuida que algunos son de take away. *Get to this point, careful cause some are take away.*
Girls	(worked quietly)
Boy₁, Boy₂:	(Returned to seats with papers marked in red by the T. A.)
Boy₁:	Yo ya te gané. *I've beat you.*
Boy₂:	No, yo te gané. *No, I beat you.*
Boy₁:	Yo agarré este extra. *I got this extra one.*
Boy₂:	Oh yo también quiero. *Oh, I want that one.*
Girl₃:	(She came to the boys table and saw the two girls working. She stood by the table for a second then told the 2 girls they were doing the ditto incorrectly and she said:) ¿Te ayudo? (At that point the teacher saw the girls copying from girls and she came to their table.)
Teacher:	(to girl₃) Tu no les debes darles las respuestas. Ahora tu tienes que hacerlo otra vez. (Looking at G_1 and G_2) Y ustedes también. *You're not supposed to give them the answers. Now you're gonna have to do it again. And you too.* (looking at G_1 and G_2)
	(G_1 and G_2 looked at each other and when the teacher walked away, they put their paper in the bin and began to draw dolls.)
Teacher:	OK recess. Clean-up para salir al recreo. *Clean-up to go to recess.*

There's a fairly congenial atmosphere in this classroom. Respect for each other has high importance as we see by the teacher's comment to the child who threw the box of crayons. However, the prevailing attitude about individual work is rather competitive between the boys. In the group, the boys make a game out of filling in their math ditto sheets as they ask each other for answers then race against each other to finish first with almost no regard for the concepts on the paper. The two girls in the group, on the other hand, do not participate in the competition to finish first, but work alone until G_3 shows up and advises them of the wrong answers. Her willingness to assist them costs all of them to repeat the assignment. This teacher practices what she revealed in an interview, that each child has to learn how to do their own individual work and if anyone is caught "cheating," they have to repeat the assignment.

A different type of competition in the classroom is exhibited in the following event.

Text 6.   (Following a morning recess Ms. Jones stands in front of the class and tells the children that they will play a word game in which the 5 rows compete against each other for points by reading the word correctly)

Ms. Jones: All right the first 5 people in each row stand up and I'll keep score up here and no calling out words by others in the row. (Students cheer and the first 5 stand up. The teacher begins flashing the word cards.)

Student₁: (reads the word:) LOFT. (students in row 1 cheer; the teacher moves to the second row and random comments from other rows are heard: "Oh, miss it!—miss it!"

(The teacher moves on to the 3rd row and flashes the word.)

Student₃: (hesitates) bud-dle

(row 3 moans and all the rest cheer:) "Good! Good! He got it wrong. Yeah! Yeah!"

Teacher: No, it's *bundle*. No point!

(The game proceeds for 35 minutes until every child in every row has had a chance to play the word game. Occasionally, the teacher stops the game and refuses to continue unless the students tone down their yelling. The students quieted down a bit only until the teacher continued the game.)

Even a spelling game like the one above is an opportunity for teachers to reinforce competition. The significant point here is that one child's failure is cause for elation and success of others. When, as in Text 5, the teacher threatens the students' sense of accomplishment by having them repeat the assignment, children are openly humiliated in front of their peers and their sense of failure is reinforced.

Cooperative participation in home activities allows for fairness, turn taking, reciprocal relationships, and an attitude of harmony among siblings and peers. The children in this study unquestionably have the potential to make a transition from their familiar cooperative orientation to the more competitive structures in the classroom. However, we see the defeating pressure, exclusion, and discomfort that children are subjected to when they are forced to operate alone, without support from others to accomplish tasks that could more effectively be taught in cooperative structures. Children in this study are accustomed to collectively negotiating tasks and roles in their home and play activities; these practices largely motivate their preference for interaction in the classroom. Children have learned to operate effectively in this mode, they need to have the opportunity to incorporate their diverse learning patterns in the classroom in the process of learning different independent styles of working.

VARIATIONS OF AUTHORITY

A related issue to cooperation is the uses of authority between adults and children in the home and school. This refers to the way that adults direct or command children in tasks. In the home, adults have a well-defined role in the assignment of tasks. Direct, clear, authoritarian patterns of adult behavior emerge frequently enough in the data that allows us to predict the adults' interaction in children's tasks. Parents usually assign the task to the children and they expect them to be responsible and assist around the house with family chores. Children, in turn, respond to the parameters of a task with adults by clarifying the instruction and oftentimes requesting monetary compensation of a quarter or a dime when they go to the store. Implicitly, this dismisses any notions of a passive obedience on the part of the children. How the task is accomplished is usually decided on by how the children may choose to involve friends or siblings in carrying out their task; they may also choose to do it alone, particularly if the task is minor, like emptying out the trash or changing diapers, such as in the following example.

Text 7.   (Efren's mother is busy preparing dinner and Efren and his 2 younger sisters are in the living room. His youngest sister who is 1½ yrs. begins to cry.)

Efren: (Picks up the baby and swings her around, but the sister continues crying and he calls out:) No se calla. *She doesn't stop crying.*

Mother: A ver qué necesita. *See what she needs.*

Efren: (Takes his baby sister into the bedroom and lays her on the bed and searches around the room for diapers. When he can't find any, he calls out:) "Amá no hay pañales. *Mother there aren't any diapers.* (He complains and mumbles under his breath.)

Mother: (Doesn't respond immediately, then calls back:) ¡Buscalos! *Look for them!*

Efren: (Locates a clean diaper under a bunch of other clothes and puts it on the baby. The baby struggles when he's changing her and Efren talks to her:) No hagas eso—¡No! ¡No! *Don't do that. No!*

No! (When Efren is through with the diaper change he takes the baby off the bed and walks back out to the living room to watch TV the baby follows him. Mother is still in the kitchen cooking.)

Efren's mother assigns him to care for his baby sister and totally expects and trusts that he carry out the task while she's occupied. Efren in turn requests assistance and receives further direction to proceed on his own to search for the diaper. He is expected to use his own discretion and intelligence in outlining the steps necessary to fulfill his mother's request to make his sister comfortable.

In the next event Nora again examplifies how parental authority is directive yet flexible in allowing her to assume a sense of assertiveness in accomplishing it. Certainly, the confidence demonstrated by Nora is a result of familiarity with the responsibility entrusted her and the support of her friends.

Text 8.   (Mr. Reina prepares to leave for work and gives Nora last minute instruction.)

Father:	Nora, dile a tu mamá que le deje un dinero allí para que compre pan para que tomen con chocolate. *Nora, tell your mother that I left some money there for her to buy bread so you can have it with chocolate.*
Nora:	(Stands and listens.) M m m—m m m.
Father:	Y también dile que le eche gas a la troca. A ver si encuentra la llave para el tanque. ¿Entiendes? *And also tell her to put gas in the truck. Hopefully she will find the key for the gas tank. Do you understand?*
Nora:	Sí. *Yes.*
Father:	(Exits out the door.)
Herlinda and Yolanda:	(Knock on Nora's door and go in.)
Nora:	(Locks the door and pulls the curtains.) (All four girls sit and watch television and Nora brings out a coloring book. She colors one page, then given it to Yolanda.)
Nora:	Tóma, tu pinta esa. *Here, you color this one.* (Points to an unfinished page in the coloring book.)
Laura:	(Goes to join her while Yolanda and Herlinda watch.) (A couple of minutes pass.)
Nora:	Ya Laura, Ya no. ¡Bajaté! *Ok, Laura, no more. Get Down!* (They hear the mother's truck and all of them run out the door. As mother walks up the stairs, Nora delivers the message:)
Nora:	Dice papá que dejó dinero para que nos compre pan, y que le eches gas a la troca. *Dad says he left some money for you to buy us bread and to put gas in the truck.*

Nora complies with her father's directions to deliver the message to her mother and to care for Laura. Sibling care is rarely ever considered work for the children of Los Portales since it is often in context of play with friends. Again, the familiarity of the task allows Nora to decide the best way to care for Nora in her parent's absence. Consequently, she accepted her friend's companionship while she cares for Laura.

In the following event, Yolanda chooses to have Herlinda help her with the dishwashing after her mother commands her to wash them. Here we see parental authority guiding the task and Yolanda deciding how and when she will do it.

Text 9.   (Yolanda's mother assigns her the task of washing dishes.)

Mother: Ándale Yolanda quiero que me friegues esos trastes y no me los dejes sucios. *Come on Yolanda, I want you to wash the dishes and don't leave them dirty.*

Yolanda: Ahí voy, ya voy. *I'm going, I'm going.* (She continues talking to Herlinda in the living room.)

Herlinda: Vete Yolanda porque se te va enojar tu mamá. Mira, yo te ayudo con los trastes—ok? *Go on Yolanda, because your mother will get angry. Look, I'll help you with the dishes. I'll wash and you dry and put them away—ok?*
(The two girls push two chairs up to the sink and Herlinda washes dishes while Yolanda stacks the dishes on the tile.)

Herlinda: "Mira ya acabé. *Look, I'm finished.*

Yolanda: Yo también. *Me too.*

Herlinda: Vamos afuera—¿Nos vamos afuera? *Let's go outside. Shall we go outside?*

In the above dialogue we see that Yolanda's mother establishes her authority by directing her to wash dishes; Yolanda accepts the task but controls the time factor by continuing to talk to Herlinda. Yolanda accepts Herlinda's offer to help. While the mother is vested in the completion of the task, she does not mind how Yolanda proceeds with the task. Yolanda's yelling to mother, "¡Ay voy!" indicates an intent to respect her mother's instruction, but she also negotiates the time parameters of the task.

Adult authority in the classroom differs in the home. First of all, the setting is formal, and secondly, in the Oakgrove school educators assume total authority for organizing classroom tasks, including time, space, noise level, curriculum content, work style and language of instruction, all of which contribute to the learning ambiance and process. Teachers play a significant role in deciding how each of the above factors will affect the instructional process. Individual differences exist among teachers in the amount of Spanish used for instruction and seating arrangements.

Thus far, we can see that children do not have much opportunity to negotiate with the teacher.

Text 10.   (Following a bilingual flag salute in this 3rd grade classroom the lesson begins.)

Teacher: This morning you'll practice your name in cursive writing. I'll be around to help you.

Pedro: (Sits slouched at his desk tapping fingers on desk and rolling a pencil, waiting for paper to be handed out.)

Students: (Lightly whispering—unrelated to task.)

Teacher: Stop all that talking and I'll come around.

Pedro: (Writes rows and rows of his first name, Pedro.)

Teacher: (Comes to Pedro.) OK, Pedro, let's see you make the "J." Stop right there. (And she proceeds to model for him.)

Students: (Write rows of their first names.)

Boy$_1$:   (Turns to another boy.) ¿Y el apellido? *And the last name?*

Boy$_2$:   (Whispers) No se. *I don't know.*

Girl$_1$:   (Goes up to teacher.) Like this, Mrs. Thomas?

Teacher: Well, you need some practice on some letters. (She goes back to her desk.)

Boy$_1$:   (Raises his hand.)

Teacher: Yes, Jesús—What is it?

Boy$_1$:   Do we have to write the last name?

Teacher: Yes, your last name too.
       (Moans of disappointment spread.)

Girl$_3$:   Do we put it in the same line?

Teacher: You can put it on a separate line.

Students: (Pass erasers around.)

Teacher: Finish up in a couple of minutes. You're doing beautifully on your writing. (About 5 minutes pass.)

Teacher: All right now, let's pass the papers forward.

The teacher presents a clear example of the extreme use of authority in any learning situation. She accepts that children practice their first and last name and only as she dictates without any variation. She sets herself up as the sole authority by controlling, time, concept, and by discouraging children from discussing the task. This teacher monitors up and down the isles during this total class project. Ms. Jones in this following lesson shows how she controls her authority from a distance while children work away from her in their individual seats.

Text 11.   (Ms. Jones assigned her 3rd grade reading group seatwork to complete a few pages of activities on syllables. Students sat in their own desks and worked alone as Mrs. Thomas sat up front and read with three students.)

Girl₁: (gets up from her seat and goes to girl₂.)
¿Cómo se hace esto? *How do you do this?*
Girl₂: Pones esta palabra aquí, luego acá no sé. *You put this word here and then over here, I don't know.*
Teacher: Ramona, what do you want? Why are you bothering Susana? If you need something, you ask me.
(girl₁ walks up to the front and Ms. Jones takes her workbook and looks at it.) Did I tell you to do this first?
Girl₁: Yeah, but I didn't know how.
Teacher: Well, you better listen now so you know how to do it and not bother Susana. Sound out balcony in syllables.
Girl₁: b-a-l-c-o-n-y
Teacher: Now I want you to go back and sit down and work quietly.
Girl₁: (walks back to her seat and sits with her book closed for a few moments looking straight ahead.)

Children rely on each other for assistance but Ms. Jones disapproves since she considers herself the only expert in the classroom. Her authoritarian approach dictates the way in which children engage in a task. Students do not openly consult with Ms. Jones because she conducts most of the lessons in English. Therefore by relying on each other, children subtly shape the parameters of the task and designate one another as authorities in their endeavor to comprehend the task.

In this section, we have seen examples of how authority functions in the home and classroom. Seemingly, authority is exercised less stringently by adults in home activities than in classroom tasks evidenced in more egalitarian structures as children set part of their rules for task completion. Adults at home expect that their children will obey requests and respect their authority by complying with the work. However, children are allowed to negotiate how they carry out the work; they may request assistance from adults if the task is unfamiliar, but generally children are left to decide independently the course they take in accomplishing the work. Whereas in the classroom, teachers usually dictate the *what* and *how* of each task and there is little opportunity for children to negotiate. Children are thus pressured to learn not only the academic content but also the social structure imposed on by the teacher.

MULTIDIMENSIONAL AND UNDIMENSIONAL ACTIVITIES

Educators often operate under a misconception that children from lower socioeconomic families are not given activities in the home that expand children's thinking skills; this notion is perpetuated when teachers expect that children from culturally different homes perform in the same language and learning mode as children from Anglo-mainstream culture even when Mexican children are the majority in the classes. When such expectations are not satisfied for the teacher, they are likely to perceive children as incompetent or deficient in the necessary skills for academic success (Saville-Troike, 1979). Lack of information about the children and the community in which teachers work potentially produces stereotypic misconceptions leading to lower unrealistic expectations of children (Carter & Segura, 1979). In Los Portales, as is true in most cultures, children relate to their environment; they observe, touch, examine, and transform their outdoor and indoor areas. This often requires a great deal of resourcefulness and independence to satisfy their creative appetite for adventure as demonstrated in subsequent sections.

ACTIVE LEARNING IN THE COMMUNITY

In Los Portales, parents commonly assign their children tasks which require them to draw upon their many creative abilities as illustrated in this following event.

Text 12. (At a family party at Nora's grandmother's new house, Nora, her sister, Laura, and parents visit on a Sunday afternoon. When they arrive, Nora immediately runs out to watch the neighbor children play.)

Mother: Nora, ven aquí. Llevate a Laura. *Nora, come here. Take Laura with you.*

Father: Hija, con cuidado. *Be careful, dear.*

Mother: Ve, Laura, salte con Nora, ándale. *Go on, Laura go with Nora.* (Laura follows Nora out the door.)

Nora: No quiero que me sigas mucho. *I don't want you to follow me too much.* (Laura walks close behind her as Nora goes to the backyard and she turns around and says to Laura:) A ver si hay una casita aquí atras para jugar con la muñeca. *Let's see if there's a little house back here so we can play with the doll.*

Laura: (follows Nora)

Nora: Mira, que yerbajal tiene 'buela acá. No está como la otra casa. Alla si estaba suave. *Look what a mess grandma has back here. It's not so great like the other house.*
(Laura stays close to Nora and gradually Nora forgets her upset about having Laura with her as she scouts around the backyard. Nora climbs half-way up a tree, then decides to climb back down. They walk around the backyard batting at the weeds with a stick. After a while, the girls run to the front yard and watch. Two boys on bikes stop and ask the girls if they lived there. Nora

said:) Mi abuela vive aquí. *My grandma lives here.* (She turns to Laura and says:) Vamos. *Come on.*
(Nora stops at a rose bush and tells Laura to cut the flower at the stem, not at the top.)

On this first visit to their grandmother's house, Nora assumes responsibility for Laura and together they scout around their new surroundings for a place to play house. They explore the backyard as they walk, climb a tree, beat the bushes, meet new friends, and pick flowers. Notice the adults trust and encourage the children to go outside and play away from adult supervision. This event shows how Nora and Laura discover their new physicalenvironment. The next home event exemplifies competencies in the way children's decision's involve physical, emotional and cognitive skills in dealing with new situations.

Another interesting, and different example of children's multidimensional abilities is illustrated below as they seek a solution to their problem.

Text 13. (During an early warm summer afternoon, Pedro's father had asked Pedro to care for Sabrina while he went to get his hair cut. Efren and Nora came over to visit them and invited Pedro and Yolanda to go swimming.)

Pedro:	No, no podemos porque mi papá no está. *No, we can't cause dad's not here.*
Yolanda:	Podemos esperar. *We can wait.*
Nora:	Luego cierran el pool. *But they'll close the pool.*
Efren:	Sí, luego es muy tarde. *Yeah, then it's too late.*
	(Yolanda looks at Pedro and shrugs her shoulders.)
Pedro:	(Holds Sabrina on his lap and cuddles up to her.) Yo me quedo aquí y ustedes váyanse. *I'll stay here and you guys go.*
Efren:	No, yo no voy si tu no vas. *No, I won't go unless you go too.*
Nora:	Mira, nos llevamos a Sabrina. *Look, we'll take Sabrina.*
Pedro:	Estas loca. ¿Luego que hacemos con ella allá? *You're crazy, then what'll we do with her there?*
Yolanda:	¡Yo sé! Se la llevamos a Lucy (Efren's mother) *You're crazy, then what'll we do with her there?*
	(At this point all children get up and go next door to Efren's house to see if his mother will take care of Sabrina. But, she's not home. The children return to Pedro's living room.)
Nora:	Se la llevan a tu papá en la peluquería. *You take her to your father at the barber shop.* (Then she laughs and shrugs her shoulders while the others looked at her and nodded their heads.)
Pedro:	Estas loca. Se enoja. *You're crazy, he'll get mad.*

Nora:	Mira todos nos vamos con la niña a la piscina y luego yo y Yolanda nos metemos y ustedes dos cuidan a Sabrina. *Look we'll all go with the baby to the pool and then Yolanda and I'll go in the pool, then . . .*
Yolanda:	¡Aha! ¡Y luego ellos se meten a la piscina y tu y yo cuidamos a la niña! *Yeah! Then they can go in the pool and; you and I care for the baby!* (Efren slouched on the couch and Pedro looked cautious about accepting Nora's suggestion.)
Pedro:	No se!
Nora, Yolanda:	¡Sí, sí! (At this point Pedro's father enters through the door. All the children cheer and Pedro asks his father for permission to go to the pool. They receive permission to go to the pool for a short while.)

In the above interaction we observe collective decision making and problem solving among the children. They rely on each other to arrive at a mutual decision that will allow them all to go to the swimming pool and still care for Sabrina. They verbally explore a variety of ways which would enable all of them to go swimming. An egalitarian ethic underlies this event as we see Pedro, who could presumably have all the power in this situation, negotiate with the others to research a solution.

Play events, like home tasks, are also an example of multidimensional activities. Both boys and girls draw upon their skills to gather materials and build a play house.

Text 14.   (After school, one afternoon in October the seven children Pedro, Herlinda, Yolanda, Efren, Nora, Blanca, and Juan build a play house in the front yard of the apartment building. Efren, Yolanda, Nora and Pedro sat on the front steps and Juan, Blanca, and Herminia arrived. Blanca immediately went to the dirt area and began to mix mud in a McDonald's cup and stir it with a stick. Yolanda joined her and suddenly the fence post was transformed into a stove. Nora and Herminia walked over to join them. Herlinda suggested that they get a big covering and put it over a fenced-off area to the building so they would have a "casita" *play house.* Efren and Juan pounded a stick on the cement walkway to shape the point of the stick and use it as a spear.)

Herlinda:	Si pones toda esta comidita allá parece más como casita. *If we put all this food over there it'll look more like a play house.*
Blanca:	No molestes mi sopita. *Don't bother my rice.*
Herlinda:	(to Nora) ¿A donde vas? *Where are you going?*
Nora:	Trae mis monas. *You bring my dolls.*
	(Pedro, who has been watching Juan and Efren, saw the girls collecting their sticks, cans, and paper cups and he

Blanca:

joined them by getting a piece of cardboard and covering the enclosed area. Juan ran over to see what Pedro was doing, but Efren continued sharpening the stick.)
(arranging the dolls in the playhouse:) Aquí pongo a mi hijita y le pongo esta cobijita para que no se enferme. *I'll put my baby here and cover her with this blanket so she won't get cold.* (She used newspaper that the boys had taken from the trash can.)
(Efren, Pedro and Juan went looking for big rocks to hold the cardboard like a roof over casita. Once the roof was secured, the boys stepped back and watched the girls inside the casita sit on the ground and pretend to drink coffee and eat sopita. Juan, then, picked up the stick which Efren had sharpened and used it as a balance stick to walk on the edge of the fence. Efren and Pedro followed.)

Almost instantly, old cardboards, used cans, and peper cups are transformed into parts of a "casita" for these children. Efren transforms a fence post into a sword. Their imagination and resourcefulness are active agents in creating their play activity. This type of activity is common among children in Los Portales; they find open spaces where they collectively respond to each other's fantasies in the following incident.

Text 15. (One day after school Pedro, Efren, Nora, Yolanda and Laura walked to the railroad track area where there was an abandoned flat-bed truck. They ran up on it and jumped off to see who could jump the farthest. Herminia and Juan came by on one bike and watched the others for a minute then joined the others stomping and singing, "Aye en el Rancho Grande" on top of the truck. Juan began chasing everyone who jumped off the truck; he pretended to be a monster. The other children ran from him and pretended to be scared.)

Juan:

Ahora, yo si los agarro, los voy encerrar en una jaula y ustedes se ratan de salir. *Now, if I catch you, you'll be locked up and try to escape.*
(The children scream and they begin to run. Juan captures two girls and Efren runs under the truck.)

Efren:

Aquí es mi casita, Mira parece casita. *This is my little house. Look, it looks like a little house.*
(Juan continues to chase the children and then Pedro challenges him.)

Pedro:

Yo soy el rey y yo digo que tu, monstruo, no puedes asustar a la gente. *I'm the king and I say you can't scare the people.*

Nora:

Quítese de aquí, rey, usted no sabe nada. *Get out of here king, you don't know anything.*

Laura:	Yo tengo que hacer chi. *I have to pee.* (runs around the other side of the truck.)
Herlinda:	No, Pedro es el rey, y yo soy reina y ustedes los princesa y Juan nos quiere agarrar pero tenemos poderes que el no sabe y cuando nos agarza, algo le pasa a el. Le hacemos algun dano. *No, Pedro is the king and I'm the queen and you're all princesses and Juan tries to catch us but we have powers that he doesn't know and when he catches us, something will happen to him that he doesn't know.*
All:	¡Sí, sí! *Yeah, yeah!*
	(Efren begins to chase, and he catches Yolanda.)
Herlinda:	Ándale, hazle algo. *Come on, do something to him.*
Yolanda:	No sé qué. Tu eres una rata. *I don't know what, you're a rat.*
All:	(laugh and cheer)
Laura:	¡Más, más, qué chistoso! *More, more, how funny!*

Collectively the children shape this event, as Pedro initiates the fantasy with his role as king, and the others assume their roles that sustain the activity. Much of this play event is dependent on children's listening skill, which enables them to participate actively. They need to be alert in order to continue fabricating their fantasy.

Opportunities are abundant in the Los Portals community that allow children to develop their native competencies e.g., observing, listening, manipulating, imagining, building, verbalizing, and interpreting. While all these skills are not necessarily unique to children in Los Portales, it is necessary to recognize how they utilize these abilities although classroom experiences do not usually allow children to demonstrate their diverse competencies.

Boundaries and lessons

A key point in this section is that children learn through diverse experiences; classroom tasks, unlike community activities, require children to perform a different set of competencies. Reading and writing are usually the focus of most school tasks. Teachers structure activities to accomplish these lessons; the common format is to have children copy material off the board or fill-in ditto pages. Furthermore, children are to work quickly, quietly, and individually as portrayed in this event.

Text 16.

Teacher:	Green group to that table and Mrs. Gomez, go sit with that group and work with them on counting. The group that's working on this page, S_1, S_2, S_3, S_4, come up. Do the front and

Girl₁, Girl₂, Girl₃: (Sit together and start quickly working on their addition and subtraction ditto.)

Students: (Move to assigned seats.)

Girl₁: Mira, tienes que hacer esta primero. *Look, you have to do this one first.*

Girl₂: (Accepts the suggestion.) Pati, yo la acabe. *Pati, I've finished.*

Girl₃: A mí me falta poco. (Continues counting on her fingers.) *I've got a bit to go.*

Girl₁: Hijolé, yo ya te pase. *Wow, I've already passed you.*

Girl₃: (Stands up to look at Girl₁ paper.)

Girl₁: No me copies. *Don't copy me.*

(One boy and girl join the group. Their papers are on addition and number sequence. The teacher's aide moves from table to table assisting students while the teacher works on the concept of "borrowing" with other students.)

Aide: (To Efren:) Lo estas haciendo bien. Apúrate pues. *You're doing it right. Hurry it up.*

Boy₁: Yo te voy a ganar. *I'm going to beat you.*

Aide: (To Girl₁:) Tu estas trabajando muy despacio. Tu sabes hacer esto. No tienes que ver esto. (Points to number line on their table.) *You're working very slowly. You know how to do this. You don't have to use this.*

Boy₂: (To aide:) ¿Esto esta bien? *Is this right?*
(He shows her a page with English directions that read: "Mark the numbers that are less than . . ." and eight rows appear with large numbers 5-1, 10-11, etc. Students have to circle the equations under each number whose answers would be less than that number. The teacher has written: "más chico" *smaller* next to the symbol.)

Aide: (To Efren:) ¿Qué va aquí? ¿Qué es 3 más 4? *What goes here? What's 3 × 4?*

Efren: (Erases the 5 and changes it to 6.)

Aide: No, cuenta bien. *No, count right.*

Efren: (Erases and changes it to 7.)

Irene: (Aide watches over her and she circles the 7.)

Aide: Ahora este es de más. ¿Cúal es más grande? *Now, this asks which is more. Which is largest?*

Teacher: Ok. Clean up.

Students: (Put all their papers in the bin on top of teacher's desk.)

This half-hour lesson reveals how adults enforce silence, speed, and individual behavior during the time children complete their worksheets. Some of the children themselves monitor each other's pace by challenging one another to finish first and by not allowing others to copy from them. The questions posed by the teacher assistant to Efren show an emphasis on recall-memory skills. The above event involves small group seatwork; however, whole class tasks, as described below, also exhibit the limited opportunity for the development of multiple competencies not only cognitively, but social.

Text 17.   (The lesson before lunch in Mrs. Thomas's room is math. On this day she has kept the whole class together to review 2-digit subtraction. She hands out the same ditto to everyone.)

Mrs. Thomas: I want you to try and work these out. They're not new to you, you've seen them before and you should all be able to do them without much trouble. And, no talking!
(Students quietly begin to complete their ditto. As Mrs. Thomas walks up and down answering question, other students ask each other for assistance.)

Boy₁: (leans over to the boy in front of him and whispers: Numero (inaudible). *Number (inaudible).*

Boy₂: (moves his paper to the edge of his desk while continuing to write on it then cautiously leans back to explain to B₁) *You have to borrow from here.*

Teacher: No talking (walks over to Boy₁ and Boy₂). You, turn around. If you need help, raise your hand—let's see what's the problem. (The two boys look up at her then lower their eyes back on to their papers.)

Boy₁: Here. (points to a problem)

Teacher: (explains how to borrow from the tens column then continues to walk around and answer other students' questions)

Girl₁: (leans across the isle with her paper to show Boy₃ the answer to a problem)

Teacher: Rosa, what's the problem? If Mario needs help, he has to ask for it. Now let me see it. (Mrs. Thomas explains:) Well, what's that? You know what that is now you just subtract these numbers. (She proceeds to walk around.)

Mrs. Thomas establishes the parameters of this task to have children work quickly and independently on this subtraction drill. Children are expected to sit and think by themselves, and alone produce abstract computations on this ditto page. The only cognitive competency involved in this task is memorization.

In summary, children in Los Portales participate in home cultural tasks (including play), that embody competencies e.g., collectivity competition, resourcefulness, imagination, observation, decision making, and Spanish-language proficiency. These skills, however, are not usually recognized in the classroom since the dominant ideology in the school fails to utilize children's competencies learned in the home.

Continuity-Discontinuity

The three major areas of continuity-discontinuity discussed in this paper, collectivity-competitiveness, authoritarian-egalitarian, and multidimensional-undimensional are only part of the many areas of discontinuity that exist between Mexican immigrant children's home experiences in the home and the school. Although we acknowledge that some discontinuity is natural and necessary in learning new practices, we need to understand how discontinuities result in ineffective instructional strategies.

Collectivity and competiveness are areas of continuity-discontinuity observed in Los Portales home and classroom activities. Home data show a stronger cooperative ethic in their work and play, including sharing of work load, turn-taking, collective group games, and frequent negotiation of tasks. Children in Los Portales do have experience in competitive skills in home tasks that require children to work alone or in play where only one winner is possible in a game. However, such occasions are infrequent in the home life of children observed. Their transition to a highly competitive emphasis in school does not permit the expression of their familiar collective practices at home in a way that would assist them in sharing ideas or developing language skills. Children attempt to work together whenever they are assigned independent seatwork, but usually such sharing of information is against classroom as it is considered disruptive and a form of cheating. The significance of the continuity-discontinuity of this cooperative/competitive issue is demonstrated in that collective work in the classroom results in far more favorable achievement for minority children than competitive work modes (Cohen, 1980).

Modes of authority are continuous and discontinuous. On one level there is continuity of authority between home and school in that adults at home usually instruct and direct children as to the tasks that need to be performed. However, discontinuity exists at another level, where adults at home allow children to negotiate with them and make decisions for themselves about the manner in which they will accomplish the task; the adults in the school usually organize the entire task and exclude children from the decision-making process so that alternative ways of accomplishing tasks are not an option. Furthermore, parents in the home often leave a child in charge of other siblings. This type of responsibility affords children an opportunity to feel confident about their abilities. Teachers are often unaware that this is a form of leadership potential that children can teach one another. The manifestation of authority in the classroom conceivably limits children's language expression with peers and inhibits their ability to demonstrate independent leadership skills.

The third finding involves the diverse type of competencies which children naturally develop in their home culture. Tasks in the real world require children to use multifaceted knowledge including cognitive, physical, emotional, and social competence, and the opposite is usually the case in the classroom where tasks demand that children think mostly in abstract, linear ways, and oftentimes in English, although they are limited in English proficiency. While the school emphasizes mostly textbook reading and rote arithmetic skills, children actually possess much more knowledge; they are observers, organizers, actors, decision makers, manipulators, explorers, and they are resourceful, but in the classroom teachers expect that children work quickly, quietly and individually.

Implications of Discontinuity

The Los Portales study suggests two major kinds of implication, research and pedagogical. Because this study raises more questions than it answers an appropriate recommendation is to conduct further extensive research on issues of continuity-discontinuity between home and school that explicate the heterogeneity of regional, social-class and generational stay in the U. S. All of these factors, as Ogbu (1978) hypothesizes, contribute to issues of discontinuity.

Furthermore, we must examine more closely the function of language for these children as well as closely analyze the variations within each of the three areas discussed here.

Although small in scale, the Los Portales study indicates a need to look at educational needs from a community perspective. A connection appears between the various areas of discontinuity and specific classroom learning structures. Classroom reforms are possible by integrating the students' home culture in the classroom to produce a more comfortable and productive learning environment through a wide range of learning alternatives. Although discussion on specific pedagogical implications is beyond the scope of this paper, we can recommend that teachers implement a more challenging multidimensional curriculum, and allow cooperative work structures in their instructional program.

It is important to note that Mexican children's education should not be dichotomized in relation to other ethnic groups. Rather, we need to underline that classroom alternatives are warranted to accommodate discontinuity. These types of classroom reforms require school staff training on the home culture of the children. Teachers need to learn about the culture of the community and understand how to acknowledge and utilize children's native intelligence. A major relief in all of these conclusions is that teachers are not found to be deliberately vicious, rather they express the ideology of the dominant society and are products of the teacher training programs that perpetuate ethnocentricity. The discontinuity of interactional orientations between Mexican children and teachers need not lead to antagonistic situations, but because the discontinuity is apparent in the school, we must develop and emphasize programs and policies that assure Mexican children full participation in their schooling as they learn to accept their traditions while making new social and cultural transitions.

REFERENCES

Au, K. (1980). Participation structures in a reading lesson with Hawaiian children: Analysis of a culturally appropriate instructional event. *Anthropology and Education Quarterly, XI, 2,* 91–115.

Au, K., & Jordan, C. (1980). *Hawaiian talk-story, sibling work groups, and learning to read: The culturally-congruent shaping of an educational program.* A mimeograph paper of the Early Education Programs.

Carter, T., & Segura, R. (1979). *Mexican Americans in school: A decade of change.* New York: College Entrance Examination Board.

Cohen, E. (1980). *Teacher application pamphlet: Designing change for the classroom.* Final report on the Status Equalization Project: Changing expectations in the integrated classroom. Submitted to National Institute of Education through Stanford University.

Florio, S., & Schultz, J. (1979). Social competence at home and at school. *Theory into Practice, XVIII, 4,* 234–243.

Gallimore, R., Boggs, J., & Jordan, C. (1974). *Culture, behavior and education.* Beverly Hills: Sage.

Heath, S. B. (1980, November). *What no bedtime story means: narrative skills at home and school.* Paper presented at the Terman Conference, Stanford University.

Heath, S. B. (1982). Questioning at home and at school: A comparative study. In G. Spindler (Ed.), *Doing the ethnography of schooling* (pp. 102–131). New York: Holt, Rinehart & Winston.

Heath, S. B. (1983). *Ways with words.* Cambridge: Cambridge University Press.

Ogbu, J. U. (1978). *Minority education and caste: The American system in cross-cultural perspective.* Orlando, FL: Academic Press.

Ogbu, J. U. (1981). Origins of human competence: A cultural-ecological perspective. *Child Development, 52,* 413–429.

Ogbu, J. U. (1982). Cultural discontinuities and schooling. *Anthropology and Education Quarterly, XII, 4,* 290–307.

Philips, S. (1983). *The invisible culture: Communities in classroom and community on the Warm Spring Indian Reservation.* New York: Longman.

Saville-Troike, M. (1979). Profiles of bilingual children. In H. T. Trueba & C. Barnett-Mizrah (Eds.), *Bilingual multicultural education and the professional: From theory to practice* (pp. 164–174). Rowley, MA: Newbury House.

Shultz, J., Florio, S., & Erickson, F. (1982). Where's the floor? Aspects of the cultural organization of social relationships in communication at home and in school. In P. Gilmore & A. A. Glatthorn (Eds.), *Children in and out of school: Ethnography and education.* Washington, D. C.: Center for Applied Linguistics.

The Author and His Chapter

José Macias, now assistant professor of education at the University of Utah, is an educational anthropologist with particular interests in the psychosocial development and schooling of ethnic minorities. He received an M.S.W. from the University of California, Berkeley, and a Ph.D. in educational anthropology from Stanford under the mentorship of G. Spindler.

Macias's research interests have their roots in his previous practice as a social worker. In that role, he was concerned with facilitating children's development in families and schools. Faced with what he perceived to be a lack of good, instructive research on ethnic minority issues, Macias decided to become a researcher himself. He sees his current work in educational anthropology and ethnography as a natural extension of the interactive techniques, family and community emphases, and sociocultural focus that guided much of his past work. Macias's work with the Papago community is an example of the long-term, interactive research he believes is important for analyzing the role of culture in schooling.

Macias was clinical instructor of pediatrics with the University of California, San Francisco, Fresno-Central San Joaquin Valley Medical Education Program. Currently, he is assistant professor of educational studies at the University of Utah.

Macias's chapter focuses on the Papago Indian Early Childhood Headstart Program (PECHS) and the ways in which Papago teachers and caretakers help to reduce the severity of discontinuity between home and school. The teaching and learning activities center on social roles, basic skills, and bicultural interaction. Macias shows how teachers and care-takers intervene in purposeful ways in critical areas of potential cultural conflict such as autonomy versus conformity to rules. A variety of new experiences is provided, that in themselves create discontinuity with traditional, and relatively isolated Papago lifestyles. This introduction to the kinds of discontinuity that will be encountered in more radical form when the Papago child does enter regular school appears to reduce the impact of that discontinuity.

The specific ways in which, in effect, "discontinuity reducing" teaching and learning occur in the PECHS program are the consistent focus of this chapter.

Macias established residence in the Papago community and met the criteria of a good ethnography in all respects. The results of his work have many implications for other parallel situations.

The Editors

The Hidden Curriculum of Papago Teachers: American Indian Strategies for Mitigating Cultural Discontinuity in Early Schooling

15

José Macias
University of Utah

This chapter summarizes the major findings of an ethnographic case study of Papago (Arizona) children in a tribal preschool. The entrance of Papago children into school is a transition marked by significant discontinuities between the new, structured school environment and childrens' prior experiences within their families and reservation community. These differences often contain cultural elements that, because they are not typically recognized by school personnel, contribute to the chronic school problems (i.e., poor school adjustment, achievement and retention) that Papagos share with other American Indian tribes and other subordinate ethnic minority groups.

SCHOOLING AS CULTURAL DISCONTINUITY

Discontinuity in the enculturation process is described in the anthropological literature as an ". . . abrupt transition from one mode of being and behaving to another . . ." (Spindler, 1974:308) and is accompanied by marked changes in social role assignment and expectations (Benedict, 1938). Within a culturally homogeneous society, the educational purposes of discontinuity—as in initiation ceremonies or schooling—are to impart knowledge necessary for social functioning, as well as to extract individual commitment to the group and its culture. Here, schooling is a discontinuous process, but one intended to contribute to the overall development of a child by making her a functioning part of society.

The problem of discontinuity becomes somewhat more complicated in culturally pluralistic settings. Some researchers have discussed the particular problems faced by children whose home culture is radically different from that of the social mainstream, the segment of the population generally responsible for the social and educational policies affecting these children (Laosa, 1984). For instance, in his analysis of the school discontinuity concept, Ogbu (1982) discriminates between different sources of discontinuity and argues that castelike groups in the U. S. (American Indians, Blacks, Hispanics) are especially affected by the subtle, diffuse discontinuities inherent in their school experience. While broader ecological structures are thoroughly implicated in this process (Ogbu, 1981) we cannot discount what has historically been a clear relationship between home-school discontinuity and the poor record of schooling for these groups.

For many children of ethnic minority origin, the transition from home to school in early childhood appears to be a critical period of discontinuity. The way in which cultural disparities—between what has been learned at home and what school teaches—are dealt with determines to some degree the efficacy of their schooling.

The remainder of this chapter describes some cultural discontinuities experienced by Papago preschool children and examines the responses of their Papago teachers in helping them cope with the contradictions of their first school experience. While the present discussion focuses primarily on children and teachers, another report (Macias, 1984) details a broader historical and sociocultural perspective which is essential for understanding the roots of Papago children's discontinuous experiences, as well as the bases for teachers' actions.

THE STUDY

The research was designed around two major goals. First, I wanted to describe the experience of Papago children as they made the transition from home to their first school experience. This entailed descriptions of children's home and community life, particularly their socialization experiences, and their experiences in a tribal preschool. My second goal—the focus of this chapter—was to describe instances of discontinuity in the experience of children in the preschool and the reactions of teachers in those specific instances.

The research setting was the Papago Early Childhood Head Start Program (PECHS), a tribal preschool program operated by the Papago Department of Education. The program operates several early childhood centers throughout the Papago Reservation and is headquartered in Sells,

Arizona, the tribal administrative seat. Centrally located on the reservation, Sells is over an hour's drive from the nearest town or city.

The ethnographic fieldwork was carried out primarily in Sells, where I worked in the largest early childhood center and with the PECHS central administration. I also observed the activity of other PECHS centers, made home visits and interviewed informants in various parts of the reservation and attended meetings of the Papago education department and tribal council. These activities broadened my perspective and made possible a contextual description of the events I observed in PECHS.

The people with whom I worked included PECHS children, their parents and families, PECHS center coordinators, teachers and staff, and PECHS and Papago Education Department administrators. I also had contact with PECHS consultants and service providers, staff of other tribal programs and tribal administrators.

An anthroethnographic approach (Spindler, 1982), marked by the use of cultural concepts and ethnographic field techniques, guided the research during the 2 years in which I had contact with PECHS. Specific characteristics of the study included long-term involvement in the research site (including 9 months of intensive field work), a focus on observed behavior and participant interpretations, and use of an inductive analytic approach.

The following data collection techniques were used:

1. *Participant-Observation* included working with children in classrooms, assisting teachers, accompanying administrators at meetings, etc. Visits to children's homes were made, as were appropriate efforts to partake in community life.

2. *Ethnographic Interviews* were done with administrators, teachers, parents, children and other informants knowledgeable about the PECHS program, children's home life and the Papago community. Three interview types were used:

   a. *Unstructured Interviews*—casual, spontaneous, yet purposive conversation in terms of providing data relevant to the research goals.

   b. *Semistructured Interviews*—designed to acquire information in specific domains such as socialization, parental attitudes toward schooling, teaching strategies, etc.; interview process allowed for exploration outside of an interview's planned focus.

   c. *Thematic Biographical Interviews*—concerned with the personal experiences and perceptions of individuals in areas such as family life, schooling, childrearing, relationship to PECHS, etc.

3. *Unobtrusive Measures* were strategies implemented with little or no disruption of the natural field setting and its participants.

a. *Ethnohistorical Research*—a review of the literature provided a survey of Papago history and sociocultural development; an overview of Papago culture and childhood enculturation; the history of contact with Whites, with particular reference to culture change, changes in childhood socialization, and attempts to formally educate Papagos.

b. *Sociodemographic Data*—secured from tribal offices that normally provide this kind of information, or from public government records.

THE PAPAGO EARLY CHILDHOOD HEAD START PROGRAM (PECHS)

The coming of the Head Start program to the Papago Reservation in the mid-1960s brought multiple, immediate benefits to Papago children and families. Children enrolled in the program were able to get preparation in basic skills, a social experience with a large peer group, as well as exposure to the structure and feel of being in school. Parents benefited, not only through the day care that all school programs provide, but also because the program encouraged their involvement and shared with them information about child development, parenting, and schooling.

But the success of Papago Head Start grew until, eventually, parents themselves decided to do something about their growing demand for early education. One parent says:

> In 1975 we started the Early Childhood Program . . . because (Head Start didn't have enough slots). We get to see the children in a setting other than the home . . . helping in the development of their education plus knowing they were safe.

Papago Head Start (sponsored by the Department of Health and Human Services), which had received its impetus from national policy, and the grassroots initiated Papago Early Childhood Program (funded by the Bureau of Indian Affairs) continued as separate programs for a few years. In 1980, however, the two programs began to combine into a single unit, the Papago Early Childhood Head Start Program (PECHS). With the merger now completed, some differences do remain between the two program components, but these are mainly administrative ones that do not significantly affect the program's daily operation. Today, PECHS serves over 300 children and their families in several early childhood centers throughout the reservation.

Outside observers, as well as Papagos themselves, consider PECHS a successful program. Locally, this success can be measured by the widespread support it enjoys from parents, the tribal government, and the Papago community at large. Another measure of the program's performance is its apparent success in preparing children to enter kindergarten. One parent's comment reflects a typical evaluation voiced to me by several informants:

> I know for a fact that these kids (in PECHS) already know the things (i.e., basic skills) they are teaching them over there (at kindergarten).

The program's success is confirmed further by outside parties. The National Congress of American Indians, for example, has designated the Papago Department of Education as one of six model tribal education departments nationwide, and much of the credit for this honor goes to PECHS' reputation as a showcase early education program. Due to this reputation, PECHS administrators receive frequent requests to provide consultant services to other tribes developing their own early education programs. Furthermore, university professors arrange to bring their students to tour the modern facilities of the PECHS center in Sells as a "state of the art" example in Indian early childhood education.

Teaching and learning activities take place in three major areas—the learning of social roles and rules, the teaching of basic skills, and bilingual, bicultural instruction. Although separated here for explanatory purposes, these areas of teacher concern normally overlap in the daily life of the PECHS classroom.

In the first of these areas, Papago teachers present children with norms for proper school behavior, as well as with experiences that introduce them to mainstream American society and culture. The second area of instruction focuses on the teaching of language and communication, as well as age-appropriate cognitive skills. Teachers integrate Papago language and cultural content with social activities and classroom projects (e.g., arts and crafts, Papago storyteller, fieldtrips) and, to a lesser extent, in the teaching of cognitive and language skills. English is the primary language of instruction as well as the medium of most social interaction.

DISCONTINUITY IN PECHS

> *When I went to school in (name of off-reservation town) it was hard for me to get into reading and writing because I had never been in a classroom before.*
> —recollection of a PECHS employee.

This informant's recollection of his own school entry over 20 years ago accurately portrays the difficult home-school transition that still confronts many Papago children on the reservation today. For these children, the social discontinuity inherent in any child's first school experience is compounded by entry into the culturally unfamiliar environment, expectations, and processes of schooling. The remainder of this section summarizes the three areas of cultural discontinuity I observed in PECHS.

Emphasis on Verbal Performance

A major finding of the study is that children in PECHS are taught and encouraged to be verbal, in direct contradiction to how they are socialized for language use in their own culture. Earlier research (Chesky, 1949; Dobyns, 1972; Underhill, 1942) has documented how Papago parents typically enculturate their children through nonverbal behaviors such as modeling and gesturing, as well as through economical speech such as brief comments or directives. Children themselves are often minimally verbal in the school setting. On one occasion, I observed how Papago children's verbal expressive style is in marked contrast to mainstream norms:

> She (teacher) takes out drawings of different things—a coyote, a cowboy, a cactus, a pig, a horse, etc. She asks if anyone can name the first picture. A towheaded Anglo boy (attending summer session as a visitor, because his mother is working as a program volunteer) immediately and loudly gives the correct answer. Meanwhile, none of the rest of the group, all Papagos, has responded in any way—either verbally or by raising a hand. . . . By the time the Anglo boy has answered it is too late to say if any of the Papago children were interested in giving an answer. Teacher repeats, using other cards, and every time the Anglo boy responds in the same way. After two or three times, teacher asks for the Papago name of the next picture, an apparent technique to involve the Papago children. Again, the Anglo boy gives his answer before anyone else can. This continues in the same pattern, with the boy sometimes answering wrong. By this time the Papago children appear to not even be trying, and this forces the teacher to ask the group to take turns. As she shows the next few cards, teacher must call on different children for their answers. Only two or three children give their answers voluntarily, but in no case is the answer given with the speed, volume, or apparent confidence of the Anglo boy.

This passage brings into sharp relief the modal communication style of children in PECHS. Papago children are typically reticent, and although this may be due partly to their discomfort in the new school situation, the reasons for this reticence are complex. Children are shy or restrained not only because of the new surroundings; they also feel confused and unsure of how to act because they are entering into a new culture, with new norms in many areas of behavior. New norms for language use are clearly implicated in this statement of a PECHS administrator, a Papago himself:

(the children) . . . that speak Papago are not as vocal as those exposed to English. . . . There's been instances where you get two groups (of Papago children from different centers) together and the English speakers talk more . . . they even make fun of the other (quiet) group, but towards the end of the day they're interacting with each other. We try to get them to interact.

The two preceding passages indicate that in this bilingual school setting, vocal self-assertion and social dominance are factors associated with English use, while, comparatively, social deference and restrained speech are inherent in the use of Papago. Researchers (Philips, 1983; Wax, 1972) have previously observed among other Indian groups a pattern of controlled language use in public, a trend specifically documented among Papagos by the present research.

But the development of verbal language is a major goal in PECHS. Verbal skills are taught through a variety of lessons, projects and in one-to-one as well as group contexts. A favorite exhortation of teachers is to repeatedly urge children to "speak up" as a way of encouraging their verbal skills. Teachers also present children with explicit, verbal instructions before the start of regularly scheduled classroom periods, particularly those involving cognitive skills development. In PECHS, children are confronted by both a curricular content and an instructional process that emphasize performance and elaboration in the use of language. These expectations for language use are clearly discontinuous with Papago children's language experiences at home.

Interference with Autonomy

CLASSROOM RULES
NO FIGHTING!
NO PUSHING OR SHOVING YOUR NEIGHBOR!
NO SHOUTING OR LOUD NOISES!
NO RUNNING!
NO PLAYING IN THE RESTROOM!

—Prominent sign in a PECHS classroom

A second area of discontinuity results from the increased interference of the PECHS experience with Papago children's autonomy, in comparison to what is normally acceptable within their homes and community. According to Chesky (1949), traditional socialization was ". . . informal and leisurely, attuned to the child's natural pace and accompanied with little conscious planning . . ." (p. 115), and children interacted freely with adults and were ". . . not rebuked for interfering with the work or conversation of the elders" (p. 124). Chesky also points out the traditional

Papago belief that children should not be forced to bow to an older person's demands.

The value of childhood autonomy persists today, and Papago children are not expected to conform to many explicit standards for appropriate behavior, nor are they restricted or directed by adults in their play while on the reservation. Because children are raised with very few limitations on their freedom, parents are seldom punitive, and children are not accustomed to being controlled, reprimanded, or punished.

But the teaching of school rules and roles is an integral purpose of early education, and, in PECHS, children are taught to conform to rules, follow instructions, sit quietly, raise their hands, stand in line, and so forth. Papago socialization gives children little experience or preparation for adapting quickly to this unfamiliar set of behavioral expectations.

Another way in which PECHS interferes with a child's sense of autonomy is through an increased focus on the individual, a type of action normally avoided by Papagos. Important positive effects can result from the individual attention teachers give children, including improved instruction and enhancement of self-esteem in the child. Nevertheless, an individual teaching focus is discontinuous with Papago children's experience.

Respect in the form of a deep appreciation of each child's distinctiveness is an important characteristic of Papago childrearing (Williams, 1958). But this type of respect is not dependent upon attention from adults but rather on noninterference with children's autonomy. In other words, Papagos place an emphasis on individual rights and choice rather than on the singling out of individuals from their peers or family for special recognition. In fact, Papagos generally place a negative value on calling attention to oneself, and there is a reluctance on the part of individual children to separate socially from the group. But directing attention to individual children is standard procedure in almost any classroom, and children's school success is determined largely by how well they react when they are called on to attend, speak, answer a question, or otherwise respond when they are singled out. This kind of individual attention is discontinuous and potentially traumatic to children who are accustomed to the traditional, unobtrusive Papago style of giving respect to individuals.

New Cultural Experiences

Papago preschoolers experience a third type of discontinuity in the variety of unfamiliar experiences presented by PECHS. The sheer size of the Papago Reservation (at 2.25 million acres, it is the second largest Indian reservation) results in some variability in the experiences children bring to school. Some children grow up in isolated homes or small villages. Other children live in larger villages that offer public services, such as a library, or that are close enough for easy trips to off-reservation towns like Casa Grande or Tucson. One informant, a PECHS administrator says:

> (there are) definite differences in children . . . (we have) town kinds and country kids. Many of the town children . . . (have) different kinds of learning experiences than children from the outer areas. Children from Sells speak more English; from outer villages, they speak more Papago . . . The children from the outer areas are more self-sufficient, (but) they're behind in language skills. One thing that accounts for the language lag is exposure to people and experiences. Some of the children from the outer villages are frightened of me (an Anglo) . . . or other adults not in their immediate family.

Despite these "town and country" differences, children on the reservation grow up relatively isolated from mainstream society, as illustrated by the following fieldnote:

> On the way back to Sells, Caroline points out an isolated area where some families live. The children grow up hearing only Papago. Some of them, adults as well as children, have never been in a museum, she adds. Nor a shopping center or other things typical of modern city life, I think to myself.

Reservation children in general have limited experience with mainstream environments, norms, and values, certainly much less than children brought up within or in close proximity to a mainstream context such as an off-reservation town or urban area.

By contrast, PECHS introduces children to the new world of schooling and to mainstream ways of life by providing them with a series of new experiences. Some of these experiences are typical school events planned by teachers—holiday activities, field trips to the Tucson Zoo, an adult guest invited to sing children's songs, etc. Other experiences are related to specific program goals. For example, teachers select children to help with the lunch set-up as one way of promoting social competence. Visits to the library are arranged so that children become comfortable there while receiving an introduction to the world of literacy. Even nutrition is used as a vehicle for new experiences, as the cook at one center said, ". . . to help the child feel comfortable with different foods."

The problem is that Papago children sometimes reject school experiences that seem foreign to them. This is especially common in the more isolated areas of the reservation, as the following fieldnote entry on a small village illustrates.

Donald also relates a story about his son and the recent Christmas party given for the (name of small village) Home Start children. Staff was trying to have the kids play organized games such as musical chairs and circle games, but Kevin would have no part of it. The teacher's attempts to involve the children failed, to the point that Kevin ran away from the party and "went home to his grandma." As he relates this to me, Donald shows no more concern about the incident, other than mild amusement. No attempt was made to bring Kevin back to the party. The child later said, according to his father, that he "didn't want to play what the teacher wanted them to play." Donald adds that "these kids aren't used to having teachers try to make them play in a certain way."

This passage shows how an everyday school activity can be unacceptable to a Papago child. Children's reactions are not always as dramatic as Kevin's response to organized play, but any given experience in PECHS can be potentially discontinuous with a child's prior experiences and a traumatic introduction to the conventions of the sociocultural mainstream and its program of schooling.

Teachers in PECHS intentionally present children with discontinuous experiences designed to help them acquire social behavior and academic skills necessary for school success. It could be argued, in fact, that the process of learning, in any context and with any population, involves the engagement of new information and experiences which often conflict with past learning. While it is tempting to criticize those aspects of a school program that create discomfort and stress for the child, it is equally important to recognize how critical it is for the child to acquire the requisite knowledge and skills.

In the case of Papago children, it is also crucial to acknowledge that much of their discontinuous school experience is a direct result of the superimposition of an alien culture upon an indigenous one. Whereas children experiencing discontinuity within their own culture are provided with helping persons and structures associated with the discontinuous process, children experiencing discontinuity engendered by an alien system do not enjoy the support of such built-in institutions. Thus, there would appear to be a value in helping children overcome these discontinuous experiences at an early age so that they are resolved, rather than compounded with time. The following section shows how Papago teachers in PECHS, with the support of parents and administrators, appear to have put this realization into practice.

PAPAGO TEACHER RESPONSES TO DISCONTINUITY

My focus now turns to a discussion of the strategies through which Papago teachers attempt to reduce the negative impact of discontinuity by incorporating Papago experiences, values, and ways of relating into that experience. Table 15.1 presents several examples of home-school discontinuity experienced by children in PECHS. In the first column of the table is a brief reference to a specific discontinuous experience as structured by the school context. In the adjacent columns are a brief summary of the essential purpose of the discontinuous experience in terms of facilitating school success (column two), specific areas of conflict arising from the experience (column three), and Papago teacher strategies for mitigating the negative consequences of the discontinuity for the child (column four). These instances of conflict between home and school culture illustrate both the complexity and apparent inevitability of discontinuity for Papago children being prepared for mainstream schooling. Although any example of discontinuity may reflect more than one area of culture conflict, my discussion draws upon those examples that are particularly representative of a certain type of discontinuity. Any example may also reflect additional sources of culture conflict, and a list of these possible conflicts may be found in column three of the table.

Language and Communication

Young (1983) has outlined a teaching strategy that appears appropriate for addressing the discontinuity experienced by Papago children when they are presented with increased expectations for verbal performance. Criticizing the present one-sided emphasis on verbal and decontextualized learning, Young proposes a greater emphasis on teaching through doing, rather than through talking. His suggestion is particularly applicable to the schooling of young Papago children because they are accustomed to a parental instructional approach emphasizing modeling, demonstration, and practical experience.

In PECHS, children often learn by doing, combining a physical activity, such as dancing, with a verbal activity, such as singing (example #1 in the table). During crafts projects, teachers first verbally explain to the class as a whole how the task should be accomplished and then demonstrate the task individually if children need this done. Rather than detracting from the verbal emphasis of the curriculum, these efforts to include nonverbal activities in the learning process of Papago children facilitate conversation and verbal expression. Although the actual amount of talk may be reduced during periods of activity, there is great impetus from involvement of both teacher and child in these activities to communicate clearly and perform with verbal skill.

In her ethnography of a Warm Springs Reservation elementary school, Philips (1983) describes the overstimulation of students in the classroom by teachers' encouragement of excited verbal responses, combined with too little opportunity for physical activity. Warm Springs Indian parents

TABLE 15.1
Examples of School Discontinuity in PECHS

Experience in PECHS	Value of Experiences	Nature of Discontinuity	Teacher Behavior, Strategy, or Style
1. saying own name, speaking out in group	verbal skill & self-assertion	"speaking up" vs. controlled public speech; individual vs. group focus	children may nod or raise hands; verbalization combined w/ activity & music; little direct questioning; tolerant of reticent children
2. required to be quiet & walk in file	situation-appropriate behavior	rules vs. autonomy	enforces school rules in positive, objective manner; nonpunitive
3. given verbal directions prior to starting project	attending/listening, cognitive/motor planning skills	verbal/decontextualized instruction vs. brief imperatives, nonverbal instruction	requires their attention, then helps children by repeating instructions, modeling & encouraging
4. working at planned activities & crafts	cognitive learning	verbal vs. nonverbal instruction; new vs. familiar exp; control vs. autonomy	small group; demonstration, modeling & minimal talking; one-to-one interaction
5. formal, structured social experience	learning culture & context of school	new vs. familiar experience; interference vs. autonomy	Papago teachers' comforting, parent-like attitudes and subtle, minimally directive interaction style
6. classroom rules made explicit	socialization for school role, discipline	control vs. autonomy	extreme patience, direct reprimand only after repeated, impersonal warnings
7. rest time	good health habits; situation-appropriate behavior	adherence to time schedule vs. autonomy	uses short commands to get children quiet, then pats/ comforts to sleep
8. supervised in bathroom	hygiene; proper behavior	rules vs. autonomy	doesn't hurry, but primarily observes or helps children to keep them from getting wet, hurt
9. treated as individuals	personal instruction & self-esteem; exposure to new values	individual vs. group focus	develops trust; one-to-one interaction; small groupwork still dominant teaching strategy

(Continued)

TABLE 15.1 *(Continued)*

Experience in PECHS	Value of Experiences	Nature of Discontinuity	Teacher Behavior, Strategy, or Style
10. taught to play new games	learning organized, group activity	rules vs. autonomy; new vs. familiar exp.	non-coercive; tolerant of nonparticipation, withdrawal
11. wide range of new experiences	learning the mainstream culture & instrumental behaviors	new vs. familiar experience	models, encourages new experiences; own cultural tradition emphasized; mixes new Papago experiences w/mainstream ones
12. served new foods	trying of new foods	new vs. familiar experience	encourages, but doesn't require eating of new foods; Papago food served

are reported to be very critical of their children's behavior in class, especially in regard to what they perceive as uncontrolled verbal behavior. Teachers, on the other hand, are critical only of the children's physical restlessness which they unwittingly encourage through their own verbal stimulation of students and restriction of more controlled physical activities.

In PECHS, Papago teachers encourage, but do not require, children to respond verbally during group activities (example #1). For instance, during roll call children are asked to say their names. However, if a child prefers to raise her hand or nod her head, this physical communication is accepted as a substitution for the verbal response. Likewise, during the subsequent sharing time children are invited to give reports of the happenings in their lives but are not individually asked to do so. It is significant that while these teachers do not place pressure upon the children to perform in these verbal exercises, when a child does participate he is allowed free expression, both physically and verbally.

Autonomy and Control

Teachers implement various strategies for managing the classroom at the same time that they are careful not to compromise the Papago value of individual autonomy. Classroom rules are made explicit and continually repeated in generalized warnings, such as "We don't shout in the room" (example #6). The patience of Papago teachers seems endless, and they are concerned primarily with teaching the children the new limits on their freedom rather than absolutely enforcing these limits. Even when children are required to be quiet and sit still before beginning a new activity, misbehavior is not directly punished (example #2). Rather, the Papago teachers positively reinforce good behavior by allowing those children who are quiet and still to leave first.

This same patience and reluctance to interfere with children's autonomy is evident in PECHS teachers' supervision of toothbrushing to the point that children are not hurried to finish (example #8). Whenever it does become necessary to be more directive, as when children are disruptive while settling down to nap, these Papago teachers generally give short, to-the-point commands to be quiet and go to sleep, and then physically comfort the children with pats and backrubs (example #7). In each of these ways the new structures of time and activity that are being imposed on children are mitigated by teachers' patient and caring behaviors, behaviors which seem familiar to the children because they characterize much of Papago parent-child interaction.

Papago teachers do focus on individual children, but they are careful of how they do so. For example, they typically work with groups of from three to six children at planned projects or in less structured activities. However, they consciously help each child learn to accept a focus of adult attention and to become adept at conversation by working with them in one-to-one relationships while other children are involved in their own pursuits (example #9). This type of teacher attention and individuation, a style which Erickson and Mohatt (1982) observed to be typical among Odawa Indian teachers, is less disturbing to the Papago child than attention directed to her in front of the whole class, and it is a gentle introduction to the individual focus of mainstream elementary classrooms. During all-classroom activities requiring verbal responses, however, teachers usually address a question to anyone who feels he can give an answer (e.g., Now who knows what this is?) and focus directly on an individual only after a child has raised his hand (example #1).

When a child is disruptive and needs to be reprimanded, PECHS teachers single out the child only as a last resort. On such occasions, after giving many generalized warnings to the group as a whole, a child is usually called aside and, without an audience of other children to observe, given instruction on how to behave more properly (example #6). Teachers are careful to avoid recognizing publicly a child's misbehavior even when he has already attracted the attention of his classmates. Respect for the Papago value of personal autonomy is reinforced in PECHS children by these teachers' care in focusing attention on the individual child.

New Experiences

A third type of discontinuity experienced by Papago preschoolers results from their participation in a wide range of unfamiliar activities. Within

PECHS, activities with which the children should become familiar in order to adjust to school and society outside the reservation are introduced in ways that are culturally compatible and nonthreatening.

One of the ways this is accomplished is through the integration of these new experiences with more familiar experiences (example #11). For instance, new foods are prepared for lunch on one day; Papago popovers and beans, on the next. Field trips to libraries and other "strange" places are interspersed with visits to familiar Papago places of interest. Likewise, the encouragement of verbal participation and development of verbal skill is accomplished by teaching the children to speak and sing in the Papago language as well as English, and structured group activities become less strange as a way of doing things when the children are involved in making a Papago flag or replica of a traditional home.

Another PECHS teacher strategy for reducing discontinuity when presenting new experiences is tolerance for nonparticipation. This was clearly illustrated by teacher acceptance of a child's disinterest and withdrawal from a new game (example #10). While a teacher may try to get children to try a new food or experience by talking in positive terms about how nice it might be and/or modeling the new activity (example #12), there is no coercion or punishment if a child leaves food untouched or refuses to participate in the activity.

Of course, nonparticipation can only be tolerated by teachers when the new experiences are tangential to school rules and class structure. In those instances when children must conform to school rules for good conduct and time schedules, teachers make it clear that children have no choice as to whether to participate—but they do so in their characteristic low-key, patient and minimally directive Papago style. The teaching style of the Papago staff is characterized first by attention to the immediate needs of the child, her emotional welfare and understanding of her own place in the new school environment and, second, by attention to the task of instructing the child in how to fit into the overall organization of the classroom.

COMMENTARY

PECHS teachers, in essence, have developed their own Papago "hidden curriculum" geared to minimize the negative effects of cultural discontinuity. These teachers continuously present their students with experiences which are typical of mainstream education and which necessitate the child's adjustment to culturally different ways of behaving and learning. Yet, of most importance, these same teachers act to mitigate the discontinuity of the necessary preschool experiences and ensure that the child's appreciation of his own culture is not eroded. While it may not be immediately apparent to an observer that PECHS teachers are doing any more than fulfilling the goals and established procedures of any early childhood education program, children who participate in these programs benefit from the more subtle Papago styles of presenting material and relating to students.

The conclusions to which this case study can point are necessarily limited. We cannot conclude, for instance, that children from a given ethnic group are best taught by members of that group. As Papagos, PECHS teachers do enjoy some advantage in the common cultural knowledge and experience they share with their students. However, this kind of cultural content—not all, but enough to make a difference—can be learned by interested teachers, regardless of background (Heath, 1983). At any rate, cultural congruence between teacher and child is only one part of the successful PECHS teaching formula which also requires skillful preparation and presentation of curricular content, optimal class-room management, sufficient knowledge of child development and learning processes, and a personal style that works well with children. These criteria define good teachers anywhere, and all applicants for teaching positions in PECHS are screened for their experience and potential in these areas.

Furthermore, the discontinuities experienced by Papago children do not necessarily characterize the school experience of children of other tribal or ethnic groups. Cultural variance across groups means different language styles and variable approaches to autonomy/control issues, and some groups may experience discontinuity in areas which have not been discussed here. The content of home-school discontinuity obviously reflects the cultural incongruities that exist between a given ethnic group and the mainstream.

Moreover, the successful strategies used in PECHS may not transfer easily to other school levels and contexts. Teacher flexibility in the enforcement of rules, for example, may be more problematic in later grades. By the same token, the growing complexity of cognitive and language learning tasks demands increasingly creative teacher behavior for engaging students whose learning strategies have been uniquely structured within their own cultural experience.

The strength of this research begins with its ability to alert us to the reality of cultural discontinuity in the formative experiences of young children. The basic nature of this process—a disruption in the developmental process with potentially long-lasting, negative results for many children—needs to be better understood if schooling is to contribute to the welfare of these children and of society itself. This ethnographic study contributes directly to our understanding by specifying certain discontinuities affecting one school population and also enhances a growing data base that will help educators to recognize and assess this phenomenon in the school setting.

But the uses of the present research are more than descriptive and diagnostic. The kinds of techniques used by Papago preschool teachers provide relevant content for any prescriptive dialogue in the area of ethnic minority education and serve as practical models for teachers working with similar school populations. The more important point here, however, may be that a trained participant-observer is fully capable of pinpointing—and, in the case of a teacher, responding to—cultural discontinuity across its range of expressions. In a rare example of this kind of intervention, Heath (1983) documents the successful teaching and learning taking place in the schools of a culturally diverse, rural South Carolina community. Teachers, trained as ethnographers by Heath, worked together with students on linking the students' familiar strategies of knowing to unfamiliar classroom content and tasks.

Both the Papago and South Carolina cases suggest that it is not so much the content of school learning that is unintelligible or upsetting to students but, rather, it is the new ways of learning that often contribute to their disengagement from school. Studies in this area need to continue not only to identify and describe specific discontinuities, but also to illustrate the positive interventions that experienced teachers can and do use successfully.

Future research also needs to focus on the bases of teachers' decisions and actions, the perceptions and coping strategies of students themselves, and the role of parents and family in shaping the teacher-student interaction. Ethnographic research can continue to be an important tool in the identification, description and analysis of the issues involved.

The results and discussion presented in this chapter have focused on the experience of children being prepared to enter a mainstreaming school system. The research was not designed to address the more basic question that asks what the ultimate goal of schooling should be for Papago children, a question for which Papago parents and community are continually seeking answers. The major aim of the present research has been to address a longstanding problem in ethnic minority schooling: how to present mainstream ideas, knowledge and skills in a way that is culturally meaningful for students. The issues are clearly stated by two Papago parents, Mr. Johnson and Mrs. Gomez (informants' pseudonyms), respectively:

> (education) It's important . . . in order to get along with the outside world. They have to understand (school content) . . . and the differences in the lifestyles . . . (education) sets up their future.

> To understand the history, the background of the tribe . . . of the way we are

as O'odham (Papago) people. Star Wars . . . I tell the kids 'one of these days we could be doing those things.' We tell her (a daughter) 'no one can give you those things . . . mathematics' (except school).

For these parents, and for many other Papago parents that I met, there is no contradiction between wanting both a Papago cultural identity and an enriching school experience for their children.

REFERENCES

Benedict, R. (1938). Continuities and discontinuities in cultural conditioning. *Psychiatry, 1*, 161–167.

Chesky, J. (1949). Growing up on the desert. In A. Joseph, R. B. Spicer, & J. Chesky, *The desert people: A study of the Papago Indians*. Chicago: University of Chicago Press.

Dobyns, H. F. (1972). *The Papago people*. Phoenix: Indian Tribal Series.

Erickson, F., & Mohatt, G. (1982). Cultural organization of participation structures in two classrooms of Indian students. In G. Spindler (Ed.), *Doing the ethnography of schooling: Educational anthropology in action*. New York: Holt, Rinehart and Winston.

Heath, S. B. (1983). *Ways with words: Language, life, and work in communities and classrooms*. Cambridge: Cambridge University Press.

Laosa, L. M. (1984). Social policies toward children of diverse ethnic, racial, and language groups in the United States. In H. W. Stevenson & A. E. Siegel (Eds.), *Child development research and social policy* (Vol. 1). Chicago: University of Chicago Press.

Macias, J. (1984). *Papago home-to-school transition: Overcoming school discontinuity in early childhood*. Unpublished doctoral dissertation, Stanford University.

Ogbu, J. U. (1981). Origins of human competence: A cultural-ecological perspective. *Child Development, 52*, 413–429.

Ogbu, J. U. (1982). Cultural discontinuities and schooling. *Anthropology and Education Quarterly, 13*(4), 290–307.

Philips, S. U. (1983). *The invisible culture: Communication in classroom and community on the Warm Springs Indian Reservation*. New York: Longman.

Spindler, G. D. (1974). The transmission of culture. In G. D. Spindler (Ed.), *Education and cultural process*. New York: Holt, Rinehart and Winston.

Spindler, G. D. (Ed.). (1982). *Doing the ethnography of schooling: Educational anthropology in action*. New York: Holt, Rinehart and Winston.

Underhill, R. M. (1942). Papago child-training. *Marriage and Family Living, 4*, 80–86.

Wax, R. H. (1972). The warrior dropouts. In H. M. Bahr, B. A. Chadwick, & R. C. Day (Eds.). *Native Americans today: Sociological perspectives*. New York: Harper and Row.

Williams, T. R. (1958). The structure of socialization process in Papago Indian society. *Social Forces, 36*, 251–256.

Young, R. E. (1983). A school communication-deficit hypothesis of educational disadvantage. *Australian Journal of Education, 27*(1), 3–15.

GROUP B:
MAINSTREAM

The Author and Her Chapter

Joyce Canaan received her Ph.D. and M.A. in cultural anthropology at the University of Chicago and she is presently in England on a study fellowship. She has studied teenage girls in a summer camp and researched metropolitan Chicago adults as well as the teenagers of the middle school and high school of Sheepshead, the town of 13,000 where she did the field research for this chapter. She says of herself:

> Unlike most of my peers who investigated people far from their homes, I conducted research in an American middle-class suburb near a major metropolitan area. Moreover, until the last 6 months of my 16 months of field work, I lived in my parents' house and commuted to my field site daily. My research reconstructed my earlier teenage transition; arguing with my parents over issues of autonomy eventually forced me to leave their home and live among my informants as a reconstituted adolescent—I moved in with the family organizing the community runaway program for teenagers having problems with parents. More importantly, I used my retrieved and transformed teenage experience—familiar and different from that of my informants—as a basis for anthropological inquiry about their experiences.

Canaan's chapter describes a situation with which most of us are familiar but that most of us have forgotten. The social life of the middle and high school years has not gone unchanged but there are continuities that go back for decades. The social life of the schools puts academic achievement in an American perspective—important but not everything. It is precisely the perspective that gives an immigrant youth with a high achievement drive who takes education seriously an academic edge.

Canaan's chapter demonstrates, however, that in high school the cliques that dominate social life in middle school become less explicit and the mainstream values of individualism, independence, and equality assert themselves in the wide range of choices available to students, and the choices that they actually do make.

This chapter is about schools in a small middle-class community that is quite unlike the environment of schools in metropolitan areas with large minority populations. Sheepshead's schools are mainstream schools in the most conservative sense of mainstream. The analysis of the social life within them is a useful introduction to this section on mainstream education.

The Editors

16

A Comparative Analysis of American Suburban Middle Class, Middle School, and High School Teenage Cliques*

Joyce Canaan
University of Chicago

INTRODUCTION

This is a report on recent research on teenage cliques in an American, suburban, middle-class community. This research, conducted in and through the middle school and high school of the community of Sheepshead, differs from prior studies examining only high school students' cliques.[1] It thus provides a wider framework for understanding teenagers' cliques and teenagers as a distinct age-grade.

The paper is divided into five sections. An examination of the similar structural components comprising the middle school and high school students' cliques as hierarchically organized social structures follows this introductory section. The third section focuses on ways cliques at both schools are more or less visible. A brief section considering how top clique members at both schools act as stereotypic teenagers follows. The fifth and final section specifies major differences in the structures of middle and high school cliques.

The 13,000 people of Sheepshead fall generally into the upper range of the middle class. Per capita income is third highest in the state and 73% of

---

*An earlier draft of this paper was published in the *Chicago Anthropology Exchange*, Vol. 15 (1), 1982.

[1]There is a substantial social science literature on teenage cliques to date produced primarily by sociologists who generally suggest that high school teenagers are influenced noticeably by their peers. They seek to delineate the particular ways in which peer groups affect teenagers (see, for example, Coleman, 1961; Cusick, 1973; Eisenstadt, 1956; Henry, 1963; Hollingshead, 1949; Parsons, 1942, 1963; Smith, 1962).

the community's work force holds white collar jobs. The community is predominantly white (97.1%); 1.3% of the population is Asian; 1.1% Hispanic; and 0.5% black. In Sheepshead there are eight houses of worship: five Protestant, one Jewish, one Roman Catholic, and one Ukranian Catholic. Per pupil funding for the five public schools in the community is third highest in the state. Of the 2,624 students in public schools, 937 attend three elementary schools (kindergarten through 5th grade), 634 attend middle school (6th through 8th grade), and 1,053 attend high school (grades 9 through 12) (1970 U. S. Census, *1980 Legislative District Data Book, Municipal Data Book, 1981*).[2]

A principle finding of the research was that teenagers define themselves by the cliques they form and belong to. Another finding was that in both the middle school and high school cliques provide an interrelated system whose components are located at one of the three ranked levels. Finally, the research showed that the ranked clique system operates explicitly at the middle school and implicitly at the high school.

Teenagers themselves call the cliques they form "groups." They call themselves and other teenagers "kids." In what follows, the teenagers' own terms are used.

SHARED STRUCTURAL COMPONENTS OF MIDDLE SCHOOL AND HIGH SCHOOL TEENAGE CLIQUES

Middle School

In the middle school, "top" ("popular," "high," or "cool"), "middle," and "low" groups are differentiated by appearance and demeanor. The top group is comprised of boys and girls thought to be "cool," that is, athletically skilled and socially capable of following the "rules to live by":

> Don't brag. Don't wear clothes that are too fancy.[3] Don't say you like school. Don't . . . get good grades. Don't brag about your good grades. Don't punch people out. You gotta ridicule people that are supposed to be "fags." Don't be quiet, and be crazy.

The middle group is comprised of kids who conform to these rules relatively less successfully. They conform to the expectations of their teachers and parents and those of the cool group. A middle group 7th grader describes their comportment:

---

[2]The exact names of these books have not been provided to protect community identity.

[3]Dress and overall appearance are critical elements of cool group social action believed to determine social placement.

We sometimes make fun of people in the low group, but not, not as much as they [members of the top group] do. And, oh yeah, we respect our teachers most of the time—most of the time, most of the teachers. But, like, we do what they say and stuff like that, and we don't fool around and act wild that much. Well, we act wild, but we don't do it in public like they do.

A few middle group kids are chided, primarily by top group kids, for being too compliant with adult values. Those thought to study all the time and to brag about their grades are called "brains." Those thought to follow all the rules with which adults structure their social action are called "goody goodies."[4]

In the following comment, one middle school girl illustrates her awareness that being a brain means studying all the time and displaying one's knowledge:

A lot of times what you have to do is, mm, if the teacher says, "Do you have an answer to the problem?", and it involves thinking, if you can raise your hand and give a reason, and this reason can be so valid. It's just, you know, and you don't do it too often . . . You can't always, you know, pretend to know it all because then they'll think that you're a good-two-shoes (goody goody).

Low-group kids generally are those least successful in conforming to the "rules to live by." "Scums" or "scumbags" are thought to be dirty, to look strange, or to smell bad. "Wimps" (generally boys) are physically weak and sometimes are thought incapable of appropriate social action; "fags" or "faggots" (generally boys) are wimps who also act "immature."[5] These named and unnamed low group kids are known for socially inappropriate action: bragging, acting too shy, or telling and laughing at jokes their peers do not think funny. The following description of actions of one boy considered a fag indicates how inappropriate actions distinguish low group kids from others:

[One day] he didn't have his homework and he started to cry. And we're laughing at him. And he started crying even more cause we're laughing that he was crying. The kid is such a fag. He's like, Mrs. uh, goes, "Jack, you have your homework?" "No." And so, she started talking to everyone else. He started crying, he started breaking out in tears and everything. Mrs. Hurst is like, "Jack, you okay?" He's like, [in high voice] "yes" and everybody started laughing . . . But the kid, he's like he's like really

---

[4]"Brain" and "goody-goody" are not mutually exclusive terms.

[5]"Faggot" is a stronger and more general term than "wimp." It primarily connotes a male "sissy," that is, an unathletic small boy who informs the teacher when kids make fun of him.

immature. . . . He had to read this paragraph [in science class] about the mass of gas. He started, he couldn't read the rest of the paragraph. Mrs. Hurst had to read the rest of it cause he was laughing. He fell off his seat, everything.

Although members of the middle school top and middle groups readily rank themselves as such, low group members tend to upgrade their position and call themselves middle group kids.

High School

High school kids do not so readily acknowledge their group structure, but like middle school kids have a three tiered group ranking system.[6] The highest group is comprised of the two coolest subgroups, jocks and freaks, which differ by degree rather than kind: A freak is "someone who isn't afraid to drink or smoke pot or take drugs during the week whereas a jock would tend to do it on the weekends when he's not in school." As in the middle school, the highest groups' members are considered outstanding for their cool social actions which, as an 11th grade jock girl states, include:

being up on the times, knowing what's happening, "hanging out" [spending one's free time] with a well-known group . . . [This means] like, knowing about the recent parties, who's going out with who, who likes who, who is with who, that kind of stuff. It uh, well, it all blends together, you know, being able to talk in a group, knowing who's going out with who, whatever.

Cool kids are knowledgeable about carrying themselves well in informal social interaction on weekends, out of school. In school, kids display their cool by engaging in extracurricular activities, telling jokes, teasing classmates, and dressing right.[7] Underlying the particulars of performance is self-confidence. A cool person:

has a feeling of always being right, you know, that type of thing . . . someone who, uh, doesn't make a fool of themselves, you know, or who has the power to convince people that he doesn't make a fool of himself.[8]

Coolness is manifested differently by high school males and females. As at the middle school, cool jock males are so ranked primarily for their

---

[6]The ways in which they do and do not acknowledge group structure will be discussed.

[7]Dress provides one of the major differences between jocks and freaks. Jocks dress relatively more neatly and formally than freaks. The details of these differences will be discussed in future writings.

[8]Schwartz and Merten (1972) also found cool was both constituted by having self-confidence and served as the basis for high social status (p. 329).

extracurricular athletic ability, and cool jock females are so ranked for their ability to dress and act with self-confidence, their desirability as dates of cool jock males and their ability to gossip well. (Females who are literally jocks, that is, outstanding extracurricular athletes, only are considered cool if they present themselves to others with self-confidence.) Cool male freaks are so labeled for defying adult values in and out of school while cool female freaks are so labeled primarily by associating with cool male freaks.

Of the two cool subgroups, jocks are the more positively distinguished. Jocks act as their teachers and administrators think they should in school. In athletics, the most socially esteemed and publicly noticed extracurricular activity, they follow a coach's orders. Extracurricular athletics distinguishes them in the school context in general, and provides them with greater leeway in complying with adult values in school.[9] Moreover, on weekends, jocks drop conformity with adult values. They "party" (drink alcohol, take drugs, and experiment sexually). On Monday morning jocks discuss their weekend activities among themselves and in front of other students in their classes, thereby bringing these activities to public attention, and demonstrating that they accept adult values only in school. Because jocks do as adults think they should during the week and as they want on weekends, they more than any subgroup are masters of both major contexts of social action.

In contrast, freaks are considered cool primarily because they party both on the weekend and during the week. Because their in-school partying attitude flouts adult values, and because they are less active than jocks in extracurricular activities in general, they successfully manipulate only one system of values and therefore are relatively less cool than jocks. Positive aspects to freaks' manipulation of one context enables them to be considered to have a status almost as high as that of jocks. More than jocks who have two faces—that is, one for each of their two major contexts of social action—freaks consistently present one attitude in all contexts and are believed relatively less hypocritical than jocks. One female jock remarked that:

> What's good about the freaks is that they accept a person the way they are, which is really nice . . . a lot more [than jocks do] . . . Maybe I don't go out and smoke pot, you know, thirty, every day of the month, but still, I'm like accepted to them, you know, just because of what I am, not because of what I'm not. Not because I don't go out and smoke every day.

Although high school kids do not have a group named the middle group, there are unlabeled groups known for being not as cool as jocks or

---

[9]Cusick (1973) found this to be true also.

freaks and for not exhibiting many negative characteristics of the low group.[10] Most of these groups midway between the cool and low groups model their social action after jocks or freaks, although they are neither as active in school as jocks nor do they party as much as freaks. When asked, many say they are "really" jocks or freaks. A few other middle group kids do not follow jock or freak social action and manifest instead certain characteristics deemed low.

One labeled middle subgroup, "cool band fags," comes fairly close to jocks in prestige. Cool band fags and jocks are the only subgroups in either the middle or high school which act one way during the week and another on weekends. They comply with adult values in school and teenage values on weekends. However, band fags in general are considered less cool than jocks or freaks, because they have chosen playing a musical instrument over joining an athletic team. That is, they are labeled "fags," because they are considered physically and psychologically ineffective kids. Boys in the band in particular are thought to be less masculine than athletes and are:

> put down because they're in the band . . . it's not a sport. . . . Being on a football team, which is a structure like the band, is more cool than being in the band, because it's still, I think, a little left over from being a sissy type thing. . . . It's more cool to be on the football team, because it's masculine, whereas in the band it's not much of a masculine thing to play an instrument.

Girls in the band are also considered less cool than jocks or freaks, not just because they have chosen the band over athletics (in which many cool jock girls participate), but also because band members are considered "prisses" (the high school equivalent of "goody-goodies," i.e., kids overly compliant with adult values).

Two modifiers of the noun "band fag" indicate the distinct statuses of the two subgroups. Cool band fags are in the middle group, because they overcome their band membership by acting like jocks in and out of school. "True" or "total" band fags in contrast are in the low group, because in addition to playing instruments they have little or no awareness of how to act cool in or out of school. As their name indicates they most completely fulfill the band fag image. While cool band fags may label themselves as such, true or total band fags drop the pejorative modifiers and call themselves band fags.

High school kids do not have a named low group, though they

---

[10]Schwartz and Merten also found a large unnamed middle group. However, they did not develop the implications of having an unnamed group in a named system of groups as is developed below.

distinguish several other categories of kids for their negative characteristics. These subgroups are viewed negatively, because, to a greater or lesser degree, their actions do not conform with cool notions of proper social action. "Weirdos" are judged ambivalently by their peers. They are esteemed somewhat, because they blatantly defy adult-imposed rules governing their social action in and out of school. They generally are evaluated negatively, because they dress and act in defiance of cool social norms—wearing clothes that purposefully negate cool dress and overtly expressing disdain for cool weekend social action. While weirdos and some others view this as an indication that they forge their own life style, their appearance and demeanor are determined by negating many of the rules and mores governing kids' social action in or out of school.

"Brains" are also evaluated ambivalently by their peers. Though less scorned than weirdos, brains are looked down upon, because they do not, either in or out of school, defy adult expectations. Also, brains are considered narrower in interests and actions because they seem to study so much. As one high school girl observed, "That's all there is to them . . . They have no other, no other facets to their personality. They just have a mind and that's it."

They are judged somewhat positively for their academic achievement, and, unlike their middle school counterparts, they do not hide their intellectual abilities. They view their mode of action as being appropriate and consider their peers to be misguided in their emphasis on partying to the neglect of their studies.

"Burn-outs" are a little seen and highly criticized subgroup. They are rarely seen, because they are in school as infrequently as possible. More importantly, when in school they take most courses outside of the college preparatory area where cool kids and middle group kids take most courses. They are viewed negatively, because they are thought to be interested in drugs to the exclusion of all else. While burn-outs are labeled as such by most other subgroups, they and many freaks label them as freaks.

Finally, the members of the unnamed low subgroup, unlike other subgroups, are primarily distinguished because of smell, dirty appearance, or strange physical characteristics. They are secondarily noticed for several other characteristics: their complete inability to act cool, their complete adherence to the rules with which adults structure their social action, and their membership in the AVA (Audio Visual Aids) Club. Several high school girls developed in their idiolect a term for some persons in the unnamed low group. One brother and sister are considered "scheeves" or "scheevos" (skēvz, skēvōz)—that is, so repulsive they make one want to throw up. The following graphic description points out their embodiment of the above enumerated low group characteristics:

Earl Downs . . . has got like, of my God!, he's got like 4 inches of grease under his fingernails . . . He's slimy [dirty] and he has really gross, gross [repugnant] clothes . . . I mean, like he is a scheevo. I mean, like, ya know, his parents turned off the water in the house, so they're only allowed one shower like a week. And it was like total scheevo. Betty Downes is just as bad. I wrote an English paper on her . . . We had to write something really disgusting. And I said, there she was, at Marv's Soda Shoppe, sitting at the fountain, sucking down a big banana split, in her green, lime green polyester pants . . . polka dot flowered [blouse] . . . and greasy grimy black hair all going down. And she had like all these, um, chicken pox marks on her face and her nails were really short . . . That's a scheevo, okay?

VISIBILITY OF MIDDLE SCHOOL AND HIGH SCHOOL GROUPS

In each school the groups and subgroups comprising the three-tiered ranking system are ordered in part according to how visible they are and can be placed somewhere along a continuum of visibility.[11] Each school's most visible group is recognized as being cool primarily by its members' dress and demeanor. All groups know the most and latest information about this group. While visibility is not a native term, kids perceive groups using this notion. In the following statement about popularity, a high school girl indicates that the most popular group is the most visible group because its members stand out most from and are most recognized by peers:

[Being popular is] having a lot of people know you . . . not just by, yes, I've seen that person before, but, to know who you are and come up and want to talk to you and, um, do things with you . . . [in the halls] if you don't have time to look around and people are talking, are saying "hi" to you the whole time, or you don't ever have a chance to see who it is that says "hi" before somebody else does, then you know that you've got a lot of friends, you're popular, people recognize you and pick you out of a crowd . . . If you're a bump on the log and just sit there, then nobody's gonna notice you because you're not going to make people notice you.

The second most visible group is the low group, whose members are primarily noticed for the negative aspects of their appearance and de-

---

[11]"Visibility" is not a native term but does capture how kids differentiate people into one of three ranked levels by the amount and kind of information known about them. After devising this continuum of visibility I found that Coleman (1961) characterized students most known by all others as "visible." However, he did not apply the notion of visibility systematically to all groups.

meanor. The least visible group is the middle group, which does not exhibit positive or negative characteristics.

Although groups are differentiated according to their quantity and quality of visibility, primarily the group at the top of this continuum puts most effort into maintaining its position and pointing out the discrepancies between it and other groups. Visibility is maintained in different ways by middle school and high school top groups and by boys and girls in each school's top group.

Kids in the middle school top group directly acknowledge a person's positive or negative visibility by acting upon him in the more public settings of the school (the cafeteria, halls, and locker rooms). Boys at the top publicly acknowledge their equals by physically playing with each other while walking between classes in the halls, the most public school area:

> It's mostly among your friends or the people you know. . . . We always go around the halls. We do fake boxing, or something, or we rap each other in the mouth. It's . . . like a kind of "macho" act. . . . It is to show that you can hit them, and, uh, mostly that you're friends with them . . . cause . . . they're powerful, so if you're . . . batting around with them that means that you're their friends really. That's kind of a signal that you know them and you're with them.

The boys publicly indicate to all kids around that each of them is physically and socially powerful and thus, equal to each other and superior to everyone else.

In contrast, social superiority can be expressed by having more than one top group boy gang up on one low group boy in the locker room, an area not watched over by adults as closely as the halls. There are unequal odds, and the top group boys continue to harangue the low group boy until he loses his composure:

> Nobody [in the top group] would . . . really do that among their friends. They'd have to pick someone they don't like a lot. . . . This is not a playful thing. . . . This is serious. . . . They usually stop, like, when the person gets mad and gets really, you know, "hyper" [overexcited] and then starts throwing a fit, and then they stop. "Calm down you faggot" . . . and then they can control the person.

With this final comment top group boys affirm that the low group boy loses his control and cool, while they maintain theirs.

These top group boys' physical and verbal strategies effectively place them high above the low group. Moreover, since middle group kids only infrequently "mock out" (make fun of) low group kids, and even then are unlikely to do so as dramatically as top group kids, such teasing places top group above middle group boys.

Just as top group boys manipulate their athletic ability both to affirm their coolness and other groups' uncoolness, top group girls employ gossip to acknowledge their coolness and their superiority over girls in other groups. The following incident reveals how gossip works within the top group of girls:

> In gym one day, you know, we were in the locker room, and there were these three or four [popular] girls in my locker room . . . and, um, this one girl, you know, they were all palling around and laughing and everything, and she left, and then the other girls were talking: "Isn't she such a jerk?" You know, they were just talking about her like that. . . . They want to still be friends with them [the people they talk about], but they want people to know that they don't really like them.

Sharing negative comments with one or several friends about a person's character, dress, or actions affirms the bond one has with these friends over and above the bond one has with the person discussed. This stronger bond is reinforced if these friends relay information about the girl talked about to the girl initiating conversation. In a group where all talk about each other, one must not just establish bonds with many people by talking with them about others but must also give the impression of being friendly with all others, which enables one to receive information about the person one is talking with for later use.

Such an exchange is problematic, however, for the more information one provides to others, the more likely it is that they will eventually leak this information to the girls one talks about, thereby alienating these girls from oneself. Consequently, friendships among top group girls are tenuous and explosive. These friendships fluctuate like a merry-to-round, with two girls in the forefront at each moment; one is lauded and the other degraded. The group sides with the former against the latter, and the girl in each position changes frequently.

While top group girls, like top group boys, make fun of low group kids, they publicly display their social strength and superiority primarily by their intragroup gossip. By talking about one another in the locker room and other public contexts (the halls and cafeteria), kids in other groups come to know what is going on among top group girls. Top group girls, in contrast, know very little about the activities and feelings of kids in other groups. As a result of this public one-way interchange of gossip, all kids come to know about top group girl's social actions, thereby enabling top group girls to view their intragroup relations as public drama.

High school kids' sex-specific ways of displaying cool occur primarily out of school. Here, boys demonstrate coolness by manipulating their physical and social strength in out-of-school contexts which they structure themselves. In these contexts they drink, take drugs, and become sexually involved with girls. For example, high school boys play drinking games in which each tries to beat his peers not only by physically holding more alcohol but socially controlling himself by not getting too drunk, vomiting, or passing out. In the following claim, one high school cool boy illustrates how the masculinity of cool high school males develops by maintaining physical and social control of himself when engaged in such drinking games with his peers:

> I can drink an awful lot and not get drunk. Because I won't let myself get drunk . . . It's a challenge . . . Because you're fighting with something that you don't know. How many kids do you know [that] sit around and see how many beers they can chug? . . . It's a challenge to see how much you can drink. And you're a much better person if you can drink more than the other person . . . You're a man if you can, if you can hold your alcohol . . . If you puke, right, you're not a man.

For many cool high school girls, gossip serves as the basis of an exchange relationship and enables them to maintain their visibility much as it does for middle school cool girls. However, high school cool girls do not gossip primarily to make public negative opinions about a person's appearance or actions, but to share with others private information told to them in confidence:

> The main thing you have to do [to be popular] is know all the gossip. . . . Know what everyone else's business is, who's going out with who, what these two did and everything, so . . . you can report everything to everybody. I don't know how, like, certain groups become the popular ones, because, like, what do they do that I don't do? And I figured it out; it's gossip.

Being an effective gossip indicates one's power. Being privy to information about many people suggests that one is a good friend of and trusted by these people. By passing this information on to others, one develops an exchange relationship with them:

> If I wanted you to be my friend, I would say to you, "Oh, did you hear about so-and-so?" And [you would], . . . be, like, "No, really!" . . . [And I would reply] "Oh, yeah, well, I'll call you tonight and tell you about it."

Being an effective gossip, however, once again has its dangers. One can be found to have passed on information that one had promised not to relay. The dangers are somewhat lessened since high school cool girls have small, interconnected groups, rather than the one large circle of middle school girls. Consequently, confidences exchanged within groups generally are about girls in other groups. Having interconnected but separate groups of friends also contributes to the greater stability of high school girls' relationships. Disagreements generally remain localized within a small group. As a result, the entire group does not simultaneously give high esteem to one girl and taunt another.

Groups at the top of the continuum of visibility in each school provide the entire system with its order. By positively interacting with one another, ignoring kids in the middle group, and, either negatively interacting with (in the middle school) or publicly ignoring (in the high school) kids considered lowly, these most visible kids place themselves and all others at different positions in the system. Although most other groups believe they act independently of the top group, their social action affirms or negates top group values and thus is guided by these values.

TOP GROUP MEMBERS AS MODEL TEENAGERS

Another component comprising the top group at each school is the capacity to develop the strategy to express most adeptly in appearance and actions age-appropriate elements of teenage social action. Middle school cool kids demonstrate their coolness primarily by following the nine "rules to live by" and by experimenting, in the 7th and 8th grades, with forbidden social action outside of school—primarily smoking cigarettes and perhaps pot, drinking, shoplifting, and going out with cool group kids of the opposite sex. By doing most or all of these actions, middle school cool kids most effectively give the appearance of being teenagers. As a 7th grade middle group girl explains, she and her friends are "a stage below" top group girls who are more teenage-like than they:

> They've been going out for a long time . . . so they pretty much know how it goes and what is . . . supposed to happen . . . and that's something that . . . we don't really know, you know, so we want to find out.

Like middle school cool kids, high school cool kids' expression in dress and demeanor of the appropriate ways to be a teenager indicates their greater knowledge of things teenage than that of their peers. However, there is more flexibility in high school cool kids' dress and demeanor, and their coolness primarily manifests itself outside of school. Moreover, cool high school kids are considered more complete teenagers. Both middle school and high school kids believe that being a teenager is not acquired, but achieved through conduct (driving, drinking, going to parties, taking drugs, and dating) more commonly performed by high school than middle school kids.

While cool groups in each school best exemplify age-appropriate social actions, some middle groups and low groups in each school express all the inappropriate social actions of teenagers. For example, middle school scums or scumbags wear the wrong or dirty clothes or do not keep themselves clean, and goody-goodies comply too readily with adults' expectations. High school burn-outs take too many drugs, and true or total band fags do not participate in the cool kids' out-of-school activities.

If one knows what the cool groups do right and what those middle and low groups do wrong at each school, then one knows how to be a middle or high school teenager. Thus, the very structure of group relations at each school articulates what being a teenager is all about.

TWO SETS OF VALUES CONTRIBUTING TO GROUP PLACEMENT

Groups at each school are placed in their respective structures not just according to how well or poorly they manipulate teenage values, but also by their degree of acquiescence with or defiance of adult values. The cool groups are held in such high esteem, in part, because they moderately defy adult authority primarily in school (middle school) or out of school (high school). The middle groups are so placed, in part, because their members are fairly compliant with the adult-structured rules operating in their actions in and out of school. Low groups also are defined partially in terms of their compliance with adult values. Some purposefully defy adult values (e.g., high school burn-outs); others are overly compliant with adult values (e.g., middle school goody-goodies and high school true band fags); still others are inept at complying with adult values (e.g., middle school wimps).

Not only are middle and high school kids placed in groups in part by their degree of compliance with both teenage and adult values, but there is generally an inverse correlation between a group's compliance with teenage and adult values. Thus, just as groups can be conceptualized along a continuum of visibility, so can they be conceptualized along a continuum of compliance with teenage and adult values, ranging from those most compliant with adult values and least compliant with teenage values (e.g., wimps and total band fags) through those moderately compliant with both sets of values (e.g., cool groups), to those most compliant with teenage values and least compliant with adult values (e.g., middle school druggies and sluts or high school burn-outs). Moreover, the actions of groups near the center of this continuum are condoned, while those of groups at either extreme are criticized. Finally, the two continuums—visibility and compliance with teenage and adult values—are interrelated. The highly visible groups are most appropriately compliant with teenage and defiant of adult values; the least visible groups are moderately compliant with both sets of values, and the negatively visible groups are overly compliant with or defiant of either set. [12]

DIFFERENCES BETWEEN MIDDLE SCHOOL AND HIGH SCHOOL TEENAGE GROUPS

Contexts of Social Action

Middle school and high school kids differentially emphasize the in- and out-of-school contexts of social action. While middle school kids publicly defy adult authority primarily in school by deviating from school rules, high school kids defy adult authority primarily out of school by acting in ways opposing adult perceptions of appropriate teenage social action. From the middle school to the high school there is a shift from one to many contexts in which kids act as group members and from in-school defiance of school rules to out-of-school defiance of adult notions of proper teenage comportment in many areas of social action. Thus, for example, high school kids begin experimenting with drugs, alcohol, and sexuality, which adults believe are appropriate areas of social action only for adults.

Since high school kids are believed more complete teenagers than middle school kids—distinguished primarily by their more numerous contexts of social action and more general defiance of adult rules and values—the process of becoming a suburban middle class teenager in this locale involves an increasing defiance of adult values in expanded contexts of action. [13]

---

[12]The features of middle school and high school groups enumerated above are clearly expressed only in kids' last 2 years at each school. During the first year of middle school and first 2 years of high school students learn to manipulate the symbols of which their age-specific value systems are comprised. After that, groups take the form described herein.

This comparative analysis of middle school and high school groups raises *other* questions: How, why, when, and where does the shift from the middle school structure to that of the high school take place? This problem will be considered in another paper.

[13]While American adults in general and parents in particular lament teenage experimentation with sex, drugs, and alcohol, they provide kids with the opportunities for doing so. As Seeley, Sim, and Loosely (1956) point out, American parents encourage a child's independence from birth and are surprised when their children reach their teen years and attempt to carry their independence to its logical endpoint by developing their own values in their own contexts of social action.

Group Naming Systems

Major differences between middle school and high school groups also are indicated by their group naming systems. The middle school group system emphasizes placement in one of three ranked groups, while that of the high school focuses on placement in one of many equal subgroups and ignores subgroup placement in one of the three ranked groups. When asked, all middle school kids immediately place themselves in one group whose name relays information about its rank relative to the other two. Some subgroups within each group additionally have names primarily based on and relaying information about what they do or how they act. This information confirms subgroup placement in a ranked group. For example, middle group brains act wrong in one way—they study too much—while low group wimps more generally act ineffectually. Only the lowest subgroup in the low group (scums or scumbags) are defined by their poor physical appearance. At the group and subgroup levels, middle school group names express the explicit inequality with which they primarily are ordered.

The high school naming system is the more complex. Rather than being ordered by the single value of inequality, equality and inequality motivate placement in subgroups and groups respectively. Instead of one value operating equally at two levels, each value operates at one level, and the system in general focuses upon subgroup equality and ignores group inequality. The three group levels can only be determined inductively because:

1. No level is named explicitly.[14] To the contrary, high school kids maintain that cliques no longer exist and that they dislike using labels,[15] although they often acknowledge that cliques exist or use labels to prove their point:

> Now that I'm a junior, I mean, I feel that I know all the seniors, I know all the juniors, I get along with them all whether they're a freak or a jock or a priss or a band fag, whatever. I mean, I don't label them as much any more.

2. Jocks and freaks put little effort into asserting either their superiority or low group inferiority:

> Part of it [the reason there is more tolerance between groups now] is 'cause when you were younger, you didn't [try to understand kids in other groups].

---

[14]While jocks and freaks are known to be the two subgroups of cool kids, there is no group name encompassing them both.

[15]This finding concurs with that of Hervé Varenne (1982).

It's your maturity. Whereas, you know [in the middle school], the jocks would make fun of kids who smoked pot or something like that, partially out of the knowledge perhaps of, you know, their unawareance [sic] of it, you know, never having tried it.

Names generally signifying kinds of formal and informal social action are given to many subgroups at each group level, although the unnamed lowest high school subgroup is known for its members' poor physical appearance. For example, jocks participate in extracurricular athletics and weirdos generally look and act strange. The placement of subgroups into groups is based on its members' extracurricular activities,[16] their dress and actions, and the circles in which they "hang out" (spend time).

While social organizations generally provide identifying labels for each of their components (as does the middle school three-tiered group system), the high school group naming system does not do so. Names are given only to subgroups visible for outstanding social action, such that the system rhetorically substantiates and distinguishes only these groups.[17] Not only is there no term encompassing cool jocks and freaks, but the entire middle group and the lowest subgroup of the low group are not labeled. Middle group kids primarily manipulate the less visible actions of jocks and freaks. Even those few middle group kids acting in ways suggestive of low group kids manipulate the latter's less visible actions. The nameless middle group, which exhibits none of the distinctive actions constituting the named subgroups, signifies its ambiguous status in the system of named groups.

The nameless lowest subgroup has an ambiguous status, because its visibility, based on physical characteristics rather than social action, qualitatively distinguishes it from all other subgroups. There is a parallel between the differentiation of the lowest high school subgroup from all others and the general American differentiation of nonwhites from whites: In both cases physical characteristics ostensibly provided by nature separate the lowest level of an overtly egalitarian system from the higher and more rationally distinguished groups:

> In certain circumstances . . . a hierarchical difference continues to be posited, which is this time attached to somatic characteristics . . . The individual . . . believes in the fundamental equality of all men taken severally at the same time . . . the collective inferiority of a category of men . . . is expressed and justified in terms of what physically differentiates them from himself and people of his group (Dumont, 1970, pp. 255–256).[18]

16This point is more fully discussed below.

17Hervé Varenne suggested this point (personal communication).

18There is historical continuity to this somatic structural differentiation of the lowest high school group. The lowest group in Hollingshead's (1949) three-tiered group system is distinguished primarily by its members' physical characteristics.

The comparable treatment of the lowest high school subgroup by high school kids and of nonwhites by adult whites points to another way in which there is greater high school than middle school approximation to American adult social action. Although the lowest middle school subgroup also is differentiated somatically,[19] since the middle school group naming system only emphasizes inequality, the distinct manner of labeling this group does not set it very far apart from other unequally evaluated subgroups. In high school and in American adult culture generally, the somatic differentiation of the lowest subgroup affirms both its difference from other groups and the fundamental equality of these other groups.

Nameless groups in the system both affirm the definition and contribute to the ambiguity of named groups. Unnamed groups affirm named groups' statuses by their contrast with the latter; they lack the visible social action and an appropriate physical presentation of self characteristic of named groups. Unnamed groups obscure named groups' position, because: (1) While they inappropriately utilize the symbols with which named groups act and are defined, they remain in the group system, and (2) While they share many social actions with named groups by virtue of their common situation as high school students, their claimed difference from named groups makes questionable the performance of these actions by named groups.

The structure of the high school group naming system provides further evidence for and elaboration of Varenne's (1982) claim that among high school students, "cliques sometimes are there and sometimes are not there" (p. 215). Moreover, the differing structures of the middle and high school group naming systems provides evidence for high school kids' assertion that they no longer have cliques, another point Varenne makes in his analysis.

Whereas prior researchers specify social structural components of cliques, Varenne points out such components do not always function in teenage social action. His analysis of high school kids' speech about cliques suggests cliques provide one classificatory means operating only when kids objectify their social relations—that is, focus on those distance from them temporally, spatially, or ideologically. Cliques are absent when kids adopt a more subjective stance about their relations to others. As Varenne indicates, the presence and absence of cliques enables teenagers to construct complex means of relating to each other.

This examination of Sheepshead middle school and high schools' group naming systems specifies other ways cliques exist ambiguously for high school kids. First of all, high school kids view their overall group system

---

[19]The highest middle school group is also distinguished in part by its supposed somatically determined athletic ability.

against the backdrop of their former middle school group system. Middle school kids do not question whether or not they have a group system. From 6th to 8th grade groups develop into an increasingly hierarchized system with wider divisions between them. In comparison, fewer barriers divide high school kids' groups. At least in school, if not during some week-end activities, high school kids interact with persons at somewhat different social levels—although such interactions span only a limited portion of the group hierarchy. As one 9th grade girl observed:

> Like in 8th grade it got to the point where, like, the upper class kids, you know, didn't hardly care about the middle class kids, you know . . . They didn't hardly talk to them . . .
>
> So 8th grade is cliques, where 9th grade was like you're opening up different things, like opening up new relationships and friendships. . . . I talked with some of my friends and they don't think there's definite groups this year except for the low class, so like the middle and top are like, the middle is rising and the top is lowering, so that they're kind of, you know, weighing out each other.

Thus, the strong divisions between groups and consequently the group system seems to fade with entry to high school. When high school kids say they used to have cliques but no longer do so, they mean in part that there are more interactions between kids at different levels relative to the middle school system.

The perception of a waning and ambiguous group system is substantiated in several ways in the group naming system. High school kids previously experienced a group naming system specifying three interrelated levels. Not only do they not have three interrelated levels of groups any longer, but the subgroups they do have operating at each level are not explicitly interconnected. This can lead them to believe they no longer have groups. Moreover, unlike the middle school group naming system, not all subgroups have names. Again, the absence of names for all subgroups suggests cliques no longer exist. At the same time however, cliques do seem to exist because, among other things, some groups have names, those highest and lowest in the group system remain outstanding from their peers and there is only minimal interaction between kids in subgroups at the three levels. Thus, cliques are there and not there because kids have available for manipulation two contradictory sets of values with which they can perceive group relations.

Extracurricular Activities

Middle school and high school extracurricular activities affirm and represent their contrasting structures of group relations. Almost exclusive middle school top group participation in extracurricular athletics acknowledges and provides further evidence for top group preeminence. Since participation in extracurricular activities is voluntary, the preponderance of top group kids in such activities distinguishes them from their peers. As middle school kids consider athletic ability to be largely an innate physical capacity—especially for boys, among whom those taller and more physically developed seem most athletic—biological factors contribute to group position. Top group kids participate in athletics most frequently, while physically weak low group fags and wimps rarely participate. Predetermined and determining biological factors operating in the extracurricular context are significant features of the ranking system of middle school groups.

In contrast with the partial biological determination and almost exclusively athletic nature of middle school extracurricular activities, diverse high school groups participate in a multifaceted set of extracurricular activities.[20] These activities affirm the openness and equality of the group system and ignore its restrictions and inequality, as indicated by the reported absence of cliques and group names. Moreover, the high school extracurriculum explicitly emphasizes that kids' affiliations are based on their rational choices as free and equal individuals. The following statement in the Sheepshead 1981 *Yearbook* makes this evident:

[Sheepshead] High School offers numerous activities in which students are encouraged to participate. There is an activity to suit every personality and interest. Whether it be debating, singing, reporting or dancing, each student can find fulfillment in an activity which expresses his or her individuality.

This statement and the extracurriculum in general affirm the fundamental American values of individualism, liberty, and equality motivating the actions of high school students as well as adults (Dumont, 1970). The "numerous activities" designed to "suit every personality and interest" acknowledge and give high value to the wide variety of individuals present in the high school. Moreover, the extracurriculum encourages the further development of individualism since this activity is believed to enable one to find fulfillment" and expression of one's "individuality." Liberty is affirmed by the fact that no kid is restricted from joining any activity.[21] Because activities are open to all kids, selection of one activity over another is thought to be based on one's "personality and interest" rather than on any overt evaluative principle. Therefore, no activity is considered intrinsically better than any other and all have equal value.

---

[20]Hollingshead (1949) also pointed out the centrality of extracurricular activities to the construction of high school groups (p. 217).

[21]The sex-restricted sports and age restrictions of other activities are not considered significant.

Although Americans in general and high school kids in particular believe that participation in an activity of their choice affirms their status as free and equal individuals, they do not realize that such participation also (a) creates the system's constraints and inequalities, and (b) facilitates individual acquisition of group-mindedness. The mere act of choosing one activity over another implies that a ranked system of activities motivates one's choices (Dumont, 1970, p. 20). Moreover, individuals see themselves as group members partially by participating in extracurricular activities. Consider, for example, that kids' participating in athletics, the band, and AVA are viewed as jocks, band fags, and unnamed low group members respectively.[22] Participation by individuals in activities with other similarly oriented individuals indicates the common evaluative framework and their distinctiveness from kids choosing not to participate in such activities (Varenne, 1977, p. 85). Thus, the fulfillment of one's individuality by extracurricular participation also provides one with a group identity. Finally, the act of choosing an activity is motivated by and motivates one's position as a member of a particular informal group. The system of extracurricular activities is based on and further confirms the evaluative components constituting and differentiating informal groups—visibility and compliance with teenage and adult values. Consider, for example, the significance of participation in the AVA Club, which functions to help teachers, coaches, and administrators operate audiovisual equipment. Whereas most extracurricular activities center on student performance, receive guidance from adults peripherally, and take place in school contexts least emphasizing adult authority, the AVA Club members assist adult performances, and occupy a peripheral position in the classroom where adult authority is most emphasized. Thus, participation in the club acknowledges the negative visibility of its low group members, who are distinguished in part for their excessive compliance with adult values.

Relative Rigidity and Fluidity of Middle School and High School Group Systems

Middle school and high school group structures also differ in that the middle school structure is more rigidly organized. Middle school kids are placed and place themselves and others in sharply demarcated groups which rarely interact. Only top group kids cross group boundaries with some frequency, primarily to make fun of low group kids and secondarily

---

[22]Participation in other less visible activities contribute to placement in less visible groups. For example, brains are in chess or math clubs.

to converse with middle group kids when their own friends are not around. With the exception of 8th grade, when the top group divides—the "druggies" (boys) and "sluts" (girls) separate from the jocks—there is only one acceptable mode of social action with which all kids are evaluated and placed at one of three levels. Right social action means acting cool, as the top group does, and avoiding the uncool actions of the low group.

The high school group structure is somewhat more flexible, for there is greater intergroup interaction, less overt mocking of low group kids, and several available forms of social action from which kids may choose their preference. However, while high school kids claim to get along and spend more time than they once did with kids in other groups—in class and in the unstructured settings of the halls, cafeteria, and locker rooms—they get along best and associate most often with kids in their own group. Some parties are "open" to kids in other groups, but most weekend social life is "closed." Low group kids are not mocked but ignored, which is at least as effective as mocking in keeping them separate. Finally, because all groups are constituted with the same values—visibility and compliance with teenage and adult values—the several forms of social action constructed with these values are not as radically different from each other as group members believe them to be.

This cultural evaluation of the similarities and differences of middle and high school groups most generally suggests that:

1. one can examine not only the place of one group in a teenage group system, which has been done in almost all the literature to date, but the ways in which all groups are differentiated from and ordered relative to one another using a shared structure of meaningful action, and 2. one can compare groups over the middle school and high school years to determine the continuities and discontinuities in the experience of being an American teenager.

ACKNOWLEDGMENTS

I especially would like to acknowledge the incisive comments of Hervé Varenne both during the incipient stages of my ideas and as I have developed them. I also gained much from my insightful informants, Maria, Michael, and Fredrika Sidoroff who helped me clarify my ideas and provided me with the atmosphere in which I could do so. Finally, the staff of the *Chicago Anthropology Exchange* helped me tighten my argument and more clearly state my points.

REFERENCES

Bureau of Government Research. (1980). *1980 Legislative District Data Book.* (State name and publisher omitted to maintain the anonymity of the community in which this research was done.)

Coleman, J. S. (1961). *The adolescent society.* New York: The Free Press.

Cusick, P. (1973). *Inside high school.* New York: Holt, Rinehart and Winston.

Dumont, L. (1970). *Homo hierarchicus.* Chicago: University of Chicago Press.

Eisenstadt, S. (1956). *From generation to generation.* New York: The Free Press.

Henry, J. (1963). *Culture against man.* New York: Random House.

Hollingshead, A. B. (1949). *Elmtown's Youth.* New York: Wiley.

Parsons, T. (1942). Age and sex in the social structure of the United States. *American Sociological Review, 7,* 604–16.

Parsons, T. (1963). Youth in the context of American society. In E. E. Erikson (Ed.), *Youth: Change and challenge.* New York: Basic Books.

Schwartz, G., & Merten, D. (1972). The language of adolescence. In S. M. Clark & J. P. Clark (Eds.), *Youth in modern society.* New York: Holt, Rinehart and Winston.

Seeley, J. R., Sim, A., & Loosely, E. (1956). *Crestwood Heights.* New York: Basic Books.

Smith, E. A. (1962). *American youth culture.* New York: Teachers College Press

Varenne, H. (1977). *Americans together.* New York: Teachers College Press.

Varenne, H. (1982). Jocks and freaks: The symbolic structure of the Expression of social interaction among American senior high school students. In G. Spindler (Ed.), *Doing the ethnography of schooling:* Educational anthropology in action. New York: Holt, Rinehart and Winston.

The Author and Her Chapter

Ruth Gallagher Goodenough received her B.S. from Cornell University in 1939 and her M.A. in social psychology also from Cornell, in 1941. She married Ward Goodenough, an anthropologist, in 1941 and subsequently raised two daughters and two sons. During 1964–1965 she spent a year in Truk, Micronesia, with her husband and sons, where she did a study of adoption, which has been published. From 1966 to 1978 she taught primary grades in a private, country day school in the Philadelphia area. Following her retirement from teaching, she undertook the research reported here.

Her chapter pushes the analysis of the conditions of mainstream schooling back to preschool and kindergarten. She describes in telling detail the emergence and reinforcement of sexist behavior in those contexts. Little boys harass and reject girls in displays of male bonding and macho behavior that are all too reminiscent of the more blatant sexism one often observes among adults when conditions call forth and reinforce such behavior. Goodenough discusses the underlying predisposition towards such machoism engendered by the problems of gender identification facing males and the greater aggressiveness of males and greater nurturance of females displayed cross-culturally.

She does not, however, accept the display of sexism among children as inevitable, and points to the damaging effects such behavior has upon both sexes. She describes behavior in four children's groups and analyzes factors that seem accountable for differences in degree of sexism exhibited. It becomes clear that sexism is variable from group to group and that individual differences among children, group composition, and history can combine to produce nonsexist behavior, and conversely that these factors may also combine to produce the most radical forms of sexist behavior.

In a culture, such as mainstream America's, where sexism is deeply ingrained but increasingly discouraged, interpretive ethnographic studies such as Ruth Goodenough's can be very important. If sexism in its most virulent and destructive form is to be eradicated, or even significantly reduced, it will take more than public discussion and legislation to bring this about. The emergence of sexist behavior in the earliest years of life must be studied carefully so that appropriate ameliorative measures may be taken when they can have the greatest effect.

The Editors

17

Small Group Culture and the Emergence of Sexist Behavior: A Comparative Study of Four Children's Groups

Ruth Gallagher Goodenough

INTRODUCTION

For many adults the little boys' refrain "I hate girls" has faded into memory, resurrected occasionally by the cartoon tree house with its seemingly obligatory "Girls Keep Out" sign. Even in these liberated times, however, teachers and parents are more sharply reminded of its continued existence when they hear it on the playground or encounter it in their own children's attitudes. It was as a teacher, hearing a first-grade boy scornfully refuse to hold a girl's hand for a circle dance, that I decided to embark on the present study. When he added that he would rather hold hands with a dog than a girl, I found I had more to deal with than the immediate classroom crisis. I needed to understand how a decent, attractive little boy could so devastatingly reject a set of fellow human beings. When the girls fumbled the rebuttal, one of them saying lamely, "Some girls are good cooks, you know," I felt impelled on their behalf, as well as my own, to enlarge my perspective on the problem.

The questions that bothered me then, when confronted by this early expression of sexism, are essentially the ones that this paper addresses: when and how, in the schooling of children, does "I hate girls" appear, what is its effect on girls, and how can we account for it.

Theoretical Background

A review of the recent literature on sex differences[1] reveals general agreement on the behavioral differences between boys and girls, permitting us to draw a baseline differentiation of the two populations. In virtually all studies and across different cultures boys as a group are more aggressive and girls more nurturant. Additionally, boys are described as more competitive, impulsive, and attention seeking than girls, who tend toward greater cooperativeness, empathy, and compliance. By the age of five, when most children attend kindergarten, these characteristic differences have already emerged.

It seems reasonable to suppose that contact between any two populations discriminated by differences such as these might lead to inequalities of status and power. Barring strong counterpressures to preserve equality, or strong needs for mutual interdependence, the more aggressive, competitive group would have a clear edge in obtaining power and privilege over the more nurturant, cooperative one. But in the case of human males and females an additional twist is given to the situation by an important developmental difference between the sexes, one that frequently results in male antagonism toward females.

By virtue of being mothered by a member of the opposite sex boys face a troublesome problem in identity formation. In the psychoanalytic description of the process,[2] the primary identification of both boys and girls is with the female who mothers them. For girls, growing up as females, this primary identification presents no particular developmental hazard; their identification with mother is simply the bottom layer, so to speak, of an eventual unity of self. Boys on the other hand, as biological *others*, are obliged by society to develop an overlying or even antithetical masculine identity, whose achievement and maintenance is at some risk. In the chanciness of this identity process lie a number of possible distortions, including the gratuitous assumption of hostility toward girls and women.

If masculine identity must be acquired and maintained at the cost of suppressing primary female identification, it is unfortunate that only a short step leads from such denial to outright denigration. Given the importance of establishing a proper gender identity, boys facing the problem must find it seductive to assume a superiority over girls and to profess hostility toward them, particularly if parents encourage it as a sign of being a proper boy. Whether all boys at one time or another succumb to the temptation is an open question, but there is no doubt that this

---

[1]For thorough reviews of the extensive literature see Maccoby and Jacklin (1974), Pitcher and Schultz (1983), and Block (1983).
[2]See Stoller (1974) and Chodorow (1978).

particular developmental warp adds emotional fuel to the boys' side of the gender differences we have already noted. There is also little doubt, to judge by the literature of psychoanalysis, that the matter is high on the psychic agenda of boys by ages five and six.

Thus the characteristics that young boys bring to early classroom encounters with girls, if not restrained, would appear to lead inevitably to both inequality and to sexism. In a society like ours, where most school experiences involve children who are strangers to one another, the likelihood is greater than it would be in smaller and more stable communities, where even very young children may know each other within a defined and constraining system of relationships. If little Amy is George's sister, or the constable's daughter, or a cousin on my mother's side, it is indeed more difficult to reject her as one of an alien class. In the absence of ties that define roles and limit exploitation, however, it falls to parents and teachers to impose what restraints they can. They do so largely without the conscious aim of softening sexual conflict,[3] but as agents of society they teach the cultural values of fairness, turn-taking, and respect for others, which, if learned, promote equality and soften sexism, at least at home and in the classroom, if not necessarily on the playground.

But another important countervailing force exists, and it is to be found within children themselves. As young members of the same species they share a common ameliorating human agenda, a mixture of social and biological forces that nudge them toward accommodation rather than rejection. We know that by age five both boys and girls are caught up in a similar thrust toward autonomy and independence, and that both have the task of learning gender-appropriate behavior and consolidating it within a sexual identity; but beyond these is a developmental task whose presence and importance is less often recognized for young children. Along with autonomy and identity concerns, rudimentary courtship behaviors are a significant part of the agenda youngsters have for themselves at this age. Certainly by age five, if not before, both sexes are already embarked on the long process of attraction and adjustment that will eventually take most of them to mature heterosexual bonding. These three developmental tasks are interrelated; they posit for each sex the existence, and ideally the cooperation of the other if both are to become fully and functionally human.

That it doesn't always work out successfully, that power differentials and sexism crop up despite the efforts of socializing adults and the elemental need for male-female accommodation, is obvious at almost every level of social life. Our concern is to see how these opposing forces come together and work themselves out among certain 5- and 6-year-olds,

---

[3]A fascinating exception is described by Paley (1984). See also Borman (1978).

for this is the age not only when most children, on entering school, encounter large numbers of the opposite sex for the first time, but when, among boys, "I hate girls" begins to be said in all seriousness.

The Study

The current study began with preliminary background observations at the 3- and 4-year-old nursery school level, and was followed by year-long observations in two successive kindergarten groups. Two kindergarten-first-grade classes, each studied for a considerably shorter time, were added to the sample when they became available. Because I was interested in spontaneous boy-girl interactions I looked for groups that were together for longer periods of the day and under a looser rein than could be found in standard public school kindergartens. Consequently, the groups on which the study is based were not chosen because they were typical of kindergarten or primary groups, but because they afforded an exceptionally rich field of interaction among children of the appropriate age.

The groups designated as K1, K2, and K4 were all from the same East Coast, country-day school, which was organized some 50 years ago around the principles of the Progressive Education movement. K3 was a primary class in a West Coast public school, but it too was unusual in being part of an enclave of classes set up on the alternative education model of the Open Classroom. For reasons of educational philosophy the children of these groups were allowed more freedom of expression and choice than prevails in the usual kindergarten or first grade. As a consequence there were opportunities for them to play out significant parts of their own agendas, rather than simply to fulfill academic and social requirements set by the teacher.[4]

My original intention was to study in successive years two kindergarten groups at the same school and with the same teacher, in order to compare the kinds of cross-sex behaviors they exhibited. A period of intensive observation and recording (about 3 months in all) proved sufficient to establish the patterns of cross-sex interaction in each group, after which the behaviors became largely repetitive of what I had already observed. Although participant observation continued in both groups throughout the year, the material gathered in this period of concentrated focus forms the basis for the statistical comparison used in the study.

Later, an opportunity arose for a shorter study of a kindergarten-first-

---

[4]This does not imply an absence of rules or structure, but simply an allowance within wider boundaries for behavior initiated by the children. See Shultz and Florio (1979) for an account of operative controls in an open classroom.

grade in the West Coast public school. Although the time allowed was short, the same kind of intensive recording, now sharpened by experience, proved to be enough to establish a picture of patterned response in the area of boy-girl interaction. The West Coast group was then matched by another kindergarten-first-grade class in the school studied earlier. The material gathered for each of these two multilevel groups turned out to be just one third of that obtained for the original kindergartens, yet clear and comparable patterns of interaction emerged for both, verified in the case of one of them by available teacher observations.

As to methods, I found the making of timed, spot-observations less productive than recording behavior framed by activities, whose beginnings and ends the children set themselves. Scanning strategies helped me record the activities of most of the play or work groups as well as those of isolated children; dialogues of significant same-sex or cross-sex exchanges were recorded verbatim. I kept counts of seating and association choices, records of spontaneous responses to questions in whole group settings, and records of access to areas and materials. For the two kindergarten groups, K1 and K2, I used a kind of projective test at year's end that employed a model of the play area and school room. In the case of K1 girls only, this exercise was followed by a short interview on the general subject of boy-girl relationships.

In the analysis of the data, items of interpersonal behavior were labeled as positive or negative, depending on a judgment of inferred intention as well as observed impact. Negative behaviors included aggressive acts, verbal put-downs, tauntings, and rejections. Positive behaviors included helpful acts, compliments, acts of affection or consideration, and expressions of liking. For the total population of 85 children, 529 negative/ aggressive acts and 339 positive ones were recorded.

To compare the groups I converted the total output of negative and positive behaviors of each to ratios, and subsumed them under four categories of boy-girl interaction. In Table 17.1 we see for each classroom the ratio of negative to positive where boys are directing their behavior either to other boys or to girls, and similarly the ratios of negative to positive where girls are targeting either boys or other girls.

The whole-sample ratios at the bottom of Table 17.1 give a bland and homogenized picture that reinforces what has been reported by other studies. The boys, predictably, show more than twice as much negative or aggressive behavior for every instance of positive, while the girls exhibit slightly more positive than negative kinds of behavior. When we move from these rather prosaic whole-sample comparisons to those that characterize and differentiate the groups, however, we begin to find things we did not necessarily know before. Separating the data by groups, we see significant and surprising differences among them. Each of the four

TABLE 17.1
Ratios of Negative to Positive Response

GROUP		BOYS TO BOYS Neg. / Pos.		BOYS TO GIRLS Neg. / Pos.		GIRLS TO BOYS Neg. / Pos.		GIRLS TO GIRLS Neg. / Pos.	
K1	Responses	87	20	124	4	25	8	22	7
	Ratio	4.4 to 1		31.0 to 1		3.1 to 1		3.1 to 1	
K2	Responses	80	32	32	51	17	46	19	44
	Ratio	2.5 to 1		0.6 to 1		0.37 to 1		0.43 to 1	
K3	Responses	24	12	38	5	5	9	5	4
	Ratio	2.0 to 1		7.6 to 1		0.55 to 1		1.2 to 1	
K4	Responses	32	29	13	27	6	28	0	13
	Ratio	1.1 to 1		0.48 to 1		0.2 to 1			
Total Population	Responses	223	93	207	87	53	91	46	68
	Ratio	2.4 to 1		2.4 to 1		0.58 to 1		0.67 to 1	

appears with its own particular accommodation to male-female differences, a kind of miniculture in the areas of cross-sex interactions, whose costs or benefits we can begin to evaluate.

For our purposes the most significant column of Table 17.1 is the one that shows the ratios of behavior directed by boys to girls. Here the differences among the groups is greatest, ranging from a benign .48 to 1 for group K4 up to 31.0 to 1 for K1—a sixty-fold difference. If a 1-to-1 ratio is defined as cross-sex neutral, then K1 comes across as the most sexist of the four groups by a wide margin. In these terms, K2 and K4, each showing more positive than negative behavior from boys to girls, must be rated as nonsexist, while K3, with its ratio of 7.6 to 1, although well below that of K1, is still substantially on the sexist side.[5]

Comparing the figures for each group with the ratios for the total population, we see that K1 is farthest from the average in each category of interaction and not just in its elevated ratio for Boys to Girls. In the

---

[5]To calculate chi square tests of significance, the data on K1 and K3 were combined, as were the data on K2 and K4. They showed little difference in boy-boy behavior, which was more negative than positive throughout, although there was a somewhat higher proportion of positive behavior in the K2-K4 cluster (chi square 6.256, 1 degree of freedom, probability 0.0124, total cases 316). Otherwise, the K1-K3 cluster contrasted markedly with the K2-K4 cluster. The contrast was most dramatic in boy-girl behavior (chi square 116, 1 degree of freedom, probability 0.0001, total cases 294); but it was also highly significant in girl-boy behavior (chi square 21.908, 1 degree of freedom, probability 0.0001, total cases 144) and in girl-girl behavior (chi square 22.232, 1 degree of freedom, probability 0.0001, total cases 114).

category of Boys to Boys, it is twice the average for the population as a whole. In the category of Girls to Boys, it exceeds the average by a factor of 6, and in Girls to Girls by a factor of 5.

To account for such differences we must examine the groups more closely. To understand the sexist behavior of K1, for example, we want to see if the relatively high rate of negative behavior shown by the girls to the boys can be construed as the cause of the boy's misogyny or a response to it. Similarly, we want to look at the background for the elevated ratios of negative to positive behavior within the girl groups of K1 and K3 to see how it differs from that of K2 and K4. Our concern is to flesh out the comparisons implied in the ratios of Table 17.1 and to lay out some of the social dynamics that are involved. As a preliminary overview, Table 17.2 gives a summary of the background features of each of the four groups.

In the case study materials we shall seek answers to some of our earlier questions. Having determined that sexism does characterize some groups and not others, we shall look not only for the forms antifeminism may take among boys of 5 and 6, but for factors associated with its emergence or absence, and particularly for its effects on girls. In this more detailed account we may also hope to find whether sexism at this age is linked to the differentials of power and privilege that we associate with dominance behaviors.

KINDERGARTEN 1

K1 was the smallest of the four groups. In the fall term it consisted of only eight boys and four girls,[6] but by January an additional girl brought the total to thirteen. As we can see from Table 17.2, virtually ¾ of the members of K1 (all of the girls and more than half of the boys) were newcomers.

The four boys who had been at the school the previous year would

---

[6]In addition to these children, who were white, two black children, a boy and a girl, were with the group for 3 months in the fall but are not included in the descriptive nor statistical portion of this account. In their short stay they played mostly with each other and maintained an attitude of rather belligerent disdain for the white children. Although they contributed to the generally aggressive profile of the group and to its initial stress levels, in the area of cross-sex interaction their behavior ran counter to the sexist trends of the white majority. The boy, unlike his white peers, was equally aggressive with both boys and girls, while the girl, whom the white boys treated with wary respect, was just too tough to invite sexist treatment. Because they were with the group for only a short while and operated, in a sense, beside it rather than fully within it, the adaptations of this pair, as interesting as they are, lie outside the focus of the present study. What follows is confined to a description of what transpired within the white majority of the class, much of it after the withdrawal of the two black children.

TABLE 17.2
Background Features of Four Groups

Group	Class Size	Number of Boys	Number of Girls	Grade Level	Percentage of Children in the Core Group*	Type of School	Length of School Day	Sex of Teachers
K1	13	8	5	Kdg.	30% (Boys only)	Private	Full day	Female, with female assistant
K2	19	8	11	Kdg.	60% (Both sexes)	Private	Full day	Female, with female assistant
K3	30	16	14	Kdg.-first	Estimated 25% (Both sexes)	Public	Kdg. A.M. only 1st Grade full day	Male, with parent aides
K4	23	16	7	Kdg.-first	75% (Both sexes)	Private	Full day	Female, with female assistant

*The term Core Group designates the children who had already been members of the same school community for a least a year. For K3 it should be noted that roughly 1/4 of the 19 kindergarten children had also attended a cooperative part-time nursery school in the previous year.

hardly have qualified as a core group except that three of them quickly assumed leadership in the first days of the term. Two had been together both as 3- and as 4-year-olds but the other two had been in a separate and younger group for just a year. When school started, however, they built upon their slight acquaintance and their knowledge of the scene to establish themselves as an in-group that set the tone for the other kindergarten boys. In the absence of girls in the core group, the incoming girls were without comparable leadership, and at an initial disadvantage that grew worse with time.

Despite the evidence of the skewed ratios of Table 17.1, there were no particularly disturbed children among either the boys or the girls of the group. As individuals, any one of them might fit easily into any of the other groups of our study. It was true of them, as it was of the other children in the study, that whatever stress levels there may or may not have been in their lives outside of school none of them could be singled out as a serious behavioral problem.

The Boys' Cross-Sex Interaction

In the judgment of the adults who dealt with them, however, as well as in the evidence of Table 17.1, there was an excessive amount of antagonism from the boys to the girls of K1. The boys dominated or discriminated against the girls regularly. They rarely used force, but relied instead on small harassments and verbal put-downs. They excluded girls from choice play or sitting areas. They openly refused to hold hands with them in circle games and ostentatiously resisted sitting next to them at snack or lunch time.

During sharing times,[7] they paid small attention when the girls spoke, and on several occasions held their ears rather than listen. A boy holding a pet snake thrust it repeatedly in the faces of the girls to make them flinch. Other boys, seeing a girl write her name on the board, scribbled over it.

"I hate girls" was an explicit watchword. They scapegoated the girls for things that went wrong and banded together to chortle over the real or imagined discomfiture of a girl. They made up songs or stories that associated girls with nastiness. "Her ears were full of yellow diarrhea," or a chorus of "She went pee and pooh in her pants," were their 5-year-old versions of what might later pass as locker-room humor.

When a tone of superiority would work to intimidate the girls, they used it. Jill,[8] announcing that she wanted to join a group of boys in the

---

[7]Sharing time is a whole-class activity where the children take turns telling something of interest.

[8]Fictitious names have been substituted for real names throughout.

prized loft area, was refused permission. They told her with exaggerated patience, "Can't you see we're having a conference, Jill?" At the same time, another girl who tried to climb up was simply jostled off the ladder.

The boys exploited the belongings and the territory of the girls while jealously guarding their own. In one example a boy snatched a toy from a girl, then made a face at her. When she objected he told her coolly, "I'll give it to you when we're done with it." Another appropriated a musical toy from a girl's locker and passed it around among his friends as she watched somewhat anxiously from a distance. Only when the boys tired of it did she venture to retrieve it and return it to her locker. In contrast, when one of the boys saw the girls playing with a toy he thought belonged to a friend, he shouted angrily at them, "Hey girls! I call on you girls to get this back! It belongs to Tom."

The girls attempted to buy their way into favor by bringing treats and games from home to share with the boys. The brief detentes that followed would last about as long as the treat did. If the girls would play service roles, fetching and carrying for the boys, they were sometimes allowed to play, but the tones of voice used and the orders given, "Pick that up!" or "What are you doin' in my seat!" made it clear that they were there on the boys' sufferance.

In a common form of cross-sex activity, the boys defined themselves as Baddies, whose role was to disrupt the girls' play. Characteristically the girls would be busy with some sort of domestic play when the boys would descend on them looking for things to steal or ways to pester. They might pretend to set a fire, or actually leap down on the scene from an overhead rope, then run off with mock-villainous laughs, telling each other what they had done and what fun it was. The girls, trying to ignore or play around these interruptions, would be drawn half-reluctantly into the boys' scenario. They would go along, threatening in play to call the police or trying to recover their belongings in exasperated forays, but what had started as quiet family play would often end as a hurly-burly that required the teacher's intervention.[9]

The activities of the boys, on the other hand, were almost never disrupted by the girls. Their space-war games and building projects went on without interference no matter how much of the room they occupied nor how much equipment they monopolized. They surrounded their own activities with a forbidding atmosphere of importance, often adopting deepened voices and an air of command. One such play started with Tom announcing to Carl, "Let's play World War I. I'm General Howe and you're one of my men!" They arranged themselves in hierarchies where self-appointed leaders gave orders to various underlings, or fathers in-

---

[9]For a sensitive description of this kind of interaction in a less negatively charged atmosphere see Paley (1984).

structed their sons. One boy wrapped it up with "I'm the father. That means I'm the Captain and I tell you what to do!"

In an alternative form of organization that just as thoroughly excluded girls, the boys defined themselves as comrades or buddies. Rejoicing in being friends, groups of boys would sit or walk with their arms across one another's shoulders. In this mood they liked to sing strongly cadenced songs together and sway in exaggerated unison to the beat.

Despite rather frequent clashes and disagreements among themselves they had an obvious sense of identity as an all-boy group. To maintain it they were stern in guarding the code of manly behavior. "You're scared" was a charge that drew instant denials. "You're a girl" was another. Lesser embarrassments lay with babyish mispronunciations or not knowing the *in* vocabulary of a popular war or space play. A couple of the boys erred when they showed their liking for the most popular lad in the class by kissing him. He reacted with immediate disgust and scrubbed away at the offending spot on his face. They did not try to kiss him again.

Dependency

Correlated with their rejection of girls and their strong sense of identity as an all-boy group went a consistent rejection of dependency. A familiar start for a play for example was, "Pretend our parents are dead." They showed little interest in caring for the classroom guinea pigs, nor did they pretend to be baby animals themselves. Human babies and babyhood were a source of unease and ambivalence;[10] if they pretended to be babies at all, the boys burlesqued it by acting silly and saying "goo-goo, gaw-gaw." They reacted with "oooh sick!" at hearing of a nurse changing a newborn infant, and they became increasingly restive during a short film showing the bathing of a baby. In the follow-up discussion, when their teacher asked, "Do you think you liked it when your mother or father bathed you when you were little?" the boys answered with a defiant chorus of "I hated it!" On the way back from seeing this film several of the boys dogged the steps of one of the girls chanting, "Kathleen is a gir-rul, a pretty little gir-rul," repeating it and underlining the words sneeringly while she hurried silently back to the classroom.

Cross-Sex Attraction

If the group's macho values were incompatible with dependency or other reminders of their own recent pasts, these same attitudes produced

---

[10]That boys at all ages show less interest in infants than girls do, and that the interest of both increases with age, is reported by Blakemore (1981). It seems clear however that the aggressive rejection of infancy by the boys of K1 was more than a matter of reduced interest.

conflict about activities that pointed toward more mature heterosexual relationships. Circle games were often painfully embarrassing, while light-hearted games of chase between the girls and boys, like those we encounter in K2, were for this group compromised by the boys' rejections of the girls in other contexts. As teases, the boys of K1 came off as heavies. The best they could do was to be the Baddies who disrupted what the girls were doing. Understandably, both sexes in K1 looked with envy at the carefree chases of the then 4-year-old nursery group, and some of the kindergarten boys, particularly those of the core group, occasionally slipped off to join the younger children in a 4-year-old version of the game of "Kissing Girl" (described below).

In summary to this point, the boys of K1 rejected and denigrated the girls of their class. They denied dependency in themselves, and suffered conflict in showing heterosexual interests. Concentrating their attention on masculine pursuits, they enforced conformity to their image of masculinity and exalted male comradeship. All of the boys participated in the development of this hyper-masculine ethos, but five of the nine, including three of the four who had been at the school the previous year, were the most heavily involved. This group was the most vocal in rejecting girls and the most vigilant in holding other boys to the line.

The Girls

In Table 17.1 we saw that the girls of K1 had higher than average ratios of negative to positive behavior both in their interactions with the boys and among themselves. It is appropriate to ask whether these ratios reflect an innately higher level of negativity or whether they may be seen instead as a result rather than a cause of the boys' rejection. In the judgment of the adults who dealt with them, the girls of the group were an average set of middle-class children. They had no particular physical or psychological handicaps nor were they lacking in essential self-esteem. Their teachers ranked none of them as being particularly aggressive, negative, or trouble-making.

Table 17.3 shows the distribution of cross-sex negative behavior generated and received by individual girls. Although three of the girls received by far the largest share of negative behavior from the boys the table shows little correlation between the negative behavior the girls received and the amount they generated. To appreciate the reflexive nature of the girls' negative responses we must look more closely at the cross-sex interactions of individual girls.

In comparison with the other girls of the group, Jill's scores in both columns of Table 17.3 are high. She received four times as much negative behavior as Karen or Susan and responded in kind eight times as often as they did. Without knowing her one might assume that she was a contentious child, and that the boys might be responding appropriately in their strong negative response to her, but a closer look reveals that her negative behaviors to the boys were almost all verbal reactions in negative interchanges that they initiated.

Jill was in fact an agreeable, outgoing girl whose problem was that she was attracted to the boys and their activities, and did not try to avoid them as most of the other girls did. Compounding this, when they rejected her or put her down, she attempted to stand her ground. It did not take the boys long to learn that her defenses were ineffectual, and her efforts to defend herself often became a springboard for fresh baiting. In an incident that catches the flavor of this:

> Jill is at the sandbox with four boys. They have just taunted her and Jill chooses to ignore it. She hums a tune. Adam, coming back to the attack says, "That's a dumb song!" and Tom echoes him. Jill responds with her favorite ploy, "You're verrry, verry smart, and you are too." Tom says with scorn, "I'm smarter than you!" Carl flies his plane close to her head, causing her to duck. Jill retaliates with, "I'm not gonna invite you to my birthday party!" Tom, complacently, "Good, you have yukky parties." Adam, "yeah!" Carl threatens again with his plane. Jill tries her mollifying tack again but can't sustain it, "Well, I *am* gonna invite you to my birthday party, you creeps!" Tom, in the same complacent tone, "Good!" Jill, near tears, says "Excuse me!" and leaves. Adam turns to Carl, who despite his hectoring is known to like Jill and asks innocently, "Who's your best girl friend?" Carl walks into the trap, "Jill." Adam says unbelievingly, "You must be sick!" Carl quickly retreats with, "My *Mom* is my best girl friend."

By the second term of the school year some of Jill's ebullience and confidence were gone and she began to show signs of anxiety about the boys. In the year-end interview she confessed that their rejections made her "nervous" and she wished, somewhat plaintively, that the boys liked her.

Table 17.3 shows that Wendy accumulated negative reactions from the boys at an even greater rate than Jill, but also that she rarely if ever paid them back in kind. Curiously these rejections by the boys followed a period of initial acceptance. Coming into the group at mid-term, she was welcomed warmly by both the boys and the girls. In an unusual show of gallantry for example, the boys invited Wendy up into the loft, one of them even helping her to climb up. They structured the play to include her: "Let's pretend we're little boys," suggests Adam, and Tom adds, "And Wendy can be a little girl." On another day Peter, one of the more confirmed misogynists, announced during sharing time that Wendy was coming to his house after school. Wendy was gracious about all these

TABLE 17.3
Cross-Sex Negative Behavior

	Given	Received
Jill	17	49
Wendy	2*	44*
Kathleen	4	20
Karen	2	12
Susan	2	11

*Because she was with the group for one term only, Wendy's score was doubled to make comparison possible.

attentions but had trouble deciding which boy she liked best. She favored John, whom she invited to her home, but she also liked Tom, whose head she patted lovingly during story time, and Adam, whose company she sought out at rest time.

Within a month this honeymoon atmosphere had dramatically changed and most of the boys singled her out for vehement rejection. When a teacher remarked on how well Wendy had played the piano in assembly, Peter and Adam shouted, "We hate how she played!" John, referring to a situation in which Wendy was barely involved, said angrily, "That's why I hate her!" and Peter went out of his way to push or hit her, making her cry.

Whether jealousy was at the root of it, or the threat she posed to their solidarity, the boys began an almost unrelieved campaign of derogation and rejection. From Wendy's point of view a hornet's nest had opened at her feet. Her manner, which had been one of easy confidence, turned to confusion and anxiety. When playing with the girls she took to defining herself as sickly or lame, even dead. When questioned late in the term about her feelings, she responded, "I feel very sad, 'cause they make fun of me, 'cause they don't like me . . . all except Tom."

Kathleen got less than half as much negative response from the boys as the other two, but considering that she tried to avoid confrontation at all costs, the amount may seem disproportionate. She too was a secure child, but more reserved than some of the others. Pretty and always attractively dressed, she was popular with the girls as a peacemaker.

Yet Kathleen was the one the boys would spin on the merry-go-round long after she begged them to stop, the one whose quiet efforts at sharing time they pointedly ignored or even shut out by holding their ears. She was the one they taunted with being a "gir-rul, a pretty little gir-rull." Suppressed attraction and even envy would appear to have been part of the boys' problem with Kathleen. They worked hard at denying her appeal, at times blocking out even the sound of her voice. The derogatory songs they made up about nameless girls must have had the same motivation, blocking out appeal or value by associating it with excrement.

In the interview at year's end Kathleen claimed that the boys were just "too fighty" and she hoped that when they grew up they would be "more polite." In her words, "I know a friend, 20-years-old, who didn't get polite, but some people do."

The remaining two girls suffered the least antagonism from the boys, although this much was still six times what they themselves generated. Karen, unlike Jill, determinedly avoided the boys. She was not interested in their play, nor did she present an image of vulnerable femininity, excessive motherliness, or tenderness, as perhaps Wendy or Kathleen did. Susan, the only one with a younger brother, had few illusions about boys her own age and had set her sights on the later dating scene. Her play fantasies leaned in the direction of clothes, shopping, and entertaining, and were largely absorbed by play in the girl group.

Neither of these girls reported feelings of anxiety about the boys in the year-end interview, but we cannot assume that they escaped altogether the negative fall-out from the boys' hostility. They, along with the other girls, stayed unusually close to grown-ups, and restricted their activities to avoid confrontation. The classroom participation of all the girls suffered as they became less and less willing to speak up when the boys were around. During question periods the boys gave almost all the answers, in an extraordinary ratio of 30 to 1. When the children were choosing activities for a free period the girls invariably waited quietly for the boys to announce their choices and even to move off the scene before venturing to name their own.

There is little doubt that the playing-out of the boys' antagonism reined in the spontaneity and limited the participation of the girls. But the ratios of Table 17.1 show a further result. The girl-to-girl negativity for K1 is at least three times greater than it is for the other groups. One could argue that the girls of K1, unwilling or unable to fight back against the boys, were forced to displace their frustration upon themselves.

The Teachers

The teacher of K1 and her assistant were deeply concerned about the sexist attitudes and dominance practiced by the boys. Whenever they heard a boy call the girls dumb, or weird, or fatheads, they rebuked him. A boy who made a vomiting gesture when a girl chose him in a circle game was told it was rude and warned that he would be removed from the game if he repeated it. They reprimanded boys for refusing to listen to girls, they held discussions about hurting the feelings of others and talked repeatedly about the need for kindness and sharing, but to no avail. The boys continued their attacks on the sly or simply ignored the mild rebukes.

The teachers resorted to seating and resting charts that called for cross-sex pairings, but these failed as the boys found graphic ways to show their distaste for girl partners. On their side, the girls came to dread the charts because of the hatefulness they engendered. To bolster the position of the girls the teachers separated the group, and with the boys off the scene encouraged the girls to speak out in discussion periods. They taught the girls to use the balcony of the room, helping the more timid to climb up and encouraging them to use it for their own kind of play. When the boys returned after this session they found the girls were having a tea party in the high regions that before had rung only with Star War noises. The point was made, if only momentarily, that the area should not be solely a male bastion.

At mid-year the teachers introduced a greatly expanded dress-up corner that briefly offered some real-life alternatives to the stereotyped games of Space and War. At the same time they increased activities like cooking and exercise sessions that involved everyone. But despite these and other attempts to deal with the situation the end of the year found the teachers discouraged by the persistence of the boys' sexist attitudes. In this group the boys had welded their anti-girl sentiments into a self-perpetuating stance that was largely impervious to adult disapproval or intervention.

KINDERGARTEN 2

As kindergarten groups from the same school, K1 and K2 shared a number of common background features. They had the same teacher and curriculum for instance, and a similar socioeconomic profile. K2 was larger, however, and with eleven girls and eight boys its sex distribution reversed that of K1.

We already know from the ratios of Table 17.1 that the two groups were very different in the quality of their boy-girl interaction. Unlike K1, whose boys directed a barrage of negative behavior toward the girls, in K2 the boys gave almost twice as much positive as negative response to the girls in their class. The figures in the ratios, as dramatic as they are, hardly prepare us for the differences in tone between the two groups. The emotionally restrictive, male-dominated atmosphere of K1 stands in sharp contrast to the easy egalitarianism of K2, where it was commonplace for girls and boys to show that they liked each other, and for girls to be as free and independent in their behavior as the boys.

A too-easy assumption that the differences we find are due to the sheer preponderance of boys in the one group and of girls in the other is belied by a look ahead to K4, a group marked by an even greater proportion of boys than that of K1 but yet the least sexist of any in our sample. A more promising circumstance to investigate, as we look more closely at K2, lies in the nature of its core group, for here we have one that differs significantly in size, experience, and sexual composition from that of K1. Sixty percent of the boys and girls of K2 had been together at least one full year before entering kindergarten, with most having been in the school's nursery program since they were three. It would be difficult to understand the social dynamics of K2 without reference to the organization and strengths of this core group, for the associations and atmosphere they brought with them as 5-year-olds, and to which the newcomers adapted, was essentially formed out of their experiences together as 3- and 4-year-olds.

As preschoolers they had been part of a well-knit group that included equal numbers of boys and girls. Although their play might involve any combination of these children, three social groupings occurred more frequently than others and became an enduring pattern of association. The most cohesive was a threesome made up of Michelle, Jonathan, and Bruce, who charged about as super heroes (including Wonder Woman), pretended to be members of real or animal families, or simply wrestled and chased each other about. The five remaining girls of the class specialized in more elaborate family plays, often based on characters from the "Brady Bunch." The rest of the boys, when not playing at boy games with each other, fitted themselves in and around the activities of the girls or the mixed-sex threesome.

Among the strengths of the core group of K2 must be counted their affection for one another, as well as the social skills they had developed for minimizing or resolving conflict. In 2 years of nursery school they had picked up useful strategies from their teachers. "Did you tell him you didn't like it?" was the first suggestion to a child with a complaint, followed by "Let's talk about it," if the first did not work. There were strong-minded girls and boys in the group but they had learned to work out differences rather than prolong them. As a result the general tone of the class, if not always without friction, was easy-going and pleasant.

These patterns of association and behavioral resources were part of the culture that the core group carried over into kindergarten; as such they proved to be strong enough to absorb and shape the behavior of a sometimes difficult assortment of eight newcomers. The aspects of the culture that had to do with cross-sex interaction differed at every point from those that characterized K1. In months of observation, "I hate girls" was never heard, nor was any other putdown in terms of sex. Disagreements between a girl and a boy could arise, but they were context-specific and dealt with as such. Boys did not monopolize prized areas or toys; girls were not bullied nor ordered around in service roles. These boys did not disrupt girl activities, nor see themselves as Baddies with a mission to harass the girls.

Although boys and girls tended to clump together in same-sex groups for particular kinds of play, just as they had in preschool, members of the opposite sex were not excluded. In a fairly typical example, when a number of boys were building with large blocks, Kevin called to a girl who was standing on the sidelines, "We've got plenty of room, come on and build with us."

In this group children frequently hugged or patted each other, and it was common to see friends of the opposite sex sitting or resting next to one another. One boy seeing the chart for rest-time placement said, "Good, I get to rest next to a girl." His friend, checking the list noted, "Oh, me too." The hand-holding games and dances that caused grief in K1 were not a problem in K2. There were nearly always combinations of boys and girls who wanted to be partners.

Dependency

With K1 we saw that boys rejected symbols of dependency as being incompatible with their masculine image. In contrast, the boys and girls of K2 spent much time holding and petting the classroom rabbits, and K2 boys were interested, rather than embarrassed, when a visiting baby brother underwent a diaper change. Some of them still played that they were in animal or human families, either as babies or parents, and these roles sometimes slid over into real life, as in this episode from a music class:

> The children are playing a guessing game and Michelle wants to go out as Jonathan's partner. She can't, it's Laurie's turn. She looks unhappy, then puts her head in Bruce's lap. He pats it. Soon she recovers and sits up again. Later Bruce can't have a turn for the same reason. He says, "Oh shucks, Baby!" and hugs Michelle, who hugs him back.

Cross-Sex Attraction

In the realm of cross-sex attraction and rudimentary courting games, K2 boys and girls were predictably more at ease than those of K1. This was true, as we saw, for circle games and dances, but it was also apparent in the way they could entertain the prospect of more serious cross-sex attachment. The three friends, Bruce, Michelle, and Jonathan, were sometimes caught up in the question of which of the boys was to marry

Michelle. However they chose to resolve it, one of them had, temporarily at least, to be disappointed, as in this excerpt:

> Bruce turns to Michelle and asks, "You gonna marry me, Michelle?" She answers, "Yes." Bruce asks: "You're not gonna marry Jonathan?" Michelle, "No." Bruce turns and says, "Jonathan, she's gonna marry me, and not you." Jonathan looks unhappily to Michelle. "You're not gonna marry me?" Michelle says lamely, "I'm sorry, Jonathan, I can't help it. I *was* gonna marry my cousin."

That the field is open, and that others can play the game is clear from a later episode.

> Michelle has the record player, Bruce reaches across the table and tries to grab it. She laughs and grabs it back. Bruce explains, "It's not yours, it's the school's." Michelle just laughs. Cathy, sitting next to Bruce, says something to him ending in "Bruce, honey." Laurie, sitting across the table and enjoying it all says, "That's your honey," and she laughs. Then she adds mischievously, "Your honey had to rest next to me yesterday."

In another pairing, Andrea and Michael, one of the new boys, formed an attachment early in the year. Thanks to Andrea's persistence and sense of the dramatic, the affair lasted for several months, running through various femme fatale and Sleeping Beauty episodes. Some of these entailed the cooperation of half the class, whose job it was to lure Michael in from his affairs outdoors so that he could play his role, which was to awaken the "sleeping" Andrea. Everybody knew what was afoot, including Michael, who, to everyone's enjoyment allowed himself to be drawn into these grand awakenings.

Fewer than half the children were involved in explicit attractions of this sort but most of them enjoyed vicariously the ones that existed. When it came to games of pursuit between boys and girls however, no one held back. The classic Kissing Girl game of the older children at the school involved a chase whose ostensible purpose was the kissing of a boy when he was caught. The girls of K2 substituted perfume or chapsticks (often as not brought to school by the boys). In their version of the game the chase could go either way, as this excerpt shows:

> The girls are chasing the boys to put perfume on them. Four boys come running breathlessly around the corner of the building and compare experiences. One of them says, "Get Michael! Get Michael to help us!" (Michael is in shop.) Steve says, "They almost got me!" Jonathan adds, "They almost got me, but I got away!" Apparently Jonathan has captured the perfume bottle, for they sneak over and try to hide it in the tall grass. The girls appear by now, and seeing what is going on, one of them says firmly,

"Jonathan, it's Cathy's!" Jonathan says, "I'll give it back to you if you stop chasing us!" Cathy answers, "We will, we're havin' a little break." Jonathan passes the bottle back but then, seeing that this promises to put an end to the game he asks, "Can I have it back?" Cathy gives it to him and Laurie says, "Now it's the boys chase the girls!" Jonathan agrees, "Yeah, now it's the boys chase the girls!" They happily change roles and the girls take off, followed hotly by the boys.

Individual Styles of Accommodation

The various strands that made up the nonsexist ethos of K2 were represented in the behavioral styles of particular children, each of whom contributed in some way to the successful bridging of the differences between the two sexes. The common bridging roles are those that either minimize the differences or capitalize on them in a culturally acceptable way. One thinks of the role of *tomboy,* or those of *boyfriend-girlfriend* as examples of these; but simply being friends, or treating each other as siblings, or taking a caring parental role are forms of bridging that are possible in an environment where children feel secure with one another.

The following short descriptions are of seven children who were successful players of bridging roles in K2. They represent some of the possible styles of cross-sex accommodation that occurred in the group but by no means exhaust them.

As the bridging-girl par excellence, Michelle combined a tomboy sturdiness with an attractive, open personality. She could take part in the rough and tumble play of the boys or the quieter domestic play of the girls as it pleased her. Secure in the affection of Jonathan and Bruce, and protected by them, she moved effortlessly through her days at school, making her attachments to boys seem both easy and desirable.

Andrea's cross-sex interests were more narrowly defined, but they formed another successful bridge between the worlds of the boys and the girls. Not for her the bear-cub wrestles or the blue jeans of a tomboy like Michelle. Concentrating on romance and courtship, she was busy bringing presents of gum and pennies for her new conquest, wearing her prettiest clothes for him, and figuring out ways to involve him in her romantic schemes. We noted that the other children enjoyed these fantasy plays, which provided an early but safe look at the allurements and cliches of romantic attachment.

Maureen exploited yet another strand of the complex ties between the boys and girls. The most loving and maternal child in the group, she bridged the differences between the sexes with an unfailing supply of affectionate words, gestures, and smiles, which the boys accepted as unself-consciously as they did the pleasures of a sunny day.

After her turn at holding the visiting baby brother, Maureen says to Andrea, "I hugged him and I kissed him like this," and she kisses Bruce, who is now holding the baby. Bruce accepts the kiss on his cheek without comment, while Maureen and Andrea smile at each other over his head.

Among the boys, Bruce and Jonathan showed the widest range of bridging skills. They were affectionate and protective, particularly with Michelle, but they also played the courtship game with gusto. As large, sturdy boys, they were interested in traditional boy activities, yet they were also genuinely interested in the activities of the girls.

As one of the girls demonstrates her newly acquired skill at knitting, Bruce and Jonathan lie on the floor watching. Bruce asks in a tone of some awe, "How did you learn to do it?"

Michael, even as a newcomer, jumped into the cross-sex games with enthusiasm. As we saw, he played the role of Prince Charming in Andrea's romance, but his attachments were broader than this. He combined unmistakable macho ways with an open liking for girls, which many of them reciprocated. Although it was his first year in the group, he established himself as a hearty fellow with both the boys and the girls, and did nothing to subvert the nonsexist atmosphere of the class despite his tough-guy masculinity.

Finally, among the bridging boys, Marcus played a more gentle but just as significant role in establishing a positive cross-sex atmosphere for K2. As the affectionate brother of a younger sister he often initiated light-hearted, brotherly kinds of play with the girls. In a typical instance he and Kate spent a happy half hour changing each other and anyone else they encountered into green mushrooms; in another, where he was seen marching with a friend, he explained away the stick "guns" they were carrying:

"We're not Baddies. We're guards, really. We're guarding Andrea 'cause she's the queen."

Summary for K2

In K2, boys and girls treated each other with virtually twice as much positive as negative behavior. In such a group one would expect that both sexes would show fewer signs of stress than we encountered in K1, where negative input, particularly toward the girls, was very high.

To this observer the boys of K2 appeared to be less anxious and self-protective than those of K1. They were less critical of one another, their play options were less stereotyped, and they brought zest to a wider range of activities that included both boys and girls. The greater difference in security level, however, lay with the girls. There was far greater freedom and spontaneity in the behavior of the girls of K2, who, unlike those of K1, were free to play or sit or rest where, how, and with whom they pleased. Significantly, when teachers addressed questions to the whole group these girls answered as freely and as frequently as the boys. In their freedom from rejection and domination by the boys, they generated very little negative interaction among themselves. Their low negative ratio in Girl-to-Girl interaction reflects simply the lower aggressivity of girls and is not, as we suggested with K1, artificially high from the displacement of negative effect.

KINDERGARTEN 3

We turn now to the first of our kindergarten-first-grade classes, the one designated as K3 in Table 17.2. Its open-classroom format provided opportunities for free choice of activities and partners and was made possible by the use of parents as teacher-aides. The teacher was a young man who was experienced in this somewhat unusual form of classroom organization, which entailed the daily use of four or five parent helpers.

Of the thirty children of the class, sixteen were boys. The kindergarten was the larger group, with ten boys and nine girls; six boys and five girls made up the first grade. All were from white, middle-class families not unlike those of K1 and K2.

Most of the first graders had been together the year before. This, in addition to their greater maturity and their full-day attendance (as opposed to half-day for the kindergarteners) gave them a sense of themselves as an in-group. They set the tone as far as general classroom decorum went, modeling the role of involved and cooperative students for the younger children, but they were too few and too lacking in consensus to prevail in the area of boy-girl interactions. As we shall see, members of the large incoming kindergarten class developed their own patterns of cross-sex behavior into which one or two first-grade boys were drawn.

Returning briefly to the ratios of Table 17.1, we are reminded that in cross-sex interactions K3 was considerably more sexist than K2 and K4, although less so that K1. Like K1 however, its boys generated far more negative behavior to girls (some 14 times more) than the girls returned, and they gave more negative behavior to girls than they did to their fellow boys by a ratio of 3 to 1. As with K1, the girls of K3 also showed a similar, if smaller, displacement factor in the elevation of the ratio for Girl-to-Girl negativity.

Despite the difference in scale, the results from the girls' point-of-view were similar. Whether they were kindergarteners or first graders the girls of K3 suffered exclusion from at least one of the choice areas of the classroom. They showed diminished responsiveness in question periods and lower spontaneity in whole-group activities, just as the girls of K1 did.

The favored sitting place in the room, for example, was a large, comfortable couch at the edge of the rug area. During whole group gatherings the boys preempted the couch to the almost total exclusion of girls, who used it freely only during work periods when they were not in competition with the boys. Similarly, when line-ups for various activities were announced, the boys were five times more likely to occupy the first third of a line than girls were. The boys of K3 did not blanket the verbal scene as thoroughly as those of K1, but they answered questions put by the teacher twice as often as did the girls.

Quite striking, though unquantifiable, was the disappearance of the girls' spontaneity, the suppression of their laughter and lightness, when they moved from all-girl to mixed-sex groups. Girls' contributions during sharing time, unlike those of the boys, were given in the smallest of voices and often accompanied by lowered eyes or shy glances to a friend or the teacher for support.

Seating and association choices were a good index of the division between the sexes. More than 60% of these were exclusively with same-sex partners, as only two girls and three boys broke through the pattern of segregation to assert a preference for cross-sex association. One kindergarten boy, Terry, often played with the girls; one kindergarten girl, Patricia, would occasionally sit with boys she had known at nursery school. Another kindergarten girl, Heidi, who was the butt of much hostility from some of the boys, became the friend of two otherwise unconnected first-grade boys.

K3 differed most significantly from K1 in that only a small group of boys actively contributed to the sexist atmosphere. Although they were a somewhat noisy and visible bunch in classroom affairs this group of five boys was not strong enough to impose a sexist code on the whole group of sixteen. Four of them were only kindergarteners, and coming in as newcomers they lacked cohesion. Whatever their success in creating an atmosphere that intimidated the girls, they lacked the clout to set an overall tone of discrimination like that of K1.

As one might suppose, their targets were fellow kindergarteners, and for the period under observation they had narrowed it down to four or five girls who had in common only what seemed to be a total harmlessness.

Heidi, for example, who received the most negative attention, was a waifish but appealing child who remained quite spirited in the face of ongoing harassment. It was she who was the friend of the two first-grade boys, one of whom she joined at recess/snack time for a sharing of treats brought from home. Whether it was these friendships that some of the boys found unsettling, or her independent spirit, is difficult to say. Whatever it was, she, like Jill of K1, pulled down most of the negative reaction. Of the other three girls there was even less that was exceptionable. At most, one appeared to be somewhat awkward, another shy, and the third very gentle.

As we noted, most of the children of K3 dealt with cross-sex differences by separation, essentially staying out of each other's way. The group of boys responsible for sexist or harassing behavior reversed this strategy, and like the boys of K1 when they were intent on being Baddies, these lads appeared to go out of their way to engage themselves with girls, albeit negatively.

Of the boys who contributed to the picture of cross-sex negativity, Terry's input was the least threatening. Although he played with groups of girls most of the time, he spent much of that time mildly teasing. When a group of kindergarten girls would go off to build blocks or draw pictures Terry would often be among them, hiding the blocks or magic markers, snatching their papers and holding them out of reach. Generally his teasing was good-natured, a nuisance that the girls had no reason to fear except when he was drawn into more aggressive behavior by other boys.

Douglas was as preoccupied with girls as Terry, although his behavior was not meant to tease but to intimidate. He rarely missed a chance to kick out at the targeted kindergarten girls when they passed his chair. If he encountered one in passing he would make mocking faces or threatening gestures at her. Heidi was his particular bête noire, and it became clear when he spoke of his coming birthday party that his conflicted acquaintance with her went beyond school.

> Sitting at a table with a group of boys, with Heidi sitting across the way, Douglas holds his nose and says disgustedly, "Heidi's gonna be there." He explains that because her mother had phoned his, he *had* to invite Heidi. Raymond, Heidi's special snack-time friend, says mildly, "I'm gonna be there, Douglas." With exaggerated relief Douglas says, "Okay, you're the only one that can blow the wind away," indicating by holding his nose that the bad smell from Heidi will have to be blown away. Heidi sits impassively, working on a drawing. When Douglas sees her looking at his picture he makes a face at her and holds it so she cannot see it. Raymond says with some satisfaction, "Heidi saw the back!" Douglas responds, "Who cares?"

It was not only Heidi and the other kindergarten girls that Douglas found offensive. Significantly, he also rejected Terry.

When Terry stands behind his chair Douglas says loudly, "Get outta here, Herve! You stink! Get outta here, you stink!" He holds his nose dramatically and, as Terry moves to another table, he announces to the boys around him, "Stink's outta here now!"

Like Douglas, Joshua and Gary also had trouble leaving the girls alone, but where he was threatening, they were more mischievous in their teasing. They contributed their share of fingers poked at the girls' eyes, however, and admitted that they chased the girls "to scare them." Something of this comes through in the following episode:

The scene is the playground during recess and snack time. Four kindergarten girls and Terry are sitting on the blacktop with their lunch boxes open in front of them. In the background one of the mother aides is reciting from a book of rhymes as six girls and two boys take turns jumping rope. Joshua and Gary run mischievously at the group and jump over Janice's lunch box. The girls close up the circle. When the boys do it again, and then again, Patricia stands up and says firmly, "I don't want you guys doin' that. It's not fun for us!" Terry adds, "Yeah, you fucka!" He gets up and chases after Joshua and Gary who kick at each other and laugh. Terry returns to the circle and sits down, saying "I really chased him! I really got 'im!" He gets up and goes back to running after the boys, and then all return to the girls' circle. Joshua jumps over Janice's lunch box. Terry is excited and he shouts, "Now do it at her!" Joshua jumps again, then chases Terry and on his return kicks the lunch box. Janice stands up and laughs unconvincingly. Then she kicks her own lunch box and tells the girls, "I like to kick lunch boxes." Joshua comes back and stands with his feet on the sides of the open box, bending the metal. He looks triumphant. Janice comes over to where I am standing. She moves in very close. I say, "You need a little protection?" She huddles and says unhappily, "Just because Joshua kicks my lunch box and . . ." Her words trail off. I say, "Why don't you tell Joshua you don't like it?" Joshua has come up by now and hears her small defeated statement, " 'Cause boys don't listen to girls." Joshua says loudly, "Yeah, 'cause boys hate girls, that's why!" Terry and Gary both push at Janice, who cringes against me. Nearby, the aide reads out the counting rhymes to the jumpers: "I like coffee, I like tea. How many boys are crazy for me . . ."

Dependency

With the two previous groups, dependency rejection by the boys was associated with the down-grading of girls and not with sexual egalitarianism. For K3 there is little evidence upon which to make such a judgment. Babies and animals were not part of the scene, nor were there rest periods that might encourage regressive behavior. The occasional chance to sit on the teacher's lap or the privilege of joining one's own mother when she was there as an aide were the only visible concessions to dependency. Whatever the needs of the children in this area, they were deemed by adults and children alike to be inappropriate for school.

Courtship Games

Chasing and courtship games also took a different turn in this group, where they were more traditionally defined or controlled by adults. As we have seen, both boys and girls jumped rope, and thanks to the rhymes taught by the adults the activity carried messages of conventional boy-girl attraction. In a similar way, one boy's chasing of girls held elements of aggressiveness that were not always welcome but they were reinterpreted for him in positive terms. When he came up breathlessly from such a pursuit he reported, "I used to chase Peggy, now I like to scare Beth!" The aide defined it conventionally for him, "Is she your girl friend? 'Cause you chase her?" But the boy ran off without responding.

On another day the older girls brought perfume to the classroom intending to confront the boys with it. They showed it first to their teacher and asked him to smell it on their wrists. He told them firmly to put it away or have it confiscated for the day, thus short-circuiting the girls' plans to use it in a boy-girl chase.

Summary of K3

In its cross-sex behavioral profile, K3 was more like K1, showing a much higher ratio of negative to positive responses from boys to girls than either K2 or K4. Its chief difference from K1 was that the boys' anti-girl behavior was not an established feature of group culture, but rather the work of a small number of boys. This group targeted the more vulnerable of the kindergarten girls for their negative attentions, which appeared to have a conflicted base of attraction and rejection.

The girls of the class showed some of the same patterns of repression as the girls of K1, including their muted contributions in whole group discussion. They confined spontaneity to all-girl situations, and like the girls of K1 their ratio of negative to positive responses within the girl group was somewhat elevated, although less dramatically than that for K1.

There were no apparent ties between the sexist behavior of the boys and dependency concerns, and the role of courtship-type attractions was blurred by adult presence and definitions.

KINDERGARTEN 4

Like the previous group, K4 was a combined kindergarten-first grade with roughly twice as many kindergarten as first-grade children. Despite its having almost twice as many boys as girls, the children of K4 matched or bettered even those of K2 for nonsexist behavior. In its percentage of children who knew each other well from previous nursery or school experience K4 surpassed all the preceding groups. At the beginning of the year only five of the twenty-three had come in as strangers. Most of the children who made up the core group had been at the same school for at least 2 years and many of them had attended the school's extended day-care program or summer camp.

The word *family* comes to mind to categorize the relations among these children. There were in fact two sets of real brothers in the group and half a dozen whose parents were friends or colleagues, but for the majority it was the shared and extensive school experiences that had created family-like bonds among them. Being with each other from 9 to 3 throughout several school years, sharing lunch and nap times as well as long, leisurely play periods, some of them indeed saw more of each other than of their own real siblings.

The children themselves were aware of the close feelings they had for their classmates. A parent reported that her son had surprised her one night by saying that he hated girls. Her reply was one of disbelief: "Come on, you're always telling me how much you like Carla and Nina and Sally" (naming girls in his class). "What's this 'I hate girls' stuff?" He answered in all seriousness, "Oh, not them, they're my sisters."

With this family feeling went a great tolerance, particularly for those idiosyncracies that might reflect immaturity. Eight of the core group for example unabashedly sucked their thumbs at rest or story times, a form of regression that children of the other groups rarely if ever permitted themselves at school. They were patient with one of the kindergarten boys who cried rather noisily over minor hurts, and none of them blinked to see some of the older boys playing *house* or animal family with the kindergarteners. When Barry, a competent and popular boy, asked a male teacher to tie his shoe, the teacher demurred, saying that he found it hard to believe that Barry couldn't tie his own shoe. A chorus of friendly voices from his classmates assured the teacher that indeed Barry couldn't. They were not taunting, simply reporting an interesting fact.

As one might expect, this tolerance did not extend to those who mistreated one of their own. In an incident where a new boy knocked a child off her perch on a pole,

> Edward yells at him, "Stop that! She can be on it if she wants to!" A bit later, Bart comments, "I hate him for what he did to Sally," and Benjy concurs, "Me too!"

They showed affection for each other in many ways. Girls and boys leaned companionably against one another when they listened to a story. More exuberantly, they lifted each other off the floor, or patted or hugged one another when they were assigned to work with favorite friends. In shop they were quick to help when a classmate needed an extra pair of hands; in the classroom they were generous in their appreciation of another's stories or art work.

> Clifton hands his journal to Lewis, who reads the story Clifton has written and smiles his appreciation. Clifton, watching for his reaction, smiles and says, "I told you you'd like it!"

The sheer number and variety of friendships in K4 was impressive, as was the fact that as many involved cross-sex as same-sex pairings. Although each child seemed to have someone who was a favorite friend there were no two-somes that were totally exclusive. Barry and Carla for instance had been best friends from the age of three, yet each also had a number of other good friends of both sexes. John and Jim were similarly close, yet both were affectionate with Nina and Sally, and often teamed up with other boys, and Carla, for play.

Even the most tightly bonded group, that of the three first-grade girls, did not exclude others. So long as they could be together, these three were happy to include their classmate Clifton as a kind of perennial suitor-satellite, and they reached out as well to include younger children at reading or play time.

For the newcomers this openness was a help, for although two of them suffered some rejection at the start, all five gradually worked their way into full acceptance over the course of the year. One suspects that this was as much a matter of acculturation on their part as it was gradual acceptance by the majority. An incident from early in the fall term shows how the core group communicated its values to a new boy who was starting off with a more sexist view of boy-girl relationships than suited them.

> At a table where four boys and two girls are building with Lego blocks, Charles is the new boy. He looks across at Carla and Sally and says, "Girls aren't allowed at this table with boys." Barry, building a tower with Carla, says earnestly, "I really want Carla here!" Inexperienced with such grounds for exclusion, Carla reads it as age discrimination and says stoutly,

"I'm five and a quarter!" The talk turns to age and they compare their ages. Charles, commenting on Barry and Carla's construction says, "That looks more like a monkey cage." Barry responds placidly, "You look more like a monkey cage." Sally, harking back to the earlier issue, says "Anyway, there are *two* girls here." Eric, looking to add some mischief says, "No, you mean there are *three* girls here. Charles is a girl." They all laugh, including Charles. Benjy chimes in, "No, calm down. *Barry's* a girl." They laugh again. Barry makes a silly face at Benjy, then he and Carla chat as they build. Eric says, "I have a great joke!" and the rest of the period is spent in building and telling jokes.

The joke telling in this last episode was not an isolated occurrence, for jokes, puns, and humorous sallies were a favorite currency in their dealings with one another. Many a sharing time was spent in telling old "knock knock" jokes or updated versions of "Why did the chicken cross the road?" but verbal play was also a part of even the most casual comments.

In shop, Carla says, "I'm makin' a ruler." Barry, "To rule your house?" He laughs and adds, "I like to make jokes. It's a pun, actually." Then he asks if she knows what a pun is. Carla, "Yes." Barry explains anyway.

In another episode Betsy, the new kindergarten girl, uses humor skillfully in dealing with one of the older boys.

She comes into shop with a smile and says "Here I am!" to the teacher. She walks over to Lewis, who announces to the group at large that he is making a bath tub. Betsy smiles and comments dryly, "It's a *bath tub* he wants to make!" managing a bit of flattery laced with humor. This is not lost on Lewis, who smiles back at her.

To this mix of affection, tolerance and humor, bred in long association with each other, the children of K4 also brought the kinds of interpersonal skills that we encountered in K2. They too had been schooled in communicating their wants or needs to one another and were similarly used to resolving differences by talking them out. With such a battery of positive attitudes and social skills it is little wonder that the boys and girls of K4 created a benign environment for themselves, where positive responses significantly outweighed negative ones in three out of four of our categories of interaction.

In the area of boy-girl interaction we see not only the absence of sexism, but its very opposite, for which, perhaps unfortunately, we have no comparable term. The boys of K4 gave more than twice as many positive responses to the girls as they did negative ones. They were like K2 in this, only more so. K4 boys appeared to see themselves as protectors and helpers of the girls, and the girls of their class reciprocated with more positive responses to them than even the girls of K2 generated.

Boys and girls chose to sit, or play, or work with one another more than they chose to be in same-sex groups. Girls took part in all the outdoor activities that boys did, and a couple of them matched the best of the boys in team sports. They spoke out in group gatherings, answering questions as freely as the boys. They used all parts of the room and its equipment without interference. Boys listened with interest when girls spoke, even paying attention to the new girl, Betsy, who was initially very diffident.

Although the ambience of both K2 and K4 was egalitarian and nonsexist, each group had its own distinctive pattern for achieving it. For K4, protectiveness, affection, helpfulness, and mutual respect made up most of the spectrum of positive behavior, while the children of K2 had put together a possibly more robust mix that included respect and liking but also overt heterosexual attraction as well.

The courtship games and chases of K2 were almost nonexistent in K4, perhaps because the strong family feeling among the children muted or even precluded expression of cross-sex interest. They played games of chase almost daily, but little of it could be described as (in the words of a K2 boy) "something between the girls and the boys." They were comfortable with each other in a broad range of activities, including for some of them playing mother and father, but apparently not in playing at boyfriend and girlfriend. It is interesting that what little of this there was, emerged late in the year and involved would-be liaisons with Betsy, the new girl.

The children of both nonsexist groups appeared to be comfortable with aspects of dependency and immaturity, with K4 perhaps even more so than K2, given the number in that group who sucked their thumbs. Babies or small children appeared to be as welcome in the one group as in the other. As a parallel to the little brother who was enjoyed in K2, the baby sister of one of the older girls in K4 often visited and was affectionately welcomed by both girls and boys.

A description of K4 would not be complete without a brief look at the individual children who played a key role in establishing its non-sexist atmosphere. The children who most successfully played bridging roles, like their counterparts in K2, were all popular among their classmates.

Of the girls, Carla had far and away the most cross-sex ties, more than double the average for all the girls. Her ease with the boys of the class was extraordinary. Bright, athletic, and forthright, there was no game she could not play nor any group that was not glad to have her. In sharing time she spoke up clearly, with suggestions that were usually fair and well thought out. They were often taken up and acted on by the others. Although on good terms with the girls in the class, she usually chose to sit or play with the boys.

Sally was also a universal favorite but, unlike Carla, she played or sat with girls as often as with boys. She was young and appealing, and the others watched out for her interests and welcomed her as a partner. She had a number of favorites among the boys, but for several months she and George, a first grader, had a special relationship in which they played rather gentle games at her level. Her special position in the class was expressed by the delight with which one of the new boys greeted the news that he and Sally were to be partners. "Oh," he said happily, "Me and Sally!" as he ran to join her.

Of the boys, Barry and Clifton played bridging roles significantly more than the others, Barry with his friendship for Carla, Clifton with his attachment to the three first-grade girls. Barry was something of a leader among the kindergarten boys, and his open preference for Carla's company did nothing to undermine his position. Clifton, quieter and more introspective, related without difficulty to the other first-grade boys but just quietly preferred to be near the first-grade girls much of the time.

These four children accounted for at least a third of the cross-sex choices that were made by the whole class, and because of their general popularity they contributed substantially to the positive feeling that each sex had for the other.

Summary

We are left to summarize what was a very benign set of interactions, and a design for cross-sex accommodation that was impressively free of dominance and hostility. The model for K4 was that of a family of affectionate siblings. Overall, far more positive than negative behavior marked their interchanges, but the excess of positive response was most apparent in the behavior of the boys to the girls. Here the protectiveness, affection and goodwill of the boys created a totally non-threatening environment for the girls. In turn the girls responded with warmth and attachment to the boys, and over the period of observation, without a single recorded incident of negative behavior among themselves.

K2 and K4 were alike in having little or no sexist behavior, as well as in their tolerance for dependency, but they differed in the amount of explicit boy-girl attraction that they displayed. By virtue of its family feeling, K4 exhibited little of the incipient courtship behavior that was a conspicuous feature of K2.

ANALYSIS AND CONCLUSION

Several of the questions raised in the introduction have been answered in the review of our four groups. We have seen some of the forms that antifeminism may take among 5- and 6-year-olds, from the culturally sanctioned "I hate girls" to various kinds of put-downs and attempts at intimidation. In our data, sexist attitudes and behaviors also appear to be linked to rudimentary differences in power and privilege between boys and girls at the kindergarten level.

More importantly, we have found that sexist behaviors adversely affect the feelings and performance of girls. In a classroom dominated by sexist attitudes, girls answer fewer questions; they are more timid, and far less spontaneous in what they say and do. Where sexism is severe, as with K1, some girls react with signs of anxiety and depression.

We would predict reactions like these if the target of the negative behavior were children of another race. The curious thing is that we shield ourselves from knowledge of such consequences when sexism rather than racism is involved. Like the mothers in K3, we say of boys' harassment, "It shows he really likes you" or we dismiss it with "Boys will be boys." With the former, we may be contributing to a false and damaging linkage between mistreatment and love; with the latter we accept sexist behavior as inevitable.

That sexism is not inevitable, at least at the kindergarten level, is the most promising finding of the current study. It is always there as a latent possibility, thanks to the greater aggressiveness of boys and the emotional vulnerability inherent in masculine gender identification, yet we need not expect it inevitably to appear. The boys of K2 and K4, with their affectionate regard for the girls in their class, demonstrated other and more benign possibilities.

How are we to account for such differences as we have found in the groups studied? An easy assumption would be that a significant number of boys in K1 and K3, for various personal reasons, were simply more prone to sexism than those of the other two groups. One could plausibly argue that certain cultural or psychological differences in their backgrounds predisposed them to greater sexism, or equally, that they were experiencing greater stress in their personal lives outside of school and taking out their frustration on the girls. We would then have to assume that such factors were absent in the boys of K2 and K4. Unfortunately, there is no way within the framework of the present study to evaluate or rule out these possibilities. On the other hand, certain aspects of the data, as well as a bias in favor of contextual explanation, encourage us to look beyond them for other kinds of contributing factors.

Against the circular argument that the boys acted the way they did because that was the way they were, is our observation that even the most misogynous of them were not always and everywhere so. Even a group of K1 boys protectively rescued a tearful 4-year-old girl and returned her to her teacher, hovering around as she regained her composure and returning later to see that she was all right. We know that these same boys were pleased to accept Wendy in her first month at school and, for this while at least, exempted her from sexist treatment. In K3, even Douglas, who aimed kicks at the other kindergarten girls, did not pick on Patricia, whose self-confidence was unassailable. None of the kindergarten boys in that group, moreover, directed negative behavior toward the first-grade girls.

That girls of higher status or out-of-the-ordinary toughness or self-respect do not suffer sexist treatment is easy enough to understand. Superior power or prestige are known to discourage discrimination at any level of encounter. But again, opting for a situational rather than a characterological explanation, we must remind ourselves that the girls of K2 and K4 were not uniformly of higher status or tougher mien, yet none of them were subjected to sexist put-downs in their groups. Why should vulnerability in one context elicit protectiveness and in another bring on harassment? Or how was it that the same girl could go from acceptance to rejection in just a few weeks? We have already indicated that to answer questions like these we need to examine more closely the background feature that most clearly differentiates our two nonsexist groups from the others, that is, the extent to which the children knew each other before entering kindergarten.

In Table 17.2, we saw that the two groups with the least sexism had the most substantial core of well-acquainted children. Where more than half of both sexes had been together in nursery school for a year or longer there was an associated reduction in negative cross-sex behavior.[11]

The nonsexist cultures of K2 and K4 did not spring up overnight; they were the product of a long previous association in nursery school. Built into them was a rich mixture of cross-sex interactions going back to when some of the children were barely three. In the school's daily 9-to-3 nursery program boys and girls played, ate, napped, toileted, worked, and joked together much as members of a family would. They had seen each other in intimate and vulnerable situations and had learned to support and trust one another; they were not threatened by the disclosure of dependency, nor did they need to deny cross-sex friendships they had

---

[11]The work of Doyle, Connolly, and Rivest (1980) points to peer familiarity as a salient variable in children's play, while the study of Lamb, Easterbrooks, and Holden (1980) points to peers as important influences on the development of sex-stereotyped behavior in preschoolers.

formed. The boys continued to be comfortable with the nurturing behavior of girls that they had first experienced as 3-year-olds. The girls were unintimidated by the rough and tumble play of the boys, which they had learned they could join or sidestep on their own terms.

The cultures set in motion within these earlier experiences were strong enough to absorb newcomers as they came along. Whatever their own psychic bents or needs, the children who joined later took on the prevailing nonsexist cultural ways, in a process made easier by the tolerance that was also part of the ethos of both groups.

With K1 there was no such preexisting culture of accommodation. The four boys who had been in the nursery school had experienced the intimacy and sharing we have described, but the girls with whom they had interacted as 3- or 4-year-olds had either left the school or were still in one of the younger groups. When they came together in kindergarten, the most important thing the four of them had in common was their identity as boys, and this was what they fell back upon. When the new boys looked to this small group of "old hands" for leadership, they responded with a bluff of the most macho behavior they could command, thus setting the sexist course of the year in motion.

Playing to one another as audience, these boys increasingly isolated themselves from the girls, whom they saw as an alien lot, and then worked to find rationalizations for rejecting them. They knew other more positive ways of behaving, as we have seen, but these ways were cognitively dissonant within the snowballing Macho culture, and they could not sustain them in the classroom. The brief acceptance of Wendy in the middle of the year was followed by a crashing rejection as they returned to their earlier, full-blown, sexist stance.

There were heady rewards for the boys in playing out the full macho scenario. The pleasure of exercising power and seeing themselves as superior, as well as the reassurance of close bonding with one another, provided enough positive reinforcement to override any latent sympathy they might feel for the girls or any guilt that the teachers might appeal to. The costs to the boys themselves were obvious only to the adults who were monitoring the scene. Among these would have to be counted the blunting of their capacity for empathy, the narrowing of their experience and the frequent use of shame to control one another's behavior.[12]

Analysis of our three private school groups thus suggests that sexism is more likely to emerge as an organizing principle of a kindergarten in the absence of a prior sense of community. Unfortunately it is rare for

---

[12]In a work devoted to the study of sexism among older children, Raphaela Best (1983) argues that a strong sexist ethos in the classroom may be associated not only with strictures such as these but also with the reading difficulties suffered by some boys in the middle elementary grades.

children in our society to experience the kind of community we have been describing. Few of them come from small, stable, social worlds, fewer still move from nursery school to primary grades with the same cohort of friends. The more common experience is like that of K3, where of the nineteen kindergarteners only a small handful had had even a limited nursery school acquaintance. For this reason the picture that K3 presents (despite its unusual concentration of supervising adults) is a much more likely one than those of our three private school groups.

The new and the strange provoke insecurity at any level, but for children at the age of five the start of formal schooling may be particularly stressful. In the average kindergarten, children who find themselves among strangers react by retreating to the familiar haven of same-sex groupings. Unfortunately such withdrawal fosters polarization and as they increasingly draw apart girls become stereotypically more girlish and boys more boyish, thus consolidating their views of each other as different and potentially threatening. The boys find it easier to identify the girls with the dependency they are trying to leave behind, as well as with precocious heterosexual interests they are not ready for. The girls, for their part, are threatened by the boys' exaggeratedly rough and boisterous ways. When polarization has reached such a point, talents and interests that might serve a cross-sex bridging function themselves come under attack on sexist grounds.

Yet we have seen in all the groups that boys and girls are drawn to one another. What is the outcome of such attraction when so much uneasiness prevails among them? Judging by what we observed in K3 the girls and the shyer boys hold back from expressing their interest, leaving the initiative largely to the more aggressive boys. The emergent pattern then becomes the familiar one of unprovoked harassment practiced by Douglas, Terry, and their friends in K3. Under the protection of an "I hate girls" formula, these more aggressive boys bully the girls and disguise their ambivalence toward them at the same time.

Conclusion

The contrasts we have found among our groups allow us to isolate two polar organizing principles for cross-sex interaction. The first, characteristic of the nonsexist groups, is based on the possibility of a gradual development of complementary relationships through time. It is a mode of organization that allows for the orderly fitting together of emerging differences between the sexes, within the larger context of what we have called their common human agenda. It is the thesis of this paper that where such organic development is possible boys and girls provide each other with a richer and more fully human base of experience from which to work out their common problems of dependency, sexual identity and heterosexual attraction. Freedom from cross-sex tension and hostility ideally allows them to get on comfortably with the developmental tasks that lie before them.

Using this mode as the baseline, we see that as an organizing principle sexism comes off as a stress-related distortion[13] that interferes with the natural processes of growth, rather than enhancing them. The results, as we saw with K1, are like those of sexist or authoritarian societies everywhere, wherever males try to shore up a shaky sense of sexual identity at the expense of females. When boys or men use their greater aggressiveness to create a ghetto of restraints and subservience for girls or women, both sexes suffer a loss of full human potential. Even at the kindergarten level, we are reminded that when the latent possibilities of sexism and dominance become the realities of social life, they provide a poor climate for growth.

REFERENCES

Best, R. (1983). *We've all got scars: What boys and girls learn in elementary school.* Bloomington: Indiana University Press.

Blakemore, J. E. O. (1981). Age and sex differences in interaction with a human infant. *Child Development, 52,* 386–388.

Block, J. H. (1983). Differential premises arising from differential socialization of the sexes: Some conjectures. *Child Development, 54,* 1335–1354.

Borman, K. (1978). Social control and schooling: Power and process in two kindergarten settings. *Anthropology and Education, 9,* 38–53.

Chodorow, N. (1978). *The reproduction of mothering: Psychoanalysis and the sociology of gender.* Berkeley: University of California Press.

Doyle, A. B., Connolly, J., & Rivest, L. (1980). The effect of playmate familiarity on the social interaction of young children. *Child Development, 51,* 217–223.

Lamb, M., Easterbrooks, M., & Holden, G. (1980). Reinforcement and punishment among pre-schoolers: Characteristics, effects and correlates. *Child Development, 51,* 1230–1236.

Maccoby, E. E., & Jacklin, C. N. (1974). *The psychology of sex differences.* Stanford, CA: Stanford University Press.

Paley, V. (1984). *Boys and girls: Superheroes in the doll corner.* Chicago: University of Chicago Press.

Pitcher, E. G., & Schultz, L. H. (1983). *Boys and girls at play: The development of sex roles.* New York: Praeger.

Shultz, J., & Florio, S. (1979). Stop and freeze: The negotiation of social and political space in a kindergarten/first grade classroom. *Anthropology and Education Quarterly, 10,* 166–181.

Stoller, R. J. (1974). *Sex and gender.* New York: Jason Aronson.

---

[13]Not unlike that which crops up in later life under some of the same kinds of stress, as with the anti-coed sentiments of young college men or the sexist barracks humor of new recruits.

The Author and Her Chapter

Reba Neukom Page is assistant professor in education at Bowdoin College. She has a Ph.D. in curriculum and instruction from Wisconsin, an M.L.A. in literature from The Johns Hopkins University, a B.A. in history from Washington University in St. Louis, and secondary school teaching credentials in English, history, and special education. She was a participant in the training seminar in the ethnography of schooling conducted at Wisconsin by the Spindlers. For 8 years prior to her work at the UW-Madison, Page taught English and history to academically unsuccessful and emotionally disturbed adolescents in public high schools and at a large state mental hospital. The teaching experience generated and reflects her interest in the interrelated processes of curriculum and social differentiation.

Combining concepts from social interactionism, language analysis, organizational analysis, and cultural anthropology, Page describes how people in one largely college-preparatory high school construct educational meanings about what a lower track student, teacher, and curriculum are. They draw on stable, even formulaic themes of differentiation, membership, and the social order provided by educational institutions and the wider culture. The result is a chaotic, desultory classroom that is a prime expression of the ambivalence these lower track students hold about school. The situation is made particularly dramatic because these students are not characteristically minority or lower class youths.

She couples a microanalysis of classroom interactions and language with a broader ethnographic analysis of the contexts within which local communication is meaningful. Her perspective implies the possibility of

445

practical school reform. The utility of interpretive ethnography, embodying the anthropologist's focus on specific contexts, but applying theoretical perspectives in analysis, seems apparent. Dr. Page's dissertation from which this chapter was drawn, received recognition as a "best dissertation" at the annual meetings of the American Education Research Association in San Francisco in 1985.

The Editors

18 Lower-Track Classes at a College-Preparatory High School: A Caricature of Educational Encounters

Reba Page
Bowdoin College

Southmoor High School[1] is one of six, large (2000 students), well-funded, public high schools in the medium-sized, middle-class, midwestern city of Maplehurst. The school enjoys a reputation as an educational institution of excellence. Its buildings are well-equipped, its staff is experienced, its support services are generous, and its curriculum is comprehensive. Students, most of whom are white and middle class, may choose from an array of over 200 courses, ranging from civilization to music theory to welding. This array of courses is officially undifferentiated, formal tracking by ability having been discontinued in the late 1960s. Despite its wide range of courses, Southmoor perceives itself to be and operates as a preeminently academic, college-preparatory institution. Over half the seniors plan to attend 4-year colleges or universities. A large coterie of academically able students regularly wins top honors in state and national competitions, and Southmoor is often ranked with exclusive private schools, rather than with public high schools.

Teachers take pride in the students' academic accomplishments and are credited with contributing to the students' success. Thus, teaching at Southmoor High School is an important and prestigious occupation, perhaps the most important role in the school. The powerful faculty takes seriously its responsibility to run the daily life of the school and preserve thereby a sound tradition of academic excellence. Teachers' enthusiasm for their jobs translates into a seniority system in which "being a teacher

---

[1]All names are pseudonyms.

at Southmoor for 15 years is still to be a newcomer."[2] Teachers stay because, as one remarked, "coming to teach at Southmoor was like arriving in heaven." Students are typified as coming "from upper-middle class, professional families." They make Southmoor "heavenly" because they are "motivated; they are *easy* to teach, *easy* to relate to. You don't have to *work* to relate to them." Most staff members also feel they, themselves, are "treated like professionals. Nobody's running around checking up on you, seeing if you've done your job. Oh, there are a few that are not professionals, even here. But, I mean, no place is *perfect*."

At Southmoor, the "heavenly" ethos, constituted by the institution's definition of its students and its mode of organization (Schlechty, 1976; Waller, 1932), sets parameters within which individual teachers enact their role in classrooms. Despite the diversity produced by different academic disciplines, different ages and enthusiasms of students, and idiosyncratic styles of teaching, the school culture shapes the individual enactment of the teacher's role, and, consequently, the classroom climate, even when the classroom door closes.

Relying on a definition of the student body as high achieving and on organizational features that allow teachers to teach as they, as professionals, deem best, teachers at Southmoor express their right and obligation to be academic experts. They guide "easy-to-teach" students to think critically, broadly, and with enthusiasm about traditional academic subjects which they present as important to students' present and future educational success. As a consequence of teachers' serious and enthusiastic role enactment, the classroom climate in individual courses at Southmoor reflects and re-creates the "perfection" of the institutional culture. It is orderly, but informal, purposive and academically demanding, but also exploratory and spontaneous.

As a public institution, Southmoor draws students with a variety of interests from diverse neighborhoods. The comprehensive curriculum is designed to provide for these differences without partiality. In fact, courses are not all equal, and leveling of students occurs informally, through student choice. Various teachers acknowledged this differentiation of the curriculum and, hence, of the students: "Students earn an English credit whether they elect a *hard* course like Shakespeare or an *easy* course like Sci-Fi." In addition, some curriculum differentiation

---

[2]Quotation marks denote statements by staff members and students in the Maplehurst school district. I also indicate some characteristics of talk, using these symbols: overlapping utterances by [brackets]; short, untimed pauses by —, slightly longer pauses by ———, and timed pauses by (seconds); emphasis by underlining and greater emphasis by *ITALICS*; omissions of parts of quotations by . . .; and descriptions regarding the situation in parentheses.

occurs more formally. Southmoor has students who are not academically successful, who are not economically and culturally advantaged, and who, thus, do not fit the faculty's definition of the typical Southmoor student. Such students, evaluated as having additional needs, are defined as unable to succeed in regular-track courses but ineligible for placement in special education classes. To "meet their individual needs," in 1982–83 Southmoor offered a total of ten Additional Needs classes in English, social studies, math, biology, and distributive education. Approximately seventy-five academically unsuccessful students, mostly freshmen and sophomores, were referred to the program, most at the beginning of the school year, but some during the year. The courses are designed to reduce educational failure and dropout rates by addressing designated students' academic and social needs in smaller classes, using adaptive curricula.

How such academically unsuccessful students fare in this "heavenly" school is an important educational question, raising issues of educational equity and excellence. If Southmoor's regular-track classrooms exhibit so much purpose, academic stimulation, and easy but respectful camaraderie between teacher and students, does a similar atmosphere prevail, with salutary educational results, in the school's few Additional Needs classes? In short, what does academically oriented Southmoor make of its academically unsuccessful students?

To investigate this question, I spent 6 months at Southmoor as an educational ethnographer, observing what classroom participants do and asking what they know that makes their actions understandable (Spindler, 1982).[3] As a participant-observer, I regularly attended five lower-track classes in English or social studies, documenting the ordinary, and sometimes extraordinary, daily life in lower-track classrooms. In particular, I paid attention to the form and content of classroom talk, and the educational relationships between teacher, student, and curricular knowledge reflected and re-created therein. I recorded some of the talk in field notes and some on audiotapes. I also observed teachers and students in regular-track classes. Moreover, to understand their perspectives on classroom events, I interviewed teachers and volunteer students from lower-track classes. I also interviewed staff throughout the high school and the school district to comprehend the wider organizational contexts within which lower-track classrooms operate. Thus, I used three theoretically and methodologically linked strategies—extensive observation, interviews, and microanalysis of talk—to form a holistic analysis of the production of educational meanings in lower-track classrooms at Southmoor.

---

[3] I conducted parallel research during the same period at a second high school in the Maplehurst district for purposes of comparison. See Note 7.

To convey a sense of life in lower-track classrooms at the college-preparatory high school, I begin by describing and analyzing the explicit and implicit principles governing educational and social relationships in one Additional Needs classroom. The classroom climate in the Additional Needs course is wildly chaotic and very different from the relaxed, academic, orderly climate in regular-track classes at Southmoor. In the second section of the essay, I scrutinize the form and content of 3 minutes of talk in an Additional Needs lesson. Using as my unit of analysis the participation structures that teachers establish and direct, I identify the processes through which the chaotic climate is produced by classroom participants. I compare the processes to those in other equally riotous Additional Needs classes and to regular-track classes, and show that the climate is not simply different from that in regular-track classes, but a caricature of regular-track educational encounters. Thus, the informal but purposive relations between students and teachers in regular-track classrooms become ironical and aimless in Additional Needs classes. Finally, in a brief closing section, I relate the production of a differentiated educational climate within Additional Needs classrooms to the teachers' unconscious mediation of the wider culture of the academically-oriented institution. Experiencing conflict as they integrate the Southmoor teacher and the lower-track teacher roles, teachers distance themselves from the lower-track role, mocking themselves, the students, and the educational enterprise in which they are jointly engaged. Significantly, therefore, the chaos in Additional Needs classes at Southmoor cannot be attributed simply to a few obstreperous adolescents or inept or uncaring individual teachers, but is a function of the ethos of an institution which gives educational excellence extraordinary emphasis.

THE DISORDERLY CLIMATE IN CLASSROOMS FOR ACADEMICALLY UNSUCCESSFUL STUDENTS

Teachers and support staff cite a constellation of student traits to explain the chaos in Additional Needs classes. The enunciation of characteristics begins educationally: Lower-track students "lack basic skills," "are close to illiterate," or "are frustrated and can't make it academically." The litany then moves to social history. Additional Needs students have "poor family backgrounds," "are from single-parent homes," or "have nobody who gives a damn about them at home." Most adamantly, staff members insist that students are "behavior problems." They exhibit a pattern of truancy, "off-the-wall" actions in class, or discipline problems of theft, drugs, or fighting. The order and emphasis of the characterization reflect teachers' overriding concern with controlling, not educating, lower-track students.

A similar constellation is used to characterize lower-track students in other schools (Keddie, 1971; Rist, 1973), and a similarly chaotic classroom climate has been described (Furlong, 1977; Hargreaves, 1967; Hargreaves, Hester, & Mellors, 1975; Lacey, 1970; Leacock, 1969; McDermott & Aron, 1978; Metz, 1978; Schwartz, 1981; Willis, 1977). However, unlike most lower-track students described in the literature, Southmoor's academically unsuccessful students are not grossly underskilled, uniformly impoverished, or isolated from the mainstream culture. Instead, they demonstrate a wide range of academic skills, with most exhibiting middle-school proficiencies in reading and math. Lower-track classrooms include many students from middle-class families, and even a few from "upper middle-class, professional families," as well as students from working-class families. Minority students are overrepresented in Additional Needs classes, but because minority students constitute only 10% of the student body, few classes are noticeably segregated racially. (In two lower-track classes, nonetheless, minority students make up over half the students.) Lower-track students at Southmoor are like those described in the literature, and unlike their regular-track peers, in their fundamental ambivalence toward schooling (see Metz, 1983). They underscore the importance of a high school diploma, but feel that school is "so boring." Most want to get better grades, but express considerable insecurity about their ability to learn. Because of their ambivalence, the institution's definition and treatment of lower-track students becomes crucial.

Thus, at Southmoor, Additional Needs students do present some differences from white, affluent, college-bound students. Moreover, the staff perceives that they are troublesome anomalies that challenge the prevailing definitions of Southmoor's student body, its methods, and its general purpose as a college-preparatory high school. The concomitant challenge presented by academically unsuccessful students to teachers' definitions of themselves is met by putting them off the scale, "at the bottom" of an educational hierarchy. Adults describe lower-track students as "your, you know, your basic bottom." They are "the dregs," both intellectually and behaviorally. Worse yet, this educational hierarchy is nearly permanent: to enter Southmoor as an academically unsuccessful student is not simply to be different from the majority of the students, but to be irremediably different.

This extremely negative perception of academically unsuccessful students at Southmoor has significant effects. They are so far below their peers in the hierarchy that their instruction is deemed impossible and teachers are not held accountable for it. Moreover, teachers' low expectations for these students and the teachers' low expectations for their own efforts to educate them result in a consistent pattern of confused and uncertain encounters in an educational setting.

Confused and uncertain educational encounters abound in Mr. Ellison's Additional Needs class, social studies for 9th graders. During the first semester, a total of sixteen freshmen were referred to the class, either by their 8th grade teachers the previous spring, or by their 9th grade teachers or their high school counselors during the fall semester. Even though an aide rounds up students at the local hangouts, attendance is erratic and usually, only four or five students are present. Sometimes students saunter in desultorily halfway through the class period. Students scatter around the perimeter of the sea of forty desks that fill Mr. Ellison's classroom, sitting where they will. Boys generally sit singly, against the back wall or in the front row. Girls array themselves in pairs in the outer aisles near the windows or along the blackboard. Mr. Ellison usually sits at the desk at the front of the room.

Academic Aspects

Class activity in Mr. Ellison's course is organized around daily, in-class worksheets. Teacher-made, the worksheets consist of four or five questions about a two-page reading selection, and a puzzle. The questions require an answer of several words or a sentence or two. The puzzle usually relates to the reading selection; for example, students find and circle important words mentioned in the text in a grid of letters. Worksheets are also personalized; students' names or upcoming school events are often included in the word search. As Mr. Ellison explains, he uses games to motivate academically unsuccessful students: "Puzzles make class interesting enough to the students so they can't say, 'It's boring,' without you having a good reason to say, 'Hey, I never had puzzles in school; it'd have been better if I had.' That's really giving in to them." With his regular-track students, Mr. Ellison's use of a puzzle is limited to "Oh, maybe the day before Thanksgiving."

Additional Needs classes have small enrollments so that each student's needs can be met, but there is very little individualized instruction. Indeed, worksheets are identical, not individualized. Although students complete worksheets at varying rates, and Mr. Ellison says he uses discrete worksheets to accommodate the varied attendance and performance patterns of students, class time is often spent going over each question as a group. Thus, even though Mary may be working on question five, Mr. Ellison will loudly discuss question two with Carl. He may ask for information about question two to which Mary, even though she has finished question two, will respond. Furthermore, Mr. Ellison rarely assigns new worksheets until everyone has completed most of an old one. Instead, students who finish early are given passes to the library or cafeteria.

Academic work in Mr. Ellison's room proceeds slowly. As one student notes to another, "Ever notice how slooow this class is?" When they enter the room, students may receive an uncompleted worksheet from the previous class period. Once or twice a week, they get a new worksheet, related to the next short reading selection in the history text. Continuity between reading selections, and therefore, between worksheets, is only broadly chronological; the text is not thematically organized. Nor does Mr. Ellison lecture or conduct cogent recitations about the readings or arrange them into units. Rather, class time is spent working through the worksheets, question by question, with accompanying discussions ranging far beyond the academic work.

Thus, progress during the semester is marked only by a series of grades on a small number of discrete worksheets. On the one day when Mr. Ellison scheduled a test, no students came to class. Mr. Ellison hypothesized that "they'd rather have just taken a *miss* than turn around and flunk it." The next day, students took the test and, indeed, did poorly. Mr. Ellison argues that with students' erratic attendance, their range of academic skills, and the in-and-out referral process of Additional Needs classes, he can not make or give a fair test. For the same reasons he does not assign oral reports, research projects, book reports, or quizzes.

In general, interruptions plague Mr. Ellison's class. The teacher's interruptions of students' individual work, in the form of demands for group recitations, is paralleled by other interruptions. During the test, for example, a counselor dropped by to check on Melissa's attendance and stayed to chat with her for several minutes. In addition to their absences, students' own late arrivals interrupt class:

May:	(loudly, stumbling against several desks) TEN MINUTES LATE!
Sue:	TEN MINUTES AND ONE SECOND LATE! I'm here, but could I go get some water, my throat is sooo sore.
Mr. E:	Well, ma'm, I suggest you hurry.
May:	WHERE'S MY WORK? I want to get it done!
Mr. E:	You won't finish the work I have today.
May:	Sheeeit! You just give it here. (She snatches the worksheet out of Mr. Ellison's hand and looks at it.) Why we do this BABY work! (Then, wheedling) You got a pencil, Mr. Ellison?
Sue:	I'M BACK!

In sum, academic progress is the least important aspect of Mr. Ellison's class. His worksheets offer "games," rather than lessons, to motivate students who cannot learn. Progress toward academic goals is slow and uncertain. Talk about personal affairs, simple gossip, and fortuitous chatter compete with talk about the academic lesson.

Social Aspects

Mr. Ellison describes many of his classroom efforts as attempts to address students' personal and social needs. He justifies the placement of Mary, "who could get B's and C's in regular classes," on the basis of "building her self-confidence." He explains that he knows "that Carl and Marvin just sit in the back of the room and talk a lot of the hour. But Marvin, especially, needs a friend, so I let it go. If I made a seating arrangement and had him up front and Carl in back, what would be accomplished?" In the classroom, Mr. Ellison often prompts students to show concern for each other. When a student is absent, he asks those present if they know if the student is sick. He encourages and joins conversations about students' personal affairs. When Cheryl was suffering from a bronchial infection and coughed through most of a class period, he solicitously advised her to "drink orange juice—I do, this time of year, and it really helps."

However, Mr. Ellison's attempts to "befriend students" and "establish a little family" often backfire. Students perceive his questions about an absent student's whereabouts as attendance-taking, for example. For them to answer would be to "rat" on a fellow student. Mr. Ellison himself often blurs his personal interest and his authority as the teacher. After advising Cheryl to drink orange juice, he comments further that "some students call it 'Hi-C' and they wish that were their grade." Similarly, when Mary enters class saying she is "in a good mood," Mr. Ellison responds personably, saying he is glad to hear it. But then he adds a teacherly admonition, hoping the good mood would "translate into some of your work today."

Students in the class, despite its small size and Mr. Ellison's intent, perhaps in part because of erratic attendance patterns, do not form a cohesive group. Although they usually work together on class assignments, students do not always know each other by name. Carl and Marvin worked together several days, but when Carl was absent and Mr. Ellison asked Marvin if he had seen Carl, Marvin did not know to whom Mr. Ellison was referring. During school hours, in addition to attending classes, students may frequent the near-by candy store together, share a smoke, or, occasionally, get drunk or "high" together. However, they do not call each other after school or share week-end activities. When Dawn, a seemingly well-liked student in the class, left Southmoor for a residential drug treatment center, students paid little attention and did not write to her.

Order By One-Ups-Manship

Students' academic progress and the class's social cohesion is further undercut by the implicit rules governing behavior in Mr. Ellison's class.

Instead of teacher-directed rules and order, the overriding rule is one of one-ups-manship. Each person attempts to satisfy her or his individual needs as they become apparent. Consequently, if Sue needs help on question 5 of the worksheet, she blurts out a demand for assistance, even when discussion on another question is in progress. If her demand is not acknowledged, it is repeated, usually more loudly: "I can't find this word!———Ellison! (3.0) I CAN'T FIND THIS WORD, I SAID! I'm gettin' MAA-AD! (warningly)." Mr. Ellison himself interrupts students in their work. Once, moving rapidly back and forth among four students, giving 15–30 seconds of attention to each, Mr. Ellison monitored students' progress and provided encouragement, as teachers providing individual instruction are encouraged to do, even though his attention was unsolicited and distracting. Such competitiveness for the floor feeds the isolation of the students from one another and from Mr. Ellison as each classroom participant tries to out-bid the other for attention.

Classroom participants not only compete with each other in getting and giving academic assistance, but they seek to out-trump each other in efforts to enliven the class. May responds to Mr. Ellison's question of why she is so loud by explaining, "I'm just making it fun—It's so *dead* in here." Personal anecdotes, dirty jokes, and word play compete with talk about the lesson. For example, Mr. Ellison maintains a nonstop stream of talk, much of it a witty and ironic commentary on the academic and extraacademic activities of the students. When a student gets up to sharpen a pencil, Mr. Ellison remarks: "Fifteen minutes into the period and you just realize you need to sharpen your pencil?" The teacher-made worksheets are full of puns, some of which are quite difficult. On a crossword puzzle, one clue reads: "A word used in baseball, jewelry, and cards." Another clue is: "A vital organ or someone who hasn't died yet."[4] Such clues stimulate strings of additional jokes or disparaging comments from students. Similarly, a favorite trick of Mr. Ellison's is to wad up pieces of paper and fire hook shots at the wastepaper basket. His success or lack thereof provokes a stream of interruptions of the class's progress through the worksheets.

Students add to the mayhem as they belch, break wind, and throw pencils at each other. They blatantly share answers on worksheets, despite Mr. Ellison's rebuke not to "over-hintify." During one class, Dawn and Sue discussed how to sneak a stick deodorant onto a teacher's desk: "He stinks so bad I can't hardly stand it. We'll tape a note on the bottle—'hint.' How you spell hint?" At that, Sue unscrews the bottle top, lifts her sweater above her armpit, and begins to apply deodorant, much to the bug-eyed amazement of everyone in the classroom. Students who

---

[4]The answers are "diamond" and "liver."

are newly referred to the class take in these antics quietly, at first, but within a day or two become participants. Clearly, the one-ups-manship principle effectively undercuts the order and academic purpose expected in an educational encounter.

Mr. Ellison bases his strategy for managing the Additional Needs class on "flexibility. I never do anything normal and that way I keep them off-guard. If they think they know what I'm going to do, they sabotage it." Consequently, Mr. Ellison responds phlegmatically to interruptions of the lesson from within and without the classroom. Rather than try to limit an interruption, Mr. Ellison often prolongs it. For example, if a principal enters the classroom to check on a student's attendance, Mr. Ellison asks how he is, describes what the class is doing, or asks if the principal can guess a crossword puzzle clue.

Paradoxically, by flowing with interruptions, Mr. Ellison achieves the appearance of control. With his mild, "flexible" manner, he simply waits for an interruption to complete itself, or even encourages it to run its course. If he tried to limit the principal's interference, by briefly noting that Carl is present and accounted for, students might prolong the interruption by shouting out questions about the reason for the principal's visit or by volunteering information about their studies. Furthermore, by flowing opportunistically with classroom events, rather than trying to direct them, Mr. Ellison can select those on which he *will* take action, yet not appear powerless when he does not attend to all. Although Mr. Ellison gives the illusion of control, the random development of the lesson and the extraordinary attention paid to interruptions of all kinds precludes the coherent, ordered development of instruction.

A Caricature of Education

The unspoken principle of one-ups-manship that governs much of the behavior of classroom participants promotes a sense of gaminess in the class. The relationship between Mr. Ellison and his students is of a teasing or lightly sarcastic nature, dominated by exchanges of jokes, insults, and anecdotes. When Mary complains rather bitterly that "this class is stupid," Mr. Ellison challenges her to write down her suggestions for improving it. Taking his challenge to heart, she quickly composes a list of eight remedies. Mr. Ellison pantomimes reluctance as he reads the list aloud to the gleeful class. The list includes many items directed at Mr. Ellison: no more "rotten" jokes, no more sports talk (football season was at its height), no more puzzles or worksheets, and "don't talk so much," to which another student amends, "That's the truth!" Mr. Ellison pretends to be crushed, but Mary pertly points out, "You asked!" However, having read the list, Mr. Ellison routinely redirects the class to the worksheet. Reading and joking about the list consume one-third of the class period, and Mary continues to comment on the stupidity of the class throughout the hour, but no changes result from Mary's suggestions.

Blatantly hostile outbursts, whether by teacher or students, are rare in Mr. Ellison's class. He works hard to respond to students with equanimity: "My rule for survival is, 'Never let them get me mad.' If I do, it's all over." He does occasionally get "het up," as students call it, and demands obedience (accusing students of the very gaminess he himself presents in class): "All you're doing is playing *games* with me and I don't like it. If you want to get out of this class, FOR ANY REASON, you're going to have to change your behavior. I can't just *babysit* you."

Students maintain their equanimity as well. One day when Sue arrives 5 minutes late, without a textbook she was supposed to return, Mr. Ellison suggests sarcastically that "perhaps we should flush your brains." Softly, seriously, almost tearfully, Sue replies, "Don't make me hate you." The minority counselor, who escorted Sue to class, defuses the situation by commenting, "Sue's cool." The girl rebounds with this support, and begins to chatter about one of her latest escapades at the candy store. Mr. Ellison tells her to "quiet down." This time she playfully echoes, "Don't make me hate you." Equally gamey, Mr. Ellison responds, "I haven't done anything yet. Wait till next semester. Then I start kicking your desk."

Mr. Ellison "joshes" lower-track students to establish a less-authoritarian, easy-going relationship with them. His paper wad tosses and stretched puns demonstrate that Additional Needs students should not judge him strictly as a teacher, since those are not teacherly behaviors, but should consider him a "good fellow." Nevertheless, like his attempts to be friendly, such a strategy to establish good will and control often goes awry. While it may allay openly hostile and antieducational confrontations, it creates an atmosphere of irony in which genuine educational encounters are difficult to define. Mr. Ellison's gamey, jocular behavior certainly leads to confused classroom encounters. His expressions of personal concern are undercut by their teasing tone. His evaluations of students' work are often back-handed compliments:

> How'd you do on this worksheet? Uh, I would say, uh, A minus or B plus—
> (teasingly) What I'd probably do, I'd flip a coin up in the air and if it comes down with a head, you know, I give you an A minus, and, uh, tails, a B (1.0)
> No, I think you did pretty good. I'll have to give you that. This one's much better than the one I gave you to fix up. Can't even tell the same person did 'em, in fact.

The climate in Mr. Ellison's class, like that in other classrooms for academically unsuccessful students at Southmoor, has a curious ambiguity. It represents a strange mixture of educational order and chaos, one in which classroom activities become a game, and both teacher and students go through the motions of teaching and learning. Making academic progress on basic skills, one of the formal goals of the Additional Needs class, vies in importance with the interruption of a principal, getting in a good joke, or tossing wads of paper at a wastebasket. Although students always have a worksheet before them, making a friend sometimes takes precedence over its completion. Even so, there is little cohesion among students or between students and teacher but, instead, considerable competition and bickering. Classroom participants work hard to maintain a veneer of light sarcasm in which encounters, whether academic or social, are rarely taken seriously. As a consequence, despite special funding, the sincere concern of teachers like Mr. Ellison, students' reasonably competent academic skills, and ostensibly adaptive educational and social practices, Additional Needs students drop out of high school at a rate of over 50%.

PARTICIPATION STRUCTURES IN REGULAR-TRACK CLASSROOMS AT SOUTHMOOR

Participation structure is a concept used to define types of social encounters according to the patterned allocation of participants' interactional rights and obligations (Erickson, 1982; Philips, 1983). In classrooms, participation structures vary according to the number of students interacting with the teacher, the academic task, and the ways in which turns at talk are allocated (Erickson, 1982; Philips, 1983). Teachers direct participation structures and students respond, identifying the often implicit rules by which they are to enact their reciprocal roles.

In regular-track classrooms at Southmoor, a participation structure in which a single teacher interacts with all the students in the room predominates. In this participation structure, which finds expression in the recitation and lecture, the teacher is the central director of classroom talk. Posing questions and assessing responses, the teacher retains control of the floor (Bellack, Kliebard, Hyman, & Smith, 1966; Edwards & Furlong, 1978; Mehan, 1979; Philips, 1983). Thus, she or he may choose who will talk from among the thirty participants in the recitation. The teacher's central position also allows control of the topic, its meaning, and the pace of the lesson. Thus, the teacher-whole group participation structure, which is the norm at Southmoor, allows the academic goals of the teacher's choosing to be reached through verbal means, yet in an orderly, efficient fashion.

Although classroom participants act reciprocally, taking into account the actions of others (Sacks, 1972), they are not equals. Teachers have some interactional prerogatives that students do not have. These derive from the teacher's possession of the knowledge students are deemed to need and from their adult status. Consequently, teachers direct the topic of talk; they can interrupt students; they assess students' responses (Bellack et al., 1966; Edwards & Furlong, 1978; Mehan, 1979; Philips, 1983).

However, at Southmoor, particularly in classrooms for upper classmen and/or able students, teachers modify the usual participation structures to encourage student direction of classroom talk. Challenging queries to teachers' explanations are expected, invited, and common. Students sometimes respond to the talk of peers directly. Students may introduce new topics which the teacher incorporates into the lesson. These rights, and the informal teacher-student relationships that they reflect and recreate, suggest that teachers perceive older and/or abler students as not so different from themselves and, therefore, as able to acquire some of the prerogatives of a teacher and an adult.

Furthermore, in Southmoor's regular-track classes, it is unusual for teachers to establish more than one participation structure per class period. Except for a few minutes devoted to opening procedural matters, students and teacher interact in business-like fashion through the 50 minute period. Use of only one participation structure increases the time spent on academic matters, since changing participation structures itself uses time, and it minimizes confusion about students' and teacher's interactional obligations in a specific classroom encounter. Furthermore, using only one participation structure, and particularly the teacher-whole group structure, reflects positive assumptions about regular-track students' age and academic ability: They are expected to have longer attention spans than children and the ability to learn through listening, rather than doing. Individual seatwork, like reading or writing, is usually reserved for homework. By way of contrast, in the early elementary grades, participation structures change about 20 times per day and exhibit considerable variety, including teacher-small group, teacher-individual, and seatwork structures. Yet, by the upper elementary grades, participation structures change only 10 times per day and are more restricted in type (Philips, 1983).

In sum, in Southmoor's regular-track classes, teachers authoritatively establish one participation structure during a class period. Most often, the teacher and the whole class verbally explore an academic topic together. Thus, students learn that they are educationally competent and maturing adolescents, successfully maneuvering through the rite of passage (Henry, 1963; Kett, 1977) that is high school.

PARTICIPATION STRUCTURES IN LOWER-TRACK
CLASSROOMS AT SOUTHMOOR

In contrast, in Additional Needs classes, the participation structures, while of the same type as those found in any educational setting, differ in their arrangement. They shift more frequently and with less clear marking; topics are entertaining or "relevant," rather than academic. The shifts reflect uncertain direction by lower-track teachers, to which students then respond confusedly. Often their responses appear communicatively incompetent or, as teachers say, like those of "naughty 4th graders," rather than like those of intellectually competent adolescents. This unintended result is produced in the talk in Mr. Ellison's lessons and those of other Additional Needs teachers.

One November day Mr. Ellison and five students in the English/social studies class continued to work on worksheets begun the previous day about the bombing of Pearl Harbor. Like all of Mr. Ellison's worksheets, this one consisted of several questions and a puzzle. The class spent the first half of the period discussing the first question, their talk punctuated by lengthy personal asides, jokes, and loud bantering. Then, Mr. Ellison left the room briefly to speak to a teacher in the hall. Students continued work on the next question or chatted among themselves. When Mr. Ellison returned, he entered the classroom speaking loudly.

1	*Mr. E:*	Uh, ANYBODY HAVE ANOTHER QUESTION. BE—
		[
2	*Tina:*	(reading from the worksheet) "What—
		[
3	*Mr. E:*	—SIDES
		[
4	*Tina:*	"WI
5		DID WE DO ABOUT IT?"
6	*Mr. E:*	UH, I was just going to ask if you had another question.
7		another question.
8	*Tina:*	Heh, heh.
9	*Mr. E:*	Well—
10	*Tina:*	We went over there and beat 'em up;
11		we hit 'em in the jaws!
12	*Mr. E:*	Well, in other words, I would say—
13	*Ss:*	(beginning to chatter loudly among themselves)
14	*Mr. E:*	I WOULD SAY that if you would talk about
15		what the Japanese are doing. In other words,
16		they were conquering huge areas of Asia, just taking
17		'em, and, uh, adding it to their own
18		territory, uh—
19	*Ss:*	(continuing to chat with each other)
20	*Mr. E:*	Do any of you know what they called that

21		(pointing to the four circles he had drawn on
22		the board earlier to represent the Japanese
23		empire), that whole thing there. I betcha one
24		person in here at least knows what they
25		called it when . . . they took all this.
26	*Tina:*	They borrowed it.
27	*Mr. E:*	No, when they *took* the Empire. What'd they
28		call their Empire? (1.0) You know what
29		they called their Empire?
30	*Bill:*	King China.
31	*Mr. E:*	King China, yeah.
32	*Ss:*	(giggling)
33	*Mr. E:*	Uh, Louis, you know what they called their
34		Empire, you know, what the Japanese called their
35		Empire, right up here? (pointing to board)
36	*Louis:*	No.

[

37	*Tina:*	No.
38	*Mr. E:*	Do you know what they called it?
39	*Mary:*	No.
40	*Mr. E:*	Do you know what they called it?
41	*Mary:*	They called it "theirs."
42	*Mr. E:*	(to Cheryl) Aren't you working on
43		this (the worksheet)?
44	*Cheryl:*	I told you.
45	*Mr. E:*	You told me what?
46	*Cheryl:*	I've already done it.
47	*Tina:*	Pearl Harbor?
48	*Mr. E:*	Uh! Uh, anybody, uh, nobody has an idea
49		what the Japanese called this thing, other people
50		were adding to Japan. In other words, if you
51		tried to draw Japan's boundary it would
52		look . . . very unusual. It would go way
53		out here in the Pacific, like that (drawing
54		on the board). They said this big area
55		here was theirs (pointing to one circle).
56		Nobody in here knows what they called it? (2.0)
57		Not a single one of you has ever heard this?
58	*Bill:*	Nooo.
59	*Mary:*	Probably have.
60	*Tina:*	Probably didn't tell us anything about it.
61	*Mr. E:*	I just don't believe this, that nobody—

[

62	*Mary:*	WELL TELL US!

63	*Mr. E:*	What?
64	*Cheryl:*	Tell us so we do know.
65		(3.0)
66	*Mary:*	We already know.

67	Mr. E:	But nobody's telling me something they know.
68		I have to believe some of you must know this . . .
69		Well, the—
		[
70	Mary:	WELL, WHAT!

71	Mr. E:	Well, okay, what they called it, they called
72		it the Greater (writing on the board) . . . East . . .
73		Asia . . . Co-prosperity . . . Sphere. (2.0) There.
74	Mary:	What a stupid name.
75	Mr. E:	No, that was, well, I thought it was very
76		official on their part, to call, to call all this
77		taking of an Empire and everything. That's
78		what they called it. They said that everybody
79		in Asia—
		[
80	Bill:	Who cares?

81	Mr. E:	EVERYbody in Asia would prosper. Cro, er,
82		CO-prosperity. And then of course it is a sphere,
83		makes it "greater." That's what they called it,
84		Greater East Asia. What a nice way to call
85		something that's, you know, they're probably
86		killing people, taking their goodies, and then,
87		what a nice idea to call it that. (1.0) I, uh,
88		really think that that was very clever on their part
89		to give it a name.
90	Mary:	"Taking their goodies?"
91	Mr. E:	Greater East Asia . . . And none of you knew that.
92	Mary:	(louder, looking disgusted) "TAKING THEIR
93		GOODIES?"
94	Mr. E:	You mean there's nobody here ever heard that?
95	Cheryl:	Well, (reading from the worksheet, but
96		missing the first word) "Why did we do about it?"
97	Mr. E:	What?
98	Cheryl:	What'd we do about it?
99	Mr. E:	What? I thought somebody would have heard
100		of it.
101	Cheryl:	Forget it.
102	Mr. E:	(turning to a late-arriving student) Here's
103		Tom. Did you, uh, run into trouble getting here,
104		uh, this morning?

This 3-minute segment of talk divides into three sections. In the first, Mr. Ellison reenters the classroom and, after several exchanges with one student, Tina, eventually establishes a teacher-whole group participation structure which takes the form of a recitation (lines 1–23). In the second, the recitation itself unfolds (lines 24–101), its topic, the name the Japanese gave their empire. In the third, the late arrival of a student interrupts the recitation (lines 102–104). In the 3 minutes, several types of confusion are evident: confusion about what kind of participation structure is operating, about the academic task, or topic, and, fundamentally, about how class-room participants should be acting.

Unclear and Shifting Participation Structures

One of the basic ambiguities in the talk in Mr. Ellison's classroom, and one of the sources of the disorderly classroom climate, concerns whether the participation structure in operation is that of the recitation, of individual seatwork, or of small group seatwork. Although each of Mr. Ellison's students has a worksheet and is responsible for completing it, the rules by which students are to accomplish this are uncertain because of Mr. Ellison's unclear direction.

Sometimes Mr. Ellison comes around to a student to help with a particular question, or a student goes up to his desk for help with an individual problem. If the participation structure is that of individual seatwork, teacher and student should relate on a one-to-one basis, with talk allocated on a first-come, first-served private basis according to individual needs, with students filling in worksheets. (In this description of classroom structures, I rely on Philips, 1983). Under such a structure, talk occurs between individuals; other students are not to attend to the talk of Mr. Ellison and another student. On the other hand, some students in Mr. Ellison's class sit near friends and work together on the worksheet. If the participation structure in operation is that of small group seatwork, the teacher should relate to two or three students at a time, as requested. However, students would also rely on each other for information, and the worksheet's completion is a joint venture. Finally, Mr. Ellison's class operated a considerable part of the time under the participation structure of the recitation. Mr. Ellison addresses one question from the worksheet to the group at large for an answer, for example. If operating under this participation structure, teacher and student should relate in a one-all ratio, with turns at talk allocated by the teacher. Talk is public, but it assists individual students in filling in the answers of the worksheet independently.

Yet, in the opening 18 lines of the segment of talk from Mr. Ellison's class, Mr. Ellison appears to direct the operation of all three participation structures at once.[5] For example, when he reenters the classroom from the hallway, students are already working independently or in pairs on the

---

[5]As Philips, 1983, suggests, more than one participation structure can and often does operate within a class at one time. For example, a teacher can help an individual student, while others work on seatwork. However, the teacher must speak quietly to the individual if other students are to "pretend" not to hear. Such is not the case in Mr. Ellison's class.

worksheet. Loudly, Mr. Ellison interrupts the seatwork to ask if "ANY-BODY" has another question about the worksheet (line 1). His question may be an invitation for individuals—"ANYBODY"—to raise hands if they need his assistance. If one did not have a question, presumably one could continue working independently and ignore the question. Or, it could be an indication that seatwork is over and a change to a different participation structure is imminent. Perhaps the class, acting as a group, as it had with question one, should now turn its attention to the review of "ANOTHER" question. Mr. Ellison's loud tone of voice supports this interpretation, but who is to respond and how is not clear from Mr. Ellison's question.

Tina provides one response, by reading aloud the next question on the worksheet: " 'WHAT DID WE DO ABOUT IT (the bombing of Pearl Harbor?' " (lines 4–5). Her response continues the ambiguity, however. She announces that, an an individual, she needs help with the second question. However, by speaking loudly (and thereby matching her reply in volume to Mr. Ellison's), she suggests that the question is problematic for and deserves the attention of the whole class.

Mr. Ellison's assessment of Tina's response, since he already has asked for questions, is an ironic reprimand: "I was just going to ask if you had another question," he says (lines 6–7). His sarcasm marks Tina's loud and persistent overlaps of his talk (lines 2 and 4). Thus, it shifts the topic of talk from the question "any" student has about the worksheet to how one student, Tina, should voice hers. The shift of topic also suggests that Mr. Ellison and Tina are now engaged in a one-to-one interaction. However, it is also unclear whether Mr. Ellison will return to Tina's question (" 'WHAT DID WE DO ABOUT IT?' "). Perhaps, having disapproved of her overlapping of his talk, he will again broadcast an appeal for questions to the group at large. To ensure that her question from the worksheet will not be passed over, Tina blurts out an answer to it, thus continuing her topic (lines 10–11). Again loud and public, Tina's answer revives the ambiguity about whether the participation structure involves the teacher and the whole group or the teacher and one student.

At this point (line 12), Mr. Ellison begins a series of moves which eventually establishes a participation structure involving the whole group. By lines 20–23, he asks one direct question to the whole class, to the persons "in here": "Do any of you know what they called that (the empire), that whole thing there?" The participation structure thus established, in the form of a recitation, lasts almost 2 minutes, when there is yet another shift (lines 102–104).[6]

---

[6]Some confusion lingers in lines 42–46. This inconclusive interchange does not establish whether the student's or teacher's expectation of what the student should be doing is correct.

In lower-track classrooms at Southmoor like Mr. Ellison's, participation structures shift much more frequently than in regular-track classrooms, and the structure in which classroom participants are to operate is often ambiguous. In a 3-minute segment of talk, for example, participation structures shift twice (lines 20 and 102). This rapid fluctuation is not peculiar to the particular segment of talk transcribed or to Mr. Ellison's class. Shifts are equally frequent in one other Additional Needs class at Southmoor. In the other three Additional Needs classes in which I observed, the rate of change was lower (4 to 5 shifts per class period), but was still decidedly higher than in regular-track classrooms.

Furthermore, these ambiguous curricular practices produce some of the very "immature" or "unthinking" behaviors of lower-track students of which teachers complain. When Mr. Ellison provides worksheets for independent seatwork but interrupts students with a loud appeal for questions, students may either shout back a response or ignore him and continue working. Both the shout, as in the case of Tina (lines 4–5), and the failure to attend to group activities, as in the case of Cheryl (lines 42–46), are subsequently sanctioned.

Ambiguous Classroom Topics

The climate in classrooms for academically unsuccessful students is also disorderly because the topic of the lesson is not clearly academic and, therefore, the basis for a relationship between teacher and students is unclear. In general, an academic topic in lower-track lessons at Southmoor is replaced or undercut by entertaining games or jokes, as in Mr. Ellison's class, by topics "relevant" to students' personal lives, or by unconnected daily exercises. For example, Mr. Ellison's question about the name of the Japanese empire diverts attention from Tina's legitimate topic, which was how to answer question two. It relates, at best, very tangentially to the day's academic lesson on Pearl Harbor. Mr. Ellison has no logical reason to introduce it, given the reading selection, the questions on the worksheet, or previous discussion.

In fact, Mr. Ellison's question is, like the entertaining puzzles on the worksheets he prepares, a joke or trick, exemplifying one-ups-manship. Mr. Ellison does not really expect students to know the name, "Greater East Asia Co-prosperity Sphere." The name is not in the reading and is not common knowledge. Yet Mr. Ellison insists that the students consider the question. His repetitions of the question both mark a "joshing" relationship with the students, yet make students uneasy about the answer. However, the joke culminates in the students' hostile rejection of it and of its academic content. As Mr. Ellison belabors the question, forcing students to take it seriously, students respond angrily: they blame their memories (line 59) or the teacher (line 60) for their inability to answer. Finally, exasperated, they demand the answer: "WELL, TELL US!" (line 62).

This climactic moment in the recitation quickly dissolves into bitter rejection, when students are at long last told the answer to Mr. Ellison's question. They assess the academic information, "The Greater East Asia Co-Prosperity Sphere," as of no value: "What a stupid name" (line 74) and "Who cares?" (line 80). Their assessment is related to the double-nature of the question. Students took seriously the expectation that they, as students, should know the answer, but this was a trick. Rejecting the position of having been the butt of a joke, they reject the knowledge offered by the teacher, as well as his subsequent attempt to explain why the name is "official" and interesting (lines 75–89). Indeed, Mr. Ellison himself turns away from the topic and students' angry rejection of it at the first opportunity (lines 102–104). Tom's late arrival provides a "flexible" shift to a new topic and a new participation structure.

Interactional Prerogatives in an Ambiguous Encounter

In such ambiguous classroom situations, generated by frequently shifting and unclearly marked participation structures as well as bewildering mixtures of academic and nonacademic topics, the interactional preroga-tives of classroom participants themselves become confused and unclear. To communicate competently in a situation, a person must first under-stand what the situation is. Yet, in Southmoor's lower-track classrooms, the situation is above all not clear. It is not clearly educational, and the rules for how students should act, both in terms of their intellect and their age, are confused. Consequently, students' actions often appear stupid or immature, but their confusion mirrors the teacher's uncertain role enact-ment.

In the 3 minutes of talk transcribed earlier, Mr. Ellison's enactment of the teacher role is decidedly curious. On the one hand, by line 20, he does have an educational point to make: The Japanese choice of a name for the empire shows their skill as propagandists. Moreover, Mr. Ellison's enact-ment of his role appears very teacher-ly: he asks 15 questions, that most common form of teacher talk (Bellack et al., 1966; Edwards & Furlong, 1978; Mehan, 1979). On the other hand, Mr. Ellison makes his *educa-tional* point in as *entertaining* a way as possible: He teaches by perform-ing an elaborate trick or joke. The joke is produced through the repetition of one question (9 of Mr. Ellison's 15 elicitations are virtually identical) on a topic that is rather extraneous to the day's lesson. Usually, when teachers ask a question to which students don't rather quickly respond correctly, they offer prompts, or repairs, in the form of rephrasings or simplifications, or they give the answer themselves (Mehan, 1979; Philips,

1983). Instead, Mr. Ellison's question assumes a mocking cast which grows more onerous for the students as the recitation proceeds. Eventually, when Mr. Ellison does not modify the question to give the students a better chance to respond correctly, they reject their obligation to answer, and turn the tables. They demand point-blank that Mr. Ellison himself answer: "WELL, TELL US!" (line 62).

Mr. Ellison's strange enactment of his role as teacher/trickster initiates confusion in students. The students and teacher shift into a very unusual relationship (Bellack et al., 1966). The students become the questioner and, especially unusual, the evaluator, of the teacher, who becomes the respondent. The usual social relations in the classroom—between students and teacher and between adolescents and adult—are momentarily inverted. For instance, the students insist, three times, that Mr. Ellison tell them the name of the empire (lines 62, 64, and 70). When he finally does honor their request, his answer appears so banal that they negatively assess the information. It is dismissed as "stupid" (line 74) or not worth caring about (line 80). Eventually, Cheryl, using another teacher/adult prerogative, changes the topic entirely, rejecting Mr. Ellison's topic and reintroducing Tina's original question from the worksheet (lines 95–96). However, the inversion of the social relations produces the subversion of the educational enterprise. Mr. Ellison fails to understand (line 97), then, to credit Cheryl's question (lines 99–100), just as he refused to credit students' demands that he "tell (them) so (they) do know." In essence, Mr. Ellison makes visible his power to ignore Additional Needs students, as students and as maturing adolescents. This time, however, Cheryl, already duped once in being asked to answer a trick question, exerts *her* ultimate power, in response. She withdraws from the academic task, muttering disgustedly: "Forget it!" (line 101).

When a disorderly classroom climate is constructed, in part as the result of the confused direction of the teacher, the interactional prerogatives of students also become unclear. As a consequence, students exhibit behaviors that are deemed "out-of-control"; they seem not to care about, even to reject, classroom knowledge. Thus, they act toward the teacher, not as high school students should, but as "naughty 4th graders." Yet their actions are taken in account of the teacher's (Sacks, 1972).

Mr. Ellison's low expectations for the students is communicated in his offering them an entertaining trick, rather than a serious academic topic and purposive direction. They respond, reciprocally, with a lack of seriousness, which, cyclically, confirms Mr. Ellison's low expectations. Furthermore, Mr. Ellison's direction of the talk reflects his own sense of uncertainty regarding the success of his professional efforts. Students respond, first, by attempting to make him teach: "Tell us so we do know!" However, ultimately, they reject him, their own role as students, and the educational encounter: "Forget it!" Cheryl says scornfully. Failing to act according to the prerogatives and obligations of students, they again confirm Mr. Ellison's expectations and keep the cycle of low expectations in motion.

ROLE INTEGRATION AT SOUTHMOOR

Given that the chaos in Additional Needs classes, while fed by students' confused responses, begins with the teacher's uncertain direction of participation structures, the next question is why the Additional Needs teachers I observed enact their prerogatives as teachers with such confusion and ambiguity.

Mr. Ellison is not an incompetent or uncaring teacher, one who "just can't or won't control the kids." His three regular-track classes are orderly and purposive (if still full of "bad" puns!). Also, Mr. Ellison demonstrates sincere concern for the well-being of the individuals in his lower-track class. Moreover, the chaotic atmosphere in Mr. Ellison's class is uniformly present in all Additional Needs classes at Southmoor. It echoes, yet is strikingly unlike, the easy, academic atmosphere maintained by the same teachers in their regular-track classrooms. Therefore, to analyze an individual classroom's climate, the culture of the whole institution as it is mediated by the classroom teacher must be considered.[7]

When teachers enter lower-track classrooms at Southmoor, they must integrate two roles: teacher at Southmoor and teacher of lower-track students. In attempting to integrate the two roles, teachers, like other persons, experience much conflict (Goffman, 1961). Many of the norms for their behavior as regular-track teachers shift or are distorted in lower-track classrooms. The conflict, expressed in their inconsistent direction in the classroom, is evident in their instructional practices, the formal curriculum they adopt, and their relationships with students.

For example, as in Mr. Ellison's class, the contradiction in roles affects

---

[7]Marshall High School, the site of my parallel study, is very similar to Southmoor in size, funding, equipment, staffing patterns, and expertise of faculty. However, its ethos and, consequently, the classroom climate in lower-track courses, is dramatically different from Southmoor's. At Marshall, the mode of organization is bureaucratic, rather than professional, and the faculty characterizes its typical student as "your typical blue-collar kid," not as "from upper-middle class, professional families." Hence, the school provides a disciplined, instrumental, skills-based education, one deemed appropriate for "blue-collar kids." Furthermore, the climate in Additional Needs classes at Marshall is not just disciplined, like that in regular-track classes, but regimented. Moreover, this climate contrasts with the chaos in Southmoor's Additional Needs classes. An interaction between the social order and the educational order is visible in the comparison of the two high schools and the comparison of their regular and lower-track classrooms.

the participation structures that teachers direct in lower-track class-rooms. Lower-track teachers use daily worksheets in class, explaining that this allows an academically unsuccessful student to work at her or his own pace. If a student is very slow, obstinate, or frequently absent, other students can proceed without her or him holding them back, as might be the case with a class discussion or group project. In addition, pedagogical theory supports the use of a variety of class activities for students with short attention spans, so teachers try to provide many activities. None-theless, because the prevailing participation structure at Southmoor is teacher-large group, Southmoor teachers in lower-track classes also feel compelled to direct students as a group ("ANYBODY HAVE AN-OTHER QUESTION?"). Moreover, the varied activities often bear little relationship to one another, so that while students are busy, their work has little coherence. Thus, teachers' performances in classrooms for academically unsuccessful students borrow elements from both the Southmoor teacher role and the lower-track teacher role, often with contradictory and confusing effects on students.

The contradiction between roles also affects the formal curriculum teachers devise for Additional Needs classes. Sometimes the broad topics from regular-track classes are studied, but at a much slower pace, in less depth, or using an elementary school text, as befit less able and less mature students. Frequently, teachers provide lower-track students with "relevant" subject matter. Teaching students to read national newsmaga-zines is appropriate because "They see their parents reading them; they're around the home." Games are often part of the curriculum because the students "can't complain about lessons that are fun." Thus, teachers in Additional Needs classes do not abdicate their professional responsibility for the design of a curriculum appropriate to students' needs. However, they also act as lower-track teachers; i.e., they provide curricular topics that assume such students are incapable and/or unwilling to take intellectual work seriously. Nevertheless, neither they nor the students who complain continually about "this baby work" see the differentiated curricula as "real," or valid. For example, when a teacher told me a lower-track student had gone on to a state university, I asked if this didn't seem odd, given his lower-track status in high school. But the teacher explained easily: "Well, you have to consider the college—he's only at the state university. And, you know, he's not, he's not aiming for any great big huge job in the academic life, I'm sure." At Southmoor, only the traditional academic curriculum counts.

The easy give-and-take between regular-track classroom participants is caricatured in lower-track classrooms in a veneer of harmony. Teachers joke with students, but, as in Mr. Ellison's class, such jokes can go awry. To maintain the veneer, and control, teachers limit face-to-face interactions, using many films and "structured," individualized worksheets in their stead. When recitations do occur, they are full of arrhythmic shout-outs and interruptions. With such interactional dissonance, teachers' expectations come into play. Academically unsuccessful students are viewed as hostile or immature children, not as near-equals, and their present or future commitment to the educational values of teachers is deemed impossible. Therefore, their questions are not treated as important emendations to the topic, as regular-track students' questions are, but are autocratically rejected as nonsensical, off-the-topic, or un-welcome challenges to the teachers' authority. Interactions between teachers and students who are "your basic bottom" cannot be based on an intellectual exchange.

The give-and-take teachers do institute in lower-track classrooms centers *not* on academic matters, as in regular classrooms, but on matters of behavior and, thus, reflects the importance lower-track teachers give to the issue of behavior. No longer claiming authority on the basis of the important knowledge they can communicate, lower-track teachers seek to establish their authority largely on the basis of an exchange of time and classroom rules for students' good will. By easing up on behavioral requirements, as well as academic standards, teachers act the part of the nice guy, rather than that of the academic director.

The concessions teachers make to academically unsuccessful students exemplify their judgments of them. For example, lower-track classes at Southmoor rarely begin and end with the bell. Almost all start late and end early, and students are allowed to talk, find their notebooks, arrive late, eat, go to their lockers, or relax generally. This relaxation of the teacher's expectations for classroom behavior reflects her/his view of academically unsuccessful students as both needing or demanding child-ish indulgence and as non-learners. Importantly, as teachers make such implicit or explicit exchanges, their facial expressions signal a fundamen-tal disapproval or dismay. They feel compelled to make such allowances as lower-track teachers, but they distance themselves from that role because, as Southmoor teachers, they must condemn such tactics as "silly" or as bribes for persons unable to control themselves.

In sum, the teacher's performance in a classroom for academically unsuccessful students is a contradictory one, reflecting the variance between the requirements of the lower-track teacher role and those of regular teacher at Southmoor. As a regular-track teacher, she or he is to be a subject matter expert, with the wit and poise to accept the intelligent challenges of able and maturing students committed to the educational enterprise. However, as a lower-track teacher, expertise in a discipline is not required. Furthermore, one's charges are not near-equals but often obstreperous children with whom one exchanges indulgences, not ideas. As one teacher succinctly described his history class, "Sometimes we're historical; sometimes we're hysterical."

Goffman (1961) explains that social actors may resolve conflicts between roles by distancing themselves from one. Lower-track teachers resolve the conflict between the Southmoor teacher role and the lower-track teacher role by distancing themselves from the latter. They adopt this solution because, at Southmoor, the educational success of Additional Needs students is only marginally important to the college-preparatory institution. Teachers are not rewarded for their efforts with the "hard-to-teach" by the students themselves in terms of exemplary academic achievement. Faculty members may gratefully praise and commiserate with the teachers of lower-track students since, through their efforts, they are spared the "hard" work of dealing with such students themselves. But regular teachers also do not actively support such efforts because the provision of classes for less-able students takes scarce resources away from the main business of Southmoor and challenges the institution's definition of itself as an elite institution and their prestigious role in it. Finally, teachers can distance themselves from the lower-track role because, as part of Southmoor's powerful and professional faculty, they are not accountable for students' educational progress. One administrator voiced the prevailing ambivalence toward Additional Needs classes this way:

> Could we give them a diploma if we expanded the Additional Needs classes and they stayed in it for 4 years and got the twenty credits needed for graduation? That brings up the question of standards. We expect a lot of students at Southmoor. But there are no standards in Additional Needs classes. We're just trying to get the kid in class; we're not worrying about what he does while he's there.

Teachers of academically unsuccessful students at Southmoor thus become mere "babysitters," maintaining control of the "hysterical," in an institution that values only high academic achievement by self-disciplined students.

Teachers accomplish the integration of the contradictory demands of their position by distancing themselves from the lower-track teacher's role. They act with unconscious mockery toward themselves and the students. Academic tasks become games; shifting and unclearly marked participation structures reflect uncertain direction and require confused responses; teacher-student relationships are informal, as with regular-track students, but also ironical; and teachers' distancing prompts students' negative attitudes toward schooling and themselves. The overall atmosphere is therefore chaotic and purposeless, and encounters in Additional Needs classes become caricatures of the excellent education provided the college-bound.

REFERENCES

Bellack, A., Kliebard, H., Hyman, R., & Smith, J. (1966). *The language of the classroom.* New York: Teachers College Press.

Edwards, A., & Furlong, V. (1978). *The language of teaching.* London: Heinemann Education Books.

Erickson, F. (1982). Classroom discourse as improvisation: Relations between academic task structures and social participation structures in lessons. In C. Wilkinson (Ed.), *Communication in the classroom* (pp. 153–181). New York: Academic Press.

Furlong, V. (1977). Anancy goes to school: A case study of pupils' knowledge of their teachers. In P. Woods & M. Hammersley (Eds.), *School experience* (pp. 23–44). London: Croom Helm.

Goffman, E. (1961). *Encounters.* Indianapolis: Bobbs-Merrill.

Hargreaves, D. (1967). *Social relations in a secondary school.* London: Routledge and Kegan Paul.

Henry, J. (1963). *Culture against man.* New York: Random House.

Keddie, N. (1971). Classroom knowledge. In M. F. D. Young (Ed.), *Knowledge and control* (pp. 133–160). London: Collier-MacMillan.

Kett, J. (1977). *Rites of passage: Adolescence in America, 1790 to the present.* New York: Basic Books.

Lacey, C. (1970). *Hightown grammar: The school as a social system.* Manchester: Manchester University Press.

Leacock, E. (1969). *Teaching and learning in city schools.* New York: Basic Books.

McDermott, R. P., & Aron, J. (1978). Pirandello in the classroom: On the possibility of equal educational opportunity in American culture. In M. Reynolds (Ed.), *Futures of education for exceptional children: Emerging structures* (pp. 41–64). Minneapolis: National Support Systems Project.

Mehan, H. (1979). *Learning lessons.* Cambridge: Harvard University Press.

Metz, M. (1983). Sources of constructive social relationships in an urban magnet school. *American Journal of Education, 91,* 202–245.

Metz, M. (1978). *Classrooms and corridors: The crisis of authority in American secondary schools.* Berkeley: University of California Press.

Philips, S. (1983). *The invisible culture.* New York: Longman.

Rist, R. (1973). *The urban school: A factory for failure.* Cambridge, MA: MIT Press.

Sacks, H. (1972). An initial investigation of the usability of conversational data for doing sociology. In D. Sudnow (Ed.), *Studies in social interactions* (pp. 31–74). New York: Free Press.

Schlechty, P. (1976). *Teaching and social behavior: Towards an organizational theory of instruction.* Boston: Allyn and Bacon.

Schwartz, F. (1981). Supporting or subverting learning: Peer group patterns in four tracked schools. *Education and Anthropology Quarterly, 12,* 99–121.

Spindler, G. (Ed.). (1982). *Doing the ethnography of schooling.* New York: Holt, Rinehart and Winston.

Waller, W. (1932). *The sociology of teaching.* New York: Wiley.

Willis, P. (1977). *Learning to labour.* Westmead, England: Saxon House.

The Author and Her Chapter

Susan Jungck has her doctorate from the University of Wisconsin-Madison in the curriculum and instruction department, and was also a participant in the Spindler ethnography seminar there. She has been a lecturer in the elementary education program at Madison, a visiting professor at Chulalongkorn and Chiang Mai Universities in Thailand and is currently a professor in the curriculum and instruction department at the National College of Education in Evanston, Illinois. Her focus on Computer Literacy in the schools has provided an opportunity to examine the relationship between the day-to-day curriculum practices in schools and the social pressures on schools to develop more technologically relevant curriculum. She has used an ethnographic perspective as a means of observing classroom and school district curriculum processes in an evolving, natural, and holistic context.

Her interests in schools are informed by her many years as a classroom teacher in various grade levels in Minnesota, Florida, Massachusetts, and New York as well as by her academic preparation in curriculum theory, sociology of education, and anthropological ethnography.

In this chapter Jungck describes in telling detail what happens in classes and labs as computer literacy curriculum is enacted in a middle school and a high school in the same school district in a midwestern town. Her ethnography of attempts to develop, implement, and achieve "computer literacy" raises important issues and questions that are especially critical if the computer does play the dramatically influential role in our society, and in education, forecast by many educators and social scientists. Who learns programming rather than just data processing? Is a new

473

stratification among students and the faculty consequent to this division? How does the introduction of computer courses in general affect the priorities in education, teacher professionalization, and the culture of the school? What effect does the addition of these electives have on the elective areas in art, music, and even advanced science courses? Is there depersonalization in the instructional process due to prepackaged curriculum materials?

These kinds of questions are raised and tentative answers provided using the ethnographic evidence from these two schools.

The Editors

19 Computer Literacy in Practice: Curricula, Contradictions, and Context

Susan Jungck*
University of Wisconsin-Madison

INTRODUCTION

Advertising campaigns claim that the computer will become as common as the telephone for the home market and will be as revolutionary as the invention of writing. Television specials, newspapers, popular magazines, education journals, and conferences, as well as recent national reports such as *A Nation at Risk* (1983), have all advocated "computer literacy" as the new basic skill to complement reading, writing and arithmetic. The popular message and the fear of many educators is that those who remain uninformed will be computer illiterates and at an educational and occupational disadvantage.

Schools have thus procured microcomputers at an astonishingly fast rate. A 1982 survey indicated that over 60% of the U.S. school districts and 53% of the school buildings had computers, and the numbers were increasing at an annual rate of 56% (Market Data Retrieval, 1982). However, a recent survey found that between 1983 and 1985, "The number of computers in use quadrupled from about 250,000 to over one million" and that, "By the Spring of 1985, almost all secondary schools and five-sixths of the elementary schools in the U.S. had begun to use computers in their instructional program" (Becker, 1986). These and other surveys have also revealed that the computers are distributed unequally relative to the size, location, and wealth of school districts;

---

*The author is presently a faculty member of the National College of Education in Evanston, Illinois.

"Whereas two-thirds of public schools in the better-off districts have microcomputers, only 41 percent of the schools in the least wealthy districts have any" (Becker, 1983).

Henry Jay Becker's (1983) survey on *School Uses of Microcomputers* also documents inequities by type of use:

> Predominantly minority elementary schools use drill-and-practice activities much more (30%) than they use programming (10%) activities with their students. In contrast, low SES predominantly white elementary schools do programming with students (49%) much more often than they use their micros for drill work (9%).

Computer literacy, or teaching about the computer, which usually includes such topics as the history, technology, applications, and social implications as well as the programming of computers is most often associated with affluent school districts. Computer Assisted Instruction, the use of the computer as an instructional medium, is commonly used in less advantaged districts to drill students in the "basic facts." The latter use of computers does not prepare the user to understand computers or use them independently. These uses have different implications. This study focused on the development and implementation of computer literacy in one white, middle class, suburban school district.

Although this chapter is limited to an ethnographic analysis of computer literacy as practiced in a middle school and high school setting, it is important to emphasize that the interpretation and analysis of this research must be situated in the broader social context in which we are experiencing an overall transformation of the labor process. Two statistics are relevant here. One is the projected 50% rate of growth in computer related occupations between 1980 and 1990, a statistic often used to justify the introduction of computers into the school curriculum. The implications of this become obscured however, when one realizes that in absolute numbers, "no high-tech job even makes the top 20 in terms of total numbers of jobs added to the U.S. economy" (U.S. Labor Department Projections as cited in Nielsen, 1983), and most jobs will be in service occupations like "janitors, nurses aids, orderlies, fast food workers, and kitchen helpers." In addition, most of the jobs that do occur in the high-tech industries occur in office areas and production which require minimum skills and pay low wages.

Another trend relates to the proletarianization of existing jobs. Here "The new technologies provide opportunities to further simplify and routinize work tasks and to reduce the opportunities for worker individuality and judgement" (Rumberger & Levin, 1984). For example, many clerical workers, nearly 85% of whom are female, are experiencing, with the use of word and data processors, increased, rationalized and depersonalized work loads.

As the introduction of high technology works through the labor force, attention is also focused on reevaluating schools' curricula according to national priorities for international technological superiority. One response has been the rapid development and implementation of a new curriculum area called computer literacy.

LAKESIDE-MAPLE GLEN

This study was grounded in an ethnographic foundation in order to observe and analyze the development and implementation of a computer literacy curriculum in Lakeside-Maple Glen, a small, midwestern suburban/rural school district. The purpose was to observe the process through which the district developed theoretical and practical meaning for the term computer literacy. Ethnography of course, is more than a methodology, it implies a holistic perspective about observing and describing people as they interact in a natural context. Because I wanted to understand how historical, cultural, and organizational factors in the Lakeside-Maple Glen district affected the use of computers and how the introduction of computers then came to affect them, an ethnographic perspective was most appropriate because it allowed me to observe the anticipated and unanticipated events and describe them within the meaning structures that participants gave to them.

I spent over a year in the small district, which consisted of one 4-year high school, one middle school and six geographically dispersed elementary schools, and became a familiar person, generally trusted, and as it often seems to happen when one spends so much time with people, an informal participant. I spent all my days and many evenings in the district observing courses taught, attending teacher, school board, parent, and computer committee meetings, interviewing people either formally or informally as well as reading historical and current curriculum documents. Long-term familiarity meant that people shared an accumulation of deeper meanings with me. Much of what the computers came to mean to some participants would not have been learned through brief or less intrusive means. For example, while most teachers in Lakeside-Maple Glen supported the goals of computer literacy, they were far less likely to speak openly or superficially about it in terms of what it was coming to mean for their work. Furthermore, the development of computer literacy was a process in the district and its effects were subtle and developmental in nature, best examined in context and over time.

This chapter describes three initial computer literacy related programs in the district as practiced in the high school and middle school. The research was conducted during the second year of the high school Computer Programming course which was the first year of the Data Processing course and the first year of the 7th grade Computer Literacy Unit.

THE HIGH SCHOOL

Considering the social and economic pressures on all schools in general, and in upwardly mobile middle class schools in particular, it is not surprising that two new course additions, Computer Programming as a math department elective and Data Processing as a business department elective, were quickly approved and widely supported by the Lakeside-Maple Glen School Board, community, and students. Two new labs were developed and equipped with about 12 computers each, teachers were recruited to develop the curricula, 3 sections of each course were filled each semester, and the whole process occurred very matter of factly. These popular additions to the curriculum seemed sensible to most and, as the curriculum expanded, district administrators proudly announced, "we're one of the first districts in the state to have a K through 12 Computer Literacy Curriculum."

But the nature and effects of these courses was not as unproblematic as their smooth introduction would imply. Observation and comparison of these courses led to the analysis of the implicit curriculum, and to the nature of the relationship between students and computers. An examination of the school context in which these new courses appeared led to an analysis of what the courses meant to other teachers in the school, and the reciprocal effects between their introduction and the culture of the high school. The nature of these two courses and their broader school context is the focus of this section.

Computer Programming Course

After the first year of the Computer Programming course the instructor and the guidance counselor decided to increase the prerequisites for the course from just algebra to algebra and geometry. They did this because many students who first took the course had difficulty and the teacher essentially wanted to limit the course to more capable students, because, in the words of the current teacher, "The course is a rigorous one and students have to be strong students, with good work and study habits." When asked, "Why the geometry prerequisites?" the teacher went on to say that it "emphasized doing logical proofs and it's those problem-solving strategies and skills that are required in order to be successful in the programming course." The official course description now reads, "Strong logic skills and considerable out-of-class work will be required."

Essentially, the students who took the programming course were college oriented students who did well in school and many of the school's academic and social leaders were among them. The teacher claimed that this course was "good preparation for those who will go on and do more with computers in college." The classes enrolled many more males than females.

November 18, Period 1. There are 12 males and 7 females in class. The students are working on a programming assignment. Some students are working on the computers and others are sitting at desks planning their programs. Some students walk around examining what the students at the computers are writing, they make comments, tease, or give suggestions in a low key and generally friendly manner. The teacher is also walking around helping those that need it. As program "bugs" arise students gather around and offer suggestions, "try putting in a GOTO after . . . ." These informal problem-solving sessions happen spontaneously as students become interested in overheard conversations and walk over to observe and participate. Despite an informal appearance, there are firm expectations and general "on task" behaviors.

Today students were working on a banking program that would give $11.00 for every 3 and 7 rolled on a dice and subtract $2.00 for every other number. The students were to determine "Why can you always win in this banking program?" As they worked and discussed it comments such as, "Why does it do that?", "How does this work?", "Well, it won't factor out the . . . ." Although students were individually responsible for the assignment, they were free to converse and share information and strategies.

November 22, Period 1. The students were very busy completing an 'interactive program,' which means that the student had to program the computer to respond differentially to specific user input. The computer was to display questions or options to a user and would then process the user's responses and display appropriate output. The students were free to develop any content within this format. Some wrote "dating questionnaires" which asked users for their preferences in a date, and then suggested someone who would meet those qualifications. One student wrote a program in which the user could select a quiz, survey, or a bibliography based on science fiction or fantasy books, another developed a personal interest inventory and yet another wrote a mathematics program that would calculate and graphically display lines and shapes based on input coordinates. Students were given much discretion in designing their programs. The students and teacher laughed and conversed as they wrote and tested programs, the casualness of which belied the complexity of the programming task.

Business Data Processing Course

Data processing was being offered for the first time and was a popular elective in the Business Education department. About the students, the teacher said, "Over half of them are vocationally oriented and they are not college bound." The guidance counselor said that "Primarily these are kids who are interested in secretarial, technical-vocational, Business without advanced education, or a 2-year business course at a vocational/technical school." Many of these students are from the surrounding rural areas and take the course because they feel that any job they get will probably involve computer use. When comparing her students with those in the programming course, the teacher said that the business students generally have lower grades than the former. There were more females than males in the classes.

She said that this course is "taught just the opposite from the computer courses. In data processing you teach all the hardware first, the vocabulary is extremely important, in fact one of the fathers is going to come in and talk to the group about how important it is. I won't get to basic programming skills and flow charting until the end." The main purpose of the course is to prepare the students to use a computer to process information. The official description of the course reads, "Each student will develop a basic understanding of the principles involved in preparing information for input into memory bank hardware." The prerequisite for the course was completion of or current registration in the typing/keyboarding course.

The course curriculum was centered around the coordinated use of a textbook, a workbook, and some business data computer programs.

November 11, Period 3. Today was a lecture day; the students had their textbooks open to Chapter 7. The teacher keeps a lively pace with questions and probes intended to provoke discussion. There are some responses, especially by a few boys seated together near the front of the room. There are no overt distractions, but from the back of the room I notice many private conversations occurring and one girl knitting. Midway through the class the teacher divides the students into small groups and gives each group a controversial question, which they were to debate later in the period. She intensifies the controversial nature of the topic by interjecting money and profitability as powerful motivators of what businesses and corporations do. Student debate occurs without much intensity and with only a few students actually contributing. After class the teacher said that, "They don't do the homework," if she assigns a chapter maybe "two will have read it" and "I've gone back to more lecturing . . ." She said that there is "a group of boys who do all the talking and dominate and others who just sit."

November 22, Period 3. Today is a lab day, students are working in groups of two or three at a computer and filling in the answers to workbook pages using a computerized airline reservation program. The program is intended to make and confirm reservations, scan passenger lists, and assign seats. A few students were interested in using the program and were actively using the computer, however, most students were conversing socially and made no attempt to use the computer until the student intern would come near, when they would then appear to work. Because only one student could actually run the computer program at a time, the others were to watch, help, and take turns; however, most typically one student would do all the work while the others would copy later the information into their workbooks.

This was very common for all lab work in the data processing course and during an interview with the teacher in February, she said that she had made some curriculum changes based on her experiences from last semester. She said that she does not want students sharing computers in the lab because, "If one does the work, the other doesn't know what to do . . . some couldn't boot a program" and she felt that they should have been able to do so by the end of the course. She decided to impose more structure on the form of the course, for example, she decided to have a test directly follow the workbook days in order to help students focus more. She later commented that, "I don't have the knitting problem as much!" Her typical schedule now is:

First: Introduce new chapter, lecture
Next: Half the students work in the lab while half work in their workbooks.
Next: Reverse groups
Last: Test on chapter

A Comparison

Both of these courses were focused around an introduction to computer technology. In the programming course college-bound students were learning the technical skills necessary to control the computer to their own specifications. The programming students worked on tasks until they got the computer to do what they wanted and the group dynamics facilitated a collaborative and problem-solving atmosphere. Students assumed problems could be solved and they experimented until they solved them. Their assignments were relatively open and allowed them a substantial degree of choice in topics and problem-solving approaches. Some cooperative behavior developed around group problem-solving strategies.

In contrast, the data processing course was more text and workbook structured, and used computer programs that focused on getting predetermined information from and into the computer. There was little room for student initiative or interest. The students were learning to manipulate programs conceived by others and for purposes not their own. The general difference between these courses was that one group was becoming independent users of computers and the other group was using computers to manipulate information through preexisting programs.

Because the computer programming course was essentially a high track course with a majority of males and the data processing course was essentially a vocationally and technically oriented course with a majority of females, we must ask if these divisions represent old patterns in a new facade? Work in recent years has made us aware of sex-role socialization patterns in school math and science programs; perhaps the same types of divisions are also occurring with computers. Certainly the difference between the two courses prefigures a future in which some new jobs will be in the areas of sophisticated technologies while most will require workers with minimal skills exercising minimal degrees of individual discretion.

The School Context

The introduction of these courses occurred within the broader context of some major and controversial changes in the high school's administration, philosophy and organization. Gradual changes in the school's philosophy from an open and modularly scheduled school in the 60s and 70s to a much more traditionally organized school in the 80s, had resulted in a much narrower approach to the definition and form of the curriculum and student discipline. For teachers, recent changes in the administration had resulted in a more centralized approach to decision making than had been traditionally granted to this faculty. In addition to losing the right to decide class scheduling, teaching assignments, and departmental budgeting, some faculty were also experiencing enrollment declines in their elective courses due to the recently increased graduation requirements in English, social studies and health. In emphasizing the "drastic change in elective areas" the guidance counselor took out her calculator and said, "This is real, not perceived." She went on to calculate:

3 semesters more of social studies
1 semester more of English
+ 1 semester of health
5 additional semesters of requirements

5 semesters * 1200 students = 6000 students
6000/26 (class average) = 230 new sections

Therefore, 230 class sections were lost from the electives area. With the addition of the two new computer courses, each with three sections a semester, there was an additional six sections of students not enrolled in the other elective areas.

The combined effects of the increased graduation requirements and the addition of six new sections of computer course options meant decreases in the art, industrial arts, and music departments as well as in some advanced level electives in science. The fine arts department has gone from five and a half faculty positions to two; one dismissed teacher had taught for 9 years. Thus departments and individual teachers were competing for students, who were now regarded as scarce resources. One teacher said, "We have even promoted our courses in classes, that maybe isn't fair, students are quite impressionable, but it means course offerings and jobs!" A social studies teacher referred to a past practice of teachers advertising their courses on posters and of the competition as "dog eat dog."

Teachers felt that courses were now valued on the basis of numbers, not quality, as one agriculture teacher lamented:

It's no longer the case that what happens depends on a teacher's competence, dedication and good work. If courses don't go, enrollment declines, programs are cut, regardless of what a good job that teacher may have been doing . . . that is what is discouraging to me. If I wasn't making it, couldn't cut the cake anymore, I could deal with that, I could leave or something, but now any program could be cut, regardless of how hard you work and how good the program is.

The agriculture program is down to one faculty member and after 10 years of teaching he doesn't feel very secure. He said, "I have begun to get a sense of what's the use. I slip into an unmotivated mood . . ."

An industrial arts teacher said that they were cut one faculty member and now they are playing "the numbers game." He said that classes are loaded now, they pleaded to keep the faculty, but, "it all fell on deaf ears, they'll listen if a kid gets hurt only." He went on to express his discouragement with a system in which the quality of the program and the teacher's work "doesn't count."

A science teacher complained that students who would have taken his advanced level science course instead took the computer programming course. He went on to say that, "I can teach more about problem solving in 2 weeks in my lab than they can teach in the programming course." With a sweeping gesture toward the well-equipped computer lab near his office he said, "We need analytical balances, not computers!"

Some school board members and parents did not feel that teacher competition was all that bad. One board member explained that students still had plenty of electives to take and that "It's up to teachers to make their courses interesting enough so that kids will want to take them!" When the subject of declines in the elective areas came up at a high school Parent/Teachers committee meeting, one influential parent dismissed the concern with, "That's how it works in the market place, a little competition isn't bad." Neither did competition seem to be an issue for most administrators who tended to view course competition as a stimulus for developing and maintaining a form of quality control.

One consequence of this competitive atmosphere was that teachers and departments tended to isolate themselves and play the numbers game. A business teacher claimed:

> It is very divisive, teachers stick close to their departments. In fact if you did a sociogram among the teachers to see who talks to who you would see that there is minimal communication among people in different departments, in fact sometimes even within a department you have to keep your mouth shut!

Most of the teachers of electives experienced this as a loss of professionalism. For them competition did not promote quality; it promoted a mentality to compete for students' attention and advertise courses as you would grocery specials, to substitute trendy for substantial courses and to exchange easy grades for rigorous course standards. The principal sensed some "grade inflation" and conducted a survey in order to document its occurrence. Thus, teachers who wanted to maintain rigorous elective courses were experiencing multiple and contradictory pressures.

The introduction of the computer courses have to be seen as threatening as they are associated with and intensify a situation where the jobs of many teachers are in jeopardy. Although most teachers supported the concept of computer literacy, the accomplishment of that objective had far broader implications.

THE MIDDLE SCHOOL

Lakeside-Maple Glen intended that its computer literacy curricula be one that empowered users. The goal was for all students to understand computers, "to control the computer and not be controlled by it." The district's first nonelective computer literacy curricula was a 2 week unit developed and taught in the middle school math department for all 7th graders. Two male middle school math teachers who had some computer experience, prepared the unit for the department. Three female math teachers were unaware of the required unit until school began in the Fall.

Although the men seemed to have discussed the unit before Fall, they had not specifically developed the curriculum and this time consuming task occupied much of their attention during the first 6 weeks of school. While observing the process of planning the computer literacy unit, and its subsequent implementation in all the 7th grade classrooms, a basic contradiction emerged between the goals of the computer literacy unit and the form of its implementation. During the curriculum planning stage the teachers identified characteristics of the school organization, resources, and teacher capabilities that to a significant degree shaped the form of the curriculum that they developed. During the implementation stage it became apparent that the form of the curriculum severely limited teacher involvement and student interest. The computer literacy unit, its form, content, implementation process, and effects is the subject of this section.

Planning for Computer Literacy

It was late August and on the board in Mr. Nelson's room was a planning chart which specified days 1 to 10 and the daily topics such as input, output, flowcharting or test. During September and October Mr. Nelson and Mr. Miller, the two math teachers responsible for developing the unit, met periodically to develop the curriculum and get the necessary materials assembled. Although they met frequently, the task was a comprehensive one and the unit was not ready or even distributed to the other teachers until its implementation date. While observing Mr. Nelson and Mr. Miller during this period, I was made aware of several factors that influenced the development of the unit. The abilities of teachers who had to teach the unit, the available resources and the time schedules in the math department, became the givens of the situation, and the unit was developed to accommodate these givens. The curriculum development process proceeded as a series of solutions to these givens.

One major obstacle they faced was the fact that, although the school had seven computers, they were in the computer lab and being used for the 8th grade computer elective course. Therefore, the computers were not conveniently available for 7th grade use. That meant that most of the unit had to be taught without the use of computers and this was a major obstacle for the planners because a major goal of the unit was to provide maximum hands on computer time. Through elaborate rescheduling the teachers were able to schedule three days in the computer lab, not very much considering that there would be about 25 students sharing seven computers on those lab days. Therefore access to computers was a major problem, only minimally resolved. This affected the curriculum content because concepts best taught at the computer had to be developed in more vicarious ways.

Probably the biggest consideration in planning the unit was stated by Mr. Miller, when he said, "You have to remember that we have faculty in this department who don't know much about computers. We needed a program that everyone could teach." Mr. Nelson also claimed that in developing the unit a crucial factor was that teachers who knew nothing about computers would be able to teach it and, as he explained, "We were trying to develop a canned Unit." The other teachers were all women, one was newly graduated and just hired, one was returning from a year's leave of absence and the other was an experienced teacher with no computer experience.

A third factor related to the scheduling of the unit. It was a practice in the department to test all 7th graders after the first 10 weeks of school and transfer those with demonstrated ability to the 8th grade math classes. This meant that in order for all 7th graders to participate in the unit, it would have to be taught in two shifts, beginning the 7th week of school. This schedule placed tremendous pressure on Mr. Nelson and Mr. Miller to plan the unit quickly and, because the unit was not completed beforehand, the women teachers did not get an opportunity to examine it until time to teach it.

A fourth consideration was the fact that given the time pressures, Mr. Nelson and Mr. Miller were not able to write an original curriculum, develop the materials themselves, or consult the other teachers. What they did was to examine some commercially prepared computer literacy curricula:

We really looked hard for materials to use . . . this program we found, covers the material we wanted, we left out a lot of it . . . I think we would have done about the same thing.

The material they selected was a prepackaged curriculum consisting of filmstrips, tape recordings, and worksheets. They added two lab days for using instructional computer programs and one lab day for copying and writing a computer program. The 10th day consisted of a written test (for which the students could bring and use all their notes and worksheets), and a film about the social implications of computers. Most days were spent in the classrooms completing worksheets according to the information and directions given from the commercial tape recordings. Therefore, each day of the unit was planned in detail and daily plans came with ready made activities.

The canned unit seemed to be an efficient, practical and sensible way to accommodate inadequate computer access, teacher expertise, and planning time. Due to the bulk of all the necessary worksheets and equipment, the materials were rolled around from room to room on a cart.

Implementing Computer Literacy: The Curriculum on a Cart

Students and teachers seemed excited about studying computers for the next 2 weeks. It represented a new and exciting topic. Because there were five teachers and eleven math classes, there were some individual variations by teacher and class in the implementation process; however, what became most interesting was just how little variation there was. The unit appeared very similar as it was implemented in these various classes as were the behaviors and reactions of the teachers and the students. Because the unit was implemented immediately after it was written, and some teachers were seeing it for the first time as they taught it, I was able to observe spontaneous reactions in context, which were then followed by interviews after the completion of the unit. It is these typical behaviors and reactions across classrooms, teachers, and students resulting from this highly structured curriculum package that is now characterized.

The unit began with a filmstrip, some enthusiasm and two worksheets. Students were shown a filmstrip that focused on the history and development of computers and were given a timeline of events for notetaking. For homework they were given a WordSearch worksheet with names of computer parts. The content emphasized dates of events such as the invention of the transistor and names of parts of a computer. There was little discussion as the filmstrips took the whole period.

Day five represents a composite of the classroom lessons and characterizes some of the common reactions to the accumulating impact of routine use of cassette tapes and worksheets.

Day 5

Equipment needed: Cassette recorder, cassette tape "Getting Information Out of a Computer," student booklets

Objectives: To introduce students to the variety of ways that
                           information can be output from a computer. To
                           introduce students to the PRINT command as
                           used in the computer language BASIC.

Lesson Plan: I.   Play cassette, stopping when directed to do
                           so.

                     II.   Students will fill out response booklet as
                           directed to do so by the cassette.

                     III. Discuss and answer questions as necessary.

As the students came into class today, one boy shouted, "Are we going
to the lab today?" The teacher responded, "We've got those sheets again
and the tapes. . . ." Invariably when hearing that it was a worksheet day
students would start to grumble, some very loudly: "That man's de-
jected," "I hate this, this is boring," "Do we have to do this all the
time?", "I can't stand this class," "This isn't computer class, this is
worksheets . . . what do we learn, nothing . . . how to push a button"
(referring to the tape recorder). One student turned to the researcher and
gesturing to the worksheets and tapes angrily said, "We know this stuff
already, maybe not these fancy words . . . but we know this stuff."

The first procedure in every class was the distribution of worksheets
which took about 10 minutes because there were usually several of them.
A stapler was passed around and this was the occasion for much fooling
around as students dawdled, withheld it from the next students, slid it on
the floor and generally used it to divert attention from getting on with the
task.

The teacher began the lesson by turning on the first tape recording and
students were expected to follow using their first worksheet. A man's
voice on the tape read and explained the worksheet to the students, then
he said, "Now turn off the tape and complete the worksheet." Often the
teachers, who had not been listening missed this and the students
shouted, "Turn off the tape!" After a few minutes the teacher turned the
tape back on and the man read the answers while students supposedly
checked their papers. Many students, however, just waited for the
answers to be read and filled in their papers at that time. The man then
introduced the next worksheet with, "If you want to continue . . ." In
several classes students mumbled, "But we don't!" After a few days of
this one teacher singsonged, "Oh we do, we do. . . ." This same teacher
told the researcher after one of the first classes, "I don't think this was a
good day, the kids didn't really get much out of this." This seemed
surprising at first because the students had been very attentive, the day
went smoothly as far as the equipment and the lesson plans. It was,

however, the teacher's sense that this material was not too meaningfully conveyed to the students through tapes and he could have done a more effective job.

As the tape recorder droned on teachers and students found many quiet diversions. Students combed their hair, cleaned dirt from their sneakers, poked each other, daydreamed, and chipped pencils. One girl worked all period getting a piece of candy out of her pocket and unwrapping the crinkly paper quietly enough not to be noticed.

Teachers also seemed bored; some used this time to correct papers from other classes and take care of other routine paperwork. But they would run out of diversions and one teacher paced around the room, stared at a poster for 5 minutes, then stared out the window and finally stopped near me and said, "I'm so sick of these tapes!" One teacher dozed off during a tape. Teachers had very little involvement other than distributing the worksheets and turning on and off the tapes.

At times, however, the teachers would disrupt the planned lesson, and interject in order to clarify a concept. Mr. Miller turned off the tape one day to explain a concept, he said, "We have to discuss and clarify some to smooth the rough edges of these worksheets." However, he never did get back on schedule because the unit was too tightly paced. Ms. Wilson missed a day because of a school assembly and tried to consolidate 2 days by talking through some of the material herself, "We have to catch up today, so we can go to the lab tomorrow." They couldn't catch up, however, and ended up skipping some tapes. Ms. Linder stopped a lesson because it referred to some mathematical formula that she knew her students did not understand. She was irritated and later said, "If I had seen the lesson first . . . I would have taken that out, 7th graders don't know that, it shouldn't be in there." But by increasing their own involvement and disrupting the planned lessons, teachers had to rush and invariably fell behind.

In later interviews teachers talked about how they felt during the unit. Mr. Nelson, one of the developers said, "I felt hamstrung, I would probably do things differently, but I felt that I had to pilot it. I would like to have used computers more." Mr. Miller said, "Oh those tapes, well there were times when you'd want to throw the tape recorder across the room, with the 'now turn the tape off . . .'." Ms. Linder resented not being given the unit in time to examine it, she said, "I kept asking to see the unit, but it wasn't ready and I was told, 'Don't worry, there isn't much to do, just tapes.' But I didn't like those 2 weeks at all, I knew when I was out those days, the sub would be able to do it, she just had to turn on the tape recorder!" Ms. Smith told Mr. Miller that there was too much information, but his reply was, "Better too much than too little" and the subject was dropped.

The 3 days in which the classes met in the computer lab were quite a contrast to the classroom days, in that the students were active and enthusiastic computer users. They mainly used different types of educational computer programs. Students worked in groups, three or four to a computer, and their main frustration was that many did not get to try as much as they would like in the brief period. During the lab period half the students worked with the teacher using one computer and a popular simulation game while the rest of the class was given a worksheet with a simple program to copy into the computer. The students working on programs were expected to write a program of their own, a task which the majority could not do, since the teacher was occupied with the large group and could not give them individual help. The computer lab days were by far the most favored by teachers and students, but there was insufficient time for individual students to work with a computer.

The final test summarized the worksheets, tapes, and filmstrips and the students could use their notes and worksheets to complete the test. The test consisted of matching, listing, and fill-the-blank short answer items:

> Name 3 ways of putting information on printouts _____
> The first computer was built in Philadelphia and was named _____
> Put the outcome of each program on the output line.

Most teachers said that the students "did well" on the test.

The Effects of the Unit

Although the goal of computer literacy, and to some extent the content of the 7th grade unit, focused on producing students who would be in control of the computer, the form that the curriculum took rendered them passive receivers of information. Teachers modified the rigid form of the unit when they interjected to "round off the edges of the tapes," and stopped to add or explain a concept, but when they did this they got off schedule. While students and teachers were at first excited about computers and the new unit in general, their excitement gradually diminished as the rigid form of the curriculum marginalized and regimented their involvement. The routine use of the impersonal tape recordings established a fast paced form of one-way information transmission.

In the process computer literacy was reduced to technical information processing; the input was a barrage of information on worksheets, tape recordings, and filmstrips that stressed computer vocabulary, equipment, and logic. The output occurred on the last day when the students reiterated this information on the unit test. How much processing went on in the students' heads is questionable. The teachers spent most of their time turning on and off tapes and managing the hundreds of worksheets, a role they subverted at times but with consequence. To compensate for "the rough edges of the tapes" the teachers had to abandon the routine and fall behind in the 10-day sequence. Most of the teachers did not do this as their own computer backgrounds were limited, they had not had sufficient time to preview the unit and were on a rigid schedule in order to complete the unit in 2 weeks. Therefore the form and conditions of the unit worked against the teachers inclinations and good sense about what the students were and were not understanding. The teachers were cast in the role of managers of the instructional process while the students acted as information processors. The unit as a whole was a seeming contradiction to the spirit of hands-on activity and control that was to be the foundation of computer literacy in Lakeside-Maple Glen.

CONCLUSION

The pressures to develop computer literacy curricula are especially great among middle class school districts today. Observing what computer literacy means in practice, however, is more complex than more common pretest, posttest forms of assessment can reveal. In those terms, Lakeside-Maple Glen has an effective program; there is a computer literacy curriculum and students are taking the courses and passing exams. But there are other meanings and consequences of the new curriculum that are not readily observed or explicitly intended, and ethnographic research is especially powerful in illuminating these deeper, more subtle and consequential effects. The meaning of computer literacy curricula therefore cannot be viewed in isolation from its organizational and cultural context and the long-term consequences it has for the teachers and students who participate in it.

The current trend in many school districts to increase graduation requirements in the basics and add computer courses will have consequences for faculty who teach in other areas. With these additional requirements, there will be significant declines in other course enrollments, especially in the arts. In Lakeside-Maple Glen, these changes combined to erode enrollments in music, art and other advanced-level courses. Teachers in elective areas felt embarrassed at having to sell their courses, a de-professionalization of their role. As a more tangible consequence of enrollment changes, some teachers were placed on lay-off and other jobs were subject to a process of competition where survival was based on "the numbers game." The computer became the latest symbol of the classical dichotomy between the arts and sciences and popular choice was now largely on the side of the computers. The introduction of the computer courses contributed to competition, division, and isolation among departments and faculty members.

There are other effects on faculty as they are pressured to quickly develop mass computer literacy curricula. Teachers who have had minimal computer experience themselves may be more vulnerable to the use of impersonal and alienating prepackaged curricula. In the interest of what may be called the "quick and dirty" computer literacy unit, computer literacy may be reduced to trivial and technical competencies, vocabulary, and information. In the process curricular goals intended to empower individuals, mediated through a rigid and fast paced curricular form that constrains the agency of teachers and students, may in the long term be contradicted in practice.

More contradictions are evident when we examine the purposes of introducing computer literacy into the schools. Popular opinion is that everyone must be computer literate, but just what that means as a consumer and a future worker is ambiguous. Certainly the implication of the labor market projections introduced at the beginning of this chapter are that the world of work will become even more polarized as fewer and fewer actual jobs require technological expertise because most jobs will be in routinized and less skilled service occupations. Even at Lakeside-Maple Glen, a relatively homogeneous middle class school district, we see evidence of this dichotomy between the programming and data processing students; the former actively engage the computer through problem solving and programming requirements, and the latter are more passive observers of computer application systems developed to be used by vocationally trained data processors to increase efficiency and managerial control in business and industry. The dichotomy is as much one of an approach to computers and technology as it is one based on particular content. Although the ability to program in BASIC is probably a temporary asset at best, it is the programming student's independent position as a computer programmer and problem solver that contrasts with the data processing student's more passive role. For the programming students, the computer becomes less mystical and intimidating because of their real or at least potential ability to control it.

Computer literacy is theoretically an empowering concept; its development in practice can have contradictory effects.

REFERENCES

Becker, H. J. (1983). *School uses of microcomputers: Reports from a national survey.* (Issues 1–6). Baltimore, MD: Center for Social Organization of Schools, The Johns Hopkins University.

Becker, H. J. (1986). *Instructional uses of school computers: Reports from the 1985 national survey*, (Issue 1). Baltimore, MD: Center for Social Organization of Schools, The Johns Hopkins University.

Market Data Retrieval. (1982). *Update on the school market for microcomputers*. Westport, CT: Author.

National Commission on Excellence in Education. (1983). *A nation at risk: The imperative for educational reform*. Washington, DC: U.S. Government Printing Office.

Nielsen, R. (1983, March). Consensus: We must educate, not train. *On Campus*, p. 16.

Rumberger, R. W., & Levin, H. M. (1984). *Forecasting the impact of new technologies on the future job market* (Project Rep. No. 84-A4). Stanford: Stanford University, School of Education, Institute for Research on Educational Finance and Governance.

Author Index

Subject Index